THE MASTER MUSICIANS

HANDEL

Series edited by Stanley Sadie

The Master Musicians

Titles available in paperback

Berlioz *Hugh Macdonald*
Brahms *Malcolm MacDonald*
Britten *Michael Kennedy*
Bruckner *Derek Watson*
Chopin *Jim Samson*
Grieg *John Horton*
Handel *Donald Burrows*
Liszt *Derek Watson*
Mahler *Michael Kennedy*
Mendelssohn *Philip Radcliffe*
Monteverdi *Denis Arnold*
Purcell *J.A. Westrup*

Rachmaninoff *Geoffrey Norris*
Rossini *Richard Osborne*
Schoenberg *Malcolm MacDonald*
Schubert *John Reed*
Sibelius *Robert Layton*
Richard Strauss *Michael Kennedy*
Tchaikovsky *Edward Garden*
Vaughan Williams *James Day*
Verdi *Julian Budden*
Vivaldi *Michael Talbot*
Wagner *Barry Millington*

Titles available in hardback

Bach *Malcolm Boyd*
Beethoven *Barry Cooper*
Chopin *Jim Samson*
Elgar *Robert Anderson*
Handel *Donald Burrows*

Schubert *John Reed*
Schumann *Eric Frederick Jensen*
Schütz *Basil Smallman*
Stravinsky *Paul Griffiths*

In preparation

Bartók *Malcolm Gillies*
Dvořák *Jan Smaczny*

Musorgsky *David Brown*
Puccini *Julian Budden*

THE MASTER MUSICIANS

HANDEL

Donald Burrows

OXFORD UNIVERSITY PRESS

OXFORD

UNIVERSITY PRESS

Great Clarendon Street, Oxford OX2 6DP

Oxford University Press is a department of the University of Oxford.
It furthers the University's objective of excellence in research, scholarship,
and education by publishing worldwide in

Oxford New York

Athens Auckland Bangkok Bogotá Buenos Aires Calcutta
Cape Town Chennai Dar es Salaam Delhi Florence Hong Kong Istanbul
Karachi Kuala Lumpur Madrid Melbourne Mexico City Mumbai
Nairobi Paris São Paulo Shanghai Singapore Taipei Tokyo Toronto Warsaw

and associated companies in Berlin Ibadan

Oxford is a registered trade mark of Oxford University Press
in the UK and in certain other countries

Published in the United States
by Oxford University Press Inc., New York

British Library Cataloguing in Publication Data
Data available

Library of Congress Cataloging in Publication Data
Burrows, Donald
Handel/Donald Burrows.
p.   cm.—(The Master musicians)
Includes bibliographical references and index.
1. Handel, George Frideric, 1685–1759. 2. Composers—Biography.
I. Title II. Series: Master musicians series.
ML410.H13B94 1996   780'.92—dc20   [B]   93–15279
ISBN 0 19 816649–4

1 3 5 7 9 8 6 4 2

Contents

Illustrations

Figures

Preface

Any biographer of Handel quickly discovers an imbalance in the surviving material about the composer. We can document Handel's public and professional life with fullness and precision: there are periods when we can even account for his movements day by day. Yet there is surprisingly little firm evidence about his private life and many aspects of his personality. That Handel had a strong personality is clear from the reactions of his contemporaries. In his youth he seems to have gained almost immediate favour with such diverse patrons as Roman cardinals, German princes and Electors, and Queen Anne of Great Britain. In his later years he emerges as rather excitable and impatient, yet generous and an entertaining companion. However, we know virtually nothing about his opinions on the political, religious or philosophical issues of his day. His letters, which are few in number in any case, are mostly business-like, though a liveliness of style is evident enough. He was not, apparently, given to writing official memoranda, and we must conclude that a large part of the management of his career in the London theatres was conducted verbally. As to the identities and characters of his personal friends, the evidence is again surprisingly thin.

I offered that view of Handel as a biographical subject in 1985, in an introductory chapter ('Handel: his Life and Work') in the catalogue of the National Portrait Gallery exhibition that celebrated the anniversary year (Simon, *Handel*, p. 9). Nearly a decade later, I remain sceptical about the extent to which inferences about Handel's personality can be drawn from the content of his musical output, beyond the obvious one that he could probably identify with a wide range of human emotions and situations. But I do not think that the position I described is necessarily regrettable, nor that it undermines the possibility of coming to a sympathetic, imaginative and perhaps even empathetic understanding of Handel and his music. Handel was one of the most professional of composers. If, in its outward form, his biography seems largely controlled by his annual routines of theatre performances, that is because his life was like that. It does not mean that his life was uneventful, for various crises, artistic and (in the broadest sense) political, rocked the boat fairly frequently; we may imagine that Handel would from time to time have welcomed the prospect of a period of dull, routine success.

Handel's outward biography is complemented by the inner biography of his creative life. In the end, although he had a significantly high profile in the political and social circles in which he moved, it is his creative life, visible to us in its musical products, that makes him a compelling subject for biography. In this volume I have chosen to focus on the development of his style and repertory from one period to another rather than to treat the operas, oratorios, concertos etc. in discrete chapters; consequently the 'musical' chapters (3, 5, 7, 10, 13) are interleaved with the biographical ones. This decision was partly affected by the fact that Handel's career breaks down into a number of fairly well-defined phases, each with its own characteristic repertory. So, in general, chapters outlining the biographical framework are for each stage followed by chapters dealing with the music from the appropriate period, except in Chapter 14, where Handel's last major creative works are more conveniently dealt with in the context of the biographical chapter. I am aware of, and make no apology for, a certain amount of 'leakage' elsewhere: there are areas where it is neither desirable nor efficient to banish musical discussion from Handel's biography.

Within the confines of this book it is clearly impossible to deal with every one of Handel's works. Accordingly, I have chosen a handful of the major works from each period as representative examples for rather more extended investigation, and in doing so I hope I have at least managed to convey some of the character of the works concerned, and of the compositional skills and imagination that they display. For many people coming to this volume Handel will, in the first instance, be the composer of *Zadok the priest,* the *Water Music* and *Messiah.* But Italian opera was central to his career for more than 35 years, and an understanding of the operatic genre that he absorbed and developed is fundamental to an adequate appreciation of his musical thinking. In Chapter 7 I have dwelt at some length on a single work (*Giulio Cesare in Egitto*) in order to provide an introduction to the span of a complete opera.

In dealing with Handel's works I have sought to place them as to their periods and circumstances. There are various ways of approaching Handel's musical style: one might, for example, follow through the influence of national, regional or 'genre' styles, or of dance rhythms, or of Handel's 'borrowings' from his own music and from that of other composers. Any of those approaches, taken in detail, would require books as long again as this one, but I have attempted to draw attention to at least some relevant influences in each area. In the end, it perhaps matters less that labels are attached to musical influences than that due attention is given to the way that they were used and converted by Handel to his own purposes. It is Handel's ability to match music to context, and to extend and integrate the musical materials with which he worked, that places him among the most remarkable composers.

A number of basic technical and bibliographical matters, explained more fully in the introductions to Appendices B and F, need to be mentioned here. The standard thematic catalogue for Handel's works is that prepared by Bernd Baselt and published in vols. 1–3 of the *Händel-Handbuch*. It is from this source that the identification of Handel's works by HWV numbers is taken. For the music, there are two collected editions of scores: the near-complete edition of the *Händel-Gesellschaft* series, masterminded in the nineteenth century by Friedrich Chrysander, and the modern complete edition, the *Hallische Händel-Ausgabe*. Neither is perfect: Chrysander's work was limited by the knowledge (and opportunities) of his time, while the new edition is still very much 'in progress'. Other editions of specific works are mentioned in this book where they significantly augment or correct the materials available in the collected editions. Where a familiar short title for a German or Italian work by Handel (e.g. *Almira, Rodrigo* or *Il trionfo del Tempo*) is used in the text, its full form will be found in the List of Works (Appendix B). I have retained a number of familiar descriptive titles (e.g. *Birthday Ode for Queen Anne, Ode for St Cecilia's Day* and *Foundling Hospital Anthem*) that were not used by Handel himself. In general, Handel's spellings (where consistent) have been adopted as standard for work titles.

All modern Handel biographers have had cause to be grateful for the impressive collection of contemporary documents that Otto Erich Deutsch transcribed in *Handel: a Documentary Biography,* published in 1955. A revised version of Deutsch's collection, incorporating much new material but omitting English translations of documents whose originals were in other languages, was published in 1985 as vol. 4 of the *Händel-Handbuch*. References in footnotes to 'Deutsch' or to '*HHB*' (without a qualifying volume number) are to these collections of documents. References to 'Mainwaring' are to the *Memoirs,* published anonymously in 1760.

A considerable problem arises over the consistent recording of dates. In London Handel experienced a kind of double life until September 1752, when Britain caught up with continental Europe and adopted the Gregorian Calendar. The Gregorian (or 'New Style') computation was 11 days ahead of the Julian ('Old Style') Calendar that was current in London for most of Handel's career. I have adopted the calendars in the forms in which Handel 'experienced' them. The German Protestant states generally adopted New Style in 1700: Prussia had done so in 1583, but Handel's baptism in Halle was recorded in Old Style, and that form of the calendar no doubt covered the first 15 years of his life. From 1700, only Britain was out of step. Germany, Italy and Holland were all ahead, in 'New Style'. Inevitably, the difference in calendars produces some apparent anomalies with regard to the dates of Handel's travels from London, and I have endeavoured to provide additional clarification where there might be ambiguity. Dated documents are recorded according to their own dates, though where letters are 'double dated' in both styles I have generally suppressed the less relevant one, especially when the original form is accessible through 'Deutsch' or *HHB*. I have, however, revised year-counts to conform to modern convention, with the year beginning on 1 January: in older conventions the new year was often reckoned from 25 March, which put the first three months one numerical year behind.

Finally, it is my pleasure to record my thanks to those who have helped in the creation of this book. Stanley Sadie, as General Editor, encouraged the work; for the publishers, Malcolm Gerratt, Julia Kellerman, Judith Nagley and Audrey Twine persisted and saw it to a conclusion. Bernd Baselt and Anthony Hicks read and commented on material in draft, and Terence Best supplied the translation that formed the basis for Appendix D and assisted with the English translations for those music examples with Italian texts. Winton Dean supplied many useful comments on points of detail. Hildegard Wright and Rosemary Kingdon turned my text into publisher-readable form. I thank the owners of the collections involved for giving permission for the use of the Illustrations and Figures. There is also a wider debt, diffused but active and significant, to Handelian friends in many countries with whom I have shared ideas, good times and good music. Long may this continue.

D. B.
Milton Keynes, 1993, 1996, 2000

1

Germany, 1685–1706

Handel was born on 23 February 1685 in Halle, a German city on the river Saale, a substantial tributary of the Elbe. The birthdate is not recorded on the entry in the register recording his baptism (as Georg Friedrich Händel)[1] on 24 February at the Ober-Pfarr-Kirche zu Unser Lieben Frauen (the Rectory Church dedicated to Our Lady, which stands in Halle's market-place), but it is attested by other biographical sources from Handel's lifetime.[2] Halle lies about 100 miles south-west of Berlin, almost exactly bisecting the distance from Berlin to Eisenach, where Johann Sebastian Bach was born less than a month later. Handel had no reason to undertake a journey to Eisenach at any time during his life, but other places associated with Bach's life certainly impinged on Handel's early experience. Weissenfels and Leipzig are each about 20 miles from Halle, the former to the south and also on the river Saale, the latter to the south-east and on a tributary of the same river.

Halle itself was a fundamentally prosperous city, with a historical source of wealth from its salt industry, but it had seen many setbacks during the seventeenth century. The social and economic life of the city was generally at its most lively when it played host to a resident court. In the early part of the seventeenth century the Margrave of Brandenburg, the Protestant administrator of the former archiepiscopal territories of Mainz, held his court in Halle; there he employed a number of musicians of distinction, including Samuel Scheidt, the Englishman William Brade and Michael Praetorius.[3] Unfortunately Halle suffered badly during the Thirty Years War: the city was occupied by General Wallenstein in 1625 and the court broken up. From 1638 Halle came under the administration

---

[1] The baptism register (Deutsch, p. 1; *HHB*, p. 8) gives his second name as 'Friederich', as does Mattheson in *Grundlage* and in the *Lebensbeschreibung* but 'Friedrich' is the form used by Handel in his signatures on the matriculation register at the University of Halle (1702) and on letters written in German (1731, 1733, 1750). In Italy Handel signed himself with the phonetic equivalent 'G[iorgio] F[ederico] Hendel' and in Britain he used the form 'George Frideric Handel'. The anglicized form will be used in this book: the form 'Georg Händel' is used in this chapter for Handel's father.

[2] Most authoritatively, in the funeral sermon for Handel's mother (*HHB*, p. 186; Deutsch, p. 265).

[3] Praetorius held an honorary post, as 'Kapellmeister von Haus aus'.

of Duke August of Saxony,[4] and it is perhaps not surprising that, once the war had ended, its musical life was in the hands of the court musicians Philipp Stolle and David Pohle, both of whom had studied with Heinrich Schütz in Dresden, the centre of influence for the Saxon court.

The presence of a Saxon court in Halle was limited by one of the terms of the Peace of Westphalia that terminated the Thirty Years War in 1648, which stipulated that on the death of Duke August the city of Halle would pass to the possession of Brandenburg-Prussia. Duke August died in 1680, and the Saxon court duly moved out from Halle to Weissenfels under the new duke, Johann Adolf. Further depopulation of the most unpleasant sort followed, as epidemics during 1681–3 reduced the city from about 11,000 inhabitants to about 5000. The new Brandenburg-Prussia administration encouraged immigration: a French Huguenot settlement was organized in 1686 (the Huguenots were granted the use of Halle's sixteenth-century cathedral church, the Domkirche), and restrictions on residence for Jews were lifted in 1692. While there was no active court presence as such in Halle, the new administrators provided some compensation by founding a university in the city in 1694, using buildings that had formerly been the site of the court riding academy. Under the leadership of Christian Thomasius the university quickly gained a reputation for 'progressive' thinking on theology, philosophy and law, involving a rejection of the old 'scholastic' methods and an encouragement of tolerance and freedom of thought. This policy naturally attracted controversy, and brought Thomasius into conflict with the pietistic Halle pastor August Hermann Francke, University Professor of Theology and Classical Languages. Francke was a man of deeds as well as words. He founded an orphanage and schools in Halle, and his activities had direct musical consequences: a boys' choir was one of the by-products of his foundations, and Johann Freylinghausen's hymnbooks, the first of which was published in 1706, were another.

Handel was therefore born into a city that had seen, and was still seeing, great changes. Strictly he was born a Prussian, but he seems to have regarded himself as a Saxon by geographical and social origin: at the end of his life he still described his birthplace as 'Halle in Sachsen'. His father Georg Händel had been born and bred in Halle, the son of a coppersmith who had migrated there from Breslau in the first decade of the seventeenth century. Georg was born in 1622, and his earliest years must have been troubled by the war, compounded (when he was 14 years old) by the death of his father. Instead of following in the coppersmith business, which passed to his elder brothers, he chose to follow a career as a surgeon, a profession that traditionally also carried with it that of

---

[4]The Elector of Saxony, with a court in Dresden, distributed parts of his country to his younger brothers (including Duke August) as fiefdoms: Halle was therefore host to a 'second-class' Saxon court.

barber. He was apprenticed successively to Andreas Beger (who was a son-in-law to William Brade) and Christoph Oettinger: on the death of the latter, he married his widow Anna and took over Oettinger's medical practice. Karl, the youngest son of this union (born 1649), followed his father's profession and became a surgeon at the Saxon court in Weissenfels (for the relationships in Handel's immediate family, see Fig. 1*a* and *b*).

Georg Händel's career must have prospered, for in 1666 he bought a substantial house in Halle's city centre, less than five minutes' walk from the market square.[5] As an additional diversification of his activities, the barber-surgeon applied for a renewal of the licence to sell wine from the building, which was known as the 'Yellow Hart'.[6] In the document recording the house purchase, Georg Händel is described as 'Geheimer Cammerdiener und Leib-Chirurgo' (Privy Chamberlain and Personal Surgeon) to the Prince of Saxony. When the Saxon court left Halle in 1680 he obtained a parallel position from the Brandenburg-Prussia authorities, as 'Cammerdiener und Chirurgus von Haus aus' (Chamber Servant and Honorary Surgeon). This was advanced to 'Wolbestalter Cammerdiener' in 1682, a higher office of servant carrying an annual pension of 100 thalers and granted in recognition of his work during the epidemics. These largely honorific indicators of status accompanied an expanding career, which already included medical responsibility for the northern suburb of Giebichenstein.[7] With its elevated riverside *Burg*, Giebichenstein was probably a quite attractive area, in contrast to the rather smoky city with its crooked, narrow and badly paved streets. Thus the elder Händel had an agreeable working location and a domestic base in the heart of the city. The doctor was not immune from the epidemics: in 1681 Georg fought off a serious attack, but the next year his eldest son and his wife were not so lucky. The widower was speedily re-married, to Dorothea, the daughter of Giebichenstein's pastor Georg Taust: the groom was 60 years old and his wife 32. Their first son was born in 1684 but died almost immediately: Georg Friedrich, born early the next year, fared better, as did his sisters, born in 1687 and 1690.

For a record of the events of Handel's early years we are indebted to John Mainwaring's *Memoirs of the Life of the Late George Frederic Handel*, published the year after the composer's death. More than half of the biographical section of the memoirs is devoted to the years before Handel settled in London, and the material must have come, directly or indirectly, from Handel himself. While there is no way of assessing how much distortion may have been introduced by imaginative expansion on the part of Mainwaring, or by the introduction of spurious anecdotes from

[5] The purchase-price was 1310 Meissen guilders: as part of the purchase agreement, Georg Händel took over the previous owner's mortgage from the Domkirche.

[6] The case for the renewal of the licence included reference to a 'wine-pole ... found on the house as an inn-sign'.

[7] Probably from 1645, and 'confirmed' in 1689 (*HHB*, p. 10).

Fig. 1 Handel's family

(a) Lineage of Handel's father (Georg Händel) and children of his first marriage

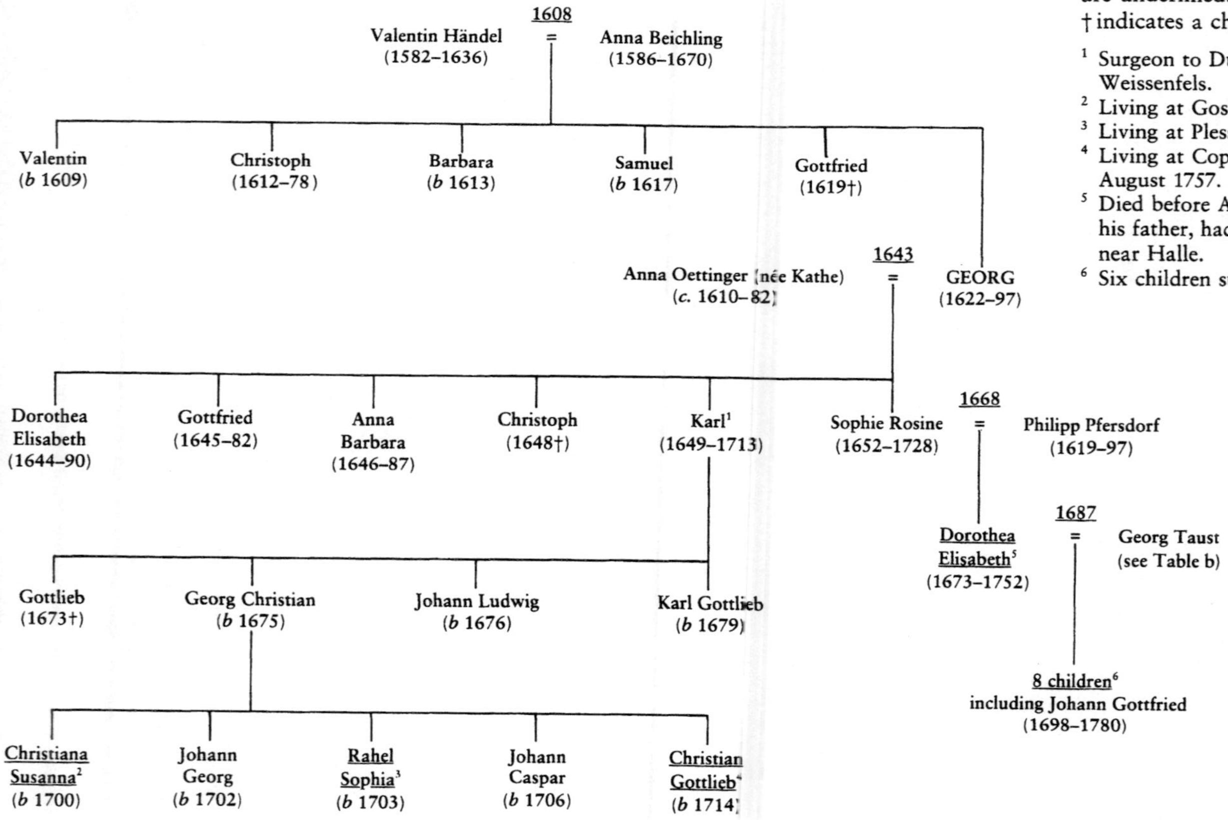

The tables show only Handel's immediate family and the lineage of relations mentioned in his will; the names of the latter are underlined.

†indicates a child that died during infancy.

1 Surgeon to Duke Johann Adolf I of Saxe-Weissenfels.
2 Living at Goslar in 1756.
3 Living at Pless in 1756.
4 Living at Copenhagen in 1750: died before August 1757.
5 Died before August 1756: her husband, like his father, had been pastor of Giebichenstein, near Halle.
6 Six children surviving in 1750, five in 1756.

(b) Lineage of Handel's mother (Dorothea Taust) and children of Georg Händel's second marriage

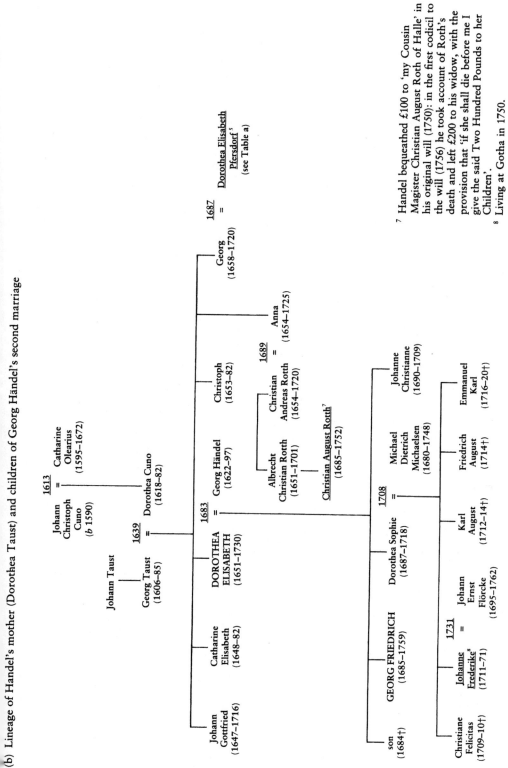

[7] Handel bequeathed £100 to 'my Cousin Magister Christian August Roth of Halle' in his original will (1750); in the first codicil to the will (1756) he took account of Roth's death and left £200 to his widow, with the provision that 'if she shall die before me I give the said Two Hundred Pounds to her Children'.

[8] Living at Gotha in 1750.

other sources, the tone of the prose lends plausible support to the idea that Mainwaring was writing up the autobiographical reminiscences of the blind composer in his last years. From Mainwaring comes the story (pp. 2–9) of the child Handel's persistence on two fronts. His determination to meet his half-brother Karl led Handel to run after his father's coach as it set out on a visit to the court at Weissenfels, and to resist attempts to send him home again; his answer to his father's ban on music-making in the house was to have a little clavichord 'privately convey'd' to an attic room so that he could practise secretly when the rest of the family were otherwise engaged. It seems probable that Mainwaring's account gives a rather exaggerated portrait of the insensitivity of Handel's father,[8] though it may still convey the child's perception of the force of adult restrictions, but we need not doubt Mainwaring's reports that Handel's father 'always intended him for the study of the Civil Law' (a profession as 'safe' in its prospects as medicine) and, as he approached 70 years of age, found some difficulty in coping with his son's 'uncontroulable humour' towards music, manifested by 'getting at harpsichords' whenever possible. There is no reason to doubt, also, that a critical factor in ameliorating Georg Händel's resistance was the strong advice that he received from the Duke of Saxe-Weissenfels to encourage and develop the youngster's talents: again, we have no good grounds for disbelieving the story that the situation was triggered when the duke heard young George playing the organ in the court chapel at Weissenfels. Perhaps his step-brother even connived in bringing the two together. According to Mainwaring's account, the duke had a higher opinion of the musical profession than Händel senior, and sent the son off with money as well as encouragement.

In consequence of the legitimization of young George's interest in music, he was sent for training around 1692–3 to Friedrich Wilhelm Zachow, the organist of the Marienkirche, the market-place church at which Handel had been baptized. Zachow was a native of that region of Germany, having been born in Leipzig and brought up in Eilenburg. No doubt the training that Handel received from Zachow was on the lines of a practical apprenticeship, with an emphasis on keyboard playing and repertory, and composition. And no doubt also Zachow soon passed on some of his routine duties to his talented apprentice: Mainwaring tells of Zachow's 'inclination to be absent ... from his love of company, and a chearful glass'. In the course of the next ten years Handel also seems to have become proficient on the violin (and possibly the oboe), though these probably received less attention than organ and harpsichord. For the important matter of Handel's early experiences as a singer we have no record. The Marienkirche employed a Kantor, Gebhard Riemschneider,[9]

---

[8] See B. Baselt, 'Handel and his Central German Background', p. 46. Baselt's article provides the most accessible account in English of the early musical influences on Handel.

[9] His son, Johann Gottfried, who may have been educated in Halle at the same time as Handel, became a solo bass singer and performed in Handel's opera season of 1729–30.

but, beyond the fact that the liturgical language of the services at the church was German from 1699 onwards, there appears to be no definite record of the nature of the music performed at the services, nor of any duties that Handel might have undertaken with the choir. Zachow's surviving music includes more than 30 German church cantatas, and many more seem to be lost. Their dates of composition and performance cannot be tied to the period of Handel's youth with any certainty, but in 1695 some pietistic members of the council complained about 'the excessively long unedifying and unintelligible performance of elaborate music' in the churches,[10] which shows that something of the sort was to be heard in Halle.

We are on rather firmer ground in our knowledge of the activities of another influential musician, Johann Philipp Krieger, who was organist to the Saxon court from 1677 and later Kapellmeister, living first in Halle and then moving to Weissenfels with the court in 1680. Krieger, brought up in Nuremberg, had received a wide-ranging musical education first in Denmark and then in Italy, where he made contacts with composers such as Cavalli, Ziani, Legrenzi, Carissimi and Pasquini. At Weissenfels Krieger was responsible for performances of many works by Italian and German composers, and his list of his own compositions performed there amounts to more than 2000 pieces, including italianate sacred vocal concertos, German church cantatas,[11] operas, trio sonatas, overture-suites and keyboard music. It seems likely that Handel heard some of Krieger's performances at Weissenfels. At Leipzig, the other urban centre relatively close to Halle, Nikolaus Adam Strungk had the musical direction of the opera house, and Johann Schelle was Director Musices of the principal churches and Kantor of the Thomasschule. Both of these were significant composers and musicians in their generation: Strungk died in 1700 and Schelle in 1701.

Of Handel's musical training, as distinct from the experiences which may in a broader sense have constituted his education, we have only slight hints. Zachow's own compositions show an agreeable mixture of 'Italian' and 'German' influences. On one hand, there are vocal movements using Italian forms (recitative, aria) and styles, displaying operatic influence in the vocal parts and the italianate 'violin' style prominently in the orchestral accompaniments. This Italian influence Zachow had probably received in Leipzig and from Schelle in Eilenburg. On the other hand, there are choruses and keyboard works employing contrapuntal imitation, and several works based round German chorale melodies. Zachow followed in a tradition of Halle organists who had been well trained in imitative techniques: Scheidt had been a pupil of Sweelinck. The French Baroque

---

[10] Baselt, 'Handel and his Central German Background', p. 51.
[11] Some were to texts by the fashionable poet-pastor Erdmann Neumeister, who was in residence at Weissenfels, 1704–6.

influence of Lully and his successors is less apparent in his music. An amiable vignette of Handel's training under Zachow is given by Mainwaring (p. 14):

> The first object of his attention was to ground him thoroughly in the principles of harmony. His next care was to cultivate his imagination, and form his taste. He had a large collection of Italian as well as German music: he shewed him the different styles of different nations; the excellences and defects of each particular author; and, that he might equally advance in the practical part, he frequently gave him subjects to work, and made him copy, and play, and compose in his stead.

This is entirely convincing, and just as we would have expected. Zachow followed a firm grounding in harmony (presumably taught from figured bass) and imitative counterpoint with stylistic analysis and composition:[12] and, like his contemporary Johann Sebastian Bach, Handel absorbed the techniques of stylistic composition by copying out other people's music. He may even have created his own pieces by developing some of the ideas he copied, perhaps laying the foundation for his later 'borrowing' practices.

Mainwaring's report can be supplemented from two other pieces of evidence that originated several decades after the event. Towards the end of his life Handel presented to his friend Bernard Granville a copy of *Anmuthige Clavier-Übung*, a printed collection of keyboard pieces (preludes, fugues, fantasias, toccatas and a chaconne) by Johann Krieger, the younger brother of the Weissenfels Kapellmeister. The collection was printed in 1698, though the pieces were composed somewhat earlier and Handel may have known them first through manuscript copies. Handel's copy of the collection does not survive, but Granville's comment about it does:[13]

> The Printed Book is by one of the celebrated organ-Players of Germany. M[r] Handel in his Youth formed Him Self a good deal on his Plan & said that Krieger was one of the best writers of his time for the Organ, & to form a good Player, but the Clavicord must be made use of by a beginner, instead of organ, or Harpsichord.

One of the common-place books into which the young Handel copied the works of other composers apparently accompanied him to London: its cover bore the date 1698 and Handel's initials. Unfortunately, once again, the book is now lost, but the names of some of the composers represented within were recorded at the end of the eighteenth century: predictably,

---

[12] A general idea of the nature of Handel's training may perhaps be reconstructed from the teaching materials that Handel prepared for his own pupils some 30 years later: see Mann, *Händel: Aufzeichnungen zur Kompositionslehre*.

[13] Granville wrote this on the end of a Handel autograph that he owned, which was presumably bound at the time with the Krieger edition: see Burrows and Ronish, *Catalogue*, p. 267.

they include Zachow and Krieger, but also Strungk, Froberger and Kerll.[14]

On 14 February 1697, shortly before Handel's 12th birthday, his father died. The funeral sermon for Georg Händel was published, and to it was appended a collection of mourning poems, most of them by relatives of his widow. The youngest generation was amply represented: three of the poems came from Johann Georg Taust and Johann Christian Taust (aged six and four respectively) and 'Georg-Friedrich Händel'. Handel's poem, which he signed as 'der freien Künste ergebener' ('dedicated to the liberal arts') consisted of seven four-line verses beginning:[15]

> Ah! bitter grief! my dearest father's heart
> From me by cruel death is torn away.
> Ah! misery! and ah! the bitter smart
> Which seizes me, poor orphan from this day.

The language seems rather extravagant, but it bears comparison with that used when the subject of death is dealt with in many of Bach's cantata texts. Perhaps the literary style is conventional: perhaps the poem was 'ghosted' for Handel by one of his relations. We can only speculate on the effect that Georg Händel's death had on his son. Perhaps the event was so traumatic for the 11-year-old that it produced a psychological insecurity that explains the apparent celibacy of his adulthood. If indeed Mainwaring recorded, however imperfectly, Handel's own feelings about his early years, it is clear that his father was a dominant force in Handel's life. No doubt young George was a favoured child of his father's old age, but according to his tombstone Georg senior lived to see 28 grandchildren and two great-grandchildren, and those must have diluted his emotional impact on his immediate family. Georg Händel had himself been left fatherless at 14 years of age, an event which clearly had not inhibited the development of his own relationships.

Nevertheless, the death of Georg senior must have had practical consequences for the Handel family which may well have put a brake on the son's musical ambitions. The family, no doubt supported by the widow's relations, continued to live in the town house, but resources may have been tight, and there was doubtless every reason to look forward to (and to hasten) the time when the son would be self-supporting and the daughters safely married off. No doubt it seemed prudent to keep young Handel's career options open as long as possible. He enrolled himself as a student at the University of Halle on 10 February 1702, just before his 17th birthday.[16] It is not known which faculty he attended. He may well

---

[14] Coxe, *Anecdotes*, p. 6. All the composers named by Coxe are Germans: 'Alberti' probably refers to Johann Friedrich Alberti, from Merseburg, near Halle.

[15] Deutsch, pp. 6–7; *HHB*, p. 15.

[16] Handel identified his place of origin after his signature as 'Hall Magdeburg', that is, Halle within the archbishopric of Magdeburg. Two other students enrolling the previous month had used the form 'Hallens[is]', that is, 'of Halle'.

have studied law, though this did not necessarily imply the inevitable prospect of a legal career. The fact of his registration at the university reflects that Handel's general education had not been neglected in the course of his musical training: he must have been sufficiently literate to come to terms with the discourse of a lively university community. The church had provided careers on his mother's side of the family, which supplied pastors to several parishes in the Halle region, and it is not surprising that young George was also initiated into Lutheran conformity: he is recorded as taking communion at the Marktkirche for the first time in April 1701, and again at the comparable time in the next two years.

Fortunately Handel's training as an organist enabled him to take a church appointment, which would not conflict with his university studies. A vacancy came up at the Domkirche in 1702, to which he was appointed as organist on 13 March for a probationary year in the first instance. His attendance was required on 'Sundays, Thanksgiving Days and other Feast Days, to play the Organ fittingly at Divine Service, and for this purpose to pre-intone the prescribed Psalms and Spiritual Songs, and to have due care to whatever might be needful to the support of beautiful harmony'.[17] The record of appointment enjoins Handel to arrive at church in good time, to take responsibility for the care and maintenance of the organ, to co-operate with the church officers and to lead a Christian and edifying life. For this post Handel received 50 thalers a year[18] and had the use of free lodgings in the Moritzburg, a fifteenth-century castle[19] that had sadly been depleted from its former splendour by fire during the Thirty Years War. Whether Handel continued to live in the family home we do not know. What is quite clear from the terms of appointment is that orches- trally accompanied cantatas were not regularly required at the Dom, which it will be remembered had a congregation dominated by Huguenot refugees. Nothing seems to be known about the repertory of psalms and hymns whose performance constituted Handel's main musical duty.

As a student who was probably simultaneously pursuing twin goals in law and music Handel was not unique: Georg Philipp Telemann, four years his senior, was in precisely the same situation at Leipzig, where Kuhnau had succeeded Schelle as Director Musices in 1701. Telemann recalled 40 years later that[20]

The writing of the excellent Johann Kuhnau served as a model for me in fugue and counterpoint; but in fashioning melodic movements and examining them

[17] *HHB*, p. 18; Deutsch, p. 9.
[18] The cathedral was a royal church within the 'Erzbistum Magdeburg' (the property of the former Archbishop of Magdeburg, since 1680 administered by Brandenburg-Prussia, and Handel's salary was paid from the Prussian court purse.
[19] The Moritzburg was established by Cardinal Albrecht, Archbishop of Magdeburg, who fled to Mainz when the Reformation reached Halle.
[20] Mattheson, *Grundlage*, p. 359 (in the article on Telemann); *HHB*, p. 17.

Handel and I were constantly occupied, frequently visiting each other as well as writing letters.

Assuming that at least some of their meetings were in Leipzig, Handel probably accompanied Telemann to performances there, at the opera house and possibly at various semi-domestic performances of the university community (Telemann had founded a student 'collegium musicum' in 1702 and became a conductor at the opera house in the same year). By the time he was 18 years old, it seems likely that Handel's musical experiences at Leipzig and Weissenfels had made him dissatisfied with the long-term prospects of a life in Halle and that he felt the need to look at the world that lay beyond the middle-German region. If he were not to stay in Halle, what career opportunities were open to him elsewhere?

One obvious line to investigate was a career with the principal court of Brandenburg-Prussia in Berlin, which was after all the political overlord of the Halle region: the honour that Georg Händel had received from the court could be used to gain an entry there. One of the incidents in Mainwaring's *Memoirs* that has been most puzzling to Handel's biographers is a story (pp. 18–21) of a visit to the Prussian court, where Handel met the Italian composers Giovanni Bononcini and Attilio Ariosti (both of whom were to feature in Handel's later career) and where Georg Händel turned down the offer of a court appointment for his son.[21] On the face of it, a single visit encompassing both of these elements is chronologically impossible: Bononcini and Ariosti were not in Berlin during the period before Georg Händel's death in 1697, though Handel might have met them there in the years just after the turn of the century. Perhaps Mainwaring's account (and Handel's memory) conflated more than one visit: it may also be significant that the story comes at the end of the narrative of Handel's years in Halle, and it is possible that the weak link in Mainwaring's story is not the mention of the Italian composers but the reference to Handel's father. Certainly, from the historical point of view, the wrong part of the story has received too much attention. Mainwaring inflated the importance of Handel's meeting with Bononcini and Ariosti in order to emphasize the impression that the youth's technical expertise made on established professional musicians whose reputations stood high in the world of Italian opera. Handel's contact with that world at first hand was no doubt important in stimulating his own musical ambitions, and these composers were probably the most renowned musicians that Handel had yet met.

But the main point of the story is the embarrassment that was caused by the prospect of a 'successful' outcome to the visit from the career point of view (pp. 23–4):

The King [Frederick, Elector of Brandenburg, who took the title 'King in

---

[21] On p. 18 Mainwaring places the visit in 1698, but Georg Händel died in 1697; in the same passage he says that Handel had a 'friend and relation' at the Berlin court.

Prussia' from 1701] ... frequently sent for him, and made him large presents
... His intention was to send him to Italy, where he might be formed under
the best masters, and have opportunities of hearing and seeing all that was
excellent in the kind. As soon as it was intimated to HANDEL's friends (for he
was yet too young to determine for himself) they deliberated what answer it
would be proper to return, in case this scheme should be proposed in form. It
was the opinion of many that his fortune was already made, and that his
relations would certainly embrace such an offer with the utmost alacrity.
Others, who better understood the temper and spirit of the court at Berlin
thought this a matter of nice speculation, and cautious debate. For they well
knew, that if he once engag'd in the King's service, he must remain in it,
whether he liked it, or not; that if he continued to please, it would be a reason
for not parting with him; and that if he happened to displease, his ruin would
be the certain consequence. To accept an offer of this nature, was the same
thing as to enter into a formal engagement, but how to refuse it was still the
difficulty. At length it was resolved that some excuse must be found.

Having rejected the generosity of his political masters, Handel probably
had no choice but to seek his fortune elsewhere, assuming that he was
not content instead to take on the role of a provincial lawyer, or to wait
for an indefinite period until the posts presently filled by Zachow and
Krieger became vacant.

Here we may pause for a moment to speculate a little on Handel's
character. According to Mainwaring, the final decision to reject the
prospect of a job with the Prussian court was taken by Georg Händel,
and it was surely the correct one. Although both Georg Händel and his
youngest son held various court appointments, they both seem to have
seen themselves as following their professions in a court context, rather
than as servants in the strictest sense: neither in fact seems to have held
any office which demanded a compulsory period of service or 'waiting'.
We may guess that Handel (and many of his 'friends') found the ambience
at Berlin less attractive than that at Weissenfels: the Prussian court
expected German servants to behave like servants. This was no doubt all
the more galling if visiting foreigners, whose technical abilities Handel
probably thought he would be able to match in time, were treated more
like honoured guests. Handel seems to have returned to Halle with both
a desire to retain his independence and a sense of his own importance.
Again Mainwaring's account (pp. 26–7) seems to hit the mark:

> On his return to Hall, he began to feel himself more, to be conscious of his
> own superiority, to discover that spirit of emulation, and passion for fame,
> which urged him strongly to go out into the world, and try what success he
> should have in it. His acquaintance with the eminent masters at Berlin had
> opened his mind to new ideas of excellence, and shewn him in a more extended
> view the perfections of his art. After his friends had refused such offers as the
> King had made him, he never could endure the thought of staying long at
> home, either as a pupil or substitute to his old master ZACKAW. He had heard
> so high a character of the singers and composers of Italy, that his thoughts ran

much on a journey into that country. But this project required a longer purse than he was as yet provided with, and was therefore suspended till such time as it could be compassed without hazard or inconvenience. In the mean while, as his fortune was to depend on his skill in his profession, it was necessary to consider of some place less distant, where he might employ his time to advantage, and be still improving in knowledge and experience. Next to the Opera at Berlin, that of HAMBURGH was in the highest request.

And accordingly it was to Hamburg that he went to seek his fortune. Soon after the completion of his contractual year at the Dom he left Halle, and he was in Hamburg by July of 1703.[22] Possibly he initially made the visit during a summer leave of absence from Halle, but he evidently soon decided that the auguries at Hamburg were good enough for him to sever his previous links with his home city: the Dom appointed a new organist in September. Hamburg was a 'Free City', a longstanding member of the Hanseatic League and without a court. Its power, influence and wealth came from trade, as Germany's foremost port; shipbuilding, too, was a major industry. As such it attracted attention as a cultural and diplomatic centre. The city supported a successful opera company, founded in 1678 (against a certain amount of opposition from Hamburg's religious authorities) by a group of German musicians including Strungk and Johann Theile. The Hamburg churches were, at the turn of the century, about to gain lasting significance for musicians as centres for annual devotional musical performances of the Passion: Telemann, like Handel, was later to find Hamburg more congenial than the Halle-Leipzig axis.

If Handel temporarily lost contact with Telemann at this point by moving to Hamburg, he gained another friend in Johann Mattheson, a tenor soloist and composer at the opera house and Handel's senior by some four years. They apparently met in the organ loft of Hamburg's Marie-Magdalenen-Kirche, both presumably having a curiosity about the instrument (though for us it is hardly the most interesting of the historical instruments in Hamburg). In the summer of 1703 the two young men had several outings together: they took an excursion 'on the water' in Hamburg, and they went off to Lübeck to examine the prospects at the Marienkirche there, where Dietrich Buxtehude was on the point of retiring.[23] The main advantage to the post would have been the residual *cachet* from the reputation that Buxtehude had built up in his performances of organ music and church cantatas: for Handel and Mattheson these were outweighed by other disadvantages – the severance from the opera house that would

[22] Handel is last recorded in the communion lists of the Halle Marktkirche on 6 April 1703. Mattheson's accounts of meeting Handel in the organ loft of the Marienkirche in Hamburg (*Lebensbeschreibung*, p. 22, and *Grundlage*, p. 191) are contradictory, giving the date as 9 June and 9 July, respectively.

[23] Mattheson gives the dates of the water party and the journey to Lübeck as 15 and 30 July 1703 respectively (*Grundlage*, footnote to p. 93): however, in another article he gives 17 August as the date for the Lübeck visit (*Grundlage*, p. 191).

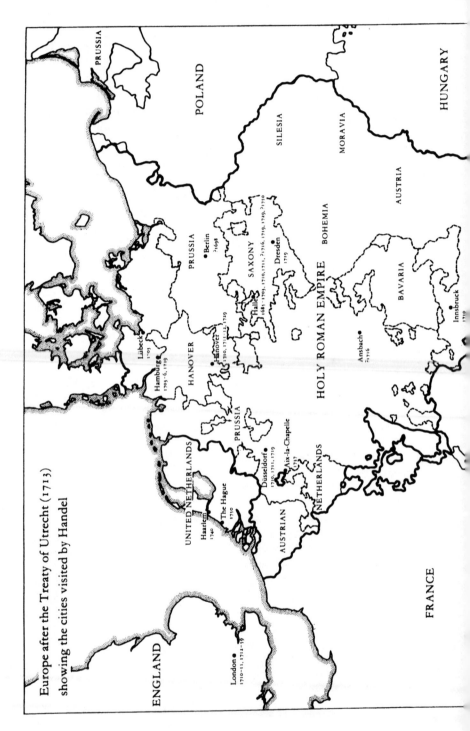

Europe after the Treaty of Utrecht (1713)
showing the cities visited by Handel

ENGLAND

London ●
1710–11, 1712–19

UNITED NETHERLANDS

Haarlem
1740

The Hague
1710

AUSTRIAN
NETHERLANDS

PRUSSIA

Düsseldorf ●
1710, 1711, 1719

Aix-la-Chapelle
1737

Lübeck ●
1703

Hamburg ●
1703–6, 1719

HANOVER

Hanover ●
1710, 1711–12, 1719

PRUSSIA

Berlin ●
?1698

SAXONY

Halle ●
1685–1703, 1710, 1711, ?1716, 1719, 1729, ?1710

Dresden ●
1719

HOLY ROMAN EMPIRE

Ansbach ●
?1716

BOHEMIA

BAVARIA

Innsbruck ●
1710

POLAND

SILESIA

MORAVIA

AUSTRIA

HUNGARY

FRANCE

14

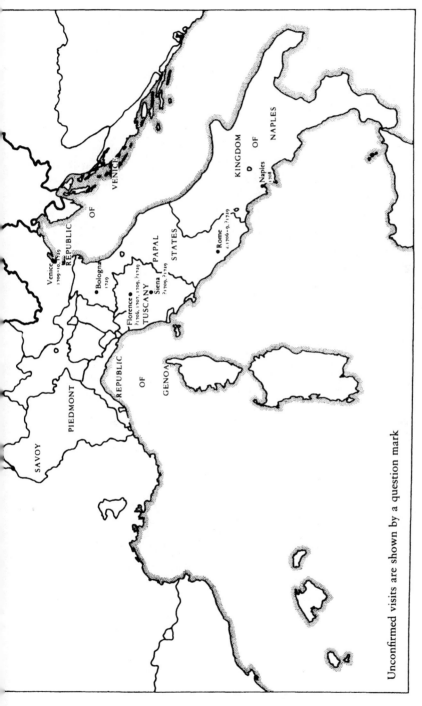

SAVOY

PIEDMONT

REPUBLIC OF GENOA

REPUBLIC OF VENICE

VENICE

Venice
1709-10, 1729

Bologna
1729

Florence ●
?1706, 1707, 1709, ?1729
TUSCANY
Siena
Siena ?1709, ?1729

PAPAL STATES

TUSCANY

● Rome
c.1706-9, ?1729

KINGDOM OF NAPLES

NAPLES

Naples
1708

Unconfirmed visits are shown by a question mark

Fig 2

15

ensue, and the expectation that the successor would marry Buxtehude's daughter.[24]

For details of Handel's life in Hamburg we are indebted to Mattheson, who in later publications included several biographical vignettes of their experiences together. These publications included a German translation of Mainwaring's *Memoirs*, accomplished in Mattheson's 80th year, and including various footnotes of his own amplifying Mainwaring's record. Mattheson's own later historical accounts have to be read in the knowledge that the easy bonhomie of his first encounters with Handel gave way to professional rivalry and a personal estrangement that Handel seems to have been anxious to maintain. Handel's letters written to Mattheson later in life reveal that he wanted to keep their contacts formal and at arm's length, in contrast to the warmth of his continuing correspondence with Telemann, to whom he sent a collection of exotic plants as late as 1750. That Mattheson was sensitive about the coldness that he still received from Handel may be apparent below the surface of passages such as this, published in 1740, which seems to over-emphasize their personal familiarity:[25]

> I know well that he [Handel] will laugh to himself (for he rarely laughs outwardly) when he reads this. Especially if he remembers the pigeon-seller who travelled with us at that time in the post-chaise to Lübeck, or the pastry-cook's son who had to blow the bellows for us when we played the organ in St. Mary Magdalen Church [in Hamburg].

Mattheson also says that during their journey to Lübeck the two musicians passed the time improvising double fugues. While it is true that Mattheson's record of his friendship with Handel is rather self-serving, these rare glimpses of the pranks enjoyed by the youthful Handel probably would not have been preserved at all had it not been for the subsequent imbalance in their relationship.

For Handel's progress in his first opera season in Hamburg, 1703–4, we rely on Mattheson again:[26]

> Handel came to Hamburg in the summer of 1703, rich in ability and goodwill. I was almost the first with whom he made acquaintance. I took him round to all the choirs and organs here, and introduced him to operas and concerts, particularly to a certain house [the English Resident's?] where everything was given up to music. At first he played back-desk violin[27] in the opera orchestra,

---

[24]Buxtehude himself had married a younger daughter of Franz Tunder, his predecessor at the Marienkirche, Lübeck. Schieferdecker, Buxtehude's eventual successor in 1707, did indeed marry his daughter.

[25]*Grundlage*, footnote to p. 93.

[26]*ibid.*, pp.93–4.

[27]Mattheson's phrase is 'die andre Violine', which may also mean 'second violin'; in *Lebensbeschreibung*, p. 29 (a passage in which Mattheson comments on Mainwaring's original text), he describes Handel's position in the orchestra as 'no better than a ripieno player's', saying that he played 'andre oder zwote, doppeltbesetzte Violin'.

and behaved as if he could not count to five, being naturally inclined to a dry humour. But once when the harpsichord player failed to appear he allowed himself to be persuaded to take his place, and showed himself a man – a thing no one had before suspected, save I alone.

At that time he composed very long, long arias, and really interminable cantatas, which had neither the right kind of skill nor taste, though complete in harmony, but the lofty schooling of opera soon trimmed him into other fashions.

He was strong at the organ, stronger than Kuhnau in fugue and counterpoint, especially *ex tempore*, but he knew very little about melody till he came to the Hamburg operas. ...

During that period he went most of the time for free meals at my late father's house, and in return for that he introduced me to some special techniques in counterpoint. Since I rendered him no small service as regards the dramatic style, each hand may be said to have washed the other.

Handel was fortunate in that he came to the Hamburg opera at one of its most successful periods, artistically speaking. The resident manager-composer Reinhard Keiser had a flair for producing the best results from the circumstances of an opera house in a prosperous (though sometimes turbulent), mercantile and cosmopolitan city. Keiser's task was to produce a good night out at the theatre from a diverse collection of elements – a musical mixture of 'high style' Italian arias (of which he was no mean composer) with German recitative and aria, on the basis of librettos whose main plots had to be stretched to accommodate humorous or homely sub-plots and spectacular scenes. The last were reminiscent of the style of French opera, though of course their introduction into the plots had no connection with the French need for scenes designed to flatter the current king. The orchestral resources were also rather French-influenced, with due prominence being given to oboes and bassoons.

Keiser's opera *Claudius*, first produced early in 1703 shortly before Handel's arrival, was the first Hamburg opera to include Italian arias: the following season featured two 'biblical' operas by Keiser, *Salomon* and *Nebucadnezar*,[28] but the season terminated early, for reasons that are not clear but which were probably connected with city politics. Keiser's response was to leave the city: he apparently spent several months in Brunswick and at Weissenfels, where his opera *Almira* was produced for the court in July 1704. Keiser, in fact, had strong connections with Weissenfels: he had been born nearby and his mother still lived in the district (his father had left the family during Keiser's youth). Furthermore, in 1685 Keiser had commenced his education at the Thomasschule, Leipzig. With such connections to the Halle area, it is not fanciful to suggest that Keiser's influence was the critical factor that led Handel to go to Hamburg in the first place: perhaps Handel's initial career move was not so speculative as it appears. As manager and conductor in Hamburg, Keiser

[28] The librettos were by Christian Friedrich Hunold ('Menantes'), from Weissenfels.

would have been the person most responsible for appointments to the opera orchestra.

Handel was concerned about the future of the opera company after Keiser's departure: in March 1704 he wrote to Mattheson (then in Amsterdam), encouraging him to return quickly because 'nothing can be done at the Opera in your absence'.[29] By the time the next season was under way, the 19-year-old Handel seems to have risen from a back-desk violinist to a position as harpsichordist-conductor, and the tone of his letter to Mattheson suggests that he might have been involved in management plans for the opera season. It was but the next logical step that Handel would soon be directing an opera of his own composition. For the first time, however, Handel's ambitions landed him in a power-struggle, though the immediate cause was an argument over precedence at the harpsichord, and it took place before Handel's opera had received its first performance. Here is Mattheson's version of the story:[30]

> On 5 December [1704] ... when my third opera, *Cleopatra*, was being per-
> formed, with Handel at the harpsichord, a misunderstanding arose: such a
> thing is nothing new with young people who strive after honour with all their
> power and very little consideration. I, as composer, directed, and at the same
> time sang the part of Antonius, who, about half-an-hour before the end of the
> play, commits suicide. Now until that occasion I had been accustomed, after
> this action, to go into the orchestra and accompany the rest myself; which
> unquestionably every author can do better than anyone else; this time, however,
> I was prevented [by Handel] from doing this. Incited by several people who
> were present, we fought a duel at the exit of the Opera House, in the open
> market place and with a crowd of onlookers. Things might have passed off
> very unfortunately for both of us, had God's guidance not graciously ordained
> that my blade, thrusting against the broad, metal coat-button of my opponent,
> should be shattered. No harm came of the affair, and through the intervention
> of one of the most eminent councillors in Hamburg, as well as of the manager
> of the Opera House, we were soon reconciled again; and I had the honour, on
> the same day, 30 December, of entertaining Handel to dinner at my place, after
> which we went in the evening to the rehearsal of his *Almira* and became better
> friends than before.

The version in Mainwaring's *Memoirs* (pp. 33–7), which may reflect Handel's perception of the situation, suggests that the real motive for the dispute was rivalry between the two composers for the succession to Keiser as the principal opera-house composer. Mattheson is not named as Handel's duellist in the *Memoirs*, where the account may have been affected by self-censorship (to the point of distortion) on Handel's part, knowing that Mattheson was still alive to read it should it come to publication. In the event, the question of permanent succession to Keiser

[29] The letter was published by Mattheson in *Grundlage*, p. 94; Deutsch, pp. 11–12; *HHB*, p. 22.
[30] *Grundlage*, pp. 94–5.

did not arise: although he was not active during the 1704–5 season (his next Hamburg opera was not performed until August 1705), Keiser afterwards returned to manage the company. The opportunities for Handel's first attempts at opera were perhaps the consequence of the vacuum left in Keiser's absence. Mattheson's last year as a soloist with the Hamburg opera was 1705, and in that year he sang tenor leads in Handel's first two operas: since the Hamburg company had no castratos, the leading male characters were played by (and written for) tenors.

Handel's first opera, *Almira*, came to performance at the Hamburg opera house on 8 January 1705 and ran successfully for about 20 performances: more successfully, one may suspect, than Mattheson's *Cleopatra*, a comparison that may not have improved relations between the two composers. The cast's leading lady, who took the part of Almira, was the soprano Conradin: she is referred to by both Mattheson and Mainwaring as if she were a well-known singer, but little seems to be known about her today. A second opera by Handel, *Nero*, followed hard on the heels of the first, opening on 25 February. It only received three performances before the theatres were closed for the Lenten period. By then, the opera company had once again run into difficulties and, beset by financial problems and an unstable relationship with the Hamburg citizenry, the theatre did not re-open after Easter: the next production was Keiser's *Octavia* in August 1705. No operas by Handel were produced in the 1705–6 season, and it is not even certain whether he took his place in the orchestra pit: he may well have spent the year in other ways, perhaps giving music lessons.

Even though Handel was notable for his speed and fluency as a composer in later years, the proximity of the opening dates of *Almira* and *Nero* suggests that both operas had been composed in 1704: it seems unlikely that the second opera was composed while Handel was still in the midst of the excitement of the opening nights of the first. (We have, of course, also to allow space in the timetable for a period of production rehearsals of *Nero* while *Almira* was running.) In 1723 Mattheson recalled how Handel 'used to bring me his earliest opera scenes every evening for my opinion',[31] and Handel may well have built up a reserve of operatic compositions during 1703–4 when his friendship with Mattheson was at its strongest. Not that Handel was greatly influenced by Mattheson's stylistic preferences, which, as is apparent in the score of his *Cleopatra*, leaned more towards the French operatic style. Handel, on the other hand, followed the more italianate model favoured by Keiser, though including the obvious 'French' elements that were the consequence of the Hamburg opera company's tradition of balletic interludes in the plots. Although Handel's works were not represented in the 1705–6 season at Hamburg, he composed one more opera there. According to its librettist Heinrich

---

[31] *Critica musica* i, p. 243.

Hinsch, it was so excessively long that it had to be split into two, as the separate three-act operas *Florindo* and *Daphne*. Since these operas together contained more than 100 musical numbers, it seems more plausible that Handel planned the work as a 'double' opera from the first: there were precedents in Hamburg for such presentations of linked operas. The turbulent insecurity of the Hamburg opera company during 1706–7 was such that Keiser gave up the unrewarding struggle as manager at Easter 1707, and by then Handel had already left Hamburg. *Florindo* and *Daphne* were produced in January 1708: it is just possible that Handel returned briefly from Italy for the occasion.

As a major port and trading centre, Hamburg was open to the international community, in contrast with the inward-looking German courts where foreign visitors were honoured intruders. Since a trading city has a shifting population of foreign nationals, diplomatic offices for foreign countries necessarily follow. One diplomatic official who probably played a significant part in Handel's life in Hamburg – though the documentary record is sketchy – was John Wych, the Resident representing the British court. In a passage already quoted, Mattheson claimed to have introduced Handel to a series of concerts in a household where 'everything was given up to music': this is very likely to have been Wych's. Handel apparently gave some music lessons to Wych's son during his first months in Hamburg: Mattheson became the boy's tutor and, later, secretary. Some of Handel's 'lost' Hamburg music may well survive in lute arrangements that Lord Danby acquired through the Wych family.[32] It is also likely that through the Wych household Handel made contacts that were later useful in London: influential visiting Englishmen no doubt called at the Wych household in Hamburg (and attended concerts there), and the family was related to the Carterets, at the centre of political life in London.[33]

Of more immediate influence on Handel's career was another foreign visitor to Hamburg, Gian Gastone de' Medici,[34] Prince of Tuscany. We rely on Mainwaring's *Memoirs* (pp. 39–41) for the details:

> The Prince was a great lover of the art for which his country is so renowned. HANDEL's proficiency in it, not only procured him access to his Highness, but occasioned a sort of intimacy betwixt them: they frequently discoursed together on the state of Music in general, and on the merits of Composers, Singers, and

[32] See Crawford, 'Lord Danby's Lute Book'.

[33] John Wych's son Cyril, who succeeded his father as Hamburg Resident, married Anne von Wedderkopp, daughter to the Duke of Holstein's first minister: Mattheson named Wedderkopp senior as the person who invited him to apply for Buxtehude's post in Lübeck.

[34] 1671–1737. Mainwaring (*Memoirs*, p. 39) incorrectly identifies him as Ferdinando de' Medici (1663–1713), Gian Gastone's elder brother, who is not known to have visited Hamburg. Mainwaring also describes him as Grand Duke (of Tuscany), but Gian Gastone did not hold that title during Handel's Hamburg years; he succeeded his father Cosimo III in 1723, his elder brother Ferdinand having died. See Braun, 'Georg Friedrich Handel'.

Performers in particular. The Prince would often lament that HANDEL was not acquainted with those of Italy; shewed him a large collection of Italian Music; and was very desirous he should return with him to Florence. HANDEL plainly confessed that he could see nothing in the Music which answered the high character his Highness had given it. On the contrary, he thought it so very indifferent, that the Singers, he said, must be angels to recommend it. The Prince smiled at the severity of his censure, and added, that there needed nothing but a journey to Italy to reconcile him to the style and taste which prevailed there. He assured him that there was no country in which a young proficient could spend his time to so much advantage; or in which every branch of his profession was cultivated with so much care. HANDEL replied, that if this were so, he was much at a loss to conceive how such great culture should be followed by so little fruit. However, what his Highness had told him, and what he had before heard of the fame of the Italians, would certainly induce him to undertake the journey he had been pleased to recommend, the moment it should be convenient. The Prince then intimated, that if he chose to return with him, no conveniences should be wanting. HANDEL, without intending to accept of the favour designed him, expressed his sense of the honour done him. For he resolved to go to Italy on his own bottom, as soon as he could make a purse for that occasion. This noble spirit of independency, which possessed him almost from his childhood, was never known to forsake him, not even in the most distressful seasons of his life.

The report of Handel's dismissal of Italian music appears to conflict with what Mainwaring says of his education under Zachow: but perhaps, ten years on, Handel felt that he could write music as good as the Italian models that were presented to him.

In Hamburg we may guess that Handel had become confirmed in his ambitions to work in the theatre and to seek a career that would not sink him in some German provincial court. For the moment he wanted to see more of the world. His taste for cosmopolitan experience and for opera naturally led him to Italy: Gian Gastone de' Medici, in recommending a visit to Italy, was only confirming advice that had already been given in Berlin. A rather unhappy period had led to the conclusion of Keiser's management of the opera company in Hamburg, and it was obviously time for Handel to move on. Nevertheless, the prospect of severing links with familiar territory must have brought some apprehension to him. Though he may have met some sympathetic Italians in Berlin and Hamburg, Handel may not yet have become fluent in the Italian language. He would be leaving the Protestant lands where he had been brought up for a Roman Catholic area, and one which furthermore was deeply involved in the War of the Spanish Succession. It is true that by 1706 most of the war's military activity was concentrated on the Low Countries, though the Mediterranean still saw some important naval action. But a large part of Italy, including that over which the papacy had direct influence, was in alliance with the French side of the dispute, and thus in opposition to most of the north German and middle German states. Nevertheless, the musical attractions of Italy outweighed the possible drawbacks. According to Mainwaring (p. 42), Handel had saved 200 ducats, a sufficient purse to embark on the journey 'on his own bottom'. Mainwaring also mentions that this saving was clear of the money that he sent back to Halle for the support of his mother: whatever Handel had been doing in Hamburg during 1705–6, it had not left him impoverished.

2

Italy and Hanover, 1706–10

Handel's time in Italy during 1706–10 saw the forging of his mature musical style, redressing the imbalance between the learned and lyrical aspects that Mattheson had noted in the early Hamburg years. He must have travelled to Italy in 1706 and left in 1710, but the precise dates of neither his arrival nor his departure are known. In Mainwaring's words 'it was his resolution to visit every part of Italy, which was anyway famous for its musical performances' (p. 51), and we know that he was based at various times in Florence, Rome, Naples and Venice. The music that Handel composed in Italy is plentiful, but documentary records, in the way of diary references or musical autographs bearing the date and place of composition, are sparse, and we have to fall back on informed guesswork concerning the places or nature of Handel's activities at some periods. His motivating principles are easy to guess: Handel wanted to be where the music was, and where the patrons were. Mainwaring's account (pp. 49–66) suggests that he spent blocks of time successively in Florence, Venice, Rome and Naples, but it seems more plausible that he travelled more than once between these centres, following the kind of timetable that would take him back to Florence and Venice for their annual opera seasons, in the autumn and winter respectively. Thus he would have the chance to hear as much music as possible, and would achieve the maximum contact with other musicians. In Florence he may have heard operas based on librettos that he himself was to set later,[1] and another at Venice in 1708.[2] Among the composers, he would have met Alessandro and Domenico Scarlatti, Francesco Gasparini and Antonio Lotti.

Mainwaring's suggestion that Handel went first to Florence makes both biographical and geographical sense: he had already received promises of a good reception from Prince Gian Gastone, and Florence lay first on the land route into Italy – assuming, that is, that Handel went over the Alps and not by sea, which might have been as easy a journey at the time. The first fixed place and point on our calendar, however, is Rome on 14

[1] In 1706 Alessandro Scarlatti's *Il gran Tamerlano*, in 1707 Giacomo Perti's *Dionisio* (*Sosarme*), in 1708 Perti's *Ginevra* (*Ariodante*) and in 1709 Perti's *Berenice* (the titles of Handel's operas are given in parentheses where they differ substantially).
[2] Antonio Caldara's *Partenope*.

January 1707, when Francesco Valesio recorded in his diary the presence of a 'Sassone' who was an excellent harpsichord player and composer, and who had been heard playing the organ at the church of St John Lateran.[3] Clearly Handel's professional self-confidence had soon overcome any barriers to his acceptance in Catholic Rome. Mainwaring's account of Handel's dealings with Gian Gastone de' Medici (quoted at the end of Chapter 1) seems to reinforce the suggestion that he was no respecter of persons when it came to discussing music, and he may have treated his patrons with a certain levity. Nevertheless, there was something in Handel's personality that quickly carried him to the top, to the very centres of influence whether in Hamburg, Rome or London. In Rome he not only gained an entrée to the church establishment, but soon secured his position with the leading musical patrons, Cardinals Ottoboni and Pamphili and Marquis Ruspoli. He also probably made contact there with Cardinal Vincenzo Grimani, the Venetian ambassador to Rome. Grimani's power and influence in Rome were at a low ebb, because Venice had taken the opposite side from Rome in the current war, but he was important to Handel: not only was he influential in the Venetian operatic fraternity, but he could make the necessary passport arrangements for Handel's visits to Venice, an important consideration in the complex political turmoil of contemporary Italy. Handel's professional ambitions were such that he needed to keep in good favour with all sides, in order to obtain the diversity of experience that he desired.

In one respect his experience in Rome was limited. Opera there had suffered under a papal ban since 1698; the ban was not lifted until 1709, by which time Handel had gone elsewhere. But the musical style and forms of opera were practised at concert performances, in the secular Italian cantata. Cantatas fell into three broad types. The largest were orchestrally accompanied, with two or three vocal soloists – effectively miniature operas, relating a drama between interacting characters. Other orchestrally accompanied cantatas involved only one singer and might be regarded as equivalent to an operatic *scena*. Continuo-accompanied cantatas for a single singer might also be regarded as dramatic monologues, but the chamber scale of performance must have produced an effect closer to that of the continuo-accompanied instrumental 'solo sonata': indeed, the common structural design of recitative-aria-recitative-aria may be seen as a close parallel to the slow-fast-slow-fast arrangement of movements that was common in sonatas. The Italian preference in cantatas, particularly in Rome, was for texts couched in a fashionable pastoral convention: the soloist in continuo cantatas is almost always a disappointed lover, a 'shepherd' assuming the conventional title of Tirsi or Fileno (these

---

[3] There are two Handel signatures from Rome accompanied by the year '1706', but these were probably written in the early months of 1707 according to the old-style convention, by which the year ended on 25 March. See Hicks, 'Handel's Early Musical Development', p. 83.

roles, with the solo part written in the soprano or alto clef, were presumably sung by castratos). Somewhere between two and four arias produced a piece of about the right length for a continuo-accompanied cantata; orchestrally accompanied cantatas were usually on a much bigger scale and, although the texts were again mainly in the pastoral tradition, they sometimes drew on stories from 'classical' mythology. In these larger cantatas women were included as soloists, a fact more significant than at first appears. At times when opera was allowed in Rome, there was frequently a papal ban on women appearing on the stage in public theatres, where the female roles were played by men, but such regulations could not extend to private concerts or 'academies'.

Unfortunately, contemporary diarists have apparently left no eye-witness accounts of any of these concerts from the period 1707–9, and, since the musical performances in Rome with which Handel was associated were essentially private ones (though they could be on a quite large scale), they were not documented in any public announcements or media reports. But we do know that some of the best singers and orchestral musicians were employed by the Roman patrons, and our best sources of information are the patrons' domestic accounts, which record payments to musicians and, more consistently, to music copyists. (The difference in coverage may have been accounted for because the performers were often retained on a regular salary, in which case individual performances would not be indicated, or because guest soloists sometimes received another form of gratuity, such as jewellery or a snuff-box; copyists, on the other hand, were paid piece-work for each assignment.) The first work of Handel's for which such payment is recorded – in the accounts of Cardinal Pamphili for 12 February 1707 – was an orchestrally accompanied cantata *Il delirio amoroso* (HWV99). There was only one vocal soloist (soprano clef), but the orchestral accompaniment was ambitious for a private performance, including oboe, recorder and strings with violins divided into three parts; one movement includes a rather extravagant violin solo, apparently written for Antonio Montanaro, a pupil of Rome's most famous resident instrumentalist, Arcangelo Corelli.

Pamphili wrote the text of *Il delirio amoroso*, and he was also responsible for the text of Handel's next, more ambitious, musical production, *Il trionfo del Tempo* (HWV46a), for which Pamphili received a copyist's bill in May 1707. As far as we know, this was Handel's first venture into oratorio, but the event can hardly have seemed portentous at the time. The musical component forms of the oratorio – recitative and aria – were familiar to Handel from operas and cantatas, and, in all but the absence of stage action, the work was a two-act opera in which the allegorical characters of Piacere, Disinganno and Tempo (later in Handel's lifetime given English equivalents as Pleasure, [Good] Counsel and Time) play out their conflicting influences on Bellezza (Beauty), who nevertheless rejects Pleasure with a decisiveness that would have been approved by John

25

Calvin. The libretto of *Il trionfo* was the first really extended Italian text that Handel had set, and it seems in retrospect providential that he had this staging-post before meeting the demands of a full three-act opera. As a text for musical setting, Pamphili's libretto is not at all bad, but the cardinal was prone to flights of literary extravagance: nowhere is this more apparent than in a cantata text praising Handel (*Hendel, non può mia musa*, HWV 117), which the composer set to music without being impressed by the attempted flattery[4] (see Plate 1).

Between the dated records for *Il delirio amoroso* and *Il trionfo del Tempo* comes Handel's first dated musical autograph, of a work that provides one of the surprises of his career. At the end of *Dixit Dominus* the composer signed himself 'G. F. Hendel', and recorded the place and time of composition as Rome, April 1707.[5] Georg Friedrich Händel had become Giorgio Federico Hendel (though he signed himself 'G. F. Hendel'), and he retained the form 'Hendel', which is a phonetic Italian equivalent to the German form of his name, throughout the Italian years.[6] Within a few months in Rome Handel had been accepted as a composer of Latin church music for the Roman Catholic liturgy: [7] the work itself shows a complete command of orchestrally accompanied choral writing. *Dixit Dominus*, a setting of Psalm cix,[8] was followed by other similar psalm settings, the D major *Laudate, pueri* (Psalm cxii) and *Nisi Dominus* (Psalm cxxvi), completed on 8 and 13 July 1707, respectively.[9]

From the same period (though the autographs which might have borne composition dates are lost) come some other sacred works of a rather different sort: a brilliant six-movement motet for voice (soprano clef, possibly castrato) and orchestra, *Saeviat tellus inter rigores*; and three cantata-style antiphons for the alto voice and orchestra, *Te decus virgineum*, *Haec est regina virginum* and *Salve regina*. From the text of *Saeviat tellus* it is apparent that the motet has some connection with the Carmelite Order, and a nineteenth-century annotation to a copy of the music links it with services held 'at the expense of the Colonna family' in the church of the Madonna di Monte Santo in the Piazza del Popolo, Rome, on the Festival of Our Lady of Mount Carmel, which was celebrated on 16 July. A set of performing parts, apparently used by Handel himself,

[4]The cantata, which was not included in *HG*, was first published in Handel, ed. Burrows, *Songs and Cantatas for Soprano and Continuo*. For Handel's later recollection of his reaction to Pamphili's text, see Dean, 'Charles Jennens's Marginalia', pp. 163–4.

[5]British Library, RM 20.f.1, f.82*v*.

[6]Probably in Hanover as well. 'Hendel' is also a form often found in London newspaper reports from his early years in London.

[7]The sacred cantata *Donna, che in ciel* (HWV 233) may have been composed in February 1707, in which case it would have preceded *Dixit Dominus*; however, its date is uncertain: see below, n.26.

[8]Handel used the psalm numbers from the Latin Vulgate Bible; for the numbering in the Authorized Version and Book of Common Prayer, add 1.

[9]Handel wrote the date for *Nisi Dominus* at the end of the autograph: this section is now lost, but the information is preserved elsewhere.

links *Saeviat tellus* with *Te decus virgineum*, *Haec est regina virginum* and *Laudate, pueri*, and it seems probable that at least these works were composed for a service of Vespers on the Carmelite festival, 16 July 1707. The other psalm settings, *Dixit Dominus* and *Nisi Dominus*, were also appropriate for Vespers and might have been used on the same occasion, and even *Salve regina* could be squeezed into the liturgy.[10] But the loading of all of these works on to a single occasion is uncertain: *Dixit Dominus* was composed three months earlier, perhaps for a different occasion, while *Salve regina* (which is in a rather different style from the other two antiphons) was composed in the first place for a different patron. Nevertheless, the service of Vespers that Cardinal Colonna mounted to celebrate the Carmelite festival in 1707 must have been a very remarkable occasion. Presumably the soprano-clef solo parts in *Haec est regina virgineum* and *Saeviat tellus* were sung by a castrato, as women would not have been permitted to sing at such a service in Rome: the motet demands a soloist with a top *d'''* and also considerable agility and sustaining power in the area around *a''*.

The 'other patron' mentioned in connection with Handel's *Salve regina* was the Marquis Ruspoli: on 30 June 1707 Ruspoli's accounts record a payment to a music copyist for 'due Motetti' and 'una Salve'.[11] Ruspoli passed the summer on his summer estate at Vignanello, near Rome, and Handel's sacred works for him no doubt had their first performances there, in the church dedicated to St Antony of Padua within the abbey of S. Sebastiano. It seems most likely that Handel's motets *O qualis de coelo sonus* and *Coelestis dum spirat aura* were performed on 12 June (Whit Sunday) and 13 June (the Feast of St Antony of Padua) respectively, and the *Salve regina* on 19 June (Trinity Sunday): all are for soprano-clef voice and strings without viola, and organ continuo. However, sacred motets were not the main area for Ruspoli's musical patronage of Handel. Ruspoli was an enthusiastic member of the 'Arcadian' Academy, a gentlemen's club devoted to the literary pastoral style, and he seems to have had a particular penchant for secular cantatas. He employed a regular team of chamber musicians, ample for performing continuo-accompanied cantatas, and a nucleus around which a small orchestra could be gathered for larger cantatas. (Two of the musicians, the soprano Margherita Durastanti and the violinist Pietro Castrucci, were to join Handel in his London opera company a dozen years later.) Payments to music copyists reveal that Ruspoli had virtually a standing order to Handel for cantatas.[12] From the

---

[10] The evidence concerning the vesper music is summarized in Shaw and Dixon, 'Handel's Vesper Music', and in the prefaces to Handel, ed. Dixon, *Three Antiphons and a Motet*.

[11] The principal Roman copyist associated with Handel's works was Antonio Giuseppe Angelini, named in both Ruspoli's and Pamphili's account-lists. Another copyist named in Pamphili's accounts is Alessandro Ginelli.

[12] The works copied for Ruspoli may well include some composed originally for other Roman patrons.

accounts for May, June, September and October 1707 it appears that 12 continuo-accompanied cantatas and five orchestrally accompanied cantatas were supplied in that year. These include *Clori, Tirsi e Fileno* (HWV96), a large-scale dramatic cantata (in two parts, comprising 17 musical numbers plus recitatives) for three solo voices and an orchestral accompaniment of two recorders, two oboes, archlute and strings, including divided violas. The continuo-accompanied cantatas included two to non-Italian texts: a French cantata (*Sans y penser*, HWV155), cast in the normal form but with concessions to the French musical style as well as to the French language; and a Spanish cantata (*Nò se emenderá jamás*, HWV140), with an obbligato part for guitar and partly written in an old-fashioned form of rhythmic notation. Ruspoli's Sunday afternoon *conversazioni*, at which the cantatas were probably performed, would most likely have received foreign visitors (apart from Handel), and the languages of these unusual cantatas are significant reminders of the papacy's support for the French-Spanish side in the War of the Spanish Succession: there are no cantatas in German, English or Dutch. The performances presumably took place variously at Ruspoli's Bonelli palace in Rome or at Vignanello.

Of Rome's musical patrons, we have least information about Handel's connection with Cardinal Ottoboni, an expatriate Venetian who had taken up residence in Rome because he supported the French-Spanish side of the war. A letter from Rome dated 24 September 1707 describing the activities of a young prodigy mentions that 'the famous Saxon ... has heard him in the Casa Ottoboni and in the Casa Colonna has played with him'.[13] Mainwaring probably gives too much prominence to Ottoboni's role in Handel's Roman career (by contrast, he does not mention Ruspoli at all) but, in connection with Ottoboni's patronage of Corelli, he gives one anecdote (pp. 56–7) that cannot be omitted:

Among his [Handel's] greatest admirers was the Cardinal OTTOBONI, a person of a refined taste, and princely magnificence. Besides a fine collection of pictures and statues, he had a large library of Music, and an excellent band of performers, which he kept in constant pay. The illustrious CORELLI played the first violin, and had apartments in the Cardinal's palace. It was a customary thing with his eminence to have performances of Operas, Oratorios, and such other grand compositions, as could from time to time be procured. HANDEL was desired to furnish his quota; and there was always such a greatness and superiority in the pieces composed by him, as rendered those of the best masters comparatively little and insignificant. There was also something in his manner so very different from what the Italians had been used to, that those who were seldom or never at a loss in performing any other Music, were frequently puzzled how to execute his. CORELLI himself complained of the difficulty he found in playing his Overtures. Indeed there was in the whole cast of these compositions, but especially in the opening of them, such a degree of fire and force, as never could consort with the mild graces, and placid elegancies of a genius so totally

[13] *HHB*, p. 31; Eng. trans. from Streatfeild, *Handel*, p. 33.

dissimilar. Several fruitless attempts HANDEL had one day made to instruct him in the manner of executing these spirited passages. Piqued at the tameness with which he still played them, he snatches the instrument out of his hand; and, to convince him how little he understood them, played the passages himself. But CORELLI, who was a person of great modesty and meekness, wanted no conviction of this sort; for he ingenuously declared that he did not understand them; *i.e.* knew not how to execute them properly, and give them the strength and expression they required. When HANDEL appeared impatient, *Ma, caro Sassone* (said he) *questa Musica è nel stylo Francese di ch'io non m'intendo* ['But, dear Saxon, this music is in the French style which I don't understand'].

As a footnote Mainwaring adds:

The Overture for IL TRIONFO DEL TEMPO was that which occasioned CORELLI the greatest difficulty. At his desire therefore he made a symphony in the room of it, more in the Italian style.

The fact that *Il trionfo* was produced under the patronage of Cardinal Pamphili need not devalue the anecdote; no doubt Corelli's relationship with Ottoboni was not an exclusive one. In any case, Mainwaring does not say specifically that the anecdote describing Handel snatching the violin from Corelli's hands occurred at a rehearsal for *Il trionfo*: the incident may have taken place on some other occasion. Corelli's presence may have given Ottoboni's musical 'academies' an emphasis on instrumental music, and works such as the *Sonata a 5* for violin and orchestra (HWV288) may possibly have been composed for such an occasion. It has also been suggested that the orchestrally accompanied cantata *Ero e Leandro* (HWV150) may have been associated with Ottoboni – and, indeed, that he may have been responsible for the text.

The last music copyist's payment of Ruspoli's from 1707 that unquestionably refers to Handel's music is dated 22 September,[14] and the letter mentioning Handel's attendance at the concerts of Colonna and Ottoboni is dated two days later: assuming that Handel was still in Rome then, the period of his first Roman residence – at least nine months – was substantial. Indeed, in spite of the drawbacks arising from the lack of opera performances, Handel spent longer in Rome during his Italian visit than in any other centre. But by the autumn of 1707 Handel's attention was moving elsewhere. He had probably received promises from Gian Gastone de' Medici, either in Hamburg or in Florence, that Florence should see a performance of a Handel opera. The period of the Florentine opera season of 1707 was now approaching, and for it Handel composed his first all-Italian opera, *Rodrigo*. It seems fairly certain that most of the initial composition took place in Rome, where Handel must have already had a copy of the libretto to hand: in Florence, he then only had to make

[14] Another, dated 14 October, may also relate to Handel's music; both probably refer back to work done during July and August.

the necessary revisions to put the show on the stage. He was in Florence by 19 October when, almost predictably, his harpsichord playing gained the attention of a contemporary correspondent.[15] The dates of the performances are not documented, but they probably took place during November and December 1707. The theatre that mounted *Rodrigo* was not the Pratolino court theatre (whose programme was already committed to the works of Alessandro Scarlatti and Perti, composers who had served the Medici family for several years) but the 'city' theatre, the Teatro Civico Accademico in the Via del Cocomero.

It seems symbolically appropriate that the first Italian opera by one of the greatest Baroque opera composers should have taken place in the city which had seen the creation of opera itself at the hands of the Camerata just over a century before. Unfortunately, we know nothing about how *Rodrigo* was received: it might just have been seen as a routine repertory piece and accorded a polite reception. Even Mainwaring (p. 50) had transparently to resort to guesswork on this subject:

> At the age of eighteen [*recte*, 22] he made the Opera of RODRIGO, for which he was presented with 100 sequins, and a service of plate. This may serve for a sufficient testimony of its favourable reception.

Mainwaring's information may have been limited by the fact that apparently none of the leading musicians that performed in *Rodrigo* re-entered Handel's career in London, so the composer's memory was not stirred by any later reinforcing stimulus.

However, Mainwaring did pick up the scent of the only rumour of a sexual liaison during Handel's career for which there is sufficient evidence to deserve serious consideration (pp. 50–1):

> VITTORIA, who was much admired both as an Actress, and a Singer, bore a principal part in this Opera. She was a fine woman, and had for some time been much in the good graces of his Serene Highness. But, from the natural restlessness of certain hearts, so little sensible was she of her exalted situation, that she conceived a design of transferring her affections to another person. HANDEL's youth and comeliness, joined with his fame and abilities in Music, had made impressions on her heart. Tho' she had the art to conceal them for the present, she had not perhaps the power, certainly not the intention, to efface them.

In June 1710 the Electress of Hanover reported Handel's arrival at her court with the comments that 'he is quite a handsome man', and 'rumour has it that he has been the lover of Victoria'.[16] The soprano Vittoria Tarquini did not perform in *Rodrigo*, but she was engaged at the Pratolino

[15] Letter from Antonio Maria Salviati to Pier Antonio Gerini, 19 October 1707: see Vitali and Furnari, 'Händels Italienreise', p. 62.

[16] *HHB*, p. 45 (14 June 1710); see Burrows, 'Handel and Hanover', p. 39. Vittoria Tarquini was the wife of the Hanover Konzertmeister Jean-Baptiste Farinel, whom she had married in 1689.

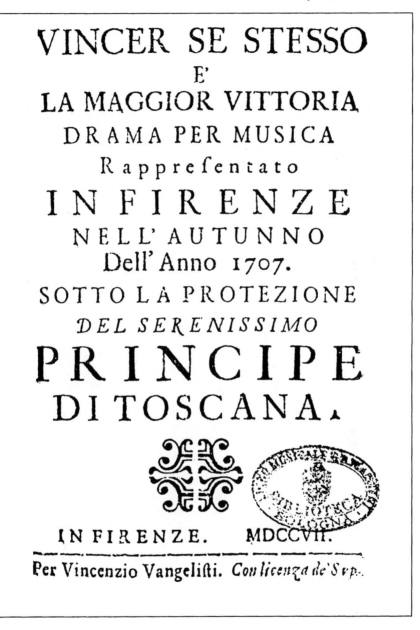

Fig. 3 Title-page of the printed word-book for Handel's first opera in Italy: *Rodrigo* (*Vincer se stesso*), Florence, 1707

theatre: as has already been noted, the fact that Handel later set librettos from the Pratolino productions of the period is strong circumstantial evidence that he took an interest in attending the performances there.

From Florence Handel may have moved on at the end of 1707 to the carnival season in Venice, and this may have been the occasion behind another of Mainwaring's anecdotes (pp.51–2):

> VENICE was his next resort. He was first discovered there at a Masquerade, while he was playing on a harpsichord in his visor. SCARLATTI happened to be there, and affirmed that it could be no one but the famous Saxon, or the devil. Being thus detected, he was strongly importuned to compose an Opera. But there was so little prospect of either honour or advantage from such an undertaking, that he was very unwilling to engage in it.

Two years later, Handel successfully engaged with Venetian opera. It is not clear which of the Scarlattis Mainwaring is referring to in this passage, though on the face of it Alessandro seems to be implied. However, he does link Handel with the younger Scarlatti in Rome (pp.59–60):

> When he came first into Italy, the masters in greatest esteem were ALLESANDRO SCARLATTI, GASPARINI and LOTTI. The first of these he became acquainted with at Cardinal OTTOBONI's. Here also he became known to DOMINICO SCARLATTI, now living in Spain, and author of the celebrated lessons. As he was an exquisite player on the harpsichord, the Cardinal was resolved to bring him and HANDEL together for a trial of skill. The issue of the trial on the harpsichord hath been differently reported. It has been said that some gave the preference to SCARLATTI. However, when they came to the Organ there was not the least pretence for doubting to which of them it belonged. SCARLATTI himself declared the superiority of his antagonist, and owned ingenuously, that till he had heard him upon this instrument, he had no conception of its powers. So greatly was he struck with his peculiar method of playing, that he followed him all over Italy, and was never so happy as when he was with him.

This story was probably rather inflated under the influence of the fashion for Domenico Scarlatti's music that grew in London in the later 1730s, but at least one feature of the story is consonant with other evidence: Mattheson's account of their joint visit to Lübeck suggests that Handel excelled on the organ while Mattheson made a better showing at the harpsichord. Unfortunately, Handel left little to show for this renowned facility, but some of the meagre evidence comes from 'Roman' works. Both *Il trionfo* and the *Salve regina* include movements with concertante organ parts. Pamphili's texts for the aria and recitative that followed the 'organ sonata' in *Il trionfo* seem to refer directly to Handel's organ playing:[17]

---

[17] The translation, by George Oldmixon, is taken from the printed word-book to the 1737 version of *Il trionfo*: the Italian text survived the 30-year transition, though not to the same music.

A youth with more than Magic Might,
The Souls awakens to Delight,
  With his harmonious strains.
And as his Bloom inchants the Eye,
The Hearing, by his Harmony,
  Its share of Pleassure gains.
His artful Fingers seem to fly,
So well the Sounds his Touch obey,
'Tis more than Mortal Harmony.

Perhaps Handel's Italian was not sufficiently fluent in 1707 for him to be embarrassed by the extent of Pamphili's flattery. But Pamphili's reaction was not unique: the report of Handel's organ playing at St John Lateran in February 1707 said that he played to the amazement of everyone ('con stupore di tutti'). Nevertheless, it is a pity that there remains little evidence, beyond the sonata in *Il trionfo*, of Handel's talent as a keyboard player at this period: no other surviving solo keyboard music can be firmly dated to this period to feed our imaginations about the nature of his improvisations.[18]

Handel returned to Rome in the early months of 1708: on his autograph of the cantata *Lungi dal mio bel nume* (HWV127a) he conveniently provided the place and date of completion – Rome, 3 March 1708.[19] No doubt this cantata was composed for Ruspoli, who was undoubtedly Handel's principal Roman patron during 1708:[20] in that year Ruspoli's household accounts even record payments for Handel's bed and board (we do not know who had supported his physical necessities in Rome the previous year). The chief composition from the period was an oratorio, on a larger scale than *Il trionfo* and composed for Ruspoli: *La Resurrezione*. This was first performed on Easter Sunday 1708, at Ruspoli's Bonelli palace in Rome, following a performance at Ottoboni's the previous Wednesday of an Italian passion-oratorio by Alessandro Scarlatti to a text by Ottoboni. Earlier in Lent another oratorio, dealing with the martyrdom of St Catherine, had been performed under Ottoboni's patronage. Its composer, Antonio Caldara, probably had some contact with Handel: in the longer term, he succeeded Handel as Ruspoli's most important musician, taking up the formal post of *maestro di cappella* in July 1709.

Fortunately, the records of the Ruspoli household give us an unusually detailed picture of the circumstances under which *La Resurrezione* was

---

[18] The Allemande in A (HWV477), ascribed to the period in Best, 'Handel's Harpsichord Music', p. 174, is now known to date from *c.* 1724–6. The sonatas HWV579 and 580 may date from Hanover or from Handel's early London years: their earliest sources are non-Italian and date from the period after 1720.

[19] British Library, Add. 30310, f.2*r*.

[20] *Il trionfo* was revived at Pamphili's expense in March 1708 (see *HHB*, p. 33, 27 March 1708), but perhaps not with Handel's participation: indeed, it may have included a new overture by Cesarini. Similar revivals may have followed during Lent and summer 1709.

produced.[21] Although stage acting was not allowed, the hall where *La Resurrezione* was performed was decorated with a stage setting incorporating elaborate painted backcloths depicting scenes from the story. The performance enjoyed the luxury of three full rehearsals, and the orchestra was substantial: Ruspoli's accounts cover 21 violins (led by Corelli), four violettas, five cellos, five double basses, two trumpets, four oboes and a trombone.[22] Handel's score also calls for various other instruments: a flute and two recorders (probably doubled by the oboe players), a bassoon and a viola da gamba (this player may have doubled on another orchestral string instrument, or perhaps he was one of the regular domestic musicians and did not feature in the accounts). Five good singers were employed, but one attracted a certain amount of controversy: the soprano Durastanti sang the role of Mary Magdalene, and thereby earned Ruspoli a papal rebuke for allowing a woman to take part in the performance. A castrato was hastily engaged to take her part for a repeat performance on Easter Monday: the soprano roles of Mary Cleophas and the Angel were already taken by castratos. Ruspoli had 1500 copies of the libretto printed, so the oratorio presumably attracted as large an audience as a couple of nights of full houses at the opera. The text was by Carlo Sigismondo Capece (1652–1728), the court poet to Queen Maria Casimira of Poland who was living in exile in Rome.

Handel seems to have spent most of 1708 in Rome, possibly until as late as November, after which we may guess that he went to Florence (and possibly Venice) for the winter opera season, though there is no certain evidence for this. The year was, however, broken up by one expedition southwards, to Naples in June and July. There he composed the extended dramatic cantata *Aci, Galatea e Polifemo* (HWV72), for the wedding of the Duke of Alvito, and the vocal trio with continuo accompaniment *Se tu non lasci amore* (HWV201).[23] The wedding cantata was probably instigated by the bride's aunt, Aurora Sanseverino, the wife of the Duke of Laurenzano.[24] *Aci, Galatea e Polifemo* is a totally different version of Ovid's story, both in text and music, from the one that Handel set ten years later in England. Handel's music for Polifemo reveals that in Naples he had the services of a bass singer of remarkable range and vocal agility: the cantatas *Cuopre tal volta* (HWV98) and *Nell'africane selve* (HWV136a) may well have been composed for the same singer. Cantatas

[21] See Kirkendale, 'The Ruspoli Documents on Handel', pp. 233–9, 256–64.

[22] No trombone is mentioned in Handel's score, but one was regularly used to support the orchestral bass line (in movements involving trumpets) in the oratorios of this period. The player may have doubled on bassoon, or the bassoon (required only in one aria) may have been doubled by one of the oboe players.

[23] The autographs are dated on completion 16 June (British Library, Egerton 2953, f.101*v*) and 12 July (Basle, Floersheim Collection, f.15*r*), respectively.

[24] See Vitali and Furnari, 'Handel's Italienreise': the identification of this patroness (who appears in Mainwaring, *Memoirs*, p. 66, as 'Donna Laura') is based on her activities in relation to two weddings in the Naples area in 1711 and 1713 at which Handel's 'serenata' was revived.

were still in demand in Rome as well. In August 1708 Ruspoli faced two substantial music copying bills, in which some of the items seem to be second copies of cantatas already performed the previous year: perhaps a new copy was a standard perquisite for music copyists (the equivalent of a modern repeat fee for performers). In the course of the year Handel travelled between both camps of the European war. The Duke of Alvito supported the emperor, and indeed Naples had passed from Spanish to Austrian control during 1707. On the other side, Ruspoli himself was involved as the leader of a mercenary expedition against the Habsburgs in 1708: Handel's cantatas *O come chiare e belle* (HWV143) and *Mentre il tutto è in furore* (HWV130) seem to make specific reference to Ruspoli and the pope as protectors of Rome, the former cantata casting Ruspoli in the uncomfortably combined role of a shepherd-warrior.

We lose sight of Handel for most of 1709, but he was probably in Rome by the late summer.[25] It is remarkable that Handel appears never to have seriously followed up the magnificent church music that he produced in Rome in 1707. Only one work, the sacred cantata *Donna che in ciel* (HWV233), appears to fall outside the main body of the Latin and Italian church music from that year. Its text seems to refer to the deliverance of Rome from an earthquake on 2 February 1703, and it might have been performed on the anniversary of that date in 1709; but it has also been suggested that it might have been given in 1707, in which case it would have preceded even *Dixit Dominus*.[26] During 1709 the output of secular cantatas from Handel, composed and performed, continued unabated: Ruspoli's last Handelian copying bill, from the last day of August 1709, lists 21 continuo-accompanied cantatas, ten of which were 'repeats'.

Not long after the date of that account Handel probably headed north, presumably to Florence and eventually to Venice. He must have decided that, for the moment, his career in Rome had finished. Perhaps he had learnt all that he wanted to there, and he may have decided that, in the long term, he needed to seek out a career in some place that combined Italy's musical excellences with a culture more similar to that in which he had been brought up. Perhaps, in the end, religious culture also was significant (Mainwaring, pp. 64–5):

> As he was familiar with so many of the Sacred Order, and of a persuasion so totally repugnant to theirs, it is natural to imagine that some of them would expostulate with him on that subject. For how could these good catholicks be supposed to bear him any real regard, without endeavouring to lead him out of the road to damnation? Being pressed very closely on this article by one of

[25] The evidence for Handel's composition of *Giunta l'ora fatal* (HWV234, but spurious) for performance at Siena on Good Friday 1709 (see *HHB*, p. 41, 29 March 1709) is now discredited.

[26] See Hicks, 'Handel's Early Musical Development', pp. 87–8. The cantata might have been commissioned by Colonna. Its musical style and the involvement of the copyist Angelini slightly favour the earlier date.

these exalted Ecclesiastics, he replied, that he was neither qualified, nor disposed to enter into enquiries of this sort, but was resolved to die a member of that communion, whether true or false, in which he was born and bred. No hopes appearing of a real conversion, the next attempt was to win him over to outward conformity. But neither arguments, nor offers had any effect, unless it were that of confirming him still more in the principles of Protestantism. These applications were made only by a few persons. The generality looked upon him as a man of honest, though mistaken principles, and therefore concluded that he would not easily be induced to change them.

Conceivably, some attempted pressure for 'conversion' to Catholicism might have accompanied an offer to Handel of a permanent job in Rome that would have entailed the regular provision of church music. Perhaps we do not have to take Mainwaring's words too seriously: they were, after all, projected to a readership of good Anglicans. But the lifelong influence on Handel of his mother's strongly Lutheran side of the family, with its plentiful pastors, should not be underestimated: Mainwaring's last sentence seems entirely in accord with Handel's apparently uncomplicated acceptance of the religious outlook of his family.

We may assume, though again not on any very firm evidence,[27] that Handel spent part of the autumn in Florence, but his most important destination was Venice. Here at last he was able to see another opera on to the stage. In view of the political situation, it might not have been diplomatic hitherto to accept a commission from an opera house in the powerful city that so obviously took the opposing side to Rome's in the war: but now such considerations were irrelevant, as Handel was not planning to return to Rome again. The consequence was *Agrippina*, Handel's second Italian opera and, as far as such judgments may be attempted with any degree of objectivity, his first operatic masterpiece. Even allowing for some exaggeration, Mainwaring's report (pp.52–3) no doubt reflects the good reception accorded to the opera:

> ... in three weeks he finished his AGRIPPINA, which was performed twenty-seven nights successively; and in a theatre which had been shut up for a long time, notwithstanding there were two other opera-houses open at the same time; at one of which GASPARINI presided, as LOTTI did at the other. The audience was so enchanted with this performance, that a stranger who should have seen the manner in which they were affected, would have imagined they had all been distracted.
>
> The theatre, at almost every pause, resounded with shouts and acclamations of *viva il caro Sassone!* and other expressions of approbation too extravagant to be mentioned. They were thunderstruck with the grandeur and sublimity of his stile: for never had they known till then all the powers of harmony and modulation so closely arrayed, and so forcibly combined.

The libretto of *Agrippina* was by Cardinal Grimani, whom Handel had

[27] Ferdinando de' Medici's letter of 9 November 1709 (*HHB*, p. 43) does not necessarily imply that Handel was then in Florence.

almost certainly met first in Rome. From 1708 Grimani was Viceroy of
Naples, and may have arranged a passport for Handel's visit there in
1708. But Grimani's real centre of influence was in his native Venice. As
an operatic centre, Venice was well worth the conquest for Handel: not
only was there a lively tradition of opera performances, but the city itself
was, by virtue of its importance as a trading centre, a magnet for foreign
visitors and diplomatic activity, on a scale that exceeded Hamburg and
even Rome. The world came to Venice, and maintained boxes at the
opera houses. *Agrippina* was probably composed in December 1709: it
was presented at the S. Giovanni Grisostomo theatre, which Grimani
owned (Plate 2), as the second opera of the autumn-winter season, and
the first of the carnival season, which traditionally began on 26 December.
The cast, with eight important principal roles, included some singers who
featured elsewhere in Handel's career. The role of Agrippina was taken
by Durastanti, already a colleague from Rome and later to re-appear in
London: at some later performances her place seems to have been taken
by Elena Croce, who also had a subsequent career in London, as did the
bass Giuseppe Maria Boschi, who played the part of Pallante.

Though not a member of the cast, one other singer features in Mainwaring's account (pp.53–4) of *Agrippina*:

> This Opera drew over all the best singers from the other houses. Among the
> foremost of these was the famous VITTORIA, who a little before HANDEL's
> removal to Venice had obtained permission of the grand Duke to sing in one
> of the houses there. At AGRIPPINA her inclinations gave new lustre to her
> talents. HANDEL seemed almost as great and majestic as APOLLO, and it was
> far from the lady's intention to be so cruel and obstinate as DAPHNE.

It is a singular coincidence – unless Mainwaring knew more than seems
possible – that Handel seems to have begun an orchestrally accompanied
dramatic cantata on the subject of Apollo and Daphne at Venice (*La terra
è liberata*, HWV122). It is also possible that Handel composed some Italian
continuo-accompanied cantatas and duets there, though the circumstantial
evidence for this is based on the 'north Italian' paper types of the
autographs, which might also have been available in Florence.

Presumably Handel stayed long enough in Venice to see his opera enjoy
a good run of performances, but we may guess that by mid-February 1710
he was a psychological, if not an actual, absentee from Italy. His journey
northwards from Rome to Venice had been only the start of a longer
northward journey back to Germany. Since Venice was a meeting-place for
political and diplomatic representatives of both 'northern' and 'southern'
Europe, with many regular German residents and visitors, Handel no
doubt prepared the way for his return to Germany there. However, it is
unlikely that his return was a sudden whim originating at the end of 1709:
if he had indeed visited Venice at carnival time in either or both of the
previous seasons, then he would doubtless have formed some useful

contacts and kept himself informed of likely openings. Among the people who, metaphorically speaking, exchanged calling-cards with Handel were the British ambassador in Venice (Charles Montagu, Earl of Manchester) and two representatives from the court of Hanover – Prince Ernst, the elector's younger brother, and Baron Kielmansegge, the elector's deputy Master of the Horse.[28] Both countries maintained strong contacts with Venice: the Hanover court even retained permanent boxes at the opera.[29] Handel chose Hanover as the most promising German centre for immediate investigation: he had arrived there by the beginning of June 1710 and was appointed Kapellmeister to the elector on the 16th of that month. Handel's path between Venice and Hanover is not well documented, and perhaps he made some detours for social reasons or to prospect for job opportunities. He travelled back to Germany via Innsbruck: a letter from Prince Karl of Innsbruck to Ferdinando de' Medici reveals that Handel had left that city by 9 March. He may have paid a visit to his family in Halle, where changes had certainly taken place. His elder sister had in September 1708 married Michael Michaelsen, a doctor of law and a Halle resident who held a court office with Brandenburg-Prussia[30] (see Fig.1*b*). Sadly, his other sister had died at Halle in July 1709.

Mention has already been made of one of the letters in which the Electress Sophia refers to Handel's arrival in Hanover. The first letter, dated 4 June 1710, reveals that no definite appointment at the court had been made in advance on the basis of contacts made in Italy:[31]

> I go almost every day to see our Electoral Princess. ... She is entertained by the music of a Saxon who surpasses everyone who has ever been heard in harpsichord-playing and composition. He was much admired in Italy. He is very suitable to become Kapellmeister: if the King took him on, his music would be in better shape than it is at present. He is going to Düsseldorf to compose an opera there.

Ten days later Sophia was able to report that the appointment had been made: in fact the news seems to have been so significant that she referred to it in letters two days running:

> 14 June 1710
>
> There is not much news from here except that the Elector has taken on a Kapellmeister named Hendel, who plays marvellously on the harpsichord, which gives the Electoral Prince and Princess much pleasure.

[28] On Kielmansegge's relationship to the electoral family, see below, Chapter 4, n.1.

[29] This practice continued even after the elector became King of Great Britain: see Timms, 'George I's Venetian Palace and Theatre Boxes in the 1720s'.

[30] Michaelsen eventually became a Prussian war councillor; he died in 1748 while a hostage for the Prussian side in the War of the Austrian Succession.

[31] The letters appear with English translations of the complete relevant passages in Burrows, 'Handel and Hanover', p. 39; the translations have been slightly revised here. The electress was at Herrenhausen, the summer palace about two miles from Hanover.

15 June 1710

The Elector has taken into his service Henling [*sic*], who plays the harpsichord so well and who is (so they say) so clever in music. The Electoral Prince and Princess are charmed with him and delighted that the Elector has kept him. For myself, I don't take much interest: since I lost my daughter, the late Queen, music makes me melancholy.

All three letters were addressed to Sophia's grand-daughter, Sophia Dorothea, daughter-in-law of Friedrich, King in Prussia: the Electress Sophia's daughter (the 'late Queen') was Sophia Charlotte, Friedrich's second wife (the houses of Hanover and Prussia thus intermarried in two successive generations; see Appendix D). It is ironic that the electress was in the first letter apparently recommending to the King in Prussia for the post of Kapellmeister someone who had already turned down the privilege of an appointment at the Prussian court and, indeed, someone who was already a Prussian subject. It is noteworthy that Handel apparently presented himself at Hanover as a Saxon, and used the Italian form of his name. The latter seems to have confused the electress, since she could not remember the correct form on consecutive days.

Court power at Hanover was in the hands of Georg Ludwig, the elector, and a certain influence remained with his mother, the Dowager-Electress Sophia, but Handel appears to have formed a stronger immediate bond with his own generation: the electoral prince Georg August and his wife Caroline were only two years older than Handel. Circumstantial evidence is strong that Caroline had a genuine interest in music, and developed into one of Handel's most important supporter-patrons. No doubt she was influential in making sure that Hanover secured Handel's services. Another powerful voice in Handel's favour might have been Agostino Steffani, the Hanoverian court's leading musician in the 1690s, who had subsequently followed an ecclesiastical career and, as Bishop of Spiga, was by 1710 attempting to extend the influence of the Roman Catholic church in the Hanover area. According to Mainwaring (pp. 69–70), Handel had already met Steffani in Italy,[32] and Steffani features in the recollections that, some 65 years later, John Hawkins claimed to have received from Handel himself:[33]

'When I first arrived at Hanover I was a young man, under twenty; I was acquainted with the merits of Steffani, and he had heard of me. I understood somewhat of music, and', putting forth both his broad hands, and extending his fingers, 'could play pretty well on the organ; he received me with great kindness, and took an early opportunity to introduce me to the princess Sophia and the elector's son, giving them to understand that I was what he was pleased to call a virtuoso in music; he obliged me with instructions for my conduct and behaviour during my residence at Hanover; and being called from the city to

---

[32] Mainwaring's subsequent statement (pp. 72–3) that Steffani resigned the post of Kapellmeister at Hanover in order to 'oblige' Handel is, however, incorrect.

[33] Hawkins, *A General History*, ii, 857–8.

attend to matters of a public concern, he left me in possession of that favour and patronage which himself had enjoyed for a series of years.'

The office of Kapellmeister at Hanover appears to have been specially revived for Handel. It had in the past been associated with duties as a composer for the court opera. Steffani had been appointed Kapellmeister in 1688 and had produced a succession of fine operas in Hanover: on his retirement from the post in 1696 he was succeeded by Pietro Torri, but Torri's period of tenure was short because the opera company was suspended on the death of the Elector Ernst August in 1698, and the post of Kapellmeister fell with it. The reason for the sudden decline in operatic enterprise in 1698 was simple, and had nothing to do with the tastes of the new elector, Georg Ludwig: the opera company had been funded from the income from the bishopric of Osnabrück, which reverted after Ernst August's death to the Roman Catholic side of the family.[34] With an expensive European war to fight during the next decade, there was no alternative source of money in the Hanover budget for revival of the opera, and it was still in abeyance in 1710. Whether Handel's appointment was related to some long-term scheme for the revival of the Hanover court opera is not known.[35] As far as we can tell, his duties were light, and probably seasonal: his services were presumably not required, for example, during the court's regular and extended annual visits to the hunting-lodge at Göhrde. He was probably expected to continue to entertain the court as a keyboard virtuoso. The court employed a regular staff of about 16 instrumentalists, managed by the Konzertmeister, Jean-Baptiste Farinel; Handel may well have composed some music for the full ensemble or chamber music for the 'Französischen' musicians, who were presumably the best players.[36]

One area of Handel's music is specifically associated with Hanover by Mainwaring (p. 85):

Soon after his return to Hanover [i.e. after Handel's first visit to London in 1710–11] he made twelve chamber Duettos for the practice of the late Queen, then electoral Princess. The character of these is well known to the judges in Music. The words for them were written by the Abbate MAURO HORTENSIO: who had not disdained on other occasions to minister to the masters of harmony.

[34] See Hatton, *George I*, p. 21, and p. 364 n.53.

[35] The bishopric of Osnabrück reverted to the Protestant side of the Electoral family in 1715, but by then the elector was in London as King of Great Britain and there was probably little incentive to revive the court opera.

[36] The 'Französischen' musicians were the best-paid players: it is not clear whether they were the leading string players or woodwind soloists. The Hanover Konzertmeister Farinel came from a French musical family but used an Italian form of his name, Farinelli, which was also adopted by the later famous castrato.

Besides these Duettos (a species of composition of which the Princess and court were particularly fond) he composed [a] variety of other things for voices and instruments.

The association of a group of Handel's Italian duets with Hanover is plausible because Mainwaring's account draws convincing links with the personalities involved: the electoral princess may well have developed a taste for that kind of music,[37] and Mauro the poet was resident near Hanover during 1709–10. Furthermore, there is a link between the genre of the duet and Steffani: in Italy Handel had acquired a manuscript volume of Steffani's continuo-accompanied Italian duets.[38] But Mainwaring's account over-simplifies the situation. Handel had certainly composed at least 12 duets by 1711, of which ten (plus the two trios) were certainly known to a contemporary Hanover music copyist.[39] But of these probably only six or seven were composed in Hanover,[40] the rest arriving in Handel's musical baggage from Italy. No doubt the texts of some of the Hanover duets were by Mauro, though the precise extent of his contribution has still to be established.[41] As to Mainwaring's 'variety of other things for voices and instruments', the Hanover-period compositions can be tentatively identified from the types of manuscript paper that Handel may have used there, but the result is only a meagre haul of about half a dozen Italian cantatas and a few instrumental sonatas.[42] The biggest project that may be associated with Handel's period of service in Hanover is the completion of the large dramatic cantata *La terra è liberata* (*Apollo e Dafne*), commenced in Venice. From the putative 'Hanover' duets it seems that Handel had good Italian-singing soloists (one each of soprano, alto and bass) at the electoral court, and the completed orchestral accompaniment to *Apollo e Dafne* requires flute, oboes and bassoon (possibly more than one) in addition to the normal strings and continuo.

[37] This seems to be confirmed by a rather curious report in 1719 that Heidegger, the opera manager in London, took part in performances of Steffani's Italian duets for Caroline, then Princess of Wales: see Lindgren, 'Musicians and Librettists', p. 31, letter 38*a*.

[38] Now British Library Add. 37779. See Timms, 'Handel and Steffani'.

[39] British Library RM 18.b.11 is in this copyist's hand and almost certainly originated at the electoral court, *c*. 1710–12: the same repertory is found in another MS written on contemporary 'Hanover' paper, now in Hamburg (Staats- und Universitätsbibliothek MS MB/2767).

[40] HWV178, 185, 194, 197 and 199 are the most likely to have originated in Hanover, with the possible addition of HWV191 and 198.

[41] The author of only one of the early duet texts, HWV196, has been established positively, as Francesco de' Lemene.

[42] See Burrows, 'Handel and Hanover'. The identification of a Hanover repertory beyond some vocal duets and the completion of *Apollo e Dafne* is admittedly very tentative; the musical style of (for example) the sonatas HWV357–8 suggests a rather earlier date.

3

Music for Germany and Italy, 1706–10

Handel's earliest efforts at composition are lost, though we could make some guesses about their genres and style from the works of those composers that he studied during his musical education – Zachow, and the composers represented in his 1698 copy-book. His earliest surviving musical autograph is of the F major setting of *Laudate pueri, Dominum* (HWV236). This is unlikely to have been written in Halle, where Latin was banished from the major churches as a liturgical language after 1700, and in any case the autograph is written on paper types that might have been available in Hamburg but not in Halle. The motet-type setting of the text for soprano-clef voice accompanied by strings (without violas) presents obvious parallels with some of Handel's Roman compositions, and it is plausible that the work was composed in Rome not long before *Dixit Dominus*, using paper that Handel had brought with him. However, the possibility still remains open that it was composed in Hamburg, for an occasion and performers as yet unidentified.[1] That Handel did compose some substantial music in Halle is fairly certain, however. He may have tried his hand at orchestrally accompanied German church cantatas of the type that Zachow wrote: it seems that, on high festivals, Zachow had about 25 musicians at his disposal.[2] Pastor Neumeister's new-style German sacred cantata texts were reprinted in Halle in 1705, after Handel's departure, but an important literary influence in the preceding period may have been Barthold Heinrich Brockes from Hamburg, who studied at Halle University in 1700–2 and arranged weekly concerts in his apartment there. Brockes is now best known for his Passion text. Musical performances of the Passion were a particular tradition in Hamburg, to which city he returned in 1704.

The loss of much of Handel's music from his first 25 years has been lamented for more than two centuries (Mainwaring, pp. 149, 42):

A great quantity of music ... was made in Italy and Germany. How much of

---

[1] See Baselt, 'Miscellanea Haendeliana II'.

[2] See Baselt, 'Handel and his Central German Background', p. 55. Seven cantatas probably by Handel were listed in the library of the Ulrichskirche, Halle, in 1718: see *HHB*, p. 77.

it is yet in being, is not known. Two chests-full were left at HAMBURGH, besides some at HANOVER, and some at HALL.

During his continuance at Hamburgh, he made a considerable number of Sonatas. But what became of these pieces he never could learn, having been so imprudent as to let them go out of his hands.

A small harvest of music composed before Handel's journey to Italy can, however, be gathered from secondary – and sometimes much later – manuscripts. On a copy of the trio sonata op.2 no.2 (HWV387) that originated in the 1730s, Charles Jennens wrote 'Compos'd at the Age of 14', and, since Jennens was an acquaintance of the composer, the information no doubt came from Handel himself.[3] If it is correct, Ex.1 seems

Ex. 1

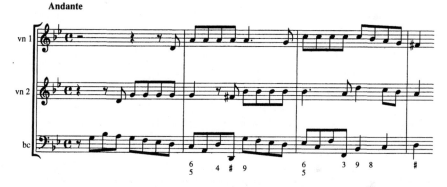

to represent our earliest surviving bars of Handel's music. A set of six trio sonatas, probably composed about the turn of the century and later brought to London by Carl Friedrich Weidemann, a flautist in Handel's opera orchestra, is reputed to have elicited the response from Handel to the effect that he 'used to write like the devil in those days, and mainly for oboe': but unfortunately the works themselves (HWV380–5), on grounds of provenance and style, do not seem very likely to be by Handel.[4] On stylistic grounds, a few keyboard works may also be attributed to Handel's early years, probably originating in Hamburg.[5]

The basis for stylistic judgments about the music of Handel's early years is his opera *Almira* (1705). Opera occupies so fundamental a position

[3]It is, of course, possible that Jennens misheard what Handel said, or that Handel's memory was not accurate on this point.

[4]Modern critical opinion is summarized by Siegfried Flesch in the introduction to the edition in *HHA* IV/9 (1976). Although the sonatas are nominally for two oboes and continuo, one of the 'oboe' parts was clearly written for violin.

[5]Suite HWV443, Partita HWV450, Allemande and Courante HWV451, Prelude HWV563, Prelude e Capriccio HWV571.

in Handel's output that a few comments on the musical structures of Baroque opera would seem to be appropriate here. Its basic musical building-blocks are recitative and aria. Recitative at this period has two major forms: 'semplice' recitative ('simple' or, less happily, 'secco' or 'dry') is the basic, fast-moving, conversational form, in which the voice is accompanied by a simple continuo bass consisting of a chord-playing instrument (usually the harpsichord), sometimes partnered by a bass instrument such as the cello. 'Accompagnato' is a more measured form of recitative, accompanied by strings and generally appropriate for soliloquies. The fundamental form for the display of solo singers' musical virtuosity was, however, the aria or air, an extended solo song with orchestral or (less frequently) continuo accompaniment. The 'classic' aria form was the so-called 'da capo' aria although there were alternative, shorter musical structures. This name relates to the return of the opening music in the final section, giving an overall *ABA* pattern. Aria texts were frequently constructed in line with this scheme: an initial self-contained idea was followed by a few lines (usually two or four) of verse extending or developing the theme or mood. These additional lines became the musical *B* section, after which the *A* section was repeated, usually providing an opportunity for the singer to display virtuosity in ornamenting the melodic lines. The da capo aria had a conventional key structure: the *A* section ended in the tonic key and was often cast in binary form with two statements of the text, one modulating away from the tonic and the second one returning to it. The *B* section usually contrasted with the *A* section in key, and sometimes in scoring and speed as well. The *A* section was usually framed with an orchestral prelude and postlude, often described as a ritornello, or (in England especially) 'symphony' (though these words are also used for orchestral interjections within sections of an aria).

The music of Handel's *Almira* survives almost complete.[6] The score is complemented by printed librettos associated with the original 1705 production, which describe the work as a 'Sing-Spiel'. Handel had a large cast in Hamburg – three sopranos, three tenors and two basses – and seven of the eight characters (including a comic servant) have arias in Italian as well as German. The arias for the two leading ladies Almira and Edilia are technically demanding, with Edilia's part requiring considerable agility above the staff, but some of the difficulties do not serve any very positive musical or dramatic ends. As a whole, the score shows Handel applying and adapting the style in which he had been trained – sometimes rather contrapuntal (e.g. 'Liebliche Wälder'), sometimes rather over-ornate (e.g. in the introduction to 'Chi più mi piace io voglio', or bars 10–11 of 'Schönste Rosen'), but generally characterized by strong harmonic

---

[6] The most complete surviving source (Staatsbibliothek, Berlin) is a score adapted by Telemann for a revival at Hamburg in 1732; Handel's autograph is lost.

progressions. Mattheson's descriptions of this transitional process in Handel's musical development, quoted on pp. 16–17, seem to fit the musical evidence, even though proper musical models from the pre-transitional period are lacking. Some of the more ornate elements may reflect French influence, which perhaps Handel did not even recognize as such since it had been integrated into the common musical habits of northern and central Germany. Conventional French-style influence is more explicit in the dance music in Acts 1 and 3. Certainly, Handel seems to have learnt in Hamburg, if not before, that Italian (or Italian-German) operas conventionally began with a 'French Overture',[7] and the understanding of its style that he brought with him from Hamburg may lie behind his subsequent reported contretemps with Corelli in Rome.

As an example of Handelian opera, *Almira* contrasts strongly with Handel's subsequent works by virtue of its origin: the Hamburg opera house provided a good night out at the theatre for an audience that expected an element of 'high-art' singing but did not necessarily give that element priority. The plot provides a romp of mistaken messages, jealousies, conflicting emotional intentions: it is finally resolved by the last-minute revelation of the royal lineage of a shipwrecked orphan. The comic servant Tabarco and the spectacular scenes (the coronation at the beginning of the opera and the Pageant of the Continents in Act 3) were important elements in an all-round entertainment, incorporating variety, dancing and spectacle. The libretto, by Friedrich Christian Feustking, has a complex history: Feustking, working in Hamburg, translated and adapted *Almira* from an Italian libretto, and it was set in various forms by Keiser in the years 1703–6, both before and after Handel's version. One of Keiser's versions was produced in Weissenfels in 1704, another in Hamburg the year after Handel's. Whether there was any actual rivalry between the two composers is uncertain, but on balance unlikely: the next production in the Hamburg opera programme seems to have fallen to whichever score was available and most appropriate to the circumstances of the moment. Handel was ready with *Almira* at the right time in the 1704–5 season, and saw it through to performance himself: the opera may even have been requested by the managers to fill a hiatus during Keiser's absence.[8] Of *Nero* and the legacy that he left behind for the 1708 Hamburg season, whose programme appears to have consisted of operas performed entirely

[7] In addition to the *Ouverture* to Act 1 and the *Entrée* to Act 3 printed in *HG* 55 a 'second' *Ouverture* to *Almira* survives in a separate manuscript at Berlin. The use of the *Ouverture* in Hamburg was an established part of Keiser's practice (e.g. in *Claudius*, 1703). Italian operas by Italian as well as 'German' composers before the end of the seventeenth century had frequently opened with a French *Ouverture*.

[8] The Hamburg company may have been expecting to perform Keiser's *Almira* in 1704 and, after Keiser's departure, asked Handel to set the text, perhaps to make full use of costumes and scenery that were already prepared. One surviving version of the printed libretto relating to Handel's production retains, probably by accident, a preface by Keiser: see Schröder, 'Zu Entstehung und Aufführungsgeschichte'.

in German, little is known. The few pieces of music that survive from *Florindo* and *Daphne* do not do much to illuminate the printed librettos, and in terms of musical style they do not modify the picture already received from *Almira*.

Someone coming to *Almira* with a knowledge of Handel's later operatic music will probably recognize some of the themes: in the most attractive movements (such as 'Liebliche Wälder', 'Ob dein Mund wie Plutons Rachen' and the 'Tanz von Asiatern') there are the seeds of greater things to come. During his journeyman period Handel recycled his best tunes at new venues without hesitation: the same thematic material may turn up in different musical contexts in operas written for Hamburg, Florence, Venice and London, and even in an aria movement in his Roman church music. This form of 'self-borrowing' is not really problematic: provided the music fits certain basic specifications (principally, that it is appropriate to the metre of the text and to the dramatic situation or mood), no-one begrudges Handel the opportunity of displaying his best wares to different audiences. However, the question of Handel's 'borrowings' from other composers is a topic that has provoked controversy among critics and music historians. There are good reasons why it needs to be aired even when dealing with music from the very beginning of Handel's creative career.

It is an accident of the historical-critical process by which Handel's music has been heard over the last 250 years that the 'borrowings' in his later music were recognized sooner than those from the earlier periods. But the fact that Handel used material from other composers has been common knowledge for most of that time. There were straws in the wind even during Handel's lifetime: as early as 1722 Mattheson published an article (in Hamburg) drawing attention to Handel's use of material from one of his own arias 'note for note' in *Agrippina* and in an opera written for London,[9] while Jennens in 1743 knew precisely why Handel wanted to borrow scores of Italian operas from his library, saying that 'I dare say I shall catch him stealing from them; as I have formerly, both from Scarlatti & Vinci'.[10] The first extensive listings of Handel's musical plagiarisms came with a magazine article in 1822[11] and, more influentially, nine years later in a published version of William Crotch's lectures as Heather Professor of Music at Oxford. Half a century further on, the extent of Handel's borrowings in such works as *Israel in Egypt* was so well documented that it provoked a most curious reaction: those that could not face the facts began to produce specious arguments that perhaps

[9] *Critica musica* (July 1722); *HHB*, pp. 105–6. In the same article (and an extensive footnote) Mattheson discusses the ethics of 'borrowing': see *HHB* and Buelow, 'The Case for Handel's Borrowings', p. 63 (with partial translation and commentary).

[10] Letter from Jennens to Holdsworth, 17 January 1743: *HHB*, p. 356.

[11] F. W. Horncastle in *The Quarterly Musical Magazine and Review*: see Buelow, 'The Case for Handel's Borrowings', pp. 66–7.

some of the works that provided thematic sources had been misattributed and were really unrecognized works by Handel. *Israel in Egypt* was composed in 1739, and most of the borrowings identified during the nineteenth century related to works composed at that period or subsequently. In the mid-twentieth century a hypothesis was evolved to the effect that a stroke in 1737–8 sapped Handel's creative powers, so that he began to rely heavily on borrowings thereafter. Research in the late twentieth-century has, however, undermined that hypothesis by unearthing many more examples of borrowings in works composed before 1737. It now looks as if Handel borrowed musical ideas from other composers all the time, throughout his creative career; and, furthermore, one of the composers who provided a substantial quantity of material for Handel's creative bank was Keiser, his musical model and employer in Hamburg.[12] The extent of Handel's borrowing will probably always remain controversial in the smaller details, for it is difficult to separate slight, half-remembered echoes, or well-integrated petty larcenies, from the common property of musical language in a style so well defined by harmonic and melodic convention as the late Baroque: but the overwhelming case for a musical input from composers such as Keiser throughout Handel's creative career is not in doubt.

The more fundamental question of 'why did Handel borrow?' cannot be addressed here in any depth, and indeed a proper answer would depend on knowledge of Handel's creative psychology and motivations that could have been gained only at first hand from the composer. But it is possible at least to make some intelligent guesses about the origins and historical significance of the borrowing process. Handel was trained under Zachow on the basis of models – he was given other people's music to play and, inevitably, to copy out. Probably pastiche composition played its part: Handel's regular student assignments no doubt included improvising or composing on a given theme. The musical technique that he thus acquired may be seen as a form of rhetorical elaboration – that is, he learned how to make the given elements of musical 'speech' more effective; and what he certainly learnt (and continued to learn, when he was well away from Zachow's influence) was an art of composition that involved control of formal construction and the manipulation of the component elements of rhythm, melody and harmony. This was the substance of Crotch's tribute to Handel as early as 1805,[13] in terms of

the greatness of his mind, the accuracy of his judgement, the variety of his styles & his skill in adopting the thoughts of preceeding & coeval composers. – Bird might be as sublime, Hasse as beautiful – Haydn more ornamental – But Handel united grandeur, elegance & embellishment with the utmost pro-

[12] See Roberts, 'Handel's Borrowings from Keiser'; also Roberts (ed.), *Handel Sources*, i–iii.
[13] In a letter to Charles Burney, 4 March 1805: printed in Appendix I to Burney, *A General History*, ii, 1038.

priety, & on this account I ventured to pronounce him, upon the whole, the greatest of all composers.

It is the development of Handel as a composer in this sense (whether or not he was working on materials derived from other musicians) that constitutes his creative history.

However, the development of Handel's style did not move at an even speed: it shows a number of spurts onwards and plateaux of consolidation. One of the biggest advances seems to have come during the period 1706–7, probably during his first months in Italy: his church music and cantatas of mid-1707 show a style altogether more fluent and more controlled than that displayed in *Almira*. There is nothing to prepare us for the surprise of *Dixit Dominus*, where Handel as a composer of concerted music for choir[14] and orchestra springs out at us fully armed. The elements of his grand style are all there—the chordal outbursts on 'Juravit Dominus'

Ex. 2

(The Lord hath sworn)

and a variety of choral textures: straightforward imitation ('Judicabit'); counterpoint on two subjects ('Tu es sacerdos'): the interplay of answering and combining voices ('Et non poenitebit'); closely overlapping vocal entries ('Dominus a dextris tuis'); and one voice versus the rest ('Donec ponam', Ex.3 – a passage that seems to look both backwards, to the cantus firmus and chorale training that Handel received in Halle, and forwards, to the technical consummation of this texture in the 'Hallelujah' chorus in *Messiah*). The music for the solo voices in *Dixit Dominus* displays the beginning of a move towards a suaver style – but only the beginning, for much of the strenuous and rather angular earlier manner is still in evidence. No matter: if *Dixit Dominus* is still rather rough-and-ready, there is ample compensation in the sheer zest with which the 22-year-old composer flung himself into the task. The choral works that

[14]The size of the original performing forces for *Dixit Dominus* is not known, but the entry of the lower voices under the soloists in 'De torrente in via' is marked 'capella' by Handel, indicating that there would have been more than one singer per part.

Ex. 3

(...until I make thine enemies [thy footstool])

followed a couple of months later are no less assured, and perhaps just noticeably more lyrical in expression. The arias of the D major *Laudate, pueri* are certainly rather better conceived than the solo music in *Dixit Dominus*, and, although the later works are shorter, their choruses are no less grand: *Laudate, pueri* has a magnificent outburst at 'Quis sicut Dominus', and *Nisi Dominus* ends with a Gloria for antiphonally distributed 'double-choir' forces of singers and orchestra. The motet *Saeviat tellus inter rigores* and the three antiphons that partner the choral works stand musically in the line of Handel's orchestrally accompanied Italian cantatas. *Saeviat tellus* is a somewhat flashy vocal concerto, while *Te decus virgineum* and *Haec est regina virginum* are more restrained and lyrical; *Salve regina* (Ex.4) is more subjective in tone than the others, and indeed it marks the closest that Handel ever came to succumbing musically to the charms of sentimental Catholicism. There are also two Italian cantatas from the period with sacred texts, *Ah, che troppo ineguali* (HWV230, for soprano and strings, possibly a fragment from a larger work) and *Donna, che in ciel* (HWV233, for soprano, chorus and strings).

Between *Dixit Dominus* and the church music written in July 1707[15] comes Handel's first oratorio, *Il trionfo del Tempo e del Disinganno*. With

---

[15] The chronology of these works is outlined in Chapter 2.

Ex. 4

(To Thee we cry, the banished children of Eve)

this work, the distance that Handel's style had advanced since *Almira* can really be measured, both in the fluency of the arias and in the management of a complete libretto. Admittedly, the allegorical nature of the drama, in which Tempo, Piacere and Disinganno put forward their respective arguments to Bellezza, gives no opportunity for the portrayal of complex human relationships: the drama lies in the conflicting claims of these forces and in the choice that has to be made between them. But Pamphili's libretto gave Handel the opportunity for some splendid 'character pieces' encapsulating the cases put forward by the four contestants, and he achieved a good balance in the variety and placing of the arias – a pleasing arrangement of fast and slow, major and minor, and contrasted moods. There was even an opportunity for a lively quartet where the rival claimants attempt to elbow each other out ('Voglio tempo'). Some movements (e.g. the rather pecky 'Tu giurasti') still display the old *Almira* style, though with a rather more expansive treatment; 'Io sperassi' presents a fascinating combination of old-style filigree work in the oboe obbligato with a more italianate vocal line. As befits the nature of the drama, all four characters have a substantial and equally balanced loading of da capo arias.

Disinganno's aria 'Crede l'uom' (Ex.5) perhaps gives us the most rounded example of the new, smoother lyrical style that Handel was assimilating (it is perhaps all the more ironic that it is based on a thematic idea from Keiser[16]).

Ex. 5

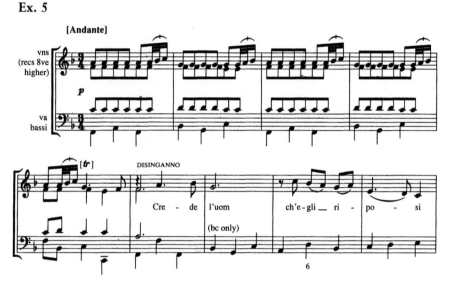

Mortals, that *Time*'s asleep, believe,
When unseen he spreads his Wings;
But tho' they can't his Strokes perceive,
They see the Ruin that he brings.[17]

It begins with a six-bar ritornello, setting the musical scene with a 'sleep' motif, and material from this punctuates the *A* section of the aria. Handel constructs a musical paragraph extending from the singer's first entry to the dominant cadence 18 bars later, a masterly construction of melodic and harmonic organization using the simplest means (and a vocal compass within an octave), which does not let the interest sag at any point. Built into the structure is a repetition of the first phrase, bringing with it an inevitable early tonic cadence: but in context this clearly signals the scale of the movement to come, and is not an absentminded early gravitation to the tonic. To adapt a description from one of the most perceptive accounts of Handel's compositional genius, 'the composer who gets as far as bar 13 of "Crede l'uom" must be intending to go much further, and

[16] *Octavia* ('Ruhig sein').
[17] Translation from the word-book for Handel's 1737 London version of the oratorio.

51

shows every sign of being able to do so'.[18] Having reached the dominant, and marked this landmark with a ritornello statement, Handel constructs an equally balanced return to the tonic, extending one-bar motifs sequentially in a harmonic arc that delivers a climax for the tonic cadence (bar 41). That should be the end, but Handel weaves a coda out of more sequential figures, once again keeping the music 'in the air' for a span that constitutes nearly a third of the A section. Throughout the A section both the picturesque ritornello material and the vocal figuration serve the flow and structure of the movement. Even so, this aria is not the most 'modern' movement in *Il trionfo*: that distinction goes to the 'Sonata' with concertante organ part (referred to in Chapter 2), which is constructed as a clearcut Vivaldian ritornello movement with well-defined episodes (it turns out to be a 'one-off', however, for Handel hardly ever followed that formal path later).

It is difficult, and perhaps none too fruitful, to make comparisons between *Il trionfo del Tempo* and *La Resurrezione*. Though completed only a year later, *La Resurrezione* shows an almost complete assimilation of the Italian manner: apart from 'O voi del Erebo' (based on another idea from Keiser's *Octavia*), the '*Almira* style' is hardly in evidence at all, and even in that movement the balanced phrases and skilled melodic and harmonic extensions produce an effect far distant from the cramped manner of Handel's earlier work. Between the two oratorios Handel had had plenty of experience of the Italian style, both as a listener and as a composer: he had developed his own work through an opera and many cantatas. A good case has been made that Handel was much influenced by Alessandro Scarlatti,[19] and certainly the results of various impressions from music encountered in Italy during 1707–8 are in his scores for all to see, in his treatment of melody and harmony and his confident management of the da capo aria.

La Resurrezione is fundamentally different from the earlier oratorio, however, in that the whole framework of the libretto is more operatic. Although the central character of the drama does not appear (and, indeed, any representation of Christ would probably have been forbidden), *La Resurrezione* proceeds through normal dramatic conventions. The story begins during the second night after the Crucifixion, as an Angel demands admittance for Christ into Hell, in order to defeat the power of death: Lucifer responds by summoning his own troops for battle. In Jerusalem, Mary Magdalene and Mary Cleophas mourn the death of Christ, and St John reminds them of Jesus's promise to return on the third day; meanwhile the Angel calls up the souls of the prophets and patriarchs, releasing them from Hell to follow Christ. Part 2 begins with the dawn of the third day: St John reflects on the earthquakes of the previous night.

[18] Tovey, 'Handel: "Israel in Egypt"', p. 85.
[19] Dean and Knapp, *Handel's Operas*, pp. 86–93.

The Angel appears to the women as they find the empty sepulchre and tells them of the Resurrection, which is confirmed by reports of Jesus's appearance to his own mother and Mary Magdalene: meanwhile Lucifer, defeated, has returned ignominiously to Hell. Given the visual stimuli of the lavish pictorial decorations that were provided for the first performances, it probably needed only a small effort for the audience to interpret the action in 'stage' terms, and Handel provided the appropriate aural cues: a swaggering, defiant role for Lucifer, and an eerie representation of the sepulchre in 'Per me già di morire', with an obbligato part for recorders and muted oboe ('oboe sordo'). Each part of the oratorio ends with a cheerful ensemble movement for the soloists – an operatic 'coro', not the 'chorus' characteristic of Latin church music.

In quantitative terms, the principal music from Handel's considerable period of residence in Rome was neither church music nor oratorios, but Italian cantatas. These remain among the least-known areas of his output in the English-speaking world, partly because concert conditions provide few equivalents to the *conversazione* (though recordings might perhaps create such conditions in the modern home) and partly because the texts, in the relative obscurity of Italian, were written to literary conventions that are out of tune with the modern world-view. However, much fine music is buried under the verbiage of the Arcadian pastoral language that Ruspoli's circle affected; and the instrumentally accompanied cantatas in particular present some miniature dramas that are worth a hearing. Their conclusions are not always predictable: in *Clori, Tirsi e Fileno*, for example, the two men at the base of the eternal triangle finally agree that love must be enjoyed lightly in view of woman's inconstancy; while in *Il duello amoroso* unrequited love is given a new twist when Amarilli tells Daliso that if he had not taken her maidenly modesty at face value he might have made some progress with their relationship before her father appeared. In these cantatas there are, along with the conventional nymphs and swains, some characters and incidents from classical mythology, serving either as the central subject (as in *Apollo e Dafne*) or as references for elaboration. While nearly all the continuo-accompanied cantatas are devoted to expressing the woes of poor Tirsi – a shepherd deserted, rejected or betrayed by his nymph – some of the instrumentally accompanied solo cantatas cast the woman as protagonist: in *Il delirio amoroso* and *Armida abbandonata*, Clori and Armida respectively lament their dead or faithless lovers. Where the plot is conventional, or where a single situation is explored, the interest obviously lies in the musical and literary treatment. The 'simile aria', familiar from opera, plays its part here, and among the cultivated Roman audience an apt simile, well realized in music, was no doubt an object of pleasure rather than impatience: the nautical helmsman, for example, provides a useful image in both *Il duello amoroso* and *Clori, Tirsi e Fileno*. Perhaps the least tractable cantatas for the modern listener are those that are tied closely to contemporary political references: they form only a small corner of the repertory, but they include O *come chiare e belle*, an ambitious and interesting work rather fettered to its time and place of origin.[20] The largest of all, *Aci, Galatea e Polifemo*, is on a time-scale that begins to call into question Handel's own use of the word 'cantata'; because of its association with wedding celebrations it soon came to be described as a 'serenata'. It contains entirely different music from Handel's later working of the story as *Acis and Galatea* and is written to different conventions that seem slow-moving by comparison, but all three soloists have fine arias. The bridal couple in Naples in 1708 received a musical treat.

While many instrumentally accompanied cantatas are virtually operatic scenes (or even sometimes miniature operas), the continuo-accompanied cantatas for solo voices are a genre of vocal chamber music. In the absence of operatic-scale gestures and the interaction of characters, there can be no fudging of musical issues here: the chains of recitatives and arias stand or fall by their treatment of melody, harmony and form, as surely as do the chains of slow and fast movements that constitute instrumental sonatas. These cantatas are a treasure-house of musical invention. While the standard patterns of melodically formulaic common-time recitative and da capo aria are endlessly repeated, the musical material is not: Handel produced a range of different, yet appropriate, themes for his arias that bears comparison with the variety of musical material in Schubert's songs, and the themes are extended and developed with scarcely a falter. The cantata autographs support an impression, which is gained from most of Handel's other Italian-period autographs, that in Italy he quickly acquired not only a new style but also a technical facility that gave his work speed as well as fluency: once he was into the flow of a cantata, he covered the pages with hardly a hesitation. It is true that there were a few dropped stitches in the process: the Italian-period works include a number of tantalizing passages with isolated 'wrong' notes in the harmony, in which Handel's brain was clearly out-running his pen. Mainly these seem to have occurred because he was momentarily thinking along different harmonic tracks for the voice part and the accompaniment. There are very few examples of actual technical incompetence, and the image of Handel as a slapdash composer who did not care about consecutive fifths and octaves in partwriting is ill-founded. Throughout Handel's career there are examples in his autographs of passages that he amended during composition to avoid such errors, and indeed there are many improvements to details that are very minor in terms of the music's total effect. The revision process did not stop with the autographs: the

---

[20] Another Italian cantata that refers, explicitly, to current diplomatic politics is *Echeggiate, festeggiate, numi eterni* (HWV119), but this was apparently composed in London; it is incomplete and is sometimes mistakenly known by the title of one of its movements, 'Io languisco fra le gioie'.

scribal copies of Handel's Italian-period works now at Münster[21] have several alterations, both substantial and minor, in Handel's hand. It is interesting that the texts of the French and Spanish cantatas composed for Ruspoli – *Sans y penser* (HWV155) and *Nò se emenderá jamás* (HWV140) – were entered into these copies by Handel himself, presumably because he felt that this task should not be entrusted to the Italian copyists. At the same time, in the Spanish cantata he altered some rhythms in the music of the first movement, to give better textual accentuation. The French cantata stands apart from its Italian companions in that, although it contains a couple of da capo movements, Handel made in it a conscious attempt at French-style melodies and 'measured' recitative in the Lullian tradition: he headed the first movement 'Chanson' and two of the subsequent arias 'Air'.

If the continuo-accompanied cantata is counterpart to the instrumental 'solo sonata', the duet with continuo (and the closely related trio) is similarly comparable in style and texture to the trio sonata. Mention has already been made of Handel's own manuscript copy of Steffani's chamber duets that he apparently acquired in Italy in 1706–7. In general terms this volume seems to have formed a model for Handel's own works, and as such it was perhaps a false model: Steffani's works include solo movements for the singers as well as duet movements, but it so happens that Handel's copy was one that did not include the former. Not that we have any reason to complain about the result: Handel's Italian duets are some of the best vocal chamber music ever composed, though they are 'connoisseur's music'. Henry Purcell's description of his own trio sonatas as being appropriate to such as 'carry Musical Souls about them'[22] seems entirely apposite here. As the texture is mainly contrapuntal, with the voices working in imitation or antiphony above the continuo bass, the music is largely continuous, falling into discrete movements (without recitatives): there is no place for startling dramatic gestures. But the medium suits the aphoristic poetry – more akin to the sonnet than the *scena* – that called forth the duets.[23] The duets and Italian cantatas that were composed in Hanover do not call for special comment, because they extended the genres and styles that Handel had already been developing in Italy: there was no major stylistic break when he moved north.

The instrumental music from Handel's Italian and Hanover years is not

---

[21] The Münster collection (described in Ewerhart, 'Die Händel-Handschriften') was mainly acquired from the collector Fortunato Santini in Rome in the mid-nineteenth century. Its previous provenance is unknown, but it may well be an amalgamation of library collections that originated with Handel's Roman patrons, possibly including the very cantata copies that feature in Ruspoli's domestic bills.

[22] Preface ('To the Reader') to *Sonnata's of III Parts* (London, 1683).

[23] I owe to Anthony Hicks the suggestion that Handel's duets may be regarded as two-part madrigals with continuo.

plentiful. There are a couple of Italian orchestral works: a violin concerto (HWV 288, called by Handel 'Sonata a 5', placing it within a recognized Italian tradition of five-part orchestral 'sonatas') and an ouverture (HWV 336).[24] The first appears to be an independent work, possibly written for Corelli; the second may have been attached to some other work from the Italian period. In spite of the electress's enthusiasm for Handel's harpsichord playing in Hanover, there are no keyboard works that can be attributed with certainty to this period.[25] The autographs of two solo sonatas (HWV 357, 358) and a trio sonata for recorders and continuo (HWV 405) can, on the evidence of their paper, be attributed to the Hanover period, though their musical style is such that they might well have been Handel's fair copies of pieces composed earlier. Perhaps there are other works from the Italian and Hanover years lurking in the Trio Sonatas op. 2, which were published in London in the 1730s but certainly contain some earlier music, but in the absence of manuscript sources or clear stylistic indicators it is difficult to assign dates. Another work published at the same period, the Concerto Grosso op. 3 no. 1, might also have been composed for Hanover: its scoring, which includes two viola-range parts in different clefs, links it with surviving works by Francesco Venturini, a leading Hanoverian court musician who eventually succeeded Farinel as Konzertmeister there in 1713. One other work whose date is uncertain is the overture to *Rodrigo*, which may have originated as an independent orchestral piece. Consisting of an ouverture, seven dance movements and a *passacaille*, it is out of scale with the needs of the opera, and its obviously French lineage suggests that it might even have been composed for Hamburg (though the autograph is written on north Italian paper).[26]

There remain for consideration the two largest works from Handel's Italian period, the operas *Rodrigo* (1707) and *Agrippina* (1709). Both are landmarks in Handel's career – *Rodrigo* on account of its position and *Agrippina* on account of its quality. Coming as he did from the world of Hamburg opera, it was probably a considerable discipline for Handel to attempt in *Rodrigo* an opera relying on recitative (in vast quantities) and aria, with scant opportunity for spectacular scenes or comic characters. There is indeed nothing comic about the story of intrigue and warfare in

[24] Although the autograph of HWV 336 is lost and its date uncertain, it has a strong thematic resemblance to the overture to *Il trionfo del Tempo* and may date from Handel's Italian years. See also n. 26, below.

[25] Two possible candidates are the G major Sonata for two-manual harpsichord HWV 579, which resembles thematically the organ sonata in *Il trionfo*, and the G minor Sonata HWV 580, which similarly echoes the *Sonata a 5*: more probably, however, these were at least committed to paper after Handel left Italy (autographs of neither survive).

[26] Marx, in 'Italienische Einflüsse', suggests that the *Rodrigo* overture may have chronologically followed the Ouverture HWV 336, which he suggests may have been associated with *Florindo* or *Daphne* in Hamburg; but the minim-beat movement in the inner parts of the *Rodrigo* overture (see Marx, p. 390) seems to represent the earlier style.

Rodrigo, the libretto of which was a revision of one set by Marc'Antonio Ziani for Venice in 1700.[27] The plot concerns the fortunes of the royal family of Aragon, whose heir Evanco has been beaten and captured by Rodrigo, King of Castile: Evanco is eventually restored to the throne, and Rodrigo's baby son by his mistress Florinda is named as the eventual heir to Castile. At the dénouement Esilena, Rodrigo's wife, saves her husband from execution at the hands of Florinda (who has turned against him) by thrusting the baby into his arms. The story, which has only a tenuous basis in eighth-century history, may have been chosen because it could be interpreted in a way that was relevant to the dynastic struggles of the current European war.

Handel's score is uneven in quality, more so than that for *Il trionfo del Tempo*, but it provided good experience for him. The arias rely quite heavily on self-borrowings, some of which seem to have been thrown together with an uncritical lack of concern for dramatic context, which was uncharacteristic of the later Handel. But there are some good things too. Handel transformed an idea from *Almira* ('Quillt, ihr überhäuften Zähren') into something better for *Rodrigo* ('Sommi dei'), discovering in the process the dramatic effectiveness of interrupting an aria before the expected da capo cycle is complete. The best aria is Esilena's 'Empio fato',[28] where Handel strikes an effectively tragic note for the first time in his operas. But, perversely, this aria was replaced before the first performance: whether its replacement was the result of pressure from a librettist-arranger or from a singer, or whether Handel himself decided that something different was needed in that particular context, we do not know, but this is only the first example among many of good music being set aside by Handel before performance.

Although the characters in *Agrippina*, like those in *Rodrigo*, are propelled by ambition and amorous intrigues, the whole tone of Handel's second Italian opera is lighter, and the action moves much faster. The libretto is a good one and may well have been written specifically for Handel. It is loosely based on events from Roman history as mediated through the stories by Tacitus and Suetonius. Agrippina, wife of the Emperor Claudio (Claudius), attempts to secure the succession for Nerone (Nero), her son by a previous marriage. Her designs are complicated by Claudio's own wishes and by the seductive powers of Poppea (Poppaea), who succeeds in attracting Claudio, Nerone and Ottone (Otho), the Roman lieutenant preferred by Claudio to succeed as emperor. In Act 3 the two younger men are concealed in Poppea's room when Claudio visits her, and Agrippina's schemes are temporarily foiled when Poppea exposes both Nerone's presence and his ambitions. Claudio orders Nerone to

<hr>

[27] *Il duello d'amore, e di vendetta*, libretto by Francesco Silvani.
[28] The string figuration at the beginning seems to derive from an aria in *Florindo/Daphne*: see Dean and Knapp, *Handel's Operas*, p. 75.

marry Poppea and names Ottone as his successor, but Ottone and Nerone exchange roles: Ottone wishes to marry Poppea and is therefore willing to cede the succession to Nerone. Agrippina's ambitions are thus fulfilled, albeit somewhat accidentally.

Librettist and composer combined happily to give credibility to the characters and zest to the situations: the text's treatment of the story in a spirit of ironic detachment does not lessen the realism of the ambitions and the passions of the characters. *Agrippina* contains a large number of arias, but few long ones: Handel's music keeps pace with the general raciness of the drama. 85% of the arias are based on known self-borrowed or borrowed musical material,[29] but the patterns in Handel's re-use of earlier music are varied and complex. Some arias were lifted from other works with hardly any alteration, and a couple even managed to carry forward their original texts – notably 'Ho un non sò che nel cor' (Ex.6), transferred from *La Resurrezione*, a sprightly and tuneful piece that any theatre composer would regard as a 'hit number'.

Ex. 6

(Something in my heart invites me to joy instead of sorrow.)

Most often, however, Handel re-worked his movements as he wrote them into the new score and, in view of the particular needs of the fast-moving *Agrippina*, the general direction of the revisions was towards compression. To take an example from an aria already described, the 61-bar *A* section of 'Crede l'uom' from *Il trionfo del Tempo* became in *Agrippina* a 36-bar aria, 'Vaghe fonti', sung by Ottone as he approaches a peaceful scene by a garden fountain where Poppea is feigning sleep. The

[29] See Buelow, 'Handel's Borrowing Techniques', p. 107; to Buelow's inventory of borrowings may now be added 'Il tuo figlio' from *Agrippina*, which is accompanied by a string figure derived from Handel's Roman antiphon *Te decus virgineum* HWV243.

first vocal phrases were telescoped to provide a shorter path to the
dominant, and the new returning binary 'half' was based on ideas from
the third part (or extended coda) of the *Trionfo* aria. It is difficult to
judge which version is the better: the *Agrippina* aria provides a good
opening cavatina for Ottone's scene with Poppea, but something more
expansive was appropriate for the full da capo aria of the oratorio. In
some cases of re-use only an initial thematic idea was adopted, or a
number of ideas from different sources were re-combined and developed
in one aria: a particularly complex example is Poppea's 'Vaghe, perle',
which draws on material from arias in four separate earlier works by
Handel, in addition to some source-ideas that can be traced back to
Keiser's *Octavia*.[30] In the end, it is sufficient to recognize that here, as in
other arias, Handel's music is entirely apposite to its context, and that
the resulting movement is skilfully composed. But, yet more important,
the re-composition process as applied in *Agrippina* produced not only
some fine arias but also entire scenes and acts that are well constructed
in musical and dramatic terms. The opera coheres as a whole: as Handel's
first operatic masterpiece, it well deserved its success in Venice.

[30] See Roberts, 'Handel's Borrowings from Keiser', pp. 68–9.

4

London: The first decade, 1711–19

According to Mainwaring, Handel had secured his post at the court of Hanover in 1710 through the support of Johan Adolf Freiherr von Kielmansegge, the elector's deputy Master of the Horse (and husband of the elector's half-sister).[1] On receiving the offer in Hanover, Handel thanked Kielmansegge, but (pp. 71–2)

> also expressed his apprehensions that the favour intended him would hardly be consistent either with the promise he had actually made to visit the court of the Elector Palatine, or with the resolution he had long taken to pass over into England, for the sake of seeing that of LONDON. Upon this objection, the Baron consulted his Highness's pleasure, and HANDEL was then acquainted, that neither his promise nor his resolution should be superseded by his acceptance of the pension proposed. He had leave to be absent for a twelve-month or more, if he chose it; and to go whithersoever he pleased. On these easy conditions he thankfully accepted it.

The Electress Sophia's first letter referring to Handel had concluded: 'He is going to Düsseldorf to compose an opera there',[2] and we need not doubt Mainwaring's word that Handel obtained some formal privilege at Hanover along the lines stated.

At Düsseldorf was the court of the Elector Palatine,[3] and Steffani had served there from 1703 to 1709, pursuing mainly a diplomatic-ecclesiastical career but also contributing to the court opera. His last opera, *Il Tassilone*, was performed at Düsseldorf in 1709, though Steffani had spent most of the period between November 1708 and April 1709 in Rome, involved with papal war politics: on his appointment as Apostolic Vicar in Northern Germany, Steffani chose Hanover as his base and moved there in November

---

[1] Mainwaring (p.71) states that Handel was offered an annual pension of 1500 crowns at Hanover: Handel was, in fact, employed as Kapellmeister with a salary of 1000 thalers (see Burrows, 'Handel and Hanover', p.40). As noted in Chapter 2, Kielmansegge may have met Handel in Venice. In London, Kielmansegge's wife's relationship to the elector (now King George) was interpreted as that of mistress, perhaps in ignorance of their family relationship.

[2] Letter of 4 June 1710; see Chapter 2.

[3] Johann Wilhelm (1658–1716). After his death, his successor as elector moved the court first to Heidelberg and then to Mannheim. The Electress Sophia of Hanover came from a senior branch of the Palatinate family.

1709. Assuming that Handel and Steffani had at some time previously met in Rome, it seems very likely that Steffani provided introductions for Handel at both Hanover and Düsseldorf, and it is possible that he had also laid the ground for Handel to compose an opera for the Elector Palatine. That plan did not come to fruition, but Handel no doubt visited Düsseldorf in the autumn of 1710, after a brief return to Halle for a reunion with his mother and his old teacher Zachow.[4] Mainwaring says that the Elector Palatine was disappointed to learn that Handel was 'engaged elsewhere', but presented him with 'a fine set of wrought plate for a desert', presumably in return for musical services of which we now have no knowledge. Düsseldorf, to the west of Hanover, lay in the geographical path of Handel's career. According to Mainwaring (p.74), 'from Düsseldorf he made the best of his way through HOLLAND and embarqued for ENGLAND', presumably on the basis of hopes for musical employment in London that had been raised through his contacts in Italy.

The primary attraction of London for Handel was the Italian opera company at the Queen's Theatre in the Haymarket.[5] The first decade of the eighteenth century had been a turbulent period in the history of the London theatres, with rival theatre companies and entrepreneurs fighting between themselves for audiences, but also competing for physical and institutional bases in the patent theatres licensed by the Lord Chamberlain. Major factors in the situation were the building of John Vanbrugh's new Queen's Theatre and the gradual introduction of all-sung opera in the Italian manner. London's own composers were active in the early stages. As the construction of the Queen's Theatre moved towards completion towards the end of 1704, Daniel Purcell and Thomas Clayton were both working on operas 'translated from the Italian by good Hands',[6] and John Eccles composed *Semele*, a genuine all-sung English opera to a libretto by William Congreve (it was, however, not performed; Handel set the libretto nearly 40 years later). The theatre manager Christopher Rich somehow slipped Clayton's opera, *Arsinoe*, over to his own theatre at Drury Lane, where it opened on 16 January 1705. For the opening of the Queen's Theatre on 9 April 1705 John Vanbrugh responded with an opera sung at least partly in Italian, Jakob Greber's *Gli amori d'Ergasto*. The 'Foreign

[4] Mainwaring (*Memoirs*, p.73); but Handel's family re-union may have taken place during his second Hanover period in 1711–12. If Mainwaring is correct, Handel would have had a very busy year of travelling in 1710. Mainwaring describes Handel's mother as being 'in extreme old-age, and total blindness' at the time, but she lived for another 20 years.

[5] It was known as the King's Theatre after the accession of George I in 1714. Subsequent references to a Haymarket theatre are to this building, unless indicated otherwise. The opera theatre was on the west side of the Haymarket, on the site now occupied by Her Majesty's Theatre; the present-day Haymarket Theatre is on the opposite side of the street.

[6] *The Diverting-Post* (28 October 1704). The tortuous early history of the opera companies can be followed through Hume, 'Opera in London', and Dean and Knapp, *Handel's Operas* (Chapter 9), and further references given there.

GIULIO CESARE.

ATTO I.

SCENA I. *Campagna d' Egitto con antico Ponte sopra un Ramo del Nilo.*

CESARE e CURIO, *che paſſano il Ponte con ſeguito.*

CORO *di Egizzi.*

VIVA viva il noſtro Alcide,
    Goda il Nilo in queſto dì.
    Ogni ſpiaggia per Lui ride,
    Ogni affanno già ſparì.
Ceſ. Preſti omai l'Egizzia Terra
    Le ſue palme al Vincitor.

Curio Ceſare venne, e vide, e vinſe:
Già ſconfitto Pompeo, invan ricorre
Per rinforzar de' ſuoi Guerrier lo ſtuolo
D' Egitto al Re.
   Cur. Tu quì Signor giungeſti
A tempo appunto a prevenir le trame:
Ma! Chi ver noi ſen' viene?

B 3   SCENA

Fig. 4 The opening scene of *Giulio Cesare in Egitto*, from the original London word-book (1724)

62

JULIUS CÆSAR.

ACT I.

SCENE I. A Plain in *Egypt*, with an old Bridge over a Branch of the *Nile*.

CÆSAR *and* CURIUS *paſſing over the Bridge with Attendants.*

CHORUS of *Egyptians.*

LIVE Great Alcides, let Nile rejoice
(this happy Day :
 Each Shore appears to ſmile,
Our Troubles vaniſh,
 And our Joys return.
Caſ. Let Egypt's Laurels wreath the Con-
(queror's Brows.

*Curius : Caſar no ſooner came, but ſaw and conquer'd :
Pompey now ſubdu'd, in vain endeavours to ſupport him-
ſelf, by joining with the King of Egypt.*
 *Cur. You timely interpos'd to croſs his Purpoſe ; but who
comes toward us ?*

SCENE

Opera' was not very successful: a contemporary description tells us that it was[7]

> Perform'd by a new set of Singers, Arriv'd from *Italy*; (the worst that e're came from thence) for it lasted but 5 Days, and they being lik'd but indifferently by the Gentry; they in a little time marcht back to their own Country.

In 1706, however, Rich scored a major success with an English-language version of Giovanni Bononcini's *Camilla* at Drury Lane: this was a full-length Italian opera, with a racy plot and newly composed English recitatives. But British composers had lost the initiative in the course of these two productions.

During the 1706–7 season a truce agreement between the theatre managers left Rich with operas at Drury Lane and Vanbrugh with plays at the Haymarket, but towards the end of 1707 Vanbrugh manoeuvred for the situation to be reversed: on 13 January 1708 the Lord Chamberlain ordered that henceforward the Drury Lane company was forbidden to perform operas, and the Haymarket company forbidden to produce plays. Vanbrugh probably believed, perhaps on the strength of the success of *Camilla*, that there was a fortune to be made from opera, but events developed in a way that changed the economic basis for opera in London. Although the Italian singers had been 'lik'd but indifferently' in 1705, Rich's introduction of the castrato Valentino Urbani into the cast of the opera *Thomyris*[8] in April 1707 was successful. Opera productions saw a gradual multiplication of Italian singers, singing in Italian: problems of dramatic communication were resolved by dual-language word-books, with texts in English and Italian on facing pages (Fig. 4), which were on sale for the theatre audience (contemporary conventions of theatre auditorium lighting probably allowed the books to be read during the performances). Vanbrugh's successor as manager of the Haymarket company, Owen Swiney,[9] signed up in the cast for the 1708–9 season the first-rate, but fabulously expensive, castrato Nicolini (Nicolò Grimaldi), who arrived in London with the Earl of Manchester (the diplomat who in Venice had probably invited Handel). The final logical step came in March 1710 with *L'Idaspe fedele*, an opera sung throughout in Italian and arranged by Pepusch from Francesco Mancini's *Gl'amanti generosi* (1705, Naples; Nicolini, who sang Idaspe (Hydaspes), had brought the score to London). Thereafter the Haymarket theatre became the London home for all-sung Italian opera in Italian.[10] Artistic integrity for opera was thus

[7] Downes, *Roscius anglicanus*, p.48.

[8] The operas of this period were variously adapted and assembled from Italian originals: *Thomyris* had music by Alessandro Scarlatti and Bononcini.

[9] The theatre was still owned by Vanbrugh: Swiney, as manager, leased the building from him. In November 1710 Swiney sub-let to William Collier and Aaron Hill.

[10] There was only one look backwards: *Calypso and Telemachus*, an English opera in the Italian style by Galliard (libretto by John Hughes), ran for five performances in 1711, when Handel was in Hanover.

achieved, but at the expense of financial security. Hitherto musical drama in London had succeeded as part of mixed theatre seasons, in which companies produced both plays and masque-type musical dramas, and under such circumstances it was possible to balance the books over the course of a season. But the Italian opera stars, on which the success of Italian opera in London depended, were not versatile performers: they had no part in English plays, masques or semi-operas. Italian opera in London henceforward had to be a separate enterprise, and the financial problems of maintaining the enterprise of this expensive and isolated medium were both enormous and continuous. A body of patronage for the financial support of opera was required, and by 1710 it appeared that there was sufficient interest in London to provide this, but only just. It relied critically on a sufficient body of commitment from the rich and the powerful.

In addition to the importation of Italian opera stars, the years preceding 1710 had seen a natural migration of other musical talent to London, impelled by professional or political uncertainties in continental Europe and attracted by the opportunities that seemed to be promised by the development of London's musical life. The composers Johann Christoph Pepusch and Johann Ernst Galliard, who became significant in London as composers as well as orchestral musicians, the woodwind virtuoso Jean Christian Kytch and the Italian cellist Nicola Haym were only the most prominent names among a group of Europeans that had preceded Handel and settled permanently in London. By the time all-Italian opera was established in 1710 it could be accompanied by a regular orchestra of considerable competence, comprising a mixture of British and foreign players. The opera company had also attracted talented Italian scene designers. What was lacking, however, was an experienced opera composer: the early London operas were pasticcio works converted locally from pre-existing Italian scores. The timing of Handel's arrival in the autumn of 1710 was therefore entirely propitious: the composer's need for an operatic outlet was matched precisely by the London company's need for an adequate composer. Handel's first London opera, *Rinaldo*, was the first original work to be written for, and performed by, the Haymarket company.

Rinaldo received its first performance on 24 February 1711, one day after the composer's 26th birthday, and the score was presumably composed early in 1711: the libretto, the joint work of the Englishman Aaron Hill (effectively, the opera company's manager in the 1710–11 season) and the Italian Giacomo Rossi, was based on incidents from Tasso's *Gierusalemme liberata* and was probably supplied to Handel at the end of 1710. He worked quickly in putting the score together – re-using, as usual, a fair amount of musical material that had proved its worth in his earlier Italian operas – but the spectacular nature of the opera's staging probably entailed a fairly long lead-in period of preparation before the

65

performance. *Rinaldo* was not, however, the first music by Handel to be heard in London. At the Haymarket Theatre in January 1710 the *Rodrigo* overture had been introduced (anonymously) as incidental music into a production of Ben Jonson's comedy *The Alchemist*,[11] and on 6 December 1710 an aria from *Agrippina* was introduced into the opera *Pirro e Demetrio* there:[12] the latter may have been accomplished with Handel's connivance, soon after his arrival in London.

There was also one other intriguing performance, reported in the newspapers:[13]

> Tuesday, the 6th of February [1711], being the Queen's Birth-day, the same was observed with great Solemnity: the Court was extream numerous and magnificent; the Officers of state, Foreign Ministers, Nobility, and Gentry, and particularly the Ladies, vying with each other, who should most grace the Festival. Between One and Two in the Afternoon, was perform'd a fine Consort, being a Dialogue in *Italian*, in Her Majesty's Praise, set to excellent Musick by the famous Mr. *Hendel*, a Retainer to the Court of *Hanover*, in the Quality of Director of his Electoral Highness's Chapple, and sung by *Cavaliero Nicolini Grimaldi*, and the other Celebrated Voices of the Italian Opera: with which Her Majesty was extreamly well pleas'd.

This performance apparently replaced the court ode for the birthday celebrations, the provision of which was traditionally the principal regular duty of the Poet Laureate and the Master of the Queen's Musick.[14] Once again Handel's capacity for gaining quick access to the main centre of power and influence is apparent: he performed privately (yet semi-officially) before the queen only a couple of months after his arrival in London. The music itself cannot be identified with certainty, but the event is significant in view of the question of royal patronage for the opera. As far as is known Queen Anne never attended Handel's operas at the opera house, though the motive for her behaviour on this point is unclear: Anne's last years were dogged by ill-health and she had, in the main, retired from appearances at public entertainments of any sort after the death of her husband in 1708. But in the long term royal patronage was an important issue for the Haymarket opera, and Aaron Hill clearly made a bid for the

---

[11] It is not known how Handel's music came to London for this occasion. The *Musick in the Play call'd the Alchimist by an Italian Master* was published by Walsh in July 1710, so presumably Handel discovered how his music had been used soon after his arrival in London, if he had not known before.

[12] *Pirro e Demetrio* was arranged by Haym from Alessandro Scarlatti (1694, Naples). The *Agrippina* aria (quoted as Ex.6 in Chapter 3) was sung by Francesca Vanini, wife of the bass Giuseppe Boschi: she had also sung in *Agrippina* at Venice, though her role there did not include this aria.

[13] Quoted from Boyer, *The History of the Reign of Queen Anne*, ix, 315.

[14] Court payments to John Eccles, as Master of the Queen's Musick, for composing the court ode are recorded annually until 1709 and again for 1711, but then there is a hiatus until 1715: see Burrows, 'Handel and Hanover', p.41, n.24.

queen's support in the dedication to her that was printed at the front of the word-book for *Rinaldo*:[15]

> Among the numerous Arts and Sciences, which now distinguish the Best of Nations under the Best of Queens; Musick, the most engaging of the Train, appears in Charms we never saw her wear till lately; when the Universal Glory of your Majesty's Illustrious Name drew hither the most celebrated Masters from every Part of *Europe*.
>
> In this Capacity for Flourishing, 'twere a publick Misfortune, shou'd OPERA's for want of due Encouragement, grow faint and languish: My little Fortune and my Application stand devoted to a Trial, whether, such a noble Entertainment, in its due Magnificence, can fail of living, in a City, the most capable of *Europe*, both to relish and support it.
>
> MADAM,
>
> This OPERA is a Native of your Majesty's Dominions, and was consequently born your Subject: 'Tis thence that it presumes to come, a dutiful Entreater of your Royal Favour and Protection; a Blessing, which having once obtain'd, it cannot miss the Clemency of every Air it may hereafter breathe in. Nor shall I then be longer doubtful of succeeding in my Endeavour, to see the *English* OPERA more splendid than her MOTHER, the *Italian*.

If this was a bid for immediate personal royal patronage for the opera company, it failed: but the queen was apparently pleased enough to have the best of the opera talents performing at the palace on her birthday. As to Handel's reputation, by then there was no doubt: in their respective prefaces to the *Rinaldo* libretto, Rossi described Handel as 'Orfeo del nostro Secolo' ('the Orpheus of our age') and Hill contented himself with saying that 'Mr. Hendel, whom the World so justly celebrates, has made the Musick speak so finely for itself, that I am purposely silent on that Subject'. The combination of Handel's music, a good cast including the castrato Nicolini and spectacular staging effects produced a resounding success for Handel's first London opera. It ran to 15 performances in the first season, finishing on 2 June 1711. At the end of April a printed edition of arias from the opera was published by Walsh and Hare, London's leading music publishers, 'Compos'd and exactly corrected by Mr. George Friderick Hendell'. This publication quickly went through a number of versions, on the title-pages of some of which Handel was variously described in English or Italian as Kapellmeister to the Elector of Hanover, as indeed he was so described on the word-book for the opera (Fig. 6).

The first anniversary of Handel's Hanoverian appointment fell in June 1711, and no doubt he left London soon after the last *Rinaldo* performance to return to Hanover. He visited the Düsseldorf court again on the way back: on 17 June the Elector Palatine wrote to both the Elector of Hanover and the Dowager Electress with apologies for detaining him.[16] At the end of July Handel wrote (in French, presumably from Hanover) to the

---

[15] The opera word-books are reprinted in facsimile in Harris, *The Librettos of Handel's Operas*.
[16] *HHB*, pp.53–4.

RINALDO,

A N

O P E R A.

As it is Perform'd

At the QUEENS THEATRE

I N

L O N D O N.

L O N D O N:

Printed by THO. HOWLATT, Printer to the
Houſe, and are to be ſold at *Rice*'s Coffee-
houſe, by the Theatre in the *Hay-market.*
· M DCC X I.

Fig. 5 *Rinaldo*, Handel's first London opera (1711). The title-page from the
original word-book

Perſonaggi.

Goffredo, Capitano Genera- } La Signora *Fran-*
le dell' Armata *Chriſtia-* } *ceſca Vanini Boſ-*
na. } *chi.*

Almirena, ſua Figlia, deſti- } La Signora *Iſabel-*
nata Spoſa a *Rinaldo.* } *la Girardeau.*

Rinaldo, Heroe del Cam- } Il Signor Cavalier
po, deſtinato. Spoſo ad } *Nicolino Grimal-*
Almirena. } *di.*

Euſtazio, Fratello di *Gof-* } Il Signor *Valentino*
fredo. } *Urbani.*

Argante, Rè di *Gieruſa-* } Il Signor *Giuſeppe*
lemme, Amante d' *Ar-* } *Boſchi.*
mida.

 } La Signora *Eliſa-*
Armida Incantatrice, Re- } *betta Piloti Schi-*
gina di *Damaſco,* Aman- } *avonetti,* Virtu-
te d' *Argante.* } oſa di *S. A. E.*
 } d' *Hanover.*
Mago *Chriſtiano.* Il Signor *Caſſani.*

La Muſica e del Signor *Georgio Frederico Hendel,*
Maeſtro di Capella di *S. A. E.* d' *Hanover.*

Fig. 6 The cast-list from the original word-book for *Rinaldo*

German musician Andreas Roner in London, asking for his compliments
to be conveyed to the poet John Hughes and mentioning that he was
making some progress in the English language.[17] Early in August he was
paid his first year's salary at Hanover and he probably remained with the

[17] *HHB*, p.54; Deutsch, p.45.

Hanoverian court for about a year thereafter.[18] Mainwaring plausibly attributes Handel's 'Hanover' Italian duets to this period (see Chapter 2). In November 1711 Handel is recorded in the baptism register of the Halle Marktkirche as standing godfather to a niece, but whether he attended in person is not known.[19] During his absence from London, *Rinaldo* was performed nine times between January and April 1712. There had meanwhile been a rift in the artistic management of the London opera company, involving the temporary alienation from the company of Haym and Clayton, who set up a short-lived concert season at York Buildings.

By mid-October 1712 Handel was back in London, no doubt by prior arrangement with the opera company, and with the Elector of Hanover's acquiescence. By 24 October he had completed his second London opera, *Il pastor fido*: this had its first performance at the Haymarket on 22 November, and was described by a contemporary as 'a New Pastorall Opera ... not by Subscription but at ye usuall Opera Prices ... The Scene represented only ye Country of Arcadia ye Habits [costumes] were old – ye Opera Short'.[20] *Il pastor fido* received six performances in November-December 1712 and a further one the next February, interleaved with other works: a pasticcio *Dorinda*, assembled by Haym, opened on 10 December. By then, however, Handel was at work on yet another opera, *Teseo*, the score of which he completed on 19 December: it received its first performance on 10 January 1713 and ran for 13 performances through to the following May. Handel was by now effectively the established house composer for the Haymarket opera company, but that company saw severe managerial problems as the expenses piled up: after the second performance of *Teseo*, on 14 January,[21]

> Mr Swiny Brakes & runs away & leaves ye Singers unpaid ye Scenes and Habits also unpaid for. The Singers were in some confusion but at last concluded to go on with ye operas on their own accounts, & divide ye Gain amongst them.

Accounts kept for the company by John Jacob Heidegger show that Handel was 'cut in' to the division of incomes with the singers: he also received the last performance of the season, *Teseo* on 16 May 1713, as a benefit night. By then Handel had also probably decided that London held sufficiently attractive prospects for a more permanent career. He did not return to Hanover after the end of the season, and other events, which overlapped with the opera season, made such a return unlikely.

Handel's first visit to London in 1710–11 had coincided with a time of change in British politics, as the queen took on new ministers and the

---

[18] There was a small deduction from Handel's salary for 1711–12 (see Burrows, 'Handel and Hanover', p.40), but no reason for this is known.

[19] Mainwaring's report of Handel's visit to Halle in 1710 may have been misplaced by a year: see n.4 above.

[20] Francis Colman's 'Opera Register': Deutsch, p.50; *HHB*, p.58.

[21] *ibid.*: Deutsch, p.53; *HHB*, p.59.

balance of power fell towards a more 'Whig' outlook and towards political forces that desired British disengagement from the European war. While Handel was in Hanover during 1711–12 the first Peace Articles were agreed between Britain and France (September 1711), and at the end of the year the Duke of Marlborough was dismissed from his post as Captain-General of the Armed Forces. After nearly a decade of concerted action by British, Imperial and Dutch forces, the military alliance was broken by the 'restraining orders' given to the British troops in May 1712. Such unilateral developments were regarded with horror in Hanover, which supported the Imperial cause, and the elector made his views known to Queen Anne in the strongest terms. Yet at the same time the question of the succession to the British throne had to be considered in Hanover: assuming that there was no last-minute interruption from a coup by Jacobites, the Elector of Hanover stood next in succession to the British throne after the death of Queen Anne. A certain amount of political sparring went on between Britain and Hanover, some of it tinged with personal rivalry between Queen Anne and the Electress Sophia: the Hanoverians pressed for the Electoral Prince Georg August to come to London to take up his seat in the House of Lords as Duke of Cambridge, as a kind of advance party for the succession, but the queen would have no-one from the Hanoverian house resident in her country during her lifetime. The diplomatic benefit of having the Hanoverian Kapellmeister in London may have been one of the reasons why Handel was so readily granted leave of absence from the Hanover court. But a career in London entailed coming to terms with the British political and court establishment, and early in 1713 Handel seems to have decided that wholehearted commitment was in order, for he composed works that aligned him completely with the British foreign policy of peace with France. The text of the court ode *Eternal Source of Light Divine* is a celebration of Anne's role as a peacemaker, and was clearly intended for the queen's birthday on 6 February 1713, though it may not have been performed.[22] Around the same time he also composed a *Te Deum* and *Jubilate* in anticipation of a thanksgiving service for the forthcoming peace celebrations: the 'Utrecht' *Te Deum* was completed on 14 January.[23]

Handel's new 'Utrecht' music was rehearsed on 5 and 7 March at St Paul's Cathedral; a newspaper report said that the first rehearsal was attended by 'many Persons of Quality of both Sexes' and that the music was 'much commended by all that have heard the same, and are competent Judges therein'. A further rehearsal followed at the Banqueting House, Whitehall, on 19 March. It seems that Handel was the queen's own choice as composer for the music: in January 1713 the Hanoverian minister

---

[22] Court celebrations of the birthday in 1713 and 1714 may have been limited by the condition of the queen's health: see Burrows, *Handel and the English Chapel Royal*, i, 140–4.

[23] The date from the *Jubilate* autograph has been trimmed away; he may have completed it in mid-February, after composing the birthday ode: see Burrows, *ibid.*, i, 143.

Thomas Grote wrote to the elector from London, conveying the specific request from the queen that Handel should be given permission to remain in London until the *Te Deum* and *Jubilate* came to performance. On the word-book for *Silla*, Handel's fourth London opera which may or may not have come to performance on 2 June 1713,[24] Handel is still described as 'Maestro di Capella di. S.A.E. d'Hannover'. Grote had estimated that the Peace Thanksgiving would be celebrated about four weeks after his letter, but in the event both the international diplomacy and the ceremonial arrangements in London dragged on: the thanksgiving service, with Handel's music, did not take place until 7 July. The service itself was on a grand scale that had not been seen since the thanksgivings for Marlborough's victories some five years before: it was also the first ceremonial service of significance since the completion of the cathedral building. Parliament had declared St Paul's complete in 1711 and paid Wren off for his work, though Thornhill had still to paint the cupola. It was certainly intended that the queen herself should attend the Utrecht Thanksgiving Service, as she had done at the Victory thanksgivings until 1708:[25] but at the last minute her attendance was cancelled, apparently on account of her continuing ill-health. Nevertheless, the occasion was a landmark in Handel's acceptance in London, and in the influence of his music there beyond the opera house.

By July 1713 Handel had certainly overstayed his leave from Hanover, and indeed had passed what would have been the reporting date at the anniversary of the third year of his Hanoverian service. But by then he had been dismissed at Hanover and the circumstances of his dismissal were taken up by Kreyenberg, the Hanoverian court's diplomatic Resident in London, in a letter to Hanover:[26]

London 5 June 1713

A few days ago I wrote to you on the subject of Mr Handel, that since His Highness was determined to dismiss him, Mr Handel submitted to that wish, and desired nothing save that the affair be conducted with a good grace and [that] he be given a little time here so that he could enter the queen's service. Moreover, it seems to me from your letters that this was precisely the generous intention of His Highness. But since then M. Hattorf has informed Mr Handel via M. Kielmansegg that His Highness had dismissed him from his service, telling him that he could go wherever he pleased. In other words, he was given notice in a way which he found particularly mortifying. I will admit to you frankly that Mr Handel is nothing to me, but at the same time I must say that if I had been given a free hand for a week or two I could have resolved the whole affair to the satisfaction of both His Highness and Mr Handel, and even

---

[24] This date is given at the end of the dedicatory preface in the word-book.

[25] The history of the musical thanksgiving services of Anne's reign is outlined in Burrows, *Handel and the English Chapel Royal*, Chapter 2.

[26] Full references, and the original French texts, for the following Hanover letters are in Burrows, 'Handel and Hanover', pp.43–5. The letters are 'double-dated'; only the Old Style dates are given here. The French text of the first letter is also printed in *HHB*, p.62.

to the benefit of the elector's service. The queen's physician, who is an important man and enjoys the queen's confidence, is his great patron and friend, and has the composer constantly at his house. Mr Handel could have been extremely useful, and has been on several occasions, by giving me information of circumstances which have often enlightened me as to the condition of the queen's health. Not that the doctor tells him exactly how she is but, for example, when I have been informed by other reliable channels that the queen was ill, he has been able to tell me that on one particular night the physician slept at the queen's residence, and other circumstances of this kind which provide illumination when taken in conjunction with other information. You must know that our Whigs rarely know anything about the queen's health. [In return,] since the queen is more avid for stories about Hanover than anything else, the doctor can satisfy her curiosity when he is with her from his own information: you understand the stories to which I am referring. Afterwards they are passed on to some serious ecclesiastical gentlemen, and this has a marvellous effect. Perhaps you will not take this seriously, but I do. I arranged things so that Mr Handel could write to M. Kielmansegg to extricate himself gracefully, and I let slip a few words to inform him that, when some day His Highness comes here, he might re-enter his service.

From a second letter, written just before the Utrecht Thanksgiving Service, it appears that the Resident's efforts were effective in securing Handel an honourable severance from his Hanoverian service:

3 July 1713

I am pleased that you have written to me about Mr Handel. I had not expected that he would remain in His Highness's service, nor was I considering that, but merely the manner of his dismissal; I have done it in such a way that he is quite content, giving him to understand that he is by no means in disgrace with His Highness, and dropping a few words to the effect that he will be quite all right when the elector comes here. He will continue to tell me all he knows.

These letters cast Handel into the role of an informer in the field of international diplomacy, and perhaps on reflection this is not so surprising in view of the current political situation between London and Hanover. The question of the queen's health was, of course, significant to Hanover because of the necessity for swift action to secure the succession if the queen were to die suddenly. The medical friend of Handel's was John Arbuthnot, who held office as one of the Physicians in Ordinary to the queen. Arbuthnot is also of consequence as a literary figure in the circle of Addison and Steele: it is rather ironic that documentary evidence tells us more about Handel's literary friends in London at this period than about his relationships with musician colleagues. The most significant message of the Resident's letters, however, is that Handel had clearly decided to sacrifice Hanover to London: indeed, he had indicated to the Resident his intention to 'enter the queen's service'. The transition was completed on 28 December 1713 when Queen Anne granted him an annual pension of £200, apparently in return for undefined services: Handel had secure compensation from the British court, as far as any foreigner could, for the loss of his position in Hanover. It seems an almost perverse twist to history that the institutionalization of Handel's commitment to London bore no immediate fruit in the opera house. The Haymarket season opened late, in January 1714, and presented no Handel operas at all: indeed, there is no firm documentary record of any aspect of Handel's life in the first half of 1714. It is almost as if he, in company with London's politicians, were holding his breath and waiting for the queen's death, which came at length on 1 August.

Although the death of the queen had for some time been expected as imminent, the new king did not travel to take up residence in London immediately, probably because he had to deal with rather complex arrangements for the administration of the electorate he was leaving behind. The new royal family arrived in London in stages: first King George arrived on 20 September with his son, created Prince of Wales soon afterwards; then Caroline, the Princess of Wales, came about a month later, accompanied by her two eldest daughters, Anne and Amelia, arriving on 13 October.[27] They all took up residence at St James's Palace, where they attended services in the Chapel Royal: the first Sunday service after the arrival of each royal party (26 September, 17 October) included a performance of a *Te Deum* by Handel, and it seems likely that the short D major *Te Deum* (HWV 280, known later as the 'Caroline' *Te Deum*) was the work concerned. Naturally, the king's first task was to come to terms with the British political system, and the routines of new court appointments took some time to sort out: it took a year, for example, to identify and legitimize the status of some musicians that had been serving in the Chapel Royal during the last years of Queen Anne's reign. As far as we know, Kreyenberg's solicitations on Handel's behalf had been effective in securing his position in London when the elector succeeded to the throne: indeed, the *Te Deum* performances could not have taken place if Handel had been in disfavour. His 'Queen Anne' pension was continued, and in the initial months of the reign Handel probably stood to gain by his previous association with the new ruling house.

It was no doubt a matter of concern, to Handel as well as to other interested parties, to see whether the new royal family would support the Italian opera. Royal patronage would confirm the opera's status among the noble patrons, and the withholding of such patronage would have an adverse effect that might sink the company's prospects for good. Since King George's tastes were an unknown quantity in Britain, attempts were no doubt made to influence him, both in favour of the opera and in favour

---

[27] The Prince of Wales's eldest son, Frederick, was left behind in Hanover as the representative member of the electoral family there: the prince's youngest daughter, Caroline, was considered too young to travel in 1714 and was brought to London the next year.

of the English drama companies. One rumour was picked up by the newspapers:[28]

> Tis said his Majesty does not approve of the Performances of the Opera in the Hay-Market, and will, for the future, honour his Comedians with his Royal Presence, which will be of great advantage to them.

This turned out to be an ill-founded scare: the king, along with other members of his family, became loyal and regular supporters of London's successive Italian opera companies, and the royal family did their duty by the 'Comedians' (actors' companies) as well. On the evidence available, it seems that King George I normally attended at least half of the performances in each London opera season,[29] and his son and daughter-in-law were even more assiduous in the 1714–15 season. That season began on 23 October 1714, and ran a couple of well-tried pasticcios for the first performances, but *Rinaldo* was revived soon after Christmas, running on to 11 performances, the last in June 1715 for Nicolini's benefit. By then it had been joined by a new Handel opera, *Amadigi di Gaula*, first performed on 25 May 1715 and running to six performances ending in July. The opera season continued unusually late that year: there were even two performances of the pasticcio *Idaspe fedele* in July and August. No doubt the opera company wanted to capitalize on the new royal patronage, and this may have influenced the stretching of the season; at least one planned performance in June had to be cancelled because of the heat. But an equally significant factor was the return of Nicolini to London after an absence of three years: he probably arrived in April, and the première of Handel's *Amadigi* seems to have been delayed to accommodate him. The printed word-book for that opera bore a dedication to Richard, Earl of Burlington, signed by Heidegger, who was effectively the manager of the Haymarket company and the theatre.

The dedication includes a phrase that 'this Opera more immediately claims Your Protection, as it is composed in Your own Family', and this seems to imply that Handel lived for a time at Burlington House: according to Mainwaring's *Memoirs* (p. 93), this was his principal base for three years, presumably around 1713–16.[30] In a passage that is clearly an elaboration of Mainwaring's, Hawkins named Handel's previous host in London as 'one Mr. Andrews, of Barn-Elms [Barnes], in Surrey, but who had also a town residence'.[31] Although written in 1776, this statement must presumably have been based on some previous information, and Hawkins also gives a convincing picture of Handel's association with the

---

[28] *The Weekly Packet* (6–13 November 1714).

[29] See Burrows and Hume, 'George I'.

[30] A short reference in John Gay's *Trivia* (published January 1716) also connected Handel with 'Burlington's fair Palace': see Deutsch, p.70; *HHB*, p.69.

[31] Hawkins, *A General History*, ii, 859. Coxe, *Anecdotes*, p.16, elaborating in turn on Hawkins, describes Handel as passing 'several months' of the summer of 1714 with Mr Andrews, and the subsequent winter at his town house in London.

professional musicians in London's ecclesiastical establishments during his first years in London:[32]

> When Handel had no particular engagements, he frequently went in the afternoon to St. Paul's church, where Mr. Greene, though he was not then organist, was very assiduous in his civilities to him: by him he was introduced to, and made acquainted with the principal performers in the choir. The truth is, that Handel was very fond of St. Paul's organ, built by father Smith, and which was then almost a new instrument; Brind was then the organist, and no very celebrated performer: the tone of the instrument delighted Handel; and a little intreaty was at any time sufficient to prevail on him to touch it, but after he had ascended the organ-loft, it was with reluctance that he left it; and he has been known, after evening service, to play to an audience as great as ever filled the choir. After his performance was over it was his practice to adjourn with the principal persons of the choir to the Queen's Arms tavern in St. Paul's church yard, where was a great room, with a harpsichord in it; and oftentimes an evening was there spent in music and musical conversation.

Although the Hanoverian connection may have worked in Handel's favour during the first months of George I's reign, this was a card that had to be played with caution: it could prove a liability in times when resentment was felt in London against the 'German' court. Newspapers that took up a stance in opposition to the current administration could always make a bid for support by appealing to public xenophobia, whether by complaining that Britain's interests were in danger of being sacrificed to Hanover's, or by complaining about the extravagance of the salaries paid to Italian singers at the opera. Although Handel's music welcomed the royal family at the Chapel Royal services, it was only right and proper that the music for King George I's coronation should be provided by the senior Chapel Royal composer, William Croft, and Croft also supplied the music for the only royal thanksgiving service that was held at St Paul's Cathedral during the reigns of King George I or his son,[33] in January 1716 for 'Bringing his Majesty to a Peaceable and Quiet Possession of the Throne'. In contrast to the rapturous reception afforded to the 'Utrecht' music, the reports of Croft's music for the 1716 service carried a veiled warning for Handel about the ambiguity of his status in London:[34] 'the Te Deum comes up to the Performance of the famous Dr. Henry Purcell, who far exceeded all foreigners'.

For obvious and practical reasons, the king was careful to distinguish between his actions as King George I of Great Britain and as Georg Ludwig, Elector of Hanover. While there was no cause for reproach in Handel's relationship with the British crown, the circumstances of his termination of office at Hanover may still have required some public gesture for their resolution. It is from this perspective that we may be

---

[32] *ibid.*, ii, 859; see also ii, 852, footnote.

[33] See Burrows, *Handel and the English Chapel Royal*, i, 190–3; ii, Appendix 12.

[34] *Dawk's News-Letter* (20 January 1714/15).

able to make sense of the story, told by Mainwaring and elaborated later by Hawkins, that the *Water Music* was the occasion for a reconciliation between the king and Handel.[35] Baron Kielmansegge, named by Main-waring as the person who effected the reconciliation, was the host for the water party on the Thames on 17 July 1717 at which Handel's music was performed. However, there had also been royal water parties with music in the previous summers, and music was mentioned in connection with some in July and August 1715.[36] It may not be a coincidence that on 10 October 1715 the king, from London, ordered Handel to be paid six months' arrears of salary (relating to the period from midsummer 1712) for Hanoverian service.[37]

After the successful season of 1714–15, the opera company at the Haymarket theatre gradually fell into difficulties. Although George had made a 'peaceable' entrance to Britain, London's outlook in the later part of 1715 was dominated by the Jacobite rebellion, and the next opera season began late, in February 1716. The royal family supported the opera company, but the Haymarket opera was not in the continental sense a 'court opera': the king and the Prince of Wales were leading patrons rather than overall providers and guarantors. In view of the broad nature of the patronage that was needed for the opera, any wobble in public or political confidence, or any influence that restrained the nobility and gentry from coming to London for the winter-spring social and political 'season', had an immediate effect on the opera house. Perhaps the most remarkable feature of the programmes for the 1716 and 1716–17 opera seasons is that they saw no new opera from Handel, though *Amadigi* was revived in the first season and again, together with *Rinaldo*, in the second. Handel's creative contribution was limited to the provision of some new music for the revivals.[38] In 1716 the additional music included a new concerto (HWV315, later known as op.3 no.4), performed at *Amadigi* on the orchestra's benefit night (20 June), and in 1717 some new arias for *Rinaldo*, mainly to accommodate the role of Argante (previously sung by a bass) to the alto castrato Gaetano Berenstadt. Many of the best singers from the original cast of *Rinaldo* – Nicolini and the sopranos Pilotti and Anastasia Robinson – were still in place. But after the performance of

[35] Mainwaring, *Memoirs*, pp.91–2; in Hawkins's account (*A General History*, ii, 858–9) the violinist Geminiani shares with Kielmansegge the credit for reconciling Handel and the king.

[36] See Burrows and Hume, 'George I', pp.333–4, 341.

[37] See Burrows, 'Handel and Hanover', pp.40, 46. The payment of Hanover salary arrears may be the substratum of fact that lies behind Mainwaring's erroneous statement (p.92) that, as a result of the water party 'reconciliation', the king added a second British pension to that granted to Handel by Queen Anne: in fact, George I continued Handel's 'Queen Anne' pension from the beginning of his reign, and Handel's second court pension came with his Chapel Royal appointment in 1723.

[38] Unlike Pepusch and Galliard, Handel did not fill in this slack period, 1715–18, by writing for the English theatre companies. It is arguable, however, that works such as Pepusch's *Venus and Adonis* formed a genre model for Handel's *Acis and Galatea*.

Ariosti's *Tito Manlio* on 29 June 1717, the opera company came to an end.

While the deadweight of accumulating managerial and financial problems may have played a part in closing the company, this aspect should not be exaggerated: opera in London was always expensive, but could more or less survive while a sufficient number of enthusiastic patrons were willing to pay. The critical factor in 1717 was a political and social division among the patrons. The flashpoint for this was a family row that broke out between the king and the Prince of Wales at the christening of Prince George William in November 1717,[39] which resulted in the banishment of the Prince and Princess of Wales from St James's Palace and their separation from their children, who were retained by the king. This crisis was, however, only the culmination of a political process involving the growth of an opposition party that had been gathering around the Prince of Wales in the preceding months. The success of the opera company relied on a patronage base which, if not actually politically united, could at least sink its social divisions temporarily: this was not possible when attendance at the courts of the king and the Prince of Wales became mutually exclusive. Rival public display was the order of the day, and this motive accounts for the extravagance of the water party that the king had taken, without his son and daughter-in-law, the previous July:[40]

On Wednesday Evening [17 July 1717], at about 8, the King took Water at Whitehall in an open Barge, wherein were also the Dutchess of Bolton, the Dutchess of Newcastle, the Countess of Godolphin, Madam Kilmanseck, and the Earl of Orkney. And went up the River towards Chelsea. Many other Barges with Persons of Quality attended, and so great a Number of Boats, that the whole River in a manner was cover'd; a City Company's Barge was employ'd for the Musick, wherein were 50 Instruments of all sorts, who play'd all the Way from Lambeth (while the Barges drove with the Tide without Rowing, as far as Chelsea) the finest Symphonies, compos'd express for this Occasion, by Mr Hendel; which his Majesty liked so well, that he caus'd it to be plaid over three times in going and returning. At Eleven his Majesty went a-shore at Chelsea, where a Supper was prepar'd, and then there was another very fine Consort of Music, which lasted till 2; after which, his Majesty came again into his Barge, and return'd the same Way, the Musick continuing to play till he landed.

One intriguing biographical issue from this period concerns the possibility that Handel may have paid a short visit to Germany. Mattheson claimed to have received letters from Handel from Hanover in 1717,[41] and an authoritative later source attributes to the year 1716 a journey to

[39] The prince was born in October 1717 and died the following February.
[40] *The Daily Courant* (19 July 1717): Deutsch, pp.76–7.
[41] *Grundlage*, p.97. A continental visit in 1717 hardly seems possible: the opera season finished at the end of June, the *Water Music* party followed in July, and Handel was at Cannons by the beginning of August.

Ansbach, where Handel reputedly renewed contact with Johann Christoph Schmidt, formerly a student at Halle, and persuaded Schmidt to return to London with him, where – as John Christopher Smith – he found various musical employments and eventually became Handel's principal music-copyist.[42] If Handel went abroad, it would most likely have been during the second half of 1716, since he would presumably have been back in London by the beginning of January 1717, for the revival of *Rinaldo*. The king made his first return visit to Hanover between July 1716 and January 1717, but Handel was not part of the official party.[43] There is some circumstantial evidence to support a continental visit, in that Handel seems to have made arrangements at the end of June 1716 for the payment of a dividend on some South Sea company stock the following August, presumably on the assumption that he would not be in London at the time.[44] The fact that Handel owned £500 of stock is testimony to the fact that he must have prospered well enough in London during his first five years of permanent residence. Along with the biographical obscurity surrounding the possible German trip goes the obscurity of motive surrounding a German work composed during this period. Handel's setting of the Passion story, *Der für die Sünde der Welt gemarterte und sterbende Jesus* (HWV48), was composed by 1716, possibly slightly earlier: unfortunately the place or occasion for its first performance is not known, and the composition autograph (like that of *Amadigi*, the other major work from the same period) is lost. The text, by Brockes, was published in Hamburg in 1712 but may have been circulating earlier; Handel's work was certainly performed there at a rather later period.[45] The contemporary demands of Handel's London career seem to weigh against the proposition that he could have been in Germany during the Passiontide season in 1715 or 1716.

It may be significant that Handel apparently did not contemplate returning to a career in continental Europe after the closure of the opera in 1717: presumably by then he saw his future as continuing in London, supported by the royal pension, and he may well have regarded the current situation at the Haymarket as only a temporary hiatus in London's operatic history. By early August 1717 he had found a private patronage base with musical potential, this time from James Brydges, Earl of Carnarvon, today better known by his subsequent title as Duke of Chandos. Brydges had retired from a public career in which he had made a fortune out of his office as Paymaster for the Forces during the

[42] Coxe, *Anecdotes*, p.37. Winton Dean, in 'Handel's Early London Copyists', concludes that Smith's earliest surviving music copies for Handel date from 1718, but Smith may have come over as an orchestral player in the first instance.
[43] See Burrows, 'Handel and Hanover', p.46.
[44] Deutsch, p.71; *HHB*, p.70.
[45] See Becker, 'Die frühe Hamburgische Tagespresse', p.36; *HHB* also notes performances at Hamburg on various dates between 31 March 1719 and 5 April 1724, some in the 'Drill-Haus'.

continental war: in 1717 he was still involved in the last stages of a public investigation about the legitimacy of the acquisition of his fortune. Brydges had considerable property both in London and in the Bristol and Bath area, but his main concern in 1717 was the development of a large house at Cannons Park, Edgware. He had already paid for an elaborate reconstruction of the parish church of St Lawrence's adjoining the Cannons estate, which was completed at Easter 1716: the best Italian painters had been hired for the decoration of the ceiling and the east end, and a gallery for Brydges and his servants had been built into the west end. The decoration of the walls was to be completed during the next two decades.

Handel's presence at Cannons, in company with Dr Arbuthnot and others, was noted by a diarist on 4 August 1717, and on 25 September Brydges wrote to Arbuthnot in these terms:[46]

> Mr Hendle has made me two new Anthems very noble ones & Most think they far exceed the two first. He is at work for 2 more & some Overtures to be plaied before the first lesson. You had as good take Cannons in on your way to London.

In all Handel composed for Cannons a *Te Deum* (HWV281), a *Jubilate* (HWV246, a scaled-down version of the 'Utrecht' *Jubilate*) and ten anthems:[47] these would have seen their first performances at church services in St Lawrence's (the domestic chapel at the Cannons mansion was not completed until 1720). Handel's association with Brydges may have lasted about a year: he is recorded as dining at Cannons again in April 1718, in company with Arbuthnot and Pepusch. By then all the Cannons anthems had probably been completed and performed, but another scheme was afoot, mentioned in a letter written by Sir David Dalrymple at the end of May:[48]

> Since my Last I have been at Canons with E. of Carnarvon who Lives an Prince & to boot is a worthy beneficent man, I heard sermon at his parish church which for painting and ornament exceeds every thing in this Country he has a Chorus of his own, the Musick is made for himself and sung by his own servants, besides which there is a Little opera now a makeing for his diversion whereof the Musick will not be made publick. The words are to be furnished by M[rs] [i.e. Messrs] Pope & Gay, the musick to be composed by Hendell. It is as good as finished, and I am promised some of the Songs by Dr Arbuthnot who is one of the club of composers.

This 'little opera' was *Acis and Galatea*, which may have been staged in

---

[46] See Beeks, "'A Club of Composers'", p.210; see also Deutsch, p.78; *HHB*, p.75.

[47] The anthem *O praise the Lord, ye angels of his* (HWV257, and included in *HG* 36) is not by Handel but by Maurice Greene: see Johnstone, 'The Chandos Anthems'.

[48] *HHB*, p.76; see also Beeks, "'A Club of Composers'", p.212. The opening phrases of the letter quoted here might suggest that 'Cannons anthems' (by Handel, Haym or Pepusch) were still being regularly performed, though this is not certain, because of Dalrymple's defective punctuation.

a dramatic or semi-dramatic form for private performance at Cannons soon afterwards. Similar circumstances also probably brought forth Handel's first English oratorio, *Esther*, at much the same period, though documentary records for its performance are non-existent.

The Cannons interlude in his career was entirely fortunate for Handel. At the time Brydges was at the height of his fortune (he was soon to lose a considerable part of it in the South Sea Bubble), and he chose to devote his wealth not only to his building programme but also to the employment of a regular band of musicians, a full chamber group of singers and players that would in 1718 have been capable of performing *Acis and Galatea* and, with some augmentation, *Esther*.[49] He was the only private patron in Britain outside royal circles with both the resources and the inclination to employ a 'musical court'. As Brydges was currently out of politics – his political actions, such as they were, were directed towards securing his dukedom – they provided a safe haven away from the royal courts. Handel could not afford to take sides in the royal dispute. He needed the support of the king, but was of the same generation as the Prince of Wales: since he could not attend one court without offending the other, it suited his purpose to stay away from both, at Cannons. The extent of the material support that Handel received from Brydges is unknown. Possibly he lived for a period either at Cannons or in London at Brydges's expense, as an honoured guest rather than as a 'serving musician', since there are no payments to Handel in Brydges's surviving household accounts. This documentary silence matches that from the establishments of Ruspoli and Burlington: perhaps Handel deliberately avoided any conditions of employment that would have branded him as a servant. Other leading composers were formally employed by Brydges. Haym had composed instrumentally accompanied anthems for Cannons before Handel came on the scene.[50] Pepusch, whose presence was reported at Cannons with Handel in 1718, took on in a more formal manner the role of musical director for Brydges, and served in this capacity, on a somewhat part-time basis, until 1725.[51]

From Handel's point of view, the most important aspect of Brydges's patronage was that it provided him with agreeable circumstances in which he could develop a musical role in the period after the opera house closed. In addition to composing the church music, the 'little opera' and the oratorio, Handel probably devoted the period to extending and committing

---

[49] Winton Dean (*Handel's Dramatic Oratorios*, pp.222–3) has suggested that *Esther* was composed in two 'layers', the second requiring augmented performing forces (including horns, bassoons, harp and extra singers, that were not part of Brydges's known regular establishment); but the dated 'Malmesbury' MS copy of *Esther* proves that the work was complete in its full form by 1718 (or March 1719 at the latest, if the year was reckoned in Old Style).

[50] A presentation copy of six anthems by Haym from the Cannons library, with a dedicatory preface by Haym dated 29 September 1716, is now British Library Add. 62561.

[51] As regular members of Brydges's musical staff, Pepusch and Haym probably played violin and cello, respectively, in Handel's Cannons performances.

to paper the repertory of keyboard music that he had developed over the years, though the amiable story that one of his themes was suggested by the sounds coming from the anvil of the Cannons blacksmith must be consigned to the category of romantic fiction. The fruits of the rationalization of his keyboard music were seen in the publication of the first collection of his *Suites de Pièces* (comprising the eight suites HWV426–33) that appeared in November 1720, 'printed for the Author, And ... only to be had at Christopher Smith's in Coventry Street'. But by 1720 Handel's life had entered another chapter.

5

The music, 1711–19

The Deficiences I found, or thought I found, in such Italian OPERA's as have hitherto been introduc'd among us, were, First; That they had been compos'd for Tastes and Voices, different from those who were to sing and hear them on the English Stage; And Secondly, That wanting the Machines and Decorations, which bestow so great a Beauty on their Appearance, they have been heard and seen to very considerable Disadvantage.

At once to remedy both these Misfortunes, I resolv'd to frame some Dramma, that, by different Incidents and Passions, might afford the Musick Scope to vary and display its Excellence, and fill the eye with more delightful Prospects, so at once to give Two Senses equal Pleasure.

The passage from Aaron Hill's preface to the word-book for *Rinaldo* (1711) suggests that he was attempting to accommodate Italian opera to English taste, and to a certain extent this was true: the opera is rather episodic, and has a strong emphasis on the visual-scenic element which may be related to the tradition of the masques and semi-operas that had been London's music theatre before Italian opera arrived. Handel could, however, have also interpreted this particular emphasis in terms of his previous experience in Hamburg, where scenic effects and spectacular scenes had been an expected part of the theatrical experience. To a certain extent, also, *Rinaldo* resembles the Hamburg tradition in that the dramatic discourse is not entirely heroic: while there are no comic scenes as such, Argante (the King of Jerusalem) and Armida (an enchantress) converse in a literary register that is noticeably more down-to-earth than that of the hero (Rinaldo) and heroine (Almirena). It is noticeable also that, while the opera contains a number of show-pieces for the leading singers, many of the arias are relatively short.

Above all, the music is tuneful – Handel re-used his stock of effective and memorable operatic melodies, and added to their store. The sarabande tune deriving from the Asiatics in *Almira* flowered as Almirena's lament 'Lascia ch'io pianga', and Rinaldo's warlike 'Abruggio, avampo e fremo' derived from 'Ob dein Mund wie Plutons Rachen' in the same source, both much improved on the way. Almirena's 'Bel piacere', with its single-thread unharmonized melody and jaunty metrical changes, came from *Il trionfo del Tempo* via *Agrippina* – in this case, the *Agrippina* version was transferred wholesale, text and all. The Italian cantata *Aminta e Fillide* supplied the material for the enchanting mermaids' song 'Il vostro Maggio' and for the first movement of the overture. The overture itself is a fascinating and successful synthesis of the principal Baroque national styles: the outline is that of the 'French' Ouverture, with a dotted-rhythm *entrée*, an imitative second movement and a final gigue (though not so named), but the imitative passages in the second movement behave as ritornellos to italianate solo violin episodes, and a typical Italian-style short Adagio movement precedes the gigue. Among the new music (as far as is known) were the marches for the rival armies, of which that for the Christian army (Ex.7, scored for an orchestra including four trumpets and timpani) achieved considerable subsequent popularity and was pirated 17 years later for use as a song in the *Beggar's Opera*.

Ex. 7

At the end of Act 2, Handel put himself in the limelight with 'Vo' far guerra', an aria for Armida punctuated by solo passages for harpsichord in the opening and closing ritornellos of the *A* section. This aria was apparently based on a thematic idea from a pre-existing keyboard piece,[1] but it was thoroughly 'composed-out' in its new context. In his part of the prefatory material to the *Rinaldo* word-book, Giacomo Rossi claimed (perhaps complained) that he had been hurried along by the composer, who had set the complete opera to music in a fortnight: while this seems

---

[1] The *Sonata for a Harpsichord with double keys* (i.e. two manuals) HWV579, also related thematically to the sonata for organ and orchestra in the 1707 version of *Il trionfo del Tempo*.

possible in view of the amount of re-used material, Handel nevertheless not only copied out the old music afresh but usually substantially re-composed it.

In terms of visual spectacle, Hill's scenario certainly made heavy demands. These included a large number of 'supers' on stage for the armies and a constant challenge to the scene-builders and scene-shifters, especially in the first scenes of Act 3:

A dreadful Prospect of a Mountain, horridly steep, and rising from the Front of the Stage, to the utmost Height of the most backward Part of the Theatre; Rocks, and Caves, and Waterfalls, are seen upon the Ascent, and on the Top appear the blazing Battlements of the Enchanted Palace, Guarded by a great Number of Spirits, of various Forms and Aspects; In the midst of the Wall is seen a Gate, with several Arches supported by Pillars of Chrystal, Azure, Emeralds, and all sorts of precious Stones. At the Foot of the Mountain is discover'd the Magicians Cave.

Godfrey, Eustatio and the Soldiers, having climb'd half way up the Mountain, are stopp'd by a Row of ugly Spirits, who start up before 'em; The Soldiers, frighted, endeavour to run back, but are cut off in their Way by another Troop, who start up below 'em. In the midst of their Confusion, the Mountain opens and swallows 'em up, with Thunder, Lightning, and amazing Noises. Godfrey, Eustatio, and the Soldiers who escape, return in great Confusion to the Magician's Cave.

They reascend the Mountain, while the Magician stands at his Cave Door, and sings, to encourage 'em. The Spirits, as before, present themselves in opposition, but upon the Touch of the Wands, vanish upward and downward, with terrible Noises and Confusion. They gain the Summit of the Hill and entring the Enchanted Arches, strike the Gate with their Wands; when immediately the Palace, the Spirits, and the whole Mountain vanish away, and Godfrey and Eustatio are discover'd hanging on the sides of a vast Rock in the middle of the Sea; with much Difficulty they reach the Top, and descend on the other side.

In a famous passage in *The Spectator* for 6 March 1711, Addison related (or, more likely, created) a story about overhearing a conversation in the street about 'sparrows for the opera', whereupon he purchased the word-book and found that 'the Sparrows were to act the part of Singing Birds in a delightful Grove: though upon a nearer Enquiry I found [that] ...though they flew in Sight, the Musick proceeded from a Consort of Flageletts and Birdcalls which was planted behind the Scenes'. This refers to the opening of Act 1 scene vi, where indeed a flageolet and recorders supply the birdsong (Ex.8). Although Hill's English stage direction had the birds 'flying up and down among the Trees', the parallel Italian page has them in bird-cages ('uccelliere'). But, as Addison found out from perusing the word-book:

The Opera of *Rinaldo* is filled with Thunder and Lightning, Illuminations, and Fireworks; which the Audience may look upon without catching Cold, and

Ex. 8

(O charming birds who sing, O zephyrs who breathe sweet breezes around me, [tell me where my loved one is.])

indeed without much Danger of being burnt; for there are several Engines filled with Water, and ready to play at a Minute's Warning, in case any such Accident should happen.

The *Spectator* had led the press criticism of the Haymarket's early attempts at Italian opera, but this gentle ribbing about scenic effects was as close as the journalists could get to a serious attack on *Rinaldo*: as Mainwaring put it (p. 78), Handel's opera put an end to the 'reign of nonsense' in the opera house. The papers had already recognized the stage 'presence' of Nicolini.[2]

For my own part, I was fully satisfied with the sight of an actor, who by the grace and propriety of his action and gesture, does honour to the human figure... Every one will easily imagine I mean Signior Nicolini, who sets off

[2] *The Tatler* (3 January 1710).

the character he bears in an opera by his action, as much as he does the words of it by his voice. Every limb, and every finger, contributes to the parts he acts, insomuch that a deaf man may go along with him in the sense of it. There is scarce a beautiful posture in an old statue which he does not plant himself in, as the different circumstances of the story give occasion for it. He performs the most ordinary action in a manner suitable to the greatness of his character, and shows the prince even in the giving of a letter or dispatching of a messenger.

Yet, in terms of dramatic power, the leading role in *Rinaldo* is not the name-part that was played by Nicolini but that of the enchantress Armida, written for the soprano Pilotti (Elisabetta Pilotti Schiavonetti, another artist 'on loan' from Hanover). She has a particularly fine scene towards the end of Act 2, where her frustration at her failure to attract Rinaldo (by disguising herself as Almirena, his 'intended wife') is vented first in a furious accompanied recitative ('Dunque i lasci d'un volto') and then in a lamenting aria ('Ah! crudel'), the latter featuring a bassoon solo for Kytch in the accompaniment and a Presto *B* section at 'O infedel'. Her subsequent recitative scene with Argante is a brilliant foil to this intensity. Armida, wishing to hide her disarrayed emotions from Argante, disguises herself as Almirena, only to discover that Argante (whom she had supposedly committed to her own service) has designs on Almirena. The new emotional setback, piled on her initial disappointment at failing to attract Rinaldo, precipitates 'Vo' far guerra', the aria with harpsichord obbligato already referred to.

After *Rinaldo*, *Il pastor fido* (1712) comes as a complete contrast. It is an amiable pastoral drama (darkened only by the threat, inherent in the plot, of human sacrifice, which is happily averted in the end) on almost a chamber scale, based on a play by Giovanni Battista Guarini that was regarded as a classic example of the pastoral literary mode. Once again Handel was able to re-work some of his well-tried music: the first aria has a musical ancestry going back to 'Quillt, ihr überhäuften Zähren' in *Almira*. The drama hangs together well enough, and provided opportunities for some lively characterization of the hero Silvio (who is more attracted to field-sports than to the attentions of young ladies) and of Eurilla, the jealous lover who tries to lure or trick the shepherd Mirtillo away from his intended Amarilli. The opera was mounted during the period of Nicolini's absence from London, and the musical honours are shared out fairly evenly among the five leading characters (a sixth, the High Priest, appears only in the final scene); in spite of the intimate scale of the drama, the arias are, on average, rather longer than in *Rinaldo*. Eurilla has some of the best music, with a particularly striking aria at the end of Act 2: the part was played by Margherita de l'Epine, who later became Mrs Pepusch.

With *Teseo* (1713), the artistic policy of the Haymarket programme took a new turn: an Italian opera was converted from Philippe Quinault's *tragédie lyrique Thésée*, bringing with it the five-act structure of the French original. This opera marked Handel's first collaboration with Nicola Haym as librettist-adapter. Over the next 15 years Haym produced some of the most successful London librettos for Handel. No doubt Haym's strength lay in the fact that he was a practising musician as well as a cultured Italian, so that his aural imagination identified the best musical opportunities in a pre-existing libretto, even if this sometimes appeared superficially to involve the sacrifice of some dramatic point.[3] *Teseo* was not an entirely auspicious start to the collaboration, as the dramatic conventions of Quinault's original did not convert well to those of Italian *opera seria*, in which arias function best as the climaxes of interchanges between the characters. But there are some good scenes, especially for the princess/enchantress Medea (a role played by Pilotti), who is successively cheated of marriage to Egeo (Aegeus), King of Athens, and Teseo (Theseus, Egeo's son, though not recognized as such until near the end of the opera). Not surprisingly, Medea makes various mischief, the dramatic presentation of which involved transformation scenes, so that *Teseo* saw a return to the visual spectacle of *Rinaldo*, although not on quite such a lavish scale. An imbalance in the score is apparent from the fact that Medea does not appear in Act 1 but has three arias and a duet in Act 2: nevertheless, all these arias are splendid, and still better music comes with the incantation scene (accompanied recitative and aria) at the end of Act 3 and with the final bravura aria 'Morirò' in Act 5. By the time he came to compose *Teseo* Handel had used up a considerable stock of his self-borrowable music, and this opera owes less than its predecessors to pre-existing material.

Silla (1713) is a more modest affair, having fewer arias than *Il pastor fido* (which itself had been regarded as a 'short' opera). In some respects Handel's music seems rather perfunctory, and the printed word-book is unique among the London publications in giving the Italian text without an English translation; nor does it name the singers. The opera may have been put together hurriedly (using the theatre's stock sets) for a private performance for the French ambassador, to whom the libretto was dedicated by Rossi. The plot concerns a Roman dictator who behaves with repulsive ruthlessness until the final insurrection, upon which he retires to private life and peace is restored: a satirical identification of Silla with the Duke of Marlborough may have been intended.[4]

With *Amadigi* (1715) Handel returned to top form. This time a French five-act *tragédie lyrique* was successfully converted (probably by Haym) into a three-act Italian opera. In some respects the dramatic recipe is the same as in *Rinaldo* and *Teseo*, with a sorceress vainly pursuing a hero who has attachments elsewhere. Once again the sorceress (Melissa, another role for Pilotti) has some fine scenes and dominates the action in the last

[3] For a comprehensive survey of Haym's career, see Lindgren, 'The Achievements'.
[4] See Chisholm, 'Handel's "Lucio Cornelio Silla"'.

act, but now the other roles are also strong. The concentration of dramatic force is assisted by the absence of sub-plots for minor characters. There are only four principals:[5] Amadigi and Dardano, in rivalry for the princess Oriana, and Melissa who is determined to gain Amadigi. Handel's music conveys the jealous emotional forces at work with a strength that overrides any structural weakness in the libretto. Furthermore, there is a cumulative pattern to the music, one that was to be repeated in Handel's great operas of the next two decades. The first act, although it contains some remarkable music, such as Amadigi's 'Oh notte' and Melissa's 'Ah! spietato', is mainly conventional and expository, and it remains tonally earthbound around the keys of B♭ major and G minor, in a fashion that was not characteristic of the later Handel. In Act 2, however, once the strands of the plot begin to move, the music develops in intensity. Amadigi looks into the fountain of true love, where Melissa conjures up an image of Oriana caressing his rival: he faints and Oriana, discovering him and believing him dead, sings a magnificent F minor lament, 'S'estinto è l'idol mio' (Ex.9). No less magnificent is Dardano's 'Pena tiranna' as he gives vent to the hopelessness of his love for Oriana. But Melissa disguises Dardano as Amadigi: he thus attracts Oriana, and in his next aria Dardano rejoices in the apparent success of this stratagem with the Haydnesque 'Tu mia speranza' (Ex.10). From then on, with both music and plot wound up to full tension, the drama proceeds in fine style. Burney, after examining the score of *Amadigi*, declared it to be 'a production in which there is more invention, variety and good composition, than in any one of the musical dramas of Handel which I have yet carefully and critically examined'.[6] In the original production Amadigi was sung by Nicolini, and his rival Dardano, in the absence of a second castrato, was taken by the contralto Diana Vico as a 'trousers' role. Although there were only four principals, the stage was well occupied: a dance troupe supplied 'infernal spirits' attendant on Melissa and 'enchanted knights and ladies' to accompany Oriana, and Handel provided suitable music for them.

While the Italian operas naturally stand at the centre of Handel's professional activity at this period, his compositions to English texts are both interesting and significant. Soon after his return to London in 1712 Handel seems to have made a positive decision to come to terms with, and to make some contribution to, the English traditions of church music and the court ode. His first attempt was a verse anthem with organ accompaniment, a setting of Psalm xlii (*As pants the hart*, HWV251a) to a text freely assembled from the King James Bible, the Prayer Book and Tate and Brady's metrical version of the psalms:[7] it seems likely that he

---

[5] As in *Il pastor fido*, an additional character (Orgando, the enchanter), appears in the final scene; he is not included in the cast-list in the printed word-book.

[6] *A General History*, ii, 698.

[7] N. Tate and N. Brady, *A New Version of the Psalms of David*; first published in 1696, it quickly attained popularity and by 1712 it was in its seventh edition.

Ex. 9

(If my lover is dead, I wish to die also.)

took advice about the text and its musical treatment from John Arbuthnot, who may himself have composed music for a similar version.[8] Although it is something of an apprentice effort, this anthem seems to have been a reference point – almost a means of security – for Handel: when

[8] Arbuthnot's anthem does not survive, but its text was printed in a collection of anthem texts published in 1712.

Ex.10

(You, my hope, my comfort, are the beloved treasure of my soul.)

he returned to the composition of English anthems, at Cannons five years later or at the Chapel Royal a decade later, Handel seems to have begun by re-working *As pants the hart* before extending the repertory with other works. In his later versions he was more careful to round off the tonal scheme: this first setting begins in D minor and ends in B♭ major. Large-scale tonal organization (as distinct from moment-to-moment contrasts of key or overall balance) does not seem to have been a serious concern of Handel in earlier periods in his career. The anthem contains a pleasing balance of contrapuntal choruses and solo movements written for Richard Elford, the Chapel Royal's leading alto soloist. One of the solos ('Tears are my daily food') employs ground-bass techniques, perhaps in recognition of the musical taste that London had preserved from the time of Purcell.

The 'Utrecht' *Te Deum* and *Jubilate* of 1713 – a landmark in Handel's English music comparable to *Dixit Dominus* in his Latin works – stands in a yet more ambiguous relationship to the legacy of Purcell. Purcell's D major *Te Deum* and *Jubilate*, composed in 1694, had established itself as the model work for London's grand celebratory church services: it had been revived during 1702–8 at the royal thanksgivings in St Paul's Cathedral for Marlborough's military victories. The printed score seems to have been continuously available from music sellers throughout the period up to 1712, and it seems very likely that Handel saw (and he may have owned) a copy. While he might have looked to Purcell's work[9] for general specifications – a declamatory style, emphasizing trumpets and strings and with alternating soloists and chorus – Handel's version turned out very differently. The opening verses of the *Te Deum*, for example

> We praise Thee, O God, We acknowledge Thee to be the Lord
> All the Earth doth worship Thee, the Father everlasting

generated two choral movements from Handel lasting about six minutes in all, compared with Purcell's brisk sequence of fanfare, solo voices and short chorus which is over in less than two minutes. The 'Utrecht' music set a new standard for time-scale and for musical solidity in English church music. As in Purcell's setting, there is a distinct difference in treatment between Handel's *Te Deum* and his *Jubilate*, arising partly from the literary structure of the texts: the *Jubilate* falls into discrete movements assignable to soloists and chorus, while the soloists have only short interludes in the *Te Deum*. This contrast is greatly magnified in Handel's setting, and it is remarkable that the soloists' names appear on his autograph of the *Jubilate*, but not on the *Te Deum*: the *Jubilate*, (from which the composition date is lost) may have been composed a few weeks after the *Te Deum*, and with more specific knowledge of the capabilities of the leading singers. For the Thanksgiving Service the full complement of the Chapel Royal choir and the Royal Musicians would have turned out, no doubt supplemented by as many extra performers as could be accommodated in the organ gallery at St Paul's (it is unlikely that space was squandered on timpani, which Handel did not include in his score). There were probably about 40 performers in all, perhaps more than had been assembled in one place in London since the coronation of Queen Anne in 1702.

The 'Caroline' *Te Deum* (HWV 280) is much more akin to Purcell's setting in its compact scale and shorter duration (about 15 minutes, as against the 25 minutes of the 'Utrecht' *Te Deum*): the scoring for trumpet and strings and the introductory 'verse' sections for voices also seem closer to Purcell. But where Purcell set the verses of the text as a series of short episodes, Handel welds them together into more continuous movements. In particular, Handel's continuous solo alto movement 'When thou tookest

---

[9] Possibly also to Croft's more recent setting, of which Handel might have been able to borrow a manuscript copy through his association with the singers at St Paul's Cathedral and the Chapel Royal.

upon Thee to deliver man' covers many text verses.[10] Here Handel clearly applied his experience from operatic arias: the scoring of the opening ritornello and of the first vocal phrases (with violins providing a bass) has clear parallels in the operatic repertory, and the vocal part is developed with masterly control of its long-span phrases. In the Chapel Royal Handel had singers who could do justice to the music: the 'English' altos Elford and Hughes had effectively been driven to the ecclesiastical choirs from careers on the stage as a result of the fashion for opera and castratos. Sadly, Elford died at the end of October 1714, less than a fortnight after singing the *Te Deum* at Princess Caroline's arrival in England.

The Chapel Royal had good bass soloists as well as altos, and in the 'Caroline' *Te Deum* Bernard Gates (who was to play an important role in Handel's career nearly 20 years later) was given a Lullian, triple-time solo in dance rhythm, 'Thou art the King of Glory, O Christ'. Handel's first setting of the anthem *O sing unto the Lord a new Song* (HWV 249a) appears to be a companion-piece to the 'Caroline' *Te Deum*: it includes another bass solo in similar style for Gates's colleague Thomas Baker, 'Glory and worship are before Him'. This movement is quite substantial, and makes free use of ground-bass techniques, but the overall effect is less of a tribute to Purcell in his 'French' manner than a reversion to the '*Almira* style' of Handel's Hamburg years. The anthem ends with a pair of short but powerful choruses, conveying the spirit but not the spaciousness of the 'Utrecht' and 'Caroline' works.

For the 'Caroline' *Te Deum* at the Chapel Royal Handel probably had about 25 performers, including the orchestra.[11] The musical establishment of James Brydges for which Handel composed his next English church music – the so-called 'Chandos' anthems, though they were almost certainly completed before Brydges received the Chandos title – was yet smaller. At the first performances there may have been two players on each of the violin parts and two or three trebles on the top vocal part, but elsewhere the rule was one to a part and the regular establishment did not run to violas or altos; in Handel's first anthems for Cannons the remaining forces comprised an oboe, bassoon, cello, double bass and organ (Handel himself), though extra musicians (a tenor or two, an alto and perhaps a second cello) were occasionally added to the forces, probably temporarily. The same singers performed both the 'solo' movements and the appropriate vocal line in 'choruses', which would have been one to a part in the lower voices. As an exercise in employing minimal resources this sounds similar to the circumstances that J. S. Bach complained about in Leipzig a decade or so later, but there was an important difference: while Bach's forces were made up with a ballast of students and amateurs,

[10] On the early history of this work, see Burrows, *Handel and the English Chapel Royal*, i, chap. 5.
[11] *ibid.*, ii, pp. 19–30, 48–52, 109.

all the musicians at Cannons (except the trebles) were fully professional musicians of competence and experience.[12] The anthems, performed in the area at the east end of St Lawrence's church, must have been an agreeable experience in extended concerted chamber music, and an enhancement of the liturgy that compared, in aural terms, to the visual stimuli provided by the building's decorative scheme.

From Brydges's letter to Arbuthnot (quoted on p. 80) it seems that Handel composed the first groups of Cannons anthems in pairs. It has been possible to establish a working hypothesis for four, and possibly five, pair-groupings on the basis of musical content, documentary evidence and the flow of different types of manuscript paper through the set of autographs.[13] The anthems that have been thus paired were probably not intended to be performed on the same occasions: they display no special affinities of theme or key but seem instead to contrast with each other. The first pair were re-workings, in a more extended form, of the Chapel Royal anthems *As pants the hart* and *O sing unto the Lord*. Handel began both (and all but one of the subsequent anthems) with a two-movement instrumental introduction, the materials of which were quarried 20 years later when he needed trio sonatas for publication. He quickly established a style in these anthems that combined the decorum suitable for church music with the compositional skills that he had developed in the opera house. On one hand there are extended ensemble ('chorus') movements such as 'Put thy trust in God' in *As pants the hart* (HWV251*b*) and 'Declare his honour unto the Heathen' in *O sing unto the Lord* (HWV249*b*); these are complemented by arias with picturesque touches such as the 'harpeggio' violin obbligato to 'Now when I think thereupon' in the first anthem and the stormy orchestral accompaniment to 'The waves of the sea rage horribly' in the second. Perhaps the greatest unexpected delight is the flowing duet 'O worship the Lord in the beauty of holiness' in *O sing unto the Lord*.

In the following pairs of anthems Handel, while extending the general style of this first pair and producing contrasted works in each group, seems also to have mixed one 'original' anthem with one based on pre-existing music. *Let God arise* (HWV256*a*) is on a much larger scale than its predecessors, with longer movements and a forceful style, strengthened by the addition of an alto to give a four-voice texture in the ensemble movements. Its second half is dominated by a succession of strong chorus movements, beginning with 'O sing unto God': the last movement develops a musical idea from the last chorus of the 'Utrecht' *Te Deum* into a movement that is half as long again and enlivened with the addition of florid hallelujahs. The companion anthem, *My song shall be alway*

---

[12] Beeks, 'Handel and Music for the Earl of Carnarvon', provides a complete review of the musical establishment at Cannons, based on contemporary documents.

[13] For the 'pairings' see Beeks, *ibid.*, p. 4, and further references there.

(HWV252) is more restrained in tone and indebted to musical ideas from the 'Caroline' *Te Deum* and the *Brockes Passion*. The trio movement 'Thou rulest the raging of the sea' does not survive in Handel's autograph and is stylistically rather distant from his normal style: it may have been contributed as an afterthought by Haym or Pepusch. Other anthems also seem to have undergone last-minute revisions by Handel himself: he added an extra introductory instrumental movement to *Let God arise* and a couple of vocal movements to one of the later anthems. For the third pair of Cannons anthems Handel matched a straightforward (but skilful) arrangement of the 'Utrecht' *Jubilate* (*O be joyful in the Lord*, HWV246) with a dark-toned, confessional piece, *Have mercy upon me* (HWV248). The latter re-uses some ideas from the 'Utrecht' *Te Deum*, but these are subsumed within new mateial in the middle of the anthem, and the tone of the work as a whole is defined by its minor-key outer movements.

In the fourth pair of anthems Handel matched the cheerful and well-wrought *I will magnify Thee* (HWV250a) with *In the Lord put I my trust* (HWV247), a colourful presentation of a selection of verses from Psalms ix, xi, xii and xiii in (as Handel described it) 'Tate and Brady's versification'. The former uses the opening vocal theme from *Dixit Dominus* as the basis of the first choral movement and includes an eloquent lyrical aria for tenor, 'The Lord preserveth'. In spite of its minor-key framework, Handel appears to have enjoyed himself with the whimsical text of *In the Lord put I my trust*, writing some lively chorus movements with a free and effective mixture of contrapuntal and homophonic passages: the music of the introductory sinfonia, which comprised two of his best instrumental movements to date, became familiar to twentieth-century audiences through Elgar's grandiose (but, in its way, serious and effective) arrangement dating from 1923. *O come, let us sing unto the Lord* (HWV253) may have been composed as a 'twin' with the 'Chandos' *Te Deum*. The anthem has echoes of Handel's Latin psalms in its opening and closing vocal movements, and its mood is predominantly cheerful. Although its thematic ideas are strong and its writing is fluent, as a whole it seems rather unbalanced: some prolix chorus movements dominate the first half, and a succession of three arias then precedes the final chorus.

The last two anthems for Cannons stand somewhat apart and were probably not composed as a pair. *The Lord is my light* (HWV255) is in many ways the best of the set, and the culmination of Handel's experience: it has some splendid tenor arias, and a graphic series of choruses beginning with the rhetorical 'For who is God, but the Lord'. *O praise the Lord with one consent* (HWV254) has less variety of mood but goes on its cheerful way with confidence: there is also a novel echo effect at 'to Heav'n their voices raise', as the sound of praise sails upward. This anthem is the only one without a separate instrumental sinfonia, but the extended opening ritornello to the first chorus (based on a theme very similar to that of William Croft's tune for 'O God, our help in ages past', composed at much the same period) adequately fulfils the introductory role. In the 'Chandos' *Te Deum* (HWV281), Handel spread himself with choruses even more extensive than those in the anthems. There are only momentary musical echoes of his earlier settings of the *Te Deum* text, and the work as a whole expands in a luxuriant and spacious manner that must have taxed the stamina of the Cannons performers. Brydges at Cannons could clearly afford to be more leisurely in his devotions than the king at the Chapel Royal, and he could not have wished for a more luxurious display of aural furniture in his church.

Of the two major dramatic works that Handel composed for Brydges, it is easier to match *Acis and Galatea* with the resources of the Cannons establishment that are implied by the anthems. A soprano (possibly Margherita de l'Epine) was presumably brought in to sing the role of Galatea, and the rest of the cast – three tenors and a bass – sang the ensembles as well as their solos, which must have affected the manner of the staging. The first tenor sang Acis, the bass Polyphemus: the second tenor, in the role of Damon, was given two arias ('Shepherd, what art thou pursuing' and 'Consider, fond shepherd') and the third tenor, as Corydon, one aria ('Would you gain the tender creature'). The text of the last, which was probably a last-minute addition to the score, was by John Hughes. The rest of the libretto may have been something of a committee job, perhaps evolved by the 'club' of composers and literary men sur- rounding Brydges at the period, though the testimony of Dalrymple's letter (quoted in Chapter 4) to the effect that Pope and Gay were the main contributors is not in doubt.

Acis and Galatea is remarkable, as Handel's first extended secular dramatic work in English, for its effectiveness as a compact drama. Ovid's story, about the lovers Acis and Galatea, Polyphemus's jealousy, his destruction of Acis, and Galatea's subsequent transformation of Acis into a stream, is presented with a light touch, yet it is so paced that the final scenes provide a moving culmination. In later years *Acis* was inflated by Handel into a full-length piece for the London theatre, but in its Cannons form it was played in an unbroken succession of scenes: the lovers' joyous duet 'Happy we' fell into immediate juxtaposition with the threatening chorus 'Wretched lovers'. With the limited Cannons resources, Handel managed to cover a wide picturesque range, encompassing the pastoral twitterings of 'Hush, ye pretty warbling choir' and the tragi-comic clumsi- ness of Polyphemus in 'I rage' and 'O ruddier than the cherry'. The emotional power of the drama was not limited by either the resources or the time-scale (the music lasts about an hour and a half). Handel draws the listener to share in the emotions experienced by the characters. The sensations of attraction which lead to the union of Acis and Galatea in the first half are beautifully conveyed through 'Hush, ye pretty warbling choir', 'Where shall I seek the charming fair' and 'Love in her eyes sits playing'. Galatea's sense of loss after the death of Acis has genuine tragic power: its effect is not entirely ameliorated by the consoling and sensual calmness of 'Heart, the seat of soft delight'. *Acis and Galatea* also shows what degree of drama could be achieved within the pastoral convention: there is no sillyness about these nymphs and shepherds.

It is more difficult to get *Esther* into focus. It may have been performed on some special occasion, for which the 'Cannons concert' must have been considerably augmented: the score calls for (at least) a soprano, an alto, two tenors and two basses, and an orchestra including two bassoons, two horns (with implications perhaps of more string players to balance), viola and harp. A copy of the score from the 1730s carries a prefatory note that *Esther* was composed 'for the most noble James, Duke of Chandos, by George Frederick Handel, in the year 1720', and it has been suggested that the work might have been composed in 1718 and then revised in an expanded form in 1720; but a manuscript dated 1718 (which, like all the earliest sources, calls the work not 'Esther' but 'Oratorium') gives the oratorio in its 'final', that is largest, form.[14] *Esther* in its 'Cannons' version, however, is clearly the same sort of work as *Acis*, even though it requires larger forces – a chamber drama, designed to be played through as a succession of six contrasted scenes without a break. And, as with *Acis*, some form of semi-staged presentation may have enabled the soloists to sing also as the 'chorus'. The heavier scoring is imaginatively used in some spectacular movements that perhaps take *Esther* strictly out of the range of chamber drama: the aria with harp obbligato 'Praise the Lord with cheerful noise' just remains within that category, but the grandiose movements with horns 'Jehovah, crowned with glory bright' and 'He comes to end our woes' imply an altogether larger musical canvas. 'Large' is also apt for the enormous, episodic, final chorus of 316 bars, though Handel may have cut this down to something rather more modest before the performance.[15]

The authorship of the libretto for *Esther*, like that for *Acis and Galatea*, remains uncertain, though it was variously attributed during Handel's lifetime to Gay and Arbuthnot: there is again the possibility that a Cannons literary syndicate may have been at work. As with *Acis*, the libretto gave Handel opportunities for some fine arias and also for a gradual accumulation of dramatic tension: the high point comes as Haman's 'Turn not, O Queen, thy face away' is answered by the aria 'Flatt'ring tongue, no more I hear thee', Esther's reply bursting in without a formal opening ritornello. In the first half of *Esther* the drama develops slowly, as various Israelites lead the people's devotions or bewail their

---

[14] See Beeks, *ibid.*, pp. 16–19; also Chapter 4, p.81, n.49.

[15] Handel's autograph includes a musical linking passage that he wrote some time after the original composition in order to shorten the movement. The shorter form thus produced does not appear in any secondary manuscripts of *Esther* and was apparently not related to the various revised versions of the movement that Handel produced for his later London theatre productions of *Esther*: it still awaits publication.

collective sins, but the arias along the way are attractive, notably 'Tune your harps to songs of praise': it is curious that Handel chose for this a pizzicato string accompaniment, reserving the harp for the next aria. Taking the Cannons anthems, *Acis and Galatea* and *Esther* together, it is clear that by 1718 Handel had developed a 'feel' for setting the English language. His treatment of texts is sometimes idiosyncratic but none the less competent: in particular, he knew how to set up melodic vocal lines with words and music in order to achieve the maximum lyrical or percussive effect, as circumstances required.

'Idiosyncratic' also describes the style of Handel's harpsichord music. He gained a reputation as a keyboard virtuoso, but the music that he committed to paper is rarely audibly flamboyant; some of it is, nevertheless, technically quite demanding, without sounding so. The well-wrought suites that he published in 1720 contained some of his latest harpsichord music. Only a couple more suites and a handful of other pieces were composed later, and the suites published in a second collection in 1733 were mainly composed before those in the 1720 set. The inclusion of the words 'Premier Volume' on the title-page of the 1720 publication suggests that Handel had intended to produce a further collection quite quickly: perhaps his good intentions were overtaken by new demands in the opera house that were already upon him by the time the suites appeared.

The 1720 publication included a prefatory note over Handel's name:

> I have been obliged to publish Some of the following lessons because Surrepticious and incorrect copies of them had got abroad. I have added several new ones to make the Work more usefull which if it meets with a favourable reception: I will Still proceed to publish more reckoning it my duty with my Small talent to Serve a Nation from which I have receiv'd so Generous a protection.

The 'Surrepticious' copies may have been manuscripts, or possibly a collection entitled *Pieces à un & deux clavecins composée par Mr Handel* published by Roger of Amsterdam at about the same time:[16] this included 16 of the 38 movements that make up the eight suites of the 1720 set. In preparing his suites for publication, Handel furnished some of them with fully written-out preludes in place of the 'harpeggio' movements (written in minim or semibreve chords, but to be played in a more decorated manner) that had opened several of the suites in their earlier, less formal versions. Some of the suites that were not included in the 1720 collection retain such 'harpeggio' openings, to the tantalization of the modern performer. All but one in the 1720 collection include at least one traditional dance-rhythm movement of the 'French' suite type – Allemande, Courante, Sarabande or Gigue – and when more than one is included they appear in the 'correct' order. But these dance movements are freely embedded in

---

[16] The publication date of the 'Roger' collection (which was actually printed by Walsh in London) is uncertain: it may not have appeared until 1721.

schemes that also involve other types of movement such as passacaglia, theme-and-variations and fugue. Handel made something of a speciality of writing harpsichord fugues during his first years in London (especially during the Cannons period): even when five of them had been used up in the suites, enough remained to form a separate set of six fugues, which was published in the 1730s.

The wider repertory of Handel's harpsichord music includes a large and rather amorphous collection of pieces composed before 1720, some grouped into suites (or with movements that apparently float in and out of them) and others surviving as isolated pieces. Many movements exist in several versions. One movement with a very complex history is the Chaconne in G, published in the second set of suites in a version with 21 variations: in fact, it had gone through five identifiable variant forms before 1718. The miscellaneous pieces (many of them preserved through the manuscript collections formed by patrons such as Elizabeth Legh around 1720 and Charles Jennens some 15–20 years later), contain some agreeable and companionable music. As well as suite-type movements, they include capriccios, chaconnes and the like, marches and a large number of minuets.[17] Another important genre, whose significance came to be recognized afresh in the 1980s, was the keyboard overture. London music publishers produced regular collections of these, to fulfil the needs of the market in which keyboard players could re-capture at home some of the experiences that they remembered from the opera house. Most of the published keyboard versions of Handel's opera (and, later, oratorio) overtures were straightforward hack arrangements, but Handel arranged some of them himself, and these qualify as original keyboard works: a few survive in his autograph, others in copies that show (by their recomposition of material from the parent orchestral versions) that they are authentic Handelian keyboard versions.[18] In all, some 20 keyboard overtures, arranged from works stretching from *Il pastor fido* in 1712 to *Semele* in 1743, seem to have seen the touch of the master. An early manifestation of the 'keyboard overture' even appeared in the first movement of the seventh suite in the 1720 set: this movement is a keyboard version of the overture to Handel's Italian-period cantata *Clori, Tirsi e Fileno*, though its roots may go back even further, to a lost work composed during the Hamburg period.

Overture-type works form the bulk of Handel's concerted instrumental music from this period. The orchestral concerto in F major HWV 315 (later published as op.3 no.4) was composed as the 'second overture' (i.e. to be played before one of the later acts of the opera) for the opera orchestra's benefit performance of *Amadigi* in June 1716. 'New' concertos by Handel were also advertised in connection with public concerts in

---

[17] The minuets and several of the miscellaneous pieces are published in *HHA* IV/19.
[18] See Handel, ed. Best, *Twenty Overtures*, and Best, 'Handel's Overtures for Keyboard'.

London in May 1718 and February 1719, but these cannot be identified. The attractive Concerto in B♭ HWV313 (op.3 no.2) was surely also written for the players of the Haymarket opera orchestra, and there was some interchange of its music with the overture to one version of the *Brockes Passion*. At Cannons, James Brydges spoke of Handel's 'Overtures to be plaied before the first lesson': it is difficult to make sense of this, but most of the Cannons anthems begin with chamber overtures that (as already noted) were later quarried by Handel for trio sonatas. The concertos HWV314 and 316 (op.3 nos.3 and 5) also contain a lot of Cannons music but may have been adapted as orchestral concertos by Handel himself. A couple of sonatas for oboe and basso continuo (HWV363a, 366) seem to have originated in Handel's early London years, or possibly at Hanover in 1711–12.

Two further categories of music from this decade require brief notice. Some mystery attaches to Handel's setting of an English cantata by John Hughes, *Venus and Adonis*. Its text appeared in a posthumous collected edition of Hughes's poems that was published in London in 1735 with the title 'Venus and Adonis, A Cantata set by Mr. Handel'. Two song-settings to words from this text survive in a manuscript copied in London about 1710, and, rather by default, these are generally regarded as 'possibly' Handel's work (HWV85). Handel specifically mentioned Hughes in a letter written from Hanover soon after his first visit to London,[19] and it is entirely plausible that he set Hughes's cantata, perhaps as his first ever exercise in dealing with an English-language text. But whether the surviving arias are by Handel is uncertain.[20]

No problems of authenticity attach to the *Brockes Passion*, even though the autograph is lost and secondary manuscripts transmit two slightly varying versions. In this work it is fascinating to see Handel – at approximately the '*Amadigi* stage' in his stylistic development – applying the lessons of the opera house to the Passion story as told in Brockes's words, some of which are familiar to the modern listener through their use by J. S. Bach in his *St John Passion*. (Bach also certainly knew Handel's Passion setting: one surviving manuscript was partly copied out by Bach himself.) The combination of some music that is now familiar, through its re-use to English texts in the Cannons anthems, *Esther* and other works, with other original music (including settings of German chorales) can at first be disconcerting to the English-speaking listener; but once Handel's Passion-oratorio is accepted on its own terms it proves to be an entirely worthy contribution to the repertory of its genre. Perhaps rather surprisingly, it is slower-moving and less dramatic than Bach's *St John Passion*. While Bach's work uses Brockes's texts as one of several elements in the composition, Handel set Brockes's complete text as it stood,

[19] See Chapter 4, n.17.
[20] The arias (HWV85) are published in Handel, ed. Burrows, *Songs and Cantatas*.

including a substantial number of 'commentary' movements which give the work a somewhat sprawling character: the longest arias fall to Tochter Zion (Daughter of Zion), who is a non-dramatic character. In view of Handel's procedure in later oratorios, it is perhaps curious that the 'crowd' scenes do not seem to have inspired him particularly, though he obviously gave his full attention to the arias that form the work's main musical substance. Although some of the short arias – for example, Jesus's 'Ist's möglich, dass dein Zorn sich stille' ('If it is possible, that your anger can be calmed') – have an emotional urgency, Handel seems in general content with a fairly leisurely, contemplative pace. The work surely was intended for complete, self-standing concert performance during Lent (probably Holy Week), conceivably by the singers from the Hamburg opera house. It was probably given as one continuous piece, without any division into parts: there are no indications for such division in the musical sources, and it is difficult to imagine a sermon being inserted midway, as happened with Bach's Passion settings, though performance in church rather than in the theatre seems entirely appropriate.

6

The 'Academy' years, 1720–32

I ask you not to judge the strength of my wish to see you by the delay in my departure: it is greatly to my regret that I find myself kept here by unavoidable business on which, I may say, my future depends, and which has been extended longer than I could have believed.

Thus Handel began a letter from London to his brother-in-law in Halle on 20 February 1719.[1] The 'unavoidable business' on which Handel's future depended was the formation of a new opera company at the King's Theatre, Haymarket, plans for which had been under discussion in London for some time.[2] If Handel felt impatient with progress in February 1719, he probably did not foresee the long haul that lay ahead: the first performance from the new company did not take place until April 1720, and it was another six months after that before it was running with the intended cast of first-rate Italian stars.

Unlike the rather hand-to-mouth management of the earlier Haymarket company, that of the new one was planned from the start on a formal constitutional basis, and the construction of the managerial institutions prolonged the lead-in period, with several rounds of documentation and meetings. Royal patronage was seen early on as one of the cornerstones of the new arrangement, and this was to be reflected in the title: a document was drafted, probably about a month after Handel's letter, as 'Heads of a Charter for Incorporating...The Royal Academy of Musick'. (The name of the company was no doubt chosen as an equivalent to Louis XIV's *Académie Royale de Musique*, established 50 years previously.) This was followed about a month later by a prospectus, a 'Proposall for carrying on Operas'. In early May 1719 the king formally granted an annual subsidy of £1000 for five years and commanded the incorporation of the Academy.[3] The result was a royal charter dated 27 July 1719. This

[1] Original in French, Deutsch, pp. 84–6; *HHB*, pp. 78–9; date presumably Old Style.
[2] See Berenstadt's letters in Lindgren, 'Musicians and Librettists', p. 20 (letters 18, 19), p. 24–5 (letters 24, 26); these letters might be interpreted in terms of an attempt by Heidegger to revive the old company.
[3] The chronological outline given here is based on the conclusions in Milhous and Hume, 'New Light', pp. 150–3, and Gibson, *The Royal Academy of Music*, chap. 3.

named 58 'subscribers', including seven dukes (Chandos among them), 13 earls (including Burlington) and three viscounts: the last name in the list is 'John Arbuthnot'. No doubt this records the subscription list only at one particular moment, other subscribers joining in while others fell away from time to time or defaulted on paying their 'calls', a problem that was a recurring theme in the Academy's business records.

Although the Academy was set up under royal patronage, with the Lord Chamberlain as its perpetual governor, its structure was that of a joint stock company.[4] A year later (and for some time afterwards) this feature provided an opening for ridicule in the press, for comparisons could be drawn with the dubious enterprises that were exposed with the bursting of the 'South Sea Bubble'. As a way of financing an opera company, the method was certainly unusual: but, far from producing a 'bubble', it was probably intended to provide financial security. With £1000 a year promised from the king, and each subscriber obliged to the extent of a £200 share, there was some predictability to the company's capital: it was recognized from the start that the opera could not survive on box-office receipts alone. The charter certainly established the company on a long-term basis:

> the Corporation hereby Established shall from henceforth for and during the Term of one and Twenty years be and be called One Body Corporate and Politick for Carrying on Operas and other Entertainments of Musick within this our kingdom of Great Britain

In practice, the company made a profit only in one year (the season of 1721–2, after which it declared a dividend of 7%), and after eight years it had run out of money, having called in all of the capital provided for at the foundation; even so, this represented a history of success and stability compared with the fortunes of the previous Haymarket enterprises. Handel had correctly assessed the significance of the project in his letter of February 1719.

By the time the charter for the Royal Academy had been prepared, Handel was no longer in London. One London newspaper on 21 February (the day after Handel's letter to his brother-in-law) reported that Handel had 'gone beyond Sea, by order of his Majesty, to Collect a Company of the choicest Singers in Europe, for the Opera in the Hay-Market'. But this announcement was premature: three days later he was still in London, writing to Mattheson in answer to a letter seeking his opinion on subjects of early music theory (solmization and the Greek modes) and deflecting a request for an autobiographical essay.[5] In his letter to his brother-in-law Handel had in any case anticipated that opera company business would keep him in London for another month. As the same letter reveals, he was planning a continental visit in any case, probably motivated by family

---

[4] See Milhous and Hume, 'The Charter'.
[5] Letter in French, date presumably Old Style: Deutsch, pp. 86–8; *HHB*, p. 79.

business: his sister had died in Halle in August 1718, and Handel was no doubt anxious to see his mother and his widowed brother-in-law. There may have been financial affairs to sort out as well: Handel mentions in his letter the failure of a merchant at Magdeburg to honour a letter of exchange, probably in connection with some money that Handel had sent back to his family.

On 14 May 1719 an official warrant was issued by the Lord Chamberlain, as governor of the (then still prospective) Royal Academy of Music, to 'Mr Hendel Master of Musick', 'forthwith to repair to Italy Germany or other such Place or Places as you shall think proper, there to make Contracts with such Singer or Singers as you shall judge fit to perform on the English Stage'. This was accompanied by a specific schedule of 'Instructions to Mr Hendel':[6]

Instructions to Mr Hendel.
That Mr Hendel either by himself or such Correspondenc[e]^s as he shall think fit procure proper Voices to Sing in the Opera.
The said Mr Hendel is impower'd to contract in the Name of the Patentees with those Voices to Sing in the Opera for one Year and no more.
That Mr Hendel engage Senezino as soon as possible to Serve the said Company and for as many Years as may be.
That in case Mr Hendel meet with an excellent Voice of the first rate he is to Acquaint the Gov[erno]^r and Company forthwith of it and upon what Terms he or She may be had.
That Mr Hendel from time to time Acquaint the Governor and Company with his proceedings, Send Copys of the Agreem[en]^ts which he makes with these Singers and obey such further Instructions as the Governor and Company shall from time to time transmit unto him.

It is interesting that, while this document in general gave Handel a free hand in the negotiations, the only singer whom he was specifically directed to secure (at any cost) was the castrato Senesino.

It seems probable that Handel was already abroad, en route for Halle, by the time the Lord Chamberlain's instructions were issued.[7] By mid-July he had travelled on from Halle to Dresden, which was currently a centre of considerable activity in preparation for the celebrations of the marriage of Friedrich August, Crown Prince of Saxony, to Maria Josepha, daughter of the Emperor Joseph I. This marriage, which took place in Vienna on 20 August, was a significant political event, marking the conclusion of nearly 20 years' conflict with Sweden over the succession to the Polish throne, and Friedrich August I, the Elector of Saxony, supported lavish celebrations for the event. The cultural background was already in

---

[6] Deutsch, p. 90; *HHB*, p. 81.
[7] According to *HHB*, p. 82 (elaborating Deutsch, p. 92), Handel travelled to Halle in May 1719 via Düsseldorf, where he engaged the castrato Baldassari; but Baldassari was already in London. After the death of Johann Wilhelm in 1716, the next Elector Palatine had moved the court to Heidelberg; the opera musicians were discharged, and Baldassari went to England.

place: since 1711 Dresden had seen the construction of the Zwinger as a cultural and sporting centre, and the crown prince's taste for Italian opera had led to the hasty construction of a large opera theatre, which was nearing completion when Handel arrived in Dresden. The human resources for the opera house were already established there: the crown prince had lured the composer Antonio Lotti away from Venice, and – most important from Handel's point of view – Senesino was one of the principal singers.

In addition to Senesino, the Dresden company included the sopranos Durastanti and Salvai, the castrato Berselli, the tenor Guicciardi and the bass Boschi. In a letter from Dresden dated 26 July,[8] Handel reported to the Earl of Burlington that he was hoping to conclude negotiations with Senesino, Berselli and Guicciardi in a few days but, perhaps because the Dresden authorities had sniffed out what was going on, the Saxon opera pre-empted his negotiations by signing up most of the singers for another year's contract. In the short term, Handel secured only Durastanti – who had sung the title role in *Agrippina* in Venice – for immediate release to London, but the negotiations with the others bore fruit in 1720 when the elector dismissed his singers early in the year after a dispute, and in the autumn Senesino, Berselli, Salvai and Boschi were to join Durastanti in London. It seems fairly certain that Handel stayed in Dresden for the first opera performances, in September 1719: of the three Lotti operas that opened the season, two provided him with librettos that he was later to set in London, as *Ottone* and, less directly, *Jupiter in Argos*.

In the autumn of 1719 the constitutional process of the Royal Academy ground slowly into action: general meetings were held, at which a board of directors was elected. Serious activity may be said to have begun with the directors' meeting on 27 November, from the minutes of which it is apparent that the company intended to open with performances in the spring: singers' contracts were to commence on 1 March 1720, initially for a short season of three months. Handel, presumably still in Dresden, was instructed to make an immediate offer to Durastanti, and it was agreed 'That Mr Hendell be Ordered to return to England'; the two other singers mentioned in connection with Handel's negotiations, Grunswald and Orsini, were never followed up. Meanwhile Heidegger was deputed to ask the castrato Baldassari and the soprano Caterina Galerati (both of whom were in London) to state their terms for performing with the Academy, and to prepare estimates for the cost of running the opera house: Arbuthnot was detailed to negotiate with the English soprano Anastasia Robinson.[9] Robinson and her colleague Galerati were the only principal singers from the old Haymarket company to be carried forward into the new one. Matters then proceeded quite quickly, and the directors

---

[8] New Style. Deutsch, pp. 93–4; *HHB*, p. 83; the letter is 'double dated' 26/15 July.

[9] Deutsch and *HHB* print only extracts from the minutes of the meetings of the Academy directors on 27 and 30 November and 2 December 1719: the full texts are given in Milhous and Hume, 'New Light', pp. 151–3, and Gibson, *The Royal Academy of Music*, pp. 327–30.

met again on 30 November and 2 December. The singers' contracts were advanced further, and Riva, the Modenese Resident in London, was asked to take up negotiations abroad with Senesino for the Academy's second projected season. A number of trails were started: Monsieur L'Abbé was approached for the provision of dancers; and the Italian poet and librettist Paolo Rolli was brought in to serve as secretary, libretto-arranger and adviser on matters Italian. A parallel series of documents from this period (now preserved in the papers of the Duke of Portland, who was one of the directors), shows that a sub-committee was also working on the establishment of an orchestra of about 35 players.[10] At the directors' meeting on 30 November it was agreed that 'Mr Hendell be Master of the Orchester with a Sallary', though there is no record of the size of this salary or how it was paid. It is quite clear, however, that Handel was not regarded as exercising a monopoly as a composer: the directors decided that 'Seignr Bona Cini [Bononcini] be writ to, To know his terms for composing & performing in the Orchester', and Heidegger was 'desir'd to propose to Seignr Portou [Giovanni Porta] the composing of an Opera'. Porta, whom Handel may have met in Rome, was already in London in the service of the Duke of Wharton, and other patrons had also collected around them musicians that would be useful to the opera: in particular, Burlington had returned from his Italian trip in 1715 with three musicians who had been in Ruspoli's service – the cellist and composer Filippo Amadei and the violinist brothers Pietro and Prospero Castrucci. Pietro Castrucci became leader of the orchestra for the Royal Academy.

Handel presumably returned to London at the end of 1719, or early in 1720, and set about composing an opera, *Radamisto*, for the new company. Although the Academy's contracts ran from the beginning of March, it was obviously going to take some time to prepare the productions, allowing for rehearsals[11] and the construction of scenery designed by the Academy's 'engineer' Roberto Clerici. During March such activity probably had to be fitted in around the regular theatre programme at the King's Theatre: at the time, French 'comedians' (actors) were booked to perform harlequinades. When the Academy opened on 2 April it was with Porta's new work, *Numitore*: no doubt the choice of story, concerning Romulus and Remus, was intended to suggest suitably elevated parallels between the founders of Rome and the founders of the Academy. Rolli arranged the libretto for *Numitore*, but (according to Burney) it was Haym who collaborated with Handel in arranging the libretto for *Radamisto*.

It may seem surprising that Handel did not have the honour of the first opera to be performed, but the delay in producing *Radamisto* may have

[10] See Milhous and Hume, 'New Light', pp. 157–61.

[11] One rehearsal, on 18 April, is known from an incidental reference in a contemporary letter: see Deutsch, p. 102; *HHB*, p. 88.

been the result of a deliberate manoeuvre on his part.[12] At the beginning of April 1720 the king and the Prince of Wales were still estranged, and their courts mutually exclusive: neither attended the opening of the Academy. But behind the scenes at court a reconciliation was being effected, though this was apparently known only to a small circle of courtiers and Whig politicians. On St George's day (23 April, the day of the fifth performance of *Numitore*), the prince went to St James's Palace, where a formal reconciliation was stage-managed. The next day, Sunday 24 April, the king and the prince attended the Chapel Royal together for the first time in more than two years, and after the service there followed the political deal that went with the reconciliation: Robert Walpole and Charles Townshend were accepted into the government. The king and the prince made their first appearance at the Royal Academy on 27 April – the first night of Handel's *Radamisto*. It is difficult to believe that the timing was accidental: an obvious possibility is that the Lord Chamberlain, as governor of the Academy, knew what was going on and advised (or commanded) the sequence of the opera programme in Handel's favour. In broader terms, the first performance of *Radamisto* marked the reunion of the patronage base that had been severed to dire effect in 1717.

No doubt the fact that the première of *Radamisto* turned out to be an important court occasion played its part in enhancing the reputation of the opera itself. Mainwaring (pp.98–9) gives an enthusiastic report of the opera's reception, but perhaps we now know more than he did of the reasons why the first performance was so crowded:

> If persons who are now living, and who were present at that performance may be credited, the applause it received was almost as extravagant as his AGGRIPPINA had excited: the crowds and tumults of the house at Venice were hardly equal to those at LONDON. In so splendid and fashionable an assembly of ladies (to the excellence of their taste we must impute it) there was no shadow of form, or ceremony, scarce indeed any appearance of order or regularity, politeness or decency. Many, who had forc'd their way into the house with an impetuosity but ill suited to their rank and sex, actually fainted through the excessive heat and closeness of it. Several gentlemen were turned back, who had offered forty shillings for a seat in the gallery, after having despaired of getting any in the pit or boxes.

The word-book for *Radamisto* included, uniquely, a dedication to the king in Handel's own name: the dedication refers to 'the particular Approbation Your Majesty has been pleased to give to the Musick of this Drama'. A couple of months later, when the songs from *Radamisto* were published, they were accompanied by a royal privilege dated 14 June 1720, giving '*George Frederick Handel*, of our City of *London*, Gent. ...Our License for the sole Printing and Publishing the said [his own] Works for

---

[12] The implications of the following course of events were first elucidated in Burrows, *Handel and the English Chapel Royal*, i, 236–8.

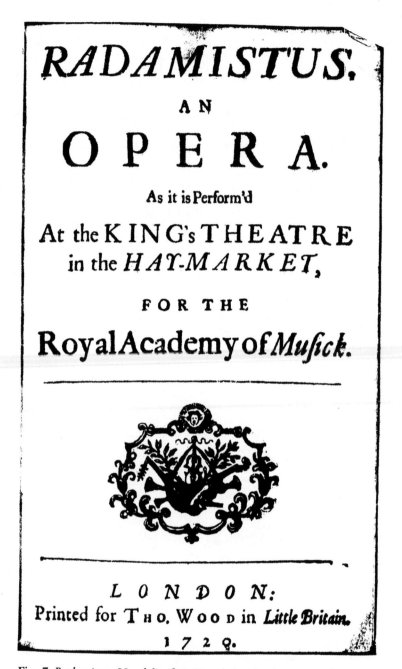

RADAMISTUS,

AN

OPERA.

As it is Perform'd

At the KING's THEATRE
in the *HAY-MARKET*,

FOR THE

Royal Academy of *Muſick*.

LONDON:
Printed for Tho. Wood in *Little Britain.*
1 7 2 0.

Fig. 7 *Radamisto*, Handel's first Royal Academy opera. The title-page from the original word-book

the Term of Fourteen Years'.[13] Handel presumably exercised this copyright privilege by entering into exclusive agreements with London's major publishers, the houses of Meares, Walsh and Cluer, for the publication of specific works. The scores of his operas that Cluer published in 1724–5 were particularly attractive, and the advertisements for them claimed that they had been 'Corrected and Figur'd' by the composer himself'. The reference to Handel as 'of the City of London' in the copyright privilege may be a geographical approximation: the houses of Handel's patrons lay mainly in the City of Westminster, but we do not know where Handel himself was living in 1720.

Since the Academy season had begun late it was, as expected, relatively short: in addition to *Numitore* and *Radamisto*, only one other repertory opera was given – Domenico Scarlatti's *Narciso*, arranged (and possibly directed) by the London musician Thomas Roseingrave. The season finished on 25 June. At the beginning of March, Richard Steele's paper *The Theatre* had had some fun comparing 'Opera Stock' and 'South Sea Stock': in one spoof report 'Signior Nihilini Beneditti rose half a Note above his Pitch formerly known', pushing opera stock up six and a half points. The autumn of 1720 was dominated by the less comical reality of the financial disasters accompanying the South Sea Bubble: the resolution of this crisis was one of the factors that strengthened Walpole on his path to becoming King George's chief minister. Many of the subscribers to the Academy were severely hit by financial losses, but the company nevertheless survived and, most important, now acquired the Italian stars that raised the performances into a new international class: in September Senesino, Berselli, Salvai, Boschi and Bononcini arrived. The first full season of the Academy ran from November 1720 to July 1721, consisting of 57 opera performances and three concerts.

Handel's life for the following years was controlled by the routine of the opera seasons. During the first seasons his creative input was, surprisingly, rather slender: in fact, the performances – in terms of both quantity and popular success – were dominated by Bononcini. For December 1720 Handel completely re-worked *Radamisto* to suit the new cast, but his only other contribution to the season was to *Muzio Scevola*. The latter, as a three-act opera with one act each composed by Amadei, Bononcini and Handel, was a novelty for London (there were Italian precedents); if the idea was to give opera enthusiasts something to talk about by comparing the music of the three resident composers, it produced little tangible result, for opera-goers were probably more interested in the singers. In terms of measurable popularity, Handel was way behind Bononcini this season: *Radamisto* saw only seven performances against 23 of Bononcini's *Astarto*, and demand for the latter was so high that the directors had to take measures against gate-crashers and overcrowding in

[13] Deutsch, pp. 105–6; *HHB*, p. 89.

the theatre. The season was enlivened by Durastanti's pregnancy, which apparently did not provide the expected interruption to her stage career: the king stood godfather to her daughter in March. Presumably Handel was on duty as 'Master of the Orchestra' (at the harpsichord) at every Academy performance; it is not known whether he took any part in training the singers for performances of operas by other composers. It would also be interesting to know how his salary compared with that of Senesino, who commanded more than £1000 for the season.

The 1721–2 season was slightly hampered by the absence from London (through illness) of Durastanti (which promoted Anastasia Robinson to the position of leading lady) and by public attacks from the clergy in sermons against the masquerades at the opera house. Although masquerades and opera performances were formally separate, they attracted the same sort of patrons (including the royal family), and attacks on 'high living' no doubt provided fuel for anti-opera journalists; it is possible also that profits from the masquerades were fed back to support the opera company. But in the end none of this affected the success of the season. A new subscription system was introduced – 20 guineas for the complete season – and the accounts ended up in profit: after the declaration of what was to be the Academy's only dividend, a London newspaper commented:[14]

> it is thought, that if this Company goes on with the same Success as they have done for some Time past, of which there is no doubt, it will become considerable enough to be engrafted on some of our Corporations in the City, the Taste of the Publick for Musick being so much improv'd lately.

Once again, the season saw a revival of *Radamisto* (four performances), as well as a new opera from Handel, *Floridante*. The word-book of *Floridante* carried a dedication by Rolli to the Prince of Wales: this was perhaps intended to balance the dedication to the king in *Radamisto*, but it may accidentally have helped to stir the embers of political controversy. The plot of the opera involves a Prince of Thrace whose jealous father tries to deprive him of the throne, and the possibility of a contemporary interpretation did not escape one section of the audience:[15]

> Some things have happened at a new opera which have given great offence. It is called *Floridante*. There happens to be a right heir in it, that is imprisoned. At last the right heir is delivered and the chains put upon the oppressor. At this last circumstance, there happened to be a very great and unseasonable clapping, in the presence of great ones.

Taking the season as a whole, Handel was again outshone in popularity by

[14] *The London Journal* (16 February 1723): Deutsch, p. 150; *HHB*, p. 115.
[15] Letter from Dr William Stratford to Lord Edward Harley (19 December 1721), quoted in Gibson, *The Royal Academy of Music*, pp. 155–6.

Bononcini. Against the 15 performances of *Floridante*, the new Bononcini productions of *Crispo* and *Griselda* totalled 34. *Crispo* had been written by Bononcini before he came to London (though he no doubt adapted it to the needs of the Haymarket cast), but *Griselda* was custom-built and provided an excellent vehicle for Anastasia Robinson in the title role. There was a fascinating autobiographical parallel between Robinson and Griselda, the low-born heroine who ends up as queen, for Robinson secretly married the Earl of Peterborough: whether the opera assisted or mirrored the real-life rise to nobility is not clear.[16] By the end of the season Bononcini was at the apogee of his fame and popularity in London, amplified by two successes outside the opera house: the publication of his *Cantate e duetti*, with a dedication to the king and a subscription list longer than any that Handel ever achieved; and the invitation to compose the funeral anthem for the Duke of Marlborough, which was duly performed in circumstances of great magnificence in August 1722. The next two seasons saw the scales tip against him.

Durastanti returned to the cast for the 1722–3 season, which also incorporated (as 'second man') Gaetano Berenstadt, a castrato who had played in the Haymarket company during 1716–17 and had taken over the role of Argante in the 1717 revival of *Rinaldo*.[17] The season was again enlivened by some clerical propaganda against the masquerades, strengthened by a powerful spokesman in Edmund Gibson, the new Bishop of London. There was even a petition in February 1723 to the House of Commons by the Grand Jury of the County of Middlesex, against the 'Ridottos' at the Haymarket. But the main event of the season was the arrival of a new prima donna, Francesca Cuzzoni, in December 1722. She made her début, with sensational success, in Handel's new opera *Ottone* on 12 January 1723. The libretto of *Ottone* was based on that of *Teofane* (with music by Lotti), which Handel had seen in Dresden in 1719: although they received new music, Senesino, Durastanti and Boschi played the same dramatic roles for Handel in 1723 as they had for Lotti in 1719. The cast as a whole was the most brilliant yet heard in London, adding the talents of Durastanti, Robinson, Berenstadt and Boschi to those of Senesino and Cuzzoni (Plate 3). In his score Handel brought off the trick of maintaining Durastanti's musical dignity (in the part of Gismondo) against the bright light of Cuzzoni's presence: to find a third, convincing, large dramatic role for Anastasia Robinson was more difficult, and Robinson entreated her friends to use their influence with Handel because she considered herself miscast. Two letters from her provide an unusually vivid insight

---

[16] For a lively account of the marriage, derived from Mrs Delany, see Burney, *A General History*, ii, 691–3.

[17] Berenstadt had maintained frequent correspondence contacts with London. Lindgren, *Musicians and Librettists*, includes many letters from him to Zamboni in London; see also Lindgren, 'La carriera di Gaetano Berenstadt'.

into the relationship, professional and personal, that she had with Handel:[18]

> The Musick of my Part is exstreamly fine, but am as sure the Caracter causes it to be of that kind, which no way suits my Capacity: those Songs that require fury and passion to exspress them, can never be performed by me according to the intention of the Composer, and consequently must loose their Beauty. Nature design'd me a peacable Creature, and it is as true as strange, that I am a Woman and cannot Scold. My request is, that if it be possible (as sure it is) the words of my Second Song Pensa spietata Madre should be changed, and instead of reviling Gismonda with her cruelty, to keep on the thought of the Recitative and perswade her to beg her Sons life of Ottone. I have read the Drama and tho I do not pretend to be a judge, yet I fancy doing this would not be an impropriety, but even suposing it one, of two evills it is best to chuse the least; in this manner you might do me the greatest favour immaginable, because then a Short Melancholly Song would be proper. I have some dificultys allso in the last I Sing, but for fear that by asking too much I might be refus'd all, I dare not mention them.

> You have hear'd my new Part, and the more I look at it, the more I find it is impossible for me to sing it; I dare not ask M[r] Hendell to change the Songs for fear he should suspect (as he is very likely) every other reason but the true one. Do you believe if I was to wait on Lady Darlinton to beg her to use that power over him (which to be sure she must have) to get it done, that she would give her self that trouble, would she have so much compassion on a distressed Damsell that they are endeavouring to make an abomminable Scold of (in spite of her Vertuous inclinations to the contrary) as to hinder the wrong they would do her; you might be my friend and represent, tho the greatest part of my Life has shew'd me to be a Patient Grisell by Nature, how then can I ever pretend to act the Termagant.

As far as we know, the composers and performers got on with each other well enough in their professional dealings, but the spirit of faction was abroad: a letter written three days after the opening of *Ottone* reported the existence of parties, 'as much at loggerheads as Whigs and Tories', 'one supporting Handell, the other Bononcini, the one for Cenesino, the other for Cossuna [Cuzzoni]'.[19] The partisanship apparently spread even to the directors of the Academy and manifested itself in a number of disorderly scenes among the audience; it was a reflection, if not actually an expression, of the opera company's high profile in London's cultural life. As Gay complained in a letter to Swift,[20]

---

[18] The letters are printed in full in *HHB*, pp. 112–13, probably with some errors of transcription, e.g. 'Framagent' for 'Termagant': Lindgren reads this word as 'Tarmegant' in *A Bibliographic Scrutiny*, pp. 268–9. 'Lady Darlington' was the Countess of Darlington, the title currently held by Kielmansegge's widow; Robinson had, of course, played 'Patient Grisell' in Bononcini's *Griselda*.

[19] Letter from Fabrice to Count Fleming; original in French, *HHB*, p. 113; English translation in Deutsch, pp. 147–8.

[20] Letter (3 February 1723): Deutsch, p. 149; *HHB*, pp. 114–15.

As for the reigning amusements of the town, it is entirely music; real fiddles, base-viols, and hautboys, not poetical harps, lyres and reeds. There is nobody allowed to say, 'I sing', but an eunuch, or an Italian woman. Everybody is grown now as great a judge of music, as they were in your time of poetry, and folks, that could not distinguish one tune from another, now daily dispute about the different styles of Handel, Bononcini, and Attilio. People have now forgot Homer, and Virgil, and Caesar, or at least, they have lost their ranks; for, in London and Westminster, in all polite conversations, Senesino is daily voted to be the greatest man that ever lived.

For the first performances of *Ottone*, half-guinea tickets were changing hands at four to six times their face value.

Ottone was Handel's first major public success since the opening run of *Radamisto*, but he did not have the field to himself. A new composer, Attilio Ariosti, came in to replace Amadei, and his *Coriolano* ran for only one performance fewer than *Ottone*. Like Berenstadt, Ariosti had served briefly in the previous Haymarket company, so he was not entirely new to London, and his new opera was not deficient in musical qualities.[21] Bononcini had been dismissed from the Academy before the season started for his 'extravagant demands'.[22] Rolli had lost his job as secretary at the same time, to be replaced by Haym, who took over responsibility for the libretto adaptations. But some rapprochement must have been achieved between Bononcini and the Academy. There were revivals of two of his operas, and towards the end of the season two new operas were presented, one by Bononcini (*Erminia*) and one by Handel (*Flavio*). *Flavio* is slightly shorter than most of Handel's Academy operas, and it has been suggested that both works may have been composed in anticipation of repeat performances in Paris:[23] no complete Academy opera performances materialized there, though groups of the soloists went to Paris (without Handel) in the summers of 1723 and 1724 and in the latter year performed substantial concert versions of *Ottone* and *Giulio Cesare*.[24]

The season of 1723–4 continued the artistic mixture as before, with two new operas each from Ariosti and Bononcini: Handel's contribution was a revival of *Ottone* and a new opera on a grand scale, *Giulio Cesare in Egitto*. The season began a little late, probably because the theatre interior had been given a major redecoration 'by some of the best Masters'. At the end of the season Durastanti made her farewells, possibly discontented with living in Cuzzoni's penumbra: she received the privilege – apparently unique in the Academy period – of a 40-guinea gratuity from

---

[21] See Dean and Knapp, *Handel's Operas*, pp. 315–16.

[22] This was the reason given in Lady Bristol's letter to her husband (7 October 1722), cited in Gibson, *The Royal Academy of Music*, p. 171: according to Lindgren (*A Bibliographic Scrutiny*, pp. 296–7), the context suggests that Bononcini's Catholicism was the real reason for his dismissal, given London's current sensibilities over the 'Atterbury Plot' (see below).

[23] Dean and Knapp, *Handel's Operas*, p. 471: the word-book of *Flavio* is certainly unusual among Handel's operas from this period in omitting the names of the cast.

[24] See Lindgren, 'Parisian Patronage'.

the king at the time of her last benefit performance.[25] More significantly still, the season saw the end of Bononcini as a house composer for the Academy. Factions rose high: a letter of 10 March 1724 reported that[26] 'the squabbles between the Directors and the sides that everyone is taking between the singers and the composers, often provide the public with the most diverting scenes'. At the end of the season Bononcini took up an offer from the junior Duchess of Marlborough of an annual stipend of £500 to serve as her private musician, provided that 'he will not compose any more for the ungrateful Academy'.[27]

Bononcini's departure from the Academy marked a turning-point in Handel's London operatic career: it left him unquestionably with the artistic reins at the Haymarket and in a position of dominance as the principal house composer. The nature of his status in relation to Bononcini in the previous years is uncertain, but the issue had two dimensions, a professional one and a public one, the latter entwined with developments in London's political life and Handel's own personal circumstances. The professional aspect is the more easy to deal with. John Byrom's famous epigram on the opera factions ran:[28]

> Some say, compar'd to Bononcini,
> That Mynheer Handel's but a Ninny;
> Others aver, that he to Handel
> Is scarcely fit to hold a candle:
> Strange all this Difference should be
> 'Twixt Tweedle-dum and Tweedle-dee!

In fact, it was not a case of 'Tweedledum and Tweedledee': Handel and Bononcini had clearly distinct musical styles that could co-exist in the opera programmes, with Bononcini's strength lying in a lighter, tuneful vein (particularly in the pastoral style) as against Handel's strength in large canvases demanding strong musical characterization and sustained compositional skill.[29] Furthermore, practical realism supported the case for the services of more than one competent house composer at the Academy: a season of 50 or more performances from a repertory of half a dozen or more works, of which half would be new productions, was an unrealistic load for one composer-impresario. Nevertheless, the presence of two or three house composers inevitably increased the potential for a

[25] See Burrows and Hume, 'George I', pp. 329–30.

[26] Fabrice to Fleming; original in French, *HHB*, p. 122; English translation in Deutsch, p. 160.

[27] Letter from Mrs Pendarves (16 May 1723 [*recte* 1724]), cited in Lindgren, 'Parisian Patronage', p. 25. Bononcini had been dismissed by the Academy before he was offered the stipend: see the newspaper report dated 23 May 1724 (Deutsch, p. 163; *HHB*, p. 124).

[28] This is printed under May 1725 in Deutsch, but the evidence for the date is uncertain. The epigram was printed in *The London Journal*, (5 June 1725): see Lindgren, *A Bibliographic Scrutiny*, p. 328.

[29] The distinction in style was well described by Burney in *An Account*, 'Sketch of the Life of Handel', pp. 17–18.

battle for artistic dominance, and Bononcini was unquestionably the senior partner in terms of age, experience and European reputation. Bononcini presumably played continuo cello in his operas, perhaps in dangerously close proximity to Handel as 'Master of the Orchestra'. As a repetiteur-trainer of the singers, Handel's reputation as a domineering force is attested by a number of anecdotes. Most famously, he is reputed to have threatened to drop Cuzzoni out of the window when she refused to sing 'Falsa imagine' (*Ottone*) and to have countered a threat from the tenor Alexander Gordon to jump on the harpsichord and smash it, as a protest against Handel's accompaniment in 'Fato tiranno' (*Flavio*), with 'Let me know when you will do that and I will advertise it: for I am sure more people will come to see you jump than hear you sing'.[30] No doubt Handel's relationship with his fellow composers also had its volatile moments, if they were forced together day after day in the orchestra during the Academy seasons (Ariosti may have played the viola da gamba for opera performances).

Public perception of the relationship between Handel and Bononcini was influenced by the circumstance that they could be taken as symbols of different foreign forces in London. While Handel was tarred with the brush of Germany and Hanover, Bononcini might be stereotyped as a Catholic Italian. There was an understandable cliquishness about the social circle that gathered around Bononcini: this included, in addition to the expected Italians Senesino and Riva, a group of English Roman Catholics (including the Earl of Peterborough, accompanied by Anastasia Robinson) and the Duchess of Buckingham. Although there was a distinction between British perceptions of 'Italian Catholics' and 'French Catholics', nevertheless there was something irritating and, in adverse political circumstances, threatening, about such cliques: unhappy memories of the secret foreign policies pursued under Charles II and James II still ran deep in British political consciousness. This channel of mistrust could most easily rise to the surface, for example, over the Jacobite issue. In practical terms, the prospect of a successful Jacobite bid for the throne lay dormant while peace with France was maintained, for France was the obvious supplier of the necessary military support. But Jacobitism was not only a matter of explicit rebellion: the community of sentimental Jacobites and non-Jurors (who could not accept the legitimacy of the present succession) in Britain was quite substantial, and such people were open to anti-government influences.[31] It was in the government's interests

[30] The source of the first anecdote is Mainwaring, *Memoirs*, footnote to pp. 110–11; the earliest source for the second is uncertain.

[31] Non-Jurors usually suffered under at least two internal contradictions in their position: they were often strongly Anglican, while supporting the legitimacy of a Catholic line, and they were often opposed (for reasons of both principle and personal economics) to the means by which the Stuart line could be restored. The tensions are well described in Colley, *Britons*, particularly pp. 71–85 (unfortunately, the treatment of Handel's oratorios on pp. 31–2 of that book is simplistic).

to attempt to discredit this community by magnifying the gravity and seditious nature of such activities as they could discover, and to deal severely with its most threatening manifestations.

A genuine Jacobite plot, involving the plan for an uprising and for the assassination of leading members of the Hanoverian family, was exposed in 1722, thanks to the efficiency of Walpole's intelligence services. While it is unlikely that the plot had any practical chance of success, its discovery gave Walpole enormous political capital by throwing a suspicion of treason over a broad range of his political opponents. Genuine public outrage at the plot was skilfully magnified and manipulated for political purposes. Most important of all, the process led to the downfall and banishment of Francis Atterbury. Walpole's procedure for destroying Atterbury was on the borders of the legally possible, but his instinct that Atterbury was a dangerous man was sound.[32] Atterbury, at the very centre of London's life as Bishop of Rochester and Dean of Westminster, had for years been organizing a Jacobite 'cell' and collecting money for the cause under a very elaborate cover: furthermore, Atterbury was immensely influential as a spokesman for 'country Tory' clergy.

In the reaction provoked by the melodramatic revelation of the Jacobite plot, and sustained by Atterbury's trial, any social nexus that looked like a gathering of papists fell under suspicion, and Bononcini almost certainly suffered under this shadow. The political mood also favoured Handel's advancement in another musical area. Ceremonial royal public thanks-givings had ceased after 1715, but a new opportunity had arisen for orchestrally accompanied church music in the Chapel Royal on the first Sunday after the king's return from his visits to Hanover.[33] William Croft, the Chapel Royal's leading composer, took up this opportunity in 1720, and the event seemed to signal the occasional introduction of such music without the excuse of the king's return: a *Te Deum* by Greene (who at that stage held no office at the chapel, but was doubtless hoping to succeed in the leading offices) followed in July 1721. In October 1722, probably triggered by sympathetic sentiments towards the Hanoverians following the exposure of the Jacobite plot, a similar celebration with orchestrally accompanied *Te Deum* and anthem marked the king's return to St James's after the summer season at Kensington. It seems fairly certain that the composer of the music, though not named in the newspaper reports, was Handel. On 25 February 1723 the Lord Chamberlain issued a warrant to admit 'Mr George Hendall into the place and quality of Composer of Musick for his Majesty's Chappel Royal'.

No doubt because of his alien status, Handel did not take up a place in the regular Chapel Royal establishment, which already included two

---

[32] See Fritz, *The English Ministers and Jacobitism*.

[33] For a full documentation of the relevant Chapel Royal events during this period, see Burrows, *Handel and the English Chapel Royal*, i, chap. 7.

composers (Croft and John Weldon) who had to serve the Sunday and weekday services of the chapel for £73 per year: Handel was rewarded with an additional £200 court pension (£200 was also the annual salary that John Eccles received as Master of the King's Music). Handel provided the music for the subsequent Chapel Royal services after the king's returns from Hanover, in January 1724 and January 1726. Yet another court emolument seems to have come his way by 1724. On 29 August it was reported that[34]

> On Monday last [the 24th] the Royal Highnesses, the Princess Anne and Princess Caroline, came to St. Paul's Cathedral, and heard the famous Mr. Hendel, (their Musick Master) perform upon the Organ; the Reverend Dr. Hare Dean of Worcester attending on their Royal Highnesses during their Stay there.

It seems very likely that Handel had received an official appointment as music master to the princesses by this time: a document of 9 June 1723 that apparently specifies the daily régime of Princess Anne includes 'from 4 to 5 [p.m.] either practice clavecin or read; after that, play music with Hendel'.[35] In spite of the reconciliation between the king and the Prince of Wales in 1720, George I had kept his grand-daughters with him at St James's Palace, granting them an establishment under the control of the Duchess of Portland; accounts that were prepared following the king's death in 1727 show that Handel received another £200 a year from this establishment. This brought his total income from the court up to £600 per year: £200 from the continuing 'Queen Anne' pension, £200 by virtue of his Chapel Royal post and £200 as music master to the princesses. It is not known whether the duty of teaching the princesses was regular or onerous, but a set of exercises in figured-bass realization and contrapuntal technique written in Handel's hand survives from the mid-1720s and may plausibly be taken as royal course-work.[36] Circumstantial evidence is strong, from the behaviour of the princesses in Handel's favour in later years, that he formed a positive relationship with the royal daughters. Apart from the princesses, Handel had another pupil at much the same period in the 1720s – the young John Christopher Smith, the son of his music copyist of the same name. Pupils probably featured more in Handel's life at this period than at any other time in his career: he was perhaps temperamentally unsuited to a sustained career as a music teacher.

Strengthened by the tide of fame and fortune that was running in his favour, Handel took the significant step of establishing himself in his own

[34] *Applebee's Original Weekly Journal* (29 August 1724): Deutsch, p. 173; *HHB*, p. 129.

[35] Original in French: see King, 'On Princess Anne's Lessons'. King suggests that the lessons may have begun *c*.1718, but this is implausible in view of the diplomatic problems at that time within the royal family. 1723–4 is a plausible period for the commencement of Handel's duties (and salary), but documentary evidence is lacking in the absence of any itemized accounts from the princess's establishment before 1727.

[36] Handel, ed. Mann, *Aufzeichnungen zur Kompositionslehre*.

London house. During July 1723 he moved into the house in Brook Street (now no.25), near Hanover Square, that was to remain his home for the rest of his life. The house was one in a terrace of four built on a new development by George Barnes, a slater, from whom Handel held the lease.[37] As a foreign national Handel was at the time debarred from either owning a freehold property or undertaking a long lease, and the initial agreement was for seven years: thereafter it seems likely that Handel renewed the tenancy annually. At the back of the house lay Horse-Shoe Yard, with stables and coach-houses, but whether Handel himself ever owned a carriage is doubtful: perhaps he undertook his journeys around London by (sedan) 'chair'. With his busy professional schedule (and, no doubt, the normal encumbrances of musical scores to carry), the opera house, more than three quarters of a mile distant, may have been sufficiently far away to justify the employment of a carriage. Assuming that Christopher Smith senior ran his music-copying activities from his own home, Smith's bases in the Soho area were nearly as far away, and Walsh's publishing-house at Catherine Street in the Strand much further. On the other hand, Hyde Park was within easy reach: Brook Street was near the edge of the built-up city of Westminster. This probably had environmental advantages, apart from the proximity of the recreational park: the smoke pollution would have been less dense than in the city centre, and the new properties may have enjoyed the luxury of water supplied from the new Chelsea waterworks. The area attracted rich and noble residents, but their houses were much larger than Handel's: his bachelor residence was a relatively modest house in a 'good' area. His immediate neighbours over the years included a couple of knights (one of them a Member of Parliament) and a colonel.

From time to time London saw outbreaks of satirical or laudatory essays and verses relating to the musical life of the capital. Daniel Prat's *An Ode to Mr. Handel, on his Playing on the Organ* of 1722 is disappointingly unenlightening, but *The Session of Musicians* published two years later includes some engaging ironical vignettes of contemporary musicians.[38] 'all Berenstadt, gaping o'er the Crowd with hideous jaws' features incidentally (see Plate 3), 'soft Galliard, shewing his hautboy' is contrasted with Pepusch with his cartload of songs, solos and sonatas, and similarly the lighthearted oboist Loeillet is set in relief against the graver violinist Geminiani. Bononcini appears: 'Two Philharmonick Damsels [one of them Anastasia Robinson] grac'd his Train, Whilst his strong Features redden'd

[37] See Greenacombe, 'Handel's House'.

[38] Reprinted in Deutsch, pp. 163–70; *HHB*, pp. 124–7. Another satirical poem, *A full & True Account of the Proceedings of the Royal Academy of Musick anno 1723* (printed in Gibson, *The Royal Academy of Music*, pp. 105–6) also has some lively touches, including

'Up Burlington started, & made a new Confusion;

For in he brought Berenst[adt] – head, shoulders and all,

And swore that he could sing well, because he was tall.'

with Disdain'. Apollo, looking for a worthy recipient for the presentation laurel bays, 'In vain look'd round, but Handel was not there' – a reference that may suggest Handel's skill in avoiding sites of controversy; in the end, however, Handel (though not so named) appears and is suitably rewarded, to the grudging admiration even of Satan.

There was no doubt about Handel's dominance in the 1724–5 opera season, which saw, in addition to a revival of *Giulio Cesare*, the production of two major new operas from him, *Tamerlano* and *Rodelinda*. Ariosti provided two operas, but even with these there was not enough material to fill up the programme (revivals of Bononcini's repertory would have been out of the question), and for the first time Handel was responsible for a pasticcio, *Elpidia*. This included arias taken from the most recently fashionable Venetian operas by Vinci and Orlandini, along with arias by a variety of other composers: Haym worked up the libretto and Handel composed new recitatives to sew the scheme together. Out of the season's 62 performances, 36 were of Handel's original operas and another ten of the pasticcio. The subjects of the operas were probably chosen with some care. *Giulio Cesare* (with Haym's libretto bearing a dedication to the Prince of Wales) was perhaps intended to make flattering comparisons between Hanoverian and Roman leaders and may also have been a riposte to the Bononcini group, who had failed to bring the late Duke of Buckingham's plays *Julius Caesar* and *Marcus Brutus* to the public stage but had mounted a private performance of *Marcus Brutus* (with choruses by Bononcini) for the Duchess of Buckingham in January 1723. *Tamerlano* may have been interpreted by the audience with reference to Nicholas Rowe's play *Tamerlane*, which had for some years enjoyed a slot in London theatre programmes around the beginning of November to accompany political anniversaries that were interpreted as marking the deliverance from Catholic tyranny: Guy Fawkes's night, and the anniversaries of William III's birthday and his landing at Torbay in 1688.

The libretto for *Elpidia* had been obtained for the Academy by Owen Swiney, the former manager of the Haymarket company who had absconded in 1713 and was now living in Venice; during the next period he acted as the Academy's agent for securing singers and materials (such as scores and librettos) from Italy, though his own opinions on artistic policy were not always accepted in London.[39] He suggested that Nicolini should be approached as a potential substitute for Senesino, who was proving vain and quarrelsome, but this never came about: Senesino always had a strong lobby in London. By the spring of 1725, however, Swiney was empowered to undertake the important task of securing another leading lady, Faustina Bordoni, for London. He accomplished this successfully, but not immediately, as Faustina was already committed to the winter carnival season in Venice: she arrived in London in March 1726 (Plate 4).

[39] See Gibson, 'Owen Swiney'.

By then another London opera season was past its zenith, having seen revivals of *Ottone, Rodelinda* and *Elpidia*, plus a new pasticcio (*Elisa*, probably arranged by Ariosti).

The prospect of two prima donnas (in itself a contradiction in terms) in the company set Handel the task of providing an opera that would give even-handed opportunities for Cuzzoni and Faustina, and give them a chance to show off their contrasted vocal and dramatic strengths. The chosen vehicle was *Alessandro*, based on a libretto that had been written for Steffani in the heyday of Hanover court opera: the libretto was selected by Haym and Handel but adapted by Rolli, now apparently in favour again. Handel probably began composing *Alessandro* and then had to set it aside because of the delay in Faustina's arrival. A new opera, *Scipione* (for which Rolli also prepared the libretto) seems to have been rushed into the gap: Handel completed the score on 2 March and it was first performed ten days later. *Alessandro* was completed on 11 April and first performed on 5 May, needless to say 'with great Applause'.[40] A play involving some of the same historical characters was already familiar to London's theatre-goers in Nathaniel Lee's *The Rival Queens*, a title that might have given the more circumspect directors of the Academy pause for thought. The season ran to 7 June, with 13 performances of *Alessandro*, the same number as for *Scipione*: a further performance had been planned but was cancelled because Senesino was unwell. Cluer published collections of the songs from both operas with unusual promptness, and with subscription lists that included Arbuthnot and Charles Jennens – old and new supporters of Handel. Even before the flurry caused by Faustina's arrival, Handel's music had seen some popularity: a newspaper reported of the *Ottone* revival that[41]

> Handel had the Satisfaction of seeing an Old Opera of his not only fill the House, which had not been done for some time, but above three hundred turn'd away for want of room.

But one swallow – or even two human nightingales – did not make a summer. At the end of the season Senesino left London, partly in order to improve his health with a continental vacation, and his continued absence during the autumn meant a late start to the next season, which did not begin until January 1727. Meanwhile, Bononcini's *Camilla* had been revived at Lincoln's Inn Fields Theatre in November 1726 with great success, and this seems to have stimulated the Academy's directors into luring the composer back: at a directors' meeting on 21 January 1727 an approach to Bononcini was proposed and soon afterwards, at a subsequent meeting, it was reported:[42]

[40] *The Daily Journal* (7 May 1726): cited in Gibson, *The Royal Academy of Music*, p. 233.
[41] *The Universal Mercury* (February 1726): cited in Gibson, *ibid.*, p. 232.
[42] *The Flying-Post* (4 February 1727): Deutsch, pp. 201–2; HHB, p. 147.

The Directors of the Royal Academy of Musick have resolved, that after the Excellent Opera composed by Mr. Hendel [*Admeto*], which is now performing; Signior Attilia shall compose one; And Signior Bononcini is to compose the next after that. Thus, as this Theatre can boast of the three best Voices in Europe, and the best Instruments; so the Town will have the Pleasure of having these three different Stiles of composing.

The scheme sounds like an expanded re-run of the *Muzio Scevola* gimmick. In fact, the season had already begun with Ariosti's *Lucio Vero* and continued with Handel's *Admeto* (first performed on 31 January):[43] the reference from the directors' meeting may be to Ariosti's next opera, *Teuzzone*, which could have been composed for this season but was not performed until the next. *Admeto* ran successfully for 19 performances during January–April (all apparently attended by the king),[44] and was followed by short revivals of *Ottone* and *Floridante*, leading into Bononcini's new opera *Astianatte* (nine performances in May and June).

Unfortunately, the 1726–7 season ended with serious trouble. Whether the arrangement of the timetable was accidental or not, Handel came out of it well by leaving the last production to Bononcini. The chief feature of the season, which was also the cause of the trouble, was the rivalry between the two leading ladies, and between their supporters: this was both reflected and intensified by a spate of pamphlets published in the spring of 1727.[45] Even before the season began, one observer reported that Cuzzoni and the Faustina were 'not perfectly agreed about their parts'.[46] The opening of *Astianatte* was apparently delayed by illnesses among the leading ladies: at the first performance Cuzzoni's voice was still 'prodigiously out of order and Faustina's Partisans say very confidently that she will never recover it'.[47] A certain amount of boisterous behaviour from partisans was tolerated, and indeed was not unusual, in the London theatres: it became news only when it led to an interruption of the drama or gave offence to any royalty that were present. At the performance of *Astianatte* on 6 June 1727 both conditions were fulfilled. There had already been some disturbance at a performance of *Admeto* on 4 April, for which a public apology in Cuzzoni's name was written to Princess Amelia. No incidents were reported at the first performances of *Astianatte*. The king left London for Hanover on 3 June, the day of the eighth performance, and the serious trouble came at the very next performance, which was attended by the Princess of Wales:[48]

[43] The autograph of *Admeto* is lost, but an annotation on another manuscript copy shows that Handel completed the score on 10 November 1726.
[44] See Burrows and Hume, *George I*, pp. 332–3.
[45] See Gibson, *The Royal Academy of Music*, p. 250.
[46] Letter from Mrs Pendarves (27 November 1726): Deutsch, p. 199; *HHB*, p. 145.
[47] Letter from Robert Hassell to Robert Cotesworth (10 May 1727): cited in Gibson, *The Royal Academy of Music*, p. 251.
[48] *The British Journal* (10 June 1727): Deutsch, p. 210; *HHB*, p. 151.

On Tuesday-night last [6 June], a great Disturbance happened at the Opera, occasioned by the Partisans of the Two Celebrated Rival Ladies, Cuzzoni and Faustina. The Contention at first was only carried on by Hissing on one Side, and Clapping on the other; but proceeded at length to Catcalls, and other great Indecencies: And notwithstanding the Princess Caroline was present, no Regards were of Force to restrain the Rudenesses of the Opponents.

The season came to an abrupt halt, though the controversy continued:[49]

As to Opera feuds, they are hotter than ever. I suppose you have heard already that both Cuzzoni and Faustina were so hissed and cat-called last Tuesday that the Opera was not finished that night: nor have the Directors dared to venture the representation of another since...No Cuzzonist will go to a tavern with a Faustinian; and the ladies of one party have scratched those of the other out of their list of visits. I was t'other night upon the water, and heard nothing till three a clock in the morning but invocations of one and execrations upon the other. The next night I went again, and heard the same ceremony performed by another company, with the names reversed; so that these transient deities, like the Egyptian ones, are alternately sacrificed to one another.

Lord Hervey wrote that letter on 13 June. The death of the king, which occurred on the journey to Hanover on 11 June, would have closed the theatres in any case, but it did not put an end to the controversy, which continued in a couple of scurrilous pamphlets published over the next couple of months.[50]

One of George I's last constitutional acts in Britain had been to sign a naturalization bill to which Handel's name had been added.[51] Thus, just before his 42nd birthday in February 1727 Handel became a British subject. No doubt he had been encouraged to adopt British nationality by his personal successes in the opera house over the last couple of seasons, but it is unlikely that he was influenced only by short-term success: he must have realized that the London theatre public was volatile. His naturalization was therefore presumably the result of a rational judgment that his future lay in London, and it was doubtless influenced by the security provided by his current royal pensions. The timing of Handel's naturalization was a happy coincidence for him, in that it enabled him to take part in the coronation of King George II (no-one had anticipated George I's imminent death in 1727, for he had apparently been in good health on leaving London in June). Although Handel received a pension as Composer to the Chapel Royal, this was a court title independent of the Composers in the chapel's regular establishment, and the lines of

[49] Letter from Lord Hervey to Stephen Fox (13 June 1727): cited in Gibson, *The Royal Academy of Music*, pp. 252–3.

[50] Gibson, *ibid.*, p. 253.

[51] Handel's petition for naturalization and the relevant parliamentary committee proceedings are covered in Deutsch, pp. 202–5; *HHB*, pp. 147–8. The Act is illustrated and transcribed in Simon, *Handel*, pp. 284–5.

demarcation over his duties up to 1727 seem to have been quite clear. Handel had made his mark with the 'Utrecht' music in 1713, but the music for the coronation of George I a year later had been composed by Croft. Native composers then took over the ceremonial church music for the court as required, but an exception was made for the Chapel Royal services marking the king's return from Hanover, which could be regarded as semi-public domestic occasions. Handel's naturalization now made him available for any opportunity that, by law or custom, was open to a British citizen.

William Croft, the Chapel Royal's leading Composer and its Organist, died on 14 August. His obvious successor was Maurice Greene,[52] but (according to a later note by King George III) for the coronation music the new king 'forbad...that wretched little crooked ill natured insignificant writer Player and musician...and ordered that G. F. Hendel should not only have that great honour but...choose his own words'.[53] A historical fact is probably embedded in the verbiage of the later king's prejudices, and certainly the newspapers carried reports early in September 1727 that Handel had been ordered by King George II to compose the coronation music.[54] The consequence was a repeat of the 'Utrecht' experience. The coronation of King George II and Queen Caroline took place at Westminster Abbey on 11 October, preceded by two public rehearsals of the music on 6 and 9 October. Reports commented both on the numerical strength of the forces gathered together and on the effect of the music itself – 'the best performance of that kind that ever was'. At the time of the next coronation in 1761, William Boyce described the 1727 music as 'The First Grand Musical Performance in the Abbey': perhaps this was not strictly true, as the coronation of James II in 1685, for example, had made a similar splash in terms of the resources and styles of its own period. But it was the 1727 coronation anthems that established a permanent niche for Handel in the English-speaking world as a composer of striking choral music, described in such terms as 'grand' and 'sublime'. The coronation anthems were to have a tangible effect on the course of Handel's career five years later: taking a longer view, Handel bequeathed *Zadok the priest* to every subsequent British coronation. One contemporary newspaper report told of 40 voices and 160 instruments at the 1727 coronation. This was probably an exaggeration, but certainly a fair number of 'supernumerary' performers were brought in to strengthen the royal musicians and the choirs of the Chapel Royal and Westminster Abbey. The full potential of Handel's music may not have been perfectly realized

[52] Handel was an unlikely contender for the posts: the salary was substantially less than his current 'Chapel Royal' pension, and the posts implied a regular commitment to chapel duties that would probably have been incompatible with the timetable of his theatrical routine.

[53] See Smith, W. C., 'George III', p. 790. The copy of Mainwaring's *Memoirs* containing the annotations that Smith records was apparently lost in the Second World War.

[54] For a full account of the background see Burrows, 'Handel and the 1727 Coronation'.

at the coronation service itself: the Archbishop of Canterbury annotated his order of service with various comments, including 'The Anthem in Confusion: All irregular in the Music' against the words for *The king shall rejoice.*[55]

Even before the first rehearsal of the coronation anthems, the next opera season had begun, early, on 30 September, with a revival of *Admeto*: no doubt the Academy was quick to capitalize on the unusually large number of patrons who were in London in anticipation of the coronation (announced for 4 October but postponed for a week because of possible flooding). The Academy had certainly one, and probably two, new operas on the stocks ready to follow *Admeto*. Ariosti's *Teuzzone* (first performed on 21 October) might have been composed during the previous season, as Handel's *Riccardo Primo* had certainly been – Handel completed his draft of the autograph score on 16 May. Both operas had probably been elbowed out of the 1726–7 season by Bononcini's *Astianatte*, but now, following the scandal in June, Bononcini was gone from the programme for good. As with the timing of his naturalization before the coronation, Handel enjoyed another fortunate coincidence in that the subject matter of his as yet unperformed opera was entirely appropriate as a theatre celebration of the new reign. The story of *Riccardo Primo* was suitably flattering to the British monarchy in that the hero, King Richard I of England, defeats the tyrant Isacio and wins the lady: embarrassingly precise contemporary parallels with the new king could not be drawn from the opera, since the action was set in Cyprus. No doubt a few people might have remembered that the historical Richard the Lionheart did not speak English (though this would hardly have been a significant message to be derived from an Italian opera): King George II seems to have been nearer to fluency in English than his father, but he conducted at least some of his court and personal business in French. A special effort seems to have been made with the scenery for the production of *Riccardo Primo*, which was designed by the painter Joseph Goupy.[56] With or without the specific stimulant of *Riccardo Primo*, royal support for the opera company and its performances continued as before under the new king.

The season, which ran through to 1 June 1728, must have revealed to Handel both the pleasures and the trials that were consequent on his triumph as the Academy's principal composer. 63 performances were

[55] Winton Dean ('Handel', in Sadie (ed.), *The New Grove*) suggests that the Archbishop Wake's annotations might have been made during a rehearsal. I think this unlikely: the newspaper reports suggest that Handel's rehearsals were musical (rather than liturgical), Wake's surviving diaries do not suggest that he had any interest in attending musical events, and Wake's annotation to the front page of his order of service (illustrated in Simon, *Handel*, p. 142) says that he recorded 'what was done or omitted at that coronation'.

[56] Perhaps in collaboration with Peter Tillemans: see Gibson, *The Royal Academy of Music*, pp. 262–3. Goupy was apparently close to the centre of the diplomatic intrigues that surrounded the formation of the 'Handel-Heidegger' company; see Rolli's letter of 4 February 1729: Deutsch, p. 237.

given[57] (on Tuesday and Saturday nights), and Ariosti's *Teuzzone* accounted for only three of them. Handel's music was therefore before the public for 60 performances, which meant that he had to sustain, single-handed, the interest of the audiences and the company for nearly the whole season. *Riccardo Primo* (first performed on 11 November 1727) was followed by revivals of *Alessandro* and *Radamisto* and then by two new operas – *Siroe* (score completed 5 February 1728, first performed 17 February) and *Tolomeo* (score completed 19 April, first performed 30 April). The new operas must have been composed during periods when Handel was engaged with the normal routines of performing other repertory works. Handel had begun his round of new compositions with an attempt at another opera, to have been called *Genserico*: he wrote a substantial portion of Act 1 before abandoning the attempt, and he re-used most of the music in *Siroe* and *Tolomeo*. The two completed operas present something of a contrast: *Siroe* is a rather formal opera to a Metastasio libretto, while *Tolomeo* is lighter and more varied, though by no means lightweight.

While Handel's fluency in composing opera scores continued unabated, the day-to-day running of the company was fraught with problems that many informed observers saw as threatening its future. The partisanship between the two leading ladies' supporters was apparently quiescent, but accumulated strains in the relationship between Handel and Senesino were probably becoming more insistent. More serious, however, was the fact that the Academy's capital was simply running out: the final calls had been made on the subscriptions promised under the system set up in 1719. During the spring of 1728 appeals to those whose payments were in arrears were coupled with reminders that 'the Royal Academy stands very much indebted to the Performers & others ingaged in their Service which in Honour and Justice must be paid'.[58] As early as November 1727 pessimistic predictions were the order of the day:[59]

> I doubt operas will not survive longer than this winter, they are now at their last gasp; the subscription is expired and nobody will renew it. The directors are always squabbling, and they have so many divisions among themselves that I wonder they have not broke up before; Senesino goes away next winter, and I believe Faustina, so you see harmony is almost out of fashion.

As it turned out, the 'last gasp' was protracted and, musically speaking, of good quality. But attendances at performances in 1728 were smaller than before: the whole Academy enterprise seems to have lost public

[57] The run of surviving newspapers carrying opera advertisements is defective for early 1728; this figure is based on the assumption that the performances continued their normal weekly routine.

[58] 'Notice to Subscribers' (25 May 1728): cited in Gibson, *The Royal Academy of Music*, p. 268.

[59] Letter from Mrs Pendarves (25 November 1727): Deutsch, p. 218; *HHB*, p. 156.

confidence. Furthermore, a new external hazard appeared. At Lincoln's Inn Fields Theatre on 29 January, John Rich followed a successful revival of Bononcini's *Camilla* with a new work that proved even more popular – *The Beggar's Opera*. By late March the latter had been played 36 times and was as full as it had been on the first night;[60] it was not strictly an opera at all, but a play with incidental songs, a couple of them derived from Handel's music. It was no doubt part of the production's satirical intent that the ballad songs were primitive if compared with the full arias of Italian opera, though in the prologue to the play the Beggar informed the audience that he had nevertheless incorporated the fashionable conventions of opera – 'the Similes of the *Swallow*, the *Moth*, the *Bee* [etc]', a prison scene and equal roles for two rival ladies. At the end of the real opera season, the stars had made their own judgments about the Academy's future prospects:[61]

> There is to be but four opera nights more, and then adieu to harmony of that kind for ever and ever. Senesino and Faustina have hired themselves to Turin and to Venice for the next winter and the carnival following.

Cuzzoni went to Vienna.[62]

An attempt was made to keep the Academy going. There were enough interested patrons to keep the company alive, and 35 of them declared themselves willing to subscribe £200 each for a season beginning in October 1728.[63] But no plans could be advanced without a prospective cast. Heidegger left London for Italy in June to look for singers, but found that few were available. A general meeting on 18 January 1729 was a turning-point in the history of the Academy, and its business was reported very fully in a letter from Rolli to Senesino in Venice (though from the author's jaundiced viewpoint):[64]

> London, 25th [January] 1729
> Heydeger returned and said that he had not found any singers in Italy; he protested that he did not wish to undertake anything without the two ladies; he spoke only of them and proposed Farinello. In the end, hearing that your friends desired you back, he gave way, and you are once more on good terms with him. He was thinking more of a lucrative subscription than of anything else and he was calculating well, for in this way the two parties and your friends in each would be helping to fill up the annual subscription with 20 pounds per head. This was the scheme, on the basis of which, already known to you, I wrote you the first letter. But Handel was not to be duped by such a paltry stratagem. He revealed his rival's rascally deceit: the only aim of his useless and ridiculous voyage was to profit himself alone. So he [Handel]

---

[60] Letter from John Gay (20 March 1728): cited in Gibson, *The Royal Academy of Music*, p. 270.
[61] Letter from Mrs Pendarves to Ann Granville (11 May 1728).
[62] See Gibson, *The Royal Academy of Music*, p. 276.
[63] See Gibson, *ibid.*, pp. 278–9.
[64] Original in Italian; *HHB*, pp. 168–9; English translation, Deutsch, pp. 235–6.

declared that there was need of a change and has renewed the old system of changing the singers in order to have the opportunity of composing new works for new performers. His new plans find favour at Court and he is satisfied. Faustina is not required, but they have lent quite a favourable ear to you. They want Farinello and Cuzzona, if she does not remain in Vienna, and the promoters are such as can pay. Mylord Bingley is at the head of the project, but the theatre has still to be found [i.e. paid for]. So they called in Heydeger and they have granted him 2200 pounds with which to provide the theatre, the scenery and the costumes.

Handel will have 1000 pounds for the composition, whether it will be by himself or by whomsoever else he may choose. The subscription will be 15 guineas per person, and so far it is thought sufficient. A total of 4000 pounds is proposed for the singers – two at a 1000 pounds each with a benefit performance, and the rest, etc. Handel will shortly depart for Italy, where he will select the cast. Three representatives of the subscribers will go with him, in order to examine them, etc. That is the new system. Riva is already suffering from it, for you can well see what a very ill wind is blowing for Bononcino. So do tell Faustina that her dear little Handel will be coming to Italy, but not for her. Have I not already written to you that she would after all have found him quite contrary to her opinions?

Poor dear! I am so sorry! This treatment – and I say it for all to hear – is well deserved by all who sacrifice their friends, in order to make the most base advances to their enemies. Expenses must, as I fear, now exclude you: otherwise I would not doubt that sooner or later I should find you here once more, in despite of the Man whose aim it has been to prevent your return. Farinello will come, attracted perhaps by the bait of a benefit performance, for no one – except you – has ever refused him [Handel], so brazen is his begging for charity.

Viscount Percival's more succinct account adds some details about the business arrangement:[65]

I went to a meeting of the members of the Royal Academy of Musick: where we agreed to prosecute the subscribers who have not yet paid; also to permit Hydeger and Hendle to carry on operas without disturbance for 5 years and to lend them for that time our scenes, machines, clothes, instruments, furniture, etc. It all past off in a great hurry, and there was not above 20 there.

Beyond the facts that Handel and Heidegger were granted the use of the Academy's capital effects for five years,[66] and that their enterprise had the Academy's blessing (or at least a guarantee of non-interference), it is difficult to make sense of the relationship between Handel, Heidegger and the continuing institution of the Royal Academy. It was presumably the job of the new composer-manager combination to raise their own subscriptions, but some sort of financial promises must have come from

[65]Percival's diary (18 January 1729): Deutsch, p. 234; *HHB*, p. 168.

[66]Mainwaring, *Memoirs*, pp. 112–13, refers to a three-year agreement, though five years seems more plausible in view of the fact that 1734 was the year in which Handel had to leave the King's Theatre (see also Chapter 8, n.14). See Hume, 'Handel and Opera Management', pp. 347–50.

the Academy meeting, since Rolli says that 'the promoters are such as can pay'.

The immediate result, of course, was that it was now Handel's turn to set off to continental Europe in search of singers. The newspapers reported the date of his departure as 26 January,[67] but a slightly later date is suggested by a second letter (with a postscript giving subsequent news) from Rolli to Senesino in Venice:[68]

L[ondon]. 4th February 1729.

The new Handel-Heidegger system is gaining ground. A general meeting was held, at which it was discussed. There were few present and only six or seven of these subscribed; others did not refuse to do so, and others requested that they should first be notified who the singers were. The Royal wishes on this matter were made known and it was announced that Handel would soon leave for Italy in search of singers. By unanimous consent the two managers were granted the use of the Academy's dresses and scenery for five years. Handel is in fact departing today, and ten days ago Haym despatched circular letters to the professional singers in Italy, announcing this new project and Handel's arrival. Farinello comes first in estimation, and all the more so as news has recently arrived from Venice...that all throng to the theatre at which Farinello is singing, and that the theatre where you and Faustina perform is nearly empty. The declared opinion of this King on the two singers is certainly as follows: that he would contribute the sum promised, if both Cuzzona and Faustina returned here, that he would contribute the same amount if Cuzzona alone returned, but that if only Faustina returned, he would contribute nothing at all. It is very uncertain whether Cuzzona is returning or not... The purpose of this new scheme is to have everything new. Dear little Hendel, as a result of personal experience and from a desire to give everyone his due, detests that lady, the promoter of *Siroe*.

Riva is furious, because he sees Bononcino excluded by his own pride and by that of the Chief Composer, on whom everyone else will have to depend.

7th [February]

They say that Farinello has already been engaged for next year here, and you also but elsewhere ...They are still talking of Carestini as second singer. It will not be difficult to obtain subscriptions, because cheap prices are popular with the majority. However, good sponsors never did any harm. I hear for certain that neither of the two ladies will be engaged – and both parties agree as to this. Thus, unless Cuzzona returns of her own accord, she will certainly not be invited to come. You will without doubt see Handel before the end of the Carnival, because, for sure, he is going directly to Venice for Farinello. I shall be curious to know how he will behave with you and with the celebrated prima donna [Faustina]; who, I fear, in her anger against the unfaithful man, may have him *thrown into the Canal*.

While Handel was away, Heidegger put on seven masquerades at the

---

[67] *The Daily Post* (27 January 1729): Deutsch, p. 236; *HHB*, p. 169.
[68] Original in Italian, *HHB*, pp. 169–70; English translation adapted from Deutsch, pp. 236–8.

King's Theatre, presumably to raise money to subsidize the operatic venture. Several of these were advertised as including instrumental pieces from Handel's operas as incidental music.[69]

By 11 March (28 February, Old Style) Handel was in Venice, which he used as a centre: writing to his brother-in-law, he gave the name of an English banker there who would forward letters to 'the various places in Italy where I shall be'. By 30 March (19 March, Old Style) Handel had been to Bologna and was on his way to Rome, and by then he had apparently become resigned to the fact that the great castrato Farinelli was not interested in joining his company. As the English Resident in Venice reported after the event:[70]

This is certain, when Mr Hendel was here last winter, Farinello would never see him in particular, or ever return'd him a visit, tho' Mr Hendel was three times at his door to wait on him.

But he had gained instead another castrato in Bernacchi, who had previously sung for the Haymarket company in 1716–17. Bernacchi and the contralto Merighi were lucky acquisitions, being at the end of their commitments in Naples: in general, Handel was running dangerously late in trying to put a company together so late in the season, when most singers would already have been booked ahead. Handel must have pursued his business briskly. He returned from Italy via Germany, passing through Hanover in June: he had probably by then also paid a short visit to Halle, where he is reputed to have met Wilhelm Friedemann Bach, Johann Sebastian's eldest son.[71] Handel arrived back in London on 29 June, and the newspapers reported the successful completion of his mission by listing the singers that he had put under contract.[72] He had solved the Faustina-Cuzzoni problem by engaging neither of them but instead Strada (Anna Maria Strada del Pò) as his new leading soprano; according to Rolli (who did not concur),[73] Handel thought Strada sang 'better than the two who have left us, because one of them never pleased him at all and he would like to forget the other'.

The new season, and new company, opened on 2 December 1729 with Handel's opera *Lotario*, the score of which he had completed on 16 November.[74] There was a public rehearsal on 28 November 'before a great

[69] See Gibson, *The Royal Academy of Music*, pp. 280–1.

[70] Letter from Colonel Burges to the Duke of Newcastle (9/20 January 1730): cited in Gibson, *ibid.*, pp. 282–3.

[71] Handel's visit to Hanover was reported in the London papers: see the entry for *The London Gazette* of 24 June 1729 in Deutsch, p. 243 and *HHB*, pp. 172–3, and the accompanying commentaries concerning Handel's possible meeting with W. F. Bach and his (less likely) visit to Hamburg. In 1729 W. F. Bach was still a student at Leipzig; he later (1746) became organist of the Marienkirche, Halle.

[72] Newspaper references for 2 and 4 July 1729: Deutsch, pp. 243–4; *HHB*, p. 173.

[73] Letter of December 1729: translated in Deutsch, p. 249.

[74] On 10 October at least one opera soloist, accompanied by Handel on the harpsichord, had performed privately before the king and queen at Kensington (see Chapter 7, n.34).

Number of the Nobility and Quality', including Mrs Pendarves, who wrote:[75]

> Bernachi has a vast compass, his voice mellow and clear, but not so sweet as Senesino, his manner better; his person not so good, for he is as big as a Spanish friar. Fabri has a tenor voice, sweet, clear and firm, but not strong enough, I doubt, for the stage: he sings like a gentleman, without making faces, and his manner is particularly agreeable; he is the greatest master of musick that ever sang upon the stage. The third is the bass,[76] a very good distinct voice, without any harshness. La Strada is the first woman; her voice is without exception fine, her manner perfection, but her person *very bad*, and she makes *frightful mouths*. La Merighi is the next to her; her voice is not extraordinarily good or bad, she is tall and has a very graceful person, with a tolerable face; she seems to be a woman about forty, she sings easily and agreeably. The last is Bertoli, she has neither voice, ear, nor manner to recommend her; but she is a perfect beauty, quite a Cleopatra, that sort of complexion with regular features, fine teeth, and when she sings has a smile about her mouth which is extreme pretty, and I believe has practised to sing before a glass, for she has never any distortion in her face.

Before the season began Handel was (as we may imagine) saddened, on both personal and professional grounds, by the loss of Nicola Haym, who had died in August. In consequence Handel no doubt had to make peace with Rolli, but he could still call on the services of Giacomo Rossi (the librettist of *Rinaldo*), who probably arranged the text of *Lotario* for him.[77] Ariosti had also died, in the summer of 1729, and for diplomatic reasons Bononcini was unacceptable to the new management: so Handel had to take on the complete burden as his own composer-impresario.

He moved into the routine for which the last season of the Academy had prepared him. Each season was to have a couple of new operas and some revivals of his own works, and if this repertory did not prove sufficient the programme would be completed with pasticcio operas (using arias from his own works or those of contemporary Italian composers) which Handel would arrange himself. In the first season, *Lotario* was followed by the new opera *Partenope* in February 1730, forming a contrasted pair – a rather conventional work succeeded by a more lighthearted one. The programme was completed by revivals of *Giulio Cesare* and *Tolomeo*, and by the pasticcio *Ormisda*, which drew on music from Orlandini, Vinci, Hasse and others: Handel apparently had a large stock of material from scores to hand in London, probably including some he had collected in Italy. It is perhaps perverse that *Ormisda* proved very

[75] Letter of November 1729 to Ann Granville: Deutsch, p. 247; *HHB*, p. 175.
[76] Johann Gottfried Riemschneider from the Hamburg opera company, son of the Kantor at the Marienkirche in Halle and reputedly a schoolfellow of Handel's; but he only sang a single season with Handel in London.
[77] Following Haym's death, Rolli described Rossi in a letter to Riva (3 September 1729: *HHB*, p. 174) as 'il poeta dell'Handel': Deutsch (p. 245), following Streatfeild (*Handel*), translates this as 'Handel's accredited bard'.

popular, receiving twice as many performances as *Partenope* during the season. The pasticcio's musical contents were fluid: Strada's benefit performance on 21 April was advertised as having '12 songs changed'. At the end of the season Rolli grudgingly commented that the operas 'succeed no better than they deserve. The musicians will be paid, and that is all that can be done'.[78] In July 1730 Heidegger duly received the £1000 from the king that had formerly been paid to the Royal Academy. It may not be a coincidence that the songs from the operas composed for the new company were given to a different publisher, John Walsh: Cluer may have been in some sense the Academy's publisher.

In the summer of 1730 Francis Colman, the British Envoy in Florence, was charged with the task of negotiating to bring Senesino back to London. No doubt Bernacchi had been signed on for only a year, and Handel had eventually conceded that Senesino's popularity with the London audiences outweighed his disadvantages. The negotiations were successful, though at a price: 1400 guineas for the season. Senesino was back in London by October 1730. In view of his return, it is perhaps surprising that the 1730–1 season saw only one new original opera, though a substantial and colourful one – *Poro*. Perhaps, on the other hand, both the composer and his leading man were content with revivals of operas that included proven roles composed for Senesino, *Scipione* (which opened the season) and *Rodelinda*. But Senesino also had to come to grips with revivals of the more recent operas *Ormisda* and *Partenope*, suitably revised to accommodate him. Most remarkable of all, Handel and Heidegger decided that one way of keeping the interest alive was to return to Handel's London origins with a revival of *Rinaldo*, heavily revised to suit the new cast but still recognizably the same in musical outline. It seems very unlikely that the original scenic effects and costumes would have survived the 14 years since the previous production. Finally, the programme was completed with another pasticcio, *Venceslao*, again drawing on arias by a variety of composers. The opera season as a whole seems to have been successful: Colman's 'opera register' recorded that *Poro* and *Rodelinda* 'took much' and, having completed the 50 performances for the season successfully in May, the 'Undertakers for the Opera' presented two extra performances to make up for the previous year's shortfall. Probably life was too hectic during the season to allow Handel to dwell too much on the death of his mother in December 1730, which was the subject of an emotional letter, written on black-edged notepaper, to his brother-in-law the following February. Although his letters to his brother-in-law were usually written in French, this one is in German, with a mixture of odd words in other languages (principally Latin).[79] In the

---

[78]Letter to Riva (12 June 1730): *HHB*, pp. 179–80; English translation in Deutsch, pp. 254–5.
[79]Deutsch, pp. 268–70 (with English translation); *HHB*, p. 188. The letter is dated 23/12 February 1731 (which was not Handel's 46th birthday; he presumably kept this anniversary, if

summer Handel wrote two further letters to his brother-in-law, one to thank him for clearing up his mother's estate and the second to inform him that Handel was sending a watch and some jewellery as a present for the forthcoming wedding of his niece: transfers of family property between London and Halle were effected through a Hamburg merchant, Sbüelen.[80]

In March 1731 the London newspapers had picked up a rumour that Cuzzoni would be returning to London, but nothing came of this: Strada was now established, and remained, as the company's first lady. Senesino also seemed to have settled back in again – or resigned himself – to a few more years in London. There were some minor changes to the company before the next season, including the acquisition of a fine new bass singer, Montagnana. The season began on 13 November 1731 with a revival of *Tamerlano*: the choice probably reflects the fact that Handel had also gained a good tenor in Pinacci, who could do justice to the part of Bajazet. Revivals of *Poro* and *Admeto* followed, and Handel's first new opera of the season, *Ezio*, was not heard until 15 January 1732. The delay might well have been caused because Handel was late finishing the opera.[81] He had already made an abortive attempt at a 'Tito' opera based on Racine's *Bérénice* (he headed the autograph 'Titus l'Empéreur', though the work was, of course, in Italian), completing three scenes in Act 1 before abandoning it and reaching for his third (and last) libretto by Metastasio as an alternative[82] (he had already set Metastasio texts for *Siroe* and *Poro*). The rather conventional Roman story of *Ezio* went down less well with the London audience than the more colourful *Sosarme*, completed on 4 February 1732 and first performed 11 days later. Handel began *Sosarme* on the basis of a libretto that set the story in Portugal, but halfway through he changed the character names and moved the location to 'Sardis, in the Kingdom of Lidia'. The change to a politically insignificant location might have been undertaken to prevent unwelcome identifications with contemporary events. The story concerns a disagreement between the father and the son of a ruling house, and relations between King George II and his son Prince Frederick were by 1732 beginning to boil up in a manner familiar from the previous generation (though a literal interpretation of the plot of *Sosarme* would lay the blame on a leading politician).

Sandwiched between *Ezio* and *Sosarme* came a modest revival of *Giulio Cesare*. *Sosarme* was followed, remarkably, by a revival of an Academy opera by another composer, *Coriolano* by Ariosti, a repertory opera from

---

at all, on the Old Style date). One other letter in German from Handel to Michaelsen survives, from August 1733.

[80] Letters of 10 August/30 July and 28/17 August 1731 (both in French), the year of the second mistranscribed as 1736 in some publications: Deutsch, pp. 275–6, 413–15 (with English translations); *HHB*, pp. 191–2. Handel sent greetings in both letters to Michaelsen's wife: since the death of Handel's sister, his brother-in-law had remarried twice.

[81] The end of the *Ezio* autograph, which probably carried the completion date, is lost.

[82] Handel had probably brought the libretto of *Ezio* back from Italy in 1729.

1722–4. Staying with operas that had originated at that period, possibly because their scores matched his present cast fairly well, Handel followed *Sosarme* with his only revival of *Flavio*. The performance of *Flavio* on 29 April was the company's 41st of the season, and was the last in the continuous run of operas. Four performances of the pasticcio *Lucio Papirio* (arranged by Handel, from an earlier opera by Giacomelli) followed between 23 May and 6 June. Before them came *Esther* and after them *Acis and Galatea*: and with the introduction of these works on the end of the opera season Handel's career in London entered a new phase.

The music of the 'Academy' years

Operas

The period 1720–33 saw 18 new operas from Handel, plus one act of *Muzio Scevola* and two substantial fragments. For a rounded view of Handel's creative achievement in the opera house there is also a case for taking the pasticcios into account, but even without them (and discounting other movements that were composed for the operas but never performed) there exists more than 55 hours of music. It is difficult to deal concisely with such a body of works. Although the musical conventions of all the operas are standard, proceeding through the formal structures of recitative and aria, one striking feature of the complete repertory is its variety. This is not always immediately apparent from a casual glance at the scores, which the English-speaking listener needs to take in conjunction with the original printed word-books, that have facing-page translations of the Italian text:[1] while these translations may sometimes be rather free or literally inaccurate, they at least explain the stage action at any moment and give the original descriptions of the settings – Asia Minor for *Radamisto*, Persia for *Floridante*, Rome for *Ottone*, Lombardy for *Flavio*, and so on (see Fig. 4, pp. 62–3). The historical locations, like the styles of the costumes, were no doubt interpreted through the eyes of the eighteenth century, but we may be sure that each opera did not look the same as the next. It is necessary, therefore, to bring a certain amount of visual imagination to the musical scores.

The practical stagecraft of the eighteenth century also needs to be considered. There was no director/producer in the modern sense: the blocking of positions and moves on stage was evolved by the principals at rehearsals, on the basis of the formal training they had received and their accumulated stage experience, in collaboration with the theatre manager and within the constraints and opportunities imposed by the scene designer. The singer was dominant: during an aria he or she would not have countenanced any distracting stage business in the vicinity. The physical resources of the theatre also have to be taken into account. Deep

---

[1] Copies of such word-books survive for nearly all Handel's productions, including revivals: a comprehensive collection, in facsimile, is in Harris, *The Librettos of Handel's Operas*.

stages and perspective sets were elements in the definition of Baroque opera,[2] and the soloists always sang from the front apron stage. There were no mid-act curtain drops: transformation scenes with sliding flats were a speciality of a well-equipped Baroque theatre. It was both cost-effective and popular to re-use in a new opera any elaborate setting or complex piece of stage machinery, duly adapted and re-decorated to its context: the Academy obviously owned a breachable city wall, for example, which fell down to order in *Alessandro*, *Riccardo Primo* and *Lotario*.

Given both the quantity and the variety of Handel's operas, they legitimately deserve detailed studies that are beyond the scope of this biography.[3] They may be judged from a number of different standpoints. An obvious one is dramatic coherence, which may be assessed to a large extent from the libretto: but that gives only a partial view, as music drama follows different rules from the spoken theatre – *The Magic Flute* would fail any known test if judged on its libretto alone. (Allowance must also be made for different operatic conventions – a late Baroque opera, *Don Giovanni* and *Tosca* represent different kinds of 'dramatic' experiences for the audience.) Alternatively, the score of an opera may be evaluated from a purely musical standpoint, on the constructional quality of the concerted movements: but that obviously misses the point of dramatic appropriateness and the contribution of each aria to the building-up of character portraits. Some Handel operas may, from either point of view or from both taken together, be deemed better or worse than others. But the tantalizing fact is that even the apparently weaker operas invariably include a couple of fine arias, a good character portrait or a stirring and striking dramatic scene. Descriptions of individual operas naturally tend to concentrate on novelties (such as an unusual turn in the orchestration or harmony) or on such momentary strengths as have been indicated above, without giving a feel for the complete work. In the present context I have chosen to examine one work in some detail, as a general introduction to Handel's mature Italian operas.

One period presents itself as a starting-point in the search for an 'exemplary' Academy opera: during 1723–5 Handel produced three works in succession that, on a dual assessment of musical and dramatic qualities, must be regarded as the masterpieces of his Academy years – *Giulio Cesare*, *Tamerlano* and *Rodelinda*. Each has different qualities. On sheer musical and compositional power, *Rodelinda* (1725) might be preferred: one beautiful aria follows another in an immensely well-balanced succession of contrasts. Although Baroque opera is more than a 'concert in costume', *Rodelinda* would stand up well against any other

---

[2] See Lindgren, 'The Staging of Handel's Operas', p. 93.
[3] The two most substantial studies in English are Dean, *Handel and the Opera Seria*, and Dean and Knapp, *Handel's Operas*.

three-and-a-half-hour concert work.[4] *Tamerlano* (1724) has both good music and an interesting drama, with some remarkable scenes. There is a particularly fascinating climax to Act 2, where the conventional final aria for one of the leading soloists is preceded by a chain-ensemble in which the characters in turn admit to misjudging the heroine Asteria, who had feigned submission to the tyrant Tamerlano (Tamerlane) in order to make an attempt on his life. For illustration of the widest range of Handel's techniques, however, the best exemplar is *Giulio Cesare* (1724), which has a fast-moving plot, full of incident, and some of Handel's best arias, as well as scenes that are spectacular from both musical and dramatic standpoints.

It is necessary to deal first of all with a preliminary crisis of identity that is frequently found in Handel's larger works but is here rather more urgent than usual: what exactly constitutes Handel's *Giulio Cesare*? During composition Handel subjected Act 1 to a series of massive revisions: there were at least seven stages in the composition and re-arrangement of the complete draft score.[5] Some of the changes were made to accommodate changes in the casting (probably more than six months separated the beginning of the composition from the première in February 1724), but it also seems probable that the upheavals in Act 1 were due to running revisions to the libretto. Circumstantial evidence suggests that Haym, working closely with Handel, gradually developed the libretto, modifying it as he did so, drawing on more than one literary source and paying careful attention to dramatic coherence. *Giulio Cesare* was entirely typical of the London operas in that it was based on a pre-existing libretto that had seen service in Italy – twice, in fact, at Venice in 1677 and, revised, at Milan in 1685.[6] Haym and Handel drew on both versions. Beyond the completion of the original draft score, it was normal for further revisions to follow as an opera proceeded from rehearsal to performance, and indeed there could be further thoughts as the first performances settled down into the normal routine of a short run (*Giulio Cesare* had 13 performances in 1724 and ten in the next season). For revivals in later years, there would certainly be more changes to accommodate new casts, as happened with *Giulio Cesare* when it was presented again in 1725, 1730 and 1732. Some of the alterations after the completion of the draft composition score might be regarded as running repairs, but most were serious responses to the musical capabilities of the performers and to the opportunities for improvements in dramatic presentation. It is impossible

[4] Most of Handel's operas comprise, in their complete and authentic forms, about three hours of music each; some (including *Il pastor fido* and *Flavio*) are rather shorter, others (including *Giulio Cesare*, *Rodelinda* and *Alcina*) rather longer.

[5] See Dean and Knapp, *Handel's Operas*, pp. 508–16.

[6] The original libretto was written by Giacomo Francesco Bussani and set to music by Antonio Sartorio. On the details of its conversion for London, see Dean and Knapp, *ibid.*, pp. 486–9, and Monson, ' "Giulio Cesare in Egitto" '.

to separate the dramatic and musical motives behind such revisions: the dramatic force of a character depended on how the performer could convey it musically. The version to be regarded as standard for the present purpose is the one as performed in 1724.[7]

In accordance with Handel's normal practice, *Giulio Cesare* begins with a 'French Overture': it opens with a grand *entrée* (Ex. 11a) whose harmonic and rhythmic strength lies in the interplay between the outer orchestral voices, followed by a faster contrapuntal movement (Ex. 11b).[8]

Ex. 11
(a) Ouverture

(b)

Once the faster movement is under way, its melodic subject dissolves into more fragmentary counterpoint, elaborated with sequences, modulations and melodic extensions: no subsequent statement gets as far as the final trill-cadence of bar 3, but there is plenty of bustle and excitement. The French-overture scheme could include a dance movement, and here a minuet-type movement does appear to follow on the end of the Allegro:

[7] An authoritative edition of the score of *Giulio Cesare*, clearly presenting all of Handel's performing versions, is in preparation, ed. W. Dean and S. Fuller.

[8] Normal fugal procedure presented a 'subject' in the tonic followed by an 'answer' (second entry) on the dominant. Ex.11b shows that Handel reverses this procedure: the first movement has ended on the dominant, and the fugal Allegro begins with a 'dominant' subject. The two movements thus form a binary arch: Handel had used this scheme even more explicitly elsewhere, e.g. in the overture to *Rinaldo*.

but it turns out also to be the opera's first vocal number, a *coro* (i.e. a concerted movement sung by the soloists) welcoming Cesare (Caesar) to Egypt. The entry of the voices comes as something of a surprise: Handel makes as if to repeat the minuet theme, but the voices enter in mid-phrase. The repeat of the theme had in any case introduced a striking musical effect with the entry of four horns, and the surprising entry of the voices follows this up. Handel sustains our attention in what at first had seemed a conventional minuet movement. The use of dance metres and styles (though not necessarily their strict formal schemes) is a significant and typical feature of Handel's music: however elaborate his aria structures became, many retained the rhythmic sturdiness and forward harmonic thrust derived from Baroque dance genres.

At the time of *Giulio Cesare* horns were still relatively novel in London (they seem to have arrived about 1717): Handel had introduced a pair of horns into the *Water Music* and (for the first time at the opera house) into *Radamisto*. In order to provide a range of possibilities in the construction of chords, Handel combined two pairs of them in different keys in *Giulio Cesare*. They were pitched in A and D in the *coro*, a movement in A major: in Act 3 he used horns in G and D for a movement in G major which accompanies the entrance of Cesare and Cleopatra at Alexandria – the stage direction mentions 'con trombe e timpani', but Handel's score includes neither. This was Handel's only experiment with mixed-key horn combinations.

Cesare's first aria ('Presti omai l'Egizia terra') is relatively short, as is appropriate to its introductory function within the scene: da capo show-piece arias come later, when the dramatic tension had built up sufficient power to justify the release of musical display on a larger scale. 'Presti omai' can in fact be regarded as being comparable to the A section alone of a da capo aria. The thematic material is similar to that of 'Ev'ry valley shall be exalted', an aria that occupies a comparable position in *Messiah*, written nearly 20 years later: in the opera, Cesare is announcing his arrival in Egypt; in the oratorio, the coming of the Messiah is prepared for. A bold opening theme, introduced by the orchestra (Ex. 12*a*) is taken up in a different form by the voice (Ex. 12*b*) and extended by decorative

Ex. 12a
(*a*) Opening

Ex. 12
(*b*) Vocal entry

(Let the Egyptian land now lend its palms to the victor)

melismas that are characteristic of the vocal style of the day, extending the vowel in the word 'palme'. Such extensions can serve a number of functions: they may give rhetorical force to a significant word in the text; they may function as a form of word-painting (though it is uncertain whether Handel had waving palms in mind here), or they may be largely decorative—which, of course, does not negate their usefulness in the skilful construction of a melodic line. The structure of the aria follows the binary scheme that was Handel's normal procedure for the A section of major-key arias: two statements of the text, the first modulating to the dominant and the second returning to the tonic. The join is effected by a one-bar re-introduction of the opening theme by the orchestra (bar 19), something that could hardly be dignified by the title 'ritornello'. As the second 'binary half' comes to its natural close in the tonic, Handel veers off with another statement of the text, moving the music towards the subdominant, and this develops into an extended coda section, longer than any of the previous ones and modifying the conventional binary balance: Handel keeps the music of the coda in the air for 17 bars (the previous binary sections had been 11 and 13 bars respectively), avoiding a tonic cadence until the music clearly signals 'the end' (Ex. 13). The reduction in texture in the last vocal phrase is the clearest possible invitation to the soloist for a short cadenza (the simple continuo accompaniment could easily adapt to the singer's caprices).

Cesare has defeated Pompeo (Pompey) in Greece and pursued him to Egypt (the historical background to the beginning of the opera was usually included in the 'Argument' printed at the front of the word-book). Pompeo's wife and son, Cornelia and Sesto (Sextus), appeal for a peaceful settlement, and gifts arrive from Tolomeo (Ptolemy), who rules Egypt jointly with his sister Cleopatra. The gifts, brought by his general Achilla (Achillas), include the severed head of Pompeo: Cesare, far from appreciating the gift, sends Achilla back with a message of contempt and disgust. All this action takes place in the opera through *recitativo semplice*[9] and culminates in Cesare's second aria 'Empio, dirò, tu sei'. This aria is a full da capo movement: the texture looks thin on paper (with only a single violin stave above the voice and a bass one below), but Handel achieves a degree of force through piling all the violins on to one lively melodic line, in counterpoint with Cesare's indignation.[10] In this minor-key number (C minor) Handel adopts a tripartite scheme for the A section – three statements of the text, marked by final cadences successively in E♭ major,

[9] *Recitativo semplice* is accompanied by basso continuo alone (harpsichord or lute, possibly with cello); *recitativo accompagnato* is accompanied by full strings. Though conventionally notated in common time, *semplice* recitative was intended to be flexible in the speed of its delivery, according to the dramatic action. (See also p. 44.)

[10] Handel's effective use of scoring for unison violins was one of the features noted by Fougeroux: see below and Appendix E.

Ex. 13

le sue pal-me al vin-ci-tor, _____ le sue pal - me al vin - ci - tor!

[45]

G minor and C minor; the *B* section has two subsections, beginning in E♭ major and cadencing successively in B♭ major and G minor.

The text of this aria provides a good example of the principle of literary construction followed by *opera seria* librettists whereby the second part of the text (musically, the *B* section) extends the topic of the first:

Empio, dirò, tu sei,	I will say [to Tolomeo]
Togliti a gli occhi miei,	'You are an impious wretch,
Sei tutto crudeltà	Take yourself from my sight,
	You are all cruelty'.
Non è da re quel core,	That heart is not worthy of a king
Che donasi al rigore,	Which gives itself to cruelty,
Che in sen non ha pietà.	And does not have pity in its
	bosom.
Empio [etc.] (da capo)	I will say [etc.] (da capo)

In the first section Cesare rehearses the firm line with which he is going to denounce Tolomeo, while the second section gives the philosophical justification for the denunciation. The return to the *A* section reinforces the expression of Cesare's anger (we may imagine him winding himself up to confront Tolomeo) and would have been heightened musically by vocal ornamentation. The aria comes as the climax of the scene, at a landmark in the plot, and, given that any extended solo movement will necessarily introduce a pause in the action, the da capo structure does not in itself retard the development of the drama.

Cesare has two further arias in Act 1.[11] The first occurs at the climax of a scene which begins with Cesare meditating on the transitoriness of human power, standing next to Pompeo's military trophies and the urn containing the ashes of his head. This soliloquy is an accompanied recitative that twists with Cesare's thoughts through a succession of tonalities (Ex. 14). Burney described it as[12]

> the finest piece of accompanied Recitative, without intervening symphonies, with which I am acquainted. The modulation is learned, and so uncommon,

Ex. 14

(...and you are a shadow. Thus finishes human splendour in the end. He who but yesterday spread over the world his victorious arms is now contained in the narrow limits of an urn.)

[11] As already noted (n.4 above) *Giulio Cesare* is one of Handel's most extensive scores: Senesino (as Cesare) received eight arias (compared with four in *Flavio*) and Cuzzoni (as Cleopatra) had the same number.

[12] Burney, *An Account of the Musical Performances*, 'Second Performance', p. 36.

that there is hardly a chord which the ear expects; and yet the words are well expressed, and the phrases pathetic and pleasing.

In the scene that follows, Clèopatra, in the guise of 'Lidia', a noble Egyptian maiden whose fortune has been stolen by Tolomeo, appeals to Cesare for justice: Cesare is captivated by her and promises redress, concluding the encounter with an aria declaring that her beauty exceeds that of the spring flowers ('Non è si vago e bello'). The aria slips in on the end of a recitative, without even the conventional double bar, and it dances along with violins largely doubling the voice an octave higher. The comparison between Lidia and the blooms, though conventional, suits the moment in the action: though captivated, Cesare is not giving too much away at this first encounter. It is therefore perhaps no accident that the aria follows Handel's most straightforward tonal scheme for major-key arias: the *A* section is a standard binary movement (two statements of the text, cadencing successively in dominant and tonic), while the *B* section begins in the relative minor and modulates to its dominant minor, which is Handel's most favoured scheme in major-key arias. It may seem strange that the *B* section in Handel's arias does not normally end in the relative minor, but such a scheme would have entailed an unfortunate juxtaposition of the chromatically altered leading-note of the minor key with the dominant note of the tonic key for the return of the *A* section.[13] The juxtaposition of keys favoured by Handel in many arias at this point is anticipated in the recitative cadence that precedes the aria. Cleopatra's next aria ('Tutto può donna vezzosa'), for example, is in A major, but the preceding recitative cadences in C♯ minor: the *B* section of the aria also ends on C♯ minor, to return to A major for the da capo.

Cesare's final aria in Act 1, 'Va tacito e nascosto' (the opening of which is shown in Ex.15), once again follows the conventional tonal pattern, with a binary-form *A* section in F major and a *B* section modulating from D minor to A minor. Its interest lies in the sinewy counterpoint and harmonic thrust of the theme and its accompaniment, and in the horn obbligato, which provides 'hunting' motifs that are taken up by the singer: at this point in the story Tolomeo has invited Cesare to take up the royal apartments prepared for him at the palace, but Cesare, wary of potential traps, knows he must move with the stealth of a hunter. The thematic material, which seems so apt in its context and so idiomatic for a movement with horn obbligato, may be seen as a new elaboration of a melodic idea that can be traced back, through 'The flocks shall leave the mountains' in *Acis and Galatea*, to Handel's reputedly earliest surviving trio sonata (quoted as Ex. 1 in Chapter 3). The music of Cleopatra's final aria in Act 1, 'Tu la mia stella sei', has an even more explicit ancestry from Handel's earlier works, through an aria for the version of *Radamisto*

---

[13] E.g., the D♯ at an E minor cadence would 'fight' with D♮, the dominant of G major, on the return to the *A* section.

Ex. 15

given in December 1720, movements from the Queen Anne birthday ode of 1713 and a cantata written in Italy, and thus to a movement from Keiser's *Claudius* of 1703.

Having followed Cesare through Act 1, let us similarly follow Cleopatra through the rest of the opera. At the beginning of Act 2 she arranges an elaborate set-piece entertainment for the seduction of Cesare: 'A Garden of Cedars, with Prospect of Mount Parnassus on which is seated the Palace of Virtue'. Her aria 'V'adoro, pupille', one of Handel's great sarabande-type themes, is accompanied by the strings in the orchestra pit and a stage band of oboe, first and second violins, viola, viola da gamba, theorbo, harp, bassoons and cellos.[14] No doubt the theatre provided a scenic setting as attractive as the aural one. The aria is in the same key, F major, and has the same general tonal scheme, as Cesare's 'hunting' aria from Act 1, but there are differences. This time Handel craftily slides over the central 'binary' join in the middle of the *A* section, without any form of orchestral intrusion, extending the dominant cadence to turn the chord back into the dominant seventh of F (Ex. 16, bar 18). And, although the *B* sections of both arias move from D minor to A minor, Cesare's has a central cadence in B♭ major, while Cleopatra's moves to G minor.

The scene achieves its desired result, and Cesare is granted an assignation with 'Lidia'. As she prepares to meet him in the garden, Cleopatra has an A major aria ('Venere bella'), with unison violins accompanying the voice: the form again is conventional, the interest lying in the lighthearted triple-time rhythms and in the melodic skill with which the musical paragraphs are constructed and sustained. Curio, a Roman tribune, then announces that Cesare is betrayed and that people are calling for his murder. 'Lidia'

[14]It has been suggested that this combination was intended to represent the nine Muses.

Ex. 16

(I adore you, O beautiful eyes; arrows of Love, your sparks are delightful in my breast.)

reveals her true identity, saying that she will use her royal presence to quell the tumult; but she fails, and urges Cesare to seek safety in flight. Cesare refuses and goes off to face his assailants: his exit aria, 'Al lampo dell'armi', runs into an offstage *coro* as the conspirators chant 'Morà, Cesare' ('Let Caesar die'). In Cleopatra's ensuing accompanied recitative, which is in its way as powerful as that of Cesare's in Act 1, She asks Heaven to protect Cesare – otherwise 'Unhappy Cleopatra too must die'. This leads to an intense, plangent aria for Cleopatra in F♯ minor, 'Se pietà', beginning with an orchestral ritornello (Ex. 17) in which bassoons

Ex. 17

provide a sustained, tenor-register counter-melody to the violins.[15] The conventionality of form and tonal scheme in no way diminish the aria's power and dramatic effectiveness: it is a great set-piece for the heroine, and marks the first time that Cleopatra's relationship with Cesare has

---

[15] Although the bassoon was used in some later traditions for whimsical or comic effect, during the Baroque period it was more often associated with tragedy or mourning.

gone deeper than flirtation. Taking up a musical hint from the ritornello, the voice begins in broken phrases, gradually building up to a sustained line that is achieved only in the second half of the A section. Yet it is clear that even the broken phrases of the first half contribute to a larger melodic arc: Handel's skill in constructing sustained melodic paragraphs is again in evidence. In technical terms, the success of this procedure is ensured by treating the voice and the answering violin phrases as a single melodic thread over a harmonically well-propelled accompaniment in the lower strings. The violin writing itself shows a keen appreciation of the possibilities for dramatic contrast inherent in the instrument's different registers. In sum, the movement is rewarding for both singer and orchestra.

In due course it is reported that Cesare has been drowned after trying to escape from the soldiers of the treacherous Achilla and that Cleopatra has sought safety with the Romans. At the beginning of Act 3 Tolomeo's army is victorious over Cleopatra's protectors: his aria of triumph over his sister, 'Domerò la tua fierezza' seems to begin (Ex. 18) with a distorted version of the music at the opening of Cesare's 'Presti omai'. Cleopatra,

Ex. 18
Vocal entry

(I will conquer your haughtiness, which abhors and despises my throne, [and I will see you humiliated.])

alone and imprisoned by her brother, bewails her fate in an aria ('Piangerò la sorte mia'; Ex. 19) that conveys pathos through the major mode. It is the more remarkable for beginning without orchestral introduction, the only aria in the opera to do so:[16] it bursts forth as the natural climax to the preceding recitative. The A section opens as if it were a short binary structure, reaching a dominant cadence after 15 bars, but the second half is wondrously lengthened, with excursions through the relative minor and a tonic 'recapitulation' that begins in the orchestra but is taken in a new direction by the voice. The tonal landmarks are highlighted by the

---

[16]This description might also seem to apply to 'V'adoro, pupille', but there the preceding sinfonia acts as orchestral introduction, interrupted before Cleopatra's entry by a short recitative from Cesare.

Ex. 19

(I will bewail my fate, so cruel and so harsh, while I have life in my breast.)

recurrence of a descending bass. Presumably Handel cannot have known 'When I am laid in earth' from Purcell's *Dido and Aeneas,* but it is intriguing that he hit on similar musical symbolism for a comparable mood: no doubt the descending bass figure carried the same musical-rhetorical associations for both composers. (The descending tetrachord had a substantial history as a constructional device appropriate for laments). Cleopatra's aria has a faster *B* section (with a change of metre but a conventional tonal scheme), in which she determines that her ghost will haunt Tolomeo: the agitated mood is assisted by broken chords in rushing semiquavers in the cello.

After Cleopatra has been led away, it transpires that Cesare is not dead after all: he reappears, having escaped by swimming from the harbour, but he has lost contact with his troops. The soliloquy in which he tells his tale is set by Handel as a cleverly conceived sandwich of accompanied recitative and aria, taking in the 'recitative' text that follows the aria and resulting in the following scheme:

Orchestral ritornello → *accompagnato* 'Dall'ondoso periglio' →
aria *A* section 'Aure, deh, per pietà' (F major) →
aria *B* section 'Dite: dov' è' (D minor, A minor, G minor) →
accompagnato, interrupting *B* section, 'Ma d'ogni' (ending in B♭ major) →
reprise of aria *A* section without opening ritornello.

Cesare thus recounts his story in the first *accompagnato* and then launches into the aria, which is arrested in mid-flight (as the *B* section approaches its close) by the second *accompagnato* as he notices the slain bodies from the battle; he then takes up the aria again and completes it.

Cesare goes off to reassemble his forces; an official seal taken from the dying Achilla gives him the authority to command Achilla's troops as well. Cleopatra, knowing nothing of this, tells her 'women that weep' that her brother will shortly kill her. She conveys this through a forceful *accompagnato*, 'Voi, che mie fide ancelle', which opens with a short orchestral sinfonia that might otherwise have been taken as an introduction to another plaintive aria. Towards the end of the *accompagnato* she hears a 'clashing of arms within' and fears the worst, but Cesare appears with his soldiers and drives out Tolomeo's guards. After reunion with Cesare, Cleopatra gives vent to her joy and relief in a *simile* aria, comparing her condition with that of a ship gaining port after a storm at sea, 'Da tempeste il legno infranto' (Ex.20). Once again the rhythmic contours of the opening – and here the melodic contours as well – seem to refer back to 'Presti omai': this time the victory is Cleopatra's, won through Cesare's

Ex. 20
Vocal entry

Allegro

CLEOPATRA

Da tem - pe - ste il le - gno in-fran - - - - to,

(The ship damaged by the storms, [if it arrives safely in port, has gained its immediate desires.])

support. The nautical *simile* is a conventional one, and the musical development also conventional, though nonetheless skilful: Handel constructs his musical paragraphs from diverse thematic figures that seem to flow into one another in an entirely logical manner. In terms of the drama, everything is now in favour of Cesare and Cleopatra: Pompeo's son Sesto kills Tolomeo, and Cornelia gives Cesare Tolomeo's crown and sceptre, which he bestows on Cleopatra as a 'tributary queen' to the Roman emperor. Cesare and Cleopatra declare their undying love in a duet, a gigue-like affair in full da capo form: joyous as it is, it does not plumb the depths as some similar duets do in similar circumstances in the other operas. Perhaps Handel was trying to indicate here that, in spite of their declared devotion, the two would soon be following separate paths again. Nevertheless, Cesare and Cleopatra have another opportunity to reaffirm their commitment in the central section of the final *coro*: in the outer sections the full cast (including the two 'dead' characters, singing offstage to enrich the sound) celebrate the return of peace in a breezy, strongly rhythmical number whose accompaniment includes the four horns.

Although Cesare and Cleopatra clearly dominate the opera, they do not have a monopoly of the good music. Cornelia, a tragic figure widowed at the beginning of the opera, has some moving music expressing not only her grief but also her personal qualities of courage and fortitude. She comes into her own particularly towards the end of Act 1, first with a short but powerful aria as she views her husband's funeral urn ('Nel tuo seno') and then in the full da capo duet with Sesto which ends Act 1. The duet, as Sesto is about to be led away a prisoner (whereupon Cornelia faces the prospect of losing her son as well as her husband), is to some extent a musical genre piece, because such minor-key Largo movements in siciliano rhythm run through Handel's career in theatre music, but it is remarkably well executed here and ideally suited to its context. Apart from his participation in this duet, Sesto's music is limited by his dramatic role: he determines on vengeance for his father's death early in the opera, and re-affirms his intention from time to time. His best aria is 'L'angue offesso' in Act 2, though his first aria in Act 1 is also striking for its contrasted *B* section, in which he derives strength from his dead father's spirit. In some ways Ex.18 is typical of Handel's music for Tolomeo, which is restless and angular, a musical representation of a character who has been described as a 'crafty and treacherous aristocrat, a petulant adolescent of criminal propensities'.[17]

It clearly requires some imaginative effort for us to gain full value from the theatrical experience inherent in a Handel opera. We have to come to terms not only with contemporary musical conventions but also with eighteenth-century theatrical practices – from an age before the forward picture-frame proscenium or the theatre in the round, an age before electric lighting and the easy employment of the drop curtain, but one in which labour (apart from opera soloists) was relatively cheap and the budget was not constrained by limitations on the number of stage carpenters or of stage-hands to operate elaborate scenic transformations. We can gain some idea of what it was like to attend an Academy opera

[17] Dean and Knapp, *Handel's Operas*, p. 498. The consistency of the musical characterization is the more remarkable because, as Dean and Knapp point out, all Tolomeo's arias were first written for other characters.

from the account written in 1728 by Pierre-Jacques Fougeroux, a French visitor to London. He recorded his impressions of the city in the course of six extended letters, one of which deals with theatrical matters. Fortunately, he was interested in opera, attended performances during the Royal Academy's last season, and was sufficiently well informed to make comparisons with other operatic centres. His account, which is given in full in Appendix D,[18] is a fascinating vignette from a member of the audience: we can imagine him, for example, craning his neck in an attempt to identify the instruments in the orchestra pit. His report is incidentally – and perhaps predictably – inaccurate in this area (24 violins is an approximation, and he missed the oboes, for example), but he was obviously impressed by the ensemble that 'fait un grand fracas', as he was also by the German composer and director 'Indel'. The value of Fougeroux's account lies not only in his lively reporting but in the wealth of incidental detail that reveals contemporary musical and theatrical practices – for example, his description of the scoring for recitative accompaniment,[19] and his remark that a small bell was used (instead of the conventional whistle) as a signal to the stage-hands to change the scenes.

Some comments on other operas from the Academy years were offered in Chapter 6;[20] the brief review of the repertory given below follows the same chronological order as in that chapter. In some ways *Radamisto* (1720) set the tone for the operas of the period by the nature of its subject, which concerns dynastic warfare (among the ruling families of Asia Minor) and exhibits contrasting behaviour in the principal characters – on one hand the fidelity and heroism of Radamisto and his wife Zenobia, and on the other the capriciousness of Tiridate, Radamisto's brother-in-law, who makes war on account of his 'unjust Amours' for Zenobia. The opera is constructed on a conventional framework of da capo arias. There are effectively two distinct performing versions from 1720, the second arising from the re-casting that took place after Senesino's arrival. Handel's other contribution to the 1720–1 season was Act 3 of *Muzio Scevola*: Handel's music was the strongest of that from the three participants. Considering the background to its composition, the work coheres reasonably well, though the necessary even-handedness of the scheme makes for three rather long acts.

Handel's new operas for the 1721–2 season continued the general theme of conflicts among ruling families. Although, as noted in Chapter 6, one aspect of *Floridante* (1721) was momentarily interpreted in terms of the

[18] A transcription of the original French is in Dean, 'A French Traveller's View', pp. 177–8, and reprinted in *HHB*, pp. 166–8; Dean's article provides a valuable commentary on the passage.

[19] His description of the use of two harpsichords, cello and archlute for continuo accompaniment need not imply that they were all used simultaneously and continuously.

[20] Accessible introductions to each opera, with plot summaries for most, are in Sadie (ed.), *The New Grove Dictionary of Opera*, and in Holden (with Kenyon and Walsh), *The Viking Opera Guide*.

current political situation between King George I and his son, it is unlikely that specific political messages were intended to be conveyed in the Academy operas: this would have given offence to one or other essential sector of the patronage base, and the support for opera in London required some sort of consensus. Certainly, contemporary British resonances might be derived from the plots – which dealt with the succession of rightful heirs (relevant to Jacobite concerns), as well as family conflicts – though these could not of course have been foreseen by the original Italian librettists. In a more general way, however, dramatic parables about the behaviour of people at the centre of political power (from whom actions motivated by self-interest or sexual possession could have considerable practical consequences) were of interest to the Academy audience. In *Floridante* the principal conflict revolves around the fate of Elmira, the only surviving daughter of the murdered King of Persia: her natural love-match is threatened by the fact that, as a desirable heiress, she is also a valuable political pawn. The opera included the first of Handel's prison scenes for Senesino. There is some delightful music for two pairs of lovers, who are eventually both united after the resolution of political obstacles. *Ottone* (1723) has a more complicated plot than *Floridante*, and one that is hard to follow because Haym drastically compressed Pallavicino's original libretto (Pallavicino had in any case produced a fairly complex text for Dresden, based on historical events of the tenth century when 'German' kings had territorial power in Italy). Ottone (historically Otho II, though the role incorporates some actions of his father Otho I) has been promised Teofane, daughter of the emperor in Constantinople, as a bride, but Adelberto (son of the overthrown 'Italian tyrant' Berengario) and his mother Gismonda plot to subvert the plan, first by passing off Adelberto as Ottone when Teofane arrives, and then by kidnapping Teofane. Cuzzoni made her début with the Academy in the role of Teofane, but her music is lyrical rather than virtuoso. In general, Handel's arias in *Ottone* seem less dramatically forceful than usual, though they make up that deficiency by musical attractiveness: as concert items, many of them (according to Burney) became 'national favourites'.

Flavio, Handel's new opera for the 1722–3 season, deals like the previous operas with conflicts of love and honour, but its tone is less serious: although the consequences of the plot are no less grave than usual (indeed, one of the principals, unusually, is killed off before the end of Act 2), neither the libretto nor the music dwells extensively on the high issues involved. This does not mean that personal tragedies are ignored: Emilia has two powerful arias in Act 2, and Guido's 'Amor, nel mio penar' in Act 3 is a striking set piece in tragic vein. The combination of such moving music with a deft and rapid plot makes *Flavio* attractive to modern audiences, but it did not receive many performances from Handel. In some ways *Flavio* represents Handel's attempt to accommodate the lighter touch of Bononcini, whose operas were popular enough with the Academy audience; but perhaps that audience expected something more heavyweight from Handel. If so, they were not disappointed in the next two seasons, which saw *Giulio Cesare*, *Tamerlano* and *Rodelinda*.

In *Tamerlano* (1724) the title role of the self-made ruler of the Tartar Empire was sung by the castrato Pacini, and Senesino took the role of his 'confederate', the Grecian prince Andronico. The two castratos had to share the vocal honours in this opera with a tenor, however, for the major role of Bajazet the Turkish sultan (Tamerlano's main adversary) was sung by Borosini, for whom Handel composed one of the most significant tenor roles in all *opera seria*. Borosini had previously sung Bajazet in a revised version of the Gasparini opera that had provided Handel with his source libretto: Borosini brought with him to London materials connected with the 1719 production which influenced Handel in his final (and quite substantial) revisions to the role before performance. Bajazet, having defiantly preserved his integrity against Tamerlano, finally dies in captivity, an event that forms the climax of the opera, in place of the more dramatically conventional *lieto fine* (happy ending); remarkably, Handel cut a fine aria from the last scene, apparently to avoid weakening the impact of Bajazet's death. As with *Giulio Cesare* (its immediate predecessor), *Tamerlano* has an ample quota of excellent arias, dramatically powerful as well as musically outstanding; in addition, a novel final scene to Act 2 includes a succession of short exit arias, as Asteria, Bajazet's daughter, is praised by various characters in turn for her part in opposing Tamerlano. *Rodelinda* (1725) was written for the same cast and also has a substantial tenor role, though not as remarkable as that of Bajazet. The plot returns to the style of the complex dynastic stories of the earlier Academy operas, treating a topic from seventh-century Lombard history (which had also provided the background for *Flavio*), but this time the subject receives more heavyweight treatment. Like *Tamerlano*, *Rodelinda* has a succession of first-rate arias, and Rodelinda herself is a full-scale dramatic heroine. The complications of the plot (most of which are faithfully preserved in Handel's libretto) necessarily make for a rich opera, testing the audience's stamina. But in both musical and dramatic terms *Rodelinda* is among Handel's best operas, with consistent and credible characters and a wealth of glorious music.

After three large-scale masterpieces, *Scipione* (1726), though routinely good, is something of an anti-climax. It is effective enough on the stage, however, and has some attractive music, including the famous march which accompanies the arrival of Scipione (Scipio), the Roman proconsul, at New Carthage. Scipione falls in love with one of his Spanish captives, who is betrothed elsewhere, but in the end he sacrifices his feelings in true Roman fashion. Like *Scipione*, *Alessandro* was drafted in the spring of 1726: indeed, it seems probable that Handel began work on *Alessandro* first, but then held up its completion to compose *Scipione*. It is not difficult to guess why: *Alessandro* was to be Handel's first opera in which Cuzzoni and Faustina appeared together; Faustina's arrival in London was delayed, so *Scipione* was needed to fill the gap in the programme. In *Alessandro* the arias return to the quality of those in *Tamerlano* and *Rodelinda*, though the score is a little over-burdened by the need to provide equally substantial parts for the two leading ladies. The plot concerns the exploits of Alexander the Great in India, and the opera opens with a spectacular scene involving the breaching of the city walls at 'Ossidraca'. Rolli's libretto was adapted from one that had seen service, to music by Steffani, at Hanover in 1690, so it is possible that its choice was encouraged, or approved, by the royal family.

With *Admeto* (1727) Handel's operas appear to have taken a new turn, away from historical-political subjects and towards classical mythology: in addition, *Admeto* contains some spectacular scenes reminiscent of Haymarket practice in the previous decade. The opera opens with Admeto (Admetus) on his deathbed. His life is saved because his wife Alceste (Alcestis) sacrifices hers, and she is in turn rescued from the Underworld by Ercole (Hercules). Admeto has meanwhile renewed a former relationship with another woman, but he and his wife are finally reunited. *Admeto* provided Handel with the opportunity not only for good arias but also for more extended continuous scenes, as in the opening sequence and in Ercole's rescue of Alceste. As noted in Chapter 6, *Riccardo Primo* became, through the accidental timing of King George I's death, the first Academy opera of King George II's reign, for which its subject (the exploits of Richard the Lionheart) made it particularly appropriate. The action, on Cyprus, begins with a lively scene representing a stormy sea, calling for the orchestral use of timpani without trumpets. Riccardo comes to Cyprus to meet and marry Costanza (historically Berengaria of Navarre), but Isacio (Isaac), the island's ruler, attempts to pass off his own daughter Pulcheria as the intended bride: the plot gave obvious opportunities for the effective deployment of Cuzzoni and Faustina (Plate 5).

Handel's final two operas for the Academy returned to more traditional-style Italian librettos. *Siroe* (1728) was his first setting of a Metastasio libretto and, viewed alongside his more recent operas, appears somewhat conventional in that it proceeds almost entirely through recitative and regular da capo arias. Its strong plot involves the disputed succession to the throne of Persia; vivid characterization seems to have been sacrificed to the intricacies of the story line, and the music is on the whole efficient rather than inspired. *Tolomeo* (1728), a more flexible drama, is set like *Riccardo Primo* on Cyprus, but this time the dynastic conflicts involve Egyptians. The music is nicely varied, with effective use of *accompagnato* recitative and two fine duets, and each act ends with particularly strong scenes. Senesino, as Tolomeo, had much of the best music, with a well-contrived scene at the end of Act 3 including 'Stille amare', an aria whose da capo is never completed because Tolomeo is overcome by a sleeping potion.

When Handel resumed after the hiatus of 1728–9, it seems to have taken him a little while to return to top form in his operas. *Lotario* (1729) is rather uneven. The drama (dealing with events in Italian history immediately preceding those of *Ottone*) is straightforward enough: the plotting of Berengario the usurper and his wife Matilda against Lotario is lively almost to the point of caricature, but some of the best music went to Berengario. The best set-piece arias are not tied to the advancement of the plot, so it is not surprising that Handel salvaged such fine movements as 'Scherza in mar la navicella' and 'Se il mar promette calma' for insertion into other operas. *Partenope* (1730), on the other hand, to a racy Venetian libretto of a type that Handel had not attempted since *Agrippina*, is surefooted and engaging throughout. The plot concerns Queen Partenope (Parthenope) and three rival princely suitors, one of whom (Arsace) is pursued by his former fiancée Rosmira, who has followed him to Partenope's court disguised as a soldier, 'Eurimene'. One of the other suitors, facing rejection, declares war, and at the start of Act 2 Partenope leads her army against him. Act 3 culminates in a duel between Arsace and 'Eurimene', which is abruptly curtailed when Arsace insists they fight bare-chested. There are some engaging extended arias for Partenope (and also for Rosmira), but Handel also provided a number of lively ensembles, including a 'quartet of perplexity' at the start of Act 3 and *coro* movements interspersed with *sinfonie* in the battle sequence.

For *Poro*, the new opera for the 1730–31 season, Handel turned again to a libretto by Metastasio – indeed, a very recent one, written for Vinci's setting in Rome only a year before. The subject matter returns to the same area as *Alessandro*: Poro (Porus), an Indian prince, has been defeated by Alessandro (Alexander), whom he continues to oppose and indeed tries to assassinate. The actions of Cleofide (Cleophis), an Indian princess in love with Poro, lead him mistakenly to suspect her of infidelity and disloyalty. At the end of Act 1 the pair bitterly quote back the vows that the other partner has made, culminating in a duet of disagreement: their reunion is celebrated in another duet in Act 2. *Poro* marked the return to Handel's company of Senesino, in the title role; the tenor Fabri sang Alessandro and Strada Cleofide.

The result was altogether more successful than Handel's previous Metastasio opera *Siroe*, and he returned to the same librettist for *Ezio* (1732). The plot, based on incidents in fifth-century Rome, concerns the general Ezio (Aetius), whose military success inspires jealousy in the Emperor Valentiniano (Valentinian) encouraged by the treacherous patrician Massimo (Maximus). The situation is complicated by the mutual devotion of Ezio and Fulvia, Massimo's daughter, whom Valentiniano also wishes to marry. Although the opera is formally contrived, the characters are well drawn, and Handel's arias are of a high quality: there are some outstanding pieces for the new bass, Montagnana, who sang the minor role of Varo. Senesino, as Ezio, received an affecting 'prison' aria in Act 2 and a magnificent showpiece aria with recorders and horns in Act 3. Fulvia's role is also musically significant: its peak is her declaration of fidelity, 'La mia costanza', in Act 2. *Sosarme* (1732) returns to more conventional patterns of dynastic strife: warfare between members of the ruling family is encouraged by the treacherous counsellor Altomaro. The original libretto placed the action in Portugal, but the London adapter, perhaps out of sensitivity to Britain's continental ally, moved the action to the Kingdom of Lidia. The colourful story in its new setting was matched by some attractive music from Handel, and the opera proved popular with the first audiences. Its crowning glories are two duets for Sosarme and Elmira (Senesino and Strada), one of which ('Per le porte del tormento') was even taken up as a concert item and performed in the intervals of London plays in 1733–4.

Other works

After opera, Handel's most significant area of musical development in the 1720s was church music. For Chapel Royal services (mainly celebrating the king's return from Hanover) he re-worked pieces composed in the previous decade.[21] It seems most likely that, when the first opportunity arose for him to re-enter the musical life of the chapel, probably in 1722, Handel returned to the anthem *As pants the hart*, producing a new version of his first 'verse-anthem' setting of the text from ten years before. He retained the three choruses from that original version, tightening them up in detail and transposing the last movement to give a more rounded tonal scheme to the whole anthem (it now began in D minor and ended in A major), but he composed new solo movements, drawing on ideas from the 'Cannons' version of the anthem. The result was a new verse anthem with accompaniment for organ and continuo cello (HWV251*d*), but it may never have come to performance: most likely, Handel discovered (or so arranged it) that the Royal Musicians would be on duty for the service in prospect, so he re-worked the anthem again with orchestral accompaniment (HWV251*c*), this time in a form suited to the Chapel Royal forces (including violas and a solo oboist, as well as a full choir, though of chamber dimensions). When composing the new orchestrally accompanied version Handel must have had before him both the recent verse anthem and the 'Cannons' anthem to the same text. The first two choruses were scored up from the verse anthem, while the last chorus was based on the parallel movement in the 'Cannons' version. The opening sinfonia and the solo 'Tears are my daily food' were re-composed from the Cannons anthem, while the following recitative came from the verse anthem. The duet 'Why so full of grief, O my soul?' was developed from

---

[21] For the basis of the chronology of the Chapel Royal music, see Burrows, *Handel and the English Chapel Royal*, i, chaps. 7–8; the versions of HWV251 are also dealt with in Burrows, 'Handel's "As Pants the Hart"', and in the Preface to Handel (ed. Burrows), *As Pants the Hart*.

musical ideas derived from both source versions. The result was more than a mere jackdaw-like assembly of the best parts of earlier versions. It was necessarily more compressed than the Cannons setting: Chapel Royal anthems were normally shorter because the total length of the Chapel Royal service was constrained by the fact that the royal family dined 'in public' after the Sunday morning services. For the same service in 1722, or a similar one in January 1724 (or possibly both), Handel also revived his 'Caroline' *Te Deum*, with 'Vouchsafe, O Lord' re-composed as an aria, with flute obbligato, for the chapel's leading alto Francis Hughes. At about the same period he composed a lively and substantial Latin motet, *Silete venti* (HWV 242), for an occasion and soloist as yet unidentified.

For the Chapel Royal services in January 1724 and January 1726 Handel produced three more works, again using earlier material but re-composing it to suit changed circumstances and adding, or substituting, new movements. Where he worked from 'Cannons' materials he tightened up the structures: the movements are less prolix (usually to their advantage) but more substantially scored. The Chapel Royal works from this period are, in fact, perfectly geared to the small, professional Chapel Royal choir, comparable in size to present-day collegiate and cathedral choirs. The music was conceived in terms of the relatively small building at St James's Palace in which it was performed. The extra players brought in for the performances did not include trumpeters, and they were not catered for in the new scores:[22] the trumpet music in the revived 'Caroline' *Te Deum* was probably transferred to the oboe. The oboist was Kytch, and he may well have played an instrument specially constructed or adapted for use in the chapel, where the pitch was probably higher than that used in the opera house or at St Lawrence's at Cannons (much of the related Chapel Royal music is transposed to a notationally lower pitch than that used in the Cannons sources). In the opera house Kytch's special Chapel Royal instrument became a 'transposing oboe': in *Flavio* and *Tamerlano* it allowed Handel to write arias in B♭ minor (notated for the solo oboe in A minor), a key that would otherwise have been restricted against the instrument.

The bassoonist employed for the services must also somehow have managed to cope with the chapel pitch: that instrument features particularly in the A major *Te Deum* (HWV 282) and *Let God arise* (HWV 256b), both probably composed for a Chapel Royal service in 1726. These works are particularly rewarding products of Handel's association with the Chapel Royal in the 1720s. In *Let God arise* Handel retained, in modified form, only the outer choruses of his Cannons anthem, filling the

[22] The 'Caroline' *Te Deum* and the anthem HWV 249a, composed for the Chapel Royal in 1714, had included trumpets: perhaps, second time round, Handel thought better of the idea (which may have been derived from the Purcellian model).

centre with fine, new music that includes solos for Hughes and one of the chapel's leading basses, Samuel Weeley. The A major *Te Deum* begins with a movement re-worked from the Cannons *Te Deum* but largely goes its own way thereafter, with only occasional references to its predecessor. Many of the sections are short but effective – for example, the new setting of 'Day by day we magnify thee'. One of the more extended numbers is Hughes's solo (with oboe and bassoon obbligatos) 'Vouchsafe, O Lord'. In setting this text as a substantial movement for alto (as in the revised 'Caroline' *Te Deum*) Handel was perhaps reverting to a hint in Purcell's D major setting, but the music is of Handel's own stock, a re-working of materials from 'Amor, nel mio penar' in *Flavio*. In a reciprocal interchange, the music of 'O sing unto God' in *Let God arise* re-appears later to good effect in *Arminio*, and later still in movements held in common by *The Choice of Hercules* and *Alceste*. This transference of thematic material between theatrical and liturgical contexts does not diminish its effectiveness in both contexts and does not undercut Handel's presumed seriousness of purpose.

Handel's Chapel Royal compositions were necessarily heard by only a small group of people, even allowing for those who attended public rehearsals at St James's.[23] In terms of both public impact and musical style the Chapel Royal works were naturally overshadowed by the coronation anthems. These were conceived as grand music for a grand occasion, making advantageous use of large forces and of the wide expressive possibilities of late Baroque musical vocabulary. One or two opening vocal entries in the coronation anthems were specified by Handel for a semi-chorus of the leading singers, presumably for practical reasons in circumstances where the performers may have been crowded into galleries (perhaps several galleries, separated from one another)[24] which would have made it difficult to establish common ensemble. But the major spectacular effects were choral, in the nineteenth-century sense of the word: they depended on the weight of sound available from the combined vocal forces, supported by comparable orchestral riches. The first vocal entry in *Zadok the priest* (Ex.21) is, with good reason, one of the Handelian gestures that has made a permanent mark on the English-speaking world, along with the opening of the 'Hallelujah' chorus in *Messiah*. There would have been no problems of ensemble here: the long orchestral prelude, like a slow parting of theatrical curtains, established the beat for the singers. It has not escaped the notice of music theorists that between the first and second bars of the vocal entry Handel committed consecutive 5ths between the first alto and first bass parts (and con-

[23] Mrs Pendarves attended one such rehearsal, of music by Greene, in the Chapel Royal in 1729; cited in Burrows, *Handel and the English Chapel Royal*, ii, 128, n.356.
[24] A memorandum written by William Boyce at the time of the next coronation (1761) suggests that in 1727 the physical arrangements at the Abbey had militated against good ensemble; see Burrows, 'Handel and the 1727 Coronation', p. 471.

Ex. 21

secutive octaves between the second soprano and first bass), which those judging by their eyes rather than their ears might take as evidence that Handel did not care about such things. But Handel was not 'thinking' in seven real parts: the vocal harmony is an enriched version of four (or, arguably, five) real parts, in which the first bass is clearly strengthening the tenor-bass register in the most effective way. Handel was mainly concerned about spacing and texture here, and the result amply justified the means. In other contexts Handel was as finicky as any pedagogue about the avoidance of consecutives, and revised his music accordingly.[25]

Zadok the priest was performed at the Anointing in the coronation service: the 'God save the King' with which it concludes provided an appropriate transition to the Crowning itself that followed. The Recognition section of the service, at which the king was presented to the assembled company and greeted with 'God save King George the Second', came earlier in the service. There is a conflict between the order of Handel's anthems according to the printed Order of Service and that recorded in the Chapel Royal memorandum book,[26] but, taking the latter as being more probably in accordance with the facts,[27] it seems likely that *Let thy hand be strengthened* was performed at the Recognition and *The king shall rejoice* at the Crowning. The former is the only coronation anthem whose scoring does not include trumpets (they may have been engaged elsewhere in the Abbey at the Presentation ceremony), but it nevertheless ends with a rousing 'Allelujah'. *The king shall rejoice* returns to the full scoring of *Zadok the priest* and extends the rejoicing to twice the length of the previous anthem, with some substantial movements (including another final 'Allelujah') and a midway choral outburst at 'Glory and worship hast thou laid upon him'.[28]

According to an anecdote related by Burney, Handel was brought texts for the coronation anthems by 'the bishops' – presumably during the final drafting of the 1727 coronation liturgy – and responded with 'I have read my Bible very well, and shall chuse for myself'.[29] In fact, Handel's 'chusing' seems to have been influenced by the coronation liturgy from 1685, the most recent British one to include the coronations of both a king and a queen consort.[30] The anthem for the queen's coronation in 1727, *My heart is inditing*, is on the same scale, as regards both scoring and length, as *The king shall rejoice* and is, if anything, even finer. It also benefits from some internal variety, with more lyrical moments in the movements 'King's daughters' and 'Upon thy right hand'. The themes in the first movement are also more flowing than their rather more conventional counterparts

[25] There are many examples in Handel's autographs of alterations that were motivated by sensitivity to consecutives. It is significant, by contrast, that his alterations to the last chord in the first bar of the vocal entry in *Zadok the priest* (alto 2 and tenor 1 parts) amended the spacing of the chord.

[26] See Burrows, 'Handel and the 1727 Coronation'.

[27] The Order of Service was published in advance, but the Chapel Royal record was probably written down after the event.

[28] Text as in Handel's autograph; some authoritative secondary manuscripts have 'Glory and *great* worship'. The passage has cross-relationships with the Gloria of the 'Utrecht' *Jubilate*, 'Glory to God' in *Messiah* and other pieces. Purcell's setting of the text in the anthem *O sing unto the Lord* (Z44) and other passages in that anthem are sufficiently Handelian to suggest that it was available to Handel as a general stylistic model soon after he came to London.

[29] Burney, *An Account of the Musical Performances*, 'Sketch of the Life of Handel', p. 34.

[30] An edition of the 1685 liturgy was published in London in 1727, presumably out of topical and antiquarian interest; see Burrows, 'Handel and the 1727 Coronation', p. 470.

in the king's anthems, while in the last movement ('Kings shall be thy nursing fathers') Handel mixed chordal, contrapuntal and motivic elements to masterly effect, in a vein that he was to develop further in his later oratorio choruses.

Like the previous decade, the 1720s saw the composition of some Italian cantatas by Handel which, though constituting a relatively minor activity, were no doubt stimulated by his association with the soloists at the opera. One substantial cantata with orchestral accompaniment, *Crudel tiranno Amor* (HWV97), was probably composed for Durastanti's benefit concert at the King's Theatre on the end of the 1720–1 opera season. Handel purloined all the arias from the cantata for operatic use when he strengthened Durastanti's role in the revival of *Floridante* in December 1722 – in itself perhaps adequate testimony to their musical quality. The cantata as a whole deserved better than the single performance that it received at Handel's hands. There is also a quite considerable repertory of contemporary continuo-accompanied Italian cantatas, some perhaps dating from the 'Cannons' period or the early days of the Academy, while another group seems to have originated in the later 1720s.[31] The autographs of two cantatas from around 1722–3 (HWV103 and 118, both to texts by Rolli)[32] are now bound with scribal copies of arias from *Ottone* and *Floridante* dating from the same period which certainly came under the composer's hand, for he added ornamentation to the vocal lines – a rare example of such first-hand evidence.[33] About 1722 Handel also composed two more Italian duets, *Langue, geme* (HWV188) and *Se tu non lasci Amore* (HWV193). Unfortunately, the documentary record of the occasions for which Handel composed the cantatas and duets is sparse. In October 1729, when the soloists for Handel's new opera company had arrived in London ready for the first season under the Handel-Heidegger management, there was a musical 'private view' for the royal family.[34]

On Friday last [10 October] several of the Italian Singers lately arrived from

[31] From paper studies of the autographs, the cantatas from *c*.1717–1723 seem to include HWV103, 109*a*, 118, 121 and 164*b*; those from the later 1720s include HWV127*c*, 139*c*, 158*c*, 160*b*, 161*c* and 164*a*.

[32] Oxford, Bodleian Library, MS Mus. Don.c.69. The autograph of HWV118 is incomplete there: in the nineteenth century it was owned by Dragonetti, the famous double bass player, who apparently divided it at some time. The fragment missing from the Bodleian manuscript is now at the British Library, Zweig MS 36. I am grateful to Anthony Hicks for drawing my attention to the authorship of the texts.

[33] See Handel (ed. Dean), *Three Ornamented Arias*; in his preface Dean presents a case for dating the ornamentation to 1727.

[34] *The Norwich Gazette* (18 October 1729): Deutsch, p. 245; *HHB*, p. 174, from an earlier, London newspaper. The performance is also referred to in a letter from Princess Amelia to her governess the Duchess of Portland, dated 11 October 1729: 'We had yesterday twice the new singer her name is Strada it is a charming voice and think her beyond all her predecessors ... the others a[re]nt come yet but indeed if they proove but half as good we shall be very happy this winter'. On 23 October Princess Amelia reported 'We have heard now all the singers'. I thank Richard G. King for drawing my attention to the letters.

Italy, who are to perform at the Opera's, had the Honour of a private Performance before their Majesties at Kensington; when the Harpsichord was played upon by Mr Handell, and their performances were much approved.

The performance may have included cantatas, as well as arias from operas: no doubt Handel's cantata repertory was extended by similar performances (before various patrons), of which we know nothing.

The record is similarly imperfect as regards instrumental music. In August 1730 Handel 'made Trial of the new Organ in Westminster Abbey' (a rebuild of the instrument provided specially for the 1727 coronation) but nothing is known of the music he played on that occasion nor on his visit to St Paul's with the princesses six years previously. Both organs were probably unusual (for Britain) in that their resources included pedals.[35] Of Handel's harpsichord music written during the 1720s there is one substantial suite, in D minor HWV436. There are also a number of individual keyboard pieces, some probably associated with Handel's teaching activities.[36] Handel seems to have put as much effort into creating keyboard works from versions of opera arias or overtures as he did into 'original' keyboard works. There are five authentic aria arrangements (HWV482[1-5]), four of them based on arias from the early Academy repertory, and the majority of the authentic keyboard 'overtures' are related to operas written between *Radamisto* and *Partenope*.[37] The overtures provide a rewarding repertory for keyboard players; the keyboard arrangements also provide some hints about the extent to which 'double dots' may have been used in the opening *entrée* movements.

Independent orchestral compositions figured little in Handel's activities during this period. A concerto for horns, woodwind and strings (HWV331), consisting of two newly composed movements based on themes previously used in the *Water Music*, may have been the 'New Concerto for French Horns' that was performed at the Drury Lane theatre in March 1723. A concert at Hickford's Room in February 1719, in the period before Handel set off for Italy to secure singers for the Academy, included 'A new Concerto, Compos'd by Mr. Hendel, and perform'd by Mr. Matthew Dubourg'.[38] This concerto cannot at present be identified.

[35] This does not mean a full-compass pedalboard in the modern sense: the precise ranges are uncertain at this date. According to Burney (*An Account of the Performances*, 'Sketch of the Life of Handel', note to p. 33) Handel was specially attracted to the organ at St Paul's in his early London years 'for the exercise it afferded him, in the use of the pedals': but the pedal provision would have been much inferior to that of the German organs among which Handel grew up.
[36] There seem to be two groups of miscellaneous pieces, one including HWV457, 460, 479, 483, 559, 582, 585) from the period *c.*1720–2 and another (including HWV462, 464, 468, 477, 492) from the mid-1720s, *c.*1724–8. The first group includes some technically elementary pieces (HWV457, 460, 559), which may suggest teaching activity somewhat earlier than is otherwise documented.
[37] See Chapter 5, p. 99 and n. 18.
[38] See Deutsch, pp. 83–4; *HHB*, p. 78. One of the beneficiaries of the concert was Linike, one of Handel's principal music copyists from the period; see Dean, 'Handel's Early London Copyists', pp. 78–80.

It may have been the concerto later published as op.3 no.2, which was extended from movements that Handel had used in the overture to the *Brockes Passion* – but the solo violin part in that concerto is hardly sufficiently prominent to justify Dubourg's separate billing. The most interesting new concerto of the period seems to have been a three-movement work in D major, with a central B minor Adagio featuring solo flute and violin, accompanied by a continuo group of archlute, cello and double bass. It was probably composed in the early 1720s, perhaps even for one of the concerts on the end of the 1720–1 season; Handel later split off the first movement for use in the first act of *Ottone* and re-worked the music of the last movement into the overture to that opera.[39] A single-movement Ouverture in D (HWV337), composed some time around 1722–5, is probably a detached or discarded section from another work.

Some of the trio sonatas subsequently published in Handel's 'op.2' set may have been composed in the early 1720s, though they may alternatively have originated in the Cannons period, or at Dresden during his visit there in 1719. They were published with catch-all titles, giving violins, flutes and oboes as alternative treble instruments. Most were composed for two violins in the treble, though a couple involve flutes or recorders; the only one in which oboe participation might have been intended is the early C minor version of op.2 no.1 (HWV386a).[40] It is easier to date a group of 'solo' sonatas with continuo accompaniment, later included in various forms in a published collection, the so-called 'op.1.'[41] The paper of the autographs indicates that these were composed in the mid-1720s (HWV359–62, 364–5, 367, 369, 377, 379), and they include sonatas for violin (one with a 'gamba' alternative), recorder and flute. Most are cast in the four-movement scheme (slow-fast-slow-fast), and some, such as the recorder sonata HWV369 (Ex.22), have justifiably gained some popularity with instrumentalists and audiences. It is rather surprising that Handel did not at this period write oboe sonatas for Kytch (unless Kytch was the original interpreter of the recorder sonatas): perhaps Handel regarded the recorder as a more appropriate chamber instrument than the oboe, whose volume and tone were better suited to the bigger spaces of the concert room and opera house, or to outdoor military music.[42] The violin sonatas

---

[39] The original three-movement concerto has been included in three recordings of Handel's op.3 concertos but is not published as such. The opening movement can be found as the first movement of op.3 no.6 (HWV317); the other two movements, as HWV338[1–2]; appear in *HHA* IV/15.

[40] See Best, 'Handel's Chamber Music', pp. 487–94.

[41] See Best, *ibid.*, and Best, 'Handel's Solo Sonatas'; see also Chapter 10, p. 253 and n. 44.

[42] Handel had, of course, written oboe sonatas at an earlier period (HWV357, 363a, 366). HWV366 appeared in the Roger/Walsh editions published in the early 1730s, which also included the violin sonata HWV364a (composed *c.*1724) with the solo instrument specified as 'Hoboy': the latter was no doubt the consequence of Walsh's desire to broaden the market for his publications by including two sonatas for oboe, and its instrumentation probably had no immediate authority from Handel.

Ex. 22

were composed around 1724–6:[43] the A major sonata HWV361 makes considerable technical demands in the way of contrapuntal passages involving double-stopping. Unfortunately, the corpus of Handel's violin sonatas has been confused by the presence of four spurious ones in the early printed editions (HWV368, 370, 372–3), among which the F major sonata (HWV370) has attained a popularity with violinists that has obscured the genuine Handelian repertory.

---

[43] HWV359*a*, 361, 364*a* and possibly (on grounds of style, as no instrument is specified on the autograph) HWV367*a*; the most likely soloists were Castrucci (who left London for Rome in 1722, but probably returned soon after), Dubourg (who visited Dublin in 1724 and emigrated there in 1728) and Geminiani.

The transitional decade I: Competition, 1732–7

Until April 1732 Handel's London theatre programmes, which were the centre of his career, had consisted entirely of Italian operas. After 1741 he never gave another Italian opera in London: his theatre programmes were based on English works performed in the oratorio manner. The transition from one genre to the other was not a straight line of artistic development, and coincidences and historical accidents played their part. In some respects Handel was not in control of the process: he reacted to the situation developing around him, abandoning lines that seemed to have no immediate future and taking new opportunities as they presented themselves. But it would be wrong to regard him as a victim of circumstance, an unwilling participant at the mercy of the buffets of fortune: while he may have felt some nostalgic regret for his best days with Italian opera, he eventually accepted the new direction of his career wholeheartedly.

Nowhere was the influence of external accidental forces more apparent than in the case of *Esther*. Handel included *Esther*, performed without the normal stage attractions of special costumes and scenery, in his theatre programme at the end of the 1731–2 opera season. For a record of the chain of events leading up to the performance we are indebted to Burney, writing half a century later:[1]

> A copy of the score having been obtained, it was represented, in action, by the Children of his Majesty's Chapel, at the house of Mr. Bernard Gates, master of the boys, in James-street, Westminster, on Wednesday, February 23, 1731. Soon after this, it was twice performed by the same children, at the Crown and Anchor, by the desire of William Huggins, esq. a member of that Society ... who furnished the dresses. Mr. HANDEL himself was present at one of these representations, and having mentioned it to the Princess Royal, his illustrious scholar, her Royal Highness was pleased to express a desire to see it exhibited in action at the Opera-house in the Hay-market, by the same young performers; but Dr. Gibson, then bishop of London, would not grant permission for its being represented on that stage, even with books in the children's hands. Mr. HANDEL, however, the next year, had it performed at that theatre, with

[1] *An Account of the Musical Performances*, 'Sketch of the Life of Handel', p. 22, and 'Fifth Performance', pp. 100–1.

additions to the Drama, by Humphreys; but in *still life*: that is, without action, in the same manner as Oratorios have been since constantly performed.

There is no reason to doubt the main outlines of Burney's story, which was partly based on information from John Randall (the chorister who took the role of Esther in the Chapel Royal performances), but some additional commentary is required.

There is no independent confirmation of the preliminary performance at Gates's house, but *Esther* was certainly performed on 23 February 1732 (Handel's 47th birthday) at the Crown and Anchor Tavern in the Strand, and repeated there on 1 and 3 March. The first two performances were given under the auspices of the Philharmonic Society and the third under those of the Academy of Ancient Music: the tavern was a regular meeting-place for such societies.[2] The performances were undertaken against the background of a dispute among London's musicians that came to a head in 1731. The Academy of Vocal Music was founded in London in 1726, drawing most of its performing membership from musicians employed in the choirs of the Chapel Royal, St Paul's Cathedral and Westminster Abbey. All ran smoothly for a few years, but jealousies and divisions gradually appeared. In the light of subsequent events, it seems likely that the greatest antipathy was between Gates, Master of the Chapel Royal Children,[3] and Greene, who was from 1727 the principal composer and organist to the chapel and also organist at St Paul's. Tensions mounted until 1731, when they culminated in a public dispute over the authorship of an Italian madrigal by Lotti, *In una siepe ombrosa*, which had been presented to the Academy as a composition of Bononcini's. The evidence for Lotti's authorship was gathered together in a substantial published pamphlet, and the conclusion of the dispute in Lotti's favour seems to have been one of the factors that persuaded Bononcini to leave London for good.[4] Greene similarly fell under a shadow for having taken Bononcini's side in the affair. A split in the Academy was the inevitable consequence: Greene left, with the St Paul's component, and the remaining members re-formed the society as the Academy of Ancient Music. During the most controversial period in the dispute Gates appears to have promoted performances of Handel's music in an attempt to outface or annoy Greene: he was responsible for an Academy programme in January 1731 that included the 'Utrecht' canticle settings in addition to the contentious madrigal (attributed to Lotti in the public notice), and it is significant that the newspapers included the event in their 'news' sections

[2] The largest taverns would have a meeting-room, often equipped with a harpsichord: Hawkins (*A General History*, ii, 852, note) describes Handel playing through Mattheson's harpsichord suites to the vicars choral of St Paul's Cathedral at a tavern in 1714. In 1732 there was a further performance of *Esther*, on 20 April at 'the Great Room in Villars-Street, York Buildings'.

[3] As a bass singer, Gates had sung in all Handel's Chapel Royal music.

[4] See Lindgren, 'The Three Great Noises', pp. 564–70, and, on the general background to the dispute in the Chapel Royal, Burrows, *Handel and the English Chapel Royal*, i, 398–402.

rather than among the advertisements.[5] The *Esther* performances in 1732 were therefore the product of Gates's pre-existing commitment to Handel's music: he sensed that *Esther* would make a good evening's performance at the Academy and that it would be a practical proposition, thanks to the timely coincidence of an exceptionally talented group among his choristers.

The Chapel Royal choristers had historical associations with drama in London, though not within living memory in 1732.[6] Although Edmund Gibson, Bishop of London and Dean of the Chapel Royal, was no friend to the theatres – he had been vociferous in the ecclesiastical lobby against Heidegger's masquerades in the 1720s – his reluctance to allow his charges to act on the London stage is understandable on administrative grounds. The chapel choir's professional function was to perform the daily liturgies, and the prospect of Gates committing his choristers to the performances of a London theatre company constituted a threat to the performance of the choir's regular duties, perhaps already rather undermined by unpredictable attendance among the Gentlemen. If Gibson foresaw that Gates might be starting a permanent connection with Handel's theatre enterprises, he was remarkably prescient.[7] Although he failed to put a ban on the Chapel Royal singers taking part in the theatre performances of *Esther*, his actions did influence the manner of performance: while the Cannons and Academy presentations of *Esther* had probably been given with normal stage conventions, Handel's theatre performances of 1732 were, as Burney reported, given in 'still life'.

In spite of Burney's hints to the contrary, there was probably never any serious question of Handel bringing to the opera house Gates's Chapel Royal production as it stood. Handel used the best members of his opera company for the leading roles – Senesino, Strada, Montagnana and the contralto Bertolli, adding to them two English sopranos, Mrs Davies and Ann Turner Robinson. The Chapel Royal singers (or some of them)[8] joined these soloists in the concerted movements, and advertisements for the performance (Fig. 8) hinted at one particular feature that compensated for the lack of stage action:[9]

[5] Another consequence of Gates's triumph may have been to influence those who arranged the annual festival charity service for the Sons of the Clergy at St Paul's Cathedral to adopt Handel's 'Utrecht' music and coronation anthems: see Burrows, *Handel and the English Chapel Royal*, ii, Appendix 4.

[6] See Baldwin, *The Chapel Royal*, chap. 5.

[7] Gibson's involvement may have been an accidental consequence of a staffing problem within the Chapel Royal; see Burrows, *Handel and the English Chapel Royal*, i, 406–8.

[8] The full Chapel Royal choir probably never took part in oratorio performances; the priests among the Gentlemen would surely have been barred from singing in theatres. For the Foundling Hospital *Messiah* performances in the 1750s the Chapel Royal typically supplied half a dozen boys for the treble line and a few men for the chorus.

[9] *The Daily Journal* (9 April 1732): Deutsch, pp. 288–9; *HHB*, p. 200.

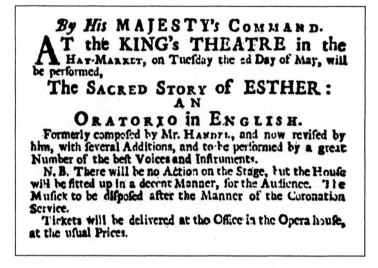

Fig. 8 Advertisement for Handel's first theatre performance of *Esther*, from *The Daily Journal*, 19 April 1732

NB There will be no Action on the Stage, but the House will be fitted up in a decent Manner, for the Audience. The Music to be disposed after the manner of the Coronation Service.

The phrase 'after the manner of the Coronation Service' presumably led the audience to expect (in contemporary terms) serried ranks of performers, and hinted at a musical style to match. Handel filled out the score not only with new arias but with music from two of the coronation anthems. He created in all a full, three-act evening's entertainment at the theatre that combined the attractions of the opera stars with those of the grand anthem style that had made its mark at the 1727 coronation – and all sung in English. Thus, accidentally, and without its being realized at the time, Handel hit on the recipe for his future success.

Handel's performances of *Esther* at the King's Theatre, Haymarket, between 2 and 20 May, were popular. Part of their success may have been due to the fact that English music drama was a topic of contemporary interest, as English opera was currently being attempted in productions by the Arne family and Lampe at the 'Little' Haymarket Theatre across the road from Handel's opera house. These had drawn a considerable audience, attracted partly by the success of a young singer, Susanna Arne (she became Mrs Cibber on her marriage two years later). Happily, a contemporary description of the situation is preserved in a pamphlet:[10]

[10] *See and Seem Blind*, pp. 14–16, partly quoted in Deutsch, pp. 300–1 and *HHB*, p. 206.

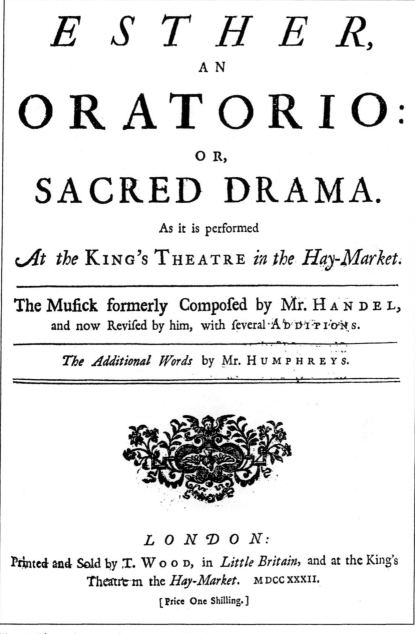

ESTHER,

AN

ORATORIO:

OR,

SACRED DRAMA.

As it is performed

At the KING'S THEATRE *in the Hay-Market.*

The Muſick formerly Compoſed by Mr. HANDEL,
and now Reviſed by him, with ſeveral ADDITIONS.

The Additional Words by Mr. HUMPHREYS.

LONDON:

Printed and Sold by T. WOOD, in *Little Britain,* and at the King's
Theatre in the *Hay-Market.* MDCCXXXII.

[Price One Shilling.]

Fig. 9 The title-page from the original word-book for Handel's first theatre
performances of *Esther*, 1732

169

I left the *Italian* Opera, the House was so thin, and cross'd over the way to the *English* one, which was so full I was forc'd to croud in upon the Stage, and even that was throng'd: Is not this odd, I say, for an English Tradesman's Daughter to spring up all of a suddain, and rival the selected Singers of *Italy*?

This alarm'd *H—l*, and out he brings an *Oratorio*, or Religious *Farce*, for the duce take me if I can make any other Construction of the Word, but he has made a very good *Farce* of it, and put near 4000 l. in his Pocket, of which I am very glad, for I love the Man for his Musick's sake.

This being a new Thing set the whole World a Madding; Han't you been at the *Oratorio*, says one? Oh! If you don't see the *Oratorio* you see nothing, says t'other; so away goes I to the *Oratorio*, where I saw indeed the finest Assembly of People I ever beheld in my Life, but, to my great Surprize, found this Sacred *Drama* a mere Consort, no Scenary, Dress or Action, so necessary to a *Drama*; but *H—l*, was plac'd in a Pulpit, I suppose they call that (their Oratory) by him sate *Senesino Strada Bertolli*, and *Turner Robinson*, in their own Habits; before him stood sundry sweet Singers of this our *Israel*, and *Strada* gave us a *Hallelujah* of half an Hour long; *Senesino* and *Bertolli* made rare work with the *English* Tongue you would have sworn it had been *Welch*; I would have wish'd it *Italian*, that they might have sang with more ease to themselves, since, but for the Name of *English*, it might as well have been *Hebrew*.

The 1732 story did not end with *Esther*. While its music was currently available only in privately circulating manuscripts, a large proportion of the arias from its Cannons companion-piece *Acis and Galatea* had been readily accessible in a published edition for ten years. Between the last two nights of Handel's *Esther* performances, the Arnes staged *Acis and Galatea* across the road. Handel's response was to prepare his own new version of *Acis*, which he performed during June 1732. This time the Chapel Royal choir was not involved as such, but the soloists were probably strengthened by a few extra singers in some chorus movement though not on the 'coronation anthem' scale. Handel's new version of *Acis* for the theatre was a conflation of movements from *Aci, Galatea e Polifemo* and the 'Cannons' *Acis and Galatea*, plus some extra movements which were mainly adapted from his other works. Only four arias (sung by two minor characters) and three choruses were in English, the rest in Italian, which involved the production of a bilingual word-book. Although *Acis and Galatea* was not an oratorio,[11] it was performed in basically the same manner as *Esther*, though with a gesture towards the use of scenery:[12]

There will be no Action on the Stage, but the Scene will represent, in a Picturesque Manner, a rural Prospect, with Rocks, Groves, Fountains and Grotto's; amongst which will be disposed a Chorus of Nymphs and Shepherds, Habits, and every other Decoration suited to the Subject.

---

[11] The printed word-book for Handel's 1732 performances described it as a 'Serenata': that for Arne's production (which was acted) called it a 'Pastoral Opera'.

[12] Advertisement in *The Daily Courant* (5 June 1732): Deutsch, p. 293; *HHB*, p. 202.

This production also proved popular, and brought Handel's 1731–2 season to a successful conclusion with four performances between 10 and 20 June 1732. Presumably Heidegger, Handel's co-manager, approved.

The contemporary pamphlet already quoted contained one reference that had rather ominous implications for Handel:[13]

> As for *Lincolns Inn* Play-house, I am inform'd her Grace the D[uche]ss of M[arlboroug]h, has advanc'd very largely towards a new Subscription for Italian Opera's, to be there under the direction of *Bononcini* and *Arrigoni*; and a new set of Singers, are to be sent for from *Italy*, for that purpose.

The pamphleteer had picked up some important gossip. Neither the Duchess of Marlborough nor Bononcini was involved in the final result, but the first moves were indeed being made by mid-1732 to form a second Italian opera company in rivalry to Handel's: and, since Handel still had two more years of the original five-year agreement at the King's Theatre to run,[14] the Lincoln's Inn Fields Theatre was the venue most accessible to the new company. A new generation of opera patrons was probably becoming rather impatient with Handel's established position, and the situation was fuelled by the growth of an opposition party around Prince Frederick: there was thus a young social base for the project that became the Opera of the Nobility. In fact, it took another year to set the company up, but the rumours must have been unsettling for Handel during 1732–3.

The next Haymarket opera season opened on 4 November 1732, with a new soprano in the cast:[15]

> Signora Celeste Gismondi, who lately arriv'd here, performed a principal Part with universal Applause. We hear that this Opera was not composed by Mr Handell, but by some very eminent Master in Italy.

The rumours were true: *Catone*, the first production, was a pasticcio arranged by Handel from a score by Leonardo Leo. In this case, Handel kept the framework of Leo's recitatives but not many of his arias, drawing in addition on music by Hasse, Porpora, Vivaldi and others: it is perhaps somewhat ironic that in a year's time Porpora was to be the leading composer for London's rival opera company. Soon after *Catone* opened there was a rehearsal for Lampe's English opera *Britannia* at the Little Haymarket Theatre, at which the soprano Cecilia Young made a con-

---

[13] *See and Seem Blind*, pp. 25–6.

[14] Heidegger may have pulled out after three years of the joint partnership, leaving Handel solely responsible for the performances of the last two years, though Heidegger remained manager of the theatre itself: that could explain Mainwaring's reference to a three-year partnership (*Memoirs*, pp. 112–13, 114–15).

[15] *The Daily Advertiser* (6 November 1732).

siderable impression, and a verse appeared in the newspapers suggesting that Handel had become yesterday's man:[16]

> No more shall Italy its Warblers send
> To charm our Ears with Handel's heav'nly Strains;
> For dumb his rapt'rous Lyre, their Fame must end.

In fact, at that very moment Handel was at work on the score of his next original opera, *Orlando*, which he completed on 20 November and brought to the stage the following January. Meanwhile, the opera programme was filled with revivals of *Alessandro* (with Strada and Gismondi taking the roles originally conceived for Faustina and Cuzzoni) and *Acis and Galatea*. The latter was no doubt included partly as a response to competition from English opera across the road, though it was again performed mostly in Italian. English-language dramatic works were still a subject of interest: in addition to Lampe's work in the Haymarket, T.A. Arne was currently presenting performances of *Teraminta* (with music by John Christopher Smith the younger, Handel's own pupil) at Lincoln's Inn Fields Theatre. On 5 December Aaron Hill, who had written the libretto for *Rinaldo*, even wrote to Handel to encourage him to take up English opera:[17]

> Having this occasion of troubling you with a letter, I cannot forbear to tell you the earnestness of my wishes, that, as you have made such considerable steps towards it, already, you would let us owe to your inimitable genius, the establishment of *musick*, upon a foundation of good poetry; where the excellence of the *sound* should be no longer dishonour'd, by the poorness of the *sense* it is chain'd to.
>
> My meaning is, that you would be resolute enough, to deliver us from our *Italian bondage*; and demonstrate, that *English* is soft enough for Opera, when compos'd by poets, who know how to distinguish the *sweetness* of our tongue, from the *strength* of it, where the last is less necessary.
>
> I am of opinion, that male and female voices may be found in this kingdom, capable of every thing, that is requisite; and, I am sure, a species of dramatic Opera might be invented, that, by reconciling reason and dignity, with musick and fine machinery, would charm the *ear*, and hold fast the *heart*, together.
>
> Such an improvement must, at once, be lasting, and profitable, to a very great degree; and would, infallibly, attract an universal regard, and encouragement.

There was no immediate response from Handel: *Acis and Galatea* was followed early in 1733 by his return to straightforward Italian opera, with a revival of *Tolomeo*, the first production of *Orlando* and then a revival

---

[16] *The Daily Post* (15 November 1732): Deutsch, p. 297; *HHB*, p. 204. A footnote to the third line of the verse in the original reads 'The opera of "Cato" is not Mr. Handel's'. The inclusion of pasticcios in the opera programmes had not hitherto been criticized: the newspaper references at this time may confirm the impression that the public now regarded Handel as the sole manager and impresario at the opera house.

[17] Letter, dated 5 December 1732, subsequently published in Hill's collected works: Deutsch, p. 299; *HHB*, p. 205.

of *Floridante*. But although it turned out that Handel had no intention of tackling English opera (an impossibility with his current italianate cast, in any case), he had not lost sight of English oratorio. During the run of *Orlando* he composed a new one, *Deborah*, completed on 21 February and first performed on 17 March. Meanwhile, interesting things were happening at Lincoln's Inn Fields Theatre: Willem De Fesch's oratorio *Judith* (to an English text by William Huggins) was performed in February, and Arne's English opera *Rosamond* had four performances in March. Handel may have deliberately timed his second experiment with oratorio to fall into the Lenten season: the first night of *Deborah* was on the eve of Palm Sunday. The libretto of *Deborah*, by Samuel Humphreys, was dedicated to the Princess of Wales, but royal connections did nothing to quell the discontent of the theatre audience at the management's attempt to charge higher prices: 'the subscribers being refused unless they would pay a guinea, they, insisting upon the right of their silver tickets, forced into the House, and carried their point'.[18] In a contemporary epigram Handel was compared with Walpole, who was simultaneously trying to increase the national coffers with his Excise Scheme. Of the *Deborah* performance that he attended, Viscount Percival wrote that 'It was very magnificent, near a hundred performers, among whom about twenty-five singers', so the soloists must have been supported by a chorus of about 20.[19] Handel revived *Esther* with two performances in April, followed by further performances of *Orlando* and *Floridante* and – of all unexpected things – a revival of Bononcini's *Griselda*, with which the season closed on 9 June.

Although the London season had finished, Handel's own musical season saw a remarkable extension. Two days before the last opera performance he completed the score of a new oratorio, *Athalia*. Equipped with an English oratorio repertory consisting now of three works, Handel set off for Oxford, where he gave five performances (two each of *Esther* and *Athalia*, one of *Deborah*) at the Sheldonian Theatre between 5 and 12 July. In addition, he gave one performance of *Acis and Galatea* in Christ Church Hall and contributed music to a service in the university church. This musical feast was a contribution to Oxford University's 'Publick Act'. The university's Commemoration of Benefactors was celebrated annually in the summer, including events in the theatre that were supplementary to the main ceremonies of awarding degrees at university Congregations – the ceremonies for which the theatre had been designed and built. Latin orations were a normal occurrence in the Commemoration

---

[18] Letter from Lady Irwin to Lord Carlisle, 31 March 1733: Deutsch, pp. 309–10; *HHB*, p. 211. The advertisement for the performance (Deutsch, p. 308; *HHB*, p. 210) said that tickets were a guinea for pit and boxes, and half a guinea for the gallery, and 'The House to be fitted up and illuminated in a new and particular Manner'. For details of the financial basis of Handel's season, see Milhous and Hume, 'Handel's Opera Finances'.

[19] Percival's diary, 27 March 1733: Deutsch, p. 309; *HHB*, p. 211.

programme: the 1733 occasion included one in praise of oratorios and of Handel.[20] Musical events at the theatre were relatively infrequent, and usually comprised performances of original compositions that were offered as 'exercises' for the degrees in music – Croft and Pepusch had contributed in this way (and received their degrees of Doctor of Music in consequence) in 1713. It is not clear whether there was any intended connection between Handel's performances and the award of a university degree to him: before the event London newspapers declared that Handel was to take a degree, and a pamphlet published after the event in Paris (but written by someone who was in Britain at the time) related that he had been offered the degree of Doctor of Music, but had refused.[21] However, there is no record of such an offer in the university's records, and insufficient evidence of the motives on both sides. The most straightforward account of Handel's Oxford excursion, a rather jaundiced report from the diary of Thomas Hearne, a conservative Oxonian who disliked the invasion by 'Handel and (his lowsy Crew) a great number of foreign fidlers',[22] suggests that the question of the degree may have been a red herring and that Handel's performances were simply intended to brighten up the Act:[23]

> One Handel, a forreigner (who, they say, was born in Hanover) being desired to come to Oxford, to perform in Musick this Act, in which he has great skill, is come down, the Vice-Chancellour (Dʳ Holmes) having requested him to do so, and as an encouragement, to allow him the Benefit of the Theater both before the Act begins and after it. Accordingly he hath published Papers for a performance today at 5s. a Ticket. This performance began a little after 5 clock in the evening. This is an innovation. The Players might as well be permitted to come and act. The Vice-Chancellour is much blamed for it. In this, however, he is to be commended for reviving our Acts, which ought to be annual, which might easily be brought about, provided the Statutes were strictly followed, and all such innovations (which exhaust Gentlemen's pockets and are incentives to Lewdness) were hindered.

Although Hearne objected on principle to Handel's performances, his diary does not contain any particular adverse criticisms of them: he probably did not attend, contenting himself with a certain moroseness at the fact that they seemed to be popular. Claims in the newspapers that 3700 people attended a performance of *Athalia*, and that Handel made a clear £2000 out of the Oxford visit, are probably considerably exag-

---

[20] The verses, by Henry Baynbrigg Buckeridge, are printed in Deutsch, pp. 320–2 (with English translation); *HHB*, pp. 217–18.

[21] Deutsch, pp. 316–17, 335–6, the second in English translation; *HHB*, pp. 215–16, 223–4, the second in the original French. Hearne's diary for 18 July 1733 (Deutsch, pp. 327–8; *HHB*, pp. 220–1) implies that the newspapers had reported Handel's refusal.

[22] Hearne's diary, 6 July 1733: Deutsch, p. 319; *HHB*, p. 217. Handel no doubt brought a large number of musicians from London but he used local Oxford musicians as well, including the alto soloist Walter Powell.

[23] Hearne's diary, 5 July 1733: Deutsch, p. 319; *HHB*, p. 217.

gerated,[24] but the week in Oxford may well have been very good for both his reputation and his pocket.

Handel's success was perhaps all the more remarkable because Oxford University was an acknowledged centre for those of a non-Juring and Jacobite disposition, while Handel himself was certain to be identified to some extent with Hanoverian interests. However, Handel's supporters, professional colleagues and patrons throughout his life included some non-Jurors (like Charles Jennens) and 'country Tories', and eighteenth-century British political life is not amenable to simplistic interpretation. All the same, it would be interesting to know what was going through the minds of members of the first audiences for *Athalia* as they heard Handel's affirmative setting of the text 'Bless the true church, and save the king' at the restoration of Joas. One thing is clear: the Oxford visit both established some new friends for Handel's English oratorios and confirmed some old ones. Among the converted was William Hayes, soon to become professor of music at Oxford and to be responsible for many subsequent Handel performances there. Handel himself never returned to Oxford but, in spite of the brevity of his association with the Sheldonian Theatre, that building remains of special interest for Handelians: it is the only building in which Handel performed his oratorios that has survived to the present day, substantially unchanged. None of Handel's London opera theatres remains. Most of the church sites do (Westminster Abbey, St Paul's Cathedral, St Lawrence's church at Cannons and the Chapels Royal at St James's Palace), but with some minor alterations that inhibit a precise reproduction of the circumstances of Handel's performances.

The visit to Oxford probably took Handel's mind away from the problems that beset his future in London and which certainly faced him on his return. The sponsors of the rival opera company had made considerable progress towards bringing their project to fruition, not least because they had secured most of the leading opera singers for the coming season. At the end of the last performance of Bononcini's *Griselda* on 9 June, the final one of Handel's season,[25]

> Signor Senesino made his Leave of the Audience, in a short Speech, acquainting them, as he said, with Regret 'That he had now perform'd his last Part on that Stage, and was henceforward discharg'd from any Engagement.'

If Senesino had disengaged himself from Handel's company, it was in order to re-engage himself to the Opera of the Nobility. By mid-June the founders of the Nobility Opera were in pursuit of a cast to accompany

[24] Deutsch, pp. 327–8; *HHB*, pp. 220–1. The figure of 3700 seems well beyond the possible capacity of the Sheldonian Theatre (even before the modern age of fire regulations): 1000 per performance is perhaps more realistic.

[25] *The Daily Advertiser* (11 June 1733).

him. On 16 June, the day after a meeting of the subscribers to the new venture, the Earl of Delawarr reported:[26]

> There is a Spirit got up against the Dominion of Mr. Handel, a subscription carry'd on, and Directors chosen, who have contracted with Senesino, and have sent for Cuzzoni, and Farinelli, it is hoped he will come as soon as the Carneval of Venice is over, if not sooner. The General Court gave power to contract with any Singer Except Strada, so that it is Thought Handel must fling up, which the Poor Count [Heidegger] will not be sorry for, There being no one but what declares as much for him, as against the Other, so that we have a Chance of seeing Operas once more on a good foot. Porpora is also sent for. We doubt not but we shall have your Graces Name in our Subscription List. The Directrs. chosen are as follows. D. of Bedford, Lds. Bathurst, Burlington, Cowper, Limmerick, Stair, Lovel, Cadogan, DeLawarr, & D. of Rutland, Sir John Buckworth, Henry Furnese Esq., Sr. Micl. Newton; There seems great Unanimity, and Resolution to carry on the Undertaking comme il faut.

In the end, the Opera of the Nobility gained all the personnel they wanted, having signed up all the leading members of Handel's cast except Strada for the next season, and did indeed begin negotiations to lure the famous castrato Farinelli to London. So Handel had to find a new cast (and, presumably, orchestral players) for his next season: the only strong card in his hand was that one year remained of the agreement with the Royal Academy directors for 'undisturbed' use of London's premier opera house and the Academy's physical theatrical stock. The Opera of the Nobility had to begin at the smaller, and less central, Lincoln's Inn Fields Theatre.

Handel must have expected that he would be at the centre of a war of nerves which, though directed principally towards his audiences, was likely to touch him at sensitive points from time to time. In spite of the fact that there was a new, younger circle of opera patrons, associated with the Prince of Wales's 'opposition' political grouping, London did not have, in all, sufficient resources to support two fully blown Italian opera companies for long: Handel knew from first-hand experience the effort that was needed to keep even one company afloat. In such circumstances the battle for resources was to be waged not only with rival attractions in the way of soloists and programmes but also by attempts to undermine public confidence in the other side. That process had already begun in a letter, 'ghosted' in the name of Paolo Rolli, that was published in *The Craftsman* on 7 April, which painted an extravagant picture of public reaction to the price rises for *Deborah*:[27]

> Many of the most constant Attenders of the *Opera's* resolved absolutely to renounce them, rather than go to them under such Exortion and Vexation. They exclaim'd against the *insolent and rapacious Projector of this Plan*. The

[26] Letter to the Duke of Richmond, 16 June 1733: Deutsch, pp. 303–4; *HHB*, p. 208; both mis-dated as January 1733, but Simon, *Handel*, pp. 145–6, gives the correct date.
[27] Deutsch, p. 312; *HHB*, pp. 212–13.

King's old and sworn Servants of the two Theatres of *Drury-Lane* and *Covent-Garden* reap'd the Benefit of this general Discontent, and were resorted to in Crowds, by way of Opposition to the *Oratorio*. Even the fairest Breasts were fir'd with Indignation against this *new Imposition*. Assemblies, Cards, Tea, Coffee, and all other Female Batteries were vigorously employ'd to defeat the *Project*, and destroy the *Projector*. These joint Endeavours of all Ranks and Sexes succeeded so well, that the *Projector* had the Mortification to see but a very thin Audience in his *Oratorio*; and of about two hundred and sixty odd, that it consisted of, it was notorious that not ten paid for their *Permits*, but, on the contrary, had them given them, and Money into the Bargain, for coming to keep him in Countenance.

This Accident, they say, has thrown Him into a *deep Melancholy*, interrupted sometimes by *raving Fits*; in which he fancies he sees ten thousand *Opera* Devils coming to tear Him to Pieces; then He breaks out into frantick, incoherent Speeches; muttering *sturdy Beggars, Assassination*, &c. In these delirious Moments, he discovers a particular Aversion to the City. He calls them all a Parcel of *Rogues*, and asserts that the *honestest Trader among them deserves to be hang'd* – It is much question'd whether he will recover; at least, if he does, it is not doubted but He will seek for a Retreat in his *own Country* from the general Resentment of the Town.

Handel was hardly likely to leave the country permanently when he had a year to run on his current theatre agreement, and in any case all the signs were that he had not modified his decision to make his career, whatever it might turn out to be, in London. There may have been substance in the rumour of a flying visit to the Continent, however: Handel probably knew by the spring of 1733 that he would have to gather a new cast for the next year, and from a letter he wrote to his brother-in-law during August it is apparent that he had been asked to attend to some family matters in Halle, including the arrangements for the future occupation of the family home following his mother's death.[28] But a continental expedition was for the moment impossible (as Handel explained to his brother-in-law), because his plans for the next season required his full attention in London.

He took the precaution of completing an opera well ahead of the season: the draft autograph of *Arianna in Creta* was finished by 5 October. Long before then, his agents abroad had been working to find him a cast.[29] As Strada had remained with Handel as the leading lady, the key item in the scheme was to find a new leading castrato, and this was resolved by securing Carestini, the singer that Handel had tried to attract to London in 1729. Scalzi (a second castrato) and the Negri sisters (a contralto and a mezzo) also came from Italy, and London itself provided a bass in Gustavus Waltz, a theatre singer who had, according to some

[28] Letter (in German), 21/10 August 1733: Deutsch, pp. 330–1 (with English translation); *HHB*, p. 222.
[29] *Arianna* (and the season's pasticcios) saw considerable revision once the new singers arrived in London: see Strohm, *Essays on Handel*, pp. 184–5.

anecdotes, been Handel's one-time chef. The biggest surprise was the return of Durastanti. Lady Bristol summed up her experience of the cast:[30] 'the new man, who I can find out to be an extream good singer: the rest are all scrubbs except old Durastanti, that sings as well as ever she did'.

November saw Durastanti take up again the role of Gismonda in the revival of *Ottone*, a role that she had created ten years earlier: Carestini and Strada, naturally, were accommodated to the roles formerly created by Senesino and Cuzzoni, with suitable modifications to the music.[31] *Ottone* did not open the season; it was preceded by the pasticcio *Semiramide riconosciuta* (opening on 30 October) and succeeded in December by another pasticcio, *Caio Fabricio*. This was followed by yet another pasticcio, *Arbace*, before *Arianna* came to production on 26 January 1734. Meanwhile, the Opera of the Nobility had opened on 29 December with Porpora's *Arianna in Nasso*, preceded by a rehearsal at the Prince of Wales's residence (Carlton House) on Christmas Eve.

That both companies should have run new operas on 'Ariadne' subjects – though not covering the same plot material – can hardly have been a coincidence. However, the rivalry was played out in a more subtle way as well. This was the first time that Handel had packed a season with pasticcios in such a concentrated manner, probably for the reason that they were derived from scores by composers writing in the 'modern' style – that is, the style with which Porpora was associated. *Semiramide* and *Arbace* were adapted from operas by Vinci, *Caio Fabricio* from Hasse: the last was very new indeed, having originated during the Rome carnival season of 1732.[32] Handel also took account of the fact that Scalzi and Carestini had previously sung the leading roles in *Semiramide* and *Arbace* respectively, in the original Italian productions: the new singers would thus be on familiar musical territory, while the audiences would have a first-hand taste of recent Italian music without having to go on a Grand Tour. Handel's *Arianna* itself had a very decent run of 14 performances to 12 March, and a couple more in April: in the gap came more performances of *Arbace*, Handel's 'Serenata' *Parnasso in festa* and a revival of *Deborah*, this time probably in a bilingual version, because oratorio entirely in English would have been impractical with the new Italian cast. *Parnasso in festa* was timed to the celebrations of the wedding of the eldest royal princess: it is a full evening's theatrical entertainment, but the 'plot' consists largely of conversation and reminiscence among the gods on Mount Parnassus concerning the wedding of Peleus and Thetis. Handel re-used a considerable amount of music from *Athalia* (not yet heard in London) in the score, to good effect. The Opera of the Nobility had,

[30] Letter to John Hervey, Earl of Bristol (3 November 1733): Deutsch, p. 336; *HHB*, p. 225.
[31] Handel had also apparently planned a revival of *Ottone* (with his current cast) earlier in 1733: see Dean and Knapp, *Handel's Operas*, p. 440.
[32] On the music of these pasticcios, see Strohm, *Essays on Handel*, pp. 182–96.

meanwhile, presented a new oratorio by Porpora, *Davide e Bersabea*, as their contribution to the festivities.

Further attention is given below to Handel's involvement with events surrounding the royal wedding. Two other events from the early months of 1734 deserve notice. In February a lengthy satirical pamphlet entitled *Harmony in an Uproar: a letter to F-D-K H-D-L, Esq; M-r of the O-a H-e in the Hay Market, from Hurlothrumbo Johnson, Esq.* was published.[33] This took up a stance against the Opera of the Nobility, so Handel must have had his supporters at this time. He certainly had some friends as well, and from April 1734 comes one of the rare descriptions of Handel in more relaxed surroundings, in a letter from Mrs Pendarves:[34]

> I must tell you of a little entertainment of music I had last week; I never wished more heartily for you and my mother than on that occasion. I had Lady Rich and her daughter, Lady Cath. Hanmer and her husband, Mr. and Mrs. Percival, Sir John Stanley and my brother, Mrs. Donellan, Strada and Mr. Coot. Lord Shaftesbury begged of Mr. Percival to bring him, and being a <u>profess'd friend</u> of Mr Handel (who was here also) <u>was admitted</u>; I never was so <u>well</u> entertained at <u>an opera</u>! Mr. Handel was in the best humour in the world, and played lessons and accompanied Strada and all the ladies that sang from seven o'clock till eleven. I gave them tea and coffee, and about half an hour after nine had a salver brought in of chocolate, mulled white wine and biscuits. Everybody was easy and seemed pleased, Bunny [presumably her brother, Bernard Granville] staid with me after the company was gone, eat a cold chick with me, and we chatted till one o'the clock.

After the April performances of *Arianna*, Handel ran a short revival of *Sosarme*, a single performance of *Acis and Galatea* (inevitably in a bilingual version) and then a substantial revival of *Il pastor fido*, expanded beyond its original innocent brevity with a couple of grandiose (and magnificent) new arias for Carestini, some movements (including choruses) transferred from *Parnasso in festa* and some arias derived from other operas by Handel. This ran for 13 performances, closing the season on 6 July. In spite of the competition, Handel had run a full season, with sustained runs for *Arianna* and *Il pastor fido*. Of the former, the author of a contemporary theatre record commented:[35] 'a new Opera & very good & perform'd very often – Sigr Carestino sung surprisingly well: a new Eunuch – many times performed'. Nevertheless, with the end of the season came the end of the five-year term of the Academy's agreement with Handel and Heidegger. When the next season began, the Opera of the Nobility had won occupation of the King's Theatre; Handel moved his company to the Theatre Royal, Covent Garden, a new theatre (opened

[33] Full text in Deutsch, pp. 344–58; *HHB*, pp. 230–7. The author is unknown, though the pseudonym was once used by one Samuel Johnson (not the writer who was later famous as 'Dr Johnson').
[34] Letter to Ann Granville, 12 April 1734: Deutsch, pp. 363–4; *HHB*, p. 240.
[35] Opera Register, January 1734: Deutsch, p. 343; *HHB*, p. 229.

on 7 December 1732) under the management of John Rich.

Royal patronage of the opera companies was a matter of importance to Handel; rival groups had formed within the royal family, and the subject of the opera companies was one on which the parties took sides. A first-hand account of the situation comes from Lord Hervey:[36]

> The Prince of Wales forced himself to be tolerably civil to the Prince of Orange during his stay here, but with the Queen and the Princess Royal he kept so little measure, that the one he never saw but in public and the other he hardly ever spoke to either in public or private.
>
> One of his wise quarrels with the Princess Royal was her 'daring to be married before him,' and consenting to take a portion from the Parliament, and an establishment from her father, before those honours and favours were conferred upon him. As if her being married prevented his being so, or that the daughter should decline being settled because her father declined the settling of her brother.
>
> Another judicious subject of his enmity was her supporting Handel, a German musician and composer (who had been her singing master, and was now undertaker of one of the operas), against several of the nobility who had a pique to Handel, and had set up another person to ruin him; or, to speak more properly and exactly, the Prince, in the beginning of his enmity to his sister, set himself at the head of the other opera to irritate her, whose pride and passions were as strong as her brother's (though his understanding was so much weaker), and could brook contradiction, where she dared to resent it, as little as her father.
>
> What I have related may seem a trifle, but though the cause was indeed such, the effects of it were no trifles. The King and Queen were as much in earnest upon this subject as their son and daughter, though they had the prudence to disguise it, or to endeavour to disguise it, a little more. They were both Handelists, and sat freezing constantly at his empty Haymarket Opera, whilst the Prince with all the chief of the nobility went as constantly to that of Lincoln's Inn Fields. The affair grew as serious as that of the Greens and the Blues under Justinian at Constantinople. An anti-Handelist was looked upon as an anti-courtier, and voting against the Court in Parliament was hardly a less remissible or more venial sin than speaking against Handel or going to the Lincoln's Inn Fields Opera. The Princess Royal said she expected in a little while to see half the House of Lords playing in the orchestra in their robes and coronets; and the King (though he declared he took no part in this affair than subscribing £1000 a year to Handel) often added at the same time that he did not think setting oneself at the head of a faction of fiddlers a very honourable occupation for people of quality; or the ruin of one poor fellow so generous or so good-natured a scheme as to do much honour to the undertakers, whether they succeeded or not; but the better they succeeded in it, the more he thought they would have reason to be ashamed of it. The Princess Royal quarrelled with the Lord Chamberlain for affecting his usual neutrality on this occasion, and spoke of Lord Delaware, who was one of the chief managers against

[36] Sedgwick, *Lord Hervey's Memoirs*, pp. 42–3.

1 *Hendel, non può mia musa*, HWV117, the cantata in praise of Handel, to words by Cardinal Pamphili. The first page of Handel's autograph

2 Interior of Teatro San Giovanni Grisostomo, Venice. Engraving by A. Coronelli from *Venezia festeggiante* (1709)

3 Caricature of Senesino, Cuzzoni and Berenstadt (and a page) in a London opera c.1723 (possibly Handel's *Flavio* or Ariosti's *Coriolano*). Etching by John Vanderbank

4 Faustina and Senesino. Pen and ink drawing, over pencil, by Marco Ricci, c.1728

5 The singers united in a *coro*, Act 3 of *Riccardo Primo* (1727).
'Cuzz[oni]' and 'Faust[ina]' on stave 6, 'Sine [=Senesino]' (with Baldi)
on stave 7. Handel's autograph

6   Oil portrait of Handel, *c.*1730, by Philippe Mercier

7   Covent Garden Theatre interior: riot during a performance of Arne's *Artaxerxes*,
24 February 1763. Engraving by L. Boitard, 1763

8   Vauxhall Gardens, *c*.1751. The statue of Handel is shown in its second setting,
at the centre of the box circle shown at bottom right. Etching by I.S. Müller, 1751

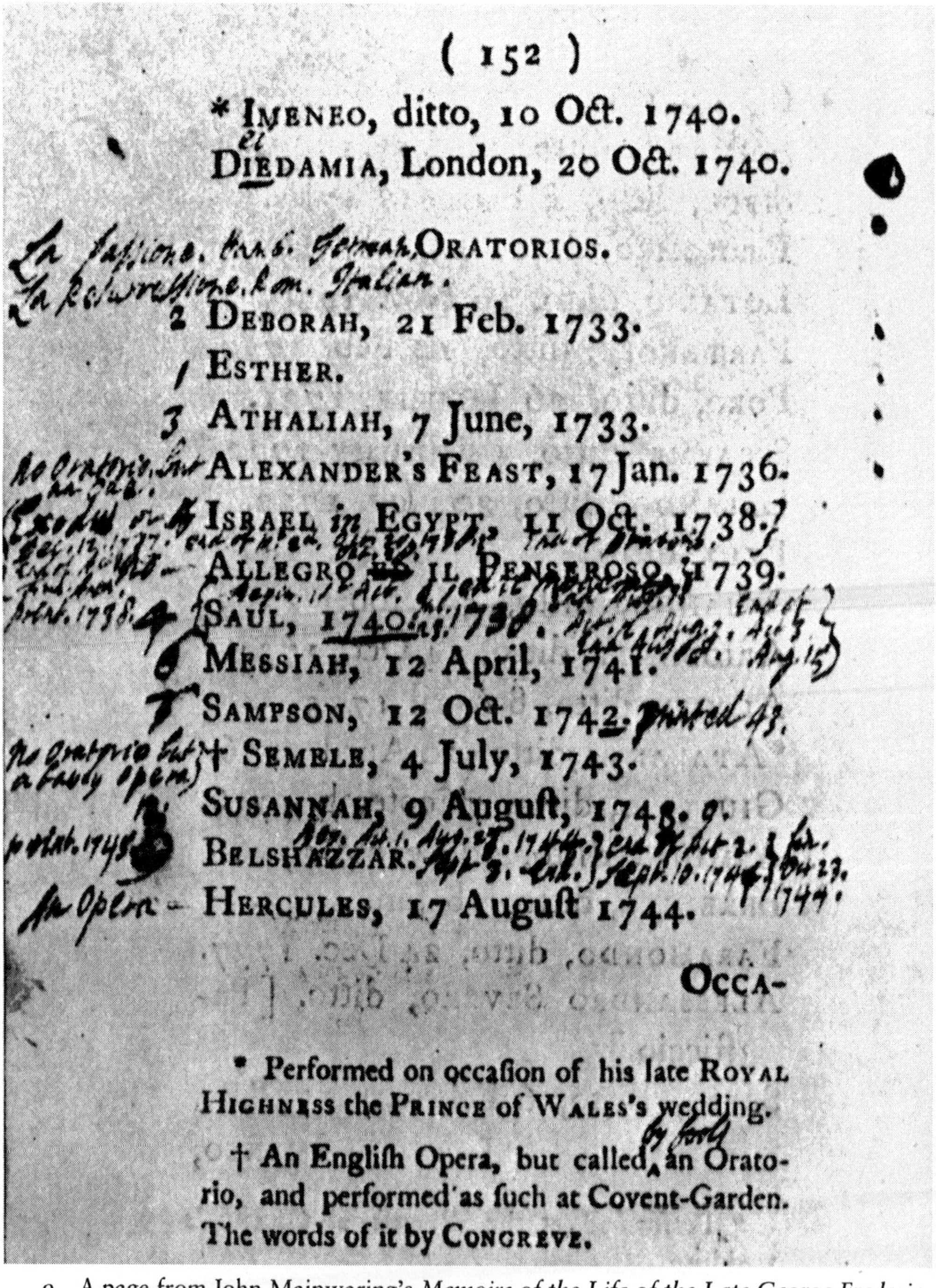

* IMENEO, ditto, 10 Oct. 1740.

DIEDAMIA, London, 20 Oct. 1740.

[handwritten: La paffione. tuud. German] ORATORIOS.

[handwritten: La Refurrettione. Rom. Italian.]

2 DEBORAH, 21 Feb. 1733.

1 ESTHER.

3 ATHALIAH, 7 June, 1733.

[handwritten annotations] ALEXANDER'S FEAST, 17 Jan. 1736.

[handwritten annotations] ISRAEL in EGYPT, 11 Oct. 1738.

ALLEGRO & IL PENSEROSO, 1739.

SAUL, 1740 *[handwritten]* 1738.

MESSIAH, 12 April, 1741.

SAMPSON, 12 Oct. 1742. *[handwritten: printed 43.]*

[handwritten: no oratorio but a bawdy opera] † SEMELE, 4 July, 1743.

SUSANNAH, 9 August, 1748.

[handwritten] BELSHAZZAR.

[handwritten: An Opera] — HERCULES, 17 August 1744.

OCCA-

---

* Performed on occasion of his late ROYAL HIGHNESS the PRINCE of WALES's wedding.

† An English Opera, but called *[handwritten: by fort]* an Oratorio, and performed as such at Covent-Garden. The words of it by CONGREVE.

---

9   A page from John Mainwaring's *Memoirs of the Life of the Late George Frederic Handel* (1760), heavily annotated by Charles Jennens

Recitative.

Jonathan.

Mysterious are thy Ways, O Providence,
But always true, & Just. — By Thee Kings Reign
By Thee they fall. — Where now is Ægypt's Boast
Where thine, O Syria? laid low in Dust.
While chosen Judah triumphs in Success
And feels the Presence of Jehovah's Arm.
Mindfull of this, Let Israel ever fear
With filial Reverence his tremendous Name,
And with obsequious Hearts exalt his Praise.

Chorus of Israelites

O Thou, ~~whose ever-righteous Ways~~
Demand ~~our Wonder, & our Praise;~~
Whose ~~Pow'r extends from Pole to Pole,~~
And ~~will ~~convulsive binds the Whole:~~
Strengthen our ~~arms~~ in War, that War may cease,
In all the Bless~~ings~~ of a glorious Peace.
Amen. Hallelujah.

Chorus   Amen.
Ye servants of the eternal King
His Pow'r and Glory sing;
And speak of all his righteous ~~deeds~~ Ways
With wonder, and with Praise.   Hallelujah

10 A page from the manuscript libretto of _Alexander Balus_,
deposited with the Inspector of Stage Plays (1748).
In the hand of Thomas Morell, with the new text for the final chorus added
by Handel and pencil amendments in another hand.

11 Oil portrait of Handel by Thomas Hudson, 1756.
Originally commissioned by Charles Jennens

Handel, with as much spleen as if he had been at the head of the Dutch faction who opposed the making her husband Stadtholder.

Hervey adds that when the Princess Royal left London on 21 October 1734 after a brief return visit to her parents:[37]

> She had Handel and his opera so much at heart that even in these distressing moments she spoke as much upon his chapter as any other, and begged Lord Hervey to assist him with the utmost attention.

The Princess Royal was, of course, Princess Anne, George II's eldest daughter and sometime music student (perhaps rather than 'singing' student) of Handel. Her wedding to Willem, Prince of Orange, at the 'French Chapel' in St James's Palace on 14 March 1734 involved Handel, as it included the performance of his anthem for the occasion, *This is the day* (HWV262). There was a rather tortuous story behind the wedding celebrations. Willem had arrived in London the previous autumn, and it had been intended that the wedding should take place in mid-November: on 20 October the newspapers reported that the French Chapel at St James's Palace was being prepared[38] and that an anthem by Maurice Greene was to be performed at the wedding. A rehearsal for Greene's anthem was announced for 27 November, but by then the newspapers carried a further announcement:[39]

> The Musick to be performed in the Royal Chapel at the Solemnity of the Princess Royal's Marriage, is now composing by Mr. Handel.

Once again Greene had been edged out by Handel, and this time we must assume that Handel was given priority at the princess's request. We may suppose that Greene was displeased by this, and indeed some chagrin would have been more reasonable than at the time of the coronation, because by 1733 there was no question but that he was the established leading regular Chapel Royal composer: indeed, he had produced orchestrally accompanied music for the Chapel Royal services marking each of King George II's returns from Hanover.[40] Anne was the eldest of the royal daughters, and her wedding set the pattern for the decade: Handel composed the music for the royal 'family' occasions, while Greene retained his duties at the other important Chapel Royal services. Princess Anne's wedding had to be postponed because Willem fell ill fairly soon after his arrival in London: the French Chapel, already specially decorated and furnished, was shut up for the winter and the ceremony finally took place the following March. With Princess Anne's marriage and consequent

---

[37] *ibid.*, p. 66.
[38] The French Chapel (now the Queen's Chapel) is a separate Chapel Royal building within St James's Palace. In the early 1730s it was not in regular use, and it underwent elaborate alterations in preparation for the wedding.
[39] *St James's Evening Post* (27–30 October 1733).
[40] See Burrows, *Handel and the English Chapel Royal*, ii, Appendix 14.

departure to live in Holland, Handel lost his favourite music pupil, though he continued to receive his pension as music master to the remaining royal daughters.[41]

From Lord Hervey's report it is clear that, with Princess Anne's departure, Handel also lost an important channel of influence at court: although he retained the formal support of the king and (perhaps more especially) the queen, the counter-balance to the influence of Prince Frederick was now light. Frederick supported both opera companies during 1733–4 (perhaps because his sister had browbeaten him into maintaining a subscription at the King's Theatre), but only the Nobility Opera in the following two seasons.[42] The king is variously reported as supporting Handel with £1000 and £500 in 1733–4.[43]

On 27 August Handel wrote to Sir Wyndham Knatchbull:[44]

> At my arrival in Town from the Country, I found my self hoñored of your kind invitation.
>
> I am sorry that by the situation of my affairs I see my self deprived of receiving that pleasure being engaged with Mr. Rich to carry on the Operas at Covent Garden.

It is clear from this that Handel was by late August gearing up for his next theatre season and had no intention of leaving London. The reference to his 'arrival in Town from the Country' is intriguing.[45] On 12 August he had begun the composition of a new opera, *Ariodante*, in preparation for next season.[46] It seems entirely possible that Handel began the composition of this opera 'in the Country', but it is doubtful whether he was able to maintain his usual serious concentration on a major composition when he was away from the domestic surroundings that he had created in Brook Street. His regular and extensive use of musical borrowings and self-borrowings implies a stock of notebooks and/or scores, of his own music and other people's, to hand: furthermore, the very intensity of his compositional activities (of which later anecdotes about untouched food outside his door may be legitimate reflections) required a control over his environment that Handel probably could not achieve elsewhere.

---

[41] Princess Anne nevertheless continued to receive news of Handel, and he visited her on his later continental journeys: see King, 'Handel's Travels'. Her payment to Handel 'for a Silver Ticket' in 1735 (King, p. 378) may have been a back-payment for opera attendance in 1733–4 rather than an example of continued patronage *in absentia*.

[42] See Taylor, 'Handel and Frederick, Prince of Wales'.

[43] Deutsch, pp. 372, 374; *HHB*, pp. 245, 246. The official payment of £1000 in October 1734 (Deutsch, p. 370; *HHB*, p. 244), paid directly to Handel, appears to be retrospective to 1733–4. See also n.48, below.

[44] Deutsch, p. 369; *HHB*, p. 244. This is Handel's earliest surviving personal letter in English.

[45] It is sometimes said that Handel had been to Tunbridge Wells, on the basis of Hawkins, *A General History*, ii, 879, but that passage clearly refers to events in 1737.

[46] The autograph of this opera is the second one of Handel's to bear a date of commencement: the first was *Tamerlano*, composed almost exactly ten years previously.

The score of *Ariodante* made fairly leisurely progress, possibly interrupted by the arrangements for setting up his opera company in the new
theatre: Act 2 was not completed until 9 September, and the final date on
the draft score is 24 October. Handel was still well clear of the opening
date for the season, which was 9 November, but the first work to be
performed also required new composition. It was a revival of *Il pastor
fido*, but expanded yet again from the form in which it had been presented
the previous May. A new attraction for this first Covent Garden season
was the inclusion of Madame Sallé's dancers, and he worked them into
his scores, providing opportunities that were attractive for both dancers
and audience, and integrating the dance elements as far as possible into
the dramas. For *Il pastor fido* he added a suite of dances at the end of
each act and an independent prelude, *Terpsicore*, that was played before
the main opera. For singers, Handel carried with him to Covent Garden
his cast from the previous season, adding to them the young English tenor
John Beard,[47] who was to figure as an increasingly important soloist for
Handel in the coming years.

At Covent Garden Handel obviously tried to make his productions
distinctively different from those at the Haymarket: the presence of dancers
helped with this, as did his employment of extra 'chorus' singers for both
operas and oratorios. As usual, he saved up his new opera for the new
year: the calendar year 1734 ended with a revival of *Arianna* and
performances of *Oreste*, a 'self-pasticcio' assembled from Handel's own
music. The latter was something of a triumph for the anonymous librettist,
who successfully adapted a Roman libretto from the 1720s to accommodate
Handel's pre-existing arias. Meanwhile, the Opera of the Nobility had
mounted a version of Handel's *Ottone*. Handel produced no pasticcio
from the works of other composers that season: apparently he had decided
that it was better to fight the rival company with his own works in his
current style than with works by 'modern' Italians. *Ariodante* came on
early in January 1735 and sustained a decent run of 11 performances. On
5 March, a week into Lent, it was followed by *Esther*: perhaps this was
not much of a surprise, but it heralded a substantial and continuous run
of oratorios, with six performances of *Esther*, three of *Deborah* and five
of *Athalia* (in a rather uncharacteristic departure from his usual practice
Handel even put *Athalia* on for three consecutive evenings). Together
these performances amounted to a quarter of Handel's presentations
during the season. As had been the case with *Deborah* in 1734, the nature
of Handel's current cast posed problems for the performance of English
oratorio, though this time it appears that only Carestini had considerable
difficulties with the language. In the performances of *Athalia*, and probably
in *Esther* and *Deborah* as well, Handel reduced the English content of

---

[47] See letter from Lady Elizabeth Compton to Elizabeth Shirley, 21 November 1734: Deutsch,
p. 375; *HHB*, p. 246. Beard would have been about 17 years old at that time.

IL

PASTOR FIDO.

O P E R A.

Da Rappreſentarſi

Nel Novo Reggio Teatro

D I

COVENT-GARDEN.

The Third E D I T I O N, with large Additions.

LONDON:
Printed for T. WOOD, in *Little-Britain*, and are to
be Sold at the THEATRE in *Covent-Garden*.
MDCCXXXIV.
[Price One Shilling.]

Fig. 10 The title-page from the original word-book for the revival of
Il Pastor fido in November 1734, Handel's first performances at Covent
Garden Theatre

184

Carestini's role to a bare minimum and introduced Italian arias. He followed the same policy when faced with similar circumstances in subsequent seasons. In the 1734–5 season Handel for the first time departed substantially from the old rhythm of opera performances on a Tuesday-and-Saturday basis (no doubt precisely because that rhythm was being maintained at the King's Theatre). At Covent Garden he played regularly on Wednesdays, giving his oratorios on Wednesdays and Fridays during Lent. During the period of the oratorio performances Handel composed a new opera, *Alcina*, which he completed on 8 April (Easter Tuesday); it was introduced on 16 April and ran with remarkable success, to 18 performances, closing the season on 2 July. The expected attendance of the king and queen at the first night of *Alcina* was noted by the newspapers.[48]

The 1734–5 season saw one other innovation, in addition to the dancers and a regular chorus, that was clearly designed to attract public interest – the introduction of organ concertos, with Handel himself as soloist, into the intervals of his oratorio performances. The innovation was noted by a newspaper correspondent in March 1735, soon after the beginning of the oratorio run:[49]

> *Handel*, whose excellent Compositions have often pleased our Ears, and touched our Hearts, has this Winter sometimes performed to an almost empty Pitt. He has lately reviv'd his fine *Oratorio* of *Esther*, in which he has introduced two Concerto's on the Organ that are inimitable. But so strong is the Disgust taken against him, that even this has been far from bringing him crowded Audiences; tho' there were no other publick Entertainments on those Evenings. His Loss is computed for these two Seasons at a great Sum...

It seems possible that the extended oratorio run, and the subsequent success of *Alcina*, did something to retrieve Handel's losses. He had probably fared very badly in the 1733–4 season: in December 1733 Jennens had commented 'How two Operas will subsist after Christmas, I can't tell; but at present we are at some difficulty for the Support of One; & M^r. Handel has been forc'd to drop his Opera three nights for want of company'.[50] Although Hawkins and Burney both state that Handel first introduced organ concertos in 1733,[51] 1735 is the more likely date: the first references to his concertos appear in oratorio advertisements from 1735. By then Handel was in need of some such novelty, and the physical

---

[48] *The London Daily Post* (16 April 1735): Deutsch, p. 386; *HHB*, p. 252. See also the report for 15 May: there is a conspicuous absence of references to the Prince of Wales. The king was reported as subscribing £1000 to Handel's season of 1734–5: Deutsch, p. 372; *HHB*, p. 245. The royal family also attended the Nobility Opera.

[49] *The Old Whig* (20 March 1735): Deutsch, p. 384; *HHB*, p. 251.

[50] See Hicks, 'A New Letter'.

[51] Hawkins, *A General History*, ii, 881 (with the reference date given in Old Style), and Burney, *An Account of the Musical Performances*, 'Sketch of the Life of Handel', p. 23 (probably derived from Hawkins).

arrangements for the Covent Garden oratorios may have used the organ as a visual centrepiece. He had used the instrument in 1732 at the King's Theatre, where it had first been brought in (on the bass line) to accompany chorus movements derived from the coronation anthem music. The next year, in *Deborah*, he had written an organ obbligato into one aria and a short passage for 'organi soli' at the end of one chorus, so to that extent Hawkins and Burney were correct in identifying *Deborah* as the first work to include organ solos. For the 1735 oratorios Handel composed four of the organ concertos later published in the 'op.4' set (nos. 2 and 3 were for *Esther*, no.5 for *Deborah* and no.4 for *Athalia*. (There are no autographs of any Handel organ concertos earlier than 1735, apart from the sonata movement in the Roman *Il trionfo del Tempo* of 1707: it is curious that it took 28 years for the idea to bear fruit.) The second of the 1735 performances of *Deborah*, on 2 March, may have marked the official début of a newly-completed 'oratorio organ': the day before, the *London Daily Post* had announced that

> to perfect the Performance, Mr. Handel designs to introduce, to-morrow night ... a large new Organ, which is remarkable for the Variety of its curious Stops; being a new Invention, and a great Improvement of that Instrument.

Handel's supporters were suitably impressed by his performances in 1735:[52]

> We were together at Mr. Handel's oratorio Esther. My sister gave you an account of Mr. Handel's playing here for three hours together: I did wish for you, for no entertainment in music <u>could exceed it</u>, except his playing on the organ in Esther, where he performs a part in two concertos, that are the finest things I ever heard in my life.

The Granville sisters were privileged to attend a rehearsal of *Alcina* a month later:[53]

> Yesterday morning my sister [Ann Granville] and I went with Mrs. Donellan to Mr. Handel's house to hear the first rehearsal of the new opera Alcina. I think it the best he ever made, but <u>I have thought so</u> of <u>so many</u>, that I will not say positively <u>'tis the finest</u>, but 'tis <u>so fine</u> I have not words to describe it. Strada has a whole scene of charming recitative – there are a thousand beauties. Whilst Mr. Handel was playing his part, I could not help thinking him a necromancer in the midst of his own enchantments.

This was clearly a read-through for the singers alone, with perhaps a continuo cellist in attendance.

In terms of musical variety and quality, the 56 performances of Handel's 1734–5 Covent Garden season constitute one of the most attractive seasons he ever mounted in London. But Handel was in no position to repeat the formula on the same scale the next year: whether or not he had the

---

[52] Mrs Pendarves to Mrs Mary Granville, 15 March 1734/5: Deutsch, pp. 383–4: *HHB*, p. 251.
[53] Mrs Pendarves to Mrs Mary Granville, 12 April 1735: Deutsch, pp. 385–6: *HHB*, p. 252.

financial base to do so, he lacked the cast. Carestini left London just over
a week after the close of the 1734–5 season. The end of July found Handel
catching up on his correspondence, writing to Mattheson to deflect another
request for an autobiography ('my continual application to the Service of
the Court and the Nobility keeps me from any other business'), and to
Jennens to thank him for an oratorio libretto.[54] In his letter to Jennens,
Handel mentioned that he was about to visit Tunbridge, no doubt to take
the waters at the Wells. After that, very little is known of his activities
during 1735. The Nobility Opera began their season at the end of October,
and a month later Handel was reported as being in the audience: 'Handel
sat in great eminence and great pride in the middle of the pit, and seemed
in silent triumph to insult this poor dying Opera in its agonies.'[55]

By that stage in the year Handel had normally started his own theatre
season, but there was as yet no sign of activity. However, it seems in the
light of later events that Handel had a plan, and had obtained Rich's co-
operation in principle for the use of Covent Garden at some time during
the season. Once the main opera seasons were over on the Continent, the
singers would be free to come to London and he might then manage a
short run of operas, after Easter 1736. In the meantime, the best that
could be done was to perform English oratorio-type works with such
singers as were to hand. Handel was probably sceptical about the number
of performances that an all-English repertory could sustain, so it was
prudent to begin late, not long before Lent, and to treat the English works
as a run-in to the operas. (The pattern of his programme may also have
been affected by the terms of his agreement with Rich for the use of the
theatre, details of which are not known; Handel had probably been the
first person to whom Rich had let his new theatre).[56] Accordingly, Handel
opened at Covent Garden on 19 February 1736 with *Alexander's Feast*,
composed early the previous month. He had a minimal cast – Strada,
Beard and the bass Erard.[57] The work itself marked a new direction, for
Alexander's Feast was a Cecilian ode by John Dryden, arranged by
Handel's friend Newburgh Hamilton: for the first time Handel was setting,
in Dryden's text, the work of a major English poet.

The only drawback was that *Alexander's Feast* was too short, equivalent
to two acts rather than the three to which theatre audiences were
accustomed. The end of the ode was extended with a short[58] epilogue, to
texts from an earlier Cecilian ode by Hamilton himself, and Handel

---

[54] Letters of 29/18 July and 28 July (O.S.) 1735: Deutsch, pp. 393–4 (with English translation
of the first); *HHB*, p. 256.

[55] Letter from Lord Hervey to Mrs Charlotte Digby, 25 November 1735. Hervey had attended
Veracini's *Adriano in Siria*, which he found very dull, at the Nobility Opera.

[56] See Hume, 'Handel and Opera Management', pp. 352–6; also Deutsch, pp. 411–12; *HHB*,
pp. 267–8.

[57] The name of the bass Reinhold also appears fleetingly on Handel's autograph, but he was
not a soloist in the first performances.

[58] Hamilton's ode, *The Power of Music*, had been written for Robert Woodcock, who set it in

made up the weight with an orchestral concerto (HWV318) and a substantial Italian cantata, *Cecilia, volgi un sguardo* (HWV89), which were played in the interval between the parts. Handel also composed an organ concerto (op.4 no.1, HWV289) for inclusion towards the end of the ode, and a concerto for 'Harp, Lute, Lyrichord and other instruments' (op.4 no. 6, HWV294) which was introduced near the beginning, at the reference to Timotheus playing his lyre. If the performance was rather light on vocal soloists, Handel made up for it with some excellent choruses and by additional instrumental solos – for himself on the organ, for the first cellist, Caporale, in the course of the work, and for the lutenist Arrigoni in the harp concerto and the cantata.[59] As to the performance:[60]

> Last Night his Royal Highness the Duke, and her Royal Highness the Princess Amelia were at the Theatre Royal in Covent Garden, to hear Mr. Dryden's Ode, set to Musick by Mr. Handel. Never was upon the like Occasion so numerous and splendid an Audience at any Theatre in London, there being at least 1300 Persons present; and it is judg'd that the Receipt of the House could not amount to less than 450£. It met with general Applause, tho attended with the Inconvenience of having the Performers placed at too great a distance from the Audience, which we hear will be rectified the next Time of Performance.

And indeed, for the next performance:[61]

> For the better Reception of the Ladies, the Pit will be floor'd over, and laid into the Boxes; and the Orchestre plac'd in a Manner more commodious to the Audience.

Alexander's Feast was followed by revivals of works that did not necessarily require an extensive cast of soloists – *Acis and Galatea* and *Esther*. For them Handel brought in a few more English singers: the soprano Cecilia Young, the tenor Thomas Salway and the young William Savage, who had performed as a boy treble in *Alcina*.[62] By mid-April, while *Esther* was running, the newspapers began to carry reports of the impending arrival of Italian opera singers to perform for Handel. Although, in terms of conventional theatrical habits, Handel had only the tail-end of the season left to him, the moment was quite opportune because another royal wedding was imminent and public festivities were appropriate at that time. By the end of April Handel had completed a draft score of a new opera *Atalanta*, on a subject that had been used in Germany at the

---

1720. Handel's accompanied recitative 'Look down, harmonious Saint' and aria 'Sweet accents all your numbers grace', did not survive to performance; they have been published as an independent cantata (HWV124). Handel re-used the aria in his Italian cantata HWV89 (see below).

[59] On the lutenist, see Dean, 'An Unrecognised Handel Singer'.

[60] *The London Daily Post* (20 February 1736): Deutsch, pp. 399–400; *HHB*, p. 260.

[61] *ibid.* (25 February 1736): Deutsch, p. 400; *HHB*, p. 260.

[62] They may already have sung in the chorus in *Alexander's Feast*. Dean (*Handel's Dramatic Oratorios*, p. 176) argues that *Acis* was given in a bilingual version, but there seems no compelling reason why the 1736 cast (*ibid.*, p. 211) required Italian texts.

time of court celebrations.[63] Handel's version ended with a spectacular scene in which Mercury descends to convey Jove's blessing on the nuptials of Meleagro and Atalanta, after which 'The Scene opens and discovers Illuminations and Bonfires, accompanied by loud Instrumental Musick'. The real wedding, between the Prince of Wales and the Princess of Saxe-Gotha, took place at the Chapel Royal on 27 April. The court was anxious to avoid a repeat of the hitch in the previous royal wedding, so the bride was hustled with all haste from her arrival in London to the Chapel Royal for the ceremony, which was certainly on a less lavish scale than that for Frederick's sister. Nevertheless, the service included a new wedding anthem by Handel, *Sing unto God* (HWV263):[64]

> There was a prodigious crowd ... The chapel was finely adorned with tapestry, velvet, and gold lace ... Over the altar was placed the organ, and a gallery made for the musicians. An anthem composed by Hendel for the occasion was wretchedly sung by Abbot, Gates, Lee, Bird [Beard], and a boy.

In a letter also written on the day of the wedding, Jennens was full of his news about Handel's plans:[65]

> Mr. Handel has made a new Opera for the occasion, but I don't hear when he will produce it; for he does not begin before Wednesday May 5th, & then with one of the last year's operas. I don't wonder you have not heard of Sign'. Conti, for they tell me he is but 19 years of Age, & perhaps had not appeared upon the Stage when you was in Italy. Those who have heard him say He is the finest Soprano they ever heard: & what is something surprising, he goes five notes higher than Farinelli with a true natural voice, & is sweet to the very top. You must have heard Domenico [Annibali], whom Mr. Handel expects next year, & very great things are said of his singing, too.

With the new castrato Conti and the contralto Caterina Negri joining the cast of Strada, Beard and two resident basses, Waltz and Reinhold (the latter making his début as a soloist with Handel), Handel revived *Ariodante* for two performances at the beginning of May and followed this with a run of eight performances of *Atalanta*, ending his short season on 9 June. It apparently took some time to integrate Conti into the operas, for Handel allowed him to substitute several arias by other composers (presumably music already in Conti's repertory) in the *Ariodante* performances. In a letter of 29 June Handel mentioned that he had just returned to London from the country ('where I made a longer stay than I intended');[66] his country visit must have lasted less than three weeks, which perhaps suggests that his summer excursions were not normally

---

[63] See Strohm, *Essays on Handel*, p. 72: a particularly influential model in the choice of subject may have been *Le rivali concordi* by Mauro (composed by Steffani, given in Hanover, 1692, and revived the next year when electoral status was celebrated).

[64] Earl of Egmont's diary, 27 April 1736: Deutsch, p. 405; *HHB*, p. 263.

[65] Letter to Edward Holdsworth, 27 April 1736: *HHB*, p. 264.

[66] Letter to the Earl of Shaftesbury: Deutsch pp. 412–13; *HHB*, p. 268.

very long. In August he was certainly in London, where he began an opera score (*Giustino*) on the 14th.

The death in March 1736 of the music publisher John Walsh, who was succeeded by his son of the same name, may have initiated a new phase in the relationship between Handel and the wider London public. The elder Walsh had published a considerable amount of Handel's music over the years, and Handel had been paid for providing him with copy-texts for opera songs.[67] But the enforceable border between legitimate publication and piracy was virtually non-existent. Around 1732–3 – just before the term of Handel's publishing 'privilege' from 1720 was due to expire – Walsh prepared sets of Handel's 'solo' sonatas (i.e. for solo instrument and continuo), trio sonatas and concertos: these were later regarded as 'op. 1', 'op. 2' and 'op. 3' respectively, though the bib-liographical situation is confused because the 'op. 1' designation was not used during Handel's lifetime. Walsh also issued a set of Handel's keyboard fugues (*Six Fugues or Voluntaries*, 1735), which was also published as 'Troisieme Ovarage' (*sic*), in a sequence following from Handel's first (1720) set of keyboard suites and the 'Second Collection' that Walsh published in 1733. It seems very likely that all Walsh's publications of Handel's instrumental works in the early 1730s were assembled and published without the composer's approval: for the solo sonatas ('op. 1') and trio sonatas ('op. 2') Walsh even took cover in the first instance behind a bogus title-page that carried the imprint of Roger (the publishing house in Amsterdam), although a 'Walsh' title-page was substituted soon after.[68] When the younger Walsh took over the family business, he came to a proper arrangement with Handel for the presentation of his com-positions. The first result was that, from *Atalanta* in May/June 1736, scores songs from Handel's operas were published by subscription. Four operas definitely appeared in this manner, and subscriptions were announced for two others, though no subscribers' lists are known for these. (Cluer had similarly published four Handel operas by subscription in 1725–7.) Better still, subscriptions for a full score of *Alexander's Feast* were solicited in 1737, and it appeared, handsomely printed with an engraved frontispiece incorporating Handel's portrait, in 1738. This was the first published complete score of a major English theatre work by Handel: previous publications had consisted only of solo and orchestral movements, without choruses or complete recitatives. Also during 1738, Walsh published a set of six Organ Concertos (designated 'Opera Quarta' on the orchestral parts), the solo part of which bore a note over Handel's name that they were 'Publish'd by Mr Walsh from my own Copy Corrected by my Self,

[67] See Deutsch, p. 468; *HHB*, p. 301.
[68] The music pages of the 'Roger' edition were the work of Walsh's engravers: see Burrows, 'Walsh's Editions'.

190

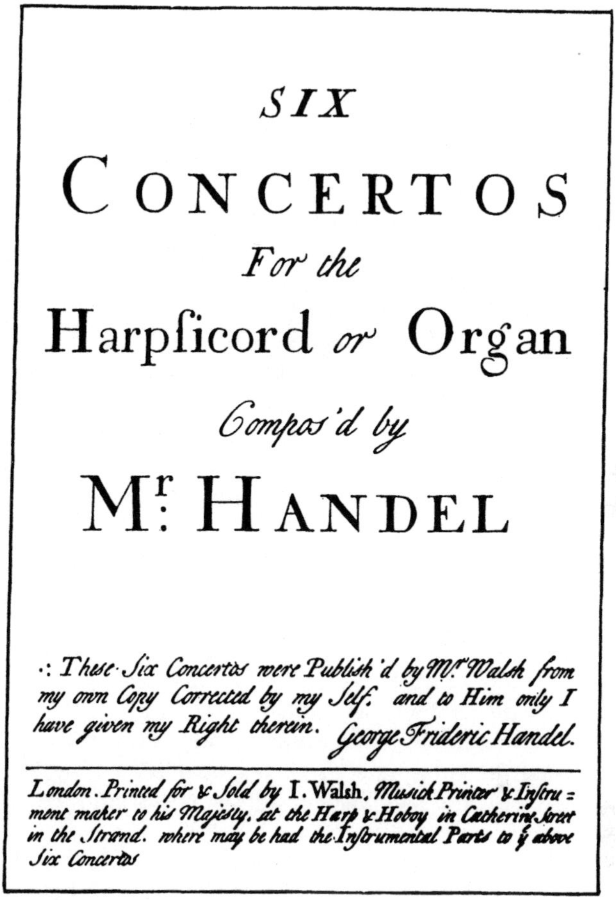

SIX

CONCERTOS

For the

Harpſicord *or* Organ

Compos'd by

Mr HANDEL

·: *Theſe Six Concertos were Publiſh'd by Mr Walſh from my own Copy Corrected by my Self. and to Him only I have given my Right therein.* George Frideric Handel.

London. Printed for & Sold by I. Walsh. Muſick Printer & Inſtru = ment maker to his Majeſty. at the Harp & Hoboy in Catherine Street in the Strand. where may be had the Inſtrumental Parts to y above Six Concertos

Fig. 11 The title-page to the first edition of Handel's Organ Concertos op.4, 1738

and to Him only I have given my Right therein'. The concertos consisted of the four composed for the 1735 oratorios, plus the organ and harp concertos from *Alexander's Feast*. In *The Session of Musicians*, a satirical poem from 1724, the elder Walsh had been represented as asking Apollo:[69]

> What are your Notes, unless you wisely join
> My brighter Name, in Print, to make 'em shine?

With the younger Walsh, Handel seems to have come to a happy agreement

[69] Deutsch, p. 168; *HHB*, p. 126. The poem is also referred to above, in Chapter 6.

that made his music more accessible to the London public – which is not to say that Walsh's subsequent editions were free from error, nor that they represented the composer's current or most considered versions.

Jennens was correct in his prediction that Annibali would join Conti in London: for his 1736–7 season Handel had two leading castratos of good quality. In fact, he had a cast sufficient to allow him to mount a full Italian opera season. Before it began he had two new opera scores ready. He finished the rough draft of *Giustino* on 7 September and worked on *Arminio* between 15 September and 3 October. At the beginning of October Annibali, recently arrived in London, 'was sent for to Kensington, and had the Honour to sing several Songs before her Majesty and the Princesses, who express'd the highest Satisfaction at his Performance'.[70] Strada also returned to London at the same period, having spent part of the summer in Holland with the Prince and Princess of Orange. Following Annibali's arrival Handel revised and put the finishing touches to his two opera scores, completing them by 20 October. He opened his season with revivals, beginning on 6 November with *Alcina*: curiously, Annibali did not appear in this production, and the word-book lists the cast as consisting of Strada, Conti, the Negri sisters, Beard and the bass Reinhold, with 'Young Mr. Savage' re-creating his treble role. Revivals of *Atalanta* and *Poro* followed: as he had done with Conti in the previous season, for Annibali Handel countenanced the inclusion in *Poro* of three arias by other composers, including two by Ristori that Annibali had sung at Dresden.[71] During this season the divided royal family took to supporting both companies (though not on the same nights). The Prince and Princess of Wales attended the first night of *Alcina*, and three new Italian ladies from the Nobility Opera had the honour of performing to the queen's circle at Kensington in November.

As in previous seasons, Handel kept his new operas back until after the turn of the year, with *Arminio* opening on 12 January and *Giustino* on 16 February. Initially these received modest runs of five and six performances respectively, though *Giustino* had a further outing with three more performances in May-June. Even while the two new operas were going into rehearsal, however, Handel was at work on a third: *Berenice* was begun on 18 December and finished on 27 January. Handel hardly even took a pause for Christmas: he dated the completion of Act 1 on 27 December. *Berenice* had to wait its turn for performance. In March and April 1737 Handel packed in revivals of *Parnasso in festa*, *Alexander's Feast* and *Esther*, and a new, expanded version of his old Italian oratorio

[70] *The Old Whig* (14 October 1736, reprinted from another paper a week previously): Deutsch, p. 416; *HHB*, p. 269. At the time the king was in Hanover, and the court at Kensington.
[71] See Strohm, *Essays on Handel*, pp. 197–8.

Il trionfo del Tempo.[72] *Il trionfo* was performed entirely in Italian, while *Esther* was given in a bilingual form with new Italian songs, and *Cecilia, volgi un sguardo*, in *Alexander's Feast* was adapted to accommodate Annibali. At the performance of *Alexander's Feast* on 16 March 'The Prince and Princess of Wales seem'd to be highly entertain'd, insomuch that his Royal Highness commanded Mr. Handel's Concerto on the Organ to be repeated'.[73] Nor was this all: in mid-April Handel returned to a former track by introducing a new pasticcio, his version of Vinci's opera *Didone*. He retained most of Vinci's music but, significantly, re-composed a couple of arias from which he had borrowed ideas for *Arminio* and *Giustino*.[74] *Berenice* opened on 18 May and received three performances in a week (and possibly another on 15 June); June saw final repeats of *Didone, Giustino* and *Alcina*, and the season closed on 25 June with *Alexander's Feast*.

On 11 March a rather curious announcement had appeared in the newspapers.[75]

> We hear, since Operas have been forbidden being performed at the Theatre in Covent Garden on the Wednesdays and Fridays in Lent, Mr. Handel is preparing Dryden's Ode of Alexander's Feast, the Oratorios of Esther and Deborah, with several new concertos for the Organ and other Instruments; also an Entertainment of Musick, called Il Trionfo del Tempo e della Verita, which Performances will be brought on the Stage and varied every Week.

By that date the calendar was more than a fortnight into Lent, and during that time Handel had performed *Giustino* and *Il Parnasso in festa* on days that had included Wednesdays and Fridays. It is uncertain whether Handel was forced to cancel further opera performances during Lent, or whether the newspaper report was a 'planted' advertisement for his forthcoming programme. As Handel now had a number of oratorios and oratorio-type works in his repertory, it was no doubt to his advantage (and that of Rich) to perform on the 'dark days' when the patent theatres were forbidden to perform plays – Holy Week (sometimes referred to as 'Passion Week') and the Wednesdays and Fridays of Lent. This gave him a competitive advantage in access to the London audience, and provided his performers with continuity of employment. Handel had performed *Deborah* during Holy Week in 1734, and at Covent Garden during the Lenten season of 1735 he went over to a regular Wednesday/Friday programme with his oratorios, finishing also with three presentations of *Athalia* in Holy Week. In 1736 he had given *Alexander's Feast* and *Acis*

---

[72] The autograph of the new version (now British Library RM 20.f.10): was begun on 2 March 1737 and finished 12 days later. The title, from the advertisements and the printed word-book (which, of course, included an English translation) appeared as *Il trionfo del Tempo e della Verità*, though the role of Disinganno (translated as 'Council', i.e. Counsel) was not renamed.

[73] *The London Daily Post and General Advertiser* (17 March 1737): Deutsch, p. 429; *HHB*, pp. 277–8.

[74] See Roberts, 'Handel and Vinci's "Didone Abbandonata"'.

[75] *The London Daily Post* (11 March 1737): Deutsch, p. 428; *HHB*, p. 277.

and Galatea on the 'dark days' of Lent: in 1737, as noted, he had slipped
an opera and a serenata (as well as *Alexander's Feast*) into his Lenten
Wednesday/Friday routine, and he gave four performances (including one
of *Alexander's Feast*) during Holy Week.

By 1737 Handel's activities may have excited a certain amount of
resentment from the actors, playwrights and managers in the patent
theatres who were forbidden to perform on the 'dark days'. This may
have been the motive behind a critical article that appeared a year later:[76]

> *Wednesdays* and *Fridays* in *Lent*, have, for several Ages, been appropriated for
> Fasting and Divine Worship, in the Churches of *England* and *Rome*, and the
> Clergy of both have always zealously recommended the strict Observance of
> them by their *pious Examples*; but those Days were never totally engrossed
> for Sacred Purposes, for Men were always allowed to pursue their proper
> Employments; and in our Days the celebrated *Handell* has often exhibited his
> Oratorio's to the Town without any Prohibition; but every Body knows his
> Entertainments are calculated for the Quality only, and that People of moderate
> Fortunes cannot pretend to them, although, as Free *Britons*, they have as good
> a Right to be entertained with what they do not understand as their Betters.
>
> Whether Mr. *Handell* has a License from the Ecclesiastical Court, or from
> the Licensers of the Stage, for playing on *Wednesdays* and *Fridays*, I can not
> tell; but if he has not, I must think the Restraint laid on the facetious Mr.
> *Punch*, from acting on those Days, seems a little partial; for he has at least as
> good a Pretence to the same Liberty, especially considering the submissive
> Remonstrance and candid Office made by him in his Petition to the Licenser
> of the Stage.

As it happened, Handel had not performed on Wednesdays and Fridays
in Lent that year, though he had had a benefit night performance on the
Tuesday of Holy Week.

During the 1736–7 season the rival Opera of the Nobility fell into
difficulties. They had lost Senesino, Cuzzoni and Porpora at the end of
the previous season, and even Farinelli was not sustaining the necessary
drawing-power with audiences: the performance on 11 June 1737 marked
the end of the company. It was perhaps the sense that he had his rivals
on the run that induced Handel to undertake such a heavy programme at
Covent Garden in 1736–7, seeking to outbid them on sheer quantity
instead of offering productions of a different sort, as he had done in
1734–5. It was the most ambitious season he had ever attempted single-
handed: a repertory of 12 works (eight operas and four oratorios), of
which five were new to the London audience. It is perhaps not surprising
that his health gave way towards the end of the season; his illness
prevented him from directing all the performances of *Berenice* and prob-

---

[76] *Common Sense* (13 May 1738): Deutsch, pp. 459–60; *HHB*, pp. 295–6. The author was
possibly Henry Fielding.

ably most of those of *Didone* as well. One newspaper reported on 14 May:[77]

> The ingenious Mr. Handell is very much indispos'd, and it's thought with a Paraletick Disorder, he having at present no Use of his Right Hand, which, if he don't regain, the Publick will be depriv'd of his fine Compositions.

In fact, this report was late: another newspaper had noted on 30 April that Handel was indisposed with 'rheumatism', and that there was some concern as to whether he would be able to direct the performance of *Giustino* on 4 May which the king and queen were expected to attend.[78] On 5 May James Harris wrote to the Earl of Shaftesbury that[79]

> It is certainly an Evidence of great Strength of Constitution to be so Soon getting rid of So great a Shock. A weaker Body would perhaps have hardly born ye Violence of Medicines, wch operate So quickly.

However, the medical advice that Handel received suggested that medicines alone were insufficient, as Mainwaring (pp. 121–3) recalled:

> The observation that misfortunes rarely come single, was verified in HANDEL. His fortune was not more impaired, than his health and his understanding. His right-arm was become useless to him, from a stroke of the palsy; and how greatly his senses were disordered at intervals, for a long time, appeared from an hundred instances, which are better forgotten than recorded. The most violent deviations from reason, are usually seen when the strongest faculties happen to be thrown out of course.
>
> In this melancholic state, it was in vain for him to think of any fresh projects for retrieving his affairs. His first concern was how to repair his constitution. But tho' he had the best advice, and tho' the necessity of following it was urged to him in the most friendly manner, it was with the utmost difficulty that he was prevailed on to do what was proper, when it was any way disagreeable. For this reason it was thought best for him to have recourse to the vapor-baths of Aix la Chapelle, over which he sat near three times as long as hath ever been the practice. Whoever knows any thing of the nature of those baths, will, from this instance, form some idea of his surprising constitution. His sweats were profuse beyond what can well be imagined. His cure, from the manner as well as from the quickness, with which it was wrought, passed with the Nuns for a miracle. When, but a few hours from the time of his quitting the bath, they heard him at the organ in the principal church as well as convent, playing in a manner so much beyond any they had ever been used to, such a conclusion

---

[77] *The London Evening Post* (14 May 1737): Deutsch, p. 434; *HHB*, p. 281. The nature of Handel's 'paraletick disorder' has naturally received some modern expert attention, though the scanty clues do not seem to provide an unambiguous diagnosis. The article in *The Craftsman* for 7 April 1733, quoted above, refers to Handel's 'deep melancholy' and 'raging fits', but I am not disposed to regard this as evidence for an earlier occurrence of his 1737 disorder. The circumstances in which the operatic rivalry developed in 1733 could well have produced a reaction of some distress from Handel; morever, the report itself seems to have an element of dramatic exaggeration.

[78] *The London Daily Post* (30 April 1737): Deutsch, pp. 432–3; *HHB*, p. 280.

[79] Deutsch, p. 433; *HHB*, p. 280.

in such persons was natural enough. Tho' his business was so soon dispatched, and his cure judged to be thoroughly effected, he thought it prudent to continue at Aix about six weeks, which is the shortest period usually allotted for bad cases.

9

The transitional decade II: Confusion, 1737–41

Handel's programmes at Covent Garden had made a significant move towards an English repertory during March–April 1735 and in the early months of 1736, but that proved to be only temporary: the English-based cast of 1736 naturally required an English-based programme, but it is very unlikely that Handel foresaw at the time that his long-term future would lie with an English repertory. The path of his career during the period 1732–7 can be explained fairly comprehensively in terms of competition with the Opera of the Nobility, which extended not only to attracting audiences but also to the challenges of assembling viable casts or of making do with such singers as were available. The collapse of the Opera of the Nobility in 1737 left Handel triumphant, if physically exhausted. It might have been expected, therefore, that he would then take up his natural place at the centre of London's operatic life, continuing to compose and perform Italian operas for another decade or two, probably in partnership with Heidegger, and perhaps regularly including English oratorios in the programme during the mid-season Lenten period. But no such thing happened. The four seasons between 1737 and 1741 saw the wildest swings yet in Handel's programmes, with ever varying proportions between Italian opera and English oratorio-type works. Far from moving steadily from one to the other, Handel seems to have kept both options open all the time, from season to season developing one line or the other according to the opportunities that presented themselves.

Handel arrived back from Aix-la-Chapelle in late October or early November 1737. The cure must have been remarkably effective. In October Prince Frederick of Prussia, writing to the Prince of Orange, expressed the opinion that Handel's great days were over, his inspiration exhausted and his taste behind the fashion.[1] But he was about to be proved wrong. Handel began the score of a new opera, *Faramondo*, on 15 November. He had not proceeded very far before his progress was curtailed by the death of Queen Caroline, whereupon he fell to the task of composing the anthem for her funeral, *The ways of Zion do mourn* (HWV264), to biblical

[1] Letter of 19 October 1737 (NS): *HHB*, pp. 284–5 (original French); Deutsch, p. 441 (English translation).

texts selected by Edward Willes, the sub-dean of Westminster Abbey. He completed the anthem on 12 December: it was rehearsed at the Banqueting House, Whitehall, four days later and then performed at the funeral, in King Henry VII's Chapel, Westminster Abbey, on 17 December. Newspaper reports, as with the coronation music of 1727, emphasized the size of the performing forces, but reports of 140–80 musicians must have been exaggerated: there would hardly have been room for them in the specially constructed organ gallery in the chapel. But Handel correctly judged the tone and size of the anthem to the occasion. The Bishop of Chichester said that it was 'reckoned to be as good a piece as he ever made',[2] and the Duke of Chandos wrote to his nephew:[3]

> the Anthem took up three quarter of an hour of the time, of which the composition was exceeding fine, and adapted very properly to the melancholly occasion of it; but I can't say so much of the performance.

An opera season had started at the King's Theatre, Haymarket, on 29 October, probably managed by Heidegger with the backing of many of the former Nobility Opera patrons. The company had only one castrato,[4] Caffarelli, a singer new to London, but basically the cast was that inherited from the Nobility Opera. Before the queen's death, which closed the theatres for a period of public mourning, the opera company had made a rather tentative start, giving only three performances:[5] it is possible that the enterprise was marking time while negotiations took place with Handel. Most probably Heidegger (as theatre manager) and the managerial rump of the Royal Academy of Music (still well within the 21-year period of its legal existence, though unable to call on further capital) were during the 1730s continuously associated with the King's Theatre and co-operated with whichever musical management seemed most appropriate—working in turn with Handel, the Nobility Opera and now, presumably, those opera patrons who were still willing to commit their time and resources to continuing a company at the Haymarket. Apart from the single payment made directly to Handel himself to clear the debts of the 1733–4 season, the king still regularly paid his annual £1000 opera bounty to the Academy: in 1735–7 this money supported the Nobility Opera's productions at the King's Theatre. After the queen's death, the king observed a lengthy period of mourning, one manifestation of which was that he did not visit the public theatres for a year, though he still paid the usual bounty for the 1737–8 season. The Prince of Wales, who had already shown some support for Handel at Covent Garden the previous year, as well as continuing his regular commitment to the Nobility Opera, supported the

[2] Letter to Francis Naylor of 18 December 1737: Deutsch, p. 443; *HHB*, p. 286.
[3] Letter to Theophilus Leigh of 18 December 1737: Deutsch, p. 443; *HHB*, p. 286.
[4] Farinelli, Conti and Annibali had left London at the end of the previous season.
[5] *Arsace* (pasticcio) on 29 October, 1 November; *Sabrina* (pasticcio, from the Nobility Opera repertory) on 19 November. The texts of both were adapted by Rolli.

1737–8 opera season at his usual level of £250. We may assume that some sort of agreement had already been reached between the current opera company and Handel, in order to bring him into the scheme at the Haymarket, before he began the composition of *Faramondo*.[6] The theatres were allowed to re-open at the beginning of January 1738, and Handel was off the mark on 3 January with his new opera.

Handel had finished writing *Faramondo* on Christmas Eve 1737. He began a new score, *Serse*, on 26 December, completing it on 14 February 1738. It seems almost as if he were trying to prove to himself that he could repeat the intensity of the previous year's creative energy after his health cure. *Serse* was held in readiness for performance later in the season, and for the opera company's second production in 1738 he put together another pasticcio opera from his own music, *Alessandro Severo*. The cast consisted almost entirely of Italians,[7] and he did not even attempt a run of English or bilingual oratorios during Lent. The first two operas ran until 11 March, and then *Serse* began on 15 April (for five performances), followed in May by isolated repeats of the earlier operas. Handel may not have had much control of the programme, for in the gaps between the runs of his operas during January–April the company performed works by Pescetti and Veracini, rather in the 'Nobility Opera' taste; and the end of the season saw repeats of operas from the company's accumulated repertory, Handelian and otherwise. In this season Handel therefore seems to have functioned as a supplier of operas, instead of fulfilling his accustomed role as impresario. Had he been in a position of executive power, he would surely have tried to find a place in the cast for the faithful Strada, who had stayed in London in the hope of employment.

As part of his agreement with the management of the opera company, however, Handel seems to have been granted a benefit night at the opera house, which took place on 28 March. Under the title 'An Oratorio', the benefit programme consisted of a concert selection of music from his anthems (including the coronation anthems and yet another working of the Chapel Royal version of *As pants the hart*) and oratorios, mainly *Deborah*. Although there were some Italian movements, most of the music was to English texts, which suggests that Handel brought in some soloists of his own choice; he also appeared as soloist in an organ concerto, a genre that had been in abeyance for a couple of seasons. The Earl of Egmont went to the performance and 'counted near 1300 persons besides

[6] According to Hawkins (*A General History*, ii, 888), Handel was paid £1000 by the Earl of Middlesex for composing operas for the 1738–9 season, but that information is most likely derived from Mainwaring (*Memoirs*, p. 124), which perhaps magnifies Middlesex's role in the 1737–8 season. The king paid his usual £1000 bounty for the season in July 1738.

[7] There were seven principals: Caffarelli (castrato), the sopranos and contraltos Francesina, Lucchesina, Chimenti and Merighi, and the basses Montagnana and Lottini; since there was no 'second man', at least one of the women had to take male roles in each production.

the gallery and upper gallery. I suppose he got this night 1,000£'.[8] Burney similarly reported later that the night[9]

> proved extremely lucrative: for, besides every usual part of the house being uncommonly crouded, when the curtain drew up, five hundred persons of rank and fashion were discovered on the stage, which was formed into an amphitheatre.

Burney associated the benefit with an attempt to rescue Handel from financial difficulties, saying that Handel's 'affairs were at this time so deranged, that he was under constant apprehensions of being arrested by Del Pò, the husband of Strada'.[10] Certainly Handel's operatic ventures in the 1730s had lacked the secure financial basis that had been provided in the previous decade by the regular royal subsidy for the Royal Academy of Music and the capital available from the Academy's corporate members. But he almost certainly managed his affairs so that he was never personally bankrupt, though the opera companies might fluctuate in their fortunes; in so far as Handel carried any responsibility for the payment of performers, there is no evidence of any failure to fulfil his responsibilities. There are records of his buying and selling annuities, and he kept accounts at the Bank of England for which records survive fairly continuously from 1732 onwards.[11] But it is difficult to relate these financial records directly to Handel's activities: it is not even possible to trace from them when he received his court pensions, still less to reconstruct the more variable receipts and expenses of the theatre companies for which he may have been responsible. In the absence of a comprehensive knowledge of his day-to-day financial affairs, our best guess must be that, although the opera companies always operated on a knife-edge, Handel's own financial circumstances were never the subject of either personal or professional embarrassment.

Aside from any financial considerations, the popularity of Handel's benefit night seems to indicate that he was at a turning-point in his reputation with the London public. Although he might still have had 'enemies' among both influential theatre patrons and rival musicians, Handel was becoming an accepted part of London life. Two events both symbolized and encouraged this. Handel took a leading role, along with musicians who would not otherwise have been sympathetic to him, in

[8] Egmont's diary (28 March 1738): Deutsch, p. 455; *HHB*, p. 293.
[9] *An Account of the Musical Performances*, 'Sketch of the Life of Handel', p. 24.
[10] *Ibid*. It is possible that Strada and her husband felt that Handel should have secured her a job in the opera company of 1737–8.
[11] The bank accounts, which were first published in Young, *Handel*, are given in full in Deutsch, pp. 835–41, and *HHB*, pp. 548–52. The only relevant section for the present period, the 'Drawing Account' for 1732 onwards, shows that by the end of March 1739 Handel had drawn on all the £2300 that he had deposited as a lump sum in 1732; it is silent about the income that he must have received during that period, which was presumably accounted for elsewhere.

founding the Fund for the Support of Decay'd Musicians, which held its first meeting at the Crown and Anchor Tavern in April 1738. His music provided the mainstay for the programmes of the fund's first benefit performances: he seems to have taken a strong personal interest in the charity, which was inaugurated in response to the discovery that the children of Kytch, his former oboe soloist, were near to destitution. More remarkable still is the celebration of Handel's status that was implied by the lifesize statue in Carrara marble that Jonathan Tyers commissioned from the sculptor Louis François Roubiliac and set up in April 1738 at his pleasure gardens at Vauxhall, just over the Thames from Westminster.[12] Quite apart from the fact that it was unusual for a living composer to be commemorated by such a statue – and Handel was not merely living but, at 53, still in mid-career – the form of the statue itself was remarkable. While kings were conventionally shown in military attire, usually on horseback, Handel was portrayed in the guise of Apollo, idly strumming his lyre and in informal dress. Such a 'humanizing' portrait was a remarkable complement and contrast to the images of Handel as Hanoverian court servant, ambitious opera director or creator of sublime church music. Through his church music he had already penetrated beyond the opera house: people still remembered the coronation music, and Handel had contributed to the royal weddings in 1734 and 1736. Since 1731 his music had featured in the well-attended annual Sons of the Clergy Festival charity services at St Paul's Cathedral, and public rehearsals or performances of his church music from time to time brought forth literary effusions in the newspapers.[13] His music also reached London's non-operatic theatre audiences: apart from the songs that were pirated in *The Beggar's Opera*, the *Water Music* appeared in miscellaneous theatre programmes,[14] and Handel even contributed an original song (*I like the am'rous youth that's free* HWV228[11]) for the actress Mrs Clive to sing in a play at Drury Lane in 1737; he was to do the same again for her three years later (with *Love's but the frailty of the mind* HWV218). The seeds of the broad appeal that was eventually to lead to the popular myth of 'The Great Mr Handel' had already been sown.

With the reunion of Handel, Heidegger and an opera company at the Haymarket, the scene appeared to be set for Handel's career to return to its main track with Italian opera in London, but the next year saw the biggest sudden swerve yet in its direction. Towards the end of May 1738

---

[12] On the history of the statue, see Hodgkinson, 'Handel at Vauxhall'.

[13] See Deutsch, pp. 339–40, 448; *HHB*, pp. 228, 288–9. 'Harmonia Sacra' in the title of the 1733 poem from *Polymnia* (Deutsch, p. 338; *HHB*, p. 228) referred to a series of performances given in aid of the Chapel Royal fund that had included a programme of Handel's church music on 13 March 1733. Many of the performers for that occasion had, of course, been involved with Handel's own performances of the works. See Burrows, *Handel and the English Chapel Royal*, i, 413–15.

[14] E.g., as an afterpiece to two plays (Cibber's *Love's Last Shift* and Fielding's *The Lottery*) at Covent Garden on 16 May 1737.

Heidegger made an appeal for an opera subscription for 1738–9, but on 25 July he had to announce the cancellation of his plans 'by Reason of the Subscription not being full, and that I could not agree with the Singers th'[ough] I offered One Thousand Guineas to One of them'.[15] Strada, who had stayed on in the hope of a better outcome, left London for Holland and Italy, and most of the other Italians had probably already gone. Of the principal singers inherited from the Opera of the Nobility, only the French singer Elisabeth Duparc (known as Francesina) stayed behind. For the moment, opera patronage in London seemed to be an exhausted seam, and Handel appears to have recognized this. By the time of Heidegger's announcement Handel was formulating plans for a season of his own and had probably already come to an agreement with Heidegger for the use of the theatre to put them into practice. He thought in terms of repeating the scheme that he had followed successfully in 1736 – a season built around English oratorio-type works, beginning in the new year and employing singers that were available in London. If Italian opera were to come into the picture at all, it would either be at the end of the season (when Italian singers might become available) or involve some modest, easily stageable works that might even be attempted with his 'oratorio' cast.

Accordingly, Handel first took up *Saul*, an English oratorio on a libretto supplied by Jennens, on 23 July[16] and worked on it through August and probably into September. Between 9 and 20 September he drafted an opera, *Imeneo*, but did not bring it to completion, presumably because he considered it impractical for his prospective resources in the next season: by mid-September he presumably knew for certain that he could not attract a cast of Italian singers. There is no mention of the opera in a letter of Jennens's dating from 19 September: Jennens had called on Handel the day before, for what turned out to be a progress conference on *Saul*:[17]

> Mr. Handel's head is more full of Maggots than ever: I found yesterday in his room a very queer Instrument which He calls Carillon (Anglice a bell) & says some call it a Tubalcain, I suppose because it is both in the make & tone like a set of Hammers striking upon Anvils. 'Tis play'd upon with Keys like a Harpsichord, & with this Cyclopean Instrument he designs to make poor Saul stark mad. His second Maggot is an Organ of 500£ price, which (because he is overstock'd with Money) he has bespoke of one Moss of Barnet: this Organ, he says, is so contriv'd, that as he sits at it, he has a better command of his Performers than he us'd to have; & he is highly delighted to think with what exactness his Oratorio will be perform'd by the help of this Organ: so that for

---

[15] Deutsch, pp. 464–5; *HHB*, p. 298.

[16] This date is given on the autograph at the beginning of Part 1 scene i, where Handel probably began work (rather than with the overture).

[17] Letter to Lord Guernsey: Deutsch, pp. 465–6; *HHB*, p. 299. Both have errors in transcription, which are corrected here.

the future, instead of beating time at his Oratorio's, he is to sit at the Organ all the time with his back to the Audience. His third Maggot is a Hallelujah which he has trump'd up at the end of his Oratorio since I went into the Country, because he thought the conclusion of the Oratorio not Grand enough; tho' if that were the case 'twas his own fault, for the words would have bore as Grand Musick as he could have set 'em to: but this Hallelujah, Grand as it is, comes in very nonsensically, having no manner of relation to what goes before. And this is the more extraordinary, because he refus'd to set a Hallelujah at the end of the first Chorus in the Oratorio, where I had plac'd one & where it was to be introduc'd with the utmost propriety, upon a pretence that it would make the Entertainment too long. I could tell you more of his Maggots: but it grows late & I must defer the rest till I write next; by which time, I doubt not, more new ones will breed in his Brain.

Following Jennens's visit, Handel revised *Saul*, bringing it to some sort of completion on 27 September: on 1 October he started another oratorio,[18] *Israel in Egypt*, which he completed a month later.

Whether Handel's 1739 season at the King's Theatre is to be regarded as a success depends on the perspective from which it is viewed. The new oratorios were remarkable works, and Handel succeeded in keeping something afloat in London, apparently financed by walk-in audiences, during the season for which Heidegger had failed to raise a subscription. But it was certainly the most unusual programme that Handel had ever mounted in London, and it must have seemed inadequate to the regular patrons of the King's Theatre who were used to about 50 opera performances in a season. Handel opened on 16 January, and finished his series on 5 May, having given only 15 performances, one of which (*Alexander's Feast*, on 20 March) was a charity benefit. The opening presentation, *Saul*, came near the beginning of the calendar year, seven weeks away from the Lenten season. The first performance was honoured by the presence of the king and his younger children; this was only the second occasion on which the king had attended public entertainments after his period of mourning, and it was, in fact, the last of his attendances at Handel's theatre performances to be unequivocally recorded by the newspapers. The Prince and Princess of Wales appeared at the second performance, and attended six more times during the season.[19]

The initial run of *Saul* (four performances) was followed in February by a revival of *Alexander's Feast* (two performances)[20] and by a single revival of *Il trionfo del Tempo* (based on the 1737 version) on 3 March. Within the Lenten period Handel gave one more performance of *Alexander's Feast*, two of *Saul* and three of his new oratorio *Israel in Egypt*.

[18] The date is unclear on the autograph – Handel may have altered '1' to '2'; he began the composition with 'Moses' Song' (Part 3 of the oratorio, as performed).

[19] On one occasion the prince attended without the princess: see Taylor, 'Handel and Frederick', p. 92. The king later attended the first performance of *Imeneo*, in November 1740.

[20] *Alexander's Feast* had been performed privately by the Academy of Ancient Music on 18 January 1739, presumably without Handel's participation and using Walsh's published score.

The subject of the last may have had a dual appeal to the audience, as it was a suitable biblical work for the Lenten season for the Christian audience and also had topical relevance to the Passover season for London's Jews. The support that Handel's oratorios received from London's Jewish community is uncertain, though a later anecdote – concerning *Theodora* (see Chapter 14) – suggests that Handel may have taken Jews into account in the 1740s. After Easter Handel gave only two performances, of the 'Dramatical Composition' *Jupiter in Argos*, which was largely a musical self-pasticcio, with new recitatives and half a dozen new movements:[21] he completed the new music on Easter Tuesday, only a week ahead of the first performance. Though performed in Italian, the work appeared as *Jupiter in Argos* (rather than the Italian *Giove in Argo*) on both the printed libretto and Handel's autograph. It is possible that Handel's working title was a German form, derived from a bi-lingual word-book that had been produced for an opera performance at a German court, and that he did not work directly from Lucchini's libretto for Dresden in 1719 (which had been printed in an Italian/French word-book) – or perhaps Handel even thought of the title in English. Whether *Jupiter in Argos* was performed with full staging is not known, but it may well have been given in the serenata manner: even so, it was as close as Handel came that season to Italian opera.

The best-received work of the season seems to have been *Saul*. Royal patronage, a good cast[22] and a number of orchestral novelties (including large military timpani borrowed from the Tower of London and the carillon that had featured in Jennens's letter about 'maggots') no doubt contributed to its appeal. After the first performance, the artist William Kent reported to the Earl of Burlington:[23]

> The oratorio's goe on well, I was there with a handsom widow fatt, which has given much diversion to the looker on & we was in the box you us'd to have – There is a pretty concerto in the oratorio there is some stops in the Harpsicord that are little bells, I thought it had been some squerrls in a cage.

The lead-up to the first performance is documented from the correspondence of Lord Wentworth:[24]

> Mr Handel rehearsed yesterday a new Oratorio call'd Saul, and Mr. Hamilton thinks it a very good one; and for a chief performer he has got one Rusell an Englishman that sings extreamly well; he has got Francisschina for his best woman, and I believe all the rest are but indifferent.

[21] On his copy of music from *Jupiter in Argos*, Jennens wrote 'Not Handel's' against one of the 'new' movements (the *accompagnato* 'Iside, dove sei?').
[22] *Saul* had a large cast of at least ten principals; *Israel in Egypt* and *Jupiter in Argos* each required six.
[23] Letter of 22 January 1739: *HHB*, p. 304.
[24] Letter to the Earl of Strafford, 9 January 1739: Deutsch, p. 471; *HHB*, p. 303. Lord Wentworth's tutor was Newburgh Hamilton, who had arranged *Alexander's Feast* for Handel and was subsequently the librettist for *Samson* and the *Occasional Oratorio*.

The other principal singers included Cecilia Young (playing Merab to Francesina's Michal) and Beard (playing Jonathan): the latter was the focus for a certain amount of contemporary gossip on account of his recent marriage to the daughter of the Earl of Waldegrave. The Lenten performance of *Alexander's Feast* attracted attention because it was a benefit performance, the first one held in aid of the Fund for the Support of Decay'd Musicians: 'Mr. Handel gave the House and his Performance, on this Occasion, gratis'.[25] For the occasion Handel composed a new organ concerto, and another soon followed to accompany the première of *Israel in Egypt*.[26] The second performance of *Saul* was also enlivened by 'several new Concertos on the Organ'.[27] *Israel in Egypt* received a rather cool reception, probably because it was largely a choral oratorio, which was not necessarily appreciated by the more opera-minded section of the theatre audience; the second performance was 'shortened and Intermix'd with Songs' in an attempt to placate the aria-lovers. A few people wrote to the newspapers in support of the oratorio, and their action was perhaps influential in having its run extended from two performances to three. If *Israel in Egypt* had been an opera, a run of three performances would have been regarded as a failure; but, as far as we can tell, Handel was now entirely free to adjust the number of performances of any work in the season, and the normal pressure on an opera to run for long enough to recoup overhead expenses from the staging did not apply to oratorios. We do not know how *Jupiter in Argos* was received, but Handel judged the effective span of his season correctly, and there was probably no serious enthusiasm for the continuance of the season beyond early May, nor demand for further performances of his 'Dramatical Composition'. A newspaper had announced the arrival of one 'Signiora Busterla' on 17 April 'to perform in the Opera's that are intended to be perform'd by Mr. Handel, after the Holydays',[28] but there is no sign that Handel planned anything to follow *Jupiter in Argos*. The score of *Imeneo* remained undisturbed, except as a quarry for *Jupiter in Argos*.

Handel's 1739 season brought a problem in semantics: what general descriptive name could be given to his theatre programme? In the past he had clearly given opera seasons, into which oratorios, odes and serenatas had been introduced in various languages and proportions, though clearly never as dominant features of the programme. If Handel's Oxford per-

---

[25] *The London Daily Post* (22 March 1739): Deutsch, p. 478; *HHB*, pp. 306–7.

[26] Respectively, HWV296a and HWV295, published (as the keyboard score, without orchestral parts) by Walsh in 1740 in *A Second Set of Six Concertos for the Harpsicord or Organ*; they were the only two genuine original organ concertos in the set, the rest being organ arrangements of op.6 concerti grossi.

[27] These cannot be identified; the reference may be to the organ solos in the overture and to a sinfonia in Part 2.

[28] *The London Daily Post* (19 April 1739): Deutsch, p. 483; *HHB*, p. 309. 'Bustterla' (correctly 'Posterla', or 'Pasterla') was the wife of the violinist Giovanni Piantanida; she presumably performed in *Jupiter in Argos*.

formances in 1733 could be dignified with the name of a 'season', then clearly the title 'oratorio season' was appropriate: the works he presented at the Sheldonian Theatre were all oratorios (*Esther, Deborah, Athalia*), though in addition he gave one other work (*Acis and Galatea*) in Christ Church Hall. The strict categorization between English-language oratorios and non-oratorios soon broke down in common parlance, and it was obviously convenient to describe the series of performances in 1739 as an 'oratorio season': the Prince of Wales paid for seven performances under the title 'the Oratorio in the Haymarket. Exhibited by George Fred: Hendell Esq.',[29] though two of the seven had been of *Alexander's Feast*. Revealing also is the fact that Mrs Pendarves needed to correct a slip of her pen: 'I go to-night to the oratorio – no I mean to Alexander's Feast – with Mrs. Carey'.[30]

The correct use of the word 'oratorio' was, in the end, probably a matter of supreme concern only for the linguistically punctilious. Among them was Jennens, who in the 1760s heavily annotated the work-list in his copy of Mainwaring's biography of Handel (see Plate 9). He rejected many works in Mainwaring's list of oratorios, and there is a clear pattern to the ones he retained: for Jennens, the use of 'oratorio' was strictly confined to librettos derived from biblical stories, supplemented by the allegorical 'morality oratorio' *Il trionfo del Tempo*, and *Theodora*, the story of an early Christian martyr. Mainwaring's original list is probably closer to the common usage of 'oratorio' by the time of Handel's death, as a general term for non-acted, English-language theatre works. It is perhaps churlish to deny Handel's 1739 series (which comprised three oratorios, one ode and *Jupiter in Argos*) the credit as his first London oratorio season. The programme was, of course, built on his experience in previous seasons, in particular the concentrated run of oratorios within the opera season during Lent 1735, and the opening of his 1736 season when *Alexander's Feast* and other English works kept the audience warmed up for the arrival of the Italians. From a present-day standpoint, the significance of Handel's 1739 season is not to be measured simply by the numerical balance between English and Italian works but by a qualitative component as well: Handel's commitment to English oratorio as the basis of his season brought forth, in *Saul*, a work that surpassed all earlier models.

From his experience of the previous two seasons Handel may reasonably have concluded by mid-1739, first, that there was no future for him in the continuation of opera under the old scheme (there were not enough willing subscribers and he probably did not have much confidence in the new generation of patrons led by Lord Middlesex), and, secondly, that it was difficult to sustain a complete oratorio-based season in London's premier

---

[29] See Taylor, 'Handel and Frederick', p. 92.
[30] Letter to Ann Granville, 17 February 1738/9: Deutsch, p. 475; *HHB*, p. 305.

opera theatre. Heidegger was still responsible for the management of the King's Theatre, but he had no regular tenants for the 1739–40 season.[31] The musicians moved out to London's smaller (and presumably less expensive) theatres. Lord Middlesex formed an opera company which performed at the Little Theatre in the Haymarket, beginning in December 1739 with serenata and concert performances and then proceeding to operas in the new year. In spite of the fact that Carestini returned to London to perform in this series, the company does not seem to have attained a very high profile. Handel, presumably somewhat encouraged by the fact that there seemed to be at least a modest regular audience in London for oratorio-type works, took Rich's smaller and older theatre at Lincoln's Inn Fields, where he gave an all-English season. A third attraction for London's musical audiences was a series of ten concerts at Hickford's Room on Fridays, beginning in January 1740. The programme there began with *Rosalinda*, a 'new Musical Drama' by John Christopher Smith the younger, who was probably in charge of the season: other works by him appeared later in the series, along with two of Handel's Cannons anthems. It is doubtful that Smith deliberately ran a series in competition with his former music-teacher (and, indeed, in conflict with his own father's interests): in practice there were very few clashes of dates with Handel's performances, and the fact that some of Handel's soloists appeared at the Hickford's Room series after the end of Handel's season suggests a spirit of co-operation rather than competition.

Furthermore, Hickford's Room had interesting Handelian associations, even though Handel is not known to have performed there. The concert room had been established by Thomas Hickford during the 1690s in Panton Street, just off the Haymarket, but in 1739 the newspapers announced that Mr Hickford had 'removed' to Brewer Street, north of Piccadilly. One of the first events in the new room in Brewer Street was a public raffle in June 1739 for an elaborate musical clock made by Charles Clay. Clay produced a number of clocks incorporating small barrel-organs with musical repertories that included several pieces by Handel.[32] Hickford's new room was decorated with a portrait of Handel that was apparently specially commissioned. It is not known whether this was part of a series of composers' portraits or whether, as in Vauxhall, Handel remained in lonely eminence, nor can the picture itself be identified with certainty. But its existence was recorded in London's principal daily newspaper:[33]

---

[31] The 1737 Licensing Act for the theatres would have prevented him from letting the theatre to non-operatic companies. Heidegger gave a number of masquerades, but no musical performances.

[32] Handel composed a set of 11 short pieces (HWV587–97) specifically for a Clay clock; a further set of seven pieces (HWV598–604) were also written as 'clock music'.

[33] *The London Daily Post and General Advertiser* (21 March 1738/9).

To an eminent Painter, seeing him drawing Mr. HANDEL's Picture, designed for Hickford's Great Room, in Brewers-street

> Whilst, from the Cloth, thou call'st the mimic life,
> And Nature, smiling, views the charming Strife;
> Handel, well pleas'd, revolves some noble Lay,
> To spread thy Fame, and thy just Art repay.
> Happy! when thus the Pencil and the Lyre
> Throw rays o'er each, and mingle Fire with Fire.

Presumably Handel spent part of the summer of 1739 negotiating with Rich over the arrangements for his next season. He took with him to Lincoln's Inn Fields his principal singers from the previous Haymarket season – Francesina, Beard and Reinhold. However, Handel vanishes from the documentary record after the last performance of *Jupiter in Argos* in May. The next fixed point in his biography comes on 15 September, when he began the composition of Dryden's *Song for St Cecilia's Day*, a work equivalent in length to a single act or part of an opera or oratorio. He finished this in ten days, and on 29 September put the finishing-date to the first of a new set of concerti grossi. A month later, 12 orchestral concertos lay completed on his desk. No doubt he foresaw that he would use them as interval music in his forthcoming season, and there is also no doubt that from the first he planned the concertos as a set with publication in mind: he must, indeed, have made a conscious decision at this juncture to give the concertos priority over the writing of an oratorio-type work for the next season. Their subsequent publication marked another stage in his fruitful co-operation with the younger Walsh, who earlier in 1739 had already printed two substantial collections of arias from *Saul* and a set of trio sonatas. After the organ concertos (op.4) of the previous year, the trio sonatas naturally fell in as op.5, and the new orchestral concertos followed as op.6. It was probably no coincidence that this sequence gave Handel's concerti grossi the designation op.6: Corelli's 12 concertos with the same opus number had achieved 'classic' status in Europe and were highly regarded among Britain's amateur and semi-professional music clubs and performing societies. Handel clearly designed his own concertos on the Corellian multi-movement model, rather than on the Vivaldian three-movement plan with virtuoso solo parts. A subscription was advertised for Handel's op.6 before he had completed the last concertos: the set appeared in print in 1740, 'Publish'd by the Author' but 'Printed for and Sold by John Walsh'. They were published under the English title of *Grand Concertos*, although Handel referred to them as concerti grossi in his autographs. As well as the list of subscribers (100 names for 122 copies), the preliminary material to the first violin part[34] included a new

---

[34] This served as the 'master copy', since the concertos were not published in score. The subscribers included the Duke of Cumberland and the royal princesses (including the Princess of Orange), but not the king or the Prince of Wales.

copyright privilege to Handel, granted by the king on 31 October 1739 for 14 years. Unfortunately, having gained the privilege (and parity with Corelli's publication record), Handel seems to have lost interest in publishing his instrumental works, and the subsequent instrumental collections (of organ concertos) were haphazard, with seemingly little input from the composer.[35]

Handel began his first season at Lincoln's Inn Fields ahead of the competition from London's other musical enterprises, opening on St Cecilia's Day (22 November 1739) with an appropriate double bill of odes with texts by Dryden: *Alexander's Feast* and the new, single-part Cecilian Ode. He thus solved the problem that had troubled him in 1736, of squaring the two-part *Alexander's Feast* with the audience's expectations of a three-act evening at the theatre. The performance also featured items from the new op.6 repertory, with 'two new Concerto's for Instruments', and also a 'Concerto on the Organ'. The Cecilian programme was followed by a revival of *Acis and Galatea*, in the only all-English theatre version that he gave in London,[36] as a new partner for the shorter Cecilian Ode. For this revival of *Acis* he composed for the end of Part 1 a chorus setting of 'Happy we' to follow the Cannons duet on the same text: the movement included an obbligato part for the carillon. Handel's season was interrupted at the turn of the year by an exceptionally hard winter: the advertisement for the first performance in 1740 (*Acis* on 14 February) reassured the audience that the theatre would be 'secur'd against the Cold, by having Curtains plac'd before every Door, and constant Fires will be kept in the House 'till the time of Performance'.[37] But the weather affected the singers: two soloists fell ill, and the planned performance had to be delayed a week. The wintry weather had not deterred Handel's creative muse, however: between 19 January and 4 February he composed *L'Allegro*, Jennens's arrangement of Milton's twin odes *L'Allegro* and *Il Penseroso*, with the addition of a third part by Jennens himself, *Il Moderato*.[38] Handel filled the slack period at the time of the cancelled performance by producing a fine organ concerto (HWV 306) to accompany the new work: later published as op.7 no.1, it was completed on 17 February. It is remarkable as Handel's only concerto requiring an organ with pedals, and

[35] The *Second Set* of organ concertos published later in 1740 contained only two original concertos (see n.26, above). The rest of his organ concertos were not published during Handel's lifetime, but a set of six (probably assembled by the younger J. C. Smith from materials found among Handel's autographs) was published (as 'op.7') in 1761, the first advertisement appearing on the anniversary of Handel's birthday.

[36] Unless he had also given an all-English *Acis and Galatea* in 1736 (see Chapter 8, n.62).

[37] *The London Daily Post* (11 February 1740): Deutsch, p. 495; *HHB*, p. 319.

[38] I use 'Il Moderato' as a convenient description for Part 3, though Jennens strictly applied it only to the 'character' who appears in that part, to bring about the reconciliation of L'Allegro and Il Penseroso. A reference in Jennens's letter of 4 February 1743 (*HHB*, p. 344) implies that Handel himself referred to Part 3 as 'Il Moderato'. I thank Anthony Hicks for drawing this to my attention. Jennens's scheme for Parts 1 and 2 originated from James Harris.

we may assume that a special instrument was available at Lincoln's Inn Fields. It seems certain that the organ, pedals and all, was in full view of the audience, because the initial musical flourish for the pedals could, from the technical point of view, just as well have been played with the left hand, and Handel presumably allocated it to the pedals so that he could be seen playing them. But the ensuing passacaglia movement contains a passage with some genuine three-stave writing, designated by Handel with the Bach-like formula 'Organo a 2 Clav e Pedale'.

L'Allegro was first performed, with the new organ concerto and two of the concerti grossi, on 27 February, by which time the advertisements were still commending the theatre's precautions against the cold. A programme of revivals followed the initial run of *L'Allegro*, with one performance each of *Saul*, *Esther* and *Israel in Egypt*: it seems remarkable that Handel should have gone to the trouble of rehearsing each work, and adapting the music to the current cast in each case, for single performances. The biblical works were performed in the fortnight before Good Friday: *Israel in Egypt* fell during Holy Week, and was accompanied in the newspapers by an appreciative essay reprinted from the previous year.[39] On 28 March Handel also performed *Acis and Galatea* and the Cecilian Ode for the benefit of the Decay'd Musicians: he had been a signatory to the fund's trust deed the previous August. The season concluded with a final performance of *L'Allegro* on 23 April: he had given 14 performances (including the charity night) in this all-English 'oratorio season'. The Prince of Wales had attended none of them, and he was a noticeable absentee from the subscription list for the op.6 concertos, which was headed by his brother and all his sisters. May 1740 brought Walsh's publication of a second selection of songs from *L'Allegro* (the first had appeared in March) and an ode in praise of Handel's music in *The Gentleman's Magazine*.[40] His works seem to have become an accepted topic for such literary exercises, but unfortunately, while they may be taken as indicators of his current cultural status, they tell us little about the performances of the music itself or the personality of the composer.

May 1740 also saw Handel's last association with music for a Royal wedding, that of Princess Mary to the Prince of Hesse-Cassel. The ceremony in the Chapel Royal on 8 May was rather unusual, in that it was one of espousal, or promise of marriage, rather than a wedding in the usual sense: indeed, it took place in the absence of the bridegroom. The wedding ceremony followed later, in Hesse, and the preceding London ceremony seems to have been the fulfilment of a diplomatic compromise: the prince would not come to London to be married, and the king would not allow his daughter to leave Britain unwed. It is perhaps not surprising, under the circumstances, that the ceremony hardly achieved

[39] *The London Daily Post* (April 1740): Deutsch, p. 497; *HHB*, p. 322.
[40] Deutsch, pp. 500–1; *HHB*, p. 322.

a high profile as an occasion for public rejoicing, and indeed the anthem that Handel supplied seems to have been a conflation of movements from his two earlier royal wedding anthems (HWV262–3). No score of it survives, and its form is known only from the text as printed in the newspapers.

Handel's activities during July and August 1740 are not known, but in late summer he visited the Continent. He was reported as passing through Haarlem in the Netherlands on 10/21 September:[41]

> The world-famous British Royal Capellmeister Mr. Hendel, when travelling through this town yesterday, took a close look at the newly-built, very elaborate, organ in the large church here; he heard the organist Rodecker [Radeker] play and afterwards himself played with great skill and artistry on this organ for half an hour, showing great pleasure in the beautiful sound and the good equipment of the organ. It is said that the above-mentioned Mr. Hendel has decided to travel to Berlin.

If he really went on to Berlin, Handel must have finished his business and returned speedily, for by 10 October he had completed, in London, a revised version of the score of his opera *Imeneo*, which he had left in limbo in 1738. It is conceivable that the visit to Haarlem was on his return journey from Germany. No further details of this expedition seem to be known: while he may have visited Hanover, Halle and possibly Berlin, it is equally possible that his travels took him no further than Holland, for a visit to his former pupil the Princess of Orange, with whom he may have maintained contact in the interim.[42]

That Handel devoted his time, on his return to London, to resurrecting his half-finished Italian opera from 1738 was a sure indication of the way things were shaping up for the next season. Once again Handel established himself at Lincoln's Inn Fields Theatre, but this time he was not planning another all-English oratorio season. The circumstances that pushed him back towards Italian opera were probably connected with the failure of Lord Middlesex's company to offer any programme in 1740–1: most importantly, this failure released the company's leading castrato Andreoni to Handel's employment, and Andreoni could not sing in English (the leading singers that were continued from Handel's previous company, Francesina and Reinhold, on the other hand, were bilingual). On completing *Imeneo*, Handel moved on to compose a second opera, *Deidamia*, to a libretto by Rolli,[43] beginning on 27 October 1740 and completing it

---

[41] The text, translated from a German newspaper report (Hamburg *Relations-Courier*, 27 September 1740, cited in Becker, 'Die frühe Hamburgische Tagespresse', p. 38) seems, apart from the last sentence, to have been derived from a Dutch newspaper report dating from 21 September (NS): see King, 'Handel's Travels', p. 374.

[42] See King, 'Handel's Travels'.

[43] The librettist appears on the original word-book as 'P.R. FRS.'; since Rolli had been elected a Fellow of the Royal Society in 1729, the identification seems correct. In subsequent seasons Rolli produced librettos for the 'Middlesex' opera company at the King's Theatre.

on 20 November. Although *Deidamia* includes a hunting-scene, both operas were probably staged with relatively modest resources. In addition to Francesina, Andreoni and Reinhold, Handel's cast for the season included William Savage (the treble soloist from the *Alcina* period, now a bass) and two sopranos – the English Miss Edwards and the Italian Signora Monza. Since Andreoni's register also lay in the soprano clef, Handel had an unusual group of voices for the season, with no fewer than four soprano-clef singers and two basses.

Handel's plan was to bring *Imeneo* on early in the season and to keep *Deidamia* for the new year: the rest of the programme would be of oratorio-type works, adapted to the needs of the bilingual cast. The first half of the season was all-Italian: a single performance of the serenata *Parnasso in festa* on 8 November, followed at a fair interval by *Imeneo* (beginning on 22 November), and then *Deidamia* beginning on 10 January 1741. The isolated performance of *Parnasso in festa* seems anomalous, and it interrupted the composition of *Deidamia*, which Handel broke off on 7 November at the end of Act 2 and resumed with the beginning of Act 3 a week later. There were only two performances of *Imeneo*, the second being on 13 December: a performance had also been planned for 29 November but was cancelled owing to the illness of Francesina, who had the leading female role.

Little is known of the audience's reaction to the new operas. One correspondent had been told, by someone who had attended the rehearsals, that *Imeneo* was 'very pretty'.[44] Monza was not included in the cast until *Deidamia* began, and she did not impress Mrs Pendarves.[45]

> Her voice is between Cuzzoni's and Strada's – strong, but not harsh, her person miserably bad, being very low, and excessively crooked. Donellan approves of her: she is not to sing on the stage till after Xmas, so I shall not lose her first performance.

The season proceeded in a leisurely way. There were three performances of *Deidamia*, on 7 January, 10 January, and 10 February 1741; between the last two Handel produced a version of *L'Allegro* adapted to his present cast. Bilingual versions of *Acis and Galatea* and *Saul* followed, the latter being the only performance in the fortnight before Easter. The season closed after Easter with a final single presentation of *L'Allegro*, accompanied by the short Cecilian Ode which apparently replaced the third part of *L'Allegro* ('Il Moderato'), on 8 April. 13 performances had been given, a comparable number to the previous season: the Prince of Wales had attended five of them.[46] In addition, *Parnasso in festa* was

[44] Letter from Mrs Donellan to Mrs Elizabeth Robinson, 15 November 1740: Deutsch, p. 507; *HHB*, p. 323.

[45] Letter to Mrs Dewes, 21 December 1740: Deutsch, p. 508; *HHB*, p. 324.

[46] Taylor, 'Handel and Frederick', p. 92. The performance of *L'Allegro* on 21 February was advertised as having been commanded by the Prince and Princess of Wales.

performed at the King's Theatre on 14 March for the benefit of the Fund for Decay'd Musicians, but it is not certain whether Handel had any direct involvement in the performance.

Handel's performance of *Deidamia* on 10 February 1741 is a biographical landmark: it was his last performance of an Italian opera in London.[47] It seems significant that the date coincided pretty well with the end of the 21-year span established in the charter of the Royal Academy of Music,[48] but there is no specific documentary evidence to illuminate the connection. It seems virtually certain that his last two seasons at Lincoln's Inn Fields had been managed by Handel himself, presumably renting the theatre from Rich on a nightly basis over an agreed period. The 1719 charter had empowered the Royal Academy to employ performers 'to Exercise and Act Operas And to Exhibit all other Entertainments of Musick within any house built or to be built where the same can be best fitted and rendred convenient and Suitable for the purposes aforesaid',[49] but in practice the Academy as an institution seems to have been specifically linked to the King's Theatre, Haymarket, which remained as the only patent theatre with a permanent licence for opera performances alone. That theatre had been dark since the end of the 1738–9 season, apart from the single charity performance of *Parnasso in festa* in March 1741, which was advertised as being 'With the Original Scenes and Habits' – a claim that was noticeably absent from Handel's performance of the same work at Lincoln's Inn Fields the previous November.[50] Such attempts as there had been in recent years to maintain an Academy-style patronage base for opera among the nobility had come not from Handel but from Lord Middlesex's initiatives. The silence of the documentary and financial record suggests that the king lost interest in opera performances after the queen's death, so the annual royal bounty to the Academy was no longer available, even as an asset that could be transferred to another company; after 1738 the Prince of Wales paid only for the performances he attended.[51] If the residue of years from the Academy's charter period affected Handel at all during 1739–41, it must have been only as a point of honour: he perhaps felt obliged to continue, so far as was possible and with whatever repertory seemed

[47] This performance was advertised for the Little Theatre in the Haymarket. It appears that Handel had for some reason to take his last ever London opera performance to a temporary venue in which he had never performed before; he continued for the rest of the season at Lincoln's Inn Fields.

[48] Strictly, the legal 21-year period expired in July 1740, but Handel might have interpreted the period as beginning from the first Academy season in April 1720.

[49] Milhous and Hume, 'The Charter for the Royal Academy of Music', p. 51

[50] The original scenery and costumes were presumably the property of the King's Theatre (or possibly of the Royal Academy), and so would not have been available for Handel's use at Lincoln's Inn Fields.

[51] His last £250 bounty payment was for the 1737–8 Haymarket season. In the 1740s the prince resumed regular opera support with bounties of £500 per year to the 'Middlesex' company. For his attendance at Handel's performances, the prince paid at the rate of 10 guineas per performance. See Taylor, 'Handel and Frederick', pp. 91–2.

most practical, to provide London with musical entertainments, though that was his profession in any case. Perhaps from time to time he was put under pressure from noble would-be opera patrons, to the effect that he still had some obligation as the Academy's house composer or 'Master of the Orchestra': such pressure may indeed explain Handel's participation in the King's Theatre season of 1737–8. There were signs in the following years that noble patrons were annoyed by Handel's refusal to serve as a matter of course in their new opera companies,[52] and he may well have considered himself entirely liberated from any obligations of that sort once the 1740–1 season had passed. In 1741–2 Handel showed his determination to sever himself from current operatic enterprises in London in the clearest possible way: soon after the new opera company opened at the King's Theatre in the autumn of 1741, Handel put himself beyond the reach of importunity by leaving London for a season in Dublin.

[52] See Taylor, 'Handel's Disengagement'.

10

The music, 1732–41

Operas

Such as are not acquainted with the personal character of Handel, will wonder at his seeming temerity, in continuing so long an opposition which tended but to impoverish him; but he was a man of a firm and intrepid spirit, no way a slave to the passion of avarice, and would have gone greater lengths than he did, rather than submit to those whom he had ever looked on as his inferiors: but though his ill success for a series of years had not affected his spirit, there is reason to believe that his genius was in some degree damped by it; for whereas of his earlier operas, that is to say, those composed by him between the years 1710 and 1728, the merits are so great, that few are able to say which is to be preferred; those composed after that period have so little to recommend them, that few would take them for the work of the same author. In the former class are Radamistus, Otho, Tamerlane, Rodelinda, Alexander, and Admetus, in either of which scarcely an indifferent air occurs; whereas in Parthenope, Porus, Sosarmes, Orlando, Aetius, Ariadne, and the rest down to 1736, it is a matter of some difficulty to find a good one.[1]

Modern revivals have proved Hawkins's judgment wrong: the operas of the 1730s work well on the stage, and even the most cursory examination of the scores gives the lie to the proposition that they are lacking in good arias.[2] It is true that in the 1730s Handel turned to new story-types and away from the old heroic love-and-duty mould: of the operas that Hawkins lists from the later period, only *Ezio* ('Aetius') is a classic example of Metastasian 'Roman' drama. *Partenope* is anti-heroic to the point of comedy, while *Orlando* is one of the masterpieces in the strain of 'magic' operas that Handel had essayed in London before the Academy period, in works such as *Rinaldo* and *Teseo*. It might reasonably be claimed, furthermore, that Hawkins ended his list in an unfortunate place, for with *Orlando* and *Arianna* Handel's creative powers were rising towards a new peak, reached in 1734–5 with *Ariodante* and *Alcina*. Whether this was perceived at the time is another matter: Hawkins's value judgments may be mirroring a set of critical opinions that were current in the mid-1730s,

[1] Hawkins, *A General History*, ii, 878.
[2] Compare Winton Dean's comment (*Handel and the Opera Seria*, p. 57) that *Siroe*, *Poro* and *Ezio* 'contain scarcely a dull aria'.

when internecine warfare between the opera companies was no doubt conducted partly by rumour. What people can be led to believe is true may be more influential than the truth itself.[3]

Comparison of the 1734–5 peak with that from a decade earlier, which had produced *Giulio Cesare*, *Tamerlano* and *Rodelinda*, dispels any notion of a simple causal relationship between commercial or social pressures and artistic quality. The fact that Handel achieved some of his best work in the mid-1730s was not a result of competition with the Nobility Opera, although the competitive situation certainly affected external features of the scores, such as the inclusion of dances and the shaping of arias for a castrato of different musical character from Senesino. A decade earlier, Handel's art had come to its full flowering only in the *absence* of competition: the great operas of the mid-1720s were the product of a situation in which Handel had a monopoly of creative opportunities in the theatre. By the time of *Tamerlano* and *Rodelinda*, Bononcini and Ariosti had departed from the scene. The competitive circumstances a decade later may have proved a distraction as much as a spur to his creative efforts. The explanation for this second peak lies more with the development of Handel's own technical invention and fluency as a com-poser – the causes of which are inscrutable – and perhaps also with some good working relationships established with his professional performing colleagues in the new company.

Orlando (1733) and *Arianna* (1734) deserve some consideration in their own right: while from the musical point of view they are rather less spectacular works than their successors, it seems curmudgeonly to withhold from them the term 'masterpiece', if such terms are to be used at all. Although *Orlando* has a fair number of da capo (and dal segno) arias, the overall impression is one of continuous dramatic flow to which shorter aria forms, *accompagnato* recitatives and ensembles (duets, trios) contribute substantially. The plot is derived from Ariosto's *Orlando furioso*, also the background source for *Ariodante* and *Alcina* a couple of years later. Like some of Handel's first London operas, *Orlando* features some spectacular scenic effects, this time involving transformations and supernatural visitations at the behest of the magician Zoroastro. This remarkable role, written for the bass Montagnana, was created by the anonymous adapter of the London libretto (whose immediate source was a libretto for a Roman opera by Domenico Scarlatti originally produced in 1711).

In the first scenes of Handel's opera, Orlando (originally played by Senesino) determines to follow Glory rather than Love, but he soon goes back on his resolve and attempts the hopeless pursuit of Angelica, a lady

---

[3] See the critical comments on *Ariodante* at the time of its first performances, reported by Queen Caroline and Princess Caroline in their letters to Princess Anne (letters of 14/25 January 1734/5, printed in King, 'Handel's Travels', pp. 384–5). It is today difficult to account for a description of *Ariodante* as 'pathetic and lugubrious'.

whose heart is given elsewhere. The consequent dissolution of Orlando's character reaches its climax with a 'mad scene' at the end of Act 2 in which Orlando imagines himself pursuing the lovers Angelica and Medoro to the Underworld. Following in the seventeenth-century tradition of such scenes, this *scena* is largely episodic, with a succession of short, apparently disconnected musical sections representing the disorder and lack of concentration in Orlando's mind. One remarkable episode includes brief passages in quintuple metre (Ex. 23), as Orlando imagines himself

Ex. 23

([In spite of Charon,] I am already cutting through the dark waters. Here are the fire-blackened shores of Pluto, and his burnt abode.)

approaching Pluto's kingdom. Hardly less telling is the recurring use of a simple gavotte-like melody (Ex. 24), which begins as just another episodic element but leads to more integrated musical material, though not to a full-blown aria: Orlando sings the gavotte-like theme only three times, but the effect is of obsessive recurrence, establishing an anchor-point in his battle for self-control. Violins and violas double the melody over a

Ex. 24

(Beautiful eyes, O do not weep.)

harmonic bass: a full orchestral harmonization comes only in the closing bars of the scene, as Zoroastro carries Orlando off to safety (according to the stage direction, 'the Magician, seated in his car, clasps Orlando in his arms and flies thro the air').

Indeed, Zoroastro's function throughout the opera is to protect the participants from the worst results of their actions: his emergency rescues involve a number of elaborate scene-changes, some of which must have been effected very quickly since Handel provides no instrumental sinfonias to cover them (a complex scene-change was also required near the beginning of the opera, when the original setting of a mountain on which Atlas supports the heavens is transformed into a tableau of the Palace of the God of Love). There is something paternalistic about Zoroastro's activities, and indeed the conclusion of the 'Argument' in the original word-book is unusually sententious in tone:

> The additional Fiction of the Shepherdess Dorinda's love for Medoro, and the constant Zeal of the Magician Zoroastro, for the Glory of Orlando, tends to demonstrate the imperious Manner in which Love insinuates its Impressions into the Hearts of People of all Ranks; and likewise how a wise Man should be ever ready with his best Endeavours to re-conduct into the Right Way, those who have been misguided from it by the Illusion of their Passions.

If the intention of the adapter had been to produce a dramatic sermon along these lines, or to persuade us that Orlando's problems would never have arisen if he had pursued his initial resolve to follow Glory (here apparently interpreted in terms of military heroism) rather than Love, then Handel's music subverts that intention: *Orlando* is in some ways a disturbing opera about the force of human passions and jealousies, whose influence Zoroastro is apparently powerless to prevent, though he can shield the characters from the worst consequences. A case has been made out for interpreting *Orlando* in terms of comic traditions in opera,[4] and

[4]Strohm, 'Comic Traditions in Handel's *Orlando*', in Strohm, *Essays on Handel*, pp. 249–67.

indeed there may be a comic interpretation of Dorinda's actions; but essentially Dorinda does not understand, or cannot accept, the force of Medoro's attraction to Angelica, which takes Medoro from her until the very end of the opera. As far as such musical signals can be read into such a stylized genre as the Ouverture, even the opening bars seem to suggest that serious subjects are to follow: the contours of the opening theme (Ex. 25*a*) resemble not only 'Amor, nel mio penar' from *Flavio* (Ex. 25*b*) but a number of related themes to penitential or supplicatory texts in Handel's earlier church music (Exx. 25*c–d*). Orlando was the last new role written by Handel for Senesino, who left for the rival Opera of the Nobility at the end of the season. Indeed, it has been suggested[5] that the opera may have contributed a last straw to the separation, if Senesino found the mad scene insufficient compensation for the normal complement of showy da capo arias.

It might be argued that in *Orlando* the arias are subservient to the greater needs of the dramatic plan, but the same cannot be said of *Arianna*, which, though it sports a strong plot and some lively scenes (including the slaying of the Minotaur), has by comparison an element of 'concert opera'. Of the six principals, only the bass (the role of Minos) might have complained of a lightweight part as regards arias; the most spectacular

Ex. 25
(*a*) *Orlando* Ouverture

(*b*) *Flavio*, HWV16/25 (1723)

(O Love, in my anguish, [tell me, may I hope to be content one day?])

[5]By Anthony Hicks, in his insert notes for the recording of *Orlando* conducted by Christopher Hogwood (1991).

Ex. 25(c)-(d)

(*d*) *Te Deum* in A HWV282/7 (*c.*1726)

arias were naturally those for the new principal castrato, Carestini. He apparently excelled particularly in energetic movements with well-articulated vocal lines accompanied by driving harmonic rhythms – the vocal equivalent, in fact, of the italianate violin concerto, and using similar decorative melodic figurations (Ex. 26). Such music needs good projection, accurate articulation and, above all, stamina. Perhaps stimulated by his new singers, Handel developed a new vein of tunefulness in his themes: the minuet from the end of the Ouverture achieved some independent popularity with the London public,[6] and many of the aria themes (e.g. 'Sdegnata sei con me', 'In mar tempestoso') are particularly attractive – shapely both in their initial contours and in their subsequent extensions. Even so, the melodies are not freestanding: their full effect relies partly on the harmonic and figural contexts supplied by the orchestral accompaniments.

Ariodante (1735) may be regarded as the apotheosis of the 'Carestini style': it has all the qualities of *Arianna,* with the addition of a better-paced and better-integrated drama. The basis of the story of *Ariodante* comes from Ariosto, and the action is set in Edinburgh: the local law against infidelity contributes to an outstanding plot (which had also been used by Shakespeare in *Much Ado about Nothing*) that focusses on human loves and jealousies. In the first scenes Ariodante and Ginevra (the King of Scotland's daughter) pledge their love for each other: the da capo of their duet is amusingly terminated by the sudden arrival of Ginevra's father (Ex. 27). Their momentary embarrassment is cleared when the king clearly approves the relationship, and Ariodante celebrates his joy in 'Con

---

[6] By 1740 the Minuet had already been published twice in song versions (to different sets of words), where it was described as a 'Favourite Air', 'Favourite Minuet' or 'Celebrated Air'.

Ex. 26

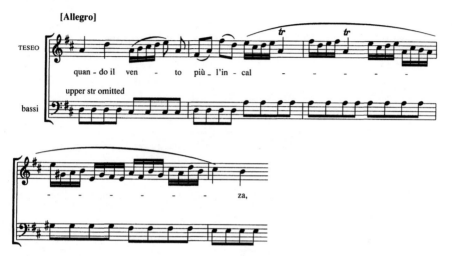

([The immovable oak tree] when the wind more furiously assails it, [gains extra strength and courage.])

Ex. 27

(Ginevra: I } from this hand receive...; Rè: Do not let me interrupt your mutual vows)
(Ariodante: You

l'ali di costanza', one of Carestini's grandest concerto-pieces (Ex. 28). This extends to more than 180 bars in all, with an *A* section running to 89 bars.[7] The excitement inherent in the material, and Handel's skill in extending it, produce an impressive aria in Handel's mature style, yet the formal plan is the same one as he was using nearly a quarter of a century previously, in the shorter arias of *Rinaldo*. The *A* section has a

Ex. 28

(With wings of constancy, Love upwards takes its flight:)

straightforward binary plan, with a central dominant cadence (followed by the usual orchestral ritornello), though this is arrived at via a complete second contrasted theme in the dominant (Ex. 29), which, were it not for the other associations of the term, could naturally be described as a second subject: it is even recapitulated in the tonic later in the *A* section, at bar 52, and is repeated in a variant form at bar 64.[8] Handel's autograph reveals that when he first began to compose the aria he used Ex. 29 as the main, opening subject, but later recomposed it into the new structure.

'Con l'ali di costanza' is matched in Act 2 by another big aria for Ariodante, but in a totally different mood. Ariodante believes that he has seen Ginevra attend an assignation with another man and reacts with anger at her supposed infidelity, in 'Scherza infida'. This is, in both time-scale and intensity, one of Handel's greatest arias. The mood is set by

---

[7] Bar-counts refer to the movement as composed: Handel subsequently shortened the aria.

[8] Handel's most interesting earlier use of a distinct 'second theme' comes in the trio at the end of Act 1 of *Orlando*, where Dorinda enters with distinctly different thematic material from the preceding duet for Angelica and Medoro: the 'Dorinda' theme then gradually takes over the initiative and dominates the *B* section. The tonal design of this trio is also unusual.

222

Ex. 29

([it makes] faith and hope triumph [in one's heart.])

muted upper strings and pizzicato basses, from the midst of which emerges a mournful cantilena for bassoons. Once the voice has entered, simple accompaniment figures in the orchestra sustain a background to long melodic arcs. Towards the end of the A section the return to the tonic (G minor) is accompanied by sinewy phrases and a careful deployment of chromatic harmony (including an augmented 6th chord) conveying Ariodante's anguish; the tonal palette of the B section is also adventurous, proceeding from E♭ major to D minor via F minor. Ariodante's main aria in Act 3, 'Dopo notte', comes at the resolution of the plot and appropriately returns to the joyous and powerful concerto manner of 'Con l'ali di costanza', but in triple time; its closing phrases (Ex.30) include a full exploitation of Carestini's two-octave range.

Ex. 30

([The sun, after the dark night,] fills the earth with joy.)

I have chosen to follow Carestini's role through *Ariodante*, but the music for Strada as Ginevra is far from negligible; she subsequently came into her own in *Alcina* (1735), as the queen whose power is gradually destroyed over the course of the three acts. Once again Ariosto provided the basis for the story and, in a return to an earlier style of plot, Alcina's power is expressed through enchantment: the principal visitors to her island are Bradamante, seeking to rescue her betrothed (the knight Ruggiero, with whom Alcina has fallen in love) and the youth Oberto, who is looking for his father (whom Alcina has transformed into a lion). The turning-point comes near the beginning of Act 2, when Ruggiero is given a magic ring that effectively breaks Alcina's power over him by exposing the harsh and barren reality that is disguised by her enchantments. Ruggiero comes to his senses and determines to escape from the island with Bradamante, though naturally he has to conceal his plans from Alcina. Towards the end of the act Ruggiero, regretting the dissolution of the island's apparent natural beauties that will follow on the destruction of Alcina's power, has a simple aria, 'Verdi Prati', that became one of Handel's best-known tunes (Ex.31). This lyrical moment forms the perfect foil for the following climactic scene, in which Alcina vainly exercises her powers in an attempt to keep Ruggiero. If 'Verdi prati' is in some ways a more mature successor to 'Lascia ch'io pianga' from *Rinaldo*, then Alcina's powerful *accompagnato* and aria that follows ('Ah! Ruggiero crudel ... Ombre pallide') is also a worthy descendant of Armida's scene at the end of Act 2 of the earlier opera.

No less impressive, in its own way, is Alcina's final aria in Act 3, 'Mi restano le lagrime', in which she recognizes that her power is broken. The cumulative phrases of the siciliana rhythm allow scarcely a break for orchestral ritornellos, as Alcina pours out her disappointment and frustration; and the aria is in complete contrast to her earlier, more concerto-like aria 'Ma quando tornerai'.

Carestini is said to have objected to the plainness of 'Verdi prati', but Handel well understood the dramatic power, in the right context, of straightforward lyrical music on a dance-rhythm foundation. Taken as a whole, *Alcina* is a remarkable showcase for a range of aria types, embracing a variety of moods and composed in Handel's most attractive 'middle-period' style: arias such as Ruggiero's 'La bocca vaga' show Handel at the height of his powers in combining tunefulness with lively musical-rhetorical construction. Carestini had little cause to complain: the score as a whole gave him plenty of opportunities to display his remarkable virtuosity, and indeed the other singers, who included the treble William Savage as Oberto, could hardly complain of short measure either. With the additional attractions of a chorus and a substantial contribution from Madame Sallé's dance troupe, it is not surprising that *Alcina* proved one of Handel's greatest box-office successes at Covent Garden.

Ex. 31

(Green meadows, pleasant woods, you will lose your beauty.)

The operas that followed *Alcina*, though not without some individual attractions, were uneven in quality, and it was not until *Serse* in 1738 that Handel achieved another well-balanced musical drama. *Serse* was not highly regarded by Burney,[9] and its return to the modern repertory may have been the result of the fortuitous popularity of the opening arietta, 'Ombra mai fù' (Ex.32), a pleasing lyrical larghetto which achieved some

[9]'Though it contains many pleasing and excellent compositions, it is by no means to be ranked with Handel's best dramatic productions' (*A General History*, ii, 823).

fame with later generations out of context as an instrumental piece entitled 'Handel's Largo'. But *Serse* deserves its relative popularity, and Burney's less-than-favourable opinion may merely reflect his own prejudices about the subject matter proper to an Italian opera. For here Handel turned away from the formalized, heroic tradition of *opera seria* towards a more ironic libretto. Admittedly, ironic elements had previously appeared in his operas – in *Partenope*, for example; but this time Handel made the break for good. His last gesture to the world of unambiguous *opera seria* was *Faramondo* (1738), to a libretto by Zeno. *Serse* is comic in its underlying situations, and includes one incontrovertibly comic character in the servant Elviro.

The ironic tone of *Serse* is apparent even in the preamble in the printed word-book, which seems to put out its tongue at the conventional 'Argument' that normally provided a libretto's historical and literary justification:

> The contexture of this Drama is so very easy, that it wou'd be troubling the reader to give him a long argument to explain it. Some imbecilities, and the temerity of Xerxes (such as his being deeply enamour'd with a plane tree, and the building a bridge over the Hellespont to unite Asia to Europe) are the basis of the story, the rest is fiction.

Presumably this paragraph was the work of the anonymous adapter of the libretto – perhaps one of the younger generation of *literati* associated with the Opera of the Nobility; it is impossible to know how far Handel chimed in with its spirit. For the most part, he did not write selfconsciously humorous music but left the humour to emerge from drama itself, as in the double dénouement in Act 3 when, as a result of a mistaken message, Serse's vassal Ariodate marries his daughter to the 'wrong' man and Serse is put in danger of execution, only to discover that his threatened executioner is his wife in disguise. Handel is generally content to provide arias in conventional forms, appropriate to the dramatic situations, but there are also scenes with more fluid structures, such as that at the beginning of Act 2, where Elviro's 'flower-selling' song punctuates the recitative.

The opening scene of *Serse* deserves brief attention, as an example of Handel's flexible musical response to the episodes of the libretto. In an accompanied recitative Serse, King of Persia, expresses the hope that fate will be kind to the plane tree in the middle of the garden: this is followed by a short, single-section aria (Ex.32) in which he luxuriates in the shade from the tree.[10]. Arsamene, Serse's brother, enters with his servant Elviro. Their dialogue is interrupted by a symphony of 'sweet musick' issuing from a summer-house which turns out to be the introduction to a song

---

[10] The praise lavished on the tree's qualities (based on a passage from Herodotus) indeed seems overdrawn; it obviously appeared so to the author of the introductory paragraph in the word-book, who was probably also the English translator of the libretto.

Ex. 32

(Never was the shade of any plant more dear, lovely and sweet.)

from Romilda, the daughter of one of Serse's vassals, who is in the summer-house; she sings about those 'who for cruel beauties sigh', citing Serse as an example. Hearing his name mentioned, Serse pays attention, only to hear the song continue to the effect that poor Serse is in love with a tree, which does not return his affection; the anti-climax comes with a change of key (at 'Un Serse mirate'; Ex.33), which is surely of humorous intent. The action then proceeds, punctuated by further short arias, as far as the first really heavyweight aria, Serse's 'Più che penso', which is well beyond the halfway point of the act. In many respects Handel's treatment follows that of Bononcini's opera on the same libretto,[11] but a comparison of the two confirms the greater expansiveness of Handel's musical language and his greater tonal adventurousness.

The operas that preceded *Serse* were a rather mixed bunch. *Atalanta*,

---

[11] First performed Rome, 1694; the libretto, by Nicolò Minato, was written originally for Cavalli (Venice, 1655). On Handel's indebtedness to Bononcini's score, see Powers, 'Il Serse transformato'. The score of Bononcini's setting is published in Roberts (ed.), *Handel Sources*, viii.

Ex. 33

(Romilda: [O ye, who for cruel beauties sigh,]
The loving Serse...
Serse: My name, I hear, is mentioned in this song.
Romilda: The loving Serse see,
[Who on a plane tree has fixed his eye,
Enamoured with a tree.])

produced in 1736 as a Covent Garden contribution to the festive season surrounding the marriage of the Prince of Wales, is a pastoral opera to the extent that the principals spend most of their time assuming conventional roles as shepherds and shepherdesses, but there is an ironic edge: the heroine, Atalanta, has declined an offer of marriage because acceptance would bring to an end her pleasure on the hunting-field, and Meleagro, King of Etolia, has to take the role of a shepherd in order to gain her interest. The opera is lighthearted and entertaining, and ends with a scene (originally enlivened by fireworks) in which Mercurio (Mercury) descends to bless the nuptial pair. The score is not without its technical difficulties: Conti had a remarkably high tessitura, and his music goes up to *c'''*. With

Arminio (1737) Handel returned to the old type of dynastic plot, with cross-currents of political and sexual motivation. There are some good arias for the leading men, Arminio and Sigismondo: the former spends much of the opera in chains, and his opening aria in Act 2, 'Duri lacci', has some of the pathos of the old Senesino days.

Handel's output for the Covent Garden season of 1736–7 included two more operas. *Giustino* has the usual extended arias (some of them featuring, as in *Arminio*, obbligato parts for the virtuoso oboe player Giuseppe Sammartini, but its real attraction lies in its fast-moving plot, matched by visual variety – no fewer than ten set-changes are called for. In a dream, the ploughboy Giustino is summoned from his lowly station by the goddess Fortuna (sung by a boy treble) and sent off to heroic deeds, which involve rescuing one lady from a bear and another from a sea-monster. *Berenice* (1737), on a political-dynastic plot, is in musical quality the most consistent opera of the group, and has an effective leavening of duets and *accompagnato* recitative. Even the conventional 'simile' arias ('Vedi l'ape' and 'Tortorella', concerning the bee and the turtle-dove, respectively) are sufficiently interesting to please us that this convention had survived the satirical references in the prologue to *The Beggar's Opera* a decade before. *Faramondo*, the companion-piece to *Serse* in Handel's contribution to the King's Theatre season of 1737–8, was his only opera to a libretto by Apostolo Zeno, Metastasio's predecessor in Vienna. It has some good musical moments but as a whole lacks dramatic cohesion: the libretto was cut and adapted almost to the point of incomprehensibility, and Faramondo appears to behave throughout with a reckless generosity that is scarcely credible.

The works from the tail-end of Handel's involvement with Italian opera are relatively modest, without the heroics or grand scale of the Royal Academy and Covent Garden works. Though scarcely chamber operas (*Deidamia*, for example, includes a hunting-scene), they nevertheless have a serenata-like quality, with relatively relaxed and slow-moving action. There must be some doubt as to the degree of spectacle that was attempted for them. The self-pasticcio *Jupiter in Argos* (1739), described as a 'Dramaticall Entertainment', may have been only semi-staged, and the Lincoln's Inn Fields Theatre, which saw Handel's last opera productions, may not have been equipped for elaborate scenic effects. *Imeneo* (1740) requires few, and *Deidamia* (1741), described in the libretto as a 'Melo-drama', may not have been played in an entirely realistic manner. Handel's treatment of the dramas hints at an ambiguity in his attitude towards *opera seria*. Like *Orlando*, *Deidamia* ends with the principal male character forsaking Love for Glory, but there is a doubt, even stronger than in the earlier opera, as to whether this is the most desirable outcome: Deidamia loses her lover Achilles to service in the Trojan War, where (as most of the audience would have remembered) he was to be killed. It would be wrong to expect Handel's last operas to display the same outlook as

Giulio Cesare or *Alcina*, just as it would be wrong to read Beethoven's last quartets from the standpoint of op.59. The comparison is not inappropriate: Handel's last operas are less direct, and less extrovert, than his earlier ones.

Imeneo provides a convenient exemplar for this period. The plot is simple. The leading lady, Rosmene, has to choose between two men, Tirinto and Imeneo: the choice is set up in Act 1 but is not resolved for another two acts. Compared with the normal multiplicity of incident in *opera seria*, decisive action is virtually suspended for much of the opera. This is partly attributable to the fact that the libretto was expanded from a two-act original: but presumably Handel's acceptance of the plan, and his musical treatment of it, indicate acquiescence in a dramatic mode that is at odds with the usual expectations of pacing. Still more significantly, Rosmene finally chooses the 'wrong' man, in terms of musical conventions: Imeneo, the successful suitor, is a baritone,[12] the rejected Tirinto a castrato. Tirinto's 'natural dominance' up to that point is established not only by his high tessitura but also by the grandiloquence of his music: arias such as 'Se potessero i sospir miei' and 'Sorge nell'alma mia'[13] are undoubtedly the musical property of an Italian opera company's *primo uomo*.

The dénouement of the drama, after all the waiting, is well managed. Rosmene decides to 'feign distraction; while, within collected, I act in Folly's Shew what Wisdom prompts'. Imeneo, then Tirinto, then both together, appeal to her to make a decision, using the same melody to express the extremity of their wishes ('Se la mia pace a me vuoi togliere'). Rosmene, assuming a trance-like state, enacts a scene in Hades where she appears before the judge Radamanto: he strikes her with his sword and her soul flies from her body. Appearing to faint, she is supported by the two men and from this position makes her choice in favour of Imeneo, providing assurances that she had not really been demented. The final *coro* – for an independent chorus instead of the more usual soloists' ensemble[14] – applauds the policy that the heart should follow the dictates of reason: presumably the castrato Tirinto was to be identified with the irrational.

'Sorge nell'alma mia', already noted as one of the opera's most striking arias, makes some gesture towards the musical style of a younger generation of opera composers, in particular the newer Neapolitan style as represented by Leonardo Vinci. Burney claimed that Vinci made music 'the friend, though not the slave, to poetry, by simplifying and polishing melody ... by disentangling it from fugue, complication and laboured

---

[12] First sung by William Savage, formerly the treble soloist in *Alcina*.

[13] Perversely, this aria was transferred to Imeneo in Handel's revival of the opera (as a serenata) in Dublin in 1742.

[14] At Covent Garden Handel seems to have employed additional chorus singers to join with the soloists; in *Imeneo*, however, the choral group appears to have been independent of the three principals.

Ex. 34

(a)

(A feeling is rising in my soul, just like a little cloud rising in the sky which then with thunder and lightning...)

(*b*)

(...goes on to shake both land and sea.)

contrivance',[15] phrases that might aptly describe the striding, chordal opening of Handel's aria (Ex.34*a*); moreover, there is a specifically 'modern' cadential figure at the midway close of the A section (Ex.34*b*). But, although Handel may have absorbed influences from Vinci, there was no question of his undertaking a thorough 'modernization' of his style. While the slow harmonic movement of this aria, elaborated by the busy string parts, certainly seems up-to-date, the movement as a whole falls into the established genre of the 'rage' aria, in which melodies that begin by outlining chords or triads are the norm. Ironically, in view of the fact that Tirinto's rival was sung by a bass, these tempestuous arias are often written for bass (e.g. Montagnana's 'Sorge infausta' in *Orlando*);[16] the obvious successor to 'Sorge nell'alma mia' is 'Why do the nations?' in *Messiah*, which is even in the same key. The string accompaniment and the vocal figurations in the *Imeneo* aria could, however, equally be regarded as precursors of the 'refiner's fire' in the famous setting in *Messiah* of 'But who may abide the day of his coming', composed as a revision for a castrato in 1750.

The truth seems to be that, when it came to matters of musical style,

[15] *A General History*, ii, 917.
[16] Bass arias sometimes brought out a contrapuntal streak in Handel: see, for example, 'Ti vedrò regnar' (*Riccardo Primo*), 'Se ti condanno' (*Arianna*) and 'Braccio si valoroso' (*Scipione*).

Handel did not feel that the latest composers such as Vinci had much to offer him. That does not mean that he had no interest in the newest operas from Italy: as noted in Chapter 8, Handel mounted operas by Vinci and Hasse in his own programme of 1733–4[17] and included Vinci's *Didone abbandonata* in 1737. Although these operas are sometimes referred to as pasticcios, they were securely constructed on the framework of the parent works by Vinci and Hasse.[18] In a different category come *Oreste* (1734) and *Alessandro Severo* (1735), complete operas constructed from pre-existing movements by Handel (with added recitatives) but on the basis of integral, pre-existing librettos of Italian origin. Their musical and dramatic coherence is a considerable tribute to the cunning of the anonymous libretto-arranger(s), who must have worked very closely with Handel.[19]

Oratorios and odes

Handel's English-language theatre works of the 1730s are clearly of momentous significance in relation to the subsequent development of his career and to the establishment of a new genre of English theatre oratorio. Their progress, however, was neither regular nor selfconscious: developments were stimulated or inhibited by the immediate needs and opportunities of particular theatre seasons. The 1732 versions of *Esther* and *Acis and Galatea* were inflated revivals of chamber-scale works written more than a decade earlier. Both lost some of their original dramatic coherence through their expansion to three acts, with extra material added to accommodate the demands of a larger cast, which included Italians; but the audiences, who had not known the works in their original forms, seem to have been satisfied with the variety and novelty of the result. As an artistic entity *Esther* probably fared better than *Acis and Galatea*, and the introduction of the coronation anthem choruses did no damage to its structure: the generalized sentiments of confidence in the Almighty (with the original texts adapted as necessary)[20] were appropriate enough to the circumstances of the drama. However, the introduction of extra choruses inevitably gave *Esther* a slower pace, a factor that clearly distinguishes Handel's theatre oratorios from his operas and incidentally presents one of the major practical difficulties in attempting to present the oratorios in staged performances for which they were never intended.

Slow dramatic pace is certainly a feature of Handel's first original theatre oratorio, *Deborah* (1733). Part 1 is devoted to anticipations of the Israelites' victory in the forthcoming conflict with the Canaanites: Deborah

[17] See also Strohm, *Essays on Handel*, pp. 182–3.
[18] This is specially true of *Caio Fabricio, Arbace, Didone, Lucio Papirio* and *Catone*: the origins of the 1720 pasticcios were more diverse.
[19] The construction of these works, and of *Jupiter in Argos*, can be followed in *HHB*, vol. iii (entries for HWV A[11], A[13] and A[14]). *Oreste* is published in *HHA* II/Sup.1.
[20] E.g. the opening movement of *Zadok the priest* became 'God is our hope'.

prophesies glory for the Israelite military leader Barak, while Jael, the wife of Heber the Kenite, is told that she will be 'divinely bless'd'. Part 2 sees a confrontation between Deborah and Sisera, the Canaanite leader, at which prospects of peace are dismissed. The battle itself is not depicted (it takes place between Parts 2 and 3), but in Part 3 Barak returns victorious, and Jael reports how she 'rivetted the Tyrant [Sisera] to the Ground'. The libretto is by Samuel Humphreys, who had provided the 'Additional Words' for the 1732 theatre version of *Esther*: he also supplied the English texts in the printed opera librettos of the period, from *Poro* to *Orlando*. A quite close collaboration between librettist and composer may be assumed. The score contains much self-borrowed music from earlier works, and Humphreys may well have moulded his choice of verse-forms to the metres of the music that Handel intended to re-use: unlike the opera arias that Handel re-used in *Oreste* and *Alessandro Severo*, however, many of the borrowed numbers in *Deborah* were largely recomposed to fit their new situations. No doubt Handel's compositional procedures were affected by the fact that *Deborah* was written in the midst of a busy opera season: in the end, he hardly saved himself much work by self-borrowing, but the arrangement probably enabled him to work at the score in odd moments, as gaps in his other commitments allowed. Furthermore, his labour was shared with assistants in those movements that required little adaptation: Handel's 'autograph' of *Deborah*[21] includes substantial sections laid out by two music copyists.

Following the formula that had been successful in *Esther*, Handel introduced more movements from the coronation anthems into *Deborah*. But he also showed himself able to match their grandeur with new choruses (some of which used thematic ideas from earlier works). The chorus that opens Part 2 (partly based on ideas from *Dixit Dominus*, composed a quarter of a century earlier) is particularly fine, though in the size of its musical canvas it is outdone by the opening chorus of Part 1[22] and by the double-choir alternations between the supporters of Jehovah and Baal in Part 2 ('All your boast'). Best of all, perhaps, is 'Lord of Eternity', a chorus in more serious vein as the Israelites implore divine assistance. Although the arias are workmanlike, the choruses admittedly put them in the shade. In one curious mis-match of words and music, Barak's vision of the slaughter that will result from the expected battle ('In the battle, fame pursuing') is set as a major-key, dance-like movement in triple rhythm, accompanied by a virtuoso obbligato part for organ: the music's character seems too lighthearted and might have accorded better with a pastoral text. Perhaps Handel simply went for a tune that would carry the words. We may similarly be misguided if we try to make too

[21] British Library RM 20.h.2.

[22] It is unclear what music, if any, was originally used for the overture to *Deborah*: the introduction to the first chorus may conceivably have been the work's only instrumental prelude.

much of a connection between Humphreys's portrayal of Deborah and his dedication of the libretto to the Queen. The choice of subject for the oratorio may have been stimulated by the fact that Maurice Greene had written an oratorio on the subject of Deborah in 1732.

Humphreys was also the librettist for Handel's next oratorio, *Athalia* (1733), which again centres on one of the formidable ladies of the Old Testament, cast here as an opponent to the forces of true religion. As a dramatic piece *Athalia* came out much better than *Deborah*, no doubt largely because Humphreys was working from a stage model (a play by Racine) instead of directly from the Scriptures. Some of the important motivations behind the opening dramatic situation are obscure: Humphreys's libretto never explains that Athalia has killed all the royal house apart from the young boy Joas, nor does it explain why Mathan the Baalite priest is an 'apostate'. But thereafter the general internal outlines are clear. The High Priest Joad and his wife Josabeth have sheltered Joas, in the face of Queen Athalia's tyranny: in Part 3 Joas's true identity is revealed and he is enthroned, whereupon Athalia's commander-in-chief Abner deserts her, and Mathan acknowledges that Jehovah has triumphed over Baal. Joad had prophesied Athalia's death at the beginning of Part 3, but she maintains defiance to the end; her final fortunes and those of Mathan are not portrayed.

Athalia achieves a rather better balance of solos and choruses than *Deborah*. Handel's departure from operatic practice is signalled by the low proportion of da capo arias (six out of 16), but the characters are lively and well-differentiated and are manifestly the fruit of his operatic experience. The arias at the start of Part 2, in particular, have characteristic motto phrases and might be described as musical pictures from an operatic gallery – 'Through the land so lovely blooming' (Josabeth), 'Ah, canst thou but prove me' (Abner), 'Will God whose mercies ever flow' (Joas) and 'My vengeance awakes me' (Athalia). There is also an extended operatic *scena* in Part 1, as Athalia, 'starting out of slumber', describes the visions she has seen: first her mother, who warned her of Joad's forthcoming vengeance ('Oh, Athalia, tremble at thy fate'), and then a youth in the robes of a Jewish priest, who plunged a dagger into her breast. These visions explain the force of her reaction when she sees Joas in Part 2, though his true identity is not yet revealed to her. Perhaps the most remarkable feature of Athalia's *scena* is the dramatic integration of two choruses ('The Gods, who chosen blessings shed' and 'Cheer her, O Baal'), which intensify rather than impede the action. Such a technique is in fact the greatest advance in *Athalia*. Sometimes it extends to physical integration within a solo movement, as when the chorus completes Joad's aria 'Jerusalem, thou shalt no more'; but mainly the relationship is less direct, the chorus commenting on or participating in the action in independent movements which are more than mere ornamental additions to the structure. Handel had used up all his transferable coronation anthem music by the time of *Athalia*, but that alone does not explain the change in the chorus's dramatic function, for he could perfectly well compose in the 'coronation anthem style' when occasion demanded, as he did in the opening of Part 2 and (most directly) in 'Around let acclamations spring' at the recognition of Joas.

Athalia, written for Oxford, has been described as 'the first great English oratorio',[23] and not without justification. Yet in some ways it is a lightweight work, weightier than the chamber-scale Cannons version of *Esther* (which might, on its own terms, have an equal claim to the title) but not of the larger-scale proportions demanded by Handel's London theatre audiences. For Oxford, Handel composed a compact work, and part of its charm lies in its status as a smaller sibling of the larger oratorios. *Athalia* nevertheless marks both the climax and the conclusion of Handel's first period of intense experimentation with English public oratorio. The experience gained was not applied directly to further oratorios but to the more literary genre of the English ode: experience with the ode, in its turn, contributed to enriching Handel's subsequent return to oratorio.

Handel's interest in setting English odes for inclusion in his theatre seasons – works of a quite different kind and purpose from the ode for Queen Anne's birthday composed nearly 25 years earlier – seems to have been the consequence of two factors: the opportunities (and limitations) provided by the circumstances of his short season in 1736; and the influence of a new literary collaborator, Newburgh Hamilton. Hamilton seems to have become a personal friend as well as a colleague.[24] We do not know whether the idea of setting Dryden's longer Cecilian Ode, *Alexander's Feast*, arose from their social contact, or whether the friendship ripened as a result of their successful collaboration. *Alexander's Feast* was a poem that had originally been intended for musical setting: Dryden had written it for the Cecilian celebrations in 1697, when it had been set by Jeremiah Clarke, and it was set again (with textual revisions) by Thomas Clayton in 1711 (the music for both settings is lost). Hamilton's preface to the printed word-book for the first performances of Handel's *Alexander's Feast* in 1736 reveals, under the conventionally inflated language, his own professional stance as a librettist-collaborator:

> The following ODE being universally allow'd to be the most excellent of its Kind, (at least in our Language;) all Admirers of polite Amusements, have with Impatience expected its Appearing in a Musical Dress, equal to the Subject.
> But the late Improvements in Musick varying so much from that Turn of Composition, for which this Poem was originally design'd, most People despair'd

[23] Dean, *Handel's Dramatic Oratorios*, p. 247.
[24] Handel bequeathed £100 to Hamilton in the first (1756) codicil to his will; see also Loewenthal, 'Handel and Newburgh Hamilton'.

of ever seeing that Affair properly accomplish'd: The Alteration in the Words, (necessary to render them fit to receive modern Composition) being thought scarcely practicable, without breaking in upon that Flow of Spirit which runs thro' the whole of the Poem, which of Consequence wou'd be render'd flat and insipid. I was long of this Opinion, not only from a Diffidence of my own Capacity, but the ill Success of some ingenious Gentlemen, whose Alterations of, or Additions to the Original, prov'd equally ill-judg'd. But upon a more particular Review of the Ode, these seeming Difficulties vanish'd; tho' I was determin'd not to take any unwarrantable Liberty with that Poem, which has so long done Honour to the Nation; and which no Man can add to, or abridge, in any thing material, without injuring it: I therefore confin'd myself to a plain Division of it into *Airs, Recitative,* or *Chorus's*; looking upon the Words in general so sacred, as scarcely to violate one in the Order of its first Place: How I have succeeded, the World is to judge; and whether I have preserv'd that beautiful Description of the Passions, so exquisitely drawn, at the same time I strove to reduce them to the present Taste in Sounds.

I confess my principal View was, not to lose this favourable Opportunity of its being set to Musick by that great Master, who has with Pleasure undertaken the Task, and who only is capable of doing it Justice; whose Compositions have long shewn, that they can conquer even the most obstinate Partiality, and inspire Life into the most senseless Words.

Musical style had indeed moved on along very different lines since 1697, but Dryden's poem was successfully moulded by Hamilton into a structure that provided for the extensive arias and choruses fundamental to Handel's new English 'oratorio' genre. It is not quite true that Hamilton did not 'add to' Dryden's poem, for he included a few lines from a Cecilian ode of his own, *The Power of Music*, which had been written for Robert Woodcock to set to music in 1720; the extraneous material was not inserted into the ode itself but was added as a kind of postscript. This was all in the cause of trying to expand the two-part piece generated by Dryden's poem into a full evening's entertainment. The Italian cantata *Cecilia, volgi un sguardo* (HWV89) and the substantial concerto (HWV318) that were inserted into the interval between the parts served the same end. Also from Hamilton's 1720 ode came the text for the sequence of accompanied recitative and aria *Look down, harmonious Saint* (HWV124), which was almost certainly originally intended for inclusion in *Alexander's Feast* but was never performed: the aria was subsumed into *Cecilia, volgi*.[25]

If the literary quality of Dryden's verse is one of the points in favour of *Alexander's Feast* it is also one of the major drawbacks. Many allusions in the text are not fully explained (it is not clear, for example, that Alexander himself was reputedly the fruit of the union between Jove, in a 'Dragon's fiery form', and Olympias, called 'Olympia' in the poem); indeed, from the information provided it is difficult to understand the

[25]See Chapter 8, n. 58.

story and, specifically, the motive for Alexander's burning of Persepolis. As a narrative drama *Alexander's Feast* would fail more miserably than any of Humphreys's librettos (which were perhaps the butt of Hamilton's phrase about Handel having set 'senseless words'); but perhaps the conventions of the ode as a literary genre carried an accepted assumption of greater background knowledge on the part of the audience. *Alexander's Feast* proved, however, to be an ideal vehicle for the development of Handel's musical strengths in 1736. Part 1 is mainly taken up with the portrayal of various states of mind – induced (according to the story) by the power of Timotheus's lyre playing to conjure up emotions in his listeners – in a pageant of fine, well-characterized arias and related choruses. The section exploring the 'pathetic' emotions ('He sung Darius great and good') underwent an interesting evolution. It originally began with a fairly conventional dal segno aria for soprano, but Handel gradually cut away and tightened up its structure to retain a modest *A* section, running into a *B* section in the relative minor ('Deserted at his utmost need'), followed directly by an accompanied recitative with a suitably colourful chromatic ending (Ex.35); the section was then rounded off with a chorus in the original tonic based on the thematic material of the *A* section. The organization of Part 1, in its final form, was along the lines of a progressive growth in formal structures, culminating in two da capo/dal segno arias: the last one is framed by an extended chorus and its repetition, producing a ternary-within-ternary structure.[26]

The sequence of emotions depicted in Part 1 had omitted an obvious one – the rousing trumpet-and-drum call to arms; this opens Part 2, summoning Alexander to action. The aria 'Revenge, Timotheus cries' has become one of the best-known movements in *Alexander's Feast*: its most striking feature is the *B* section,[27] scored for divided strings and bassoons, representing the ghosts from the battlefield who call Alexander to the act of revenge. The burning of Persepolis follows, in which Alexander is encouraged by the Grecian princes and led by the courtesan Thais, after which the ode withdraws from narrative to commentary. An accompanied recitative makes the transition from the barbarity of the preceding action – the result of the power of music in a barbarous age – to the more uplifting effect of Cecilia's loftier music:

> *Accompagnato:*
> Thus, long ago,
> Ere heaving bellows learn'd to blow,

[26] At one stage Handel also planned to repeat the chorus 'The list'ning crowd' after the aria 'With ravish'd ears', but this plan never came to performance: he probably judged, rightly so, that it would have robbed the 'chorus-sandwich' at the end of Part 1 of its effect. See Burrows, 'The Composition and First Performance'.

[27] For revivals after 1739 Handel altered the form of the movement, eliding the da capo. After 1742 he also divided the music between the voices, giving the *B* section to an alto. See Burrows, 'Handel and "Alexander's Feast"', and Preface to Handel (ed. Burrows), *Alexander's Feast*.

Ex. 35

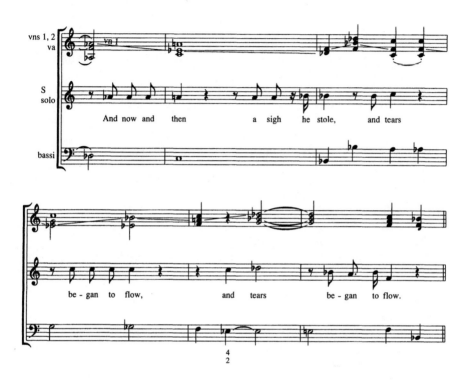

> While organs yet were mute;
> Timotheus, to his breathing flute,
>   And sounding lyre,
> Could swell the soul to rage, or kindle soft desire.
>
> *Chorus:*
>   At last divine Cecilia came,
>   Inventress of the vocal frame;
> The sweet enthusiast, from her sacred store,
>   Enlarg'd the former narrow bounds,
>   And added length to solemn sounds,
> With nature's mother-wit, and arts unknown before.

The lines beginning 'At last divine Cecilia came' drew from Handel the work's most powerful chorus – a prelude and fugue in a declamatory style that hovers between seriousness and celebration. The mood of celebration then prevails to the end of the work.

Alexander's Feast gave Handel the opportunity to portray emotional states in music, not only momentarily but also as sustained moods extending through sequences of movements. The ability to do this – always among Handel's compositional strengths – may be seen in many scene-setting episodes that open acts in his operas. In opera, however, the music serves to reinforce or complement the visual representation; in the non-staged oratorio-type works, the music has actually to substitute for the visual dimension, leaving the listener's imagination to conjure up a situation or emotion, with the help of (at most) a scenic cue in a printed word-book. Handel's success in bringing to life the emotional states described in *Alexander's Feast* was therefore a crucial step in the establishment of the musical procedures that were to crown his greatest oratorios.

In 1739, three years after composing *Alexander's Feast*, Handel produced a shorter companion work, setting Dryden's Cecilian Ode of 1687, the *Song for St Cecilia's Day* (HWV76),[28] which had originally been set by Giovanni Draghi. The shorter ode is in many ways more accessible than *Alexander's Feast*, because the 'plot' is couched directly in terms of the emotions roused by particular musical instruments. The trumpet doubles as the harbinger of war and (more spectacularly) of the Day of Judgment, but the most haunting music is associated with the softer instruments, in 'What passion cannot Music raise and quell', 'The soft complaining flute' and 'But oh! what art can teach'. There is a fine opening chorus, in which melodic ideas derived from Gottlieb Muffat are put to good use for Dryden's phrase 'through all the compass of the notes it ran'. The extended proportions of the final chorus, 'The dead shall live, the living die', may have been prompted by an extra-musical motive, since the autograph suggests that Handel for some reason deliberately set himself to write a movement of exactly 150 bars.[29] Whether Handel knew Purcell's ode *Hail, bright Cecilia* of 1692 is not known, but there are points of relevant comparison: the opening sequence of Handel's ode, depicting the creation of Harmony from the 'jarring atoms', is of comparable power and novelty to Purcell's treatment of the subject in the chorus 'Soul of the world' in the 1692 ode.

The climax of Handel's artistic association with the works of England's major poets came with *L'Allegro, il Penseroso ed il Moderato* of 1740. As with *Alexander's Feast*, Handel set the poetry in a form that had already been adapted for him by James Harris and Charles Jennens. Milton's two companion odes, *L'Allegro* and *Il Penseroso*,

---

[28] Handel copied Dryden's title at the top of his autograph: the work is now often referred to as Handel's *Ode for St Cecilia's Day* or 'From harmony, from heavn'ly harmony', the first line of its text.

[29] Handel reckoned the final 'double-length' bar as only one bar in his computation. He had to insert a section into the chorus to achieve his aim, and marked the 100-bar landmark at the end of the insertion. Elsewhere Handel's bar-counts (which are only sporadic) merely record occasional total movement lengths.

were interwoven producing a sequence of contrasting moods and images. In the libretto the contrasts alternate somewhat dizzily, but the scheme works for a musical setting in which each image is sustained for a few minutes, at least for the duration of an aria. There is thus time to accommodate each contrast: indeed, if Handel had set Milton's odes as integral units, with a complete act for each 'character', the work would surely have been indigestible in the theatre. The episodic progression of picturesque movements brought out the best in Handel: there are small-scale, momentary pleasures in the sounds of the hunting-horn, the merry bells, the cricket and the bell-man, as well as a picture gallery of successive contrasting arias, describing diverse scenes both pastoral ('Let me wander, not unseen') and urban ('Populous cities please me then'). The music of the arias is nicely varied, ranging between the concerto-like 'Sweet bird' and the introspective 'Hide me from day's garish eye'. The chorus movements, though not as extensive as in other works (perhaps reflecting the circumstances at Lincoln's Inn Fields), also contribute memorable pictorial touches – laughter holding his sides, old and young creeping off to bed at dusk and, perhaps in a direct line of descent from the shorter Cecilian ode, the sonorous chords of the 'pealing organ'.

One aspect of *L'Allegro* is controversial and, from Jennens's own testimony, seems to have been so regarded as soon as the work was performed: the addition of Jennens's own text to follow Milton's as Part 3. Jennens's letter on the subject[30] indicates that the addition of 'Il Moderato' was Handel's idea, designed to unite the 'two independent Poems in one Moral Design'. After relating contemporary criticisms of 'Il Moderato', Jennens goes on:

> But the Opinion of many others, who signify'd their approbation of it in Print as well as in Conversation, together with the account M^r. Handel sends me of it's Reception in Ireland, have made me ample amends for these random expressions of Contempt.

There is indeed something of a mismatch between Jennens's work and Milton's, both in diction ('rising reason puts to right/the fumes that did the mind involve', for example, sounds almost like a parody of Milton)[31] and in content: 'Il Moderato' presents argument – indeed, assertion – rather than images, and pours cold water over some of the scenes depicted with so much warmth in the preceding parts. Yet one can see Handel's point: the alternation of 'Allegro' and 'Penseroso' could not continue for ever, and, without some other mediation, the natural conclusion would

---

[30] Letter to Edward Holdsworth of 4 February 1742 (partly quoted in *HHB*, p. 344).

[31] I am indebted to Anthony Hicks for pointing out that these lines are in fact a parody of Shakespeare (*The Tempest*, Act 5, ll. 64–8).

leave one a winner.[32] Such a conclusion would have undercut the point of the alternation, which brought out the complementary existence of the moods in human experience. It would probably have been difficult even for Milton himself to have made the 'middle way' as attractive as the polar extremes of mood on either side; all in all, Jennens did not make a bad job of his brief. It seems likely that Handel himself was in favour of the virtues of 'Moderation', which had generated the political and cultural stability that had allowed him to flourish as a professional musician, but his music for 'Il Moderato', though worthy, seems less animated than that for the other two parts. One splendid exception, however, is the duet 'As steals the morn upon the night', which must count among the half-dozen greatest single movements that he composed, combining mastery of orchestral texture, lyrical expressiveness and skill in melodic extension with harmonic control. The duet clearly belongs in its proper context and, since the third part is fairly short, there is every reason for modern revivals of *L'Allegro* to give the work in Handel's complete, three-part 'Moral Design'. In Handel's original performing version of *L'Allegro* a considerable load fell onto the soprano soloist: the distinction between the conventions of an ode and a drama is apparent from the fact that Francesina was given arias in both the 'Allegro' and 'Penseroso' roles in the 1741 revival. In the original 1740 version, she had all the 'Penseroso' arias, and the 'Allegro' music was divided between three other soloists. At a subsequent revival in 1743, when Handel had a contralto soloist available, much of the 'Penseroso' music went to the darker-toned voice, with some gain in distinctive characterization, but by then he had also dropped 'Il Moderato'.[33] On balance, Handel's original version is still probably the best.

Two years before the composition of *L'Allegro*, the first collaboration between Handel and Jennens had marked an artistic turning-point in the development of Handel's oratorios. *Saul*, composed in 1738, was the first oratorio that realized the full potential of Handel's talents, combining opportunities for extended arias and choruses with a coherent dramatic framework and a strength of character portrayal that allowed Handel to draw fully on his operatic experience. It was arguably the first oratorio that Handel developed from first principles, in collaboration with his librettist, to suit the particular circumstances of London theatre oratorio and the particular combination of talents that Handel brought to the genre. *Esther* and *Acis and Galatea* had been re-workings of scores that

---

[32] In 1743 Handel produced a rescension without 'Il Moderato', in which 'Allegro' had the last word.

[33] As explained below, in Chapter 11, it is doubtful that Mrs Cibber performed in *L'Allegro* under Handel in Dublin, so the music that he wrote for her must relate to the 1743 London version; the form of that version can be reconstructed hypothetically from pencilled cues in his autograph. No word-book from 1743 has survived, but a similar text was printed in 1754.

originally composed for performance in different circumstances. *Deborah* was a rather hurried attempt to repeat what appeared to have been some of the popular features of the theatre *Esther*, seen in the incorporation of substantial slabs from Handel's coronation anthems, while *Athalia*, successful as it turned out to be from the artistic point of view, had (like *Esther*) a dramatic model from Racine. *Saul* represented a new start: Jennens had as a guide only his literary sources (principally the English Bible), his own dramatic imagination and his vision of how the resources of Handelian theatre oratorio might be put to good use. At the time of its composition Handel also took advantage of current circumstances: a lull in operatic productions, following Heidegger's failure to raise a subscription, which released a large cast (though a home-grown one, without a preponderance of Italian stars) and the opportunity to employ a large and varied orchestra, including exotic and unusual elements such as the carillon and large military timpani. *Saul* received Handel's full attention and was conceived on the grandest scale in every sense, with large, fully rounded characters and extensive forces.

In *Saul*, more than in any previous work, Handel used the instrumentation for dramatic ends. The carillon, which, it may be remembered, Jennens said was intended to 'make poor Saul stark mad', certainly adds a final gloss to the frenetic popular celebration in Part 1 that greets the return of David after his victory over the Philistines and thus intensifies Saul's jealousy. The supernatural events of Part 3 when Saul visits the Witch of Endor are portrayed with woodwind colouring that builds on the experience of 'Behold, a ghastly band' in *Alexander's Feast*: the Witch's invocation of Samuel is effected against a background of chords from oboes and bassoons (Ex. 36), while bassoons introduce the ghost of Samuel himself ('Why hast thou forc'd me from these realms of peace?'). The famous 'Dead March' alternates flutes, timpani and organ bass with a solemn *tutti* heavily coloured by trombone chords. A still heavier trombone-weighted *tutti* characterizes the Sinfonia that introduces Saul's decision 'at the Feast of the New Moon' that David shall die.

Saul has the clearest tonal organization of all Handel's oratorios. While others might work towards D major for a trumpet-and-drum climax, Handel here uses C major as an anchorage to which the music returns at strategic moments and in which it begins and ends.[34] The trumpets have to conform to the C major centre: the only D major chorus, the sinewy 'O fatal consequence of rage', is in any case too tortured, both in harmony and in emotional content, to admit them. David's harp-playing provides an obvious musical cue, though Handel did not take it up as directly as he had done in *Esther*: the harp has no obbligato part in David's 'O Lord,

---

[34] The participation of trombones may have influenced Handel in his choice of C major as the tonal reference-point: he also used C major for most of the large choruses with trombones in *Israel in Egypt*.

Ex. 36

whose mercies numberless', but Handel followed the air with a harp solo that repeats the same music in an elaborated form. Pictorialism is reserved for briefer gestures, such as the conclusion of the subsequent aria (Ex. 37), when David has manifestly failed to divert Saul's rage (Handel had used similar scale-gestures 30 years earlier, to represent the 'arrows in the hand of the powerful', in his psalm setting *Nisi Dominus*).

Jennens's libretto afforded Handel many such opportunities to exercise his musico-pictorial genius. In context, these devices are not gimmicks but enhancements of the plot and of the characterization. Saul's jealousy is established early on, and thereafter Handel and Jennens together created a vivid picture of his apparently uncontrollable decline. David's character

Ex. 37

is strengthened as the oratorio proceeds, and it is he that leads the moving final elegy on the death of Saul and Jonathan. The three-way relationships of Saul, David and Jonathan, and of David, Merab and Michal, are skilfully portrayed: so well-matched in weight are these roles that a performance of *Saul* requires a cast as evenly competent as that for which Handel composed it. Handel poured into the work his mature experience as an aria composer and applied all the lessons he had learnt in his earlier English works about integrating the chorus. There is scarcely a weak choral movement, dramatically or musically, in *Saul*: the role of the chorus alternates effectively and clearly between commentary (as in the opening chorus of Part 2) and active participation (as in the final choruses of Parts 1 and 3).

Soon after Handel had made his first composition draft of the score, Jennens complained about 'a Hallelujah which he [Handel] has trump'd up at the end of his oratorio':[35] in fact, Handel subsequently moved the

---

[35] Letter of 19 September 1738 (quoted in Chapter 9).

offending movement to the end of the first scene of Part 1, where Jennens had specified a Hallelujah in the libretto. Perhaps this slightly disturbs the structural balance, closing the first scene emphatically just as the action needs to get going, but we can scarcely complain about the oratorio's conclusion as it now stands: the final chorus has the Israelites united behind David's leadership, confident again after the traumatic events they have witnessed. The transference of the Hallelujah is only one example of the influence that Jennens exerted over the development of the score, between the completion of Handel's first composition draft and the form in which it came to performance. It is clear from the evidence of Handel's autograph (which contains several amendments and annotations in Jennens's hand) that composer and librettist went carefully through the score of *Saul* together in September 1738: in the end, Handel probably accepted some of Jennens's suggestions and rejected others.[36] While some of Handel's ideas may have been inhibited by Jennens's influence, on the whole the final result gained much by this close scrutiny and revision, with Handel and Jennens acting upon each other as reciprocal artistic stimulants.

One of the major changes made to *Saul* after Handel's conference with Jennens concerned the final Elegy. Handel's autograph shows that he originally intended to re-use music from the *Funeral Anthem for Queen Caroline*, composed the previous December: that plan had presumably received provisional acquiescence from Jennens, since Handel continued with Jennens's text for the subsequent movements, adding his own Hallelujah on the end. But Jennens came up with a new text for the Elegy, the setting of which formed one of Handel's principal tasks when he re-drafted the score, a task he completed on 27 September 1738. The ejected Funeral Anthem music did not go to waste, however, and indeed the idea for *Israel in Egypt* as a companion oratorio to *Saul*, using this music, may have been evolved during this same meeting with Jennens. The identity of the librettist of *Israel in Egypt* is unknown, but circumstantial evidence points to Jennens: the words are mainly taken directly from the Bible, and in a later letter Jennens implied that *Messiah* was the second 'Scripture Collection' that he had supplied to the composer.[37]

Both the concept and the scheme of *Israel in Egypt* were novel. The concept was fundamentally that of a choral oratorio that was to include solo movements, although the main narrative and expressive content were to be carried by the chorus. Variety was to be introduced not only through the usual contrasts of fugal movements with choral homophony but also by the occasional division of the chorus into antiphonal 'double choirs'. The scheme of the oratorio was probably generated by the pre-existence

[36] See Hicks, 'Handel, Jennens and "Saul"'.
[37] Letter of 10 July 1741: *HHB*, p. 334.

of the Funeral Anthem, which was entirely choral and, necessarily, sombre in tone. It was about an acceptable length for the first part of an oratorio, and it could be balanced in Part 3 by something of similar length but of a cheerful or triumphal character, rather in the manner of an extended coronation anthem. The progression between the two 'anthem' parts required, as Part 2, some form of linking narrative. The liberation of the Israelites from captivity in Egypt and the crossing of the Red Sea provided a story that was suitable for narrative treatment, and the Funeral Anthem, with an adapted text, became 'The Lamentation of the Israelites for the Death of Joseph'.

Such a reconstruction of the evolution of *Israel in Egypt*, though admittedly hypothetical, fits the known facts. On 1 October 1738, four days after finishing the re-draft of *Saul*, Handel began to write the music, under the heading 'Moses' Song. Exodus Chapter 15. Introitus', on 20-stave manuscript paper suitable for large choral movements. It seems entirely plausible that since their meeting Jennens had quickly mapped out the text of this 'anthem' for Part 3 of *Israel in Egypt* which Handel composed first, while his librettist was putting Part 2 together. (References here are to the three-part oratorio as Handel performed it: when *Israel in Egypt* was subsequently published without the 'Funeral Anthem' as Part 1, Handel's Parts 2 and 3 became known as Parts 1 and 2, respectively.) As in *Saul*, Handel availed himself of ample orchestral resources, including trombones: but this time he used these resources to vary the weight of the choral accompaniments rather than to introduce novel orchestral effects. That Handel intended his choral groups to be physically divided in the theatre as *cori spezzati* is suggested by the fact that he allocated one continuo organ to each 'choir': in some movements Handel carried the principle to its logical conclusion by also treating strings, woodwind, trombones, and trumpets and drums as independent 'choirs'.[38]

In artistic terms *Israel in Egypt* was an interesting, largely successful experiment, but it was ill-matched to its audience: a 45-minute anthem, whether sad or cheerful, might be tolerated (or even relished) at an appropriate church service, but a vast span of largely undifferentiated choral music was beyond the scope of London's relatively impatient theatre audience. The circumstances of the 1739 season meant that Handel's audience still came to his productions with operatic expectations: the 'oratorio audience' as such had not yet developed. In modern times *Israel in Egypt* has been better appreciated, but it nevertheless may always remain more highly regarded by its performers than by its audience. Given its serious-minded framework, *Israel in Egypt* has many striking features and shows Handel's mastery of the Baroque grand manner. The fine music of the Funeral Anthem in Part 1 is well balanced by Part 3, which begins

---

[38] E.g. in the chorus 'He spake the word', which provides a good example also of Handel's precise directions for the use of the two organs.

Ex. 38

with a harmonic gesture that no doubt made the audience sit up (Ex.38). The arias in Part 3 are relatively undistinguished, and the bass duet 'The Lord is a Man of War', which became popular in the nineteenth century, seems altogether too long for its material.[39] But there is ample compensation in the choruses, where Handel disports himself with every choral texture in his repertory – fugues, cantus firmus themes with faster-moving counter-melodies, antiphonal double choirs, thunderous choral homophony and so on. The chorus movements also carry most of the pictorial descriptions, to texts such as 'And with the blast of thy nostrils the waters were gathered together', 'and the depths were congealed in the heart of the sea', 'They sank into the bottom as a stone', 'The horse and his rider hath he thrown into the sea' and 'He led them through the deep'. Rough seas are a recurring image in the psalm texts that Handel had set in the Cannons anthems, an experience that stood him in good stead when faced with 'But the waters overwhelmed their enemies', where timpani are used in the accompaniment without trumpets.

Many melodic and harmonic ideas in *Israel in Egypt* were indebted to Alessandro Stradella and Dionigi Erba, who might have been surprised about the use to which they were put. The most extensive single 'borrowing' is from a keyboard canzona by Johann Kaspar Kerll, which Handel may have learnt in his youth under Zachow in Halle, and which he used note-for-note in the chorus 'Egypt was glad when they departed'. He may have been attracted to this rather undistinguished music for its

---

[39] The duet was sung, on the occasion of at least one Crystal Palace performance, by the full chorus basses, no doubt with over 100 voices on each part.

248

archaic quality, which lent a serious tone to the work (he adopted a similar style, though to much broader effect and with a more flexible use of contrapuntal material, in the chorus 'And the Children of Israel sigh'd'); alternatively, its use may be semi-ironic, the colourless modality reflecting the Egyptians' glum acceptance that they were better off without the Israelites. Elsewhere Handel brought a light touch to the description of the plagues and their consequences: the theme of 'He led them through the deep' (Ex.39) and the opening of the 'Hailstones' chorus have probably

Ex. 39

always made audiences wonder about the seriousness of Handel's intentions, while the figural orchestral accompaniments to 'And there came all manner of flies' and 'Their land brought forth frogs' are among the plainest evidence for Handel's musical sense of humour.

Church music

Handel's church music of the 1730s was produced for royal family occasions – weddings and a funeral. The timetable for these events was capricious, and often music was required under great pressure. In 1733, for the wedding of Princess Anne, Handel probably had to produce his anthem (*This is the day*) very quickly, but it was then put aside for a time, as the failure of the prospective bridegroom's health postponed the ceremony until the next year. It is perhaps not surprising that Handel turned to the score of *Athalia* as a source for the wedding anthem: the oratorio contained fine choruses and arias but had not yet been heard in London. The adaptation of the music for the anthem turned out surprisingly well: the grand chorus from the opening of Part 2 of *Athalia*, with a new text grafted on, provided the opening, and four substantial arias were used in the following sequence of movements. Only in the case of 'Her children rise up' was there a questionable match between the old music and the character of the new texts: here Handel's thinking was probably dominated by the desire to introduce some minor-key contrast into the anthem as a whole. A new chorus, 'We will remember thy name' (with thematic material that Handel had used elsewhere),[40] led with no apparent stylistic incongruity into a final 'Allelujah, Amen', transcribed from the last movement of the 'Caroline' *Te Deum* composed 20 years earlier.

It is perhaps surprising that Handel did not put more original creative effort into the anthem for the wedding of his favourite, most musical and most loyal pupil, yet this 'pasticcio-anthem' seems to cohere more success-fully than the more original *Sing unto God* that he produced for the Prince of Wales's wedding two years later. *Sing unto God* is not lacking in good music: the opening chorus and the first aria are excellent; the following bass solo with cello obbligato is worthy enough, if a little prolix; and the central chorus (derived from a movement by C.H. Graun) is effective, though stolid. The final chorus is transcribed from *Parnasso in festa*, with Carestini's original solo part in the serenata adapted for the tenor John Beard. The anthem's design seems lop-sided because, after a chain of arias, the last two choruses are separated only by a short *accompagnato*; on the other hand, the substantial chorus movements have earned for the anthem some deserved popularity with present-day choral societies.

Handel had only ten days in which to compose his Funeral Anthem for Queen Caroline, *The ways of Zion do mourn*, but it shows no sign of constriction: it is a masterpiece in its own right, and in many respects unique, since it has no exact predecessors or successors. The last state funeral in London to involve a considerable musical contribution had been that for the Duke of Marlborough in 1722,[41] for which Bononcini had contributed the anthem *When Saul was king*. Bononcini's anthem[42] was on relatively conventional lines – comparable in plan, though not in scale or mood, to Handel's wedding anthems – with outer choruses framing a duet, an *accompagnato* and an aria. Handel adopted a very different, and novel, scheme in 1737: *The ways of Zion* is entirely choral (i.e. a 'full' anthem, with no movements for vocal soloists) and is accompanied by oboes, bassoons and strings. Its character has been somewhat disguised by the fact that Arnold's printed edition of 1795 (which formed the basis for many subsequent ones) allocated two movements to soloists, probably reflecting a practice that had evolved in later eighteenth-century concert performances. There is no indication of soloists in the primary sources for the anthem: it is possible that Handel employed a semi-chorus of the best Chapel Royal singers for some important chorus entries,[43] though in the earliest sources there is no evidence even for this.

[40] The opening theme is derived from the ritornello subject of the sonata for organ and orchestra in *Il trionfo del Tempo* (1707), via a minor-key version in 'The clouded scene begins to clear' from *Athalia*. Both, however, lack the more contrapuntal continuation of 'Therefore shall the people give praise' in the anthem.

[41] There had been no state funeral for King George I in 1727: he was buried in Germany.

[42] Ed. A. Ford (Sevenoaks, 1982).

[43] In the 1727 coronation anthems Handel marked the opening entries (only) in the first movements of *Let thy hand be strengthened* and *My heart is inditing* with the names of solo

There was a striking precedent for 'full' funeral music in William Croft's setting of the Burial Service (published in 1724): but it is a far cry from Croft's relatively short, chaste (though moving) *a cappella* burial sentences to Handel's solemn, extended paean with orchestral accompaniment. The Funeral Anthem is a companion piece to the coronation anthems of a decade before, but the grand manner is now controlled by the nature of the subject and by the restrained scoring, orchestral and vocal. Handel has all four vocal parts active most of the time, relying on contrasts of texture, speed and metre to supply variety without disturbing the general mood. There is only one passage of fast-changing contrasts, at 'Their bodies are buried in peace/but their name liveth evermore' (Ex. 40) where a *piano/forte* (and implied slow/fast) contrast foreshadows 'Since by Man came death' in *Messiah*.

Ex. 40

This passage is also interesting in that the repeat of 'but their name liveth evermore' borrows (or perhaps quotes) from a motet by Jacob Gallus (or Handl; 1550–91): the effect of the chord on the flat seventh, though certainly archaic, heightens the solemnity, and it may show Handel's interest in the appropriate use of tonally 'dissociated' chords (in

singers from the Chapel Royal: the semi-chorus treatment may have been a practical way of dealing with musical communication problems in the Abbey. There is no comparable naming of singers on the Funeral Anthem; it is doubtful if the practical necessity existed in King Henry VII's Chapel.

terms of the Baroque style). In other ways, too, the Funeral Anthem's
music, while sensitive to its English texts, seems to have taken Handel
back to his German origins – to the Passion music and possibly the funeral
services that he had heard in Hamburg and Halle; he may also have been
moved by the thought that Queen Caroline had been brought up in the
same Lutheran culture as himself. His recent convalescent trip to the
Continent probably brought him into renewed contact with German
church music, and in particular with pieces using chorale-based melodies.
In the opening chorus of the anthem the cantus firmus is treated in
chorale-fantasia style, and in another movement, 'She deliver'd the poor
that cried', Handel makes a near-quotation of an actual chorale melody,
at the words 'Kindness, meekness and comfort were in her tongue'. When
he revised his Chapel Royal anthem *As pants the hart* for inclusion in his
'Oratorio' of March 1738, he added a movement that also seems to reflect
a renewed contact with the German chorale prelude tradition (Ex.41).
Although the 'chorale' element is of technical interest in the Funeral
Anthem, it is, however, only one feature in a rich work that draws upon

Ex. 41

many categories of musical idea, from conventional fugue to transformed dance rhythms. Handel succeeded in conveying the heartfelt emotions of mourning without lapsing into the melodramatically morbid, and the dignified *gravitas* of the subject without limiting himself to slow tempos and minor keys.

Instrumental music

The decade was a fruitful one for Handel's instrumental music. The publication in about 1732–3 of *Solos for a German Flute a Hoboy or Violin with a Thorough Bass* (subsequently referred to as 'op.1') and the Trio Sonatas op.2,[44] brought to the wider public collections of music that Handel had mostly composed considerably earlier. The Concerti Grossi op.3 were published in 1734:[45] the first newspaper advertisement for them appeared in December, but the set had been prepared somewhat earlier, for early versions of the title-page (possibly never issued) carry a note that 'Several of these Concertos' were performed at the royal wedding earlier in the year (if they were used for the wedding, they would probably have been played before or after, rather than during the ceremony). Like the *Solos* and trio sonatas, the concerti grossi were derived from earlier works – the overtures to the Cannons anthems and concertos composed during the preceding 20 years.[46] Rather confusingly, a collection of six of Handel's keyboard fugues (composed mainly during the Cannons period) was also published by Walsh as 'op.3' in 1735, this being the third collection of Handel's keyboard music following on from the sets of suites published in 1720 and 1733.

The 1733 collection of suites[47] contained works that predated the suites of the 1720 set but which nevertheless fully deserved publication. The first suite, in B♭, is one of the best, beginning with an arpeggiated prelude which leaves a few puzzles for the performer (a recurring problem in the keyboard music, because Handel, acclaimed as an improviser, sometimes left only shorthand traces of his intentions); it is followed by an engaging 'Sonata', which looks plain on paper but is remarkably effective in

[44] See Burrows, 'Walsh's Editions'. The form of title for the 'solos' quoted here is from the 'Walsh' title-page and is more or less a translation of the spurious 'Roger' title (see Chapter 8). The *Solos* never appeared with 'op.1' on the title-page (perhaps because they were not originally seen as part of a series), but the trio sonatas were from the start published as 'Second Ouvrage'.

[45] The wording of the main title of op.3 was based, rather inappropriately, on that of Corelli's op.6.

[46] The two-movement concerto that Walsh published as op.3 no.6 may not have any authority from the composer. Its first movement was used by Handel in *Ottone* and had been split away from a three-movement concerto (see Chapter 7, n.39); the second, for keyboard and orchestra, has a complex history and may, in its 'op.3' form, have been composed as an isolated organ concerto movement. See Burrows, 'Walsh's Editions'.

[47] 1733 is the generally accepted year of publication, but the earliest known advertisement appeared in 1734. It is possible that Walsh issued the edition on a limited scale in 1733 but did not advertise it until Handel's 'privilege' (see pp. 107, 109) expired.

performance, and an aria with five variations.[48] As published, the suite closes with a minuet which, in G minor, seems off-key, but Handel did not intend it for this suite; it is the relic of a keyboard overture whose opening movements had been used up in Suite no.7 of the 1720 collection. The make-up of the 1733 collection is rather haphazard, partly because Walsh was reliant on sources in which some of the suites appeared in earlier forms, or lacking a movement; their proper texts have to be reconstructed from manuscript sources. Two of the suites are taken up with enormous chaconnes: the G major chaconne with 21 variations that constitutes the second suite has a complex history of variant forms, one of which appeared in an organ concerto in the late 1730s.[49] By 1735 Handel's career as a composer of formally transmitted solo keyboard music was largely over, but the two suites (with conventional sequences of dance movements) that he composed for Princess Louisa at the end of the decade (HWV447, 452) are engaging; the D minor one has points of compositional subtlety (including some cross-relationships between movements) that bear comparison with some of the more innocent-looking yet complex movements in the suites of J.S. Bach.

If the years 1733–5 saw some of Handel's earlier music come into print, there was a pleasing consequence: the publications set up a train of demand (or perhaps a train of expectation – the facts of the market are difficult to determine) which led to further sets of original works. As noted in Chapter 9, Handel collected together the organ concertos that he had written for the oratorios of 1735–6 and published them as op.4; a set of trio sonatas (op.5) followed, and the sequence was crowned by the 12 Concerti Grossi op.6. The theatre organ concerto was an innovation, even though Handel had hinted at its possibilities as long ago as 1707, with the Sonata in *Il trionfo del Tempo*. The concertos are engagingly lighthearted and, Handel's own executant virtuosity notwithstanding, they came to publication in a form that could be played by other musicians, including the more competent amateurs. They were printed in independent arrangements for solo keyboard, which could be used in conjunction with the orchestral parts (see Fig. 11). To a certain extent Handel had a hand in tidying up the concertos for publication, but, even so, nos.1 and 3 seem to be less coherent than nos.2, 4 and 5.[50] No.4 is arguably the most developed of the set. It begins with a lively ritornello movement (of which the theme relates to a contemporary chorus movement in *Alcina*), followed by an Andante, which begins in the style of contemporary English

[48] More than a century later Brahms used the aria theme as the basis of his *Variations and Fugue on a Theme of Handel* op.24.

[49] See Handel (ed. Best), *Chaconne in G for Keyboard*, which gives two versions of the chaconne and elucidates its history.

[50] This is a remarkable tribute to op.4 no.5, which was arranged from the Recorder Sonata HWV369 in a very straightforward manner, with the simple addition of orchestral ritornellos.

'Diapason movement' and subsequently develops solo filigree-work in triplet semiquavers. A short Adagio (which may give some idea of the style of Handel's improvised slow movements) then leads into a vigorous finale, which opens as if promising to be a fugue but, typically of Handel, instead uses imitative techniques to impart strength and variety to the music without becoming an end in themselves (the imitative subject may have been suggested in the first place by the 'Alleluja' text of the chorus that originally concluded the movement). Op.4 no.6, though published as an organ concerto (and attaining some popularity as such), was really a harp concerto from *Alexander's Feast*: its published text even includes notes above the range of the organ of Handel's time.

The 'Second Set' of organ concertos that was published in 1740 (without orchestral parts) contained two fine and original works, followed by four direct keyboard arrangements of orchestral concertos from op.6. It is sad that thereafter Handel apparently lost interest in publishing his later organ concertos, with the result that most of them lack fully authentic performing versions; their success relies on the modern player's ability to approach Handel's powers of improvisation. In order to maximize the sales potential, Walsh named the harpsichord as an alternative solo instrument on the title-pages of his publications for organ, and no doubt most of the eighteenth-century purchasers tried out the music at home on the harpsichord. But Handel composed no original harpsichord concertos as such. The first of the 'Second Set' concertos is sometimes known as 'The Cuckoo and the Nightingale', and certainly the treble-register warblings in the organ part in the episodes of the second movement have affinities with bird-calls. Handel presumably had an attractive flute stop for this type of passage, which was not a novelty in this concerto: similar music, though perhaps not so explicitly cuckoo-like, can be found in the first movement of op.4 no.4. Handel completed the 'Second Set' concerto on 2 April 1739, early in the cuckoo season.

The seven Trio Sonatas op.5 are a mixed bag. For the collection, which was presumably assembled under his general supervision, Handel drew on two principal areas of pre-existing music, from sources that could be reduced to the trio texture without too much difficulty. The first was the music from those overtures to the Cannons anthems that had not already been used in op.3; the second was the dance music from his operas of 1734–5. The dance movements give the set a rather French aspect, though the two new, original sonatas that Handel seems to have composed specially for op.5 (nos.5 and 6) were closer to the Italian four-movement model.[51] Op.5 no.4 seems incongruous, consisting mainly of the overture to *Athalia* followed by an impressive Passacaille that had come from

---

[51] Between Handel's autograph and Walsh's publication, nos.5 and 6 became more frenchified through the addition of extra movements, probably at Walsh's instigation: see Burrows, 'Walsh's Editions'.

Radamisto via *Terpsicore*: the music is fine, but its orchestral origins are uncomfortably apparent through the trio-sonata disguise. In general, however, the individual sonatas of op.5 are successful and engaging, despite the diverse origins of their constituent movements.

There was nothing casual or haphazard about the construction of op.6: the 12 concertos that Handel produced in a concentrated burst of activity during the autumn of 1739 constitute one of the marvels of eighteenth-century instrumental music. Their status is not undermined by the fact that they were to some extent modelled on Corelli's op.6 and that in them Handel covertly re-worked a number of thematic stimulants from Domenico Scarlatti's keyboard *Essercizi*, published in London in 1738.[52] As he came towards the end of the set Handel drew more on his own recyclable material, and it is significant that he selected only music that was of good quality and recent vintage – the A major 'Second Set' organ concerto for no.11, and one movement each from the other 'Second Set' concerto and from the overture to *Imeneo* for no.9. In the first two movements of no.5 Handel also re-used, in slightly amended form, most of the overture to his *Song for St Cecilia's Day*, composed just over a month earlier. The concertos include some memorable tunes (Ex.42), but the set as a whole is a triumph of balance and compositional skill rather than of melodic invention. The multi-movement schemes generally build up around an italianate slow-fast-slow-fast plan, but each evolves in terms of the internal balance of its own material – here a dance movement is introduced, there a fugue, and so on. The music is by turns serious, witty, impassioned and lighthearted – given that such terms refer, in instrumental music, to analogies rather than to strict representations. The concertino-ripieno contrast is of varying importance, crucial in some movements but irrelevant in others. There is something of an *embarras de richesse* in op.6 that prevents any simple summary of its 60 or more carefully wrought and individually characterized movements. Handel's sensitivity and crafts-manship are readily apparent when any one of the 12 concertos is compared with the *Alexander's Feast* concerto (HWV318) of 1736, a cheerful, extrovert, unselfconscious work. The latter is theatre interval music, which subsequently saw publication; the op.6 concertos, by con-trast, are art-works that Handel incidentally used as interval music at his oratorio performances.

One of the remarkable features of the op.6 concertos is the quality of the finished article: Handel composed them quickly, but there is nothing slapdash about the musical workmanship. The extent to which the Scarlatti borrowings are buried, integrated into the Handelian style, is a measure of the compositional subtlety that was at work. The opening of the first concerto also provides a good example of Handel going one better than himself: he took an idea from the original (and eventually discarded) first

---

[52] See Silbiger, 'Scarlatti Borrowings', and Derr, 'Handel's Use of Scarlatti's '"Essercizi"'.

Ex. 42
(*a*) Menuet (op.6 no.5, HWV323/6)

(*b*) Aria (op.6 no.12, HWV330/3)

movement of the overture in the draft score of *Imeneo* and improved it
beyond recognition simply by amending the details (Ex.43). In the liveliness
of their ideas, the balance and variety of movements within each work
and fluency of compositional technique, the op.6 concertos show Handel
on top form as a composer of instrumental music.

Ex. 43
(*a*) Ouverture to *Imeneo* (HWV41, Anhang)

(*b*) Op.6 no.1 (HWV319/1)

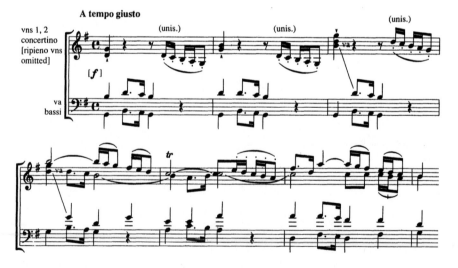

11

The oratorio composer I: Dublin and London, 1741–5

Handel says he will do nothing next Winter, but I hope I shall perswade him to set another Scripture Collection I have made for him, & perform it for his own Benefit in Passion Week. I hope he will lay out his whole Genius & Skill upon it, that the Composition may excell all his former Compositions, as the Subject excells every other subject. The Subject is Messiah.

Six extravagant young Gentlemen have subscrib'd 1000£ a piece for the Support of an Opera next Winter. the chief Castrato is to be Monticelli, the chief Woman Visconti; both of them, I suppose, your Acquaintance.

Thus Jennens, writing to a friend in July 1741, outlined his expectations for the next London theatre season.[1] Handel had finished his season at Lincoln's Inn Fields on 8 April 1741 and no doubt took some sort of break: perhaps he even went to the country to visit Jennens at his country house at Gopsall, near Coventry (though there is no evidence for this). He was certainly in London by the beginning of July, when he wrote two Italian duets (HWV 189, 192): the circumstances and performers for which he composed these (and other duets that followed in 1743 and 1745) are unknown, but they possibly indicate some continuing contact with the performers of the 'Middlesex' opera company on whose foundation Jennens's letter reports. The late summer of 1741 was devoted to the composition of two English oratorios, to librettos supplied by Jennens and Hamilton respectively. *Messiah* was drafted between 22 August and 12 September, and the details of the score 'filled up' by 14 September.[2] Handel then proceeded to *Samson*, the draft score of which he completed on 29 October. Two days later he attended the first night of the new opera company's season at the King's Theatre; from a reference in a letter quoted below, it seems that Handel was very happy to be in the audience rather than among the performers.

---

[1] Letter, to Holdsworth, 10 July 1741: *HHB*, p. 334.
[2] Handel often left recitatives and some details of scoring incomplete in the first stage of drafting a complete score; for *Messiah* (and some other works) he added a final date for the completion of the draft, using the term 'ausgefüllt' to denote the 'filling-up' of these elements.

Less than three weeks later Handel was in Dublin:[3]

> Last Wednesday [18 November] the celebrated Dr. Handell arrived here in the
> Packet-boat from Holyhead, a Gentleman universally known by his excellent
> Compositions in all Kinds of Musick, and particularly for his Te Deum,
> Jubilate, Anthems, and other Compositions in Church Music, (of which for
> some Years past have principally consisted the Entertainments in the Round
> Church, which have so greatly contributed to support the Charity of Mercer's-
> Hospital) to perform his Oratorio's.

Handel's presence in Dublin was undoubtedly the consequence of prior
negotiations conducted from London, probably through the Lord Lieutenant of Ireland (William Cavendish, 3rd Duke of Devonshire), who may
have issued an official diplomatic invitation, and through performers –
perhaps actors as well as musicians – who had performed in Dublin
recently. The phrase from Jennens's letter of July 1741, quoted above, to
the effect that Handel was not planning to perform in the next London
season, may indicate that Handel had already been planning a Dublin
season, though the resolution of his plans took Jennens by surprise:[4]

Q.Square. [London] Dec.2. 1741

> I heard with great pleasure at my arrival in Town, that Handel had set the
> Oratorio of Messiah; but it was some mortification to me to hear that instead
> of performing it here he was gone into Ireland with it. However, I hope we
> shall hear it when he comes back.

The circumstantial evidence from the scores that Handel composed
during the summer of 1741 suggests, however, that he was not certain of
his Dublin visit until October. *Messiah* is unusually lightly scored, requiring
(in its original form) only an orchestra of strings, trumpets and drums,
which Handel might reasonably expect to assemble in Dublin if necessary,
though Jennens's intention, as mentioned above, was that Handel would
perform it in London during Passiontide 'for his own benefit'.[5] *Samson*,
which followed *Messiah*, was, however, scored for much more elaborate
forces, and in one respect specifically to suit London conditions: the 'Dead
March' in Part 3 included trombones, which were apparently played by a
group of travelling performers who had been in London only since 1739
and were more likely to return to the Continent than to venture to
Dublin.[6] So Handel had probably kept open his options for a possible
London oratorio season in 1741–2. The draft of *Samson* was not 'filled
up', as *Messiah* had been, with the final details of scoring and recitatives:

---

[3] *The Dublin Journal* (21 November 1741): Deutsch, p. 525; *HHB*, p. 338. By coincidence, *The
Daily Advertiser* for the same date tardily announced that Handel had left London for Dublin.
[4] Letter to Holdsworth: *HHB*, p. 339.
[5] The significance of Jennens's phrase is obscure: the only 'benefit' occasion to provide a
precedent is Handel's single 'Oratorio' performance in March 1738. By 'Passion Week', Jennens
almost certainly meant the week before Easter.
[6] See Burrows, 'Handel, the *Dead March*'; also Herbert, 'The Sackbut in England', pp. 612–14.

presumably Handel knew by 29 October that his prospective Dublin visit was secure, and so he laid aside the unfinished *Samson* score for future use, in much the same way as he had put *Imeneo* aside in 1738. As far as we know, Handel had no specific singers in mind for the oratorios: the scores were drafted in 1741 for soloists in soprano, alto, tenor and bass clefs and could in theory have been performed by as few as four singers, one of each voice (though for *Samson* a fifth, a soprano chorus leader, is implied in the main autograph[7]). Such an even distribution of voices had not been characteristic of his casts for the previous decade: when Handel composed the oratorios he was certainly not thinking in terms of his cast from the preceding (1740–1) season, which had had four soprano-register soloists and no alto. Altogether, the 1741 scores of *Messiah* and *Samson* seem to bear testimony to the fluidity of Handel's future plans.

Dublin at this period had an active seasonal programme given by theatre companies and concert-giving societies, though one admittedly dependent on London for its style and quality. A fair number of London's best actors, singers, instrumentalists and composers found the artistic (and, presumably, financial) rewards sufficiently attractive to devote the occasional season to Dublin.[8] Politically as well as culturally, Dublin was the terminus of a significant branch line from London: the court at Dublin Castle was a smaller-scale copy of that in London and represented his Britannic Majesty's presence (through the Lord Lieutenant) in Ireland. The Dublin court employed musicians – trumpeters and string players; other professional musicians served in the theatres and in the choirs of the two cathedrals, St Patrick's and Christ Church. There were two major public theatres, in Aungier Street and Smock Alley, but Handel was to perform in neither: the venue for his season was the Musick Hall (sometimes called 'Mr Neale's Great Room') in Fishamble Street. This new concert venue, established by William Neale and the Charitable Musical Society, had opened with a concert on 2 October 1741 (it is conceivable that the timing of Handel's Dublin visit was related to the establishment of this concert room). Handel's music had preceded him to Dublin, and in particular his orchestrally accompanied church music had figured regularly in charity services at the Dublin churches. On 10 December 1741 a *Te Deum*, *Jubilate* and coronation anthem by Handel (together with a specially provided anthem by William Boyce) were given at a charity service for Mercer's Hospital in St Andrew's church: the minutes of Mercer's Hospital include an invitation to Handel to play the organ, but it is not known whether he accepted. By then Handel was presumably well occupied with the arrangements for opening his concert season, and *The Dublin Journal* on 12 December carried the following announcement:[9]

---

[7] British Library RM.20.f.6.
[8] The background is well documented in Boydell, *A Dublin Musical Calendar*.
[9] Deutsch, p. 527; *HHB*, p. 339.

Handel

On Monday next being the 14th of December (and every Day following) Attendance will be given at Mr. Handel's House in Abbey-street, near Lyffey-street, from 9 o'clock in the Morning till 2 in the Afternoon, in order to receive the Subscription Money for his Six Musical Entertainments in the New Musick-Hall in Fishamble street, at which Time each Subscriber will have a Ticket delivered to him, which entitles him to three Tickets each Night, either for Ladies or Gentlemen. – N.B. Subscriptions are likewise taken in at the same Place.

Handel's subscription seems to have filled up successfully, and the first performance took place just before Christmas, on 23 December. The letter that Handel wrote to Jennens six days later is specially informative: it contains a report of Handel's opening night in Dublin, the names of some of the friends and acquaintances in England that Handel shared with Jennens, a clear expression of Handel's lighthearted attitude towards London's new opera company, and (not least) a colloquial style that may preserve the tone and manner of Handel's conversation:[10]

Dublin Decem[br] 29. 1741.

S[r]

it was with the greatest Pleasure I saw the Continuation of Your Kindness by the Lines You was pleased to send me, in Order to be prefix'd to Your Oratorio Messiah, which I set to Musick before I left England. I am emboldned, Sir, by the generous Concern You please to take in relation to my affairs, to give You an Account of the Success I have met here. The Nobility did me the Honour to make amongst themselves a Subscription for 6 Nights, which did fill a Room of 600 Persons, so that I needed not sell one single Ticket at the Door. and without Vanity the Performance was received with a general Approbation. Sig.[ra] Avolio, which I brought with me from London pleases extraordinary, I have form'd an other Tenor Voice which gives great Satisfaction, the Basses and Counter Tenors are very good, and the rest of the Chorus Singers (by my Direction) do exceeding well, as for the Instruments they are really excellent, M[r] Dubourgh being at the Head of them, and the Musick sounds delightfully in this charming Room, which puts me in such Spirits (and my Health being so good) that I exert my self on my Organ with more than usual Success. I opened with the Allegro, Penseroso, & Moderato and I assure you that the Words of the Moderato are vastly admired. The Audience being composed (besides the Flower of Ladyes of Distinction and other People of the greatest Quality) of so many Bishops, Deans, Heads of the Colledge, the most eminents People in the Law as the Chancellor, Auditor General, &tc. all which are very much taken with the Poetry. So that I am desired to perform it again the next time. I cannot sufficiently express the kind treatment I receive here, but the Politeness of this generous Nation cannot be unknown to You, so I let You judge of the satisfaction I enjoy, passing my time with Honnour, profit, and pleasure. They propose already to have some more Performances, when the 6 Nights of the Subscription are over, and My Lord Duc the Lord Lieutenant (who is allways present with all His Family on those Nights) will easily obtain

[10]Deutsch, pp. 530–1; *HHB*, p. 341.

a longer Permission for me by His Majesty, so that I shall be obliged to make my stay here longer than I thought. One request I must make to You, which is that You would insinuate my most devoted Respects to My Lord and my Lady Shaftesbury, You know how much Their kind Protection is precious to me. Sir Windham Knatchbull will find here my respectfull Compliments. You will encrease my obligations if by occasion You will present my humble Service to some other Patrons and friends of mine. I expect with Impatience the Favour of Your News, concerning Your Health and wellfare, of which I take a real share, as for the News of Your Opera's, I need not trouble you for all this Town is full of their ill success, by a number of Letters from Your quarters to the People of Quality here, and I can't help saying but that it furnishes great Diversion and laughter. The first Opera I heard my Self before I left London, and it made me very merry all along my journey, and of the second Opera, call'd Penelope, a certain nobleman writes very jocosly, il faut que je dise avec Harlequin, nôtre Penelôpe n'est qu'une Sallôpe. but I think I have trespassed too much on Your Patience. I beg You to be persuaded of the sincere Veneration and Esteem with which I have the Honnour to be

S^r
    Your most obliged and most humble Servant
    George Frideric Handel

Clearly Handel's Dublin performances had begun well, and he hoped – on the strength of the successful first night, which was not necessarily a good indicator – that he would be able to continue there beyond his initial subscription of six performances. The mention of the royal permission necessary for an extension of Handel's stay presumably indicates that his various royal pensions carried implied duties, even though these were in practice occasional or largely fictitious. Handel's letter is quite instructive, through its silences as well as through its content, about his performers. The newspapers had reported in November that he had 'brought over several of the best Performers in the Musical Way' and had engaged an organist from England named Maclaine and his wife (presumably a singer).[11] But little of this emerges from Handel's letter: the only person that he names as having come to Dublin at his instigation is the soprano Avolio.[12] She had not sung for him before, but there seems little doubt that Handel had signed her up in London: she was the only principal soloist to come to Dublin under such an arrangement, though Handel certainly brought at least two other members of his London musical establishment with him – John Christopher Smith the elder and another music copyist (identified now only from his handwriting as 'S4') from the considerable group that Handel now employed.[13] They copied music that

---

[11] *Pue's Occurrences* (21 November 1741): Deutsch, p. 526; *HHB*, p. 338; *The Dublin Journal* (21 November 1741): Deutsch, p. 525; *HHB*, p. 338.

[12] *The Dublin Journal* (28 November 1741): Deutsch, p. 526; *HHB*, p. 339. Avolio arrived in Dublin three days after Handel.

[13] Their names are rarely known; the anonymous ones were first given sigla (such as 'S4') for their handwriting in Larsen, *Handel's 'Messiah'*.

was inserted into the conducting scores for Handel's Dublin performances, and they may well also have performed in the orchestra.

The overwhelming impression from Handel's letter is, however, that most of his performers were drawn from Dublin's resident musicians. Matthew Dubourg, formerly a violin pupil of Geminiani in London (where he no doubt maintained many links), had been Master of the King's Musick in Ireland since 1728 and would have been invaluable to the task of assembling a good orchestra. As for the singers, Handel probably worked in the first instance mainly with men from the cathedral choirs, turning them into 'oratorio' singers. The tenor whom Handel 'form'd' may have been James Baileys (or Bayly), a member of both cathedral choirs. The specific mention in the letter of chorus singers suggests that this contingent was substantial (perhaps it included boy trebles), and, furthermore, Handel's phraseology suggests that the male soloists were mainly drawn from this general pool.[14]

For his programme Handel chose works that were adaptable to the circumstances in Dublin: indeed, he had presumably selected works that would be relatively easy and versatile to mount when he sorted the scores in London that he was to take with him to Dublin. *L'Allegro*, given in full with the inclusion of *Il Moderato*, was perhaps an ambitious choice as regards length, but it made relatively modest demands on the new soloists and did not require them to sustain major dramatic roles. The heaviest part (written for Francesina in London) fell to Avolio; the other solo work could be distributed as appropriate. Baileys probably took over the music originally written for Beard, and John Mason, a bass from Christ Church Cathedral, that created for Reinhold (both singers are named in Handel's performance score). It is possible that their load was lightened slightly by passing some of the solo movements on to other 'chorus' singers. Two performances were given of *L'Allegro*, followed by two of *Acis and Galatea* in a slightly adapted version of the 1739 London revival and again partnered by the *Song for St Cecilia's Day*. This was the last time that Handel gave *Acis and Galatea*. Once again the principal parts for the evening could have been covered by Avolio, Baileys and Mason. Two performances of *Esther* completed the first subscription series, which ended on 10 February 1742.

By then, however, Handel had run into practical difficulties. On 28 January, the day after the fourth performance, Dean Swift of St Patrick's drafted a memorandum to his sub-dean and chapter, withdrawing any licence for the cathedral's vicars choral to 'assist at a club of fiddlers in Fishamble Street': if carried into immediate effect this would certainly

---

[14] As in London, many men held posts in more than one choir simultaneously. The maximum combined strength of the adults in the Dublin cathedral choirs would have been about 16, of whom four were priests and would probably not have taken part in Handel's subscription oratorios. On the practical circumstances of his performances, see Burrows, *Handel's Dublin Performances*.

have depleted Handel's chorus and removed the services of Baileys.[15] It is noticeable that the version of *Esther* that followed did not include the coronation anthem choruses, and indeed cut down some of the other chorus movements. A new tenor, Calloghan,[16] probably replaced Baileys, but the outlines of Handel's cast are obscure, the only certainty being that Avolio sang the role of Esther.

Before the first subscription ended, Handel had already launched an invitation in the Dublin newspapers for a second subscription of six concerts.[17] It was probably at this stage that a new singer, the alto Susanna Cibber, entered Handel's company.[18] Mrs Cibber had come to Dublin the previous year (about a fortnight after Handel), though this had been largely a coincidence, since she seems to have come primarily to act in the company at Aungier Street theatre. But she would certainly have been known to Handel, if only by reputation, on account of her earlier career in London. The sister of Thomas Augustine Arne, she had flourished in the London theatres in the 1730s as an actress-singer, though her recent years had been clouded by a vindictive divorce case. Handel decided to launch his second Dublin subscription with *Alexander's Feast*, in which he created a new alto part for Mrs Cibber out of sections of the former soprano and bass roles. For concert-room performance in Dublin he was apparently free of the pressures that had led him to expand *Alexander's Feast* for London audiences in 1736: the main ode now constituted Parts 1 and 2, and Part 3 was a short epilogue based on Hamilton's additional text, incorporating a new aria (of which only fragments survive) and duet for Mrs Cibber.[19]

With the inclusion of a couple of organ concertos (which had also been regularly featured in his first subscription) and the added attraction of a new singer, Handel's second subscription began on 17 February. He planned to base the programme around *Alexander's Feast* and a revival of his opera *Imeneo*, performed in Italian but in a concert version designated 'Serenata'. Unfortunately, the schedule was twice interrupted by Mrs Cibber's illness: the second performance of *Alexander's Feast* had to be postponed from 24 February to 2 March, while the première of *Imeneo* was postponed for a week; on its intended opening date, 17 March, *L'Allegro* was substituted, which seems to confirm that Mrs Cibber had not had a part in the original Dublin performances of that work. After two performances of *Imeneo*, the second subscription was rounded

[15] Baileys, however, is not among those named in the memorandum (Deutsch, pp. 536–7; *HHB*, p. 343); Mason may not have been affected, as he was not a member of the choir of St Patrick's.
[16] Probably not identifiable with James Colgan, a member of the choir of St Patrick's from 1743.
[17] *The Dublin Journal* (6, 9, 13 February 1742): Deutsch, pp. 538–40; *HHB*, pp. 344–5.
[18] As a soprano she had sung Galatea in her father Thomas Arne's production of *Acis and Galatea* in 1732; Handel's music for her, ten years later, is in the alto clef.
[19] See Burrows, 'Handel and "Alexander's Feast"'.

off with *Esther* on 7 April, presumably cutting Mrs Cibber into the cast if she had not been incorporated into the previous performances.

With Avolio, Cibber, Calloghan and a bass (of unknown identity), Handel had probably developed a quite strong cast. However, there may have been disappointment if the chorus element had been depleted by Dean Swift's edict, and it is in this context that the phrase 'the Gentlemen of the Choirs of both Cathedrals will assist' assumes significance in the advertisements for the first performance of *Messiah*. That oratorio came in as a charity performance after the end of Handel's second subscription series, though the first advertisement had been placed before the fifth performance of the series. Because of the charitable element ('For Relief of the Prisoners in the several Gaols, and for the Support of Mercer's Hospital in Stephen Street, and of the Charitable Infirmary on the Inns Quay'), it seems that the cathedral Gentlemen were allowed to take part, even though the performance took place in the Fishamble Street Musick Hall.[20] The performance was also distinguished from those of Handel's subscription series by beginning at midday instead of at the normal time of 7 p.m.

Messiah was publicly rehearsed on Friday 9 April 1742 and first performed on the following Tuesday, a day later than originally planned, 'At the Desire of several Persons of Distinction';[21] these did not include the Lord Lieutenant, who had left for London just before the second subscription series had begun. Nevertheless, the newspaper reports mention that *Messiah* was given before the 'Lords Justices, and a vast Assembly of the Nobility and Gentry of both Sexes'[22] and a capacity audience, who had been specially requested to come without swords or hooped dresses in order to maximize the seating. Handel had estimated the capacity of the Musick Hall at 600 and had sold subscription tickets for 450 seats (150 tickets), but about 700 people attended *Messiah*. The newspapers were eloquent in praise of the work, and this no doubt reflected the rapturous reception accorded to it. From the newspapers also comes confirmation that the Gentlemen of the cathedral choirs took part, and Dubourg, Avolio and Cibber are named as the leading performers.[23] Handel's conducting score also supplies the names of the male soloists drawn from the cathedral choirs – the altos Lamb and Ward, the tenors Baileys and Church, and the basses Mason and Hill.

After an interval of more than a month following the première of *Messiah*, Handel gave two final performances in Dublin, each preceded by a public rehearsal and advertised as having been produced in response

[20] At least one of the charities, Mercer's Hospital, had asked the cathedral authorities that the choirs should be allowed to take part: see Deutsch, p. 541; *HHB*, p. 346, for 4 March 1743.
[21] *The Dublin Journal* (10 April 1742): Deutsch, p. 545; *HHB*, p. 348.
[22] *The Dublin Journal* (20 April 1742): Deutsch, pp. 546–7; *HHB*, p. 349.
[23] *The Dublin Journal* (17 April 1742: Deutsch, p. 546; *HHB*, pp. 348–9) includes the estimated attendance figure and the names of the soloists

to particular requests from the 'Nobility and Gentry' – *Saul*, on 25 May, and *Messiah*, on 3 June. The audience for *Messiah* was reassured that, in order to ameliorate the summer conditions of a hot and crowded concert-room, additional ventilation would be provided by the removal of the top panes of glass from the windows. The institutional circumstances of the two performances are obscure. From the advertisements it seems that both were undertaken commercially by Handel for his own benefit (there are no hints that the charities were involved), yet it is difficult to believe that Handel could have given either without the assistance of the cathedral choirs, for both required vocal performers more numerous than for the works presented in his subscription series. *Saul* was given in a somewhat slimmed-down version, no doubt without the carillon and trombones, but it still needed a fair array of soloists: Mrs Cibber probably took on the role of David. In terms of musical content, *Messiah* was presumably a repeat of the previous performance, though perhaps with a different soprano soloist: an annotated word-book names Mrs Maclaine as the soprano (she is otherwise not mentioned on any musical source from Handel's performances), but not Avolio. Avolio was certainly still in Dublin at the time, since she announced a benefit concert a few days later, though this event was delayed because of a clash of dates with the programme of a newly arrived group of actors (including David Garrick) from London. They were not the only arrivals. By the end of June, Thomas Augustine Arne and his wife were in Dublin: a concert for Mrs Arne's benefit, given on 21 July and repeated a week later, presented many items by Handel, including several in which Mrs Cibber (her sister-in-law) sang music that she had already sung under Handel.[24] Handel may well have been present in the audience: he did not leave Dublin until 13 August.[25]

Soon after his return to London Handel wrote to Jennens, to report on the successful reception of *Messiah* and to dampen any expectations about his future plans.[26]

> It was indeed Your humble Servant which intended You a visit in my way from Ireland to London, for I certainly could have given You a better account by word of mouth, as by writing, how well Your Messiah was received in that Country ... I shall send the printed Book of the Messiah to Mr Isted for You. As for my Success in General in that generous and polite Nation, I reserve the account of it till I have the Honour to see you in London. The report that the Direction of the Opera next winter is comitted to my Care, is groundless. The gentlemen who have undertaken to middle with Harmony can not agree, and are quite in a Confusion. Whether I shall do some thing in the Oratorio way (as several of my friends desire) I can not determine as yet. Certain it is that

---

[24] For the programme, see *The Dublin Journal* (13 July 1742): Deutsch, p. 552; *HHB*, p. 351.

[25] Handel's departure was reported in Dublin newspapers dated 14 and 17 August 1742: see Deutsch, p. 553; *HHB*, p. 352.

[26] Letter dated 9 September 1742: Deutsch, p. 554; *HHB*, pp. 352–3.

this time 12 month I shall continue my Oratorio's in Ireland, where they are agoing to make a large Subscription allready for that Purpose ... I think it a very long time to the month of November next when I can have some hopes of seeing You here in Town.

That Handel was really more positive about 'doing something in the Oratorio way' than the guarded phrases of his letter reveal is suggested by the fact that he applied himself to 'filling up' the unfinished score of *Samson*, a task he completed on 12 October. This was not the end of his work on *Samson*, however. By the time he gave the first performance, more than four months later, his cast of soloists comprised three sopranos, a contralto, two tenors and two basses. The proliferation of voices required considerable expansion of the score, in order to occupy the extra sopranos and tenor as representative Israelites or Philistines, and the additional music for them was probably written in the intervening period. That the work did not lose its shape in the process of expansion is partly a tribute to the presumed co-operation between Handel and Newburgh Hamilton, because some additional aria texts were required.

Otherwise, virtually nothing is known about Handel's activities between mid-October 1742 and the beginning of February 1743, except that he composed (in London) two more Italian duets (HWV181, 190) on 31 October and 2 November 1742. Presumably this was simply a waiting period; he planned to give oratorios in London but not until the Lenten season (Ash Wednesday fell on 16 February 1743), and on a subscription basis similar to that which had proved successful in Dublin. Much of the intervening time was no doubt devoted to the practical matters of securing the theatre and a cast, the latter involving negotiations with theatre managers for the release of singers from their regular companies. On 10 January 1743 Handel presented the libretto of *Samson*, as required by the act of Parliament governing theatre licences, to the Inspector of Stage Plays: the document reveals that he had secured John Rich's co-operation for the use of Covent Garden theatre, and that the text of the oratorio was by then virtually in its final form, incorporating the additional movements required by the enlarged cast. The constitution of Handel's cast gave a clear indication of the possible future direction of his career: it consisted of 'London' singers, among whom Avolio (who had, after all, been 'anglicized' by Handel in Dublin) was the only foreign element. Mrs Cibber was re-employed, and she was joined by another actress-singer, Mrs Clive (who sang Dalila in *Samson*), for whom Handel had written occasional theatre songs a few years before.[27] Another new singer was the second tenor Thomas Lowe, who had been with the Arnes in Dublin. For the rest, Handel was able to call on soloists who had served him well in London during the previous decade: Beard (who took the role of Samson), Savage, Reinhold and Miss Edwards. Handel finished the last phase of

[27] HWV228[11] and HWV218: see Chapter 9, p. 201.

pre-season composition with an organ concerto (HWV307, later published as op.7 no.2), completed on 5 February 1743; he advertised his first six-performance subscription a week later and began the season on Friday 18 February. The subscription rate was six guineas, entitling the holder to three 'box-tickets' for each performance: walk-in tickets were half a guinea for pit and boxes ('put together'),[28] five shillings for the first gallery and 3s. 6d for the upper gallery.

The instant success of Handel's enterprise is apparent even through the jaundiced prose of Horace Walpole:[29]

> Handel has set up an Oratorio against the Operas, and succeeds. He has hired all the goddesses from farces and the singers of <u>Roast Beef</u> from between the acts at both theatres, with a man with one note in his voice, and a girl without ever an one; and so they sing, and make brave hallelujahs; and the good company encore the recitative, if it happens to have an cadence like what they call a tune.

All six performances of the first subscription were devoted to *Samson*, which ran so successfully that Handel announced a second six-performance subscription just before the first series finished on 16 March. News of his success was relayed even to the Dublin newspapers:[30]

Extract of a private letter from London, March 8

> Our Friend Mr. Handell is very well, and Things have taken a quite different Turn here from what they did some Time past; for the Publick will be no longer imposed on by Italian Singers, and some wrong Headed Undertakers of bad Opera's, but find out the Merit of Mr. Handell's Compositions and English Performances: That Gentleman is more esteemed now than ever. The new Oratorio (called SAMSON) which he composed since he left Ireland, has been performed four Times to more crowded Audiences than ever were seen; more People being turned away for Want of Room each Night than hath been at the Italian Opera. Mr. Dubourg (lately arrived from Dublin) performed at the last, and played a Solo between the Acts, and met with universal and uncommon Applause from the Royal Family and the whole Audience.

The 'Royal Family' probably included the Prince of Wales, but it is not known if the king attended any of the oratorio season. Handel's second subscription series comprised three more performances of *Samson*, a single performance of *L'Allegro* (in a revised form, omitting *Il Moderato* and substituting the Cecilian ode), and two performances of *Messiah*, announced in the newspapers not under that name but simply as 'A New

---

[28] The precise meaning of this phrase in Handel's advertisements is not clear, but some physical alteration to the theatre was involved. A newspaper announcement for a performance of De Fesch's *Joseph* at Covent Garden on 3 April 1745 referred to the practice: 'Whereas it was first intended to lay the pit and boxes together, for the better accommodation of the ladies, who are desirous of having their places kept, the boxes will be enclosed as usual'.

[29] Letter to Horace Mann, 24 February 1743: Deutsch, p. 560; *HHB* p. 358.

[30] *The Dublin Journal* (15 March 1743): Deutsch, p. 562; *HHB*, p. 359.

MESSIAH,

AN

ORATORIO.

Set to Mufick by GEORGE-FREDERIC HANDEL, Efq;.

MAJORA CANAMUS.

*And without Controverfy, great is the Myftery of Godli-
nefs : God was manifefted in the Flefh, juftify'd·by the Spirit,
feen of Angels, preached among the Gentiles, believed on in
the World, received up in Glory.*

   *In whom are hid all the Treafures of Wifdom and Know-
ledge.*

LONDON:

Printed and Sold by THO. WOOD in *Windmill-Court*, near *Weft-
Smithfield*, and at the THEATRE in *Covent-Garden*. 1743.

[Price One Shilling.]

Fig. 12 The title-page from the original word-book for Handel's first
London performances of *Messiah*, 1743

Sacred Oratorio' (though the printed word-book bore the title *Messiah*;
see Fig.12). There is evidence that Handel also planned to revive *Athalia*
this season, but eventually did not include it. The first London performance
of *Messiah*, on 23 March 1743, was preceded by an article in one of the
London newspapers questioning whether it was appropriate to perform
such a work in the theatre, and with theatre performers. While it is
difficult to assess how much this article (or the subsequent rejoinders that

270

appeared in the newspapers) reflected the views of any influential part of Handel's subscribers, Handel probably felt the pressure of public controversy, although this did not prevent the successful completion of the subscription series, nor did it prevent *Messiah* from receiving further performances on 25 and 29 March.[31] A final performance of *Samson* closed the season on 31 March (Maundy Thursday). Handel must have been somewhat taken aback by the contrast between the reception accorded *Messiah* in Dublin and in London.

In addition to suffering public controversy in the newspapers over *Messiah*, Handel also came under pressure from its librettist-compiler. Jennens seems to have developed an accumulating sense of grievance over *Messiah* because Handel had composed it quickly, because he had taken it to Dublin first, and because he had given precedence to *Samson* in the 1743 London season. Jennens's attitude manifested itself in exaggerated criticisms of the work: specifically, he directed his disapproval to the overture, to Handel's treatment of certain texts and to some features of his word-setting. Handel responded to a few of Jennens's criticisms in the revisions that he made to the score for the 1743 (and 1745) performances.[32] But Jennens's attitude seems to have been irrational, and some of his opinions may have been voiced before he had even seen a score or heard *Messiah* in performance: in the end, even he had to admit that Handel had made a 'fine Entertainment' of it.[33] After the first performance, in fact, he was quite enthusiastic:[34]

> Messiah was perform'd last night, & will be again to morrow, notwithstanding the clamour rais'd against it, which has only occasion'd it's being advertis'd without its Name; ... 'Tis after all, in the main, a fine Composition, notwithstanding some weak parts, which he was too idle & too obstinate to retouch, tho' I us'd great importunity to perswade him to it. He & his Toad-eater Smith did all they could to murder the Words in print; but I hope I have restor'd them to Life, not without much difficulty.

The combined pressures seem to have taken their toll on Handel's health, probably at the end of the second subscription series. On 11 April a newspaper reported that 'Mr. Handel, who has been dangerously ill, is now recover'd',[35] but the recovery was only temporary. Evidence of a relapse comes in two letters, from Jennens on 29 April:[36]

[31] The newspaper controversy may be followed through Deutsch, pp. 563–8, and *HHB*, pp. 359–62. See also Burrows, *Handel: 'Messiah'*, Chapter 3.

[32] See Burrows, 'The Autographs and Early Copies', pp. 205–10.

[33] Letter to an unidentified correspondent, 30 August 1745: Deutsch, p. 622; *HHB*, p. 394.

[34] Letter to Holdsworth, 24 March 1742/3: *HHB*, pp. 360–1 (with minor errors).

[35] *The Daily Advertiser* (11 April 1743). Handel's health may also have been affected by deficiencies in the available food, the result of bad climatic conditions in Britain during 1743–5.

[36] Letter to Holdsworth, 29 April 1743: *HHB*, pp. 362–3. According to an anecdote recorded some 35 years later, Handel had also had 'another Paraletic stroke ... violent and universal' while in Dublin (see Mann, 'An Unknown Detail'), but soon recovered.

I hear Handel has a return of his Paralytick Disorder, which affects his Head & Speech. He talks of spending a year abroad, so that we are to expect no Musick next year;

and from Horace Walpole on 4 May:[37]

We are likely at last to have no Opera next year: Handel has had a palsy, and can't compose.

In a letter written later in the year, Jennens even claimed, rather complacently, that he had himself contributed to the breakdown in Handel's health:[38]

I don't yet despair of making him retouch the Messiah, at least he shall suffer for his negligence; nay I am inform'd that he has suffer'd, for he told Ld Guernsey, that a letter I wrote him about it contributed to the bringing of his last illness upon him; & it is reported that being a little delirious with a Fever, he said he should be damn'd for preferring Dagon (a Gentleman he was very complaisant to in the Oratorio of Samson) before the Messiah. This shews that I gall'd him: but I have not done with him yet.

Handel must have recovered from his incapacity fairly quickly, because the summer of 1743 was exceptionally productive. He composed two scores for the next theatre season: *Semele*, between 3 June and 4 July; and *Joseph and his Brethren* during August and September. They must have been written with a London season in mind, following on the success of his *Samson*-based programme: Handel's previous plans to return to Dublin for a season in 1743–4 seem to have been overtaken by events. Furthermore, he devoted the period between these two major new works to composing the 'Dettingen' *Te Deum* and anthem (HWV283, 265), in anticipation of a later celebration in London of the victory in the continental war at Dettingen on 27 June 1743 (in which the king himself led the army.)[39]

While there is no reason to doubt that Handel was genuinely ill in the spring of 1743, he may well have tried to minimize any publicity about his recovery and subsequent creative activity in order to stave off pressure from another direction. In the summer of 1743 he seems to have faced considerable difficulty in sustaining his independence from the 'Middlesex' opera company. The noble directors of the company, which was in serious financial difficulty, applied pressures through all the available social channels in an effort to persuade Handel to compose for them: obviously they realized that a couple of new operas from Handel would give the

---

[37] Letter to Horace Mann, 4 May 1743, describing the financial collapse of the 'Middlesex' opera company: Deutsch, p. 569; *HHB*, p. 363.

[38] Letter to Holdsworth, 15 September 1743: *HHB*, p. 365.

[39] The king's reputation for glory was short-lived, especially when rumours quickly spread that the victorious charge was attributable to the bolting of the king's horse rather than the valour of its rider.

company the artistic credibility that it had failed to achieve under Galuppi. In truth, Handel wanted no more to do with the old-style opera companies and their managements, though at one stage he may have weakened and made a half-promise that he later regretted. The most accurate and graphic evidence for the situation comes from a letter written by the elder John Christopher Smith to the Earl of Shaftesbury on 28 July:[40]

It is with your Lordships kind permission that I take the Liberty to acquaint your Lordship with Mr. Handel's Health and what passes in Musical affairs, which I should have done a month sooner if it had not been that I would stay to know what Resolution He would take in what I am going to relate to your Lordship. It seems that Mr. Handel promis'd my Lord Middlesex, that if He would give him for two new operas 1000 G[uinea]s and his Health would permit, He would compose for him next Season, after which he declin'd his promise and said that He could – or would [–] do nothing for the Opera Directors, altho' the Prince of Wales desired him at several times to accept of their offers, and compose for them, and said that by so doing He would not only oblige the King & the Royal Family but likewise all the Quality. When my Lord Middlesex saw that no persuasion would take place with Him, and seeing himself engaged in such an undertaking without a Composer He sent for one from Italy, of whom nobody has any great opinion. Nevertheless He would still make some fresh Proposals to Mr. Handel, and let Him know how much regard He had for his composition, and that He would put it in his power to make it as easy to Himself as He pleased. I was charged with the Commission, and the offer was that He should have 1000 G[uinea]s for two, or 500 G[uinea]s for one new opera, and if his health would not permit Him to compose any new one at all, and would only adjust some of His old operas, that He should have 100 Guineas for each: But in case Mr. Handel should refuse all these offers, that my Lord would have some of his old operas performed without Him and to let the Publick know in an advertisement, what offers was made to Mr. Handel, and that there was no possibility to have any thing from Him. I could not in Duty but let Him know My Lord's new offers and proceedings, for fear things might be carry'd to[o] far; I wrote the contents to Mr. Goupy with the desire to com[m]unicate it to Mr. Handel (for it seems he has taken an aversion to see me, for having been to[o] much his Friend) and to have his answer, which He said He would give to the Principale, but has given none since, and has been composing for himself this two month's, and finished (as I hear) a Piece of Music from Dryden's words, the subject unknown to me, tho' they tell me that I was to do for Him as I did before, but my Son is to see Him and take his instructions. He is now upon a new Grand Te Deum and Jubilate, to be performed at the King's return from Germany (but He keeps this a great secret and I would not speak of it to any Body but to your Lordship) and by the Paper he had from me I can guess that it must be almost finish'd. This I think perfectly well Judg'd to appeace & oblige the Court and Town with such a grand Composition & Performance. But how the Quality will take it that He can compose for Him self and not for them when they offer'd Him more then ever He had in his Life, I am not a judge and could only whish that

[40] *HHB*, pp. 363–4.

I had not been employ'd in it either Directly or indirectly, for He is Ill advis'd and thinks all I do now is wrong, tho' I must say that He is persuaded in His heart to the Contrary for He had too many proofs of my fidelity within this 24 years, and I shall never be wanting to do Him still all the Services that lies in my Power, for I think it is better to suffer than to offend.

Handel co-operated with the 'Middlesex' opera company to the extent that he probably supplied them with a score of *Alessandro*, which, somewhat adapted, formed the basis of *Rossane*, the production that opened their new season at the King's Theatre on 15 November 1743. However, his refusal to give the opera company any further assistance stored up trouble for him, because he undoubtedly thereby incurred some displeasure among the noble theatre patrons – and now he had no Princess Anne or Queen Caroline to act in his defence. To aristocratic opera managers who were used to a certain deference from the musicians they patronized, it was probably yet more offensive that Handel was determined to mount his own theatre seasons without any gesture towards their controlling influence. Furthermore, one of the new works that Handel had prepared for his next season amounted in itself to a gesture of defiant competition – the libretto of *Semele* had been written by William Congreve for an operatic venture with music by John Eccles nearly 40 years previously.[41] It was the nearest thing to an 'English opera' that Handel ever produced in London, and, although the way the libretto had been adapted for him made it technically more suited to the oratorio-style medium, it certainly retained its fundamentally operatic character.

The combination of works that Handel composed in the summer of 1743 is also significant. Having established, from his success in 1743, that he could run his own subscription season with works such as *Samson*, *L'Allegro* and *Messiah*, he wanted to broaden his repertory with a view to keeping his 'oratorio' audience alert for new works while also attracting those with tastes for more secular, operatic stories.[42] In the seasons of 1744 and 1745 he was to test out the potential for this broader audience with programmes that had a dual appeal. In both years his new theatre works comprised 'pairs', one sacred and one secular, the latter based on classical subjects. For the new oratorio in the first year Handel needed a librettist, and he was probably reluctant to approach Jennens in view of their currently strained relations: hence *Joseph and his Brethren* was the work of James Miller, a literary-minded clergyman who had written political pamphlets and plays. His clerical status was perhaps Miller's least important qualification for the work: his previous experience as an

---

[41] The Congreve/Eccles version had never been performed as intended, at the period of the opening of the Queen's Theatre (see Chapter 4).

[42] Handel's choice of *Semele* may also have been influenced by Arne's setting of Congreve's *The Judgment of Paris*, which Arne had given as double bill with Handel's *Alexander's Feast* at Drury Lane in March 1742. Handel may have been bidding for Arne's audience (Arne was in Dublin in 1743–4).

author for the professional London stage and his apparently genuine interest in the oratorio genre seem to have been more significant.

When Handel was composing *Semele* and *Joseph* in the summer of 1743, the next oratorio season was still some time away. A significant event at the end of August was the publication of an almost complete full score of the Cannons version of *Acis and Galatea* – a coherent, performable version, not just a collection of 'songs'; such completeness in Handel's works had been seen before only in 1738 with the score of *Alexander's Feast*. The publication of *Acis and Galatea* signalled that Handel himself had finished with the work: he never again produced it after the Dublin performances in 1742. The autumn was mainly devoted to preparations for the performance of the 'Dettingen' music, a process that eventually stretched out over a couple of months. There was a public rehearsal of it on 26 September at the Chapel Royal before the royal princesses, in anticipation of the king's return: but the king's progress back to Britain was leisurely, and when he did return he was in no mood for an immediate celebration because the time fell close to the anniversary of the queen's death. There were further public rehearsals (in the Banqueting House, Whitehall) around the period of the king's return in November, and the Dettingen music was eventually performed at the Chapel Royal service on Sunday 27 November, officially to celebrate the king's safe return to Britain rather than to commemorate the Dettingen victory. The scale of the music suggests that Handel had originally expected a Utrecht-style thanksgiving service in St Paul's Cathedral; but the attention given to the public rehearsals may have been almost as effective in confirming his position at the centre of London's social and musical life. His influence was also spreading elsewhere, as others took up his recent music: in November, a charity performance of *Messiah* was planned in Dublin[43] and a performance of *Samson* took place in one of the college halls at Oxford.[44]

On the basis of his success in the previous season, Handel apparently felt that he had a safe audience at Covent Garden for a longer run, so in January 1744, instead of the modest six-performance series, he advertised the following: 'Mr Handel proposes to Perform by *Subscription*, Twelve Times during next Lent, and engages to play two New Performances (and some of his former Oratorios, if Time will permit)'. A different ticket 'deal' was offered for the 1744 season: four guineas for one box ticket for 12 performances, as against three guineas for three box tickets for six

---

[43] Though scheduled for December, it was delayed until February 1744: see Deutsch, pp. 576–7; *HHB*, p. 368; and Boydell, *A Dublin Musical Calendar*, pp. 95–6.

[44] Letter from Catherine Talbot to Elizabeth Carter, 27 December 1743: Deutsch, p. 577; *HHB*, pp. 368–9. This was almost certainly the performance given for the benefit of William Hayes on 22 November 1743 (advertised in the *London Evening Post* for 8–10 November); Hayes had helped present many of Handel's works in Oxford: see Burrows, 'Sources for Oxford Handel Performances'.

performances the previous year.[45] Subscriptions were collected at Handel's house and at Walsh's shop: subscribers were asked to collect their tickets from Handel's house between 9 a.m. and 3 p.m., Monday to Saturday. Handel rehearsed *Semele* at his house on 23 January, and Mrs Delany reported that it was 'a delightful piece of music, quite new and different from anything he has done'.[46] She also reported on the first performance, which she attended on 10 February:[47]

> There is a four-part song that is delightfully pretty; Francesina is extremely improved, her notes are more distinct, and there is something in her running-divisions that is quite surprizing. She was much applauded, and the house full, though not crowded; I believe I wrote my brother word that Mr. Handel and the <u>Prince</u> had quarelled, which I am sorry for. Handel says the Prince is quite out of <u>his</u> good graces! there was no disturbance at the play-house and the Goths were not so very absurd as to declare, in a public manner, their disapprobation of such a composer.

It seems quite likely that the coldness between Handel and the Prince of Wales was the aftermath of Handel's refusal to compose for the opera company.[48] Mrs Delany's invaluable correspondence also notes that[49]

> They say Samson is to be next Friday: for Semele has a strong party against it, viz. the fine ladies, petit maîtres, and ignoramus's. All the opera people are enraged at Handel, but Lady Cobham, Lady Westmoreland, and Lady Chesterfield never fail it.

If Handel's social position in London was not entirely secure, then his decision to open his season with *Semele* was a brave, or possibly foolhardy, gesture. Quite apart from the work's pseudo-operatic manner, the secular story was a peculiar choice for a theatre programme that began on the first Friday of Lent; as Mrs Delany said, her clerical husband did not 'think it proper for him to go ... it being a profane story'.[50] But the performances seem to have been well received. For his cast, Handel retained Beard, Avolio and Reinhold from the previous season, welcomed back Francesina and had two new singers in the contralto Esther Young and the alto Daniel Sullivan. Mrs Delany was not entirely flattering about the singers, after attending the fifth performance:[51]

> I was last night to hear Samson. Francesina sings most of Mrs. Cibber's part and some of Mrs. Clive's: upon the whole it went off very well, but not better

[45] *The London Daily Post* (9 January 1744): Deutsch, p. 578, *HHB*, p. 369.
[46] Letter to Mrs Dewes, 24 January 1744: Deutsch, p. 579; *HHB*, p. 370.
[47] Letter to Mrs Dewes, 11 February 1744: Deutsch, p. 582; *HHB*, p. 372.
[48] Hostility between Handel and the Prince of Wales may have been more marked than in the 1730s: in 1743 and 1745 the prince attended the 'Middlesex' opera performances and Handel's oratorios, but in 1744 he attended only the opera. See Taylor, 'Handel and Frederick', p. 91.
[49] Letter to Mrs Dewes, 21 February 1744: Deutsch, p. 584; *HHB*, p. 373.
[50] *Ibid.*
[51] Letter to Mrs Dewes, 25 February 1744: Deutsch, p. 585; *HHB*, p. 373.

than last year. Joseph, I believe, will be next Friday, but Handel is mightily out of humour about it, for Sullivan, who is to sing Joseph, is a block with a very fine voice, and Beard has no voice at all. The part which Francesina is to have (of Joseph's wife) will not admit of much variety; but I hope it will be well received; the houses have not been crowded, but pretty full every night.

'Not crowded, but pretty full every night' probably sums up Handel's degree of success in his 1744 season. Mrs Delany supplies the end of the story:[52]

The oratorios fill very well, not withstanding the spite of the opera party: nine of the twelve are over. Joseph is to be performed (I hope) once more, then Saul, and the Messiah finishes; as they have taken very well, I fancy Handel will have a second subscription; and how do you think I have lately been employed? Why, I have made a drama for an oratorio, out of Milton's Paradise Lost, to give Mr. Handel to compose to.

Handel did not take up Mrs Delany's libretto (though he accepted an invitation to dinner on 3 April), nor did he proceed beyond the 12 performances, which concluded on the Wednesday of Holy Week. The last performance was *Saul*, not *Messiah*. Handel was perhaps not yet ready to test out the state of his relationship with London's pressure groups (and Jennens) over that work. His programme had comprised the new works *Semele* and *Joseph* (four performances each) and revivals of *Samson* and *Saul* (two performances each).

Joseph and his Brethren has been adversely criticized in modern times for both its literary style and the structure of its libretto (see Chapter 13), but Handel seems to have had a better opinion of the work and revived it fairly often. *Semele*, on the other hand, was not heard after 1744, mainly because Handel abandoned using such secular works as a basis for his programmes. There is no reason to suppose that he found James Miller, the librettist for *Joseph*, an uncongenial or incompetent collaborator, and Miller for his part gave Handel the strongest support (by implication, against the 'opera party') in the dedicatory preface (to the Duke of Montagu) that was printed in the word-book:

'Tis a pity however, My Lord, that such a Genius should be put to the Drudgery of hammering for Fire where there is no Flint, and of giving a Sentiment to the Poet's Metre before he can give one to his own Melody.

Unfortunately, their collaboration was curtailed by Miller's death on 27 April 1744. Handel took almost immediate action to secure his future librettos by patching up his differences with Jennens:[53]

Handel has promis'd to revise the Oratorio of Messiah, & He & I are very good Friends again. The reason is he has lately lost his Poet Miller, & wants to set me at work for him again.

[52] Letter to Mrs Dewes, 10 March 1744: Deutsch, pp. 587–8; *HHB*, p. 374.
[53] Letter to Holdsworth, 7 May 1744.

The seasons of 1743 and 1744, based on Lenten 'oratorio seasons', had established a new pattern for Handel's professional career (the terminological confusion over 'oratorio seasons' is discussed in Chapter 13). With two sufficiently successful seasons behind him, Handel now took the logical, but still surprising, step of expanding into a much more ambitious programme: instead of the well-tried base of 12 performances, he planned for a full-scale season of twice that length. At 24 performances, this was still only about half of the number that had been conventional for opera seasons, but it represented a considerable speculative challenge in relation to the London audience. The immediate stimulant to Handel's scheme was the collapse of the 'Middlesex' opera company: Handel determined to move back into the King's Theatre, Haymarket, and offer his own programme of English works 'after the manner of an Oratorio' as a substitute for opera. It was perhaps the one aggressive competitive gesture of his career: he wanted those who had undertaken to 'middle with harmony' not merely to be beaten but to be seen to be beaten. He wasted no time in moving forward: by early June 1744, while the 'Middlesex' company was still running, he had secured the King's Theatre for the next season and was well on the way to committing singers to his company, as he related in a letter to Jennens, who was by then at Gopsall for the summer:[54]

> As You do me the Honour to encourage my musicall Undertakings, and even to promote them with a particular Kindness, I take the Liberty to trouble You with an account of what Engagement I have hitherto concluded. I have taken the Opera House in the Haymarketh. engagd, as Singers, Sig^{ra} Francesina, Miss Robinson, Beard, Reinhold, Mr Gates with his Boyes's and several of the best Chorus Singers from the Choirs, and I have some hopes that Mrs Cibber will sing for me. She sent me word from Bath (where she is now) that she would perform for me next winter with great pleasure if it did not interfere with her playing, but I think I can obtain Mr Riches's permission (with whom she is engaged to play in Covent Garden House) since so obligingly he gave Leave to Mr Beard and Mr Reinhold.
>
> Now should I be extreamly glad to receive the first Act, or what is ready of the new Oratorio with which you intend to favour me, that I might employ all my attention and time, in order to answer in some measure the great obligation I lay under. this new favour will greatly increase my Obligations.

Soon after writing this letter Handel left London, presumably to visit friends 'in the country', though there is no documentary evidence for his destination. He arrived back in London on 18 July, and the next day began the first of the new works for the forthcoming season, *Hercules*. The librettist of this 'musical drama' was Thomas Broughton who, like Miller, was a clergyman with literary experience; like Miller, too, his collaboration with Handel was confined to one work. Whether he was

[54] 9 June 1744: Deutsch, pp. 590–1; *HHB*, p. 376.

part of Handel's close circle of acquaintances is doubtful: Handel probably received a few speculative submissions of librettos from various authors during the 1740s.[55] Handel had finished and 'filled up' the draft score of *Hercules* by 17 August. Meanwhile, his mind had also been turning over the 'new Oratorio', *Belshazzar*, that had been the subject of his letter to Jennens in June. On 19 July 1744, the day he began the score of *Hercules*, Handel had written to Jennens to acknowledge receipt of the first part of the libretto of *Belshazzar*:[56]

> At my arrival in London, which was Yesterday, I immediately perused the Act of the Oratorio with which you favour'd me, and, the little time only I had it, gives me great Pleasure. Your reasons for the Lenght of the first act are intirely Satisfactory to me, and it is likewise my Opinion to have the following Acts short. I shall be very glad and much obliged to you, if you will soon favour me with the remaining acts. Be pleased to point out these passages in t[h]e Messiah which You think require altering.

On 21 August he wrote again after receiving Part 2:[57]

> The Second Act of the Oratorio I have received safe, and own my self highly obliged to You for it. I am greatly pleased with it, and shall use my best endeavours to do it Justice. I can only Say that I impatiently wait for the third act.

Two days later he set to work on the material he had to hand, and had set it by mid-September. As he was nearing completion he wrote to ask Jennens for the rest of the libretto:[58]

> Your most excellent Oratorio has given me great Delight in setting it to Musick and still engages me warmly. It is indeed a Noble Piece, very grand and uncommon; it has furnished me with Expressions, and has given me Opportunity to some very particular Ideas, besides so many great Choru's. I intreat you heartily to favour me Soon with the last Act, which I expect with anxiety, that I may regulate my Self the better as to the Lenght of it.

Jennens complained that Handel was hurrying him, but Part 3 was in Handel's hands early the next month:[59]

> I received the 3ᵈ Act, with a great deal of pleasure, as You can imagine, and You may believe that I think it a very fine and sublime Oratorio, only it is realy too long, if I should extend the Musick, it would last 4 Hours and more. I retrench'd already a great deal of the Musick, that I might preserve the Poetry as much as I could, yet still it must be shortned. The Anthems come in very proprely. but would not the Words (tell it out among the Heathen that the

[55] Among them was almost certainly one which, in altered form, was later set by Haydn as *The Creation*. See also Clive T. Probyn, *The Sociable Humanist* (Oxford, 1991), pp. 72–3.
[56] Deutsch, p. 592; *HHB*, p. 377.
[57] Deutsch, p. 592; *HHB*, p. 378.
[58] Letter of 13 September 1744: Deutsch, p. 595; *HHB*, p. 379.
[59] Letter to Jennens, 2 October 1744: Deutsch, pp. 595–6; *HHB*, p. 379.

Lord is King.) [be] sufficient for one Chorus? T[h]e Anthem (I will magnify thee O God my King, and I will praise thy name for ever and ever. vers). the Lord preserveth all them that love him, but scattreth abroad all the ungodly. (vers and chorus) my mouth shall speak the Praise of the Lord and let all flesh give thanks unto His holy name for ever and ever Amen.) concludes well the Oratorio. I hope you will make a visit to London next Winter. I have a good Set of Singers. S. Francesina performs Nitocris, Miss Robinson Cyrus, Mrs Cibber Daniel, Mr Beard (who is recoverd) Belshazzar, Mr Reinhold Gobrias, and a good Number of Choir Singers for the Chorus's. I propose 24 Nights to perform this Season on Saturdays but in Lent on Wednesday's or Fryday's. I shall open ye 3^d of Novemb^r next with Deborah.

Handel had completed the score of *Belshazzar* by 23 October,[60] although (as usual) it was to see further revisions before performance. As with their collaboration over *Saul*, Jennens and Handel seem to have conferred about *Belshazzar* after the draft was completed, probably soon after Jennens arrived in London from Gopsall (normally in November). The autograph of the oratorio contains many detailed emendations in Jennens's hand, mainly affecting the scene-descriptions, the verbal text and the musical declamation. At the same time Jennens no doubt aired the points about *Messiah* that he thought required alteration (unlike *Saul* and *Belshazzar*, *Messiah* was apparently kept away from Jennens by Handel: the autograph lacks annotations in Jennens's hand, though the performance score has minor emendations that might be his).

By the time he had finished drafting *Belshazzar*, Handel was probably well into rehearsals for his new season, which opened, as predicted, with *Deborah* on Saturday 3 November. Handel had presumably received enough subscriptions to enable him to begin the season: walk-in tickets were advertised at the same rates as for his previous seasons at Covent Garden. The immediate result was not encouraging. The Saturday performance was followed by a notice on the Monday morning:[61]

> As the greatest Part of Mr. HANDEL's Subscribers are not in Town, he is requested not to perform till Saturday the 24th Instant; but the Subscription is continued to be taken in at Mr. Handel's House ... at Mr. Walsh's ... and at White's Chocolate-House.

The performance on 3 November had also clashed with the opening night of a run of *Richard III* at Drury Lane with David Garrick in the title role (with which he had made his dramatic entry into the theatrical life of London at Goodman's Fields Theatre three years earlier). Handel accordingly held off until 24 November, when he repeated *Deborah*, and he then presented his only revival of *Semele*, on the first two Saturdays in December. These performances were remarkable because Handel appar-

---

[60] The end of the autograph is lost, but Jennens copied Handel's completion date on to his own copy of the score (now in the Henry Watson Music Library in Manchester).

[61] *The Daily Advertiser* (5 November 1744): Deutsch, p. 598; *HHB*, p. 381.

ently employed some Italian singers (possibly picked up from the debris of the 'Middlesex' opera company) who could not sing in English. This was the last occasion on which he included Italian-language arias in his public performances. The Italians then left Handel's cast again as suddenly as they had appeared.

After another pause in his Saturday-night programme, Handel resumed after Christmas with performances of *Hercules* on 5 and 12 January 1745. His strategy looks entirely sensible: *Hercules*, the secular work, was introduced at the New Year period, which in earlier years had seen the successful premières of many of Handel's operas. But *Hercules* was attended by misfortunes. Mrs Cibber was indisposed for the first performance, which necessitated some re-casting. More significantly, Handel sensed that his gamble with the season's plan was not succeeding. By mid-January, when he had performed a quarter of his intended 24 performances, he announced his doubts about his ability to complete the season in a letter published in *The Daily Advertiser*, London's principal newspaper for theatrical announcements:[62]

Having for a Series of Years received the greatest Obligations from the Nobility and Gentry of this Nation, I have always retained a deep Impression of their Goodness. As I perceived, that joining good Sense and significant Words to Musick, was the best Method of recommending *this* to an English Audience; I have directed my Studies that way, and endeavour'd to shew, that the English Language, which is so expressive of the sublimest Sentiments is the best adapted of any to the full and solemn Kind of Musick. I have the Mortification now to find, that my Labours to please are become ineffectual, when my Expences are considerably greater. To what Cause I must impute the loss of the publick Favour I am ignorant, but the Loss itself I shall always lament. In the mean time, I am assur'd that a Nation, whose Characteristick is Good Nature, would be affected with the Ruin of any Man, which was owing to his Endeavours to entertain them. I am likewise persuaded, that I shall have the Forgiveness of those noble Persons, who have honour'd me with their Patronage, and their Subscription this Winter, if I beg their Permission to stop short, before my losses are too great to support, if I proceed no farther in my Undertaking; and if I intreat them to withdraw three Fourths of their Subscription, one Fourth Part only of my Proposal having been perform'd.

This brought various gestures of support, including a letter the next day to the newspaper[63] declaring that the neglect of Handel's 'admirable Performances can no otherwise be made up with Justice to the Character of the Nation, and the Merit of the Man, than by the Subscribers generously declining to withdraw the Remainder of their Subscriptions'.

It is difficult to judge how representative these sentiments were, but apparently Handel found sufficient encouragement to respond:[64]

[62]*Ibid.* (17 January 1745): Deutsch, p. 602; *HHB*, pp. 383–4.
[63]*Ibid.* (18 January 1745): Deutsch, p. 603; *HHB*, p. 384.
[64]*Ibid.* (25 January 1745): Deutsch, p. 606; *HHB*, p. 385.

The new Proofs which I have receiv'd of the Generosity of my Subscribers, in refusing upon their own Motives, to withdraw their Subscriptions call upon me for the earliest Return, and the warmest Expressions of my Gratitude; but natural as it is to feel, proper as it is to have, I find this extremely difficult to express. Indeed, I ought not to content myself with bare expressions of it; therefore, though I am not able to fulfil the whole of my Engagement, I shall think it my Duty to perform what Part of it I can, and shall in some Time proceed with the Oratorios, let the *Risque* which I may run be what it will.

In an interesting letter dated 21 February,[65] Jennens stated that various 'ladies' (presumably of strong social influence on London's theatre-going public) were opposed to Handel's season of performances, and there may well have been a residue of ill-feeling from his refusal to co-operate with the 'Middlesex' opera company. However, Jennens did not think that this was the whole reason for Handel's ill success:

But I believe it is in some measure owing to his own imprudence in changing the profitable method he was in before for a new & hazardous Experiment. For the two last years he had perform'd Oratorios in Covent-Garden Playhouse on Wednesdays & Fridays in Lent only, when there was no publick Entertainment of any consequence to interfere with him: & his gains were considerable, 2100£ one year, & 1600£ the other, for only 12 performances. Flush'd with this success, the Italian Opera being drop'd, he takes the Opera-house in the Hay-market for this Season at the rent of 400£, buys him a new organ, & instead of an Oratorio produces an English Opera call'd Hercules, which he performs on Saturdays during the run of Plays, Concerts, Assemblys, Drums, Routs, Hurricanes, & all the madness of Town Diversions. His Opera, for want of the top Italian voices, Action, Dresses, Scenes & Dances, which us'd to draw company, & prevent the Undertakers losing above 3 or 4 thousand pounds, had scarce half a house the first night, much less than half the second; & he has been quiet ever since. I mention Hercules, because it was his first new Piece, tho' he had [previously] perform'd the Oratorio of Deborah.

Handel announced the resumption of his performances with *Hercules* on 11 February 1745, but this was called off, and thereafter he seems to have abandoned Saturday-night presentations. Instead, he waited to begin his normal Lenten Wednesday/Friday cycle, which resumed on 1 March (the first Friday in Lent) with *Samson* (two performances) and then revivals of *Saul* (one performance) and *Joseph* (two performances). The new oratorio, *Belshazzar*, followed on 27 March: there were two performances, followed by two of *Messiah* (somewhat revised) on the Tuesday and Thursday of Holy Week, and then a final performance of *Belshazzar* nine days after Easter, on 23 April, St George's Day. In all, Handel had given 16 of his promised 24 performances, and even his regular Lenten oratorio slot in

---

[65] Letter to Holdsworth, 21 February 1745: *HHB*, p. 386. Mainwaring (*Memoirs*, pp. 134–5) also describes the effects of Handel falling 'under the heavy displeasure of a certain fashionable lady', but he places this in 1743, not 1745.

London's life does not seem to have been as well attended as previously:[66]

> Handel, once so crowded, plays to empty walls in that opera house, where there used to be a constant audience as long as there were any dancers to be seen. Unfashionable that I am, I was I own highly delighted the other night at his last oratorio. 'Tis called Belshazzar.

Partly because of the paucity of surviving word-books from the 1745 season, and partly because of the complexity of the musical source materials, it is difficult to reconstruct Handel's allocation of the singers in some of his performances. There are certainly signs of a crisis or two. Mrs Cibber was indisposed for the first performance of *Hercules*, but recovered for the second: her role of Lichas underwent rapid expansion, contraction and restoration. A curious letter addressed to Handel appeared in the press after the first presentation of *Samson*,[67] complaining of the writer's

> Disappointment to see the most delightful Songs in the whole Oratorio took from one, who, by her Manner of singing them charm'd all the Hearers; Was she once instated in the Part she always used to perform, your Samson would shine with the greatest Lustre.

This seems to refer to the re-allocation of the part of Micah from Mrs Cibber to Mrs Robinson, though the tone of the letter suggests that Mrs Cibber still performed a lesser function. Mrs Cibber may have dropped out of the cast after *Hercules*, and Handel's performance score of *Belshazzar* shows a major upheaval at the last moment to cope with her absence from the planned cast for that work. It is possible, however, that this emergency took place for the performance on 23 April, after Easter: Mrs Cibber may have been given leave from her theatre company only for the Wednesdays and Fridays of Lent, when the other patent theatres were dark.[68]

Handel's Drawing Account at the Bank of England springs back to life in 1744–5, and it may now be possible to interpret the figures in terms of his theatrical activities. He deposited £900 in March–April 1744 and £650 in November–December: these major deposits were surely from subscription money. Other smaller deposits followed in 1745, but by May 1745 he had drawn on all the cash that he had deposited in this particular account. His last three payments, unusually, are itemized. They record substantial sums to the leading ladies of his company – £400 to Francesina and £210 to Robinson – and then £140 to 'Jordan', probably a payment for the organ mentioned in Jennens's letter. Presumably the instrument

[66] Letter from Elizabeth Carter to Catherine Talbot, 2 March (*recte* April) 1745: Deutsch, pp. 610–11; *HHB*, p. 388.

[67] *The Daily Advertiser* (4 March 1745): Deutsch, p. 608; *HHB*, p. 387.

[68] Mrs Cibber was contracted to the Drury Lane company for the season, not to Covent Garden (as anticipated by Handel in his letter of 2 October 1744 to Jennens). No performance was advertised at Drury Lane for 23 April.

was an 'oratorio' organ that had been tailored specially for the stage site at the King's Theatre: Jordan probably rebuilt it and adapted it for Handel's subsequent use at Covent Garden.[69]

Handel never again performed a season in his former operatic venue, the King's Theatre. His need for economy of effort and resources in the face of a dwindling audience in 1745 may be reflected in the fact that no new word-books seem to have been printed for the oratorio revivals in the Lenten season. With his plan for 24 performances Handel had overestimated the capacity of his regular audience; but that may reflect a change in London's social habits of the moment rather than a dip in his popularity. His music featured in other people's benefit concerts during April 1745 – for the Decay'd Musicians at Covent Garden, and for Miss Robinson (one of the principal members of his own cast) at the King's Theatre. That Handel's wider musical audience in London remained more or less faithful to him may be judged from the fact that Walsh published selections of arias from *Hercules* and *Belshazzar* with his accustomed promptness.

[69] This was presumably the instrument that perished in the fire at Covent Garden in 1808; a later specification for it is known, but there is no satisfactory documentation from Handel's lifetime.

12

The oratorio composer II: Towards victory, 1745–9

June 1745 found Handel on one of his few documented British excursions away from London. He went first to Exton in Rutland (now in Leicestershire), to the home of the Earl of Gainsborough. There he supplied a short cantata-epilogue for a family performance of a version of Milton's *Comus*[1] (*There in blissful shades* HWV 44), though, as the earl's brother James Noel explained in a subsequent letter, at first the family were hesitant about broaching the matter, since Handel was at Exton as a guest:[2]

> As Handel came to this place for Quiet and Retirement we were very loath to lay any task of Composition upon him. Selfishness however prevail'd; but we determined at the same time to be very moderate in our Requests. His readiness to oblidge soon took off all our apprehensions upon that account. A hint of what we wanted was sufficient and what should have been an act of Compliance he made a voluntary Deed. We laid our plan accordingly and reserved his Musick for an Eclat at this close of the entertainment. We likewise intermix'd the Poem with several of his former Compositions, as your Lordship will see by the copy I have sent you, which I think gave it great Life and Beauty. The whole scheme was concerted and executed in five Days; and that I believe your Lordship will allow was good Dispatch. It was intended to have been performed in the Garden, but the weather would not favour that design. We contrived however to entertain the Company there afterwards with an imitation of Vaux Hall: and, in the style of a news-paper, <u>the whole concluded</u> with what variety of fireworks we could possibly get.

The next section of the letter records Handel's subsequent movements:

> Mr Handel left us about ten days ago. He is gone to Scarborough and will visit us again in his return back, which he believ'd would not be long. We propose to be Fellow-Travellers to St. Giles.

St Giles's House (at Wimborne St Giles, Dorset) was the home of Noel's brother-in-law, the Earl of Shaftesbury, the recipient of the letter. The

---

[1] See Hicks, 'Handel's Music for "Comus"'; the Exton performance was based on Dalton's version of *Comus*, which had been prepared for Arne's setting. Arne's music was not performed at Exton, though other music by Handel was introduced.
[2] Letter to the Earl of Shaftesbury, 23 June 1745: *HHB*, p. 393.

autograph of a short Air (or Saraband) for keyboard (HWV425) carries an annotation in another hand that the music was 'composed at S! Giles by M! Handel extempore, & afterwards by Desire of the Company writt down in his own hand writing', and he probably went there more than once: a number of summer visits to provincial friends and patrons doubtless lie submerged behind the few documented ones. Whether Handel did visit St Giles in July-August 1745 is doubtful. At the end of August he was in London, and he had not visited his friends the Harrises in Salisbury, who might have been included in the same trip (Thomas Harris witnessed codicils of Handel's will and later was a legatee). George William Harris described in a letter to Salisbury how, in London,[3]

> I met M' Handel a few days since in the streets, & stopp'd & put him in mind, who I was, upon which, I am sure 'twould have diverted you to have seen his antic motions. He seem'd highly pleased, & was full of enquiry after you & the Counsellor. I told him, I was very confident, that you expected a visit from him this Summer. He talk't much of his precarious state of health, yet he looks well enough, & I believe you'll have him with you ere long.

On 31 August, presumably in London, Handel completed an Italian duet *Ahi, nelle sorti umane* (HWV179), his last dated composition to Italian words; the undated duet *Fronda leggiera e mobile* (HWV186), was probably completed at the same period. These pieces were his last substantial Italian works (his only known later pieces to Italian texts are the arias HWV214, 216 and 220–1, possibly copied from other composers).

It may be significant that Handel had been described as coming to Exton for 'Quiet and Retirement', and the autumn of 1745 saw some problems with his health, probably a recurrence of the nervous disorder of 1743. On 16 October Jennens wrote[4]

> I am sorry to hear of M! Handel's illness, & heartily wish his recovery; but he has acted so mad a part of late, I fear voluntarily, that I don't at all wonder if it brings a real unavoidable madness upon him, of which I am inform'd he discover'd some very strong Symptoms in his travels about the Country this last Summer.

The Earl of Shaftesbury's report, a few days later, similarly indicates that his friends took a serious view of Handel's illness: 'Poor Handel looks something better. I hope he will entirely recover in due time, though he has been a good deal disordered in his head'.[5] Whether or not he gave much thought to his immediate professional plans at this period, Handel may not have had the stamina or concentration to tackle a major work for the next theatre season. The matter would have to be faced some time, however: a new season would require forward finance from a new

---

[3] Letter, probably to Mrs Thomas Harris, 29 August 1745: Deutsch, p. 622; *HHB*, p. 394.
[4] Letter to Holdsworth: *HHB*, p. 395.
[5] Letter to James Harris (his cousin), 24 October 1745: Deutsch, p. 624; *HHB*, p. 395.

subscription, and a new subscription would require new works to attract patrons. He needed to make the subscription look particularly attractive, to compensate for the fact that he had not been able to complete the promised number of performances in 1744–5.

There was probably serious doubt in the autumn of 1745 as to whether there would be a theatre season in London at all for 1745–6. In mid-August Prince Charles Edward Stuart had raised an army of Highlanders at Glenfinnan: because of the tardiness of the military response from London and some skilful guerilla tactics and good fortune on the other side, the Jacobite cause achieved a number of victories over the next three months, and their forces moved gradually southwards. On his return to London from a trip to Hanover, King George II despatched General Wade to Scotland to counter the Jacobites, but with little success: the Jacobite army entered England on 8 November and proceeded southwards through Carlisle, Preston and Manchester, reaching Derby on 4 December. The immediate Jacobite campaign was encouraged by Britain's opponents in the European war, for whom domestic mayhem in London was useful, but it is doubtful whether in the long term the 'Young Pretender' constituted a real threat to the settlement of the Hanoverian dynasty. In Britain the uprising did not generate sufficient committed support to sustain the Stuart cause, and France would probably have been unwilling to supply the substantial resources that the permanent imposition of the Stuart line would have entailed. But the shock that the Jacobite army was apparently on an inexorable course towards London produced understandable popular apprehension in the capital, and army reserves and militia were all called out to prepare for its defence. While it is possible that contingency plans were made at court for a strategic temporary retreat to Germany, it is doubtful whether either George II or Handel ever seriously contemplated permanent withdrawal from London. Handel had by this time many roots there, professional and personal; but he had obviously also maintained his German contacts and in 1745 was elected an honorary member of Mizler's Societät der Musikalischen Wissenschaften in Leipzig.[6]. The apparent instability of the immediate military situation generated a predictable reaction of nationalistic fervour in London: Handel contributed a patriotic song, 'Stand round, my brave boys' (*Song for the Gentlemen Volunteers*, HWV228[18]), which was inserted into a performance at Drury Lane on 14 November. During December Handel probably began to look over some oratorio librettos on bellicose Old Testament themes, as being appropriate for the mood of the moment. Unusually, the autograph of the *Occasional Oratorio* bears no composition date except 'Anno 1746' at the beginning: Handel's illness probably militated against his undertaking any concentrated work on a new score (or the necessary forward management of musical performances) before January 1746.

[6]Deutsch, p. 635: *HHB*, p. 404.

The British court's more substantial military response to the Jacobite army, though delayed, was effective: it involved, first, driving the rebels back to Scotland, and then joining battle there after the worst of the winter weather had passed. William Augustus, Duke of Cumberland, the king's younger son (who, at 25, was the same age as Prince Charles), was put in command and proved an efficient choice. He was far enough from the succession to be exposed to physical danger (his elder brother, Frederick, Prince of Wales, by then had four sons), and he had first-hand experience of the military campaigns of the current European war – indeed, he had been in Flanders when Prince Charles first landed in Britain. By 20 December 1745 the forces under his command had pursued the Jacobites back to Scotland. The duke then returned to London. During the lull in the campaign the usual New Year round of public entertainments at the London theatres started, probably in circumstances of some jubilation at the current success, though tempered by the fact that the overall situation had yet to be resolved. The reconstituted 'Middlesex' opera company had brought Gluck to London to compose for them: their season opened with his opera *La caduta de' giganti* ('The Fall of the Giants') at the King's Theatre on 7 January 1746. The Duke of Cumberland was in the audience, and probably Handel as well. At the end of the month Handel's own plans were announced at last:[7]

We hear, that Mr. *Handel* proposes to exhibit some Musical Entertainments on Wednesdays or Fridays the ensuing Lent, with Intent to make good to the Subscribers (that favoured him last Season) the Number of Performances he was not then able to complete. In order thereto he is preparing a New Occasional Oratorio, which is design'd to be perform'd at the Theatre-Royal in Covent-Garden.

On 7 February the *Occasional Oratorio* was rehearsed. George William Harris reported the occasion:[8]

Yesterday morning I was at Handel's house to hear the rehearsal of his new Occasional Oratorio. 'Tis extremely worthy of him, which you will allow to be saying all one can in praise of it. He has but 3 voices for his songs – Francesina, Reinholt, & Beard. His Band of Music is not very extraordinary – Du Feche is his first fiddle, & for the rest I really couldn't find out who they were, and I [do not] doubt his failure will be in this article. The words of his Oratorio are scriptural, but taken from various parts, & are expressive of the rebels' flight & our pursuit of them. Had not the Duke carried his point triumphantly, this Oratorio could not have been brought on. 'Tis to be perform'd in public next Friday

and indeed the *Occasional Oratorio* was performed three times between 14 and 26 February. But this constituted Handel's complete 'season':

[7] *The General Advertiser* (31 January 1746): Deutsch, p. 629: *HHB*, pp. 399–400:
[8] Letter to Mrs Thomas Harris, 8 February 1746: Deutsch, pp. 629–30; *HHB*, p. 400.

subscribers from the previous venture received two free tickets for each performance, and thus Handel worked off, in principle, his six-performance deficit from the Haymarket season. The procedure seems to have restored both Handel's spirits and his finances, according to the Earl of Shaftesbury:[9]

> Handel call'd on me this morning. His spirits and genious are astonishing. He rather gets than loses by his Houses. However as he has obliged his former subscribers without detriment to himself he is contented.

Opinions of the new oratorio were mixed: the Earl of Shaftesbury thought it 'excellent', but Jennens condemned Newburgh Hamilton's libretto and had no interest in hearing the work:[10]

> The Oratorio, as you call it, contrary to custom, raised no inclination in me to hear it. I am weary of nonsense and impertinence; & by the Account Ld. Guernsey gives me of this piece I am to expect nothing else. Tis a triumph for a Victory not yet gain'd, & if the Duke does not make hast, it may not be gain'd at the time of performance. [As to the libretto,] 'Tis an inconceivable jumble of Milton & Spencer, a Chaos extracted from Order by the most absurd of all Blockheads.

In the *Occasional Oratorio* Hamilton had created a non-dramatic oratorio rather on the lines of an extended ceremonial anthem celebrating the triumph of the righteous over their opponents. It incorporated passages from *Israel in Egypt* (ironically, possibly to Jennens's text) describing the defeat of the Egyptians at the Red Sea, transferred in complete blocks. The *Occasional Oratorio* served its purpose both for Handel and for the London public. Jennens's reaction is interesting. The '45' did nothing to resolve the political-philosophical tensions in his stance as a non-Juror. On one hand, the Hanoverian succession could not meet with his approval, yet on the other the futile Jacobite initiative showed that there was no prospect of a realistic alternative, and it became apparent in 1746 (if not before) that the representatives of the 'legitimate' Stuart line had neither the statesmanship nor the command of political loyalty that a British ruler required. No wonder Jennens had no inclination to hear the *Occasional Oratorio*. In fact, his association with Handel was effectively at an end: he was not sympathetic to the type of oratorio librettos that Handel required in the next few years and he seems to have retired from prominent public activity in London. Since his father's death in 1747 he had, in any case, his inheritance of the family estate at Gopsall to look after, as well as numerous properties elsewhere.[11] Yet in the period 1744–7 Jennens for some reason seems to have decided to build up his library collection of manuscripts of Handel's music by having sets of performing parts copied,

---

[9] Letter to James Harris, 22 February 1746: *HHB*, p. 401.
[10] Letter to Holdsworth, 3 February 1746: *HHB*, p. 400; the letter was written from Gopsall.
[11] See Smith, Ruth, 'The Achievements of Charles Jennens'.

apparently without any intention of using them for performances.

Although the Earl of Shaftesbury had said that Handel's 'spirit and genious are astonishing', Handel seems not to have been very active for the next few months. He probably attended the Decay'd Musicians benefit concert on 25 March at which music by himself and Gluck (who was still in London) was performed. It is not known on what occasion, if at all, Handel made his celebrated remark to the effect that Gluck knew less about counterpoint than his cook:[12] if authentic, the remark reflects, in a whimsical way, a genuine difference in compositional manner between the two composers of 'German' origins (Gluck was born in the Upper Palatinate but grew up in Bohemia). The next fixed point in Handel's biography is his commencement of the score of *Judas Maccabaeus* on 8 or 9 July 1746 – he wrote both dates on the autograph. In the meantime, on 26 May, Walsh had published *From scourging rebellion* (HWV 228[9]), *A Song on the Victory obtain'd over the Rebels, by His Royal Highness the Duke of Cumberland. The Words by Mr. Lockman. Set by Mr. Handel. Sung by Mr. Lowe &c in Vauxhall Gardens.* Both these works were directly related to the tide of national military activity. Having at last managed to confront the Jacobites in open battle, the duke had beaten them at Culloden Moor on 16 April. The ingenuity of Prince Charles's followers, and the Highlanders' interpretation of the rules of hospitality, enabled the prince to remain hidden in the ensuing months and eventually to escape to France, but the duke was ruthlessly efficient in preventing a recurrence of Jacobite military endeavours in Scotland. This retribution was undertaken with forensic care, avoiding the many Highland parties (including some Jacobites) that had never supported the prince. Inevitably, the process was not very gentlemanly, but neither had been the Highlanders' manner of fighting at Prestonpans and Falkirk. All this military activity was now far from London, however, where the only thing that mattered was the permanent security of the realm. From the London perspective there was every reason to have the aftermath of the '45' cleared up as quickly and conclusively as possible: the Jacobite escapade had syphoned off resources from the European war, and the results were seen in the period after the battle of Fontenoy, when the French succeeded in taking Brussels. As far as London's theatre life was concerned, the situation allowed the programme of public entertainments to return to normal and encouraged celebrations of renewed national security. The composition of *Judas Maccabaeus*, a full three-part oratorio, indicated that Handel was planning a regular Lenten season in 1747: the fact that he completed the score in just over a month (finishing on 11 August 1746) signified that the composer's health, as well as that of the nation, was restored.

---

[12] According to Burney (*An Account of the Musical Performances*, 'Sketch of the Life of Handel', p. 33), Handel was responding to Mrs Cibber's enquiry about Gluck. Burney names Handel's cook as Waltz, and Hawkins (ii, 878) had previously mentioned 'Waltz, a bass singer, who had been his cook' when describing Handel's activities in the later 1730s.

The rout of the '45' rebellion, like the victory at Dettingen, received only muted official celebration. There was no state thanksgiving; King George II was probably influenced by his father's precedent, 30 years previously, of limiting the celebration of a victory that involved the king's army killing the king's subjects. A relatively small gesture was hurriedly made at the Chapel Royal: on 24 April 1746 the Dean of the Chapel had received a command from the Lord Chamberlain's office for a new anthem to be performed 'upon the Account of the Duke of Cumberland's good Success against the Rebels',[13] and Maurice Greene obliged with a *Te Deum* and an anthem – probably not entirely 'new' music, in the circumstances – which were given with an orchestra at the Sunday service on 27 April. In October a bellicose anthem by John Frederick Lampe was performed at the Lutheran Savoy Chapel in celebration of the defeat of the rebellion, but this can hardly have been regarded as an official public celebration. Therefore *Judas Maccabaeus*, though not performed until 1 April 1747, nearly a year after Culloden, probably functioned partly as a channel for the final release of public sentiment over the victory. The theatre programmes of 1746–7 had been rather less jingoistic than those of 1745–6,[14] when, for example, Cibber's play *The Non-Juror* had had a new burst of popularity and the proceeds of *The Beggar's Opera* at Covent Garden had been given, reportedly at Mrs Cibber's suggestion, to the Military Veterans' scheme. The printed word-book of *Judas Maccabaeus* began with a dedication from the librettist Thomas Morell 'To His Royal Highness Prince William, Duke of Cumberland, this faint portraiture of a Truly Wise, Valiant and Virtuous Commander, As to the Possessor of the like Noble Qualities'. It is unlikely that the libretto was written in direct response to the duke's Scottish campaign of 1746, however, since one aria text from Morell's original libretto ('O liberty, thou choicest treasure') had already been used in the *Occasional Oratorio*;[15] this implies that Handel had the libretto of *Judas Maccabaeus* in his hands by the end of 1745 and that the words had originally been written in response to the duke's provisional success in driving Prince Charles back to Scotland in December 1745. Later, however, Morell stated that the oratorio was 'designed as a compliment to the Duke of Cumberland upon his returning victorious from Scotland'.[16]

Nothing is known of Handel's activities in the latter part of 1746, after he had completed *Judas Maccabaeus*. No doubt some of his time was

[13] Public Record Office, LC5/161, p. 220.

[14] The song that subsequently became the British National Anthem was first introduced at Covent Garden and Drury Lane theatres in September 1745.

[15] In the word-book for *Judas Maccabaeus* Morell added a footnote to the aria 'Come, ever-smiling Liberty' in which he gave the text of 'O Liberty, thou choicest treasure', with an explanation that 'The following Air was design'd, and wrote, for this Place, but it got, I know not how, into the *Occasional Oratorio*'.

[16] Deutsch, p. 851; *HHB*, p. 407.

occupied with arranging performers for the next season. After the unsuccessful Haymarket venture in 1744–5, and his partial recovery with the short season at Covent Garden in 1746, he now planned a full Lenten season for Covent Garden in 1747, and the 'Lent Oratorios' were to be the basis of his professional career for the rest of his life. He put himself back on a course that had proved successful in 1743–4 and at the same time managed to stay aloof from the re-flotation of the Italian opera company. Once again, the Earl of Shaftesbury provides a first-hand account, dated 20 January 1747:[17]

> Mr. Handel call'd on me t'other day. He is now in perfect health, & I really think grown young again. There is a most absurd and ridiculous opera going forward at present, and as it is not likely to meet with success, he is delighted.

The Italian opera company had been running since November 1746, under the artistic direction of the librettist-manager Francesco Vanneschi: towards the end of February they revived *Rossane*, the version of Handel's *Alessandro* that the 'Middlesex' company had produced in 1743.

Handel's own season began on 6 March, the first Friday in Lent, and ran to the Wednesday of Holy Week. There was no previous announcement of a subscription and, as far as we can tell, Handel's theatre income hereafter came entirely from the sale of individual tickets, which continued at the rates set up in 1743; he also moved the starting-time of his performances on from 6 p.m. to 6.30. It is impossible to judge whether Handel's abandonment of the subscription system reflected a change in the type of audience that his theatre seasons attracted, or simply the composer's desire to avoid a repeat of the problems from 1745, when the subscription committed him to more performances than he could deliver. Certainly the abandonment of the subscription system left him with flexibility in the presentation of his programme from year to year. After revivals of the *Occasional Oratorio* and *Joseph* in 1747, he introduced *Judas Maccabaeus* on 1 April: the Duke of Cumberland was not present, as he was abroad for the next season of military campaigns. Writing at a somewhat later period, the Earl of Shaftesbury recalled that the new oratorio 'went off with great Applause', and Morell himself said that 'the success of this Oratorio was very great'.[18] Taken as a whole, the season seems to have restored Handel's position as a regular contributor to London's musical life. In spite of a short interruption to the season while public attention was distracted to the trial of Simon Fraser, Lord Lovat (one of the leading supporters of the '45' rebellion), Handel managed to mount 11 performances. His cast was small: it consisted of Beard and Reinhold, his faithful tenor and bass, the soprano Elisabetta de Gambarini

---

[17] Letter to James Harris: *HHB*, p. 405.

[18] Deutsch, pp. 848, 851. An incidental remark by Morell when describing the poor reception that *Theodora* received (see Chapter 14, p. 334) suggests that *Judas Maccabaeus* received particular support from London's Jewish community.

(who had sung in the *Occasional Oratorio* performances in 1746), and a new contralto, Caterina Galli. Galli had been a member of London's successive opera companies since 1742, and she continued with her independent career there while also singing for Handel, which she did on a fairly regular basis for the next seven years. According to Burney, the reputation of Galli's rendering of ' 'Tis Liberty, dear Liberty alone' in the first performances of *Judas Maccabaeus* made her 'an important personage, among singers, for a considerable time afterwards'.[19] In the opera company she undertook several male roles, thereby possibly influencing the parts that Handel created for her in his later oratorios. The third performance of *Judas Maccabaeus*, on 8 April, was announced as having 'additions', and a second (unidentified) soprano may have joined the cast at that point.

Following the end of the season, Handel moved into a new routine. Instead of taking a break in the June-July period (when he had gone to 'the country', for example, in 1745), he devoted this time to composing a couple of new oratorios in readiness for the next season: *Alexander Balus* (to a libretto by Morell) was written between 1 June and 4 July and *Joshua* (from an unidentified librettist) between 19 July and 19 August. We may deduce that he felt secure in the restoration of his 'oratorio' career and, furthermore, that the success of the 1747 season left him with a stimulus to further activity. Having completed his new scores, Handel once again vanishes from the documentary record for five months, until the beginning of the next season. Perhaps he undertook some provincial social visits in the autumn. The opera company meanwhile continued on its routine way, using Handel's music from time to time but without his direct involvement: a new Handel pasticcio, *Lucio Vero*, was produced in November 1747, and *Rossane* was revived in February 1748. Handel secured the services of two of the opera company's sopranos, Casarini and Sibilla, for his oratorio season of 1748.

That season ran from 26 February (the first Friday in Lent) to 7 April, with performances generally on Wednesdays and Fridays, but on other nights in Holy Week. It consisted of 13 performances from a repertory consisting only of Handel's three most recent works: three performances of *Judas Maccabaeus*, four of *Joshua*, three of *Alexander Balus*, and then three final performances of *Judas Maccabaeus* 'with additions' (including three arias transferred from *Alexander Balus* and *Joshua*; 'See the conquering hero comes', originally in *Joshua*, was also incorporated into *Judas Maccabaeus*, either later in 1748 or in 1750). While one can appreciate Handel's commercial wisdom in following up the success of *Judas Maccabaeus* with similar 'victory' oratorios, the programme as a whole was rather lacking in variety, being almost entirely concerned with battles and heroes. For the second half of the season Handel borrowed the large

[19] *A General History*, ii, 841; Burney says that the aria was encored every night.

military timpani from the Tower of London, which no doubt added to the bellicose effects. Just as, in the period following 1732, Handel seems to have followed through the theme of Jewish heroines (Esther, Deborah, Athalia), so now the Old Testament military heroes come to the fore. As an oratorio subject, *Joshua* was in an obvious line of dramatic succession from *Judas Maccabaeus*. *Alexander Balus*, however, was more tangential: although the Jews emerge with some victories, the story (from the book of *Maccabees*) really centres on the betrayal of the Jews' Syrian ally Alexander Balus by his Egyptian father-in-law. Nevertheless, Morell used it to develop the themes of (Jewish) patriotism and religion, balanced by a parallel dramatic thread concerning Alexander's love for the Egyptian Cleopatra (not, of course, the historical Cleopatra of *Giulio Cesare*).

In the absence of any reports on Handel's season, we may guess that it was routinely successful, without gathering the attention that *Judas Maccabaeus* had attracted the previous year. And, while the military successes of Judas had originally been displayed as paralleling Cumberland's, there is little reason to suppose that the continuing success of Handel's oratorios was attributable solely to the audience's comfortable identification of Britain with the victorious 'chosen people' of Israel: if anything, the London public probably wanted to put the '45' behind them and were wearying of the continental war. As public entertainment, the oratorios might (but need not) have been taken as political parables. Alternatively, they might have been seen as suitably serious biblical presentations for the Lenten season, and as such they may have attracted a section of London society that had been affected by the religious revival apparent in the first wave of John Wesley's influence (and in the Church of England's response to it). It is also possible that the 'Christian' audience was supplemented in this period by support from London's growing Jewish community, who would obviously identify with the oratorios' subject matter. Although no meeting between Handel and the Wesleys is documented, there was one connection around 1746–7, when Handel set to music three of Charles Wesley's hymns, as solo songs with continuo bass, following the model of the hymnbook (published in 1746, with music by Lampe) from which he took the words. One of the tunes, to 'Rejoice, the Lord is King', has retained currency to the present day, although like its companions it was composed in a genre that was probably intended for private devotions rather than public worship. Handel's hymn-settings may have been composed at the behest of Priscilla, the third wife of John Rich, the owner-manager of Covent Garden theatre, who is known to have inclined towards the Methodists: at this period Handel reputedly taught music to Rich's daughters by his previous marriage.[20]

The orchestral interval music that partnered the victory oratorios in Handel's seasons of 1747 and 1748 took a new direction. Having worked

[20] See the introduction to Handel (ed. Burrows), *The Complete Hymns and Chorales*.

through his op.6 concertos at theatre performances in the seasons immediately following their composition in 1739, Handel had reverted to presenting organ concertos with his oratorios: they had featured in his Dublin concerts and in the subsequent London seasons up to the performances of the *Occasional Oratorio* in 1746, which were presented with 'A New Concerto on the Organ', probably the one in D minor (HWV304). Apart from op.7 no.2, which was given with *Samson* in 1743, there are few surviving organ concertos from 1742–6; Handel probably performed mainly from his pre-existing repertory. *Judas Maccabaeus, Joshua* and *Alexander Balus*, however, were each given with new orchestral concertos. These were the *Concerti a due cori* (HWV332–4), which include answering 'choirs' of wind instruments (marked 'Chorus 1' and 'Chorus 2' by Handel): presumably the wind groups were spatially separated in the theatre, with the strings in the middle. HWV334 was written for *Judas Maccabaeus*, the other two for the oratorios of the next season. After an opening Ouverture-type movement, each has a miscellany of generally breezy, extrovert movements and a central slow movement: the 1748 ones include orchestral versions of movements (mainly choruses) from recent oratorios, including *Messiah, Belshazzar* and the *Occasional Oratorio*. The concertos have a grand, rather noisy effectiveness that complements the oratorios that they partnered. Presumably for these seasons Handel had more oboe, bassoon and horn players available than usual, perhaps military bandsmen from guards units that had been disbanded after the defeat of the '45'. Movements from the 'Judas Maccabaeus' concerto HWV334 were also arranged successively by Handel during 1747–8 as an organ concerto with orchestra (HWV305a) and as a solo organ work (HWV305b), but it is not known when, if at all, he performed these versions.

At the end of his oratorio season in 1748 Handel once again settled directly to composing two oratorios for the next year. The season finished on 7 April: *Solomon* was begun on 5 May and finished on 13 June, *Susanna* was composed between 11 July and 24 August. The identities of the librettists for the oratorios are unknown: both may have been the work of the same author. With these works Handel turned away from the 'Jewish victory' theme of the previous seasons and composed two contrasing works which he probably found both rewarding and diverting. *Solomon* presents a series of tableaux of the 'wise' Solomon at the height of his power, and at the height of Jerusalem's prosperity. *Susanna* is a pastoral comedy with what is effectively a secular story but, since its source was scriptural, it had a legitimate passage into the Lenten oratorio season.[21] Once again, Handel vanishes from the documentary record

---

[21] It is not known whether Handel was aware of the allegorical interpretation of the story that was offered by some Christian commentators, in terms of the church being saved from its adversaries.

during the autumn of 1748, after completing *Susanna*; there was a second performance of his *Comus* music at Exton, but in his absence. In 1748 his name appeared as one of the subscribers to the published *Lessons for the Harpsichord* composed by Elisabetta de Gambarini, his soprano soloist from the 1747 season.[22]

Presumably Handel began rehearsals for his next oratorio season well in advance: the Earl of Shaftesbury wrote on 3 January 1749:[23]

> I hear Susanna much commended by some who heard Galli and Frasi's parts. I understand there are no less than seven parts in this, that I fear the lower ones will go off bad enough, but this by the by.

Susanna opened Handel's season on 10 February 1749, the first Friday in Lent, which had by now become his customary starting-date. The Countess of Shaftesbury attended the first performance:[24]

> I cannot pretend to give my poor judgment of it, from once hearing, but believe it will not insinuate itself so much into my approbation as most of Handel's performances do, as it is in the light <u>operatical</u> style; but you will receive an opinion of it from much better judges than myself, as I saw both my Cousin Harris's peeping out of a little box, and very attentive to the musick. I think I never saw a fuller house. Rich told me that he believed he would receive near 400£.

Perhaps her doubts about whether the 'light operatical style' would go down well reflect the extent to which Handel's 'oratorio audience' differed in character and expectations from the King's Theatre audiences of the 1720s and 1730s, and indeed differed from the audience that more recently had been patronizing the 'Middlesex' opera company. The countess's fears about the reception of *Susanna* were probably not realized: Handel gave four performances, followed by two of *Hercules*, his first revival of that piece. *Samson* followed, with four performances (its first revival since 1744), then *Solomon* with three, and the season closed with a single performance of *Messiah* (Handel's first for four years) on Maundy Thursday, 23 March. The last apparently attracted no controversy. For his 1749 season Handel was able to command the services of additional string players to boost his normal complement of about 25 strings, as well as a substantial group of wind instrumentalists: he added parts for ripieno string players to the completed score of *Solomon* and also marked up the other scores with directions for them. This season probably saw Handel's most lavish performances of the decade, for the double choruses of *Solomon* imply a substantial choral force as well. The advertisements

---

[22] For a list of the miscellaneous books and musical scores to which Handel subscribed and which may reflect his personal connections as much as his tastes, see Simon (ed.), *Handel*, pp. 286–8.

[23] Letter to James Harris: *HHB*, p. 418.

[24] Letter to James Harris, 11 February 1749: Deutsch, p. 657; *HHB*, p. 419 (both omit the word 'not' from the first sentence).

announced that each oratorio would be given with 'A Concerto'. One of these was certainly the organ concerto HWV311 (op.7 no.6) – or, at least, its first movement – and the others may have included the orchestral concertos HWV335*a* and 335*b*, which have substantial wind parts. HWV335*b*, in F, includes horns but not trumpets and is arranged in the 'due cori' manner; HWV335*a*, in D, includes trumpets as well as four horns. (It is possible, however, that neither concerto reached performance). The two concertos have musical material in common, and the opening movements were developed further by Handel at the end of the 1749 oratorio season to form the grand Ouverture to the *Music for the Royal Fireworks*.

The *Fireworks Music* was composed for London's public celebrations of the Peace of Aix-la-Chapelle, and the musical preparations for the festivities kept Handel busy immediately after his 1749 oratorio season finished. The complexities of the dynastic and territorial issues involved in the War of the Austrian Succession meant that the European peace process in turn had been complex and protracted. The armistice had been agreed in May 1748, and the peace agreement was officially concluded the following October, subject to later ratifications. A celebration with a display of fireworks was planned in London, and on an elaborate scale: a ceremonial building was begun in Green Park early in November 1748 but had still not been completed when Handel finished his oratorio season on 23 March 1749.[25] Five days later the Duke of Montagu, Master General of the Ordnance (whose command of his native English seems to have come a poor second to Handel's), told the Comptroller of His Majesty's Fireworks of his anxieties about Handel's planned music for the celebration:[26]

I think Hendel now proposes to have but 12 trumpets and 12 French horns; at first there was to have been sixteen of each, and I remember I told the King so, who, at that time, objected to their being any musick; but, when I told him the quantity and nomber of martial musick there was to be, he was better satisfied, and said he hoped there would be no fidles. Now Hendel proposes to lessen the nomber of trumpets, &c. and to have violeens. I dont at all doubt but when the King hears it he will be very much displeased. If the thing war to be in such a manner as certainly to please the King, it ought to consist of no kind of instrument but martial instruments. Any other I am sure will put him out of humour, therefore I am shure it behoves Hendel to have as many trumpets, and other martial instruments, as possible, tho he dont retrench the violins, which I think he shoud, tho I beleeve he will never be persuaded to do it. I mention this, as I have very lately been told, from very good authority, that the King has, within this fortnight, expressed himself to this purpose.

In fact, at the beginning of his score Handel specified 24 oboes, nine horns,

[25] For details of the vicissitudes and delays, see Burrows, 'Handel's Peace Anthem'.
[26] Letter to Charles Frederick, 28 March 1749: Deutsch, p. 661; *HHB*, p. 422.

nine trumpets, three sets of timpani, 12 bassoons and a contrabassoon (plus a serpent), which should have been enough 'military instruments' to please the king, and he then added doubling string parts. A rehearsal was planned for Vauxhall Gardens on 17 April. Handel at first objected to the venue but, in the end, after various changes of date in order to enable the Duke of Cumberland to be present, the public rehearsal took place there on Friday 21 April at 11 a.m.: according to the *Gentleman's Magazine*, there were 100 performers, and an audience of more than 12,000 (at 2s 6d per ticket) attended – a turn-out that caused a three-hour traffic jam on London Bridge.[27]

The following week was a busy one for Handel. Tuesday 25 April was the official Thanksgiving Day, and for the Chapel Royal service on that day he revived his 'Caroline' *Te Deum* and performed a new anthem, *How beautiful are the feet* (HWV266): the anthem was based on music recomposed or transferred from other sources (including *Messiah*), but it worked well enough.[28] The music for the service had been publicly rehearsed at the chapel the previous Saturday. Thursday 27 April was the day of the Royal Fireworks in Green Park, attended by the king and the Duke of Cumberland. Handel's music was played not during the fireworks, but beforehand. As the newspapers reported: 'The whole Band of Musick (which began to play soon after 6 o'clock), perform'd at his Majesty's coming and going, and during his stay in the Machine'.[29] The firework display itself, though marred by an accidental fire at one end of the building, seems to have been enjoyable, and an eye-witness report suggests that the atmosphere was very much like that of a present-day royal festivity:[30]

> Green Park, 7 o'clock, Thursday night,
> before Squib Castle.
>
> Walking about here to see sights I have retired to a stump of a tree to write a line to thee lest anything should happen to prevent me by and by ... they are all mad with thanksgivings, Venetian jubilees, Italian fireworks, and German pageantry. I have before my eyes such a concourse of people as to be sure I never have or shall see again, except we should have a Peace without a vowel. The building erected on this occasion is indeed extremely neat and pretty and grand to look at, and a world of fireworks placed in an order that promises a most amazing scene when it is to be in full display. His Majesty and other great folks have been walking to see the machinery before the Queen's Library; it is all railed about there, where the lords, ladies, commons, &c. are sat under scaffolding, and seem to be under confinement in comparison of us [with] mobility, who enjoy the free air and walks here.

[27] Deutsch, p. 668; *HHB*, p. 426. Westminster Bridge had been completed in October 1746 but in 1747 it underwent lengthy repairs for serious subsidence; at the time of the rehearsal London Bridge may have been the only available river bridge for traffic.
[28] See Burrows, 'Handel's Peace Anthem'.
[29] *The Daily Advertiser* (29 April 1749): Deutsch, p. 668; *HHB*, p. 426.
[30] Letter from John Byrom to his wife: Deutsch, pp. 667–8; *HHB*, p. 426.

It has been a very hot day, but there is a dark overcast of cloudiness which may possibly turn to rain, which occasions some of better habits [i.e. clothes] to think of retiring; and while I am now writing it spits a little and grows into a menacing appearance of rain, which, if it pass not over, will disappoint expectations. My intention, if it be fair, is to gain a post under one of the trees in St. James's Park, where the fireworks are in front, and where the tail of a rocket, if it should fall, cannot but be hindered by the branches from doing any mischief to them who are sheltered under them, so I shall now draw away to be ready for near shelter from either watery or fiery rain.

11 o'clock: all over, and somewhat in a hurry, by an accidental fire at one of the ends of the building, which, whether it be extinguished I know not, for I left it in an ambiguous condition that I might finish my letter, which otherwise I could not have done. I saw every fine show in front, and I believe no mischief was done by the rockets, though some pieces of above one pound and a half fell here and there – some the next tree to my station, and being on the watch I perceived one fall, and after a tug with four or five competitors I carried it off.

Handel's musical activities for the year were still not finished. He embraced a new venture – one that was to have considerable consequences for him – by offering to give a 'Performance of Vocal and Instrumental Musick' at the Foundling Hospital in aid of the completion of its chapel. The Hospital for the Maintenance and Education of Exposed and Deserted Young Children had been formally set up in 1739 under a royal charter as the result of the determined efforts of a retired sea-captain, Thomas Coram.[31] The path by which Handel had been drawn towards this charity (then in its tenth year, and undertaking an ambitious building programme on a site where north London met the country fields) is not known, but the painter William Hogarth had already contributed to it, and the music publisher John Walsh had been elected a governor in 1748, so Handel's interest was probably aroused through one of these connections (or even through his own childhood memories of Francke's charitable foundation for children in Halle). Handel attended a meeting at the Foundling Hospital on 4 May, at which he offered his performance: the offer was accepted, and the hospital in turn asked Handel to become a governor, an invitation that he initially declined 'for that he should Serve the Charity with more Pleasure in his Way, than being a Member of the Corporation'. There is here a hint of the same trait of withdrawal from public prominence (in areas beyond his immediate profession) as that which may have led him to decline a doctorate at Oxford in 1733: it seems too facile to attribute both to a meanness with regard to paying the expected fees. Eventually, in 1750, he became a governor of the hospital and the usual entry fee of £50 was waived: by then the hospital had received over £1000 from the proceeds of his performances, as well as an organ that he presented to the chapel.

[31]For its history see Nichols and Wray, *The History of the Foundling Hospital.*

The 1749 Foundling Hospital performance, like the *Fireworks Music* rehearsal, saw various changes of date in order to accommodate the attendance of royalty: it finally took place on Saturday 27 May, at noon, and was attended by the Prince and Princess of Wales.[32] This royal connection was probably influential in securing a donation to the charity of £2000 from the king. Handel's concert programme for the hospital was modelled on the conventional three-part format of theatre programmes, though the total musical content was shorter, as befitted a charity matinée. The first part comprised revivals of the *Fireworks Music* (presumably with much reduced scoring) and the anthem from the recent Thanksgiving Service; the second consisted of a considerable slab of music from *Solomon*; and for the final part Handel gave the 'Foundling Hospital Anthem' *Blessed are they that considereth the poor and needy* (HWV268), another effective new anthem constructed partly from old material. The anthem concluded with the 'Hallelujah' chorus from *Messiah*, a movement that was probably still unfamiliar to most of the audience. The custom of standing up for the 'Hallelujah' chorus may have originated with the Prince of Wales on this occasion. The first reference to the audience standing up 'together with the king' dates from 1780,[33] but there is no documentary evidence that King George II ever attended a *Messiah* performance. Handel's 1749 Foundling Hospital concert took place in the chapel, which was not yet completed: the absence of window-glass was probably not unwelcome in an overcrowded chapel during the midday period at the end of May. After such unusual post-season exertions, it is perhaps not surprising that Handel did not settle down immediately to his next oratorio composition. Only one major work followed: *Theodora*, composed between 28 June and 31 July.

Handel's Drawing Account at the Bank of England revives on a regular basis between 1747 and 1751. The individual entries are not very informative, since they record neither sources nor recipients but merely say 'By Cash' or 'To Cash Him' (i.e. Handel). It is noticeable, however, that most of Handel's deposits were made during the oratorio seasons, mainly in February and March. More significant may be his Stock Accounts, which show his transactions in annuities: these reveal renewed financial activity during the period. One striking feature of the annuity accounts[34] is that most payments are to names that do not otherwise feature in Handel's biography, a reminder that very little is known of his circles of acquaintance beyond his professional colleagues and a few letter-writing patrons and supporters. The overall impression is that, however dangerously close Handel may have come to his financial thresholds during 1745–6, his subsequent oratorio seasons had restored his prosperity. It

[32] See Burrows, 'Handel and the Foundling Hospital', for details of the arrangements for the performance; for the musical programme, see also Burrows, 'Handel's Peace Anthem'.

[33] See Burrows, *Handel: 'Messiah'*, p. 28.

[34] Deutsch, pp. 836–7; *HHB*, pp. 548–9.

appears that, by giving 12–15 performances of oratorios over a seven-week period, without even the backing of an initial subscription, he accumulated more financial security than he had done in his 50-performance opera seasons.

The first half of 1749 may justifiably be regarded as one of the major peaks of Handel's career. After the uncertainties of his earlier years with opera and oratorio, he had now apparently gained a stable audience for his Lenten oratorios, his seniority as London's prime public composer was without question, and his reputation was now founded on English-language works that were potentially accessible to a wider audience in London than his Italian operas had been. A well-attended season of performances of works such as *Susanna*, *Samson*, *Solomon*, *Hercules* and *Messiah* was in itself an achievement that would have been remarkable for any composer-impresario: to it we may add the recognition, both royal and popular, that was confirmed and strengthened by the *Fireworks Music*, and the new lease of energy that was apparent as Handel took on a new enterprise for the Foundling Hospital. The prodigious and well-regarded youthful composer, keyboard player and opera composer had matured into a respected producer of sublime Lenten oratorios. With some pride, we may suspect, Handel added his age ('aetatis 62') at the end of the autograph of *Solomon* in 1748.[35] In eighteenth-century terms Handel was doing well, as both a physical and a musical survivor. Having reached the top of the mountain in 1749, his creative period on the summit was to be relatively short, though his reputation was secured and reinforced thereafter for a period more extended than he could ever have guessed.

[35] British Library RM 20.h.4.

13

The music of the 1740s

Theatre music

The first half of 1749 marked for Handel the culmination of a creative period that had seen oratorio-type masterworks follow each other with an almost predictable efficiency that bears exact comparison to his best bursts of operatic composition. It is difficult to make relative qualitative judgments between, for example, *Samson, Semele, Belshazzar* and *Susanna* – large-scale works with a close similarity of musical style, yet individual in their subject matter and in the roles they portray. Handel produced several of these major works in contrasting pairs; indeed, he seems to have relished the contrasts and probably chose his new librettos with such variety in mind. There is a close comparison with, for example, Beethoven's practice of working on two contrasting symphonies together: each oratorio represents a different 'world' (a partial exception is the combination of *Alexander Balus* and *Joshua*). We may still marvel at the physical fluency with which Handel, in concentrated bursts of activity, put so much music down on paper: a three-part oratorio, usually in itself a model of compositional fluency, perhaps took a month of work, entailing on average about 125 leaves (i.e. 250 pages) of ten-stave music paper. Equally remarkable is the instinctive concentration of musical style and technique that characterizes his treatment of each libretto.

All the theatre works produced by Handel in London during the 1740s had the same technical parameters: they employed the various forms of recitative, aria and chorus, in different proportions according to the requirements of each libretto, and were intended to be performed in 'still life'. As his programmes from 1743 onwards consisted exclusively of such works, it is not surprising that they came to be considered together in common parlance as 'oratorios', for they indeed constituted a common musical genre. At the end of the 1744 season Mrs Delany said that she had 'been at ten oratorios',[1] although four of them had probably been performances of *Semele*, which in terms of its subject matter scarcely fulfils the normal criteria for an oratorio. The reason for the common usage of the word 'oratorio' is understandable: up to 1735 Handel had

---

[1] Letter to Mrs Dewes, 22 March 1744: Deutsch, p. 588; *HHB*, p. 375.

clearly been involved with 'opera seasons' in London (into which some non-staged English-language works had latterly been inserted), and for his later programmes 'oratorio seasons' was the most obvious simple parallel description. Furthermore, it would have been awkward to have described *Acis and Galatea* separately when it was performed by Handel alongside works such as *Esther*, *Deborah* and *Athalia*. As a result, Handel's theatre programmes of English works have left a legacy of confusion over the use of the word 'oratorio' by suggesting a second, broader application of the term, in place of the older, more restrictive usage, which defined 'oratorio' in terms of operatic musical style applied to specific types of subject matter.

It is hardly surprising that, among those alert to literary and musical issues in London in Handel's day, objections were raised to this newer application of the word 'oratorio', though such rearguard actions were generally a closet activity and do not seem to have attracted sufficiently wide interest to reach public debate. A particularly instructive example of old-fashioned categorization is found in the heavy annotations that Jennens applied to his copy of the list of Handel's works in Mainwaring's biography of the composer, published in 1760 (see Plate 9). Mainwaring placed *Acis and Galatea* in a separate category of 'Serenatas' but collected most of Handel's English-language theatre works under 'Oratorios'. From the list Jennens ejected *Semele* ('No Oratorio but a baudy opera') and *Hercules* ('An Opera'), describing them as operas, although neither had been performed with stage action.[2] Out too went *Alexander's Feast* ('No Oratorio but an Ode') and *L'Allegro*, presumably also to be regarded as an ode. On the other hand, Jennens brought into the oratorio group two non-London works absent from Mainwaring's list, the *Brockes Passion* and *La Resurrezione*. (Rather curiously, he did not interfere with Mainwaring's inclusion of 'Il trionfo del Tempo, Rome' under 'Serenatas', nor did he note Handel's 1737/9 version of the work.) The resulting group of 'Oratorios', according to Jennens's stricter classification, seems to have been defined by subject matter: the stories from the Bible and the Apocrypha are extended by two works – *Theodora*, based on the story of an early Christian martyr, and *The Triumph of Time and Truth*, an allegorical 'morality' oratorio.

Handel's mature oratorios (to use the word in its broader sense) were conceived on the time-scale inherited from Italian opera: an evening's entertainment at the theatre consisted of a work in three Acts ('Parts' in an oratorio) lasting something over three hours in performance, including intervals. Handel wrote timings (probably underestimated) for each Part on the autographs of *Judas Maccabaeus* and *Solomon*, perhaps because he needed his own check to keep the length within bounds: 40 + 40 +

---

[2]The second footnote to Mainwaring's list (see Plate 9) suggests that Mainwaring defined oratorio in terms of its manner of performance, i.e. without stage action.

25 (= 105) minutes for *Judas*, 50 + 40 + 40 (= 130) minutes for *Solomon*. In his first performing version the music for *Samson* was very much longer than 130 minutes, and *Joshua* was rather shorter;[3] but these might be described as local variations. It is probably significant that for his later revivals Handel cut *Samson* down to a more conventional size, and revivals of other works that were advertised as being 'with additions' usually in practice entailed additions, subtractions and substitutions that left the work at about the same three- to three-and-a-half-hour mark. There is little evidence about the length of the intervals in Handel's performances, or about the social habits of his audiences that might have affected interval lengths. Although Handel regularly performed concertos between the Parts, his precise practice is uncertain: the concertos may have functioned as overtures to the succeeding Part.

The oratorios were not 'staged', and there is some doubt as to whether the platform arrangements even allowed the leading singers to face their interlocutors during recitatives. Pictures from a rather later tradition of oratorio performances in London suggest that the standard theatre arrangement may have placed the soloists at the front, with the chorus singers and orchestra behind. Soloists might sometimes be called on to take more than one dramatic role in an oratorio, and they also sang through the chorus movements: indeed, the 'chorus' was probably still conceived by Handel as the ensemble of soloists assisted by a handful of trebles and a number of 'bumping' chorus singers. If, as seems most likely, the Foundling Hospital accounts for the *Messiah* performances in the 1750s[4] reflect the composition of Handel's contemporary theatre forces, then the instrumental group was based on about 25 string players, and the 'chorus' support for the soloists consisted of four to six trebles and about a dozen men distributed between alto, tenor and bass voices.

While the operatic forms of the *semplice* recitative, *accompagnato* recitative and aria continued to serve Handel as basic building-blocks for his English oratorios, they underwent various metamorphoses. The proportion of recitative in Handel's London operas was already noticeably smaller than in the early operas composed for performance in Italian-speaking lands, and this trend continued into the oratorios, where *semplice* recitative was often retained in the minimum proportion necessary to support credible dramatic story-lines and characterizations. This did not, however, preclude substantial scenes being played out in recitative. The arias also continued a tendency, apparent in some of Handel's later operas,

---

[3] A modern performance of a complete reconstruction of the first version of *Samson* (given in Maryland, U.S.A., 1988) ran to nearly four hours' music; modern recordings of *Joshua* run to a little over two hours.
[4] Deutsch, pp. 751, 800–1, 825; *HHB*, pp. 481–2, 516–17, 535; the performing partbooks prepared for the hospital under the terms of Handel's will in 1759 and apparently copied from earlier performing materials also provide evidence of Handel's performing practice.

towards fewer full-scale da capo arias; proportions vary from work to work, but in the oratorios da capo (or dal segno, eliding the first ritornello) forms are usually in a minority.[5] In some works (including *Messiah*, *Judas Maccabaeus* and *Solomon*) the proportion of da capo arias is less than a quarter of the total. It may not be a coincidence that they form a majority only in the most secular-style works – *Semele*, *Hercules* and *Susanna*: these librettos were probably consciously moulded towards the operatic style, with aria verse-forms constructed so as to imply contrasted *B* sections. But Handel was not hampered by literary conventions: from time to time he set such texts either as through-composed arias or with elided recapitulations.

A partial explanation for the move away from da capo arias may lie with Handel's oratorio casts, which included a fair proportion of English theatre singers, some of whom had not been brought up in the operatic tradition. English singers of the calibre of John Beard, however (who, incidentally, had received operatic training under Handel), no doubt had the technical prowess to cope with full-scale da capo forms had Handel wished to write such arias for them; on the other side of the picture, 'English' singers did not dominate the casts, for Handel's seasons from 1743 had always included at least one Italian (or italianate) leading lady – an impressive procession, including Avolio, Francesina, Gambarini, Galli and Giulia Frasi. While some of these ladies did indeed seem to attract da capo arias (this seems to have been especially true of Francesina), it is simplistic to attribute Handel's choice of aria forms principally to the talents of specific singers: rather, the decline in the number of da capo arias reflects a difference between the parent operatic genre and the oratorio genre that Handel had developed to meet London conditions. While reports of the oratorios still gave prominence to the soloists, they also gave considerable attention to the works themselves: audiences did not attend oratorios only to hear a succession of solo arias, however well structured.

The critical factor, and one which gave a different balance to the works, lay in Handel's extensive use of the chorus, the feature that distinguishes his oratorios most clearly from his operas. Solo arias now had to share the centre of musical interest with chorus movements, and the audiences were probably as much affected by striking choruses as by fine arias. According to Newburgh Hamilton's preface to the word-book of *Samson*, the attraction of Handel's oratorios lay in the way that 'the Solemnity of Church-Musick is agreeably united with the most pleasing Airs of the Stage'. In fact, in spite of the obvious links between the chorus movements in Handel's theatre works and the English church-music tradition of the coronation anthems, Hamilton was giving only half of the picture by referring to the choruses in terms of the 'Solemnity of Church-Musick'.

---

[5] See Dean, *Handel's Dramatic Oratorios*, Appendix A (p. 627).

The chorus proved a most flexible medium for dramatic use and could depict heathen revelry as effectively as 'solemnity'. The Old Testament stories gave obvious openings for its dramatic employment, to give voice to the collective utterances of the Israelites or their enemies; but Handel and his librettists also found dramatic potential in its use for non-participant commentary on the action – like the role of the 'chorus' in classical Greek theatre.

The weight and power of tone in the chorus movements contrasted with, and complemented, the virtuoso, 'operatic' appeal of the solo arias. Even when chorus movements constituted as little as a quarter of the concerted movements, their musical weight inevitably provided a counter-poise to the arias in the total musical scheme and accordingly weakened the dominance of solo singers. Furthermore, although some chorus movements hinted at stageable, visual spectacle, the non-staged presentation of the oratorios gave Handel the opportunity for a more varied use of the chorus than would have been practical in conventional theatre. In some scenes of *Belshazzar*, for example, the chorus is a direct contributor to the action, participating with a vividness that seems to cry out for visual staging: yet the same singers have to represent Babylonians, Jews, and Medes and Persians in quick succession, which would have been impractical on the stage. It is left to the audience's imagination (assisted by the word-book) to provide the visual images: liberated from the practical constraints of stagecraft, Handel was able to employ his chorus in a versatile manner. The chorus movements obviously had an important effect on the structure of the oratorios: while some were part of the continuous action, others were 'architectural', marking the beginnings or ends of scenes. Here, again, an important change of emphasis was involved: each Part of an English oratorio ends with a chorus, not – in operatic fashion – with a big aria for a leading soloist. In addition, the effect of the chorus movements was to slow the action down. There is, in general, less action in the plots of the oratorios than in Handel's Italian operas: in Parts 1 and 3 of *Israel in Egypt* and *Solomon*, in fact, dramatic action in terms of the advancement of plot is virtually negligible.

A further distinction from opera concerns the presentation of the story, where the oratorios often seem less careful in communicating clearly every motivation or link in the plot. Here again, however, the situation is affected by the artistic debits and credits attending the non-staged medium: all motivation and action need not be covered in the musical setting, provided the links are made explicit in the word-books. A high proportion of the audience presumably purchased and consulted the word-books. If, as seems likely, the dual-language word-books for Handel's Italian operas were intended for consultation during the performances (so that non-Italian speakers could understand the stage action), then the case for oratorio audiences following word-books is equally strong (it is doubtful whether pre-electric technology allowed much variation in the level of house lighting, so that reading during a performance would have been a practical proposition). It may also have been significant that most of the biblical stories were better known to the audience than the historical opera plots.

In all, Handel's English 'oratorio' genre is one that makes its primary appeal to the more musical of listeners, for it requires from them an imaginative effort, deprived as they are of any visual stimuli beyond those provided by normal concert circumstances: the only visual assistance in any of Handel's London performances for which we have evidence was the decorative back-drop for the 1732 *Acis and Galatea*. The oratorios were presented originally to audiences who already expected certain demands to be made on their stamina: the parent genre of *opera seria* was itself relatively slow-moving because it was dominated by extended arias that froze successive climactic moments in the drama. To that extent, Handel's oratorios were a logical development and culmination of one strand of Baroque musical experience. Even so, there were limits to which Handel could carry this extension: the purely narrative form of *Israel in Egypt*, delivered largely by the chorus, failed with the London audience because it placed too many demands on their imagination and stamina – the 'Solemnity of Church-Musick' was not sufficiently leavened with 'pleasing Airs of the Stage'.

Nevertheless Handel, while mixing choruses with solo music in a more judicious manner, did make a successful return to narrative oratorio, with *Messiah*. The reason for the narrative presentation of *Messiah* relates to the nature of the subject matter, which was acceptable in the theatre only if presented in narrative form: as it was, the propriety of theatre performances was questioned in 1743, even though the role of Jesus Christ was not represented in the oratorio in a realistic manner by a specific solo singer. The unusual nature of *Messiah* also affected its musical construction: there is very little recitative, for indeed there are no dramatic 'scenes' involving conversation between dramatic characters (with one partial exception, at the angels' appearance to the shepherds). Instead, the story of the 'Mystery of Godliness' unfolds in arias and choruses, with accompanying commentary using texts adapted directly from the Bible and the Book of Common Prayer and without any attempt to clothe them in 'dramatic' verse structures. Yet the libretto is clearly structured (Part 1 dealing with prophecy and the incarnation; Part 2 relating the narrative from Passiontide to God's victory; Part 3 providing commentary), and there is a sense of musico-dramatic progression: the formal recitative-aria-chorus blocks of the opening scenes give way to more fluid structures as the 'action' gets under way, just as the music in the operas regularly gains in power as the conflicts between characters gradually charge up the plots.

Messiah is not a 'typical' Handel oratorio, but, for those with no experience of Handel's other large-scale works, its music serves as an effective introduction to the forms and styles of his arias and choruses.

The arias range from fully fledged da capo or dal segno forms ('He was despised', 'The trumpet shall sound') to extended binary movements ('Ev'ry valley') and rondo-type structures ('O thou that tellest'). Three arias provide fascinating exemplars for Handel's treatment of form. In 'Rejoice greatly' he compressed the original full da capo form by slicing the binary *A* section at its dominant-key midpoint and inserting the *B* section there, a procedure that he was to use again elsewhere (e.g. 'O sacred oracles of truth' in *Belshazzar*). 'Thou art gone up on high' was recomposed twice for different singers: comparison of the three basic versions (one of which is found in alternative keys) shows him trying out variations not only in the thematic material but also in the tonal plan. 'I know that my Redeemer liveth' begins as if it is to be a short, binary cavatina, but its tripartite text develops along subtle lines, involving ritornello landmarks in the dominant and subdominant. As for the chorus movements, the narrative at the beginning of Part 2 gave Handel his biggest opportunity since *Israel in Egypt* for an extensive vista of chorus-led music, with the choral singers taking on narrative, participatory and commentary functions in turn.

Although *Messiah* is atypical on account of its subject matter and narrative presentation, it nevertheless shares a compositional feature with most of Handel's works in that some of the musical material is 'borrowed'. The theme of 'Let all the angels of God' (complete with contrapuntal diminutions) seems to derive from a keyboard piece by Johann Kaspar Kerll, a composer whom Handel had already raided for *Israel in Egypt* and who was represented in his lost '1698' music manuscript book.[6] Porta's *Numitore* – the first Royal Academy opera to be performed in 1720 – supplied a motivic idea for 'Thou shalt break them', and, rather more subtly, another aria from the same work seems to have influenced Handel's treatment of the text in 'The people that walked in darkness'. Closer to home, Handel drew on his own Italian duets. Material from *Se tu, non lasci amore* (HWV193), composed about 20 years previously, was recomposed for the duet 'O Death, where is thy sting?', and two more recent duets provided the themes for the four choruses 'And he shall purify',[7] 'For unto us a child is born', 'His yoke is easy' and 'All we, like sheep'. The relevant Italian duets (HWV192, 189) were composed at the beginning of July 1741, some six weeks before Handel began *Messiah*, but there is no reason to regard them as being preliminary studies for the *Messiah* music: rather, it seems that in the oratorio Handel re-used themes from other recent, free-standing works because he thought them appropriate in character (and in their technical ability to carry the new words) to the new contexts. Then, having used the music for *Messiah*, in

---

[6] See Gudger, 'A Borrowing from Kerll'.

[7] Handel also used the theme, derived from Telemann, in his Italian cantata *Quel fior, che all'alba ride* (HWV154; *c*.1739–41), as well as in the duet to the same text (HWV192, July 1741).

1742 Handel re-set the words of one of the Italian duets (*Nò, di voi non vuo' fidarmi*) to different music in another duet (HWV190).

Samson, written in 1741 as the companion oratorio to *Messiah*, is more conventional in that singers represent Samson, Dalila and other characters according to normal dramatic conventions. But *Samson* is no ordinary oratorio: in terms of its richness and diversity it is one of Handel's finest achievements. The range of moods embraced by the arias is comparable to that in his best operas: each is a well-developed 'character' piece, enjoying the benefits of Handel's expansive, mature musical style. In terms of technical construction, there is hardly a weak aria. Handel's skill in creating sustained arches of phrases with firm harmonic and melodic direction is everywhere in evidence, even when he uses relatively fragmentary material, conventional formulae or word-painting (Ex.44). Par-

Ex. 44

ticularly impressive in this respect are the long musical paragraphs in the big arias. In Samson's 'Why does the God of Israel sleep?', for example, a paragraph of nearly 30 bars links the first vocal entry to the cadence in the dominant at bar 39: firm harmonic control and the overlap of vocal and orchestral phrases keep the music on the move while avoiding the closing effect of intermediate cadences. Yet the internal phrases are themselves short: none in the vocal part is longer than three bars.

Another aria in *Samson*, 'Return, O God of Hosts', is arguably Handel's finest achievement in melodic construction, moving in graceful and balanced phrases, as well as sustaining long-term melodic and harmonic interest. It presents a striking parallel to 'He was despised' in *Messiah*: it is in the same metre, key (E♭) and tempo; it makes comparable use of harmonic pedal notes; it occurs at a parallel position, near the beginning of Part 2; its mood is similar and, indeed, it marks a similar point in the dramatic conflict, when the fortunes of the virtuous seem to be at their lowest ebb. The opening phrase, with its rising 6th followed by a two-bar melodic arch (Ex.45), combines the lyrical with the impassioned: it is extended by short motifs and phrases, balanced subtly in melodic and rhythmic shape, which eventually lead to a cadence in the dominant (bar 16), though the turn to the new key is taken so late that B♭ still sounds like a dominant rather than a new tonic, and it is no surprise when the music quickly reverts to E♭. Handel has now set up a tonal 'game': there is a question as to whether the music will ever really leave the tonic and whether it can be sustained without a proper alternative tonal centre. Handel has a surprise in store for, when the expected tonal diversion comes, it is to the tonic minor (at bar 23), after which the return to the major is almost consoling. Effectively, the whole 34-bar *A* section is in the tonic E♭, yet the musical interest never flags for a moment. What follows is equally original. After a contrasted *B* section (modulating, according to Handel's lifelong, well-tried plan, from the relative minor to its dominant minor), a return to the *A* section is naturally expected, but instead the chorus enters, in C minor, with a new text, using musical material from the *B* section (Ex.46). When this eventually returns to the

Ex. 45

Largo

 MICAH

Re - turn, re - turn,   O _   God _ of hosts

Ex. 46

tonic key the soloist re-emerges with the theme of the opening *A* section,
now punctuated and complemented by the chorus with their own theme.
The result is powerful in both dramatic and musical terms, as the fervour
of Micah's prayer finds a response in the collective utterances of the
chorus. The form of this movement was the result of extensive revision:
in his first (1741) draft Handel had set the solo and chorus material as
two independent movements, in different keys; when he came to revise
the score in 1742 he initially constructed a full da capo aria to precede
the chorus, before fusing the two.

The role of Samson himself is substantial, a tribute to the musical (and,
within the terms of the oratorio medium, histrionic) powers of Handel's
tenor John Beard. His short aria 'Total eclipse' is justly well-known, for
it is a masterly piece of economic musical characterization: the emotional
power of Samson's lamentation for his loss of sight is considerable, and
it is not surprising that members of the oratorio audience in the 1750s
found it specially poignant after Handel's own sight had failed. In addition
to some fine arias, Samson has two splendid duets in Part 2 – though,
unlike most conventional operatic duets of the Baroque period, these
express conflict rather than amorous union: his partner in the first is
Dalila, in the second the Philistines' champion Harapha. Dalila was
originally sung by Mrs Clive, and Handel may have tailored the role to
her strengths as an actress rather than as a singer. The most ravishing
soprano set-piece music went not to her but to Avolio, in a dramatically
subsidiary role. Avolio sang 'With plaintive notes' in Part 2, a feigned da
capo aria which develops along quite different lines from the expected
plan, and, at the end, 'Let the bright seraphim' (probably written specially
for her), an aria whose da capo function is handed over to the chorus
after the completion of the *B* section, with the introduction of a new text,
'Let their celestial concerts all unite'. In Handel's original 1741 score the
oratorio had finished with the minor-key chorus 'Glorious hero': the new

epilogue made for a more positive ending, as well as providing a suitable aria for Avolio. The chorus movements are varied and extensive, with rollicking choruses for the Philistines (some with prominent use of horns) and more serious ones for the Israelites. Among their more unusual dramatic functions, the chorus singers represent the Philistines who are trapped at Dagon's feast when Samson brings down the building; suitably divided, they also enact a musical slanging-match between the supporters of Dagon and Jehovah at the end of Part 2. Handel's setting of the text

> Oh first created Beam! and thou great Word!
> Let there be Light! and Light was over all

contrasts simple, solemn three-part chords with a lively outburst for full chorus and orchestra, anticipating a famous moment in Haydn's *Creation*. This immediately follows 'Total eclipse', and continues the commentary on Samson's blindness (Newburgh Hamilton took the text directly from Milton's *Samson Agonistes*). Hamilton's fine libretto, drawing extensively on Milton's psalm paraphrases as well as on *Samson Agonistes*, matches the best work of Jennens and Morell.

If Handel's next pair of major works, *Semele* and *Joseph*, both composed in 1743, did not quite maintain the level of *Messiah* and *Samson*, that is largely because Handel had set the level very high. *Semele* began with the advantage of a good operatic libretto by Congreve: indeed, John Eccles's unperformed setting of it in the first decade of the century would by no means have been negligible as an opera. Handel's *Semele*, which he performed 'after the manner of an Oratorio', receives rather more expansive and slow-moving treatment than it would have done if he had intended to present it as a staged opera. The story is an engaging one, concerning Jupiter's love for Semele (the daughter of the King of Thebes) and the mortal girl's destruction when the god fulfils her request to appear in his real form. There is a particularly striking opening scene at the Temple of Juno, where the goddess's blessing is sought for the marriage of Semele to Prince Athamas. After initially favourable omens it becomes apparent that Semele is a reluctant bride and that her sister is in love with Athamas: the celebrations are abruptly terminated by the sound of thunder and the extinguishing of the fire at the altar – 'Juno assents, but angry Jove denies'. The attraction between Semele and Jupiter is celebrated in some of Handel's most sensuous music: this serves also to heighten the tragedy of Semele's eventual destruction and to give dramatic credibility to the force of Juno's jealousy, which wills that destruction. A scene at the beginning of Part 3, in which Juno has difficulty awakening the lugubrious Somnus (the god of Sleep), provides a relief from the heavier emotions of the drama. Some of the movements, such as 'Where'er you walk', 'Endless pleasure, endless love' and 'O sleep, why dost thou leave me?', have become famous independently. The last two are for Semele herself, a major soprano role created for Francesina. It was her good fortune also to gain such arias as 'Myself I shall adore' and 'No, no, I'll take no less', and she received the biggest of all Handel's set-piece arias in 'The morning lark to mine ascends his note', a worthy successor in a musical line from 'Sweet bird' (*L'Allegro*) and 'With plaintive notes' (*Samson*); yet this aria may be the work's one dramatic solecism, for it seems out of scale with its surroundings and is only tangentially linked to the action. The chorus has rather less to do than in the biblical oratorios, but 'O terror and astonishment' shows Handel on top form. In all, *Semele* is an effective musical drama, with a fine score and a well-wrought libretto.

The description 'well-wrought' is not often applied to the libretto of *Joseph and his Brethren*, which has suffered a certain amount of critical misunderstanding and, indeed, rejection. But the oratorio was well regarded by Handel: between 1744 and his death he gave ten performances, a total exceeded only by *Samson*, *Judas Maccabaeus* and *Messiah*. Certainly it is true that the librettist, James Miller, tried to force into a three-part oratorio more of the story than the structure could accommodate, and that the text, if taken by itself, leaves essential motivations and incidents without proper explanation. But the libretto as set by Handel was never intended to be taken by itself: the background and essential linking details (which were probably well known to contemporary audiences in any case) were fully explained in Miller's summary (called 'Advertisement') at the front of the printed libretto. Furthermore, research has revealed the reason for both the apparent lopsidedness of the libretto and the occasional oddities of language that have otherwise been attributed to Miller's incompetence. It transpires that Parts 2 and 3 were adapted translations of a two-part Italian oratorio libretto by Apostolo Zeno, originally set by Caldara for performance in Vienna in 1722[9]. In front of the Italian model, Miller added a Part 1 in which unities of time and place were sacrificed to the need to convey certain incidents that seemed germane to setting up the story. Miller also incorporated into Part 1 scenes that provided symmetries with the later material: the opening scene, with Joseph in prison, for example, is clearly intended to balance Simeon's prison scene in Part 2. The two prison scenes are among the work's best moments, particularly the melodramatic music for Simeon in Part 2, which seems to look forward to Act 2 of Beethoven's *Fidelio* rather than backwards to the prison scenes in Handel's operas of the 1720s that had been Senesino's speciality. Another high point is the amiable final duet, 'What's sweeter than the new-blown rose?'. Mixed with the many fine choruses and arias there are a few routine ones, and some sequences of scenes are admittedly disjointed, but modern revivals have confirmed that *Joseph* has suffered an undeserved neglect. It is perhaps unfortunate

[8] See Chisholm, 'New Sources'.

that Miller died before his collaboration with Handel had really moved into its stride.

No allowances need be made for the librettos of *Hercules* and *Belshazzar*, composed in 1744. Both Thomas Broughton (working from Sophocles and Ovid for the story of *Hercules*) and Jennens (working from the Bible, supplemented by Xenophon and Herodotus for *Belshazzar*) produced powerful and coherent dramas: Handel himself said that the *Belshazzar* libretto 'has furnished me with Expressions, and has given me Opportunity to some very particular Ideas'. *Hercules* deals with Dejanira's jealousy over her husband Hercules's (supposed) infidelity with Iole, the Princess of Oechalia, whose father he has killed during the conquest of the country. In an effort to secure Hercules' devotion, Dejanira sends him a 'rich embroidered vest' that she believes has the power to 'revive the expiring flame of love'; but the garment is impregnated with the blood of the Centaur Nessus, whom Hercules had killed, and Hercules is burnt to death by its poison when he wears the vest in the warm atmosphere of the victory sacrifice. A full appreciation of *Hercules* relies on an understanding of some details of the classical background that are not sufficiently explicit for a modern audience. Moreover, while Handel's skill in both the composition of individual movements and the construction of whole scenes is on at least a par with that in *Semele*, *Hercules* is a much heavier work; its prevailing gloom is lightened only occasionally, principally by the rejoicing (ironic, as it turns out) at the end of Part 1, instigated by Hercules at the prospect of an end to the fighting and his return to Dejanira's loving arms. The role of Lichas, substantially expanded by Handel for Mrs Cibber after the main score had been completed, poses something of a riddle: from the dramatic point of view, Lichas's arias are padding which impedes the action, but they also provide much-needed lighter contrast. Hercules and Dejanira are powerful dramatic roles, both working towards tragic ends. Gluck may have seen a score of *Hercules* while he was in London, for Dejanira's remarkable scene in Part 3 ('Where shall I fly?') seems to anticipate Gluck's 'Furies' music in *Orfeo ed Euridice* and *Iphigénie en Tauride*; the power of Dejanira's *scena* is something that could not have been predicted from its most obvious Handelian predecessor, the 'mad scene' in *Orlando*. The Sinfonia that opens Part 3, with its jagged alternations of *largo* and *furioso*, is no less markedly Gluckian, suggesting a ballet for the Furies, though without any explicit hint in the score that such an image was in Handel's mind.

With *Belshazzar* Handel composed a biblical oratorio that was a worthy successor to *Samson*. Jennens's letters hint that his libretto had been a rushed job, produced under pressure from Handel, but there is little cause for complaint in the final article. Part 1 is, as Handel recognized,[9] longer

[9] In his letter to Jennens, 19 July 1744 (quoted in Chapter 11).

than usual (at 80 minutes almost twice as long as Handel estimated for *Judas* and *Solomon*). It sets up the dramatic situation: the captivity of the Jews in Babylon; Belshazzar's plan to celebrate the feast of Sesach ("'Tis religion to be drunk on this occasion') and to make sacrilegious use of the drinking-vessels taken from the temple in Jerusalem; and the scheme of Cyrus the Persian to divert the River Euphrates during the feast and enter the city on the river-bed. The principal roles are well characterized in their arias: Cyrus the realist in 'Dry those unavailing tears', the swaggering Belshazzar in 'Let festal joy' and the Jewish prophet Daniel in 'O sacred oracles of truth'. The last is a worthy musical successor to 'Return, O God of Hosts' in Handel's gallery of lyrical arias: it is followed by a no less remarkable ground-bass aria, 'Thus saith the Lord'. Sound dramatic instinct also led Jennens to develop the character of Nitocris, Belshazzar's mother, who has only a shadowy existence in the historical sources: she serves as an essential link in the action, trying to divert her son from his blasphemy.

Part 2 carries the principal action. Medes and Persians celebrate their success in diverting the river, while in the palace itself a succession of pagan choruses depicts the feast in full swing. The appearance of the writing on the wall in the midst of the revelry constitutes one of the most stageable moments in all Handel's oratorios and, indeed, it was accompanied by elaborate 'stage directions' from Jennens:

As he is going to drink, a Hand appears writing upon the wall over-against him; he sees it, turns pale with fear, drops the bowl of wine, falls back in his seat, trembling from head to foot, and his knees knocking against each other.

The Babylonian wise men are sent for, but they can do nothing, and Daniel is eventually called in to interpret the writing: Handel enlivened the interpretation with some musical imagery (Ex. 47) for the word 'finished' and for the fall of the 'balances'. In Part 3 Cyrus duly overcomes Belshazzar, spares Nitocris, frees the Jews and promises to rebuild the Temple in Jerusalem. In the choruses of *Belshazzar*, as in the arias, Handel was once again at the peak of his powers: they include dramatic 'participation' choruses, such as those in which the feasting crowd express perplexity at the writing on the wall, and the opening chorus in which Babylonians appear on the walls of the city to deride Cyrus, and 'commentary' choruses, such as the splendid 'By slow degrees' that ends Part 1. As in *Samson*, the nations represented in turn by the chorus are well differentiated musically, with some serious, portentous numbers for the Jews in Part 1 and suitably hedonistic music for the Babylonians at the feast.

Ex. 47

'Occasional poetry must often content itself with occasional praise.' So said Samuel Johnson of one of Nicholas Rowe's plays,[10] and the sentence might equally be applied to Handel's *Occasional Oratorio*. It originated in 1746 as a tub-thumping morale-raiser just after a national emergency,

[10] *Tamerlane* (1702), in his essay on Rowe in 'Lives of the English Poets' (introduction to the section on Rowe in *The Works of the Most Eminent English Poets*, 1779–81).

and was probably thrown together fairly quickly, borrowing much raw material from *Israel in Egypt* for Part 3;[11] nevertheless, it flows along with considerable élan and contains some effective new material, both in the rousing choruses and in arias such as 'How great and many perils' and 'He has his mansion fix'd on high'. The aria-chorus sequence beginning 'To God our strength' also deserved a better fate than the limited exposure it received in Handel's six performances of the oratorio, but the festive overture has retained some hold on posterity as an independent piece (particularly as a subject for organ arrangement at a later period in Britain). The opening vocal movement provided Handel with a second chance to set the text of 'Why do the nations',[12] but the result admittedly shows the superiority of the *Messiah* setting. The oratorio deserves an occasional hearing today but it has neither the narrative-picturesque content of *Israel in Egypt* nor the individual characterizations inherent in the dramatic oratorios; its crude opposition between righteousness and rebellion is a weakness and represents an argument that can be sustained only by excluding genuine human characters.

Judas Maccabaeus, composed the same year, though also bellicose and triumphalist, is more successful from the dramatic point of view, for Judas and Simon at least are plausible characters, albeit somewhat two-dimensional. Part 1 sees Judas selected as the new leader of the Israelites; the rest of the oratorio is mainly concerned with his two military victories and culminates in a treaty from the Roman Senate granting freedom and independence to Judaea. Although the music is effective, the repeated calls to arms and the victory celebrations result in considerable stretches in a bellicose mood, and contrasting scenes such as the purging of the Temple from the heathen rites and the Jewish Feast of Lights that follows are passed over relatively quickly; furthermore, the extensive duet-and-chorus movement 'O never bow we down', which concludes the purging of the Temple, in effect sustains the defiant mood in which the Jews set off for battle. The only extended contrast comes in the opening scene, a lament over the death of Judas's father, which stands in a line of descent from the elegiac scenes near the end of *Saul* and *Samson* and picks up the mood of the lamentation chorus 'And the children of Israel sigh'd' in *Israel in Egypt*.

It is perhaps not surprising that the only clearly delineated characters in *Judas Maccabaeus* are the principal men, though the anonymous Israelite woman and man received some of the best arias, of both the

[11] In addition, the chorus 'May God, from whom all mercies spring' in Part 2 was transferred, with some adaptation, from *Athalia*; on this occasion 'Bless the true church, and save the king' would have lacked the possible ambiguity from the Oxford performances in 1733 (see Chapter 8, p. 175).

[12] The words in *Messiah* and the *Occasional Oratorio*, embodying different English versions of the same psalm verses, are not identical; the *Occasional Oratorio* version (from Milton) begins 'Why do the gentiles tumult?'.

tuneful and the virtuosic types – ''Tis Liberty, dear Liberty alone', 'Come, ever-smiling Liberty', 'From mighty kings he took the spoil', 'So shall the lute and harp awake' and 'O lovely peace, with plenty crown'd'. The last was probably replaced before performance by the duet based on the same music. Elsewhere in the score Handel seems to have had an unusually strong predilection for duets, as he provided four for soprano and alto (Gambarini and Galli, the latter also cast as the 'Israelitish Man'), of which only two seem to have been suggested by Morell's libretto, the rest stemming presumably from Handel's own initiative. Of the set-piece arias, 'So shall the lute and harp awake' is one of the most interesting in formal construction. The first section ends in the dominant, and then, after what is in effect a *B* section, music from the opening section returns, as if to suggest a dal segno structure; but, after a few phrases, music that was previously heard in the dominant slips down to the tonic, and the *B*-section material is also recapitulated in the tonic. Given the political situation in which the oratorio was introduced, it is not surprising that arias such as ''Tis Liberty alone' and 'Come, ever-smiling Liberty' gained some independent popularity early in the work's history.[13] The movement from *Judas Maccabaeus* best known today is the march-chorus 'See the conquering hero comes', but it was originally composed for *Joshua* and became associated with *Judas Maccabaeus* only in Handel's subsequent revivals.

Joshua and *Alexander Balus* of 1747 mark a return to normality in Handel's creative life, not only because they saw the revival of a composition rhythm in which he was able to tackle pairs of oratorios together, but also because they deal with individual as well as collective fortunes and contain more rounded human characters. They continue the strain of 'victory oratorios' based on stories of Old Testament heroes, but they are also something more. Both have plots that include some love interest, though this was not a prerequisite of a successful oratorio (*Belshazzar* contains no love interest, though womankind is amply represented by Nitocris). *Joshua* has two concurrent plots: the Israelites' battles, and the development of an amorous relationship between the subsidiary characters Achsah and Othniel (who, however, doubles as both lover and hero, leading the last battle; it is to Othniel's victorious return that 'See the conquering hero comes' is sung). The outcome of neither plot is seriously in doubt, although the Israelites receive one setback in Part 2, and the courtship scenes are conventional. Nevertheless, there is some enjoyable musical scenery on the way, particularly in the choral scenes that open and close Part 2. For the demolition of the walls of Jericho Handel concentrated his aural imagination not on 'the pond'rous ruin falls' but on the shock-waves that follow the collapse: 'the nations tremble at the

---

[13]E.g. as individual solo numbers in plays at Covent Garden during March-April 1748: see Deutsch, pp. 649–51; *HHB*, pp. 414–15.

dreadful sound, heav'n thunders, tempests roar, and groans the ground'. No doubt the large drums from the Tower of London assisted with the 'roar', but even without them the effect of the build-up in the orchestral parts is remarkable. The musical idea for 'The nations tremble' bubbled up into Handel's consciousness from a recollection of one of the best choral-dramatic moments in the Cannons anthems ('The earth trembled and quak'd', from HWV255), composed 30 years previously; and an idea from another Cannons anthem seems to have been in his mind when he came to set a text about 'the scattered nations' in the final chorus of Part 2. The latter comes at the climax of a movement containing one of the best aural-pictorial effects to be found in Handel's oratorios – the depiction of the sun and moon standing still in response to Joshua's command. The representation of this with a sustained high pedal *a"* is an idea that is in itself simple to the point of naivety, but Handel, with a touch as sure as that shown half a century later by Haydn in *The Creation*, integrates the idea into the music so that it makes its mark without toppling over into bathos. Here, no less than in the hammer-strokes of his assertive oratorio choruses, Handel knew both how to make his effect and (usually) the limits to which any such effect could be pushed. Bernard Shaw summed up this aspect of his genius perceptively: 'It was from Handel that I learned that style consists on force of assertion; if you can say a thing with one stroke unanswerably you have style'.[14]

The concluding choruses of Parts 1 and 3 of Joshua are perfunctory, but overall the choruses are more distinguished than the arias, the best of which is Caleb's 'Shall I in Mamre's fertile plain'. That aria comes from the same stable as 'He was despised' and 'Return, O God of Hosts' and, like the latter, leads into a chorus; but there is no combined recapitulation for soloist and chorus, and the movement is on a much more modest scale. Taken as a whole *Joshua*, since it has a few extensive arias, is a compact work. 'O had I Jubal's lyre', the final set-piece aria for soprano, is a virtuoso piece of goodly proportions, yet it is in simple binary form; its cunning lies in the extension of its musical paragraphs rather than in any structural invention, and it draws inspiration from Handel's bank of earlier melodic ideas, this time from the Roman *Laudate, pueri* (HWV237) of 40 years before.

Alexander Balus, composed in 1747 before *Joshua*, is the most interesting of the 'victory oratorios' and, like *Joshua*, develops a love story in conjunction with its political plot, though here the sexual alliance involves the principal characters and is central to the development of the plot. Neither element is straightforward: the romance ends in tragedy with the death of one of the partners and, in spite of Morell's attempt to emphasize the elements of Jewish patriotism and religion, the political story concerns incidents to which the Jews contribute as allies rather than as principals, the mainspring of the drama lying in an act of treachery by another nation. The story, from the book of *Maccabees*, is set in Syria, where Alexander has seized the throne and killed the former king. Alexander concludes an alliance with the Jews and receives the congratulations of Ptolomee, King of Egypt, with whose daughter, Cleopatra, he falls in love. Their love-match leads to marriage, but it transpires that Ptolomee has consented to the match only in order to put Alexander within his power: he means to introduce Egyptian troops into Syria under the cover of friendship and then to depose Alexander in favour of a more compliant ruler, 'the young Demetrius'. Cleopatra is kidnapped and carried off to be forcibly married to Demetrius, but she remains unshaken in her devotion to Alexander. In a series of battles the Jews win three victories, but Alexander and Ptolomee are both killed. Cleopatra commends herself to the protection of the god Isis, and the Jews sing in solemn praise of the providence of the true God.

In terms of dramatic pacing *Alexander Balus* is lopsided, with all the significant dramatic action in Part 3. Cleopatra emerges as a tragic heroine, firm in her own personal and religious devotions, a victim of her father's treachery and widowed by the consequent war. The most graphic moment comes when her pastoral reverie 'Here amid the shady woods', accompanied by muted upper strings and pizzicato basses, is interrupted (just as she is embarking on the *B* section) by the 'ruffians' sent by Ptolomee to take her away. Her final scene, with the arias 'O take me from this hateful light' and 'Convey me to some peaceful shore' (in E minor and E major respectively, the latter evoking memories of her namesake's moving music in the same key in *Giulio Cesare*), forms the climax to the oratorio; indeed, the lasting impression is of Cleopatra's tragedy rather than of the victory of true religion that Morell had no doubt intended. The text of the final chorus as set by Handel:

> Ye servants of th' eternal King
> His pow'r and glory sing;
> And speak of all his righteous ways
> With wonder and with praise

was a replacement for Morell's original:

> O Thou, whose ever-righteous ways
> Demand our wonder and our praise;
> Whose Pow'r extends from Pole to Pole,
> And Will impulsive binds the Whole:
> Strengthen our Arms in War, that War may cease,
> In all the Blessings of a glorious Peace.

Ex. 48

In Morell's manuscript libretto[15] Handel cancelled the original text and wrote in the replacement, but only after an attempt had been made to amend the first text by reshaping the opening four lines and deleting the final couplet (see Plate 10). It seems that he had raised an objection to Morell's original text and, having dismissed the attempts to amend it, demanded a replacement from his librettist. Handel probably rejected the original because he found the penultimate line offensive: though God might reasonably be asked to take sides with the righteous, total support for partisan warfare on these terms was another matter. It may be that Handel was more sensitive than Morell on this subject; perhaps he had a well-grounded suspicion of extravagant claims for the palliative effects of military enterprise, as a result of the tales that he had surely heard in his youth concerning the sufferings of Halle during the Thirty Years War.

[15] The document referred to is the copy of the libretto that was submitted to the Inspector of Stage Plays under the terms of the Licensing Act of 1737; in this case it seems that what was deposited was the final working copy of the libretto, perhaps even the one that Handel had had by him as he composed the music.

321

In a letter written about 11 years after Handel's death, Morell gave a vivid account of his technical collaboration with Handel over the text of Cleopatra's final aria, 'Convey me to some peaceful shore' (Ex.48):[16]

> And as to the last Air, I cannot help telling you, that, when Mr Handell first read it, he cried out 'D—n your Iambics'. 'Dont put yourself in a passion, they are easily Trochees.' '*Trochees, what are Trochees?*' 'Why, the very reverse of Iambics, by leaving out a syllable in every line, as instead of
>
> *Convey me to some peaceful shore,*
>
> *Lead me to some peaceful shore.*'
>
> 'That is what I want.' 'I will step into the parlour, and alter them immediately.' I went down and returned with them altered in about 3 minutes; when he would have them as they were, and set them most delightfully accompanied with only a quaver, and a rest of 3 quavers.

It seems that Handel worked quite closely with Morell, possibly involving frequent contact as a work was developing,[17] in contrast to his working relationship with Jennens, which seems to have involved more lengthy meetings at strategic stages. Morell also gives an amiable picture of the gestation of *Judas Maccabaeus*:[18]

> Mr Handell applied to me, when at Kew, in 1746, and added to his request the honour of a recommendation from Prince Frederic. Upon this I thought I could do as well as some that had gone before me, and within 2 or 3 days carried him the first Act of *Judas Maccabaeus*, which he approved of. 'Well,' says he, 'and how are you to go on?' 'Why, we are to suppose an engagement, and that the Israelites have conquered, and so begin with a chorus as
> Fallen is the Foe
> or, something like it.' 'No, I will have this,' and began working it, as it is, upon the Harpsichord. 'Well, go on', 'I will bring you more tomorrow.' 'No, something now,'
> 'So fall thy Foes, O Lord'
> 'that will do,' and immediately carried on the composition as we have it in that most admirable chorus.

Given the apparent freedom in Handel's dealings with Morell, it is perhaps surprising that Handel did not insist on a better distribution of the dramatic activity in the first two parts of *Alexander Balus*. The music here, though adequate, is not specially distinguished, one or two arias excepted; one of the most engaging features is the orchestral colour that

---

[16] Deutsch, p. 852; *HHB*, p. 413.

[17] A later anecdote of doubtful credence (from John Taylor's, *Records of my Life*, 1832) claims that Handel drove to Morell's house at Turnham Green early in the morning to ask him the meaning of the word 'billows', which occurs in 'Convey me to some peaceful shore', though he had previously set the word in the chorus 'Smiling Venus, Queen of Love' in the 1732 version of *Acis and Galatea*.

[18] Deutsch, p. 851.

Handel gave the Asiatics, whose choruses are generally lively and fully scored, with prominent horns and/or trumpets. Cleopatra's first aria, 'Hark! he strikes the gold lyre', is delicately scored, with flutes supplementing the string orchestra while the harp and mandolins are supported by pizzicato cellos and basses.[19] The scoring recalls the seductive music for Cleopatra's namesake in *Giulio Cesare*, but the contours of the first vocal phrase seem to have been suggested by a similar text at the start of the second part of *Alexander's Feast*.

With *Solomon* and *Susanna* of 1748 Handel returned to fully rounded human dramas of a quality comparable with *Hercules* and *Belshazzar*. These oratorios were to constitute his last 'pair' of large works, and the contrast between their subjects is striking: *Solomon* is set amidst the luxury and magnificence of kings and queens, while *Susanna* records the doings of humbler men and women. The contrast is reflected in the musical means that Handel employed: strings, woodwind, two trumpets and a four-part chorus suffice for *Susanna*, while *Solomon* adds flutes, horns and timpani and occasionally disposes the singers in two antiphonal four-part choirs paralleled by divided strings (supplemented by 'ripieno' players). Yet the two works also have much in common. Both deal with matters of domestic life rather than with political conflicts, and both play out their dramas through judicial scenes rather than through the clash of armies. There is also a certain similarity of language and imagery, which may point to a common authorship, though the identity of the librettist(s) is unknown.

Like *Belshazzar*, *Solomon* has one eminently stageworthy scene at the midpoint in Part 2, though once again the surrounding material is paced to concert performance rather than to operatic presentation. In this central scene Solomon judges the case of disputed ownership and parentage between two 'women' (so designated in the score, though called 'harlots' in the word-book), threatening to cut the child in two with a 'faulchion' as a device to expose the false mother. She (in F major) blandly praises Solomon's judgment without concern for the fate of the child, while the true mother (in F minor) appeals for the child to be spared. The scene is introduced with a lively trio for the two women and Solomon (in F♯ minor) and, after Solomon gives his judgment in an *accompagnato* that modulates from B♭ major to G♯ minor, it culminates in a duet between Solomon and the true mother (in E major) and a chorus celebrating Solomon's wisdom (in A major). Dramatically and musically, this is one of Handel's most colourful scenes, with a lively tonal progression.

The judgment scene contributes to the general theme of the oratorio, which is a celebration of the stability and prosperity achieved in Jerusalem

---

[19] This is the only instance of Handel's scoring for a harp in his mature oratorios; mandolins, no doubt intended as exotic colouring, were tuned in 5ths and might have been played by orchestral string players who were temporarily diverted for the purpose.

under Solomon – a golden age for the Jews (the less attractive aspects of Solomon's personality and activities are not in evidence). Part 1 begins with the completion of Solomon's Temple and continues with a scene depicting the wedded bliss of Solomon (portrayed here as monogamous) and his queen, to whom he promises a new palace. In Part 3 the splendours of Solomon's court receive the approbation of an outsider, the visiting Queen of Sheba, who is entertained with an elaborate musical masque and then admiringly tours the new temple and palace before returning to her own country. There is a symmetry in the design of the oratorio, as in the design of Solomon's Temple: the two queens in Parts 1 and 3 balance each other and frame the two women in the judgment scene in Part 2 (in Handel's performances Frasi played both queens and one of the women). In each part Solomon, originally sung by (and no doubt written for) the contralto Galli, has a duet with one of the sopranos.

Solomon is one of Handel's richest, most comprehensive and most rewarding scores. It serves as a compendium of some of the most engaging aspects of his music. The pervasive 'nature' imagery revives a strain of musical stimuli that was last displayed comprehensively in *L'Allegro*; it results in a clutch of amiable and varied arias and, perhaps best of all, in the 'nightingale chorus' at the end of Part 1. The amorous exchanges between Solomon and his queen[20] and the judgment scene in Part 2 bring out the old operatic Handel, while the masque in Part 3 produces a colourful succession of musical images that recall those evoked by Timotheus's lyre-playing in *Alexander's Feast*, moving successively through stirring military music, a despairing lover's lament, and a storm that plays itself out, leaving calm weather behind. Both for the masque and for the pageantry of the court scenes Handel's choruses are of a high order. The arias, in which he recomposed many ideas derived from earlier music of his own or of other composers (with Telemann well to the fore)[21] are well-written, in addition to being varied in type and mood. The best are not confined to the principals: the priest Zadok, for example, has lively character pieces in 'See the tall palm' and 'Golden columns fair and bright'. Handel had a happy knack in his arias of producing opening phrases (whether borrowed or not) that establish the right mood and at the same time provide a memorable and pithy setting of the text: Zadok's arias, as well as 'What though I trace each herb and flower', 'Haste to the cedar grove' and 'With thee th'unsheltered moor I tread', are some obvious examples from Part 1. The bass role of the Levite perhaps has the least interesting music but, as a flat-key foil to the surrounding excitements, it cannot be cut without damage to the balance of the work

[20] Unfortunately, some of the texts were misguidedly (and sometimes amusingly) bowdlerized in Vincent Novello's nineteenth-century vocal score.
[21] This is also true of the choruses; for Handel's predilection with Telemann as a source for borrowings at this period, see Roberts, 'Handel's Borrowings from Telemann', and Derr, 'Handel's Procedures'.

as a whole.[22] 'Praise the Lord with harp and tongue', the best of the set-piece choruses, comes near the end of Part 3 and sounds too much like a finale for the comfort of the succeeding movements (indeed, it may have been designed as such), but the valedictory music for the Queen of Sheba and Solomon that follows is magnificent and compensates for the swiftness with which Handel's eventual brief final chorus closes the work. The Sinfonia that opens Part 3 has, with its festive jollity, won deserved popularity as 'The Arrival of the Queen of Sheba', even though the music seems to have been composed originally for a different context in one of the preceding oratorios; it is a wittily constructed ritornello movement, drawing on ideas from Telemann and Porta's *Numitore*.

Susanna excels in a different way, as a domestic, human drama. Although the source for the story is scriptural (from the book of *Susanna*, a Greek addition to the book of *Daniel*, consigned to the Apocrypha in Protestant bibles), this is of hardly any significance, for the inspired intervention of the young Daniel is but one element in the unfolding of a plot which, as one commentator has remarked, 'may be worked out in reality on any day of the week'.[23] The story evolves with a deft, even comical touch (a contemporary writer commented on the work's 'light operatic style'),[24] to which a few somewhat sententious chorus movements provide the occasional foil. There is no reason to suppose that Handel was unhappy with the resulting mixture, with its contrasts of perspective. In fact the chorus, which has a relatively minor role, fulfils a number of functions. In the opening scene it depicts the oppression under which the Jews labour during the Babylonian exile: subsequently it comments on the actions of the principals, and in the judgment scene supplies the public reaction to Daniel's judgment and Susanna's innocence. The story itself is straightforward. Joachim announces that he has to go away for a week, leaving his wife Susanna behind; the way is thus left open for her to receive the unwelcome approaches of two lascivious Elders. They catch her bathing on a hot day, but their advances are repulsed by her 'self-conscious virtue'; nevertheless, when discovered in her company, they claim to have caught her in dalliance with a youthful partner. She is convicted on the evidence of the Elders and condemned to death, but Daniel intervenes, pointing out that virtue does not always accompany seniority. Questioning the Elders separately, he quickly exposes conflicts in their evidence; Susanna is reprieved to rejoin her husband, and lauded as the model of a virtuous wife.

Part 1 is expository and mainly conventional in its arias, though it includes a striking *accompagnato*, 'Tyrannic Love', in which one of the

[22]Beecham's version of *Solomon*, which was influential in the mid-twentieth century, re-arranges the score and gives no clue to the balance of Handel's original.
[23]See Young, *The Oratorios of Handel*, p. 175.
[24]Letter from Countess of Shaftesbury to James Harris, 11 February 1749 (quoted in full in Chapter 12).

Elders struggles with the conflicting demands of his public reputation and his attraction to Susanna. The dramatic action is nicely paced through Parts 2 and 3. In Part 2 Susanna's visit to the countryside is delicately depicted in 'Crystal streams in murmurs flowing', and her attendant entertains her with a couple of attractive and contrasting songs ('Ask if yon damask rose be sweet' and 'Beneath the cypress' gloomy shade'). Each of the Elders then importunes her in turn with a different approach, and her repulse generates a lively trio. The first section of Part 3 is taken up with the tragedy of Susanna's death sentence, involving a few crocodile tears from the Elders: this is balanced, after Daniel's intervention, by a celebration of her innocence (led by her father, Chelsias) and general praise for her virtue. As in *Solomon*, Handel hit upon pithy, memorable opening phrases for most of the arias and developed them in his most fluent style: it is perhaps not surprising, in view of its subject-matter, that this particular work has a larger number of operatic-style da capo or dal segno arias.

Other works

The 1740s saw Handel's last contributions to the repertory of English church music, with occasional pieces in 1743 and 1749. The 'Dettingen' *Te Deum* and Anthem of 1743 were composed on a scale that no doubt anticipated a state thanksgiving in St Paul's Cathedral, of the type that had followed the Peace of Utrecht in 1713, but the music was eventually performed in the relatively confined privacy of the Chapel Royal. The *Te Deum* is rather brash and leans heavily on D major: it matches the ceremonial of its intended occasion but is less sensitive than Handel's earlier settings of the text; only 'Vouchsafe, O Lord' provides an all-too-short reflective oasis. The last trumpet (at the words 'We believe that Thou shalt come to be our judge') quotes the fanfare opening of 'The trumpet shall sound' in *Messiah*. The Dettingen Anthem (*The king shall rejoice in thy strength, O Lord*, HWV265, clearly distinct from the coronation anthem beginning with the same text) is rather more interesting. After a workmanlike but effective opening chorus in the inevitable D major, there follows a well-contrasted sequence of movements – a minor-key duet and chorus, and an *alla breve* movement in old-fashioned strict-counterpoint style. The anthem was composed between *Semele* and *Joseph*, and there was a certain amount of musical interchange between the three works: the anthem fugue was re-written for a chorus in *Joseph*; the final chorus in Part 2 of *Semele* provided the musical basis for the following anthem movement;[25] and the anthem's magnificent final chorus, with its lively mixture of double-subject counterpoint and powerful chordal homophony, was immediately re-used by Handel to round off Part 3 of *Joseph*.

[25] See Hurley, ' "The Summer of 1743" '.

That Handel chose to revive the 'Caroline' *Te Deum*, originally composed in 1714, for the Chapel Royal service celebrating the Peace of Aix-la-Chapelle in 1749, is testimony to the quality of the earlier work and its suitability for the forces and the venue: he again incorporated the alternative, 1720s setting of 'Vouchsafe, O Lord' but felt no need to re-compose any of the music afresh. The Peace Anthem *How beautiful are the feet* (HWV267), though mainly constructed or adapted from earlier material, works well as an independent entity. When writing it in April 1749 Handel was no doubt pressed for time by his end-of-season schedule, but he devoted a surprising amount of attention to its opening movement. Possibly in an effort to break away from the *Messiah* settings of the same text, he first of all tried it as a treble solo with following chorus, using a theme derived from an aria-chorus sequence in the *Occasional Oratorio*: he was in the process of scoring up this version when he decided to revert to yet another attempt to re-work the *Messiah* material, after which the other movements seem to have fallen easily into place.[26]

The Foundling Hospital Anthem, *Blessed are they that considereth the poor and needy* (HWV268),[27] was Handel's last piece of English church music and the only one not written for performance at court or at Cannons. It went through two versions, one fully choral and the other including solo movements for a tenor (John Beard), alto (the castrato Guadagni) and two boy trebles (the treble solos were sung by Chapel Royal children, who took part in the Foundling Hospital performances, not by the hospital's own charity children). It seems most likely that the fully choral version was the one performed at Handel's concert in aid of the charity in 1749, and that the second version evolved for the subsequent dedication service for the hospital's completed chapel.[28] Like the Peace Anthem, the Foundling Hospital Anthem took in and adapted music from previous works – movements from the Funeral Anthem of 1737, a reflective chorus that had been ejected from *Susanna* and the 'Hallelujah' chorus from *Messiah*. The additional solo movements also have musical relationships elsewhere, most notably Guadagni's splendid aria 'O God, who from the suckling's mouth', which is closely related to an aria in *Jephtha* (1751). The relative chronology is difficult to establish, but internal evidence from compositional alterations suggests that the anthem movement was composed after *Jephtha* (which would, of course, mean that Guadagni did not sing it, and possibly did not take part at all, in Handel's 1749 Foundling Hospital performance). In both its fully choral version and its revised form with solo movements, the Foundling Hospital Anthem

---

[26] See Burrows, 'Handel's Peace Anthem'.

[27] Handel seems to have had a temporary problem over the syntax in 1749: he similarly began the Peace Anthem with 'How beautiful are the feet of them that *bringeth*', though he had correctly matched subject and verb in his various settings of that text in *Messiah* during 1741–2.

[28] See Burrows, 'Handel and the Foundling Hospital', and (for the two versions of the anthem), Burrows (ed.), *Foundling Hospital Anthem*.

carries conviction and is a worthy culmination to this corner of Handel's creative activities.

A further interchange of musical material took place between Handel's last Italian duets and the contemporary oratorios. That Handel used music from the 1741 duets in *Messiah* and subsequently re-set one of the Italian texts to different music has already been noted. He re-worked music from the first movement of his last dated duet, *Ahi, nelle sorte umane* (HWV179, August 1745) for the duet movement 'From the dread scene' in *Judas Maccabaeus*, and the first movement of the undated *Fronda leggiera e mobile* (HWV186), which (to judge by the paper type of the autograph) must have been completed about the same period, relates to 'See, from his post Euphrates flies', the opening chorus of Part 2 of *Belshazzar*. The undulating melody of the latter serves to represent, respectively, the waving of leaves (in the duet) and the lapping of the retreating river (in *Belshazzar*). The second movement of HWV186 was drawn on by Handel for the duet movement 'After long storms' in the *Occasional Oratorio*. In these last duets, as in his first some 40 years previously, Handel maintained fluent strands of counterpoint and combined liveliness with suavity: they are musicians' music *par excellence*.

The music of 'See, from his post Euphrates flies' reappeared in one other guise in the 1740s, in Handel's *Concerto a due cori* HWV332. These concertos, as noted in Chapter 12, were Handel's 'interval music' for the oratorios of the period 1747–9. They are extrovert and rumbustious serenade-type pieces, which incidentally incorporate music from the oratorios, in much the same way as a twentieth-century band selection might introduce 'songs from the shows'. (In this context Handel seems to have had no concern about self-borrowings being recognized, and he evidently had no scruples about including music from *Messiah* along with that from the other oratorios.) The apotheosis of these concertos comes, however, with the *Fireworks Music* of 1749. After the splendid Ouverture (which, within the technical limitations imposed by the participating wind instruments, includes no fewer than three different harmonizations of the opening theme), there follows a rather casual, suite-like assembly of short movements – lively and attractive, and apt for an outdoor summer entertainment, with or without the fireworks and with or without the 'violeens'.

Although orchestral concertos displaced organ concertos for a considerable part of the period, in the 1740s Handel did produce a few more organ concertos, some of which were published posthumously in the op.7 collection. The A major concerto (op.7 no.2, HWV307) was written for *Samson* in 1743 (its last movement, based on ideas from Muffat, was derived from a movement rejected from that oratorio's overture). Other concertos from the 1740s survive in a less complete state: particularly tantalizing is a D major movement (published as the second movement of op.7 no.4) in which Handel developed an idea from Telemann into a

breezy and attractive movement with the unusual heading 'Allegro così
così'. 'Developed' is perhaps too weak a word for the transformation that
Handel achieved: Telemann's original (from an *Air* in the second collection
of *Musique de table*, 1733) seems shortwinded by comparison. Unfortunately, Handel left the movement with several 'ad libitum' gaps for
improvisation, which pose problems for the modern performer. The
original context for the music is also uncertain: it seems to be the torso
of a concerto whose other movements cannot now be identified with
certainty. Op.7 no.4, as published, was probably a compilation by the
younger J.C. Smith, and in it the Allegro was preceded by a single-organ
version of a D minor concerto movement involving two organs (HWV303)
that Handel had written around 1738. The D minor piece, with its
spectacularly sombre opening for divided cellos and bassoons, makes a
perfect foil for the D major Allegro, and the coupling may be authentic:
a copy of the two-organ movement in the hand of the elder J.C. Smith
was marked up by Handel with an abbreviated ending that may well have
been intended to lead into the 'Allegro così così' movement.

A concerto in D minor (HWV304), based on themes from Telemann
and requiring an 'ad libitum' movement or two (presumably in a contrasted
key) in the middle, seems to date from about 1746 and may have been
the 'New Organ Concerto' that accompanied the *Occasional Oratorio*. As
noted in Chapter 12, the *Concerto a due cori* HWV334 seems also to have
gone through mutations as an organ concerto and as a piece for solo
keyboard (about 1747), while the organ concerto published as op.7 no.6
relates, in its first movement at least, to Handel's oratorio performances
of 1749. The last movement of op.7 no.6, as published, is another piece
with 'ad libitum' gaps that defy authentic completion and leave us with
regrets that Handel never prepared his later organ concertos for publication
himself.

14

The final decade I: The last major works, 1749–51

During the summer of 1749 Handel completed only one new oratorio, instead of the pairs that he had composed the previous two summers: the draft score of *Theodora* was begun on 28 June and finished on 31 July. This was not necessarily a sign of declining creative stamina. The spring of 1749 had been unusually busy, and Handel might justifiably have taken things rather more easily afterwards; in any case, his repertory of oratorios had now built up to the extent that he may have calculated on only one novelty being sufficient for the next Lenten season. He took a trip to Bath, one of England's most favoured convalescent resorts,[1] but this visit may have been more in the nature of a rest-holiday than an indicator of the onset of medical problems. Perhaps Handel savoured a sentimental connection between the Roman city of Bath and the 'Roman' subject of *Theodora*.

The documentary record for Handel's activities between August and December is thin indeed. On 7 September he bought £1000 worth of annuities (presumably financed from oratorio profits or from back-payments of court pensions) and made another, more complex, financial transaction on 9 November:[2] these place him in London during the surrounding periods. He was certainly there on 30 September, when he wrote to Jennens about the organ that was being planned as one of the furnishings of Gopsall:[3]

> Yesterday I received Your Letter, in answer to which I hereunder specify my Opinion of an Organ which I think will answer the Ends You propose, being every thing that is necessary for a good and grand Organ, without Reed Stops, which I have omitted, because they are continually wanting to be tuned, which in the Country is very inconvenient, and should it remain useless on that Account, it would still be very expensive althou' that may not be Your Consideration. I very well approve of Mr Bridge who without any Objection is a very good Organ Builder, and I shall willingly (when He has finished it) give You my Opinion of it. I have referr'd You to the Flute Stop in Mr Freemans

[1] 'Arriv'd here, Mr Handell', *The Bath Journal* (19 August 1749).
[2] Deutsch, p. 677; *HHB*, p. 431.
[3] Letter of 30 September 1749: Deutsch, pp. 675–6; *HHB*, p. 431.

Organ being excellent in its kind, but as I do not referr you in that Organ, The System of the Organ I advise is, (Vizt

The Compass to be up to D and down to Gamut, full Octave, Church Work.
One Row of Keys, whole Stops and none in halves.

Stops

An Open Diapason – of Metal throughout to be in Front.
a Stopt Diapason – the Treble Metal and the Bass Wood.
a Principal – of Metal throughout.
a Twelfth – of Metal throughout.
a Fifteenth – of Metal throughout.
a Great Tierce – of Metal throughout.
a Flute Stop – such a one as in Freemans Organ.

'Mr Freeman' may have been William Freeman of Hamels, Hertfordshire, to whom Morell dedicated the libretto of *Alexander Balus*, and he perhaps supplies another name for Handel's circle of social acquaintance. Freeman (also spelt Freman) had died in February 1749 and bequeathed the organ from his house to the Music Room in Oxford. The organ for Gopsall, though inevitably somewhat altered, survives today at Great Packington church, Warwickshire, on the estate of the Earl of Aylesford (to whose family Jennens was related). In the summer of 1749 Handel had also been involved with another organ project, having made an agreement with Morse of Barnet for an instrument that Handel was to present to the Foundling Hospital chapel. Sadly, Morse does not seem to have been a builder of the same calibre as Bridge, and the hospital organ had to be replaced within 20 years. Human beings were also subject to change and decay: we may imagine that Handel was not unmoved by the death of the 83-year-old Heidegger on 5 September.

Towards the end of 1749, instead of writing a second oratorio for his next Lenten season, Handel became caught up in a project that promised to involve him anew in the regular stage dramas of the London theatre. In February 1749 Tobias Smollett had declared that he had written 'a sort of Tragedy on the Story of Alceste, which will (without fail) be acted at Covent Garden next Season and appear with such magnificence of Scenery as was never exhibited in Britain before'.[4] The play was submitted for rehearsal in September, and Handel wrote his musical contribution at the end of the year (the autograph bears commencement and completion dates of 27 December 1749 and 8 January 1750, respectively):[5] presumably he had had discussions with either Smollett or John Rich, the Covent Garden manager, or both, during the late autumn about the nature and extent of the musical score that was required.

[4]Letter to Alexander Carlyle, 14 February 1749: Deutsch, p. 657; *HHB*, p. 419.
[5]The autograph is now divided between British Library RM 20.e.6 and British Library Add. MS 30310, the former containing those sections that were re-used for *The Choice of Hercules*. The sections with the composition dates are divided between the two manuscripts: the starting date appears on the 'Entrée' to Act 1. There are two ouvertures, presumably written after the rest of the score: one was subsequently used as the ouverture to *Jephtha*.

As things turned out, Smollett's *Alceste* never came to performance. Nevertheless, Handel's music seems to have been put into rehearsal, for he reset two of Calliope's songs, presumably at the instigation of the singer Cecilia Arne, T. A. Arne's wife. It is difficult to make sense of the musical torso that remains of *Alceste*, because Smollett's text for the complete play has not survived. The outlines of the story are clear enough (it was one that Handel had already treated, in his opera *Admeto*), and it seems that Smollett's production was conceived on the lines of a Purcellian semi-opera, with substantial musical scenes at the beginning of Act 1 and at the conclusion of the fourth (and final) act. There was a clear distinction between the principal (non-singing) actors and the actor-singers who had the roles of attendants: Calliope, Charon, a Shade, Apollo and a Siren. The singers included some of Handel's familiar colleagues, including the tenor Lowe and the bass Waltz. The play may originally have been scheduled for performance at Covent Garden in February 1750 (in which case the cancellation came at the last moment) or after Easter. Although Handel's two substantial blocks of music make some sort of sense for concert performance, the *Alceste* music remains a tantalizing fragment. But it was not wasted: Handel put nearly all of the material to good use later.

If Handel was engaged with production rehearsals for *Alceste* in January and February, he nevertheless did not lose sight of the needs of his forthcoming oratorio season. He completed a new organ concerto on 31 January 1750, intended as a companion to his new oratorio *Theodora*. This concerto (HWV310), posthumously published as op.7 no.5 includes the last, and arguably the greatest, of his ground-bass movements.[6] As written, the concerto contains some elements that would have been covered by Handel's improvisation: 'ad libitum' passages at the end of the first two movements may indicate decorative flourishes, or Handel may have intended something more substantial. As it stands in Handel's autograph, the concerto ends with a minuet: the subsequent gavotte, which may not be authentic in this context, was added for the later publication of op.7. The tone of the concerto, set by the minor mode of the outer movements, is serious and seems to match the mood of the oratorio.

There were various distractions, some of them no doubt welcome, during the lead-up period to the oratorio season, when rehearsals were presumably taking place. The Earl of Shaftesbury reported on 13 February:[7]

I have seen Handel several times since I came hither, and think I never saw him so cool and well. He is quite easy in his behaviour, and has been pleasing himself in the purchase of several fine pictures, particularly a large Rembrant,

---

[6] The first movement contains an uncharacteristic solecism – a set of consecutives, at bar 11; ironically, Handel's eye probably missed them because they occurred in a bar that he had already altered.

[7] Letter to James Harris: Deutsch, p. 680; *HHB*, p. 434.

which is indeed excellent. We have scarce talk'd at all about musical subjects, tho' enough to find his performances will go off incomparably.

There was a flurry of financial activity at this period, but once again the recorded transactions are rather puzzling. Handel deposited £8000 in his Drawing Account on 22 January, though the source for this money is not apparent and he had withdrawn it all a month later. Perhaps his picture-buying activities partly account for this: he ended up with a very substantial picture collection, rather more than could have been easily displayed on the walls of his house at Brook Street, and it seems likely that con-noisseurship of the visual arts was the principal hobby of his later years, one that presumably was tragically curtailed by his blindness.[8] Early in March 1750 Handel received an approach from the Foundling Hospital for a 'performance of musick' on 1 May in connection with the official opening of their chapel: the performance that followed was to have considerable consequences, but at the time Handel no doubt simply showed an agreeable interest, knowing that the suggested date was well clear of the end of his oratorio season.

Having made the usual preparations, as well as securing the use of the large artillery drums from the Tower of London, Handel began his oratorio season at Covent Garden on 2 March (the first Friday in Lent) with *Saul*: two performances of this were followed, on Wednesdays and Fridays, by four of *Judas Maccabaeus*, three of *Theodora* and two of *Samson*; as in the previous season, a single performance of *Messiah* on Maundy Thursday rounded off the series. *Theodora*, the new oratorio, seems to have been poorly attended and attracted little attention: this may have been an accidental consequence of a general thinness of attendance during the oratorio season, which seems to have been affected by rumours of an earthquake, though there was no interruption to the sequence of performances. The atmosphere at the time was described by one member of the audience.[9]

I was not under any apprehension about the earthquake, but went that night to the Oratorio, then quietly to bed ... The Wednesday night the Oratorio was very empty, though it was the most favourite performance of Handel's.

There is other supporting evidence for a strong disparity between Handel's own estimate of *Theodora* and the reception it received: for no other oratorio are there so many anecdotes that explicitly relate Handel's high opinion of his work. Thomas Morell, the librettist for *Theodora*, recollected the situation some 20 years later:[10]

[8]His collection (apart from the items that were the subject of bequests) was sold by auction in 1760; see Simon, *Handel*, p. 290, and McLean, 'Bernard Granville'.
[9]Letter from Elizabeth Montagu to Sarah Robinson, ?20 March 1750: Deutsch, pp. 683–4; *HHB*, p. 436.
[10]Deutsch, p. 852; *HHB* (extract), p. 436.

The next [oratorio] I wrote was *Theodora* (in 1749), which Mr Handell himself valued more than any Performance of the kind; and when I once ask'd him, whether he did not look upon the Grand Chorus in the Messiah [i.e. the 'Hallelujah' chorus] as his Master Piece ? 'No', says he, '*I think the Chorus at the end of the 2d part in Theodora far beyond it*. He saw the lovely youth &c.'

The 2d night of *Theodora* was very thin indeed, tho' the Princess Amelia was there. I guessed it a losing night, so did not go to Mr Handell as usual; but seeing him smile, I ventured, when, 'Will you be there next Friday night,' says he, 'and I will play it to you?' I told him I had just seen Sir T. Hankey, 'and he desired me to tell you, that if you would have it again, he would engage for all the boxes.' '*He is a fool; the Jews will not come to it (as to Judas) because it is a Christian story; and the Ladies will not come, because it [is] a virtuous one.*'

In 1785 Burney related the following anecdote and, in spite of the caricatured German-English accent given to Handel, there is no reason to doubt the authenticity of its spirit:[11]

In 1749 [*recte* 1750], *Theodora* was so very unfortunately abandoned, that he was glad if any professors, who did not perform, would accept of tickets or orders for admission. Two gentlemen of that description, now living, having applied to HANDEL, after the disgrace of *Theodora*, for an order to hear the MESSIAH, he cried out, 'Oh your sarvant, Mien-herren! you are tamnaple tainty! you would not co to TEODORA – der was room enough to tance dere, when dat was perform.'

Sometimes, however, I have heard him, as pleasantly as philosophically, console his friends, when, previous to the curtain being drawn up, they have lamented that the house was so empty, by saying, 'Nevre moind; de moosic vil sound de petter.'

Presumably the wooden reflective surfaces of the theatre gave a better sound-quality than the absorbent clothing of the audience. But although those who were present may have been pleased, regularly half-empty houses were of no use to Handel, who, again according to Burney, 'always employed a very numerous band, and paid them liberally'.[12]

The story of Theodora, a Christian martyr in Antioch at the beginning of the fourth century (not to be confused with the sixth-century Byzantine empress of the same name), was hardly well known, but that probably had only a marginal effect on the oratorio's reception, for the same could have been said of *Alexander Balus* and *Susanna*. Morell based his libretto on the story as found in a seventeenth-century version – effectively a short, edifying novel – *The Martyrdom of Theodora and of Didymus* by the scientist Robert Boyle. It tells of Theodora's refusal to comply with a Roman edict commanding sacrifices to Jove. She is at first condemned to serve in the Temple of Venus as a prostitute: Didymus, a junior Roman

---

[11] *An Account of the Musical Performances*, 'Sketch of the Life of Handel', footnote to p. 29.
[12] *Ibid*., p. 29.

officer, vows to free her, exchanges clothes so that she can make her escape and finally, when she gives herself up, volunteers to suffer martyrdom with her. Morell's libretto gave Handel the opportunity for some lively and characterful choruses. The Romans, for example, have a dignified opening movement to greet the imperial decree and a couple of rollicking dance-choruses in the scene at the Temple of Venus at the start of Part 2. The Christian choruses are, fittingly, more serious in tone, though not necessarily in the minor mode: the prayer in Part 3, 'Blest be the hand', is no less impassioned for being in the major. The Chorus of Heathens, 'How strange their ends', that follows soon after is a masterpiece of crowd characterization: it catches the onlookers' wondering perplexity at Theodora's willing acceptance of martyrdom, as whispers pass round the crowd in a semiquaver motif (Ex.49). Although martyrdom is presented as a beatific end to the story, the final grave, minor-key chorus, 'O love divine', is ambiguous in tone: in spite of a midpoint burst of the major key at 'That we the glorious spring may know' it subsides back into G minor and ends, like the Funeral Anthem for Queen Caroline and the final chorus of the first draft of *Samson*, with a dying fall on to the open G strings of the orchestral strings. The audience would have left the theatre thoughtful rather than jubilant.

In addition to pondering the human drama, they might have been led by the oratorio to consider the personal, religious and political cross-currents that it raised, particularly with respect to religious toleration. Didymus's lines in the second scene posed the question directly:

> Ought we not to leave
> The free-born Mind of Man still ever free,
> Since Vain is the Attempt to force Belief?

If the political threat from Roman Catholicism had ceased to be a serious problem following the defeat of the '45', British society was still wary of Papists and Non-conformists: the tensions were readily apparent in the relationship between the Methodists and the established church. There seems also to have been some hardening of opinion against the Jewish community, perhaps reflecting the success of that community in establishing itself permanently in London, leading towards the Jew Bill of 1753. Whether or not all this had an influence in attracting or repelling sectors of Handel's oratorio audiences, it does not seem to have affected the programmes of the oratorio seasons in the 1750s, which revived works on both Old and New Testament topics.

Assuming Morell's anecdote to be accurate, it seems that Handel considered the chorus at the end of Part 2 of *Theodora* to be at least as good as its counterpart in *Messiah*. 'He saw the lovely youth' is certainly a remarkable movement – more accurately, three consecutive movements – which tells the story of Christ's raising of the son of the widow of Nain. The opening B♭ minor section employs a broken-rhythm accompaniment

Handel

Ex. 49

336

over a falling bass, to plangent effect; Handel had used this element before (notably in 'Ah, crudel' in *Rinaldo*), but never so powerfully. The mood is dispelled by a brief section representing the revival of the son in response to Christ's command, again using familiar stylistic formulae (from such movements as 'Let God arise' in the church music and 'Lift up your heads' in *Messiah*), and this in turn gives place to an imitative movement. The melodic shape of the subject of the final section represents the bowing of the widow (Ex. 50*a*), but its rather jaunty syncopated rhythm also seems

Ex. 50

(*a*)

(*b*)

to refer back to the opening chorus of Part 2 (Ex. 50*b*): the pagan dance has been converted into a Christian gesture. By itself the chorus hardly seems substantial enough to justify Handel's elevation of it, but its effect in context is remarkable. It follows one of Handel's greatest duets, the sombre but impassioned 'To thee, thou glorious son of worth', which seems to sum up much of the best of Handel's art, with its vocal lyricism set against contrapuntal figural string accompaniment and coloured by a

mournful seam from bassoons in the tenor register. The duet is in F
minor, and the following chorus opens in the same key, to be dispelled
finally with the sunlight of B♭ major. Didymus and Theodora have a
further (major-key) duet at the end of Part 3, and together the two duets
provide a fitting culmination to a type of movement that, throughout a
career of opera and oratorio, had brought forth some of Handel's most
sumptuous music (one or possibly two more duets were to follow). The
arias for Valens, the Roman president of Antioch, are also in a familiar
vein, with music similar to that given to commanding rulers in Handel's
previous works. The other characters receive a rich clutch of varied arias,
some of them (such as 'Angels, ever bright and fair' and 'Sweet rose and
lily') memorable for a simple yet artful melodiousness. Theodora also has
a remarkable prison scene in Part 2, introduced by a minor-key *largo*
sinfonia which stands in dramatic contrast to the bright lights of the
preceding pagan revels. In Handel's original score the sinfonia was closely
followed by a powerful aria, 'With darkness deep', in F♯ minor and with
an opening that anticipated the musical gestures of 'He saw the lovely
youth': Handel's apparent cancellation of this aria in his performances
provides a major puzzle.

Taken as a whole, *Theodora* has a genuine sense of drama, but its pace
is leisurely and, in the broader context of Handel's complete oratorio
repertory, it marks the beginning of a new direction in his style that is
easy to recognize but difficult to describe. It is serious and introspective,
without any of the extrovert tub-thumping that had been an integral part
of *Judas Maccabaeus*, *Joshua* and even, to a certain extent, *Solomon*. For
Theodora and *Jephtha*, his two last oratorios, Morell supplied Handel
with librettos that deal with topics dominated by personal questions about
life and death, the individual's place in the historical continuum, and
alternative interpretations of events in terms of consequential accidents or
preordained destiny. It is difficult to believe that the composer himself
was not behind the change in subject matter and emphasis: Handel
certainly responded powerfully in his music to the human situations and
dramas that followed the stress-lines of these philosophical issues. In
Theodora he rejected the opportunity for an unclouded, even triumphalist,
ending that might have been implied by Morell's libretto, and in doing so
he repeated a trait apparent in several other works – *Tamerlano*, *Orlando*
and *Solomon*, for example – where he seems deliberately to have avoided
a simplistic emotional conclusion in the last movement.

The change of direction in Handel's oratorios has been attributed by
one commentator to 'the preoccupations of a man whose health and sight
were beginning to fail',[13] but there is little evidence to support a gloomy
medical prognosis in 1749–50, when *Theodora* was composed and first
performed: his visit to Bath in the summer of 1749 may have been in the

[13] Dean, *Handel's Dramatic Oratorios*, p. 556.

nature of a rest, but there are no reports of a breakdown in his health comparable to the ones he had certainly suffered in 1737 and 1743. Nevertheless, Handel no doubt began to be conscious of his seniority: his 65th birthday had fallen shortly before the opening of the 1750 oratorio season. On 1 June 1750 he made his will, in which the biggest surprise is a considerable bequest to one 'James Hunter', a social (rather than musical) acquaintance who steps unannounced out of the shadows; Hawkins[14] identified him as 'a scarlet-dyer at Old Ford, near Bow'. It is less of a surprise that Handel bequeathed some of his personal effects to his manservant (only one is named at this stage, although there were others later), his professional musical equipment (including scores) to the elder or younger J.C. Smith[15] and the residue of his estate to his German relatives (see Fig. 1). Handel seems to have followed a well-established psychological pattern at this stage in life by showing a desire to make renewed contact with his past, manifested by returning briefly to his family roots. He planned a continental trip for the summer that was to take him as far as Halle and which may well have involved conveying property or mementos that he wanted to place in the custody of his family while he was still able to do so in person: these probably included the earlier oil portrait of himself by Thomas Hudson, which is now in Hamburg.[16]

Between the end of Handel's Covent Garden oratorio season and the period in which he dealt with personal and family concerns, however, there occurred an event that, far from leading him back to his German roots, set the tone for the rest of his years in London. Having decided by 7 March that their chapel would not be ready for an official opening in 1750, the general committee of the Foundling Hospital nevertheless decided to renew their invitation to Handel for a 'Performance of Musick and Voices in the Chapel on Tuesday the first of May next' – that is, another charity concert.[17] Handel decided to offer a performance of *Messiah*, instead of a mixed programme as in 1749. The occasion was intended to be coupled with the 'opening' of the organ that Handel had presented to the chapel. The advance newspaper advertisement on 21 April included the promise that 'Mr Handel will open the said Organ', but mention of the instrument was dropped from the advertisement that appeared on the day of the performance: Morse apparently did not finish the instrument

---

[14] *A General History*, ii, 91.

[15] In one copy of the will Handel wrote 'Christopher Smith Senior', but then deleted 'Senior', which may indicate doubt as to whether at this stage Handel intended his music to pass to the father or to the son (especially as he may currently have been on bad terms with the elder Smith). Alternatively, the elder Smith may have been known as Christopher and his son as John, so that 'senior' would have been superfluous. On Handel's death his music did pass to the elder Smith, who in 1763 bequeathed it to his son.

[16] See Simon, *Handel*, pp. 43–4.

[17] See Burrows, 'Handel and the Foundling Hospital', p. 272.

in time.[18] Nevertheless, the *Messiah* performance on 1 May (beginning at noon, like the 1749 concert) turned out to be a milestone in Handel's career. The hospital authorities had made careful preparations but were overwhelmed by the size of the audience: there was an 'infinite crowd' of coaches,[19] and some of the later arrivals had to be turned away:[20]

> so many Persons of Distinction coming unprovided with Tickets and pressing to pay [for] Tickets, caused a greater Number to be admitted than were expected; and some that had Tickets not finding Room going a way.

One thousand people managed to crowd into the chapel for the performance, a number that was probably equivalent to a full house at one of the major London theatres. Handel offered a second performance on 15 May to take up the demand from those who had been disappointed the first time. In all, 1986 tickets were sold for the two performances, producing a substantial income for the hospital after expenses had been paid. Between the two performances Handel was elected a governor of the hospital (apparently without the conventional entry payment), and this time he accepted. In terms of Handel's career, the public attention generated by the *Messiah* performances was probably of greater significance than the public honour that resulted. After a season of thin houses at Covent Garden, the Foundling Hospital performances enabled him to make contact again with a large London audience: indeed, it is not implausible that the hospital performances started a new fashion for oratorio-going that fed back into his subsequent theatre seasons. The shift towards wholehearted acceptance and support of his oratorios by a substantial section of London society seems to have been sealed by the hospital performances of 1750, and it is likely that the wider public image of 'the great Mr Handel' was finally established by the successive public triumphs of the *Fireworks Music* in 1749 and the Foundling Hospital *Messiah* in 1750. Incidentally, the Foundling Hospital performances probably also killed off any lingering doubts about the propriety of *Messiah* itself: accepted and acclaimed at the hospital, it seems to have carried the associations of its success back to the theatre.[21]

1750 saw the introduction of an important new member into Handel's company, the castrato Gaetano Guadagni, then aged about 25. He had come to London with an Italian theatre company in 1748, and Burney, who probably wrote from firsthand experience, describes him thus:[22]

---

[18] Deutsch, pp. 686–7, 688–9; *HHB*, pp. 438–40.

[19] William Stukeley's diary, 1 May 1750: Deutsch, p. 688; *HHB*, p. 439.

[20] *The General Advertiser* (4 May 1750): Deutsch, p. 689; *HHB*, p. 430.

[21] There is no evidence of controversy surrounding Handel's theatre performances of *Messiah* in 1745, 1749 and 1750, but neither is there any evidence that they were particularly well received.

[22] *A General History*, ii, 875; many of Burney's 'first person' anecdotes need to be interpreted with the greatest caution. He goes on to say (possibly of a later phase in Guadagni's career) that 'neither his voice nor execution contributed much to charm or excite admiration' (*ibid.*, p. 876).

His voice was then a full and well toned counter-tenor; but he was a wild and careless singer. However, the excellence of his voice attracted the notice of Handel, who assigned him the parts in his oratorios of the Messiah and Samson, which had been originally composed for Mrs. Cibber; in the studying which parts, as I often saw him at Frasi's, whom I then attended as her master, he applied to me for assistance. During his first residence in England, which was four or five years, he was more noticed in singing English than Italian.

Guadagni's first association with Handel is sometimes attributed to the Foundling Hospital concert in May 1749, but the evidence for this is doubtful.[23] He may have been ideally cast as Micah in *Samson*, which had originally been Mrs Cibber's role (though probably not composed with her in mind in 1741), but Burney's statement about his part in *Messiah* needs correction: Handel did not simply slot Guadagni into the pre-existing alto part but composed for him new settings of 'But who may abide the day of his coming', 'Thou art gone up on high' and 'How beautiful are the feet'. This was the first time that these movements had been allocated to an alto-register voice, and the 'Guadagni' versions of the first two soon came to be regarded as the 'standard' settings, displacing the previous ones. As to the rest of the alto part in *Messiah*, Handel left most of it with the contralto Galli:[24] in fact, the presence of two excellent (though contrasted) alto-register voices may have been one of the major strengths of Handel's 1750 cast. For the rest, Frasi remained as Handel's soprano from the previous season, and indeed continued in this role until the composer's death (though a treble may have replaced her at the hospital performances in 1751–2[25]), while the veteran Reinhold was still there as the leading bass. Thomas Lowe had become Handel's principal tenor in 1748, when Beard left Covent Garden to join Garrick's theatre company at Drury Lane, and he remained so until 1751. For the top line of the choruses Bernard Gates was still supplying children from the Chapel Royal; in 1750 he probably provided seven boys for two performances.[26]

Whether from exhaustion or from the unsettling consequences of planning his forthcoming continental visit, Handel did not compose a new full-length oratorio in the summer of 1750: he seems to have decided to put off any major new work until his return to London later in the year. Nevertheless, he did safeguard part of his future programme by composing a new single-act piece, *The Choice of Hercules*. This was eventually performed as a companion to the two-part *Alexander's Feast*, and it seems not unreasonable that Handel had already begun in mid-1750 to think about reviving that work, which he had not performed in London since 1739. There were still plenty of good works stored up and ripe for revival,

[23] See Chapter 13, p. 327.
[24] See Burrows, 'The Autographs', p. 219.
[25] See Burrows, *ibid.*
[26] Deutsch, p. 692; HHB, p. 442. I assume that the boys were paid half a guinea each per performance.

many of them probably unknown to the new audience that Handel may have attracted in the wake of the Foundling Hospital *Messiah* success. *The Choice of Hercules* was constructed so as to take up as much as possible of the unused *Alceste* music and, as with *Oreste, Parnasso in festa* and the Foundling Hospital Anthem, for example, the result was a thoroughly convincing new work in which the carpentry between old and new was invisible to anyone who had not seen the original wood. The immediate source for the libretto of *The Choice of Hercules* was a narrative poem by Robert Lowth, published in a miscellaneous anthology in 1747: presumably Handel worked closely with the librettist (probably Morell), who converted the poem for setting in the 'oratorio' manner and who would have provided suitable texts for the re-use of existing music.

The Choice of Hercules is an allegorical drama in three scenes: on Handel's autograph and in the printed word-book it is described as a 'Musical Interlude'[27] The story is a temptation fable: the choice that the youthful Hercules has to make is between Pleasure and Virtue. A nice balance between Pleasure and Virtue is maintained and, although Virtue wins, the final minor-key chorus suggests that Handel had doubts about a life that followed one to the exclusion of the other. One of the best movements is the newly composed trio 'Where shall I go?', which comes at the crisis of the dramatic conflict. Another is Pleasure's newly composed aria 'There the brisk sparkling nectar drain', enlivened by horn colouring and displaying an up-to-date, galant style of harmonic rhythm. But the recycled music from *Alceste* is also apt for its new context, and one aria, 'Enjoy the sweet Elysian grove', even managed to carry forward its original text. Handel's choice of subject may have been influenced by the fact that about ten years earlier Maurice Greene had produced a masque on the same story, *The Judgment of Hercules*, but that had not been given in the public theatres and there is no musical relationship between the two works, other than their common use of a vocal trio at the climax of the drama.

Handel composed and assembled *The Choice of Hercules* between 28 June and 5 July 1750. Assuming that he was in London on 9 August, when he bought £150-worth of annuities, he probably left for the Continent soon after. On 11 August it was rumoured that he was intending to visit 'various courts in Germany and Italy'.[28] In fact, there is no positive evidence that he ever reached either Germany or Italy, although Halle is certainly a plausible destination: Handel had not mentioned a forthcoming trip when he wrote to one of his Halle cousins in June,[29] but his forward

---

[27] The manuscript libretto submitted to the Inspector of Stage Plays has the title 'Hercules's Choice of Pleasure or Virtue' but no genre description.

[28] From an Amsterdam newspaper, quoting a report from London (11 August, presumably Old Style); see King, 'Handel's Travels', p. 373.

[29] Letter, in German, to Johann Gottfried Taust, 22 June 1750 (see Marx, 'Ein unveröffentlicher Brief'), written after receiving his cousin's congratulations on the success of his music for the 1749 peace celebrations.

commitments had probably been uncertain at that stage, and the omission is not necessarily significant. The route to Germany lay through the Netherlands, and Handel seems to have stopped for substantial periods there in the course of his travels in both directions, renewing old contacts with the Haarlem organist Radeker and his former pupil Princess Anne. Handel's presence in Haarlem, where he visited Radeker and heard him play, is recorded on 27 August,[30] and again on 20 September, though on both occasions he is reported to have been 'passing through' the city. On 10 September he was in Deventer, where he played the organ in the Groote Kerk to Princess Anne, her husband the Prince of Orange, 'various nobles of the court' and 'a great mass of people, both the first and least of this town'.[31] So it seems that Handel passed at least the first month of his continental visit in the Netherlands, possibly with a view to buying Dutch pictures, and quite probably spent a considerable part of the period at Anne's court at Het Loo: she seems to have maintained at least a modest musical establishment and she doubtless entertained Handel with suitable hospitality.[32] Handel may have spent longer in the Netherlands than he had intended, and the first part of his visit may have been protracted as the result of a road accident, for on 21 August a London newspaper reported that[33]

> Mr. Handel, who went to Germany to visit his Friends some Time since, and between the Hague and Haarlem had the Misfortune to be overturned, by which he was terribly hurt, is now out of Danger.

It may be significant that there are reports of Handel playing the organ at Haarlem on 20 September, 'with great skill and art',[34] but not during the earlier visit, on 27 August, when he might have still been incapacitated as a result of the accident.

Handel reappears in the Dutch newspaper reports at the beginning of December, on his way back to London. On 2 December he played the organ at the Nieuwe Kerk in The Hague, before 'the entire court, most of the foreign ambassadors and other distinguished persons of both sexes',[35] and he played to the prince and princess again in The Hague on 7 December,[36] before leaving the next day for England via Rotterdam. The documentary record of his Dutch activities leaves a gap of more than two months, including all of October and November, during which he could easily have visited several of his old haunts in Germany. It is difficult

---

[30] Netherlands dates are New Style, i.e. 11 days ahead of the Old Style calendar used in London.

[31] From a Haarlem newspaper report (12 September); see King, 'Handel's Travels', p. 374.

[32] *ibid.*, pp. 375–6.

[33] *The General Advertiser* (21 August 1750): Deutsch, p. 693; *HHB*, p. 442, (the date is obviously Old Style).

[34] From a Haarlem newspaper report (22 September); see King, 'Handel's Travels', p. 374.

[35] Report in Haarlem newspaper (3 December); see King, 'Handel's Travels', p. 374.

[36] Report in Haarlem newspaper (10 December); see King, 'Handel's Travels', p. 374. Handel may have performed on the harpsichord on this occasion.

to guess where he might have gone in addition to Halle, and more difficult still to assess whether he attached much significance to the fact that he had missed his last chance to meet Johann Sebastian Bach, who had died on 28 July (New Style) in Leipzig. Handel presumably did not travel as far north as Hamburg, but he heard from Telemann, who wrote him a letter which the violinist Giuseppe Passerini managed to deliver just before Handel left The Hague.[37]

On his return to London, Handel replied to Telemann as soon as he had time to himself. His letter has a geniality that is perhaps surprising, considering that the two composers had possibly not met for some 40 years:[38]

> I was on the point of leaving the Hague for London when your most agreeable letter was delivered to me by Mr. Passerini. I had just enough time to be able to hear his wife sing. Your patronage and approval were enough not only to excite my curiosity but also to serve her as sufficient recommendation; however I was soon convinced myself of her rare quality. They are leaving for Scotland to fulfil concert engagements there for a season of six months. There she will be able to perfect herself in the English language; after that (as they intend to remain some time in London) I shall not fail to be of service to them in all ways that may depend on me.
>
> Moreover I was greatly touched by your most friendly expressions of goodwill; your kindness and your renown made too much impression on my heart and mind for me not to reciprocate them as you deserve. Pray be assured that you will always find in me a like sincerity and true regard.
>
> I thank you for the splendid work on the system of [musical] intervals which you were good enough to send me; it is worthy of your time and trouble and of your learning.
>
> I congratulate you on the perfect health that you are enjoying at your somewhat advanced age, and I wish you from my heart every prosperity for many years to come. If your passion for exotic plants etc. could prolong your days and sustain the zest for life that is natural to you, I offer with very real pleasure to contribute to it in some sort. Consequently I am sending you as a present (to the address enclosed) a crate of flowers, which experts assure me are very choice and of admirable rarity. If they are not telling the truth, you will [at least] have the best plants in all England, and the season of the year is still right for their bearing flowers.

It seems that a strong bond of friendship had been formed between Handel and Telemann in their student days, and this had obviously remained more durable than Handel's relationship with Mattheson. Unfortunately, the exotic plants did not reach their destination, for the sea-captain who was entrusted as courier heard a false rumour when he arrived in Hamburg that Telemann had died. When Handel eventually discovered that Telemann was in fact still alive, he sent him, in December 1754, a replacement

[37] Passerini's wife was to sing as a soprano soloist for Handel from 1754 to 1756 (or 1757).
[38] Letter to Telemann, 25/14 December 1750 (i.e. Christmas Day by the continental calendar, though not in London): Deutsch, pp. 696–7 (with translation); *HHB*, pp. 444–5.

set of plants (possibly from the Chelsea Physick Garden), having first secured a list of Telemann's requirements.

Obviously Handel's main task on his return to London was to attend to the requirements of the forthcoming oratorio season. *The Choice of Hercules* was ready, and no doubt Handel checked over the score of *Alexander's Feast*, making amendments to accommodate his cast, which was to be much the same as for the previous season and included Frasi, Galli, Guadagni, Lowe and Reinhold. The adaptation of *Alexander's Feast* was fairly straightforward, as Handel had already revised the score in 1742 to include an alto-register voice (Mrs Cibber): the duet setting of 'Let's imitate her notes above', for example, originally composed in Dublin for Avolio and Cibber, was now incorporated at the end of the work (in a slightly different position) for Frasi and Guadagni.[39] Handel also seems to have decided, at a quite early stage in his planning for the 1751 season, to revive *Belshazzar*, probably casting Galli in the role of Daniel and Guadagni as Cyrus.[40] The resulting vocal distribution was fairly close to that of Handel's original plan for the oratorio, before the 1745 cast crisis in which Mrs Cibber had dropped out: Gobrias reverted to a bass voice and Daniel to an alto. Handel re-set Cyrus's final *accompagnato* 'Yes, I will build thy city' in a longer version, incorporating sections of Jennens's text that he had omitted in 1745. In Part 3 also he re-set the aria 'To pow'r immortal' for Gobrias (Reinhold), using music from an aria, 'Peace crowned with roses on your slumbers wait', discarded from *Susanna*. In Part 2 he recomposed the final chorus in a much more extended form, again incorporating some of Jennens's text that had been cut in 1745. This involved setting some lines in 'O glorious prince' (beginning 'To all like thee were sceptres giv'n, kings were [i.e. would be] like gods, and earth like heav'n') that Handel may have deliberately avoided in 1744–5. Given that some of his performances since the *Occasional Oratorio* had topical reference, the inclusion of this passage may have been intended as a compliment to the Prince of Wales, perhaps signalling the end of a period of hostility between the prince and the composer: if so, the timing turned out to be tragic, in view of the prince's fatal accident soon afterwards. Handel now also introduced new settings that he had composed around 1747 for a revival of *Belshazzar* that never took place – the arias 'The leavy honours of the field' and 'Alternate hopes and fears' for Nitocris (Frasi) and the duet 'Great victor, at thy feet I bow'. To complete his new music for the season, he composed a new organ concerto (HWV308).

The concerto, later published as op.7 no.3, was Handel's last orchestral

[39] In the Dublin version of 1742 the duet ran into the chorus to the same text, to close the work in the short epilogue that formed Part 3; in 1751 the duet was detached and taken back into the body of the ode, to precede the final recitative and the chorus 'Let old Timotheus yield the prize'.

[40] For the 1751 version of the oratorio, see Handel (ed. Burrows), *Belshazzar*.

work, although he may not have recognized it as such at the time. It had a counterpart among his chamber music – the D major violin sonata (HWV371, sometimes known by Chrysander's spurious designation as op.1 no.13) – composed (on the basis of evidence from the paper of the autograph) around 1749–51, and quite possibly at the same period as the concerto. The sonata, arguably Handel's greatest solo sonata, was from a genre that had not seriously engaged his attention for nearly 25 years; sadly, nothing is known of the violinist or occasion for which it was intended. While it would be an exaggeration to invest the organ concerto with prophetic qualities on account of its biographical significance in Handel's creative career, there are nevertheless some forward-looking stylistic elements in the first movement. As originally conceived, the movement began with a unison motto-phrase ('x' in Ex.51) that would not have been out of place at the start of a Stamitz symphony. Its answering phrase ('y') has a galant swagger in its rhythmic and harmonic organization, while the style of the playful *piano* link ('z') to the repeat of this phrase might be interpreted in terms of either the string-orchestra idiom of Mannheim or the keyboard manner of C.P.E. Bach. After the expected excursion to the dominant, the movement returns to the tonic in the middle, displaying these motifs in a different order and extending 'z' to a two-bar component in its own right (Ex.52). The episode that follows bar 44, with its employment of motivic fragmentation, fast sequential modulation and 'non-thematic' material, is as near as Handel ever came to writing a 'development section', but the 'modern' effect is dispelled by the old-fashioned Baroque figuration and 'walking bass' of the subsequent organ solo (from bar 63). The middle movements of the concerto were left by Handel to his powers of inspiration, designated as 'adagio e fuga ad libitum' in the autograph, but there follows a *spiritoso* movement and a graceful minuet (a second minuet was added ten years later by Walsh, and may not have Handel's authority). The theme of the *spiritoso* comes from a new source of 'borrowings' for Handel at this period, the mass settings of the Bohemian composer Franz Haber-mann,[41] though the ecclesiastical origin of the music could hardly be guessed at after Handel's transformation; some of the figuration in the solo part (Ex.53) would not have been out of place in a keyboard concerto by J.C. Bach or Mozart. Handel began composing the concerto on New Year's Day 1751 and completed it on 4 January. There are two complete autographs of the first movement, because he substantially recomposed it. In the revision he decided to amplify the original ritornello with an opening 'Hallelujah' figure (Ex.54): its incorporation into the later development of the movement involved a degree of carpentry that required

---

[41] Habermann's masses had been published (in separate partbooks, op.1) at Graslitz in 1747; Handel's autograph copy of some extracts (in score) survives among his sketch material. The opening of a Habermann movement also provided the hint for theme 'x' in Ex.51, though Handel turned the idea into something much more powerful.

Ex. 51

a second copy, but Handel also took the opportunity to make other substantial alterations to improve the flow of the movement (both autographs of the first movement are dated 1 January, indicating composition and revision on the same day).[42] This 'Hallelujah' concerto is an appro-

---

[42] The first autograph (first movement only, beginning with the unison passage) is in British Library RM 20.g.14 (the detached last page is in Fitzwilliam Museum, Cambridge, MU. MS. 262); the second autograph is in British Library RM 20.g.12 (complete). The two versions of the first movement may be compared in *HHA* IV/8. The music of Ex.54 shows the thematic elements in the form they appeared in the second, revised version. In the first version of the opening, Handel introduced between 'x' and 'y' motivic material of the type seen in bars 44–7 of Ex.52.

Ex. 52

Ex. 52 (cont.)

[49]

priate celebration of a lifetime's achievement in instrumental music, showing that in January 1751 Handel was still on top form and still trying out new ideas.

The big task still lay ahead, however, for as yet Handel had no new full-length oratorio for the forthcoming season. He seems to have delayed facing this uncomfortable problem until the last possible moment. He had a libretto to hand, *Jephtha*, already supplied by Morell, perhaps after some discussion of the work's plan. He began his score on Monday 21 January. The oratorio season was to begin only a month later, on 22 February, the first Friday in Lent. In normal circumstances Handel had in the past been able to turn round the score of a new opera or oratorio within the month, though for more than a decade his bouts of large-scale composition had been undertaken at times well away from the period of a season's preparation and performance. The composition of Part 1 of *Jephtha* ran relatively smoothly, and he completed it within a fortnight, finishing on 2 February. By 13 February Handel had drafted as far as the final chorus of Part 2: at that stage it looked as if the new oratorio would not be ready for performance at the opening of the season but might be sufficiently close to completion for Handel to finish it soon after, once the performing routine was under way. But it was not to be. On 13 February Handel wrote on his score (in the relative privacy of German) that he was forced to lay the composition aside because of 'relaxation' in his left eye. His handwriting in the autograph of *Jephtha* gives ample testimony to the increasing physical difficulties under which it was composed, and there is an appalling irony in the fact that the last words that Handel set before he temporarily abandoned the score were 'all hid from mortal sight', in the chorus 'How dark, O Lord, are thy decrees'.

349

Ex. 53

Ex. 54

The affliction to Handel's sight probably developed quickly and relatively privately: on 16 February the Earl of Shaftesbury reported a very different impression of Handel's health:[43]

---

[43]Letter to James Harris: *HHB*, p. 447. The last sentence may imply that Handel had gone for another health-cure at Aix-la-Chapelle during his visit to the Netherlands in 1750.

Belshazar is now advertis'd and Smith tells me the parts will go off excellently. Handel himself is actually better in health, and in a higher flow of genius than he has been for several years past. His late journey has help'd his constitution vastly.

Clearly, Handel had recognized on 13 February that he was not going to be able to cope with the completion of *Jephtha* immediately and that he would need to conserve such strength as he had for the final rehearsals for the oratorio season; his eyesight problems presumably had a considerable effect on his general health and morale. The season duly began with two performances of *Belshazzar*, on 22 and 27 February, 'With a Concerto on the Organ'. These were followed by *Alexander's Feast*, with its 'Additional New Act' *The Choice of Hercules*, on 1 March: a 'New Concerto on the Organ', presumably op.7 no.3, was played before *The Choice of Hercules*. In the meantime Handel had taken up *Jephtha* again, feeling 'somewhat better' on 23 February (his 66th birthday), and he managed to complete the end of Part 2 four days later. Nevertheless, he did not make an immediate start on Part 3, even though a run of four performances of *Alexander's Feast/The Choice of Hercules* (which presumably needed little or no intermediate rehearsal) should have given him a breathing-space until 13 March: he had probably decided that *Jephtha* was not going to be a practical proposition for the 1751 season and so contented himself with tidying up the score as far as the end of Part 2. He would have to spin out the rest of the season with revivals.

Esther was performed on 15 March and *Judas Maccabaeus* on 20 March: these involved very little new composition (for *Esther*, the aria 'Virtue, truth and innocence' was adapted from *Solomon*) but required a number of small alterations to accommodate the new cast. This was Handel's first London revival of *Esther* since 1740. A second performance of *Judas Maccabaeus* on 22 March was cancelled when the theatres were closed following the sudden death of the Prince of Wales, and they remained closed for the rest of the season. Thus, fortuitously, the London public never knew of Handel's failure to deliver a new oratorio for 1751. Presumably Handel would have ended his season with *Messiah*, but we know nothing of his plans for the other three aborted performances: probably just one more oratorio would have been involved. However, *Messiah* was given twice at the Foundling Hospital after Easter, on 18 April and 16 May: the latter, on Ascension Day, was a 'Repetition ... at the Request of several Persons of Distinction'. As in 1750, the total audience for the two occasions approached 2000. In 1751 a tradition of annual *Messiah* performances in aid of the hospital can be said to have been established, though subsequently there was only one performance each year and the audience never again sustained such a high level of attendance. On both of the 1751 occasions Handel played the organ that he had given to the hospital, though the newspaper reports describe him as playing a 'voluntary' rather than a concerto.[44] The arrangements for the 1751 *Messiah* cast involved only simple redistributions in the score: Galli did not perform, and Guadagni took over her music as well as repeating that which Handel had composed for him the previous year; this time a boy treble took over the soprano role. Beard returned as Handel's principal tenor, displacing Lowe, and he retained this position in Handel's company for the rest of the composer's life: for the Covent Garden performances from 1752 onwards he presumably appeared under temporary release from Garrick's management at Drury Lane. Handel's faithful bass Reinhold died between the two 1751 Foundling Hospital *Messiah* performances: his place was taken by Robert Wass, the only singer to perform as a major oratorio soloist for Handel (in theatre performances as well as at the Foundling Hospital) while retaining simultaneous membership of London's major ecclesiastical choirs at the Chapel Royal, Westminster Abbey and St Paul's Cathedral.[45]

Halfway through the oratorio season at Covent Garden, a private correspondent reported that[46] 'Noble Handel hath lost an eye, but I have the Rapture to say that St. Cecilia makes no complaint of any Defect in his Fingers'. Whether or not Handel had completely lost the sight of one eye at this stage, it was obviously prudent for him to take measures to preserve his general health, once the professional demands of the spring season were over. A rest-cure at a spa was called for: on 3 June he was reported as arriving in Bath, and on 13 June he returned to London, having also 'made use of the Waters' at Cheltenham Wells.[47] He was reported as having gone to Bath with 'Mr. Smith', but whether this was the younger or the elder John Christopher Smith is uncertain. When he realized the practical difficulties that his disability would pose for the running of his oratorio seasons, Handel had appealed for help to the younger Smith, who was currently in the south of France as the companion and tutor to a Mr Waters: Smith returned in 1751 in response to Handel's request and gradually assumed the role of artistic co-manager for the oratorio seasons.[48] It seems probable that at this period Handel formed a closer relationship with his former pupil than with the elder Smith, with whom he may have maintained a certain coolness in their professional relationship until his very last years.[49]

On his return to London, Handel felt fit enough to take up work on *Jephtha* again, but he must have found the task hard: he wrote Part 3

[44] *The Gentleman's Magazine* (April 1751), *The Daily Advertiser* (17 May 1751): Deutsch, pp. 708–9; *HHB*, pp. 451–2.

[45] Some of Handel's other soloists had however been trained in the choirs, and many of the Gentlemen sang in the oratorios as chorus singers or minor soloists.

[46] Letter from Edward Turner to Sanderson Miller, 14 March 1751: Deutsch, p. 793; *HHB*, p. 449.

[47] *The General Advertiser* (15 June 1751): Deutsch, p. 710; *HHB*, pp. 452–3.

[48] See Coxe, *Anecdotes*, pp. 44, 135, and Mainwaring, *Memoirs*, p. 138.

[49] See n.15, above.

between 18 June and 15/17 July but did not complete the score until 30 August. The task took him longer than usual, probably because he found it toilsome, not because of any external interruptions. Referring to the composition of *Jephtha*, a pamphlet published in 1753 described how Handel[50]

> at the Age of *Seventy* [*recte* 65–6], with a broken Constitution, produced such a Composition, which no Man mentioned in the Essay beside, either is, or ever was (so far as it hath appeared to us) equal to, in his highest Vigour; – And, to the Astonishment of all Mankind, at the same Period of Life, performed Wonders on the Organ, both set Pieces and *extempore*.

During the summer of 1751 the question of an official opening ceremony for the Foundling Hospital chapel arose again: on 17 July the hospital's general committee resolved to consider this subject 'and the steps to be taken previous thereto; especially with respect to Mr. Handell'.[51] It was probably in response to an approach from the committee that Handel revised the Foundling Hospital Anthem, a process that included composing new movements, including a solo for Guadagni ('O God, who from the suckling's mouth') and a duet for trebles ('The people will tell of their wisdom'). The former is closely modelled on the aria 'Happy Iphis shalt thou live' from Part 3 of *Jephtha* and, while the priority of the two movements is hard to establish exactly, it seems very likely that they originated within a few weeks of each other. The opening of the hospital chapel was planned for December 1751, but many further delays followed, and the event finally took place in April 1753.[52]

Apart from some occasional transactions (five entries between 8 August and 20 December) in Handel's bank account,[53] nothing further is known of his activities until the approach of the next oratorio season: presumably he lived a semi-retired life in Brook Street, adjusting as well as he could to his disability. Close friends such as Thomas Harris foresaw the implications of his condition:[54]

> Handel, you know, has composed Jeptha: and I am sorry to say that I believe this Lent will be yᵉ last that he will ever be able to preside at an oratorio: for he breaks very much, & is I think quite blind in one Eye.

> L[or]d Brook a day or two ago bid me give you his compliments, and tell you to come up this Lent, for he feared Handel would never perform after this, and I am much of his opinion.

---

[50] William Hayes, *Remarks on Mr. Avison's Essay on Musical Expression*: Deutsch, p. 734; *HHB*, pp. 466–7.
[51] Burrows, 'Handel and the Foundling Hospital', p. 273.
[52] *Ibid.*, pp. 273–5.
[53] Deutsch, p. 841; *HHB*, p. 552.
[54] Letters to James Harris, 9 and 23 January 1752, quoted in Best, 'Two Newly Discovered References'. 'Lord Brook' was probably Francis Greville, Earl Brooke of Warwick Castle, subsequently Earl of Warwick.

The 1752 oratorio season began as usual on the first Friday in Lent, 14 February. Four days previously Handel submitted the libretto of *Jephtha* to the Inspector of Stage Plays, as required by the theatre licensing regulations, and signed the libretto at the end.[55] Handel began the oratorio season with *Joshua*, his first revival of the work: since his present cast was very similar to that of the original production (one each of soprano, alto, tenor and bass soloists – Frasi, Galli, Beard and Wass), relatively few alterations were needed. He seems to have worked out some minor revisions in his autograph and made one substantial alteration: the recomposition of the *B* section of 'Hark, 'tis the linnet and the thrush' is possibly his last complete leaf of autograph music.[56] Two performances of *Joshua* were followed by one of *Hercules*. The 1752 version of *Hercules* followed in general terms the pattern of the 1749 revival, which had omitted the character of Lichas and thus required only four principals; various items that had been performed in 1749 were now cut, but the soprano aria and chorus 'Still caressing and caressed', originally composed for *Alceste*, was added (the overture to *Alceste* had already been transferred to *Jephtha*). Then, on 26 February, close to Handel's 67th birthday, *Jephtha* received the first of its three performances. The extended gestation of *Jephtha* had left Handel with a practical problem, for when he had set about its composition at the start of the 1751 season he had written two alto-register roles appropriate to his current cast – Storgé for Galli and Hamor for Guadagni – but in 1752 he was without Guadagni, who had undertaken a season in Dublin, and so had to engage an additional principal singer. He pressed into service Charles Brent, a fencing-master who was apparently also a reasonable countertenor, though his only professional appearances as a singer in the London theatres were for Handel in 1752. Three performances of *Samson* followed the three of *Jephtha*: Brent was not needed for *Samson* (in which Galli probably took the role of Micah, as she had done in 1749) or for the subsequent oratorios. Two performances of *Judas Maccabaeus* and two of *Messiah* (the last on Maundy Thursday) rounded off the season. A single performance of *Messiah* followed after Easter at the Foundling Hospital, on 9 April: the sequence of Handel's annotations on the conducting score suggests that Frasi did not sing on that occasion and that her music was distributed between Beard and a boy treble.[57] Between 27 February and 2 April Handel deposited the more-than-substantial sum of £2290 in his bank

[55] The complete text of Handel's contribution, which comes on the end of the libretto (now at the Huntington Library, San Marino CA) in Morell's hand, is 'George Frideric Handel/London Covent Garden/February 10th 1752.'

[56] British Library RM 20.e.11, f.36 (incomplete in *HG* 17). The 3/8 version of 'Laud her, all ye virgin train' for *Jephtha* (British Library RM 20.e.9, f.125), however, may have come later.

[57] See Burrows, 'The Autographs', p. 219. 'Rejoice greatly' was allocated to the tenor, presumably to lighten the load on the treble (the boy may have been given the minor solo role of the Angel in the preceding performances of *Jephtha*).

account: it is difficult to explain this in terms of the profits from an exceptionally successful season, for there are no reports of unusual interest in the oratorios nor, as far as we know, was there any increase in ticket prices.

Jephtha is a remarkable masterpiece. It requires no special pleading on account of its position as Handel's last oratorio or on account of the circumstances of personal turmoil in which it was created. But it is implausible to deny a connection between the emotional power of some of its scenes and the composer's own circumstances, which must have led him to a strong personal identification with the work: Handel doubtless sensed by the middle of Part 2 (if not before) that this would be his last oratorio, and its subject matter – the threat of personal tragedy and the significance (religious in the broadest sense) of suffering inflicted on the innocent – surely chimed in with his own personal preoccupations. In *Theodora* the final 'victory' of martyrdom had been balanced by a regret for the lives destroyed. In *Jephtha* a similar theme is carried a stage further: Iphis faces a sacrificial death, not on account of her own actions or any choice relating to those actions, but rather because she happened to be the first person to greet her father Jephtha after his victory over the Ammonites, unaware that he had vowed to sacrifice the first living thing he saw, if Jehovah would give him victory in the battle.

Morell's treatment of the narrative from the book of *Judges* was imaginative and also drew on material from a Latin play of 1554, *Jephthes sive votum*, by the Scottish humanist George Buchanan (1506–82). From Buchanan came the character Storgé (who does not appear in *Judges*), though the additional characters of Zebul and Hamor seem to have been largely of Morell's invention. Both Hamor and Storgé contribute positively to the force of the drama's central crisis in Morell's version, as Hamor offers himself as a substitute for his beloved Iphis, and Storgé tries to prevail on her husband Jephtha to evade the letter of his vow. Zebul, who does not feature specifically in *Judges*, is something of a 'spokesman' character, but his surprise at Jephtha's reaction to the sight of Iphis is fundamental to the drama: Jephtha had made his original vow alone, unknown to anyone else. In his development of these characters Morell enhanced the main lines of the story. Rather more radical was his alteration to the ending. In *Judges*, Jephtha sent his daughter away into the mountains for two months to bewail her virginity, after which he 'did with her according to the vow which he had vowed'. In Part 3 of Morell's oratorio, however, the sacrifice of Iphis is interrupted at the last moment by an Angel, who instructs the priests to desist from the slaughter, re-interprets the vow and tells Jephtha that he must dedicate his daughter to God 'in pure and virgin-state for ever'. Jephtha is commended for his resolution in maintaining his vow, but the Angel suggests that he had erred by offering up his daughter's life to the priests as 'an holocaust to God'. The Angel's message is accepted and acclaimed by everyone, and the oratorio concludes with a chorus in which the Israelites, restored to the path of virtue, anticipate the blessings of peace and plenty.

We may nevertheless wonder why Morell, presumably in collaboration with Handel, chose to conclude the oratorio in this way. Possibly the tragic ending was considered too similar to that of *Theodora*, which had proved less than popular with the London audiences, perhaps because of its serious tone and its ending. It has been suggested that Morell's version was an attempt to 'Christianize' the Old Testament story,[58] though the specific inspiration for Morell's treatment of the dénouement surely came from the Old Testament, from the story of the sacrifice of Isaac from the book of *Genesis* where an angel interrupts the sacrifice and directs Abraham not to harm his son. Morell worked the material of Part 3 in a way that reinforced the mainspring of the action – Jephtha's resolution to follow through his duty to Jehovah as he saw it. The events of Part 2 are interpreted retrospectively as a test of Jephtha's faith, parallel to Abraham's.

Zebul's opening words, 'It must be so', set a motto for the oratorio, at least as it was interpreted in Handel's music. Certain problems about the nature of divine providence are implicit in the biblical story. If Jephtha's original vow was not merely foolish from the start, where does responsibility for the eventual tragedy lie? If Jehovah won the war for Jephtha, did he also arrange things so that the first thing that Jephtha saw on his return was his daughter? If *Jephtha* does not attempt to probe answers to these questions, it certainly presents in a powerful form the human situations that lead them to be asked. Neither Morell nor Handel regarded their oratorios as a forum for metaphysical or philosophical disquisition, but the chorus 'How dark, O Lord, are thy decrees', at the climax of Jephtha's turmoil, is presented with particular force. As already noted, it was during the composition of this movement that Handel was for a time forced to lay aside work on the oratorio because of failing eyesight, and he had good reason to feel personally involved with most of the sentiments in the movement. Pope's maxim 'Whatever is, is right' is set with particular emphasis, and it is impossible to tell whether the musical finality of Handel's setting of these words is merely the response of an experienced musical dramatist. Handel himself may have insisted on the change from Morell's original 'What God ordains, is right', and this may be of some biographical significance. Handel, like the Israelites, may have sensed that the simplistic response was reassuring in the short term but ultimately inadequate as an explanation for the workings of providence. This is not the final chorus of the oratorio. To judge by the subsequent music, which was composed as he came to terms with his condition, Handel followed his librettist through to the end of Part 3 with complete accord.

The story of Jephtha as a subject for musical setting had received the

[58] Dean, *Handel's Dramatic Oratorios*, p. 592.

attention of Maurice Greene in about 1737, and Morell 'borrowed' some phrases from its published libretto (1740), along with other quotations or near-quotations from Milton, Pope, Addison and others. It is not known whether Handel knew Greene's music for *Jephtha*, but he was certainly acquainted with the Jephtha oratorio of Giacomo Carissimi (composed before 1650), because he borrowed from its music in *Samson*. Handel's own *Jephtha* contains, in addition to a number of self-borrowings (including a substantial part of a movement from the recent D major violin sonata, for the entrance of the Angel), some thoroughly recomposed material derived from Habermann's masses, the borrowing source that had become a recent favourite in the 'Hallelujah' organ concerto.

If 'How dark, O Lord' remains in the mind as the most powerful movement in *Jephtha*, it owes some of its power to the musical context. The preceding movement, Jephtha's accompanied recitative 'Deeper and deeper still', is no less remarkable: the tensions of Jephtha's emotional crisis are conveyed in a chiaroscuro of changes of texture, speed and harmony that yet never breaks the thread of the accumulating emotions. Accompanied recitative plays a significant role elsewhere, introducing Zebul's 'It must be so', heightening Jephtha's vow, conveying Storgé's entreaties to her husband in 'First perish thou' and finally carrying Iphis's acceptance of her sacrificial role in 'Ye sacred priests'. Of all Handel's dramatic oratorios, *Jephtha* uses the smallest proportion of *semplice* recitative and relies most on arias and choruses for the development of its emotional impetus. The chorus, though nominally representing the Israelites, is mainly used to provide commentary, and Handel makes full use of this 'classical' function. There is hardly a weak chorus or aria in the whole oratorio. Handel had the imaginative resources to compensate for occasional lapses in Morell's texts – mainly in Part 1, with 'No more to Ammon's God and King' and 'When loud his voice in thunder spoke'.

To the arias in *Jephtha* Handel brought a lifetime's creative experience, and there is nothing dishonourable in the fact that some of the melodic formulae are familiar. The beatific strain from *Theodora* is magnificently repeated in Jephtha's 'Waft her, angels, to the skies' and Iphis's 'Brighter scenes I seek above'. The former is in a miniature da capo form, without even room for the dominant modulation in the A section; the latter, in context, is the second limb of a bipartite aria, its E major chasing away the valedictory shadows of the preceding E minor section ('Farewell, ye limpid streams and floods') as surely as 'Comfort ye' relieved the E minor of the *Messiah* overture.[59] Storgé's melodramatic 'Scenes of horror', at her early premonition of Iphis's tragedy, is a fully fledged aria that would not have been out of place in Handel's operas of the 1720s: however, there is

---

[59] Winton Dean makes out a good case for the careful tonal planning of Handel's score (*Handel's Dramatic Oratorios*, pp. 597–8), emphasizing the importance of the major-minor contrast, around G as a key-centre.

a breadth to the melodic and harmonic style, and a cunning to the shortening of the dal segno return, that places it firmly in Handel's later style, and the 'off-tonic' beginning to the repetition of the text of the *A* section is perhaps emblematic of the liberation in formal treatment that had come with experience. Iphis appropriately attracts dance-rhythm arias in Part 1—the first a pastoral, compound-time movement on a ritornello plan, the second a complete da capo aria in *bourrée* rhythm. There seems to be a law of natural compensation at work here: the full da capo form is applied to the most straightforward musical material, while the 'heavier' arias are mainly cast in various through-composed or shortened dal segno structures. However, Jephtha's arias before and after the central crisis demand the full formal treatment, modified only by the elision of the opening ritornellos at the return in 'His mighty arm' and 'Open thy marble jaws, O tomb'. With the placing of these arias Morell and Handel established an emotional symmetry that would have been entirely appropriate to *opera seria* in its highest dramatic manifestation: the confident energy and extended form of the first[60] is the landmark from which Jephtha's subsequent collapse, beginning with 'Open thy marble jaws', is measured. In terms of variety, formal ingenuity, and the creation of broad melodic and harmonic paragraphs, the arias of *Jephtha* show Handel still at the height of his powers. Nor was his ear for an effective dramatic ensemble diminished: the quartet 'O spare your daughter' is a worthy successor to the 'judgment' trio in *Solomon*. If *Jephtha* does not provide a complete compendium of Handel's characteristic strengths, the only omission is in the area of the duet. 'These labours past', though effective enough in its context, is not in the same league as 'As steals the dawn' or 'To thee, thou glorious son of worth': it provides, however, an interesting final example of Handel's approach towards a 'Classical' musical style in his last creative years.

[60] This aria portrays Jephtha with the vigour of a still relatively youthful military leader: he is sometimes characterized as a much older man, but that is ill-founded and perhaps too much influenced by the oratorio's position in Handel's biography.

15

The final decade II: A career completed

Handel had managed, with difficulty, to complete *Jephtha* and to run his usual oratorio season during Lent 1752. Presumably his increasing disability had been apparent at the performances, and on 17 August 1752 it was announced to the world in a London newspaper:[1]

> We hear that George-Frederick Handel, Esq; the celebrated Composer of Musick was seized a few Days ago with a Paralytick Disorder in his Head, which has deprived him of Sight.

The same newspaper reported, early in November, that Handel had received an operation from William Bromfield, the Princess of Wales's surgeon, and that there were some hopes for the recovery of his sight.[2] There were even rumours in January 1753 that he had recovered sufficiently to be 'able to go abroad'[3] (that is, to venture from his house in Brook Street), but these stories were followed by a further announcement on 27 January:[4]

> Mr Handel has at length, unhappily, quite lost his sight. Upon his being couch'd some time since, he saw so well, that his friends flattered themselves his sight was restored for a continuance; but a few days have entirely put an end to their hope.

Handel probably retained a small residue of eyesight in 1753 and may have been able to scrawl a few singers' names into the conducting scores of the oratorios that were to be performed that year.[5] But that was about the limit of his input, and any necessary revisions to the 1753 scores were no doubt carried out by the younger Smith: he (or his father) had also to deal with such practical arrangements as the application for the loan of the Tower of London drums on Handel's behalf.[6] The first performance

---

[1] *The General Advertiser* (17 August 1752): Deutsch, p. 726, *HHB*, p. 460.
[2] *The General Advertiser* (4 November 1752): Deutsch, pp. 726–7; *HHB*, p. 461.
[3] *The Cambridge Chronicle* (13 January 1753), perhaps quoting from a previous London newspaper report, now unidentified: Deutsch, p. 731; *HHB*, p. 465.
[4] Source uncertain: Deutsch, p. 731; *HHB*, p. 465.
[5] See Burrows, 'Handel's Performances', p. 332, and Burrows, 'The Autographs', p. 219.
[6] Board of Ordnance Minutes, 27 February 1753: *HHB*, p. 468. This refers to 'Christopher Smith', almost certainly meaning the father. In some years the drums were collected by Handel's timpanist, Frederick Smith (probably not related).

of the season, on 9 March, was *Alexander's Feast*, partnered by *The Choice of Hercules*, and the Countess of Shaftesbury gave a vivid description of the atmosphere:[7]

> it was such a melancholy pleasure, as drew tears of sorrow to see the great though unhappy Handel, dejected, wan, and dark, sitting by, not playing on the harpsichord, and to think how his light had been spent by being <u>overplied in music's cause</u>. I was sorry to find the audience so insipid and tasteless (I may add unkind) not to give the poor man the comfort of applause; but affectation and conceit cannot discern or attend to merit.

The rest of the season's programme repeated works performed the previous year: *Jephtha*, *Judas Maccabaeus*, *Samson* and *Messiah*. Guadagni had returned to London: he presumably took up the part of Hamor in *Jephtha*, and no doubt his roles in the other oratorios repeated the patterns established in the 1750–1 season. The official opening of the Foundling Hospital chapel finally took place on 16 April 1753, and the Foundling Hospital Anthem, presumably in its revised form, was included at the opening service. One of the London newspapers, after giving advance notice of the service, inserted a curious editorial comment:[8]

> And we hear that that Gentleman [Handel] is composing a Funeral Anthem for himself, to be performed (when it shall please God to take him hence) in the above-mentioned Chapel, for the Benefit of the Charity.

Sections of the Foundling Hospital Anthem had been adapted from movements in Handel's Funeral Anthem for Queen Caroline, but there seems to be no basis for the composition of the funeral anthem referred to in the newspapers. The newspaper report may, however, have preserved, in a distorted form, the substance of some chance remark on Handel's part. The committee of the hospital was quick to take note of the paragraph and to reassure Handel of their good wishes for the 'Continuance of his Life': the incident may also have turned the hospital authorities towards considering the future of their *Messiah* performances. In January 1754 they put together a proposition that the hospital should, by Act of Parliament, receive proprietary rights over *Messiah* as a benefaction from Handel, but the subsequent minutes record, with masterly understatement, that when the idea was put to the composer 'the same did not seem agreeable to Mr. Handel for the present'.[9] The 1753 performance of *Messiah* at the Foundling Hospital on 1 May is remarkable for the report that, on that occasion, Handel 'in the Organ Concerto, play'd himself a Voluntary on the fine Organ he gave to that Chapel'.[10]

[7]Letter to James Harris, 13 March 1753: *HHB*, p. 469; also Deutsch, p. 703, misattributed to 1751.

[8]*The London Evening Post* (3–5 April 1753), quoted in Burrows, 'Handel and the Foundling Hospital', p. 275.

[9]General Committee Minutes, Foundling Hospital, 23 January 1754.

[10]*The Public Advertiser* (2 May 1753): Deutsch, p. 742; *HHB*, p. 471.

A month earlier, the Earl of Shaftesbury had commented that 'Handel's playing is beyond what even he ever did',[11] but the 1753 *Messiah* performance is the last occasion on which the newspapers reported Handel performing in public. The wording of the report in itself is significantly ambiguous: it suggests that Handel contributed only a separate 'ad libitum' solo movement and may not have played in the concerted movements. 30 years later, Burney gave this account of Handel's continuance as a performer into his years of blindness:[12]

> HANDEL, late in life, like the great poets, Homer, and Milton, was afflicted with blindness; which, however it might dispirit and embarrass him at other times, had no effect on his nerves or intellects, in public: as he continued to play concertos and voluntaries between the parts of his Oratorios to the last, with the same vigour of thought and touch, for which he was ever so justly renowned. To see him, however, led to the organ, after his calamity, at upwards of seventy years of age, and then conducted towards the audience to make his accustomed obeisance, was a sight so truly afflicting and deplorable to persons of sensibility, as greatly diminished their pleasure, in hearing him perform.
>
> During the Oratorio season, I have been told, that he practised almost incessantly; and, indeed, that must have been the case, or his memory uncommonly retentive; for, after his blindness, he played several of his *old* organ-concertos, which must have been previously impressed on his memory by practice. At last, however, he rather chose to trust to his inventive powers, than those of reminiscence: for, giving the band only the skeleton, or ritornels of each movement, he played all the solo parts extempore, while the other instruments left him, *ad libitum*; waiting for the signal of a shake, before they played such fragments of symphony as they found in their books.

We do not know for how many seasons Handel remained able to proceed in this way, though as late as 27 March 1756 Thomas Harris could report that Handel's oratorio performances had gone 'very well, and his own on the organ as good as ever'. No doubt his health and morale fluctuated, and the variations were sufficiently unpredictable to deter any pre-advertisement of his participation.

Burney's immediately following passage, concerning the continuation of Handel's creative career, is also probably rather more optimistic than can be supported from present knowledge.[13]

> Indeed, he not only continued to perform in public after he was afflicted with blindness, but to *compose* in private; for I have been assured, that the Duet and Chorus in *Judas Macchabaeus*, of *Sion now his head shall raise, Tune your harps to songs of praise* were dictated to Mr. Smith, by HANDEL, after the total privation of sight ... Indeed, HANDEL not only exhibited great intellectual ability in the composition of this Duet and Chorus, but manifested his power of invention in extemporaneous flights of fancy to be as rich and rapid, a week

---

[11] Letter to James Harris, 3 April 1753: *HHB*, p. 470.
[12] *An Account of the Musical Performances*, 'Sketch of the Life of Handel', pp. 29–30.
[13] *Ibid.*, pp. 30–1.

before his decease, as they had been for many years. He was always much disturbed and agitated by the similar circumstances of *Samson*, whenever the affecting air in that Oratorio of "*Total Eclipse, no Sun, no Moon*," &c. was performed.

Close examination of the 'new' material inserted into Handel's oratorio seasons between 1753 and 1759 reveals that it was for the most part either derived by transcription from his earlier works or cobbled together from Handelian fragments, with joins and extensions in a rather foreign style: the obvious explanation is that the younger Smith gradually moved into the position of being the principal arranger, editor and adapter of this material, perhaps working from time to time on the basis of suggestions made by Handel.[14] At best, the additions exhibit varying degrees of 'Handel-ness': one of the most Handelian is the duet and chorus named by Burney (of which more presently). Effectively, Handel's creative career came to an end at the end of August 1751, with the completion of *Jephtha*.

The existence of the myth of Handel's constant activity as a composer, performer and impresario during his last years reflects the smoothness of the transition from Handel's leadership to that of Smith. By 1753 Handel's Lenten oratorio performances in London were an established tradition, stretching back through a decade of unbroken theatrical practice, the last seven years of which had been at Covent Garden: the wheels of the practical arrangements turned smoothly and regularly, and the performances seem to have established a loyal audience. There were plenty of scores by Handel to choose from for the oratorio seasons: the only creative task lay in selecting the works for each year and adapting the music where necessary to suit the available performers. 1752 had seen revivals of the 'victory' oratorios *Joshua* and *Judas Maccabaeus*. They were repeated in 1754, together with their companion work *Alexander Balus*: the programme was completed with revivals of *Deborah*, *Saul*, and the ever-popular *Samson* and *Messiah*. Following an established annual pattern, *Messiah* regularly closed the theatre season, now on the Friday before Palm Sunday, and the Foundling Hospital performance followed soon after Easter. The hospital's account-books for 1754 contain for the first time an intemized list of performers' expenses for *Messiah*, indicating that the arrangements hitherto conducted directly through Handel were now being put on a formal written basis. In order to safeguard the continuation of their *Messiah* performances, the hospital appointed the younger Smith as their first organist. When consulted on the matter[15]

Mr. Handel approved of the Committee's appointing Mr. Smith Organist to the Chapel, to conduct his Musical Compositions; but that on Acco.^t of his

[14] See Hicks, 'The Late Additions to Handel's Oratorios', p. 167.
[15] General Committee Minutes, Foundling Hospital, 25 June 1754: Deutsch, p. 753: *HHB*, p. 483.

Health he excused himself from giving any further Instructions relating to the Performances.

Nevertheless, the hospital continued to advertise their *Messiah* performances as being under Handel's direction up until the time of his death,[16] and he remained nominally the senior partner in the oratorio seasons: the theatre rent was paid in his name and he probably dealt with the performance receipts. In September 1754 Handel signed a letter to Telemann that he had dictated, concerning the 'exotic plants' that had gone astray between London and Hamburg: the only subsequent examples of his handwriting are signatures (of increasing uncertainty in their orthography) on the codicils to his will.

The 1755 season began with odes: *Alexander's Feast* (partnered by *The Choice of Hercules*), followed by *L'Allegro* with the shorter Cecilian ode, and *Samson*: in the programme that followed, single performances of *Theodora* and *Joseph* were relative novelties, complementing the established favourites of *Judas Maccabaeus* and *Messiah*. In 1756 *Jephtha* and *Deborah* came round again, this time accompanied by *Athalia*, which Handel had not performed since 1735. The most interesting novelty of the 1756 season, however, was a revival of *Israel in Egypt*, for which a 'new' Part 1 was created, mainly using movements from *Solomon* and the *Occasional Oratorio* in place of the Funeral Anthem. It seems as if Smith (or Handel) followed a policy of giving the more recondite oratorios a hearing by turns, as well as re-presenting the trusted favourites, but this did not stretch to the secular works: *Semele* and *Hercules* were not revived, nor was *Acis and Galatea*.

Between the 1756 and 1757 oratorio seasons Handel seems to have experienced some recovery in his spirits and in his level of activity. He re-enters the documentary record by making two codicils to his will, in August 1756 and March 1757. In addition to bringing up to date the bequests to his family and to his servants, he made bequests to his professional collaborators: an extra £1500 for Smith (probably the elder), £200 for Morell and £100 for Newburgh Hamilton. A further codicil in August 1757 added bequests of pictures (by Denner and, possibly, Rembrandt) to Jennens and Bernard Granville,[17] Handel's theatre organ to John Rich and 'a fair copy of the Score and all Parts of my Oratorio called The Messiah to the Foundling Hospital'. If the hospital governors did not receive performing rights to *Messiah*, they would at least in due course have their own performing material. On 8 February 1757 the Earl of Shaftesbury reported that[18]

Mr Handel is better than he has been for some years, and finds he can compose

---

[16] *The Public Advertiser* (7 April 1759): Deutsch, p. 819; *HHB*, p. 527.

[17] Granville (Mrs Delany's brother) had created a library collection of MS scores of Handel's works in the early 1740s.

[18] Letter to James Harris: *HHB*, p. 505.

Chorus's as well as other, music to his own (and consequently to the hearers') satisfaction. His memory is strengthened of late to an astonishing degree.

It was in the 1757 oratorio season that the 'new' duet and chorus mentioned by Burney, 'Sion now her head shall raise', was introduced, first into *Esther* and then into *Judas Maccabaeus*.[19] As already noted, this is the most substantial and stylistically consistent of the 'original' additions to the later oratorio performances, so it may be that Handel did manage to have a hand in at least one complete chorus, perhaps dictating to Smith at the keyboard and correcting the result as it was repeated to him.

If indeed Handel was able to be more active at this period, then he may also have taken more part than has usually been allowed in the creation of *The Triumph of Time and Truth*, an English version of his Italian oratorio *Il trionfo del Tempo*, produced in London in 1737 and 1739. There is an obvious and attractive biographical symmetry to the idea that Handel marked the close of his career with a revival of his first Roman oratorio of 1707, adapted to the English language and to the tastes of the London audiences and incorporating some of the music that he had added in 1737. Morell's involvement with the project also may be suggestive: perhaps Handel expressed a wish to see *Il trionfo* converted into an English repertory oratorio, but Smith realized that this would be possible only if Handel could collaborate with a sympathetic and trusted librettist. The extent of Morell's role in the creation of *The Triumph of Time and Truth* is not completely certain but is strongly suggested by his mention of the work in a subsequent letter describing his collaboration with Handel.[20] Morell took as his starting-point the 1737 libretto, using Old-mixon's English translation in the word-book as far as possible, although singing translations to fit the music of the Italian words were needed. About two thirds of the concerted movements are 'Englished' versions of movements from the 1737 Italian oratorio, including many that had been carried forward in turn from the more cantata-like oratorio of 1707, thus accounting for the relatively high proportion of da capo arias. The act-structure and 'plot' of 1737 were also faithfully followed, though there were various aria substitutions (using music from *Lotario*, the 1732 *Acis and Galatea* and *Parnasso in festa*). Choruses from a Cannons anthem and the Foundling Hospital Anthem were added, at points that were as appropriate as could be contrived, to assist with the conversion of the work into something approaching the oratorio style of the 1750s. One or two cobbled musical adaptations were probably the work of the younger Smith, but Handel may have been active in the selection and the general

---

[19] Printed in *HG* 22, and in English editions of *Judas Maccabaeus* from Randall's score (1768–9) onwards.

[20] Deutsch, p. 851. Morell must surely have known, however, that the English version was not 'entirely adapted' from Handel's Roman oratorio of 1707: his phrase suggests over-emphasis of the point.

principles of adaptation of the music; some of the new English recitatives may even have come from his dictation. The 'new' overture also seems to reflect Handel's guiding hand: the opening is reworked from the overture to Keiser's Hamburg opera *Claudius* (1703), a characteristically Handelian 'borrowing' source, but the faster movement is slung together in a rather non-Handelian manner, using a large slot of material from one of Handel's overtures to *Il pastor fido*. Although the work has some weak spots, probably not of Handel's devising, *The Triumph of Time and Truth* is coherent enough to be included in the canon of Handel's English oratorios and to deserve an occasional hearing today.[21]

For the 1757 oratorio season *The Triumph of Time and Truth* was preceded by *Esther*, *Israel in Egypt* and *Joseph*, and followed by *Judas Maccabaeus* and *Messiah*. *Israel in Egypt*, *Joseph* and *Judas Maccabaeus* received only one performance each. Obviously, the old operatic measures of 'success' in terms of numbers of performances no longer applied: no capital investment in the way of costumes, scenery and production rehearsals was required, but, even so, a proportionately higher labour factor in rehearsals must have been involved for single presentations. The performing materials and the performers' accumulated experience might be regarded as 'capital assets' that were carried forward from one oratorio season to another, but a single-performance revival nevertheless usually involved some adaptation of the score. There may now have been a 'connoisseur' element in the oratorio audience whose tastes encouraged the mixed programme of single showings and established favourites. The regular Foundling Hospital performance of *Messiah* followed after Easter. It is perhaps not surprising that there are few references to Handel himself between the oratorio seasons in his last years, as he probably lived a quiet and retired life: the only reference between the 1757 and 1758 seasons comes from a letter of the Earl of Shaftesbury, written on the last day of December 1757:[22]

I saw Mr. Handel the other day, who is pretty well and has just finished the composing of several new songs for Frederica his new singer, from whom he has great expectations. She is the girl who was celebrated a few years since for playing on the Harpsichord at eight years old.

The 1758 oratorio season began on 10 February with *The Triumph of Time and Truth*, incorporating five additional arias for the young soprano Cassandra Frederick: Mrs Delany attended and reported hearing 'a new woman instead of Passarini, who was so frightened that I cannot say whether she sings well, or ill'.[23] The 'new' movements were adapted from old thematic material and are not of a quality that suggests Handel's own

[21] Winton Dean (*Handel's Dramatic Oratorios*, p. 589) describes it as a 'tedious allegory', which seems unduly harsh and raises questions about Handel's earlier Italian versions.
[22] Letter to James Harris: *HHB*, p. 511.
[23] Letter to Ann Dewes, 11 February 1758: Deutsch, pp. 793–4; *HHB*, p. 512.

work, though he may initially have selected the themes and their treatment; the same applies to the movements added to the 1758 revivals of *Belshazzar* and *Judas Maccabaeus*.[24] The season also included single-performance revivals of *Israel in Egypt* and *Jephtha* and three performances of *Messiah*: the Foundling Hospital *Messiah* followed after Easter. By now *Messiah* had achieved more performances than any other oratorio at Handel's hands: it had clearly become an established repertory work, and a new conducting score was copied, perhaps because heavy use was taking its toll on the old one.[25] The surviving account-list from the 1758 Foundling Hospital performance[26] confirms the identities of the leading singers in the oratorio company. Frasi and Beard remained as the principal soprano and tenor respectively, 'Miss Frederick' replaced Passerini as the second soprano, while 'Miss Young' (Isabella Young, niece to two of Handel's previous soloists) had since 1755 taken over the alto-register roles from Galli and Guadagni. Wass appears in the Foundling Hospital list as the leader of the chorus basses, for the principal bass solo roles had been taken over by a new singer, Samuel Champness (who, after training in the Chapel Royal, had probably sung treble in the oratorios of the mid-1740s). During the oratorio season the barrister John Baker attended a rehearsal of *Judas Maccabaeus* in Brook Street, at which he noted the presence of Frasi, Young, Frederick, Beard, Champness and the leader of the chorus altos, Thomas Baildon.[27] The reference is remarkable because it shows that rehearsals (though presumably not orchestral ones) were still being held at Handel's house, and also that the rehearsal took place only a day before the performance: there are no surviving reports of full oratorio rehearsals from Handel's later years (though these must have taken place).

Later entries in John Baker's diary also provide the only documentary references for Handel's visit to Tunbridge Wells, where Baker met him on 26 August 1758, visiting his lodgings a week later.[28] No doubt Handel had gone to the Wells for a rest-cure, to 'take the waters': Baker mentions that Handel was in the company of 'his Dr. Murrell' (presumably Thomas Morell) and 'Taylor the occulist'. Taylor appears to have attempted an operation on Handel, but without success; a decade earlier, in Germany, he had also failed to restore J.S. Bach's sight. The next oratorio season opened at Covent Garden on 2 March 1759 with *Solomon*, in a heavily revised version that was probably the work of the younger Smith.[29] The

[24] See Hicks, 'The Late Additions to Handel's Oratorios', pp. 155–65.

[25] There is no reason to suppose that this score was intended, in anticipation of Handel's death, as the presentation copy for the Foundling Hospital that had been mentioned in the codicil of August 1757 to Handel's will.

[26] Deutsch, pp. 800–1; *HHB*, pp. 516–17.

[27] Baker, *Diary*, 2 March 1758: Deutsch, p. 795; *HHB*, p. 513.

[28] Baker, *Diary*, 26 August 1758: Deutsch, p. 806; *HHB*, p. 520.

[29] The music is described in Dean, *Handel's Dramatic Oratorios*, pp. 527–9.

other 'novelty' of the season was the first revival of its 1749 companion, *Susanna*; *Samson* also returned for the first time since 1755. It seems that a revival of *Theodora* was also planned but never came to performance.[30] The programme as a whole was summarized in a newspaper comment on 7 April, the day before Palm Sunday:[31]

> Last Night ended the celebrated Mr. Handel's Oratorios for this Season, and the great Encouragement they have received is a sufficient Proof of their superior Merit. He began with Solomon, which was exhibited twice; Susanna once; Sampson three Times; Judas Maccabaeus twice; and the Messiah three Times.
>
> And this Day Mr. Handel proposed setting out for Bath, to try the Benefit of the Waters, having been for some Time past in a bad State of Health.

On the same day another London newspaper carried a notice for the forthcoming *Messiah* performance at the Foundling Hospital, to be held 'under the Direction of *Georg-Frederick Handel*, Esq; on Thursday the Third Day of May next'.[32]

In fact, Handel was too ill to travel to Bath and never lived to see the Foundling Hospital performance. On 11 April, the Wednesday of Holy Week, he dictated and signed the fourth and final codicil to his will. He seems to have recognized that he had not much longer to live, and also that he was going to die a wealthy man. Two things are remarkable about the new bequests: the substantial gift of £1000 to the Society for the Support of Decay'd Musicians and their Families (which stood as the first item in the codicil), and then the London-based nature of the personal bequests, in contrast to the German family bequests that had dominated his previous will and codicils. There were appropriately generous provisions for servants, and for doctors and apothecaries who had presumably tended medical attention, and £200 to one of his executors, but three-figure sums also went to personal friends – 'Thomas Harris Esquire of Lincolns Inn Fields', 'John Hetherington of the First Fruits Office', 'James Smyth of Bond Street Perfumer' and 'Matthew Dubourg Musician'. £100 went to Mrs Palmer, a widow from Chelsea, and 50-guinea bequests went to some now shadowy recipients – Mrs Mayne, a widow from Kensington, and 'Mrs. Donnalan of Charles Street Berkley Square'. 'Mr. Reiche Secretary [in London] for the affairs of Hanover' received £200. Hardly less significant, in terms of Handel's own view of his relationship to the life of Britain's capital, was another clause of the codicil:

> I hope to have the permission of the Dean and Chapter of Westminster to be buried in Westminster Abbey in a private manner at the discretion of my Executor Mr Amyand and I desire that my said Executor may have leave to erect a Monument for me there and that any Sum not Exceeding Six Hundred Pounds be expended for that purpose at the discretion of my said Executor.

[30] See *ibid.*, pp. 577–8, and Clausen, *Händels Direktionspartituren*, p. 240.
[31] *The Whitehall Evening Post* (7 April 1759): Deutsch, p. 814; *HHB*, p. 527.
[32] *The Public Advertiser* (7 April 1759): Deutsch, p. 813; *HHB*, p. 527.

Handel's death was prematurely reported two days later, in a newspaper for 13 April (Good Friday), but an authoritative account of his death the next day (though not entirely accurate in its financial information) is given in a letter from James Smyth (the 'Bond Street Perfumer') to Handel's friend Bernard Granville:[33]

> According to your request to me when you left London, that I would let you know when our good friend departed this life, <u>on Saturday last at 8 o'clock in the morn died the great and good Mr. Handel</u>. He was sensible to the last moment; made a codicil to his will on Tuesday, ordered to be buried privately in Westminster Abbey, and a monument not to exceed £600 for him. I had the pleasure to reconcile him to his old friends: he saw them and forgave them, and let all their legacies stand! In the codicil he left many legacies to his friends, and among the rest he left me £500, and has left to you the two pictures <u>you formerly gave him</u>. He took leave of all his friends on Friday morning, and desired to see nobody but the Doctor and Apothecary and myself. At 7 o'clock in the evening he took leave of me and told me we "should meet again"; as soon as I was gone he told his servant "<u>not</u> to let me come to him any more, for that he had <u>now done with the world</u>". He died as he lived – a good <u>Christian</u>, with a true sense of his duty to God and man, and in perfect charity with all the world.
>
> He has left the Messiah to the Foundling Hospital, and one thousand pounds to the decayed musicians and their children, and the residue of his fortune to his niece and relations in Germany. He has died worth £20 000, and left legacies with his charities to nearly £6000. He has got by his Oratorios this year £1952 12s. 8d.

Handel was buried in the South Cross of Westminster Abbey on 20 April:[34]

> the Bishop, Prebendaries and the whole Choir attended, to pay the last Honours due to his Memory; and it is computed there were not fewer than 3000 Persons present on this occasion

The funeral was a private one, not a state one, but a full complement of singers gave Croft's burial sentences.[35] Of Handel's royal patrons, Princess Anne had died in Holland three months before him and King George II was to live just over another year.

The terms of Handel's will and codicils were duly carried out and, after the specific bequests had been met, his niece Johanne Floerke (now wife of the Rektor of the University of Halle) still received £9000. In August

[33] Letter, 17 April 1759: Deutsch, pp. 818–19; *HHB*, p. 531. Handel's executor's administration account (Deutsch, p. 838; *HHB*, p. 550) records the distribution of £17500 but may not tell the whole story.
[34] *The London Evening-Post* (24 April 1759): Deutsch, p. 821; *HHB*, p. 527.
[35] *The Public Advertiser* (20 April 1759): Deutsch, pp. 819–20; *HHB*, p. 532). The report said that the Westminster Abbey Choir would be augmented by singers from the Chapel Royal and St Paul's Cathedral: since there was considerable overlap in the membership of the choirs, this probably meant that in practice a substantial body of the best singers turned out. The funeral expenses included £8 3s. 4d. 'To the Chantor & Choir' (see Simon, *Handel*, p. 233).

1759 an inventory of household goods at Brook Street was taken (prior to their sale to Handel's servant) which, while interesting, is surprisingly unilluminating about Handel's lifestyle. More surprising, perhaps, is the extent of his picture collection which is revealed in the catalogue of its sale in 1760[36] – 67 lots, on the face of it hardly compatible with the modest wall-area of Handel's Brook Street home. In 1760 appeared the *Memoirs of the Life of the Late George Frederic Handel. To Which is added, a Catalogue of His Works, and Observations upon them.* It was published anonymously, but letters between the author and the publisher (now in the Coke Handel Collection) establish that it was written by John Mainwaring, Professor of Divinity at the University of Cambridge; it was the first full-length published critical biography of any composer.[37] The monument to Handel in Westminster Abbey was completed in 1762: it was the sculptor Roubiliac's last major work, as the Vauxhall Gardens statue of Handel 20 years previously had been his first (Plate 8). Roubiliac's work takes its place next to the portraits by Denner, Mercier (Plate 6) and Hudson (Plate 11) as preserving the most reliable physical likenesses of the composer.[38]

When Smyth described his late friend as 'the great and good Mr. Handel', he was talking about someone who was already on his way to becoming an institution, remembered as a personality and as a composer. The successful oratorio composer of the last two decades had somewhat dimmed the recollection of the opera composer of the earlier years. Handel was remembered immediately as the great benefactor to charity, the great composer of biblical oratorios and English odes, and to a lesser extent also as the composer of the coronation anthems, *Te Deum* settings, and the op.6 concertos and the *Fireworks Music*. Apart from the reputation made through his own oratorio seasons, which served to promote Handel and his music more distinctly than the multi-composer opera seasons had done, Handel's music had enjoyed an ever-widening dissemination in the composer's later years by other means. *Alexander's Feast* had been in print, complete and in full score, for 20 years, and as long ago as 1732 Arne had shown that *Acis and Galatea* could successfully be performed without recourse to the composer. The celebrations surrounding the University 'Act' at Oxford in 1749, at which William Hayes had received his doctorate, had amounted to a Handel festival promoted and conducted by Hayes; and Hayes was also engaged as a professional musician in many of the independent provincial performances of Handel's music that took place in the 1750s, at Oxford, Salisbury and the Three Choirs Festival. These regularly involved performances of church music (much

[36] See Chapter 14, n.8.
[37] Hawkins's *Memoirs of the Life of Agostino Steffani*, produced some ten years previously, was less ambitious and was printed for private circulation.
[38] See 'The Image of Handel' in Simon, *Handel*, pp. 33–47.

of which was in print) and even complete oratorios. In December 1753 the Edinburgh Musical Society had written to Handel, asking if he would supply the necessary music (additional to that found in the printed 'Songs') to enable them to perform *Messiah*: the reply was that 'Mr. Smith ... has Mr. Handel's orders to let the Gentlemen of the Musical Society at Edinburgh have any of his Compositions that they want',[39] and no doubt other similar enquiries also met with a favourable response. In 1756 Hayes similarly obtained a score of *Joshua* from the Earl of Shaftesbury for a performance in Oxford, though Shaftesbury saw fit to consult Handel on the matter and reported that[40]

> Smyth [i.e. J.C. Smith senior] has been with me just now to say, there is no objection to my lending the score of Joshua to Dr. Hayes, yet this is done under a confidence of Dr. Hayes' honour, that he will not suffer any copy to be taken or to get about from his having been in possession of the score. For otherwise both Handel and Smyth (his copiest) will be injur'd. Pray desire too, care may be taken not to spoil the Book. I only mention this particular as a caution, because very often books and especially manuscripts are much dirted by being thumb'd about.

Some of the most informative descriptions of Handel's manners and personality come from people who had known him in his later years, and are to be found in Mainwaring's *Memoirs* (1760), Hawkins's *A General History of the Science and Practice of Music* (1776) and Burney's 'Sketch of the Life of Handel' in his *Account of the Musical Performances* (1785) celebrating the Handel Commemoration of 1784. The descriptions given by Hawkins and Burney also include some amplifications of previously published material, interspersed with a certain amount of gossip. Hawkins hints that Handel's personality, and certainly his social behaviour, was considerably modified by the disability of his later years:[41]

> The loss of his sight, and the prospect of his approaching dissolution, wrought a great change in his temper and general behaviour. He was a man of blameless morals, and throughout his life manifested a deep sense of religion. In conversation he would frequently declare the pleasure he felt in setting the Scriptures to music; and how much the contemplating the many sublime passages in the Psalms had contributed to his edification; and now that he found himself near his end, these sentiments were improved into solid and rational piety, attended with a calm and even temper of mind. For the last two or three years of his life he was used to attend divine service in his own parish church of St. George, Hanover-square, where, during the prayers, the eyes that at this instant are employed in a faint portrait of his excellencies, have seen him on his knees, expressing by his looks and gesticulations the utmost fervour of devotion.

[39] *HHB*, p. 473.
[40] Letter to James Harris, 27 May 1756: *HHB*, pp. 498–9.
[41] *A General History*, ii, 910.

Clearly Handel's medical history is of some significance to his creative life, not only during his last years, when he was probably incapacitated from sustained practical activity, but also on account of the interruptions with which illness punctuated his career from the 1730s onwards. In the absence of adequate medical records, any connections between Handel's 'paraletic disorders' (some of them at least apparently involving temporary loss of function in the hands), his blindness and his reported 'fits of madness' (probably excessive tension rather than actual mental illness) must remain speculative. A case has been made out for interpreting Handel's 'strokes' as recurrent muscular rheumatism, his blindness as cataracts, and his 'madness' as the consequence of a cyclothymic personality in which over-active phases alternated with periods of depression.[42] But an alternative medical opinion has found 'little real evidence of either cyclothymia or major affective illness' and concludes:[43]

> Handel lived a generally healthy life despite his afflictions and died an easy and peaceful death. He suffered from an episodic mental disturbance that occurred for the most part and perhaps entirely in conjunction with physical illnesses of the sort most likely to be threatening to his music.

Hawkins may well be correct in suggesting that Handel had greater need for the consolations of religion in his last years, when Handel no doubt built on a foundation of faith that had been absorbed in the family circle of his youth. According to Hawkins:[44]

> In his religion he was of the Lutheran profession; in which he was not such a bigot as to decline a general conformity with that of the country which he had chosen for his residence;[45] at the same time that he entertained very serious notions touching its importance. These he would frequently express in his remarks on the constitution of the English government; and he would often speak of it as one of the great felicities of his life that he was settled in a country where no man suffers any molestation or inconvenience on account of his religious principles.

This view would not, of course, have been entirely shared by Jews or Roman Catholics during Handel's lifetime. Hawkins's report was no doubt amplified by the political context in which it was written in the

[42] See Keynes, 'Handel and his Illnesses', and, specifically on Handel's blindness, Ober, 'Bach, Handel and "Chevalier" John Taylor'.

[43] Frosch, 'The "Case" of George Frideric Handel', p. 768. Frosch has also advanced the hypothesis that Handel's health problems may have been rooted in an excessive consumption of port wine, which was cheaper and more readily available in London than French wines: some of Handel's 'palsy' may have been due to gout (which was temporarily cured when he went to Aix-la-Chapelle, away from the source of the problem), and his final deterioration may have been the result of lead-poisoning, accumulated from deposits in the vessels used in making the port wine.

[44] *A General History*, ii, 911.

[45] Such conformity was legally required as part of the naturalization procedure in 1727. Simon, *Handel*, p. 178.

1770s, when Britain might have seen itself as a model of freedom, liberty and democracy in contrast to pre-revolutionary France. But Handel may well have expressed a basic sentiment along the lines reported: the British constitution could be regarded as more liberal than most other European ones, and the Revocation of the Edict of Nantes in 1685 had provided a kind of benchmark for religious and political bigotry in Handel's youth – Huguenots had fled to Halle, as well as to London.

We have very little direct information about Handel's opinions on religious, ethical or political issues at any stage during his life. As far as any relevant evidence is available, it appears that his behaviour was generally conformist in relation to the prevailing political, social and religious cultures of the places in which he worked: that tells us nothing, however, about the all-important relationship between his opinions (and emotional allegiances) and his behaviour. There is one surviving formal record of his political participation: he voted for the Whig candidate in the Westminster Parliamentary By-election of 1749.[46] As a thoroughly professional composer and a natural dramatist, Handel knew that the theatre was not the place for sermons. Only occasionally, as in the alteration to the text of the last chorus of *Alexander Balus*, or in his refusal to label the ladies of Solomon's court as 'harlots',[47] were his librettos probably modified because he found the content personally repugnant. This does not imply a lesser degree of commitment to the religious framework in which Handel (coming from a stock of Lutheran pastors) had been brought up; but he had a wide range of sympathies and empathies with the characters that he brought to life in his operas and oratorios. It is possible to make speculations about Handel's opinions and beliefs by extrapolation from his works, but speculations they must remain. Whether deliberately or not, Handel took care to keep his own opinions and proclivities out of his work. Only when pushed to the limits of what he considered acceptable (to himself, or to his audiences) is he likely to have demanded substantial revisions from his librettists. We need have no regrets that his personality is relatively recessive in his works: his impartiality is an element of his professionalism and in no way lessens the emotional impact of his music.

In sum, Handel seems to have been a fundamentally private man, who succeeded in maintaining his privacies. This skill may have been learnt early in his professional life, when he had steered a masterly course that gained him acceptance successively with diverse political régimes in Hamburg, Rome, Venice, Hanover and London. Privacy was also useful in the theatrical world: had there been a breath of scandal it would have set him at a disadvantage against Bononcini in the 1720s and against the Nobility Opera in the 1730s. Burney picked up a scent that 'It has been

[46] Simon, *Handel*, p. 178.
[47] See Chapter 13, p. 323.

said of him, that, out of his profession, he was ignorant and dull':[48] the truth more probably was that he chose his partners in conviviality with care. There may have been a permanent barrier of personal reserve: of the correspondents who are known to have been in some degree part of his social circle, none ever refers to him by either of his first names.[49] Hawkins's comment that 'His social affections were not very strong' needs to be quoted in context:[50]

> The course of his life was regular and uniform. For some years after his arrival in England his time was divided between study and practice, that is to say, in composing for the opera, and in conducting concerts at the duke of Rutland's, the earl of Burlington's, and the houses of others of the nobility who were patrons of music, and his friends. There were also frequent concerts for the royal family at the queen's library in the Green-Park, in which the princess royal, the duke of Rutland, lord Cowper, and other persons of distinction performed; of these Handel had the direction. As these connections dissolved, he gradually retreated into a state of privacy and retirement, and showed no solicitude to form new ones. His dwelling was on the south side of Brooke-street, near Hanover-square, in a house now in the occupation of Sir James Wright, four doors from Bond-street, and two from the passage to the stable-yard. His stated income was six hundred pounds a year, arising from pensions; that is to say, one of two hundred pounds, granted him by queen Anne, another of two hundred pounds granted by Geo. I., and another of the same amount, for teaching the princesses. The rest was precarious; for some time it depended upon his engagements with the directors of the Academy, and afterwards upon the profits arising from the musical performances carried on by him on his own account. However, he had at all times the prudence to regulate his expence by his income. At the time of his contest with the nobility he had ten thousand pounds in the funds, and of this he sold out the last shilling, and lived upon his pensions, which, by an interest that he had with the minister, were punctually paid him. Some years after, when he found himself in a state of affluence, and the produce of his oratorios amounted to more than two thousand pounds a season, he continued his wonted course of living, which was equally distant from the extremes of parsimony and profusion. In the latter part of his life he forbore yielding to a temptation, which few in such circumstances as he was then in would, in these times be able to resist, that of keeping a carriage. Indeed, when his sight failed him, he was necessitated occasionally to hire a chariot and horses, especially in his visits to the city for the purpose of investing his money, which he constantly disposed of at the end of the Lent season, under the direction of Mr. Gael Morris, a broker of the first eminence, whom he used to meet and confer with at Garraway's or Batson's coffee-house.
>
> His social affections were not very strong; and to this it may be imputed

[48] *An Account of the Musical Performances*, 'Sketch of the Life of Handel', p. 37.
[49] Social conventions at this period, however, differed substantially from modern ones. There are hints, from fragmentary evidence (including the word-book for *Serse*), that when only one of his forenames was used 'Frideric Handel' was the preferred form. That may have been a convention stretching back to his youth, to avoid confusion with his father, also Georg.
[50] *A General History*, ii, 911–12.

that he spent his whole life in a state of celibacy; that he had no female attachment of another kind may be ascribed to a better reason.[51] His intimate friends were but few; those that seemed to possess most of his confidence were Goupy,[52] the painter, and one Hunter, a scarlet-dyer at Old Ford, near Bow, who pretended a taste for music, and at a great expense had copies made for him of all the music of Handel that he could procure. He had others in the city; but he seemed to think that the honour of his acquaintance was a reward sufficient for the kindness they expressed for him.

A temper and conduct like this, was in every view of it favourable to his pursuits; no impertinent visits, no idle engagements to card parties, or other expedients to kill time, were suffered to interrupt the course of his studies. His invention was for ever teeming with new ideas, and his impatience to be delivered of them kept him closely employed. He had a favourite Rucker harpsichord, the keys whereof, by incessant practice, were hollowed like the bowl of a spoon. He wrote very fast, but with a degree of impatience proportioned to the eagerness that possesses men of genius, of seeing their conceptions reduced into form ...

Like many others of his profession, he had a great love for painting; and, till his sight failed him, among the few amusements he gave into, the going to view collections of pictures upon sale was the chief.

He was in his person a large made and very portly man. His gait, which was ever sauntering, was rather ungraceful, as it had in it somewhat of that rocking motion, which distinguishes those whose legs are bowed. His features were finely marked, and the general cast of his countenance placid, bespeaking dignity attempered with benevolence, and every quality of the heart that has a tendency to beget confidence and insure esteem.

Although Handel did not keep a carriage (though he presumably travelled about London by carriage, or possibly sometimes by sedan chair or on foot),[53] by the time of his death he had an establishment consisting

[51] By 'a better reason', Hawkins almost certainly meant that the fact that Handel did not live with a woman who was not his wife could be ascribed to his blameless morals: I thank Anthony Hicks for pointing this out. It is in the highest degree unlikely that Hawkins intended to hint that Handel had homosexual orientation: eighteenth-century Britain, and that part of it that formed Hawkins's readership, would not have been sympathetic to such a hint (they certainly might not have regarded it as compatible with 'blameless morals'), and Hawkins would have undercut the personal lustre that he clearly hoped to gain by claiming close acquaintance with the 'great and good' (though eccentric) Mr Handel. In the absence of adequate social records, conclusions regarding Handel's sexual orientation must remain speculative. Revealing first-person diaries such as those from Pepys and Hervey are rare from the period before 1760 and are the products of personalities very different from Handel's. Given the structure of eighteenth-century London society, no conclusions can be drawn from the fact that most of Handel's known social and professional relationships were with men. It would certainly be wrong to read secular modern assumptions about social behaviour into the life of someone who had probably received a fairly strict Lutheran upbringing in eighteenth-century Germany.

[52] This statement seems odd in view of the fact that Goupy is normally credited with the various 'Charming Brute' caricatures of Handel, some seemingly cruel in intent, from the period around 1749.

[53] See, for example, the letter of 29 August 1745 quoted on p. 286, in which William Harris talks of meeting Handel in the street, with the implication that they were both walking. Carriages may have been available for hire from the stable-yard behind Handel's house.

of at least two manservants and a number of maids. His need for nursing may have required an expansion of domestic staff in his later years, but he no doubt maintained a regular personal establishment, at least from the time that he moved into his Brook Street home in the 1720s. Such would in any case have been in keeping with his social standing. The professional colleagues who served as music copyists must have been among those people with the closest personal access to Handel. Of Handel's personal accomplishments, Hawkins paints an amusing picture:[54]

> There seems to be no necessary connection between those faculties that constitute a composer of music, and the powers of instrumental performance; on the contrary, the union of them in the same person, seems as extraordinary as if a poet should be able to write a fine hand; nevertheless in the person of Handel all the perfections of the musical art seemed to concenter. He had never been a master of the violin, and had discontinued the practice of it from the time he took to the harpsichord at Hamburg; yet, whenever he had a mind to try the effect of any of his compositions for that instrument, his manner of touching it was such as the ablest masters would have been glad to imitate. But what is more extraordinary, without a voice he was an excellent singer of such music as required more of the pathos of melody than a quick and voluble expression. In a conversation with the author of this work, he once gave a proof that a fine voice is not the principal requisite in vocal performance; the discourse was upon psalmody, when Mr. Handel asserted that some of the finest melodies used in the German churches were composed by Luther, particularly that which in England is sung to the hundredth psalm, and another, which himself sang at the time, and thereby gave occasion to this remark. At a concert at the house of lady Rich he was prevailed on to sing a slow song, which he did in such a manner, that Farinelli, who was present, could hardly be persuaded to sing after him.

Hawkins describes Handel as 'a man of blameless morals', but he does not portray him as being without weaknesses:[55]

> Such as were but little acquainted with Handel are unable to characterize him otherwise than by his excellencies in his art, and certain foibles in his behaviour, which he was never studious to conceal: accordingly we are told that he had a great appetite, and that when he was provoked he would break out into profane expressions.

Mainwaring, Hawkins and Burney all refer to Handel's epicurean tendencies, and Mainwaring, being the earliest, is perhaps the most authoritative. He describes Handel as (pp.140–1)

> a person always habituated to an uncommon portion of food and nourishment. Those who have blamed him for an excessive indulgence in this lowest of gratifications, ought to have considered, that the peculiarities of his constitution were as great as those of his character ... Not that I would absolve him from

[54] *A General History*, ii, 913.
[55] *Ibid.*, p. 911.

all blame on this article. He certainly paid more attention to it, than is becoming in any man: but it is some excuse, that Nature had given him so vigorous a constitution, so exquisite a palate, and so craving an appetite; and that fortune enabled him to obey these calls, to satisfy these demands of Nature ... Besides the several circumstances just alledged, there is yet another in his favour; I mean his incessant and intense application to the studies of his profession. This rendered constant and large supplies of nourishment the more necessary to recruit his exhausted spirits. Had he hurt his health or his fortune by indulgences of this kind, they would have been vicious: as he did not, they were at most indecorous.

Burney takes Hawkins's hint about 'profane expressions' one stage further:[56]

He was impetuous, rough, and peremptory in his manners and conversation, but totally devoid of ill-nature or malevolence; indeed, there was an original humour and pleasantry in his most lively sallies of anger or impatience, which, with his broken English, were extremely risible. His natural propensity to wit and humour, and happy manner of relating common occurrences, in an uncommon way, enabled him to throw persons and things into very ridiculous attitudes.

And, although Burney was given to 'first-person' anecdotes of dubious authenticity,[57] the following vignette allows a glimpse of the sociable Handel, though the Germanized voice need perhaps not be taken too seriously:[58]

Besides seeing HANDEL, myself, at his own house, in Brook-street, and at Carlton-House, where he had rehearsals of his Oratorios, by meeting him at Mrs. Cibber's, and, at Frasi's, who was then my scholar, I acquired considerable knowledge of his private character, and turn for humour. He was very fond of Mrs. Cibber, whose voice and manners had softened his severity for her want of musical knowledge. At her house, of a Sunday evening, he used to meet Quin [the actor James Quin], who, in spite of native roughness, was very fond of Music. Yet the first time Mrs. Cibber prevailed on HANDEL to sit down to the harpsichord, while he was present, on which occasion I remember the great Musician played the overture in *Siroe*, and delighted us all with the marvellous neatness with which he played the jig, at the end of it. – Quin, after HANDEL was gone, being asked by Mrs. Cibber, whether he did not think Mr. HANDEL had a charming hand? replied – *a hand* madam! you mistake, it's a *foot* – 'Poh! poh! says she, has he not a fine finger?' '*Toes*, by G –, madam!' – Indeed, his hand was then so fat, that the knuckles, which usually appear convex, were like those of a child, dinted or dimpled in, so as to be rendered concave; however, his touch was so smooth, and the tone of the instrument so much cherished, that his fingers seemed to grow to the keys. They were so curved

---

[56] *An Account of the Musical Performances*, 'Sketch of the Life of Handel', pp. 31–2.

[57] As in the story of the rehearsal of *Messiah* at Chester, in which the bass singer failed to sing the music at 'first sight': see Cudworth, 'Mythistorica Handeliana'.

[58] Burney, *An Account of the Musical Performances*, 'Sketch of the Life of Handel', pp. 34–7.

and compact, when he played, that no motion, and scarcely the fingers themselves, could be discovered.

At Frasi's, I remember, in the year 1748, he brought, in his pocket, the duet of *Judas Macchabaeus*, 'From these dread Scenes,' in which she had not sung when that Oratorio was first performed, in 1746 [*recte* 1747]. At the time he sat down to the harpsichord, to give her and me the time of it, while he sung her part I hummed, at sight, the second, over his shoulder; in which he encouraged me, by desiring that I would sing out – but, unfortunately, something went wrong, and HANDEL, with his usual impetuosity, grew violent: a circumstance very terrific to a young musician. – At length, however, recovering from my fright, I ventured to say, that I fancied there was a mistake in the writing; which, upon examining, HANDEL discovered to be the case: and then, instantly, with the greatest good humour and humility, said 'I pec your barton – I am a very odd tog: – maishter Schmitt is to plame.'

When Frasi told him, that she should study hard, and was going to learn Thorough-Base, in order to accompany herself: HANDEL, who well knew how little this pleasing singer was addicted to application and diligence, says, 'Oh – vaat may we not expect!'

HANDEL wore an enormous white wig, and, when things went well at the Oratorio, it had a certain nod, or vibration, which manifested his pleasure and satisfaction. Without it, nice observers were certain that he was out of humour.

At the close of an air, the voice with which he used to cry out, CHORUS! was extremely formidable indeed; and, at the rehearsals of his Oratorios, at Carleton-House, if the prince and princess of Wales were not exact in coming into the Music-Room, he used to be very violent ...

HANDEL was in the habit of talking to himself, so loud, that it was easy for persons not very near him, to hear the subject of his soliloquies. He had, by much persuasion, received under his roof and protection, a boy, who had been represented, not only as having an uncommon disposition for music, but for sobriety and diligence: this boy, however, turned out ill, and ran away, no one, for a considerable time, knew whither. During this period, HANDEL walking in the Park, as he thought, alone, was heard to commune with himself in the following manner. – 'Der teifel! de fater vas desheeved; – de mutter vas desheeved; – but I vas not desheeved; – he is ein t-d shcauntrel – and coot for nutting.'

In the end, of course, it is Handel's music that counts most, and admittedly some of the frustrations of our imperfect knowledge about Handel's personality are generated by a natural, if often misguided, attempt to interpret the one from the other. On a more prosaic level, there is obviously an important interaction between Handel's music and his life: the course of his career defined the type of music that he wrote at any given time. But this overlooks many important things, such as Handel's own artistic imperatives, which led him to develop his music in certain ways and to try new things on his audiences, some of which (as with *Israel in Egypt*) received a less than enthusiastic reception. Handel obviously attracted some regular supporters during his lifetime, many of whom were clearly intelligent and musical. Their support did not preclude moments of criticism. Jennens wrote on one occasion: 'I am sorry I mention'd my Italian Musick to Handel, for I don't like to have him borrow from them who has so much a better fund of his own'.[59] Other musicians of the time reacted more strongly to Handel and his music. In the 1750s Charles Avison became locked in a public argument with William Hayes about the quality of Handel's music. Avison's conclusion is forcefully expressed:[60]

> Mr HANDEL is in Music, what his own DRYDEN was in Poetry; nervous, exalted, and harmonious; but voluminous, and, consequently, not always correct. Their Abilities equal to every Thing; their Execution frequently inferior. Born with Genius capable of *soaring the boldest Flights*; they have sometimes, to suit the vitiated Taste of the Age they lived in, *descended to the lowest*. Yet, as both their Excellencies are infinitely more numerous than their Deficiencies, so both their Characters will devolve to latest Posterity, not as Models of Perfection, yet glorious Examples of those amazing Powers that actuate the human Soul.

There is much justice in this assessment, provided the phrase about the 'Execution' being 'inferior' is not taken as referring to careless craftsmanship from Handel. Rather, the substance of Avison's argument is closer to Mainwaring's criticism (p. 180) that 'To speak the plain truth, HANDEL was not so excellent in Air, where there is no strong character to mark, or passion to express'. But where 'strong character' is lacking, however, Handel's sheer compositional skill nevertheless usually has a way of carrying him – and the listener – through. Handel deserves his place as one of the giants of the late Baroque. Hawkins shall have the last word:[61]

> The character of an author is but the necessary result of his works, and as the compositions of Handel are many and various, it is but justice to point out such of them as seem the most likely to be the foundation of his future fame. Many of the excellencies, which as a musician recommended him to the favour and patronage of the public during a residence of fifty years in this country, he might perhaps possess in common with a few of the most eminent of his contemporaries; but, till they were taught the contrary by Handel, none were aware of that dignity and grandeur of sentiment which music is capable of conveying, or that there is a sublime in music as there is in poetry. This is a discovery which we owe to the genius and inventive faculty of this great man; and there is little reason to doubt that the many examples of this kind with which his works abound, will continue to engage the admiration of judicious hearers as long as the love of harmony shall exist.

[59] Letter to Holdsworth, 21 February 1742/3.
[60] *Reply to the Author of Remarks on the Essay on Musical Expression*, February 1753: Deutsch, p. 736; *HHB*, p. 468.
[61] *A General History*, ii, 914.

Appendix A

Calendar

Dates for events in Britain are in Old Style (O.S.) to September 1752, and New Style (N.S.) thereafter; elsewhere New Style was in use from 1700, and in Italy before that date.

Codes for performance venues, and other abbreviations, are as in Appendix B. Theatre works 1711–34 were given at the Queen's Theatre, Haymarket (King's Theatre from 1714), unless otherwise indicated, and those from 1746 onwards at Covent Garden. From 1729, when Handel effectively took over the management of complete seasons, the overall dates of his theatrical seasons are given; between 1710 and 1741 the season normally crossed over the calendar year. In the lists of works given in these seasons, * indicates a work receiving its first performance. Works named in the 'Life' column are by Handel, unless otherwise indicated. For dates of composition etc., the conventions used in Appendix B apply.

British rulers are named without a country of identification. Figures in brackets denote the age reached by the person mentioned during the year in question, or at the time of death. The ages of a number of people relevant to Handel's London career are given under 1710, the year of his arrival.

Year	Age	Life	Contemporary musicians and events
1685		Georg Friedrich Händel born, 23 Feb., at Halle, son of Georg Händel (63), surgeon, and his second wife Dorothea (née Taust, 34). Bapt. Marktkirche, 24 Feb.	Albinoni aged 14; Ariosti 19; Blow 36; Böhm 24; G. Bononcini 15; Buxtehude c.48; Caldara c.15; Charpentier c.40; Clarke c.11; Corelli 32; F. Couperin 17; d'Anglebert 50; Fux 25; Graupner 2; Keiser 11; Kerll 58; J. Krieger 33; J.P. Krieger 36; Kuhnau 25; Lalande 28; Legrenzi 59; Lotti 18; Lully 53; Mattheson 4; Georg Muffat 32; Pachelbel 32; Pasquini 48; Purcell 26; Rameau 2; Reinken 62; A. Scarlatti 25; Steffani 31; N.A. Strungk 45; Telemann 4; G.B. Vitali 53; T.A. Vitali 22; Vivaldi 7. Death of King Charles II, 6 Feb.; succeeded by King James II.

Year	Age	Life	Contemporary musicians and events
			J.S. Bach born in Eisenach, 21 Mar. John Gay born, 30 June. Louis XIV revokes Edict of Nantes, 18 Oct.
1686	1		D. Scarlatti born, 26 Oct. B. Marcello born, 24 July or 1 Aug.; Porpora born, 17 Aug. Huguenots granted the use of the Domkirche in Halle. League of Augsburg against Louis XIV.
1687	2		Lully (54) dies, 22 Mar.; Geminiani born (bapt. Dec.); Galliard born (?).
1688	3		J.F. Fasch born, 15 Apr. French invade Palatinate, 25 Sep. William of Orange lands at Torbay, 5 Nov.; James II leaves London for France, 23 Dec. War of the League of Augsburg (–1697). Steffani becomes Kapellmeister at Hanover (–1696).
1689	4		Carey born (?). King William III and Queen Mary II proclaimed, 13 Feb.; coronation 11 Apr.
1690	5		Legrenzi (c.63) dies, 27 May; Gottlieb Muffat born (bapt. 25 Apr.).
1691	6		d'Anglebert (c.55) dies, 23 Apr.
1692	7	Visits Saxon court at Weissenfels, where Duke Johann Adolf hears him play the organ and advises his father (70) to let him have competent tuition. Begins to study under Zachow (29).	Tartini born, 8 Apr.; G.B. Vitali (60) dies, 12 Oct. Electoral status granted to Dukes of Hanover, 19 Dec.
1693	8		Kerll (65) dies, 13 Feb.
1694	9		Daquin born, 4 July; Leo born, 5 Aug. Purcell's D major *Te Deum* and *Jubilate* perf. on St Cecilia's Day (22 Nov.). Mary II (32) dies, 28 Dec. Foundation of Halle University

Year	Age	Life	Contemporary musicians and events
1695	10		Giuseppe Sammartini born, 6 Jan. P. Locatelli born. Purcell (36) dies, 21 Nov.
1696	11	? Plays at the Prussian court, Berlin.	Greene born, 12 Aug. Vinci born (?).
1697	12	Death of father (75), 14 Feb.	Quantz born, 30 Jan; Leclair born, 10 May August, Elector of Saxony, becomes Roman Catholic and is elected King of Poland, June. Treaty/Peace of Ryswick, Sep./Oct.: France recognizes non-Jacobite succession in Britain and waives claims to the Palatinate. Hogarth born, 10 Nov.
1698	13		Francke establishes charitable endowments in Halle. Ernst August of Hanover dies; succeeded by Georg Ludwig.
1699	14		Hasse born (bapt. Mar.). Racine (*c.*59) dies, 22 Apr.
1700	15		German Protestant states adopt Gregorian Calendar. Dryden (68) dies, 30 Apr. N.A. Strungk (*c.*60) dies, 23 Sep. Charles II of Spain dies, 1 Nov.; Louis XIV's grandson Philip named as his heir. G.B. Sammartini born. Second 'Northern War' in Europe (−1721).
1701	16	First communion at Halle Marktkirche, Apr. ?First contact with Telemann (20) in Leipzig.	Act of Settlement provides for eventual Hanoverian succession in Britain, 12 June. James II dies, 16 Sep.; Louis XIV recognizes 'Old Pretender' as James III. War of the Spanish Succession (−1714).
1702	17	Registers as a student at Halle University, 10 Feb. Appointed organist at Domkirche, Halle, 13 Mar., in succession to Leporin.	William III (51) dies, 8 Mar. Succeeded by Queen Anne (37). England, Holland and the Emperor declare war on France, 4 May.

Year	Age	Life	Contemporary musicians and events
1703	18	Handel's last recorded communion in Halle, 6 Apr. By June/July arrives in Hamburg, where he is befriended by Mattheson (22); they visit Lübeck together. Joins Hamburg Opera as a back-desk violinist. Compositions include arias and cantatas.	C.H. Graun born; Lampe born. St Petersburg founded.
1704	19	In Keiser's absence (1704–5), plays harpsichord at Hamburg opera house. Quarrels with Mattheson (23) during the latter's *Cleopatra* (5 Dec.); reconciled (30 Dec.). Composes first opera, *Almira* (German/Italian), and possibly second, *Nero*.	Georg Muffat (*c*.50) dies, 23 Feb.; Charpentier (*c*.59) dies, 24 Feb.; Biber (50) dies, 3 May. Battle of Blenheim, 13 Aug.
1705	20	*Almira* produced at HTG, 8 Jan.; runs for *c*.20 performances. *Nero* produced 25 Feb. Keiser (31) returns to direct opera company, Aug. Handel may have left opera and taken pupils.	Clayton's English opera *Arsinoe* at DL, 16 Jan. Greber's Italian opera *Gli amori d'Ergasto* opens QT (designed and managed by Vanbrugh), 9 Apr.
1706	21	Composes the operas *Florindo* and *Daphne* (originally one work, but divided because of its length). Leaves Hamburg for Italy, probably going first to Florence.	Pachelbel (*c*.52) dies (buried 9 Mar.). Bononcini's *Camilla* perf. (in English translation) at DL, 30 Mar. G.B. Martini born, 24 Apr.; Habermann born, 20 Sep.; Galuppi born, 18 Oct.
1707	22	In Rome by 14 Jan.: cantata HWV99 completed by 12 Feb. Composes *Il trionfo del Tempo* (*c*.Mar.–Apr.) and *Dixit Dominus* (Apr.). Composes *Laudate, pueri* and *Nisi Dominus* (July), and other music possibly for Carmelite service (16 July). Cantatas and motets composed for Ruspoli. Composes *Rodrigo*, perf. Florence (*c*.Nov.). At end of year possibly goes to Venice for	Union of England and Scotland, 1 May. Buxtehude (*c*.70) dies, 9 May. Imperial troops take Naples, Aug. Valentini, castrato, performs in London. Clarke (*c*.33) dies, 1 Dec.

Year	Age	Life	Contemporary musicians and events
		carnival season: ?meets A. Scarlatti.	
1708	23	*Florindo* and *Daphne* produced in Hamburg, ? in his absence (Jan.). In Rome by 3 Mar. (Cantata HWV127a). *La Resurrezione* perf. 8 Apr., with orchestra led by Corelli. Goes to Naples: completes *Aci, Galatea e Polifemo* 16 June (for wedding of Duke of Alvito), and Italian trio (HWV201). Probably returns to Rome (cantata HWV143 perf. 9 Sep.). Possibly goes to Florence and Venice at end of year.	Lord Chamberlain's order gives QT exclusive rights to perform operas, 13 Jan. J.S. Bach appointed organist and chamber musician to Duke Wilhelm Ernst at Weimar, June. Blow (*c.*59) dies, 1 Oct. Nicolini, castrato, first performs in London (QT, 14 Dec.).
1709	24	Possibly in Rome spring/summer, then Florence. Goes to Venice, ?early Dec. Composes *Agrippina* (perf. VSG, ?26 Dec.). Probably encouraged by Hanoverian and English visitors in Venice.	Avison born (bapt. Feb.); F. Benda born, 25 Nov.; F.X. Richter born, 1 Dec. First British Copyright Act.
1710	25	Leaves Venice, ? late Feb., and travels via Innsbruck (? and Halle) to Hanover. Arrives by 4 June, appointed Kapellmeister to elector on 16 June. Briefly visits family in Halle. Visits Düsseldorf court, ?Aug.–Sep., and is well received. Arrives in London, Nov.–Dec.	Pergolesi born, 4 Jan.; T.A. Arne born (bapt. May). Harley and St John form Tory ministry, 8 Aug.: parliament returned with Tory majority, Nov. Pasquini (72) dies, 21 Nov.; W.F. Bach born, 22 Nov. South Sea Company formed. Croft 32; John Eccles *c.*42; Galliard *c.*23; Greene 14; Pepusch 43; Weldon 34; Arbuthnot 43; Fielding 3; Gay 25; Heidegger 44; Pope 22; Vanbrugh 46.
1711	26	Composes *Rinaldo*, ? Jan.–Feb. Performs for Queen Anne (46) at St James's Palace, with singers from the QT opera company, 6 Feb. First perf. of *Rinaldo* at QT, 24 Feb. (15 perfs. to end of opera season, 2 June); songs published at end	Boyce born, Sep.; Holzbauer born, 17 Sep. Marlborough dismissed from office, 31 Dec. Wren (79) paid for 'completion' of St Paul's Cathedral. London Academy of Arts opened under Kneller.

Handel

Year	Age	Life	Contemporary musicians and events
		of Apr. Returns via Düsseldorf (June) to Hanover, where he composes Italian duets and probably completes Cantata HWV 122.	Steele and Addison found *The Spectator*.
1712	27	Jan.–Apr. *Rinaldo* perf. 9 times at QT, in Handel's absence. Returns to London before mid-Oct. Completes *Il pastor fido*, 24 Oct.; first perf. at QT 22 Nov. (6 perfs. to 27 Dec.). Completes *Teseo* 19 Dec. Stays for periods in 1712–13 with the Earl of Burlington and 'Mr Andrews of Barn-Elms'.	Peace Congress opens at Utrecht, 12 Jan. English–French truce 16 July. Zachow (48) dies, 7 Aug. J.C. Smith jr born.
1713	28	First perf. of *Teseo*, 10 Jan (13 perfs. to 16 May). Completes Utrecht *Te Deum*, 13 Jan.; soon after, completes *Jubilate* and Birthday Ode for Queen Anne. Owen Swiney leaves London mid-Jan. and Heidegger takes up management of QT opera; Handel given benefit night in May. Rehearsals for Utrecht music, Mar., well received. *Rinaldo* revived in May (2 perfs.) Handel dismissed from Hanoverian post. Probably composes *Silla*, Apr.–May; ? perf. 2 June. Utrecht Thanksgiving Service at St Paul's Cathedral, 7 July. Granted annual pension by Queen Anne, 28 Dec.	Corelli (59) dies, 8 Jan. Peace of Utrecht, Apr./June. J.S. Bach visits Weissenfels, Feb., and competes for Zachow's former post in Halle, 3 Dec. (declines offer of appointment in Feb. 1714). Couperin's first book of *Pieces de clavecin* published in Paris.
1714	29	*Te Deum* settings perf. in Chapel Royal to mark arrival of Hanoverian family, 26 Sep., 17 Oct. KT opera season begins 23 Oct.: *Rinaldo* revived 30 Dec.	C.P.E. Bach born, 8 Mar.; Gluck born, 2 July. Harley (Lord Oxford) dismissed, 27 July; Sunderland appointed Secretary of State. Whig ministry formed under Townshend, Sep. Jommelli born, 10 Sep.
1715	30	Further perfs. of *Rinaldo*, from 4 Jan. (9 perfs. to 19 Feb) Composes *Amadigi*	Wagenseil born, 29 Jan.; Alcock born, 11 Apr.; Nares born, 19 Apr.

Year	Age	Life	Contemporary musicians and events
		? Apr/May: first perf. 25 May (6 perfs. to 9 July). Also further revival of *Rinaldo*, 25 June. Royal water parties, some with music, though Handel not named as composer, July–Aug. Paid final arrears of Hanover salary, 10 Oct.	Harley imprisoned, July. Death of Louis XIV, 1 Sep.; Louis XV under a regency until 1723. Jacobite rising in Scotland, 6 Sep.; defeated at Preston and Sheriffmuir, 13 Nov.
1716	31	? Composes *Brockes Passion.* Opera season begins late, 1 Feb. *Amadigi* revived on 16 Feb. (6 perfs. to 12 July): for revival on 20 June, composes Concerto op.3 no.4. ?Travels to Germany in second half of year, possibly persuading Johann Christoph Schmidt to come to London from Ansbach. New opera season opens in London, 8 Dec.	Croft's music performed at royal thanksgiving service, St Paul's Cathedral, Jan. Old Pretender in Scotland, Jan.–Feb. J.S. Bach examines new organs at Liebfrauenkirche, Halle, 29 Apr.–2 May. Townshend dismissed, 15 Dec.
1717	32	*Rinaldo* revived, 5 Jan., presumably with Handel present, including new music (10 perfs. to 5 June); *Amadigi* revived, 16 Feb. (4 perfs. to 30 May). Opera season closes 29 June; end of the present KT opera management. Handel's music played at king's water party on Thames, 17 July. Handel at Cannons by 4 Aug.; 4 anthems for James Brydges, Earl of Carnarvon, composed by end of Sep. Anthems (and 'Cannons' *Te Deum*) perf. at St Lawrence's Church (1717–18).	Triple alliance (England, France, Holland), Jan 4. Walpole resigns, 10 Apr. J. Stamitz born (bapt. 19 June). J.S. Bach appointed Kapellmeister to Prince Leopold at Cöthen, 5 Aug. Prince and Princess of Wales set up alternative court at Leicester House, Nov., following argument at royal christening.
1718	33	Handel probably in residence at Cannons: completes anthems for Brydges. Composes *Acis and Galatea*, ?May–June, which is probably perf. at Cannons; *Esther* also possibly composed and perf. there. Begins to assemble a repertory of his keyboard music: several autographs from this period. Younger sister, Johanne (28),	New Cabinet, led by Sunderland and Stanhope, Mar. Quadruple Alliance (Emperor, England, France, Holland), 2 Aug. England declares war on Spain, 28 Dec.

Year	Age	Life	Contemporary musicians and events
		dies in Halle, 8 Aug.	
1719	34	'New Concerto' by Handel perf. at concert in Hickford's Room, 18 Feb. Formation of the Royal Academy of Music for the production of opera, Feb. onwards: royal charter, 27 July. Earl of Carnarvon (47) created Duke of Chandos, Apr. Lord Chamberlain commands Handel to visit the Continent to engage singers for the Academy, 14 May; travels, possibly via Düsseldorf, to Halle, and then to Dresden (by 15 July), where he negotiates for singers (only Durastanti is available immediately). Probably meets Lotti (*c*.52) and attends Dresden operas (as part of Saxon wedding celebrations) in Sep. Appointed 'Master of the Orchestra' to the Academy, 30 Nov. Returns to London at end of year or early 1720.	Alliance of Vienna (Emperor, Britain, Hanover, Saxony, Poland, against Russia and Prussia), 5 Jan. France declares war on Spain, 9 Jan. Unsuccessful Spanish invasion of Scotland, 13 Apr.–10 June. Leopold Mozart born, 14 Nov. Peace between Sweden and Hanover, 20 Nov.
1720	35	Composes *Radamisto*, ?March. Royal Academy of Music opens at KT, 2 Apr., with Porta's *Numitore*. First night of *Radamisto*, 27 Apr., attended by king and Prince of Wales (7 further perfs. to 22 June; season ends 25 June). Royal warrant to Handel for sole right to publication of his music for 14 years, 14 June. Keyboard suites (First Collection) published 'for the author', Nov. Second Academy season opens, 19 Nov., with *Astarto* by Bononcini (50): début of Senesino in London. *Radamisto* revived, much revised for new cast, 28 Dec.; also perf. 31 Dec.	Treaty of Stockholm (Sweden/Prussia), 1 Feb. Peace between Quadruple Alliance and Spain, 17 Feb. Reconciliation of king and Prince of Wales, 23 Apr.: Walpole and Townshend re-enter government. 'South Sea Bubble' collapses, Oct.–Dec. J.S. Bach visits Hamburg and declines post as organist at Jacobikirche.
1721	36	5 perfs. of *Radamisto* (4 Jan.– 25 Mar.). Completes *Muzio*	Death of Stanhope, 4 Feb. J.S. Bach dedicates concertos to

Year	Age	Life	Contemporary musicians and events
		Scevola, Act 3, 23 Mar.: first perf. 15 Apr. (9 more perfs. to 7 June). Academy season ends 1 July. New Handel cantata (?HWV97) sung at Durastanti benefit concert (KT), 5 July. Third Academy season opens, 1 Nov.; *Radamisto* revived 25 Nov. (4 perfs. to 6 Dec). Completes *Floridante*, 28 Nov.; first perf. 9 Dec. (6 more perfs. to 30 Dec.).	Margrave of Brandenburg, 24 Mar. Kirnberger born, Apr. Walpole appointed First Lord of Treasury and Chancellor of the Exchequer, 3 Apr.; restores public credit. Defensive alliance between Britain, France and Spain, 21 June.
1722	37	8 further perfs. of *Floridante* (3 Jan.–26 May). Academy declares its only dividend, Feb.; season ends, 16 June. Handel completes draft score of *Ottone*, 10 Aug. Chapel Royal service, probably with music by Handel, marks king's return to St James's, 7 Oct. Academy season opens late with revival of *Muzio Scevola*, 7–13 Nov. Revival of *Floridante*, 4 Dec. (7 perfs. to 26 Dec.), including new arias. Cuzzoni arrives in London, Dec.	G. Benda born, June; Kuhnau (62) dies, 5 June. Duke of Marlborough dies, 16 June: funeral (WA), 9 Aug., with anthem by Bononcini. 'Atterbury Plot' exposed: Habeas Corpus Act suspended, Oct. Reinken (99) dies, 24 Nov.; Nardini born. J.S. Bach enters candidature for cantorate at Leipzig, Dec.
1723	38	First perf. of *Ottone*, 12 Jan., and London début of Cuzzoni (14 perfs. to 8 June). Granted annual pension as 'Composer of Musick' for the Chapel Royal, 25 Feb. 'New Concerto for French Horns' perf. at DL, 20 Mar. Completes score of *Flavio*, 7 May: first perf. 14 May (8 perfs. to 15 June, ending Academy season). Established as music master to royal princesses by 9 June. Moves into London house at Brook Street in July. Fifth Academy season opens, 27 Nov. *Ottone* revived, 11 Dec. (6 perfs. to 1 Jan. 1724). *Giulio Cesare* probably drafted during	Petition against 'ridottos' (masquerades) at KT, Feb. Wren (90) dies, 25 Feb. Gassmann born, 3 May. J.S. Bach takes up posts in Leipzig, May. Treaty of Charlottenburg (Britain and Prussia), 12 Oct. Kneller (74) dies, 19 Oct.

Year	Age	Life	Contemporary musicians and events
		1723, later substantially revised.	
1724	39	Handel's music perf. at Chapel Royal service marking king's return from Hanover, 5 Jan. First perf. of *Giulio Cesare*, 20 Feb. (13 perfs. to 11 Apr). End of Academy season, 13 June. Drafts score of *Tamerlano*, 3–24 July. Plays organ in St Paul's Cathedral to royal princesses, 24 Aug. Sixth Academy season opens, 31 Oct., with first perf. of *Tamerlano* (9 perfs. to 28 Nov). London début of tenor Borosini, for whom Handel revises score before perf. Composes 'Solo Sonatas' for vn, gamba, rec and bc (*c.*1724–6).	Theile (77) dies, June. Controversy over Wood's coinage in Ireland: Carteret appointed Lord Lieutenant, 1 Apr. First perf. of J.S. Bach's *St John Passion*, Nikolaikirche, Leipzig, 7 Apr.
1725	40	*Giulio Cesare* revived 2 Jan. (10 perfs. to 9 Feb.). Completes score of *Rodelinda*, 20 Jan.: first perf. 13 Feb. (14 perfs. to 6 Apr.). *Tamerlano* revived 1–8 May (3 perfs.). Score of *Rodelinda* published by subscription, 6 May. First perf. of *Elpidia*, 11 May, Handel's first London pasticcio (10 perfs. to 19 June, ending season). Seventh Academy season opens 30 Nov., with revival of *Elpidia* (4 perfs. to 11 Dec.). *Rodelinda* revived, 18 Dec. (4 perfs. to 28 Dec.). J.C. Smith jr (13) becomes Handel's pupil around this period.	J.P. Krieger (*c.*76) dies, 6 Feb. Peter the Great of Russia dies, 8 Feb.; succeeded by Catherine I. Treaty of Vienna (Austria, Spain), 1 May. Spain guarantees Pragmatic Sanction, Austria supports Spain's claim to Gibraltar. Treaty of Herrenhausen (Britain, France, Prussia), 23 Sep. A. Scarlatti (65) dies, 22 Oct.
1726	41	*Rodelinda* revival continues (4 perfs., 1–11 Jan.). Handel's music perf. at Chapel Royal service marking king's return from Hanover, 16 Jan. *Ottone* revived 8 Feb. (9 perfs. to 8 Mar.). Commences score of *Alessandro*, but completion delayed until after arrival of	First meeting of Academy Vocal Musick, 7 Jan. Vanbrugh (62) dies, 26 Mar. Lalande (68) dies, 18 June. Austria and Palatinate agree to oppose Prussia's claims to Jülich-Berg, Aug. Philidor born, 7 Sept Cardinal Fleury becomes chief

Year	Age	Life	Contemporary musicians and events
		Faustina, Mar. Completes *Scipione* 2 Mar.; first perf. 12 Mar. (13 perfs. to 30 Apr.). Completes *Alessandro*, 11 Apr.; first perf. 5 May (London début of Faustina; 13 perfs. to 7 June, closing season). Completes *Admeto*, 10 Nov. Start of next season delayed until Senesino's return.	minister in France (–1743).
1727	42	Eighth Academy season opens 7 Jan. with Ariosti's *Lucio Vero*. First perf. of *Admeto*, 31 Jan. (19 perfs. to 18 Apr.). Royal assent to bill including Handel's British naturalization, 20 Feb. Revivals of *Ottone* and *Floridante*, 11 Apr.–2 May (2 perfs. each), followed by Bononcini's *Astianatte*: disturbance at perf. on 6 June closes season abruptly. Completes draft score of *Riccardo Primo*, 16 May. Ninth Academy season opens 30 Sep. with revival of *Admeto* (6 perfs. to 4 Nov.). Coronation of King George II and Queen Caroline (WA), with four anthems by Handel, 11 Oct. (rehearsals 6, 9 Oct.). First perf. of *Riccardo Primo*, 11 Nov. (11 perfs. to 16 Dec.); *Alessandro* revived, 30 Dec. Composes Sonata for fl, bc HWV379 (*c.* 1727–8).	War between Britain and Spain, Feb.: siege of Gibraltar. Newton (84) dies, 20 Mar. First perf. of J.S. Bach's *St Matthew Passion*, Thomaskirche, Leipzig, ?11 Apr. King George I dies at Osnabrück, on journey to Hanover, 11 June; George II proclaimed in London, 15 June. Croft (49) dies, 14 Aug. Chauvelin, leader of anti-English party, appointed French foreign secretary. Peter II becomes Tsar of Russia (–1730).
1728	43	*Alessandro* revival continues, 2 Jan., followed by revival of *Radamisto* (*c.*7 perfs.). Completes *Siroe*, 5 Feb.: first perf. 17 Feb. (18 perfs. to 27 Apr.). Completes *Tolomeo*, 19 Apr.; first perf. 30 Apr. (7 perfs. to 21 May). Revival of *Admeto*, 25 May (3 perfs. to 1 June, closing the last Royal Academy season). Heidegger travels to	*The Beggar's Opera* (Gay and Pepusch) opens at LIF, 29 Jan. Steffani (75) dies, 12 Feb. Convention of Prado ends war between Britain and Spain, 6 Mar. Marais (72) dies, 15 Aug. Frederick, eldest son of King George II, arrives in London from Hanover, Dec. Treaty of Berlin (Emperor,

Year	Age	Life	Contemporary musicians and events
		Continent in June to try to secure singers for a new season: 35 subscribers had signified their interest.	Prussia), 23 Dec. J.A. Hiller born, 25 Dec.
1729	44	Royal Academy management terminated, 18 Jan. Handel and Heidegger granted the use of KT and the Academy's capital assets (costumes, scenery etc.) for 5 years to perform operas under their own management. Handel leaves for Italy to collect a cast, end of Jan. or beginning of Feb.; arrives in Venice by 11 Mar. (N.S.) and goes to Bologna, Rome and ?Naples. Fails to secure Farinelli, but engages Bernacchi, Strada and Fabri. Returns via Germany (?Halle and Hanover) to London, arriving 29 June. Death of Nicola Haym, 11 Aug., and of Ariosti during summer. Handel and his new opera soloists perform before the king and queen at Kensington, 10 Oct. Completes *Lotario*, 16 Nov.; first perf. 2 Dec., opening first Handel/Heidegger opera season at KT (7 perfs. to 23 Dec.).	Heinichen (46) dies, 16 July. Treaty of Seville (Britain and Spain, subsequently joined by France, Holland), 9 Nov.; ends Austro-Spanish alliance.
1730	45	Completes *Partenope*, 12 Feb. Season continues with *Lotario* (2 perfs.), revival of *Giulio Cesare* (11 perfs.), *Partenope** (7 perfs.), *Ormisda** (pasticcio, 14 perfs.), revival of *Tolomeo* (7 perfs., ending season 13 June). Plays new organ (rebuilt from 'Coronation' organ) at Westminster Abbey, 8 Aug. Senesino returns to London (by Oct.). Second Handel/Heidegger season opens 3 Nov. with revivals of *Scipione* (6 perfs.), *Ormisda* (5	Dispute between Walpole and Townshend, 15 May: Townshend resigns. Vinci (*c*.40) dies, 27 or 28 May; J.B. Loeillet (49) dies (in London), 19 July. Victor Amadeus II of Savoy abdicates, 30 Sep. Senaillé (43) dies, 15 Oct. Anne, daughter of Ivan IV, succeeds Peter II of Russia (–1747). Christian VI becomes King of Denmark (–1746). Senate House, Cambridge, built

Year	Age	Life	Contemporary musicians and events
		perfs.) and *Partenope* (4 perfs. to end of year). Handel's mother dies in Halle, 27 Dec. (N.S.)	(designed by James Gibbs).
1731	46	Season continues with *Partenope* (3 perfs.), *Venceslao** (pasticcio, 4 perfs.), *Poro** (14 perfs.), revivals of *Rinaldo* (6 perfs.) and *Rodelinda* (8 perfs.), ending the season on 29 May. 'Utrecht' *Te Deum* and *Jubilate* perf. at Academy of Vocal Music, under Gates, 14 Jan. Completes *Poro*, 16 Jan. Annual festival service for Sons of the Clergy at St Paul's Cathedral, 25 Feb., includes 'Utrecht' music and coronation anthems, beginning regular perfs. of Handel's music. Writes to brother-in-law in Halle and sends jewellery for his niece as a wedding present, July/Aug. New bass soloist, Montagnana, joins cast for the next season, which opens 13 Nov. with revivals of *Tamerlano* (3 perfs.), *Poro* (4 perfs.) and *Admeto* (4 perfs. to end of year). Composes *Ezio*, ?Dec., having abandoned *Titus l'Empéreur* at Act 1 scene iii.	Defoe dies, 26 Apr. Treaty of Vienna (Britain, Holland, Spain, Austria), 22 July. *Gentleman's Magazine* first published. J.S. Bach's *Clavier-Übung* Part I published.
1732	47	Completes *Sosarme*, 4 Feb. Season continues with *Admeto* (3 perfs.), *Ezio** (5 perfs.), revival of *Giulio Cesare* (4 perfs.), *Sosarme** (11 perfs.), revival of *Flavio* (4 perfs. to 29 Apr.). *Esther* perf. by Chapel Royal at Crown and Anchor Tavern, 23 Feb. (Handel's birthday). Handel introduces *Esther* into theatre season (his first London theatre oratorio perf.) on 2 May (6 perfs. to 20 May). Handel gives 4 perfs. of	Marchand (63) dies, 17 Feb. Arne/Lampe productions of 'English operas' (including *Acis and Galatea*) at LTH, Mar.–May, Nov.–Dec. Haydn born, 31 Mar. *Teraminta* (Carey and J.C. Smith jr) produced at LIF, Nov. Gay dies, 4 Dec. Opening of Rich's Covent Garden Theatre, 7 Dec. Letters from the 'Lotti madrigal' controversy

Year	Age	Life	Contemporary musicians and events
		pasticcio *Lucio Papirio* (23 May–6 June). Introduces *Acis and Galatea* (as a bilingual 'Serenata') in his theatre season, 10 June (4 perfs. to 20 June, ending KT season). New season opens 4 Nov. with pasticcio *Catone** (5 perfs.) and revivals of *Alessandro* (6 perfs.) and *Acis and Galatea* (4 perfs.). Completes *Orlando*, 20 Nov. Aaron Hill writes to Handel, 5 Dec., asking him to attempt English operas.	published. Beginnings of division between king and Prince of Wales. Pamphlet *See and seem blind* published, including references to formation of a rival opera company to Handel's.
1733	48	Completes *Deborah*, 21 Feb. Theatre season continues with revival of *Tolomeo* (4 perfs.), *Orlando** (10 perfs.), *Deborah** (6 perfs., with controversy over higher ticket prices), then revivals of *Esther* (2 perfs.) and of Bononcini's *Griselda* (ending season on 9 June, when Senesino announces his departure). Handel completes *Athalia*, 7 June: visits Oxford and performs during the 'Act', but does not receive degree. Perfs. at Sheldonian Theatre and Christ Church Hall, Oxford, 5–12 July: *Esther* (2 perfs.), *Athalia** (2 perfs.), *Acis and Galatea* (1 perf.), *Deborah* (1 perf). Handel's church music perf. in university church on 8 July, perhaps not under his direction. Returns to London. Rival opera company (Opera of the Nobility) established, taking Handel's leading singers (except Strada) and employing Porpora as house composer. Handel gathers a new cast with Carestini, Strada and Durastanti. Completes *Arianna in Creta*, 5 Oct. Opens season	J.S. Bach visits Dresden, July, and presents MS of *B Minor Mass* to Elector of Saxony. Couperin (64) dies, 12 Sep. Preparations for wedding of Princess Anne: 'French Chapel', St James's Palace, re-furnished, Oct. Rehearsal of wedding anthem by Greene planned for 27 Oct., but simultaneous announcement that Handel is to write the wedding music. Prince of Orange arrives in London, 7 Nov., but falls ill and wedding postponed. Treaty of the Escorial (France and Spain, against Britain), 7 Nov. Opera of the Nobility opens at LIF with Porpora's *Arianna in Nasso*, 29 Dec.: rehearsed at Prince of Wales's house, 24 Dec. War of the Polish succession (–1735).

Year	Age	Life	Contemporary musicians and events
		30 Oct. with pasticcio *Semiramide**, followed by revival of *Ottone* (4 perfs.) and pasticcio *Caio Fabricio**. displaces Greene as composer of music for forthcoming royal wedding, Nov.: wedding anthem HWV262 rehearsed 5 Nov. Opera attendances fall at this period. Walsh publishes editions of 'solo' and trio sonatas (op.2), at first with spurious 'Roger' title-page, consisting of works composed in earlier years.	
1734	49	Opera season continues with pasticcio *Arbace**, *Arianna in Creta** (16 perfs.), *Parnasso in festa** (serenata, 4 perfs.) and revivals of *Deborah* (3 perfs.), *Sosarme* (3 perfs.), *Acis and Galatea* (1 perf.), *Il pastor fido* (13 perfs., ending season on 6 July). End of Handel's 5-year tenure at KT. Anthem perf. 14 Mar. at wedding of Princess Anne and Prince Willem in 'French Chapel', St James's Palace. Handel attends evening party at Mrs Pendarves's house, Apr. Begins *Ariodante*, 12 Aug. Visits 'the country', returning to London by 27 Aug., having agreed with John Rich for the use of CG theatre. Engages Madame Sallé's dancers for forthcoming season. Completes *Ariodante*, 31 Oct. First CG season opens 9 Nov. with *Il pastor fido* (revival, incorporating new prologue *Terpsicore**, 5 perfs.: London début of tenor John Beard), followed by revival of *Arianna in Creta* (5 perfs.) and *Oreste** (all-Handel pasticcio). Handel's	Empire declares war on France, 1 Jan. French, Sardinian and Spanish troops subsequently defeat Austrians in Italy. Gossec born, 17 Jan. Satirical pamphlet *Harmony in an Uproar* published, 12 Feb. Opera of the Nobility perform Handel's *Ottone* at KT, Dec. J.S. Bach's *Christmas Oratorio* perf. (Dec. 1734–Jan. 1735).

Year	Age	Life	Contemporary musicians and events
		publication privilege expires: Walsh republishes solo and trio sonatas with new title-page, issues 6 Concerti Grossi op.3 and second set of suites.	
1735	50	CG season continues with *Ariodante** (11 perfs.), then oratorios in Lent – *Esther* (6 perfs.), *Deborah* (3 perfs.) and *Athalia* (5 perfs., first London perfs.). Organ concertos introduced between acts of oratorios. Composes *Alcina* during oratorio run, completed 8 Apr.; first perf. 16 Apr. (18 perfs. to end season on 2 July). Handel thanks Jennens for oratorio libretto, 28 July, and mentions forthcoming visit to Tunbridge Wells. In Aug. Walsh publishes 6 keyboard fugues, composed 15–20 years previously. Handel attends Nobility Opera perf., Nov.	Eccles (*c.*67) dies, 12 Jan.; Arbuthnot (67) dies, 27 Feb.; J. Krieger (83) dies, 18 July; J.C. Bach born, 5 Sep. Peace of Vienna, 3 Oct.
1736	51	Completes *Alexander's Feast* 17 Jan. and accompanying concerto HWV318, 25 Jan. Begins second CG season 19 Feb. with English-based works: *Alexander's Feast** (5 perfs.), revivals of *Acis and Galatea* (?bilingual, 2 perfs.) and *Esther* (?bilingual, 2 perfs.). Completes *Atalanta*, 22 Apr. Anthem HWV263 perf. at wedding of Prince of Wales in Chapel Royal, 27 Apr. CG season continues with operas (with Conti as new castrato): *Ariodante* (2 perfs.), *Atalanta** (8 perfs., ending season on 9 June). Prepares for next full opera-based season. Drafts *Giustino*, 14 Aug.–7 Sep., and *Arminio*, 15 Sep.–3 Oct. Arrival of Annibali, second castrato, to	Maria Theresa marries Francis Stephen of Lorraine, 12 Feb. John Walsh sr dies, 13 Mar.; succeeded in business by son.; Pergolesi (26) dies, 16 Mar.; Weldon (60) dies, 7 May. Spain accedes to Treaty of Vienna, 18 May. Porteous Riots in Edinburgh, 7 Sep. Caldara (*c.*66) dies, 28 Dec.

Year	Age	Life	Contemporary musicians and events
		join Conti in CG company, Sep./Oct. Revises *Arminio*, cd. 14 Oct., and *Giustino*, 15–20 Oct. Begins 3rd CG season, 6 Nov., with revivals of *Alcina* (3 perfs.), *Atalanta* (2 perfs.) and *Poro* (4 perfs. to 5 Jan. 1737). Drafts *Berenice* 18 Dec.–18 Jan. 1737.	
1737	52	Completes score of *Berenice*, 27 Jan., and new version of *Il trionfo del Tempo*, 14 Mar. CG season continues with *Arminio** (6 perfs.), revival of *Partenope* (4 perfs.), *Giustino** (9 perfs.), revivals of *Parnasso in festa* (2 perfs.) and *Alexander's Feast* (5 perfs.), new version of *Il trionfo del Tempo** (4 perfs.), revival of *Esther* (2 perfs.), *Didone** (pasticcio) (?3 perfs.), *Berenice** (?3 perfs.), *Alcina* (2 further perfs.). Mrs Clive sings original song by Handel in comedy at DL, 28 Feb. Announcement of subscription for printed complete score of *Alexander's Feast*, c.28 May. CG season ends 25 June: final perf. of Opera of Nobility, 11 June. Handel indisposed during last weeks of season: report of 'paraletick disorder' on 14 May, and 'rheumatism' on 30 Apr. Goes for health-cure to Aix-la-Chapelle, Sep.; returns to London late Oct./early Nov. New opera company, probably managed by Heidegger, opens at KT, 29 Oct., retaining many of Nobility Opera cast and patrons: Handel agrees to compose for them. Composes Acts 1 and 2 of *Faramondo*, 15 Nov.–4 Dec. Funeral Anthem for Queen Caroline, completed	Fall of Chauvelin, French foreign secretary and leader of war party, 20 Feb. Carey (*c.*47) and Lampe (34) produce *The Dragon of Wantley*, partly a parody of *Giustino*, at LTH, May. Stage Licensing Act, 21 June. Death of Gian Gastone, last Medici Grand Duke of Tuscany, 9 July. Prince and Princess of Wales ordered to leave St. James's Palace by the King, 10 Sept. Death of Queen Caroline, 20 Nov. Göttingen University founded by Elector (King George II).

Year	Age	Life	Contemporary musicians and events
		12 Dec.; perf. at funeral (WA, King Henry VII's Chapel), 17 Dec. Completes *Faramondo*, 24 Dec. Composes *Serse*, 26 Dec.–6 Feb. 1738.	
1738	53	KT opera season continues: *Faramondo**, 3 Jan. (8 perfs.), followed by *Alessandro Severo** (all-Handel pasticcio, 6 perfs.). Full score of *Alexander's Feast* published, *c*.8 Mar. Handel benefit night ('An Oratorio') at KT, 28 Mar., reputedly earns £1000. First perf. of *Serse**, 15 Apr. (5 perfs.). First meeting of Fund for the Support of Decay'd Musicians, 23 Apr. (Handel a founder member). Roubiliac statue of Handel erected in Vauxhall Gardens, Apr. Mixed-composer season at KT ends 6 June. Heidegger advertises for a subscription for 1738–9 season, 23 May, but abandons it on 25 July after insufficient response. Handel drafts *Saul*, 23 July–28 Aug. (and possibly later), and *Imeneo*, 9–20 Sep. Visited by Jennens, 18 Sep., to discuss *Saul*; Handel revises it, finishing 27 Sep. Composes *Israel in Egypt*, using music from 1737 funeral anthem, 1 Oct.–1 Nov. First set of organ concertos (op.4) published by Walsh, 4 Oct. Handel prepares for oratorio-based season at KT, presumably having hired the theatre independently from Heidegger.	Battishill born, May. Alliance between France and Sweden, Oct. Definitive Peace Treaty of Vienna, 18 Nov. C.P.E. Bach (24) appointed harpsichordist to Crown Prince Friedrich of Prussia. Two editions of D. Scarlatti's *Essercizi per gravicembalo* published in London. John Wesley starts Methodist revival.
1739	54	KT season, 16 Jan.–5 May: *Saul**, *Alexander's Feast*, *Il trionfo del Tempo*, *Israel in Egypt**, *Jupiter in Argos**. *Saul* (16 Jan.) is last documented	Secret treaty Austria/France to support Wittelsbach claims to Jülich-Berg, Jan.; secret treaty Prussia/France to divide Jülich-Berg, Apr.

Year	Age	Life	Contemporary musicians and events
		attendance of King George II at Handel's theatre performances. Trio Sonatas op.5 published by Walsh, 28 Feb. Handel performs *Alexander's Feast* for benefit of Decay'd Musicians' Fund, 20 Mar. Completes Organ Concerto HWV295, 2 Apr.; completes *Jupiter in Argos*, 24 Apr., using many movements from previous works. Arranges with John Rich for use of LIF theatre next season. Composes *'Song' (Ode) for St Cecilia's Day*, 15–24 Sep., and Concerti Grossi op.6, 29 Sep.–30 Oct. Subscription for publication of concertos advertised, 29 Oct. Granted second 14-year copyright privilege, 31 Oct. LIF season begins 22 Nov.: *Alexander's Feast* with *Ode for St Cecilia's Day**, *Acis and Galatea* (in all-English version, and coupled with *St Cecilia Ode*).	Hickford's Concert Room moves from Poulton St to Brewer St, June: raffle of Clay (musical) clock, and picture of Handel set up in new room. Marcello (53) dies, 24/25 July; Keiser (65) dies, 12 Sep. Royal Charter for Foundling Hospital, 17 Oct. Britain declares war on Spain, 19 Oct. 'Middlesex' company opens with concert perfs. at LTH, 1 Dec.; performers include Carestini. War between British and Spaniards in West Indies.
1740	55	LIF season interrupted by severe frost in London. Composes *L'Allegro, il Penseroso ed il Moderato*, 19 Jan.–4 Feb. Completes Organ Concerto HWV306 (with obbligato pedal part), 17 Feb. LIF season resumes 21 Feb. with *Acis* and *Ode* revival, followed by *L'Allegro**, *Saul*, *Esther*, *Israel in Egypt* (to 23 Apr., completing 'all-English' season). Gives *Acis* and *Ode* at LIF for benefit of Decay'd Musicians Fund, 28 Mar. Op.6 concertos published, 21 Apr. Anthem performed at 'wedding' of Princess Mary in Chapel Royal, 8 May. Handel travels to Continent in summer: in	Lotti (73) dies, 5 Jan. J.S. Bach visits Halle, Apr. Friedrich Wilhelm I of Prussia dies, 31 May; succeeded by Friedrich II ('Frederick the Great'). Samuel Arnold born, 10 Aug. Charles VI, last Habsburg Emperor, dies 20 Oct.; succeeded by Maria Theresa. Michael Arne born, c.1740.

Year	Age	Life	Contemporary musicians and events
		Haarlem 20 Sep. (N.S.); possibly visits Hanover, Berlin and Halle. Returns to London by early Oct. Plans LIF season based on Italian opera: gains castrato Andreoni from 'Middlesex' opera company. Revises and completes *Imeneo* by 10 Oct. Composes Acts 1 and 2 of *Deidamia*, 27 Oct.–7 Nov. Second LIF season begins 8 Nov.: *Parnasso in festa*, *Imeneo**. 'Second Set' of organ concertos published 8 Nov., comprising HWV305–6 and 4 keyboard arrangements form op.6. Composes Act 3 of *Deidamia*, 14–20 Nov.	
1741	56	LIF season continues: *Deidamia**, *L'Allegro*, *Acis*, *Saul*. *Deidamia* (at LTH) on 10 Feb. is his last perf. of Italian opera in London. *Parnasso in festa* perf. at KT, 14 Mar., for Decay'd Musicians fund, possibly not directed by Handel. *L'Allegro*, but with *Il Moderato* replaced by *St Cecilia Ode*, ends his 2nd and last LIF season, 8 Apr. Completes Italian duets HWV192 and 189 on 1, 3 July. Composes *Messiah*, 22 Aug.–14 Sep. Drafts *Samson*, 29 Sep.–29 Oct. Arranges a season in Dublin. Attends first perf. of new 'Middlesex' opera company at KT, 31 Oct. Leaves London for Dublin, arriving 18 Nov.; invited to play again at charity service in St Andrew's Church, 10 Dec. Advertises forthcoming performances, 12 Dec. First subscription at DFS begins 23 Dec. with *L'Allegro* (reinstating *Il Moderato*).	Grétry born, 8 Feb; Fux (81) dies, 13 Feb. Friedrich of Prussia defeats Austrians at Mollwitz, 10 Apr. Vivaldi (63) dies, 28 July. Treaty between France and Prussia against Austria, 15 Aug.; French invade S. Germany, Austria and Bohemia, 15 Aug, and conquer Prague, 26 Nov. George II secures neutrality of Hanover from France, 27 Sep. David Garrick's London *debut* in *King Richard III*, 19 Oct. Elizabeth becomes Empress of Russia (–1762).

Year	Age	Life	Contemporary musicians and events
1742	57	DFS subscription series continues: *L'Allegro*, *Acis* with *Ode*, *Esther*. Swift, Dean of St Patrick's Cathedral, objects to cathedral singers taking part, 28 Jan. 2nd DFS subscription, 17 Feb.–7 Apr.: *Alexander's Feast*, *L'Allegro*, *Imeneo* (as a 'Serenata'), *Esther*. Mrs Cibber joins company, and her illness protracts the end of the season. Announcement, 27 Mar., of forthcoming *Messiah* perf. for benefit of charities and including cathedral choirs. *Messiah** (rehearsed 9 Apr.) perf. 13 Apr. at DFS. *Saul* (25 May) and 2nd perf. of *Messiah* (3 June) complete his Dublin performances. Benefit concert for Mrs Arne, 21 July, in Aungier Street Theatre, Dublin, includes many Handel items (sung by Mrs Arne and Mrs Cibber), though probably not directed by him. Leaves Dublin, 13 Aug., for London (by 9 Sep.). Revises, completes and adds to score of *Samson*, to 12 Oct. Completes Italian duets HWV 181 and 190, 31 Oct., 2 Nov.	Carl Albrecht, Elector of Bavaria, elected Emperor, 24 Jan. Walpole resigns, 2 Feb. Peace of Berlin between Prussia and Austria, 28 July. Anglo-Prussian alliance, 29 Nov. French evacuate Prague, 12 Dec.
1743	58	Sends *Samson* libretto to Inspector of Stage Plays, 10 Jan., in readiness for a season at CG. Completes Organ Concerto HWV307, 5 Feb. CG season, 18 Feb.–31 Mar. (two 6-perf. subscriptions): *Samson**, *L'Allegro* with *Ode*, *Messiah*. First London perf. of *Messiah*, 23 Mar., and article attacking theatre performance of the work in London newspaper. Handel has a return of 'Paraletic Disorder': recovery reported in newspapers 11 Apr.,	Boccherini born, 19 Feb. Forces led by George II defeat French at Dettingen, 27 June. Pelham appointed First Lord of the Treasury, July. Treaty of Worms (Austria, Britain, Sardinia), 13 Sep. Carey (*c.*53) dies, 5 Oct. French/Spanish alliance at Fontainebleau, 25 Oct. George II returns to London, 15 Nov.

Year	Age	Life	Contemporary musicians and events
		but a further relapse follows. Composes *Semele*, 3 June–4 July. Approached by Lord Middlesex, *c.* July, to compose operas but, after initially accepting, declines. Composes 'Dettingen' *Te Deum* and Anthem, 17 July–3 Aug. Composes *Joseph and his Brethren*, Aug.–Sep. Score of *Acis and Galatea* published 24 Aug.–19 Nov. (in 10 sections). 'Middlesex' company opens at KT, 15 Nov., with *Rossane*, a version of *Alessandro*: Handel probably co-operates only by providing score. 'Dettingen' *Te Deum* and Anthem perf. at Chapel Royal, 27 Nov. (rehearsed Banqueting House, Whitehall, 18 Nov).	
1744	59	CG season, 10 Feb.–21 Mar. (12-perf. subscription): *Semele**, *Samson, Joseph*, Saul*. Mrs Delany reports that 'all the opera people are enraged at Handel', 21 Feb. Miller (librettist of *Joseph*) dies, 27 Apr. Handel approaches Jennens for a new libretto. By 9 June Handel has arranged to take KT for next season and gathered promises from singers. Visits 'the country', returning to London on 18 July. Composes *Hercules*, 19 July–21 Aug. Composes *Belshazzar*, 23 Aug.–23 Oct. Announces 24-perf. subscription, 20 Oct., beginning with Saturday perfs. only. Opens KT season 3 Nov. with *Deborah*. 2nd perf. postponed to 24 Nov. because subscribers 'not in Town'. Perfs. of *Semele*, 1, 8 Dec., including interpolated Italian arias at one	France declares war on Britain, 15 Mar. Pope (56) dies, 30 May. Alliance France/Prussia, 5 June. 'Middlesex' opera company closes at KT, 18 June. Friedrich II of Prussia invades Saxony, 15 Aug. Leo (50) dies, 31 Oct. Carteret resigns, 24 Nov.; reconstruction of Cabinet.

Year	Age	Life	Contemporary musicians and events
		or both.	
1745	60	KT season continues with *Hercules** (5, 12 Jan.). Handel announces plans to abandon KT series, 17 Jan., but support is offered and season resumes. Planned perf. of *Hercules* on 11 Feb. cancelled. Season continues with *Samson, Saul, Joseph, Belshazzar**, *Messiah*, 1 Mar.–23 Apr. (Handel's last perfs. at KT). In all, 16 (out of 24) perfs. given. Leaves London for visit to the country, ?June–July: visits Exton, and contributes music for Gainsborough family perf. of *Comus* (*c*.9 June). Travels to Scarborough and returns to London. Completes Italian duet HWV179, 31 Aug. Return of illness ('disordered in his head'), but improvement reported in Oct. *Song for the Gentlemen Volunteers* inserted into DL play, 14 Nov.	Quadruple Alliance (Maritime powers, Austria, Saxony), 8 Jan. Emperor Charles VII dies, 20 Jan. T.A. Vitali (82) dies, 9 May. French defeat Duke of Cumberland's forces at Fontenoy, 11 May. British conquer Louisburg, May. Prince Charles Edward Stuart lands at Ericsay, 21 July; enters Edinburgh, 17 Sep.; defeats forces led by Cope at Prestonpans, 21 Sep.; enters England, 8 Nov.; captures Carlisle, 17 Nov.; reaches Derby, 4 Dec.; driven back to Scotland, 20 Dec. Swift dies, 19 Oct. Peace of Dresden (Prussia recognizes Pragmatic Sanction), 25 Dec.
1746	61	Composes *Occasional Oratorio*, *c*.Jan–Feb. CG season 14–26 Feb.: 3 perfs. of *Occasional Oratorio** (only) to make up deficiency in previous season's subscription. Music by Handel and Gluck perf. at Decay'd Musicians benefit concert at KT, 25 Mar., possibly attended by Handel. His song *From scourging rebellion* published, 26 May, previously sung by Lowe at Vauxhall Gardens. Composes *Judas Maccabaeus*, 8/9 July–11 Aug.	Re-formed 'Middlesex' opera company opens with Gluck's *La caduta de' giganti* at KT, 7 Jan. Prince Charles victorious at Falkirk, 17 Jan. W.F. Bach (36) appointed organist at Liebfrauenkirche, Halle, 16 Apr. (N.S.). Defeat of Jacobites at Culloden, 16 Apr. (O.S.) by forces under Duke of Cumberland. Carl Stamitz born, 8 May. 'Middlesex' opera company opens new season at KT, 4 Nov.
1747	62	Presents first non-subscription oratorio season at CG, 6 Mar.–15 Apr.: *Occasional Oratorio, Joseph, Judas Maccabaeus**	KT opera company presents *Rossane*, 24 Feb. Garrick becomes manager at DL, 9 Apr.

Handel

Year	Age	Life	Contemporary musicians and events
		(with *Concerto a due cori*, HWV334). *Judas Maccabaeus* (with libretto dedicated to Duke of Cumberland), proves popular. First season with contralto Caterina Galli. Composes *Alexander Balus*, 1 June–4 July; composes *Joshua*, 19 July–19 Aug. Composes 3 hymns to words by Charles Wesley, probably at request of Priscilla Rich.	J.S. Bach visits Friedrich II at Potsdam, 7–8 May. French defeat forces led by Duke of Cumberland at Lauffeld, 2 July. Bononcini (76) dies, 9 July. 'Middlesex' opera company opens season at KT with *Lucio Vero* (a 'new' Handel pasticcio), 14 Nov.
1748	63	CG season, 26 Feb.–7 Apr.: *Judas Maccabaeus*, *Joshua** and *Alexander Balus** with *Concerti a due cori*, HWV 332–3). Lowe replaces Beard as principal tenor. Handel composes *Solomon*, 5 May–13 June, and *Susanna*, 11 July–24 Aug. Subscribes to Gambarini's *Lessons for the Harpsichord*.	'Middlesex' company at KT revive *Rossane*, 20 Feb. J.G. Walther (63) dies, 23 Mar. Oxford Music Room opens, July. Preliminary Peace of Aix-la-Chapelle (Britain, Holland, France), 30 Apr., concluded 18 Oct. General recognition of Pragmatic Sanction. End of War of Austrian Succession. Celebration fireworks display planned in London, Nov.
1749	64	CG season 10 Feb.–23 Mar.: *Susanna**, *Hercules*, *Samson*, *Solomon**, *Messiah*. New leading soprano, Frasi, in cast. Handel composes *Fireworks Music*, ?late Mar. Peace thanksgiving and celebrations: *Anthem on the Peace* HWV266 and revival of 'Caroline' *Te Deum* perf. Chapel Royal, 25 Apr. (rehearsed 22 Apr.), and *Fireworks Music* perf. Green Park, 27 Apr. (rehearsed Vauxhall Gardens, 21 Apr.). Offers charity performance to Foundling Hospital, 4 May: concert 27 May in hospital chapel with mixed programme (including 1st perf. of 'Foundling Hospital Anthem,' HWV268), attended by Prince	Peace proclaimed in London, 2 Feb. *Esther*, *Samson*, and *Messiah* performed in Oxford, conducted by William Hayes, 12–14 Apr. Galliard (*c*.62) dies; Heidegger (83) dies, 5 Sep. Smollett's *Alceste* rehearsed at CG, Sep.

Year	Age	Life	Contemporary musicians and events

and Princess of Wales.
Composes *Theodora*, 28 June–
31 July. Goes to Bath (by 19
Aug.), and returns to London,
writing to Jennens (30 Sep.)
with specification of an organ
for Gopsall. Begins incidental
music for projected production
of Smollett's play *Alceste* at
CG, 27 Dec.

Year	Age	Life	Contemporary musicians and events
1750	65	Completes *Alceste* music, 8 Jan.; completes Organ Concerto HWV310, 31 Jan. Earl of Shaftesbury reports, 13 Feb., that Handel has been buying pictures. Handel approached early Mar. by Foundling Hospital governors, for a performance on 1 May. CG season 2 Mar.–12 Apr.: *Saul*, *Judas Maccabaeus*, *Theodora** (with Organ Concerto HWV310*), *Samson*, *Messiah*; cast includes new castrato, Guadagni. *Messiah* perf. at FHC, 1 May: repeat perf. 15 May needed because of overcrowding on 1 May, and Handel elected a governor of hospital, 9 May. Makes his will, 1 June. *Alceste* project abandoned at CG, without performance; much of the music re-used in *The Choice of Hercules*, composed 28 June– 5 July. Leaves London for Continent, *c.*11 Aug. Hurt in coach accident between The Hague and Haarlem. Reported as visiting Haarlem on 27 Aug. and 20 Sep. (N.S.), playing organ on 2nd occasion. In Deventer, 10 Sep. (N.S.), plays organ to Prince of Orange and Princess Anne. Probably travels to Germany, taking oil portrait	Earthquakes in London, Mar. J.S. Bach (65) dies, 28 July. Britain renounces Asiento of Negroes, 5 Oct. Giuseppe Sammartini (55) dies in London, Nov. Westminster Bridge opened.

Year	Age	Life	Contemporary musicians and events
		to family in Halle. Plays organ at The Hague, 2, 7 Dec. (N.S.) to Prince and Princess of Orange. Receives letter from Telemann; replies from London, 14 Dec.	
1751	66	Composes last instrumental work, Organ Concerto HWV308, 1–4 Jan. Begins *Jephtha*, 21 Jan., but abandons halfway through last chorus of Part 2 on 13 Feb. because of 'relaxation' of left eye; resumes on 23 Feb., finishing Part 2 on 27 Feb. CG season, 22 Feb.–20 Mar.: *Belshazzar, Alexander's Feast* with *Choice of Hercules** (and Organ Concerto HWV308*), *Esther, Judas Maccabaeus*. Season curtailed by closure of theatres following death of Prince of Wales. Private report that Handel had lost his sight in one eye, 14 Mar. *Messiah* perf. at FHC, 18 Apr. and 16 May: Handel plays a 'voluntary' on the now-completed organ. Travels to Bath (arrives 3 June): returns to London 13 June, having also taken the waters at Cheltenham. Smith junior (39) returns from France to assist with management of oratorio seasons. Handel composes Part 3 of *Jephtha*, 18 June–15/17 July. Foundling Hospital general committee, late July, considers arrangements for official opening of chapel: Handel probably composes new music for 'Foundling Hospital Anthem', though chapel opening further delayed. Completes score of *Jephtha*, 30 Aug.	Albinoni (79) dies, 17 Jan. Frederick, Prince of Wales, dies, 20 Mar. Reconstruction of Cabinet, June: Grenville, President of Council. Lampe (48) dies, 25 July. Britain accedes to Austro-Russian alliance of 1746, 13 Sep.

Year	Age	Life	Contemporary musicians and events
1752	67	James Harris reports, Jan., that Handel is blind in one eye and expects that he will not perform after the 1752 season. Handel submits libretto of *Jephtha* to Inspector of Stage Plays, 10 Feb. CG season, 14 Feb.–26 Mar.: *Joshua, Hercules, Jephtha*, Samson, Judas Maccabaeus, Messiah. Messiah* perf. at FHC, 9 Apr. Newspaper report, 17 Aug., of further 'Paralytick disorder', which has deprived him of sight: undergoes operation by William Bromfield, surgeon to Princess of Wales, 3 Nov.	Treaty of Aranjuez (Spain/Austria), 14 June. Pepusch (*c*.85) dies, 20 July. Britain adopts Gregorian calendar, Sep. J.F. Reichardt born, 25 Nov.
1753	68	Handel reported well enough to go out of doors, 23 Jan., but as having 'quite lost his sight' on 27 Jan. (he may have retained some small residual eyesight in the first half of year). CG season 9 Mar.–13 Apr.: *Alexander's Feast* with *Choice of Hercules, Jephtha, Judas Maccabaeus, Samson, Messiah.* Official opening of FHC 16 Apr.: service includes 'Foundling Hospital Anthem'. Handel, Smith (?jr) and Boyce thanked by Hospital for assistance at service. London newspaper reports (3–5 Apr.) that Handel is composing an anthem for his own funeral. *Messiah* perf. at FHC, 1 May: Handel plays a 'voluntary' on the organ. Musical Society of Edinburgh asks for copies of unpublished music for *Messiah* and other oratorios, Dec.: Smith (sr) is directed to provide them.	British Museum founded. Horace Walpole begins Strawberry Hill residence.
1754	69	CG season, 1 Mar.–5 Apr.: *Alexander Balus, Deborah,*	Pelham dies, 6 Mar.; Newcastle succeeds as Prime Minister.

Year	Age	Life	Contemporary musicians and events
		Alexander Balus, Deborah, Saul, Joshua, Judas Maccabaeus, Samson, Messiah. *Admeto* given at KT (12 Mar.–6 Apr.) by Vanneschi's opera company, possibly with Handel supplying the score. *Messiah* given at FHC, 15 May: expenses fully recorded in hospital's minute book (29 May). Smith (jr) appointed organist to hospital, 25 June, 'to conduct his [Handel's] compositions' and manage annual performance arrangements. Handel dictates and signs letter to Telemann, 20 Sep.	succeeds as Prime Minister. Society for the Encouragement of Arts founded.
1755	70	CG season, 14 Feb.–21 Mar.: *Alexander's Feast* with *Choice of Hercules, L'Allegro* with *Ode for St Cecilia's Day, Samson, Joseph, Theodora, Judas Maccabaeus, Messiah. Messiah* perf. at FHC, 1 May.	End of British alliance with Austria. Lisbon carthquake, 1 Nov. Pitt and Grenville dismissed from government, 20 Nov. Greene (59) dies, 1 Dec.
1756	71	CG season, 5 Mar.–9 Apr.: *Athalia, Israel in Egypt* (with 'new' Part I constructed from other music), *Deborah, Judas Maccabaeus, Jephtha, Messiah. Messiah* perf. at FHC, 19 May. Adds first codicil to will, 6 Aug.	Treaty of Westminster (Britain/Prussia), 16 Jan. Mozart born, 27 Jan. Alliance of Versailles (France/Austria), 1 May. Britain declares war on France, 15 May. Outbreak of Seven Years' War. Fall of Newcastle ministry, Nov.; succeeded by Devonshire and Pitt, 1757–60.
1757	72	Handel possibly more active, Jan.–Feb. Letter from Earl of Shaftesbury (8 Feb.) reports him as composing again. Possibly collaborates with Morell over adaptation of *Il trionfo del Tempo* into *The Triumph of Time and Truth* and plays some part (?by dictation) in composition of duet and chorus	Empire declares war on Prussia, 10 Jan. Russia, Poland and Sweden join war against Prussia. J. Stamitz (39) dies, *c.*27 Mar. Fall of Devonshire-Pitt Cabinet, 5 Apr.; Newcastle-Pitt coalition, 29 June. Second treaty of Versailles (France/Austria), 1 May.

Year	Age	Life	Contemporary musicians and events
		'Sion now her head shall raise'. CG season, 25 Feb.–1 Apr.: *Esther, Israel in Egypt, Joseph, The Triumph of Time and Truth*, Judas Maccabaeus, Messiah*. Adds 2nd codicil to will, 22 Mar. *Messiah* perf. at FHC, 5 May. Adds 3rd codicil to will, 4 Aug.: copies of *Messiah* bequeathed to Foundling Hospital. Earl of Shaftesbury reports, 31 Dec., that Handel has composed songs for Cassandra Frederick, a new soloist for forthcoming oratorio season.	D. Scarlatti (71) dies, 23 July. French defeat British at Hastenbeck, 8 Sep. Russians occupy East Prussia, Sep., and Swedes invade Pomerania. Friedrich of Prussia defeats French and Imperial troops at Rossbach, 5 Nov. and Austrians at Leuthen, 5 Dec.
1758	73	CG season, 10 Feb.–17 Mar.: *The Triumph of Time and Truth, Belshazzar, Israel in Egypt, Jephtha, Judas Maccabaeus, Messiah*. 'New' arias for Cassandra Frederick in these works are not very Handelian in style. One rehearsal (at least) for oratorios held at Handel's house. *Messiah* perf. at FHC, 27 Apr. Goes to Tunbridge Wells, possibly with Morell, Aug.	London Convention (British subsidies for Prussia), 11 Apr. French defeated at Crefeld, 23 June. British take Louisburg, 24 July. Friedrich of Prussia defeats Russians at Zorndorf, 25 Aug. Washington takes Fort Duquesne (Pittsburg), 25 Nov. J.F. Fasch (70) dies, 5 Dec.
1759	74	CG season, 2 Mar.–6 Apr.: *Solomon, Susanna, Samson, Judas Maccabaeus, Messiah*. Attends *Messiah* perf. on 6 Apr.; intends to travel to Bath, but is too ill to do so. Adds 4th (final) codicil to will, 11 Apr.: bequests include £600 for a monument at Westminster Abbey. Dies at his home in Brook Street, at about 8 a.m. on 14 Apr. (Easter Saturday); funeral at Westminster Abbey, 20 Apr. Contents of house sold to his former servant, 27 Aug. George Amyand, one of the executors, completes administration of estate, Oct.	Princess Anne dies at The Hague, 12 Jan. French victory at Bergen, 13 Apr.: French defeated at Minden, 1 Aug.; Russians and Austrians defeat Friedrich of Prussia at Kunersdorf, 12 Aug. C.H. Graun (58) dies, 8 Aug. British Museum opened. Alcock aged 44; T.A. Arne 49; M. Arne 19; Arnold 19; Avison 50; C.P.E. Bach 45; J.C. Bach 24; W.F. Bach 49; Battishill 21; F. Benda 50; Geminiani 72; Gluck 45; Gossec 25; Graupner 76; Grétry 18; Hasse 60; Habermann 53; Haydn 27; J.A. Hiller 31; Holzbauer 48;

Handel

Year	Age	Life	Contemporary musicians and events
			Jommelli 45; Leclair 62; P. Locatelli 64; Martini 53; Mozart 3; Gottlieb Muffat 69; Nares 44; Porpora 73; Quantz 62; Rameau 76; F.X. Richter 50; G.B. Sammartini *c.* 59; Stanley 47; J.C. Smith sr 76; J.C. Smith jr 47; Tartini 67; Telemann 78; Wagenseil 44.
1760		Handel's picture collection sold by auction, 28 Feb.	King George II dies, 25 Oct.
1762		Roubiliac's monument to Handel unveiled at Westminster Abbey, 15 July.	

Appendix B

List of works

This list adopts the numbering and, in outline, the arrangement of the *Verzeichnis der Werke Georg Friedrich Händels* (HWV) by Bernd Baselt, as set out in Eisen and Eisen, *Händel-Handbuch*, i–iii. It is arranged in the following broad categories:

1 German and Italian Operas, Italian theatre music
2 Music for English Plays
3 Oratorios, English 'oratorio-style' works
4 Secular Cantatas
5 Italian Duets and Trios with continuo
6 Arias and Songs
7 Church Music
8 Orchestral Music
9 Chamber Music
10 Keyboard Music
11 Music for Mechanical Organs in Clocks
12 Exercises in Figured Bass and Fugue

Notes
1 Dates, places or authors not firmly established by documentary evidence are preceded by '?'. A number of spurious works, otherwise attributed to Handel, are identified in the course of the list.
2 *Titles*: where a short, familiar form, differing from a simple abbreviated form, of a title is used in the book, that title is given first in square brackets, followed by the longer title.
3 *HWV variants*: some simplification and re-arrangement has been made in entries for works having variant forms; the most substantial variants are noted in the commentaries.
4 *Dates*: these follow the convention outlined in the Preface with regard to Old Style/New Style. Composition dates refer to the main drafting of a work: further composition, in theatre works at least, usually continued in the period up to performances and in the prospect of subsequent revivals. The following abbreviations are used: com. = composed; cd. = completed (usually refers to draft score); perf. = performance; fp. = first performance; r. = revival; pub. = published. Dates are given only for Handel's own performances and revivals.
5 *Places of performance*: the following abbreviations are used:
CG – London, Covent Garden Theatre
CR – London, Chapel Royal, St James's Palace
DFS – Dublin, Fishamble Street Music-Hall
DL – London, Drury Lane Theatre

Handel

FHC – London, Foundling Hospital Chapel
FTC – Florence, Teatro Cocomero
HTG – Hamburg, Theater am Gänsemarkt
KT – London, King's Theatre, Haymarket (the same building as QT)
LIF – London, Lincoln's Inn Fields Theatre
LTH – London, 'Little Theatre' in the Haymarket
OCC – Oxford, Christ Church Hall
OST – Oxford, Sheldonian Theatre
QT – London, Queen's Theatre, Haymarket
SP – London, St Paul's Cathedral
VSG – Venice, Teatro S Giovanni Grisostomo
WA – London, Westminster Abbey

6 *Voices and instruments*: the following conventional abbreviations are used:

S – soprano; A – alto; T – tenor; B – bass; pic – piccolo; fl – flute; rec – recorder; ob – oboe; bn – bassoon; tpt – trumpet; hn – horn; timp – timpani; vn – violin; va – viola; vc – cello; db – double bass; bc – basso continuo; str – strings; orch – orchestra; unacc. – unaccompanied; unis. – unison.
Continuo is not listed separately for works with instrumental ensemble or orchestral accompaniment.

7 *Keys*: capitals indicate major keys, lower-case minor keys (C = C major; c = C minor).

8 *Editions*: the relevant volume numbers in the collected editions (*HG* and *HHA* – see Appendix F) are given. *HHA* references in parentheses are to volumes not yet published. Where only a fragment or section of a work is included, this is shown by '(fr)'. For works not yet covered in the collected editions, limited references to other editions are given.

1 GERMAN AND ITALIAN OPERAS, ITALIAN THEATRE MUSIC

Names of librettists are given in parentheses. The opera librettos that Handel set were mostly adapted from pre-existing ones: the author of the 'model' libretto or other literary source is given in the form, e.g., 'after F. Briani'; in many cases, this information simplifies a more complex (and sometimes obscure) derivation of the text. All are in 3 acts unless otherwise noted.

(a) Operas

HWV	Title	HG; HHA
1	[*Almira*] *Der in Kronen erlangte Glücks-Wechsel, oder: Almira, Königin von Castilien* (Friedrich Christian Feustking, after G. Pancieri, 1691) fp. 8 Jan. 1705 (HTG)	55; II/1
2	[*Nero*] *Die durch Blut und Mord erlangte Liebe, oder: Nero* (F.C. Feustking) fp. 25 Feb. 1705 (HTG)	music lost
3	[*Florindo*] *Der beglückte Florindo* (Hinrich Hinsch) com. ?1706; fp. Jan. 1708 (HTG); composed as single opera with HWV4 but divided before performances; music mainly lost	—; IV/19 (fr)

4	[*Daphne*] *Die verwandelte Daphne* (H. Hinsch) com. ?1706; fp. Jan. 1708 (HTG); see note to HWV3	—; IV/19 (fr)
5	[*Rodrigo*] *Vincer se stesso è la maggior vittoria* (after F. Silvani, 1700) fp. autumn 1707 (FTC)	56; (II/2)
6	*Agrippina* (Vincenzo Grimani) fp.?26 Dec. 1709 (VSG)	57; (II/3)
7	*Rinaldo* (Giacomo Rossi/Aaron Hill, from T. Tasso, *La Gerusalemme liberata*) fp. 24 Feb. 1711 (QT); r. 1712–15 (QT, KT), 1717 (KT), 1731 (KT, HWV7*b*)	58; II/4.1, II/4.2
8	*Il pastor fido* (G. Rossi, after B. Guarini, 1585) cd. 24 Oct. 1712; fp. 22 Nov. 1712 (QT); r. May 1734 (KT), 9 Nov. 1734 (CG, with dances, HWV8*c*, and preceded by *Terpsicore*, HWV8*b*)	59, 84; (II/5, 31)
9	*Teseo* (5 acts, Nicola Haym, after P. Quinault, 1675) cd. 19 Dec. 1712; fp. 10 Jan. 1713 (QT)	60; (II/6)
10	[*Silla*] *L*[*ucio*] *C*[*ornelio*] *Silla* (G. Rossi, from Plutarch) fp.? 2 June 1713 (?QT)	61; (II/6)
11	*Amadigi di Gaula* (?Haym, after A.H. de la Motte, 1699) fp. 25 May 1715 (KT); r. 1716–17 (KT)	62; II/8
12	*Radamisto* (?Haym, after D. Lalli, 1710/12) fp. 27 Apr. 1720 (KT); r. Dec. 1720 (HWV12*b*), 1721, 1728 (all KT)	63; II/9
13	*Muzio Scevola* (Paolo Antonio Rolli) [only Act 3 by Handel: Act 1 by Amadei, Act 2 by Bononcini] cd. 23 Mar. 1721; fp. 15 Apr. 1721 (KT); r. 1722 (KT)	64; (II/10)
14	*Floridante* (Rolli, after Silvani, 1706) cd. 28 Nov. 1721; fp. 9 Dec. 1721 (KT); r. 1722, 1727, 1733 (all KT)	65; (II/11)
15	*Ottone, re di Germania* (Haym, after S.B. Pallavicino, 1719) cd. 10 Aug. 1722; fp. 12 Jan. 1723 (KT); r. 1723–4, 1726, 1727, 1733, 1734 (all KT)	66; (II/12)
16	*Flavio, re de' Langobardi* (Haym, after M. Noris, 1682, and ?Stampiglia, 1696) cd. 7 May 1723; fp. 14 May 1723 (KT); r. 1732 (KT)	67; II/13
17	*Giulio Cesare in Egitto* (Haym, after G.F. Bussani, 1677/85) fp. 20 Feb. 1724 (KT); r. 1725, 1730, 1732 (all KT)	68; (II/14)
18	*Tamerlano* (Haym, after C.A. Piovene, 1711/19, from J.N. Pradon) com. 3–23 July 1724; fp. 31 Oct. 1724 (KT); r. 1731 (KT)	69; (II/15)
19	*Rodelinda, regina de' Langobardi* (Haym, after A. Salvi, 1710, from P. Corneille) cd. 20 Jan. 1725; fp. 13 Feb. 1725 (KT); r. 1725–6, 1731 (all KT)	70; II/16
20	[*Scipione*] *Publio Cornelio Scipione* (Rolli, after Salvi, 1704) cd. 2 Mar. 1726; fp. 12 Mar. 1726 (KT); r. 1730 (KT)	71; (II/17)
21	*Alessandro* (Rolli, after O. Mauro, 1690) cd. 11 Apr. 1726; fp. 5 May 1726 (KT); r. 1727, 1732 (all KT)	72; (II/18)
22	*Admeto, re di Tessaglia* (after A. Aureli, 1660, and Mauro, 1679) cd. 10 Nov. 1726 (autograph lost); fp. 31 Jan. 1727 (KT); r. 1727–8, 1731 (all KT)	73; (II/19)
23	*Riccardo Primo, re d'Inghilterra* (Rolli, after F. Briani, 1710) cd. 16 May 1727; fp. 11 Nov. 1727 (KT)	74; (II/20)

24	*Siroe, re di Persia*, (Haym, after P. Metastasio, 1726) cd. 5 Feb. 1728; fp. 17 Feb. 1728 (KT)	75; (II/21)
25	*Tolomeo, re d'Egitto* (Haym, after C.S. Capece, 1711) cd. 19 Apr. 1728; fp. 30 Apr. 1728 (KT); r. 1730 (KT)	76; II/22
26	*Lotario* (from Salvi, 1722/9) cd. 16 Nov. 1729, fp. 2 Dec. 1729 (KT)	77; (II/23)
27	*Partenope* (after Stampiglia, 1699/1708) cd. 12 Feb. 1730; fp. 24 Feb. 1730 (KT); r. Dec. 1730 (KT), 1737 (CG)	78; (II/24)
28	*Poro, re dell'Indie* (after Metastasio, 1730) cd. 16 Jan. 1731; fp. 2 Feb. 1731 (KT); r. Nov. 1731 (KT), 1736 (CG)	79; (II/25)
29	*Ezio* (after Metastasio, 1729) fp. 15 Jan. 1732 (KT)	80; (II/26)
30	*Sosarme, re di Media* (after Salvi, 1707), cd. 4 Feb. 1732; fp. 15 Feb. 1732 (KT); r. 1734 (KT)	81; (II/27)
31	*Orlando* (after Capece, 1711, from L. Ariosto, *Orlando furioso*, 1532) cd. 20 Nov. 1732; fp. 27 Jan. 1733 (KT)	82; II/28
32	*Arianna in Creta* (after P. Pariati, 1721/9) cd. 5 Oct. 1733; fp. 26 Jan. 1734 (KT); r. Nov. 1734 (CG)	83; (II/29)
73	*Parnasso in festa*, serenata, includes much music adapted from *Athalia* HWV52; fp. 13 Mar. 1734 (KT); r. 1737 (CG), 1740 (LIF), 1741 (KT, possibly not under Handel)	54; (II/30)
8b	*Terpsicore*, Prologue to *Il pastor fido* fp. 9 Nov. 1734 (CG)	84; (II/31)
33	*Ariodante* (after Salvi, 1708, from Ariosto, *Orlando furioso*) com. 12 Aug.–24 Oct. 1734; fp. 8 Jan. 1735 (CG); r. 1736 (CG)	85; (II/32)
34	*Alcina* (after *L'isola d'Alcina*, 1728, from Ariosto, *Orlando furioso*) cd. 8 Apr. 1735; fp. 16 Apr. 1735 (CG); r. 1736, 1737 (all CG)	86; (II/33)
35	*Atalanta* (after B. Valeriani, 1715) com. 1–22 Apr. 1736; fp. 12 May 1736 (CG); r. Nov. 1736 (CG)	87; (II/34)
36	*Arminio* (after Salvi, 1703, from de Campistron, 1684) com. 15 Sep.–14 Oct. 1736; fp. 12 Jan. 1737 (CG)	89; (II/35)
37	*Giustino* (after N. Beregan/Pariati, 1724) com. 14 Aug.–20 Oct. 1736; fp. 16 Feb. 1737 (CG)	88; (II/36)
38	*Berenice, regina d'Egitto* (after Salvi, 1709) com. 18 Dec. 1736–27 Jan. 1737; fp. 18 May 1737 (CG)	90; (II/37)
39	*Faramondo* (after A. Zeno, 1720) com. 15 Nov.–24 Dec. 1737; fp. 3 Jan. 1738 (KT)	91; (II/38)
40	*Serse* (after Stampiglia, 1694, from N. Minato, 1654) com. 26 Dec. 1737–14 Feb. 1738; fp. 15 Apr. 1738 (KT)	92; II/39
41	*Imeneo* (after Stampiglia, 1723, 2-part 'componimento dramatico') com. 9–20 Sep. 1738; cd. 10 Oct. 1740; fp. 22 Nov. 1740 (LIF); r. 24 Mar. 1742 (DFS, as 'Hymen, a Serenata', in Italian)	93; II/40
42	*Deidamia* (Rolli) com. 27 Oct.–20 Nov. 1740; fp. 10 Jan. 1741 (LIF; final perf. 10 Feb. 1741, LTH)	94; II/41

(b) Other works

FRAGMENTARY ITALIAN OPERA SCORES (never completed)
A²   *Genserico* [*Olibrio*] (after Beregan, 1693) com.?Jan. 1728;   —
        only part of Act 1 drafted
A⁵   *Titus l'empéreur* (in Italian, ? from J. Racine, *Berenice*)   —
        com. ?–Oct.–Nov. 1731; only part of Act 1 drafted

'SELF-PASTICCIO' ITALIAN OPERAS (music entirely by Handel)
A¹¹   *Oreste* (after G.G. Barlocci, 1723) fp. 18 Dec. 1734 (CG)   48 (fr);
                                                                        II/Sup.1
A¹³   *Alessandro Severo* (after Zeno, 1717/23) fp. 25 Feb. 1738   48 (fr);—
        (KT)
A¹⁴   *Jupiter in Argos* (in Italian, after A.M. Lucchini *Giove in* —
        Argo, 1719) cd. 24 Apr. 1739; fp. 1 May 1739 (KT)

OTHER PASTICCIO OPERAS (music by other composers [listed in square brackets]
arranged and added to by Handel)
A¹   *L'Elpidia, overo Li rivali generosi* (?Haym, after Zeno,   —
        1697) fp. 11 May 1725 (KT); r. Nov. 1725 (KT) [L. Vinci,
        G.M. Orlandini, A. Lotti, G.M. Capelli, D. Sarri]
A³   *Ormisda* (?Rossi, after Zeno, 1722) fp. 4 Apr. 1730 (KT);   —
        r. Nov. 1730 (KT) [Orlandini, Vinci, J.A. Hasse, L. Leo,
        Sarri, S.A. Fiore]
A⁴   *Venceslao* (?Rossi, after Zeno, 1724) fp. 11 Jan. 1731   —
        (KT) [Vinci, Hasse, Lotti, N. Porpora, Orlandini, Capelli,
        G. Giacomelli, G. Porta]
A⁶   *Lucio Papirio dittatore* (after Zeno/C.I. Frugoni, 1729)   —
        fp. 23 May 1732 (KT) [Giacomelli, Porpora]
A⁷   *Catone* (after Metastasio, 1728/9) fp. 4 Nov. 1732 (KT)   —
        [Leo, Hasse, Porpora, A.Vivaldi, Vinci]
A⁸   [*Semiramide*] *Semiramis riconosciuta* (after Metastasio,   —
        1729) fp. 30 Oct. 1733 (KT) [Vinci, Hasse, F. Feo, Leo,
        Sarri]
A⁹   *Caio Fabricio* (after Zeno, 1732) fp. 4 Dec. 1733 (KT)   —
        [Hasse, Vinci, Leo]
A¹⁰   *Arbace* (after Metastasio, 1730) fp. 5 Jan. 1734 (KT)   —
        [Vinci, Hasse, Porta]
A¹²   *Didone abbandonata* (after Metastasio, 1726) fp. 13 Apr.   —
        1737 (CG) [Vinci, Hasse, Giacomelli, Vivaldi]

ITALIAN SERENATAS
72   *Aci, Galatea e Polifemo* – see Section 4(a), 'Italian Cantatas'
73   *Parnasso in festa* – see Section 1(a), 'Operas'
The 'Middlesex' opera company presented *Rossane* (arr. Lampugnani from
HWV21) fp. 8 Nov. 1743 (KT), and *Lucio Vero* (a pasticcio including music by
Handel) fp. 14 Nov. 1745 (KT).

2 MUSIC FOR ENGLISH PLAYS

HWV	Title	HG; HHA
228[19]	*'Twas when the seas were roaring* [*The Faithful Maid/The Melancholy Nymph*], song for S and bc, printed *c.*1715; probably sung in John Gay's 'Comic Tragic Pastoral Farce' *The What D'ye Call it*, 23 Feb. 1715 (DL); published in Handel (ed. Burrows), *Songs and Cantatas for Soprano*	—
228[11]	*I like the am'rous youth*, song for S and bc, with treble-clef intro. for ?vn, printed *c.*1741; sung by Mrs Clive in James Miller's *The Universal Passion*, 28 Feb. 1737 (DL); published in Handel (ed. Burrows), *Songs and Cantatas for Soprano*	—
218	*Love's but the frailty of the mind*, song for S and bc, with treble-clef interludes (?vn or harpsichord); autograph survives; sung by Mrs Clive at her benefit performance of Congreve's *The Way of the World*, 17 Mar. 1740 (DL); published in Handel (ed. Burrows), *Songs and Cantatas for Soprano*	—
44	*There in blissful shades and bow'rs*, 3 arias and 'chorus' for S, S, B, 2 vns, bc; written for private perf. of *Comus* (Milton, probably in version by Dalton), Exton, Rutland, June 1745; ed. C. Timms and A. Hicks, *Handel: Music for 'Comus'* (London, 1977)	—
45	*Alceste*, music for lost play by Tobias Smollett, com. 27 Dec. 1749–8 Jan. 1750; play rehearsed at CG but not produced; overture and substantial movements for Acts 1 and 4 (19 numbers, with variant settings)	46*b*; (I/30)
43	*The Alchemist*, instrumental music for revival of Ben Jonson's play, 14 Jan. 1710 (QT). 9 items (8 from overture to *Rodrigo* HWV5, 1 of doubtful authenticity); presumably a pirated arrangement	—

3 ORATORIOS, ENGLISH 'ORATORIO-STYLE' WORKS

Librettists' names, where known, follow the titles.

(a) Italian oratorios

HWV	Title	HG; HHA
46*a*	*Il trionfo del Tempo e del Disinganno* (Benedetto Pamphili) fp. Rome, ? June 1707; in 2 parts	24; (I/4)
47	[*La Resurrezione*] *Oratorio per la Risurrettione di Nostro Signor Giesù Cristo* (Carlo Sigismondo Capece) fp. 8 Apr. 1708, Bonelli Palace, Rome	39; (I/3)
46*b*	*Il trionfo del Tempo e della Verità*, revised version of HWV46*a*, in 3 parts with new material; com. 2–14 Mar. 1737; fp. 23 Mar. 1737 (CG); r. 1739 (KT)	24; (1/4)

(b) German passion-oratorio

48   [*Brockes-Passion*] *Der für die Sünde der Welt gemarterte*   15; I/7
und sterbende Jesus (Barthold Heinrich Brockes);
com. ?*c*.1715; fp. ?Hamburg, date unknown
The *St John Passion* (*HG* 9; *HHA* I/2) is not by Handel.

(c) English oratorios

50   *Esther* (? A. Pope and ? J. Arbuthnot, after Racine) com.   40, 41;
c.1718; fp. ?1718, ?Cannons; revised version for theatre   I/8, (I/10)
(HWV50*b*, with new additional texts by Samuel
Humphreys), fp. 2 May 1732 (KT); r. 1733 (KT, OST),
1735, 1736, 1737 (CG), 1740 (LIF), 1742 (DFS), 1751
(CG), 1757 (CG); perfs. in 1730s included bilingual
(Eng./It.) versions

51   *Deborah* (Humphreys, from *Judges*) cd. 21 Feb. 1733;   29; (I/11)
fp. 17 Mar. 1733 (KT); r. 1733 (OST), 1734 (KT), 1735
(CG), 1744 (KT), 1754 (CG), 1756 (CG); r. also planned
for 1737 (CG); revivals 1734–44 included movements in
Italian

52   *Athalia* (Humphreys, after Racine, 1691) cd. 7 June 1733;   5; (I/12)
fp. 10 July 1733 (OST); r. 1735 (with Italian arias), 1756
(both CG), also planned for 1743

—   *An Oratorio* fp. 28 Mar. 1738 (KT), Handel's benefit   —
performance; bilingual pasticcio, including much music
from *Deborah*

53   *Saul* (Charles Jennens, from *II Samuel* and A. Cowley)   13; I/13
com. 23 July–27 Sep. 1738; fp. 16 Jan. 1739 (KT); r.
1740–1 (LIF), 1742 (DFS), 1744 (CG), 1745 (KT), 1750,
1754 (both CG)

54   *Israel in Egypt* (?Jennens, from *Exodus* and *Psalms*) com.   16; I/14.1,
1 Oct.–1 Nov. 1738; fp. 4 Apr. 1739 (KT); r. 1740 (LIF),   I/14.2
1756–8 (CG). HWV264 adapted as Part 1, 1739–40;
replaced by miscellaneous movements, 1756–8

56   *Messiah* (Jennens, from Bible and Prayer Book) com. 22   45; I/17
Aug.–14 Sep. 1741; fp. 13 Apr. 1742 (DFS); r. 1743 (CG),
1745 (KT), 1749–50, 1752–9 (all CG), 1750–8 (FHC)

57   *Samson* (Newburgh Hamilton, from Milton) com. Sep.–   10; (I/18)
29 Oct. 1741; cd. 12 Oct. 1742; fp. 18 Feb. 1743 (CG); r.
1744 (CG), 1745 (KT), 1749–50, 1752–5, 1759 (all CG)

59   *Joseph and his Brethren* (James Miller, from *Genesis* and   42; (I/20)
after Zeno, 1722) com. Aug.–Sep. 1743; fp. 2 Mar. 1744
(CG); r. 1745 (KT), 1747, 1755, 1757 (all CG), also
planned for 1751

61   *Belshazzar* (Jennens, from *Daniel*, *Jeremiah*, *Isaiah*, Her-   19; (I/21)
odotus and Xenophon) com. 23 Aug.–23 Oct. 1744;
fp. 27 Mar. 1745 (KT); r. 1751, 1758 (both CG), also
planned for *c*.1748

62   *Occasional Oratorio* (Hamilton, from Milton, Spenser)   43; (I/23)
fp. 14 Feb. 1746 (CG); r. 1747 (CG)

63	*Judas Maccabaeus* (Thomas Morell, from *I Maccabees* and Josephus) com. 8/9 July–11 Aug. 1746; fp. 1 Apr. 1747 (CG); r. 1748, 1750–9 (all CG)	22; (I/24)
64	*Joshua* (from book of *Joshua*) com. 19 July–19 Aug. 1747; fp. 9 Mar. 1748 (CG); r. 1752, 1754 (both CG)	17; (I/26)
65	*Alexander Balus* (Morell, from *I Maccabees*) com. 1 June–4 July 1747; fp. 23 Mar. 1748 (CG); r. 1754 (CG)	33; (I/25)
66	*Susanna* (from Apocrypha, *History of Susanna*) com. 11 July–24 Aug. 1748; fp. 10 Feb. 1749 (CG); r. 1759 (CG)	1; I/28
67	*Solomon* (from *I Kings*, *II Chronicles* and Josephus), com. 5 May–13 June 1748; fp. 17 Mar. 1749 (CG); r. 1759 (CG, greatly revised)	26; (I/27)
68	*Theodora* (Morell, after Robert Boyle, 1687) com. 28 June–31 July 1749; fp. 16 Mar. 1750 (CG); r. 1755 (CG), also planned for 1759	8; (I/29)
70	*Jephtha* (Morell, after *Judges* and G. Buchanan, 1554) com. 21 Jan.–30 Aug. 1751; fp. 26 Feb. 1752 (CG); r. 1753, 1756, 1758 (all CG)	44; (I/32)
71	*The Triumph of Time and Truth* (extended English version of HWV46*b*, probably arranged by Morell) fp. 11 Mar. 1757 (CG); r. 1758 (CG); score probably assembled by J.C. Smith junior, Handel's contribution uncertain	20; (I/33)

(d) English odes

74	*Eternal Source of Light Divine* [*Ode for the Birthday of Queen Anne*] (?Ambrose Philips), probably com. for court performance, 6 Feb. 1713, but not performed	46*a*; I/6
75	*Alexander's Feast or The Power of Musick* (John Dryden, 1697, arr. Hamilton, with additional texts by Hamilton) cd. 17 Jan. 1736; in 2 parts; fp. 19 Feb. 1736 (CG); r. 1737 (CG), 1739 (KT), 1739 (LIF), 1742 (DFS), 1751, 1753, 1755 (all CG)	12; I/1
76	[*Ode*] *Song for St Cecilia's Day*, 'From Harmony' (Dryden, 1687), com. 15–24 Sep. 1739; fp. 22 Nov. 1739 (LIF); r. 1740, 1741 (both LIF), 1742 (DFS), 1743, 1755 (all CG); variously coupled with HWV75, HWV55 and HWV49 in Handel's performances	23; (I/15)
55	*L'Allegro, il Penseroso ed il Moderato* (James Harris and Charles Jennens, Parts 1 and 2 after Milton, Part 3 by Jennens) com. 19 Jan.–4 Feb. 1740; fp. 27 Feb. 1740 (LIF); r. 1741 (LIF), 1741–2 (DFS), 1743, 1755 (all CG); sometimes perf. with HWV76 in place of Part 3.	6; I/16

(e) English secular dramas

All except the first version of HWV49 were presented by Handel in oratorio style at the theatre.

HWV	Title	HG; HHA
49	*Acis and Galatea* (John Gay, John Hughes and others,	3; I/9

after Ovid) fp. 1718, ?Cannons, ?staged; revised theatre version (called 'Serenata') with additional material (HWV49*b*) fp. 10 June 1732 (KT); r. Dec. 1732 (KT), 1733 (OCC), 1734 (KT), 1736 (CG), 1739, 1741 (both LIF), 1742 (DFS); perfs. of 1732, 1734, ?1736 bilingual

58   *Semele* (William Congreve, *c.*1706, from Ovid, with texts   7; (I/19)
from Pope and other Congreve works); com. 3 June–4 July 1743; fp. 10 Feb. 1744 (CG); r. Dec. 1744 (KT)

60   *Hercules* (Thomas Broughton, from Sophocles and Ovid)   4; (I/22)
com. 19 July–17 Aug. 1744; fp. 5 Jan. 1745 (KT); r. 1749, 1752 (both CG)

69   *The Choice of Hercules* (Robert Lowth, 1743–7, adapted,   18; I/31
probably by Morell) com. 28 June–5 July 1750; fp. 1 Mar. 1751 (CG); r. 1753, 1755 (both CG); uses much music from *Alceste* HWV45; perf. in conjunction with *Alexander's Feast* HWV75

4 SECULAR CANTATAS

The Italian cantatas were mostly composed in Rome, 1707–9; known exceptions are indicated.

(a) Italian cantatas with orchestral accompaniment

Accompaniment includes continuo; obbligato instrumental parts are noted. 'Dramatic cantata' indicates an extended work with named characters. Pub. in *HG* 52*a*, 52*b* (omitting HWV79, 82, 142, 150), and *HHA* V/3–5; variants in *HG* are noted. The Spanish cantata HWV140, composed in Italy, is included here.

HWV	*Title*	*Scoring, comments*
	Aci, Galatea e Polifemo – see *Sorge il dì*	
	Agrippina condotta a morire – see *Dunque sarà pur vero*	
78	*Ah ! crudel, nel pianto mio*	S, obs, str
79	*Alla caccia* [*Diana cacciatrice*]	S + coro S, tpt, str; copied for Ruspoli, 1707
81	*Alpestre monte*	S, str (no va); incomplete in *HG*
82	*Amarilli vezzosa* [*Il duello amoroso/Daliso ed Amarilli*]	Dramatic cantata. S, A, str (no va); copied for Ruspoli, 1708
	Aminta e Fillide – see *Arresta il passo*	
	Apollo e Dafne – see *La terra è liberata*	
	Armida abbandonata – see *Dietro l'orme fuggaci*	
83	*Arresta il passo* [*Aminta e Fillide*]	Dramatic cantata. S, S, str; one section ('Chi ben ama') printed separately in *HG*, 52*b*; copied for Ruspoli, 1708
87	*Carco sempre di gloria*	A, str; variant insertion in HWV89, for perfs. of *Alexander's Feast* in 1737, including music for castrato Annibali; *HG* prints bc score (only)

		of transposed aria
89	*Cecilia, volgi un sguardo*	S, T, str; played before Part 2 of *Alexander's Feast*, fp. 19 Feb. 1736
92	*Clori, mia bella Clori*	S, str (no va)
	Clori, Tirsi e Fileno – see *Cor fedele in vano speri*	
	Il consiglio – see *Tra le fiamme*	
96	*Cor fedele in vano speri* [*Clori, Tirsi e Fileno*]	Dramatic cantata. S, S, A, recs, obs, str, archlute; in 2 parts; incomplete in *HG*; copied for Ruspoli, 1707
97	*Crudel tiranno Amor*	S, str; probably for Durastanti's benefit concert, KT, 5 July 1721
98	*Cuopre tal volta il cielo*	B, str (no va)
99	*Da quel giorno fatale* [*Il delirio amoroso*]	S, rec, ob, str; com. Rome, ?Jan 1707; text B. Pamphili
	Daliso ed Amarilli – see *Amarilli vezzosa*	
	Il delirio amoroso – see *Da quel giorno fatale*	
	Diana cacciatrice – see *Alla caccia*	
105	*Dietro l'orme fuggaci* [*Armida abbandonata*]	Dramatic cantata. S, str (no va); copied for Ruspoli, 1707, 1709
	Il duello amoroso – see *Amarilli vezzosa*	
110	*Dunque sarà pur vero* [*Agrippina condotta a morire*]	Dramatic cantata. S, str (no va)
119	*Echeggiate, festeggiate, numi eterni*	Dramatic cantata. S, S, S, A, B, recs, obs, str; partly lost: fragments printed in wrong order in *HG*; com. London, *c*.1710–12
	Ero e Leandro – see *Qual ti riveggio, oh Dio*	
113	*Figlio d'alte speranze*	S, vn(s)
	Io languisco fra le gioie – see *Echeggiate, festeggiate*	
122	*La terra è liberata* [*Apollo e Dafne*]	Dramatic cantata. S, B, fl, obs, bn, str; probably begun Venice, 1709, cd. Hanover, 1710
123	*Languia di bocca lusinghiera*	S, ob, vn(s); possibly com. Hanover, 1710; ?fragment
132	*Mi palpita il cor*	Several variant settings. A, fl, ob (HWV132*d*), com. ?London, *c*.1711–12; S, ob (HWV132*b*), com. ?London, after 1718; also a new alto version of first movements, com. *c*.1740; possibly also other variants; see also Section (b), below
134	*Nel dolce dell'oblio* [*Pensieri notturni di Filli*]	S, rec
140	*Nò se emenderá jamás*	Spanish cantata. S, 'chitarra' (= guitar, as accompaniment); copied for Ruspoli, 1707
142	*Notte placida e cheta*	S, str (no va)
143	*O come chiare e belle* [*Olinto pastore, Tebro fiume, Gloria*]	Dramatic cantata. S, S, A, tpt, str (no va); ?copied for Ruspoli, 1708

	Olinto pastore – see *O come chiare e belle*	
150	*Qual ti riveggio, oh Dio* [*Ero e Leandro*]	S, obs, str
72	*Sorge il dì* [*Aci, Galatea e Polifemo*]	Dramatic cantata. S, A, B, recs, ob, tpts, str; for wedding celebrations in Naples, July 1708; text Nicola Giuvo; cd. 16 June 1708; *HG* 53 (*HHA* I/5)
165	*Spande ancor a mio dispetto*	B, str (no va)
166	*Splenda l'alba in oriente*	A, fls, obs, str; com. London, *c*.1711–12
170	*Tra le fiamme* [*Il consiglio*]	S, recs, ob, str (gamba, no va); text B. Pamphili
171	*Tu fedel? Tu costante?*	S, str (no va); copied for Ruspoli, 1707, 1708
173	*Un' alma innamorata*	S, vn(s); copied for Ruspoli, 1707

(b) Italian cantatas with continuo accompaniment

Pub. in *HG* 51 and *HHA* (V/1, 2) unless otherwise indicated. The French cantata *HWV*155, composed in Italy, is included here.

HWV	*Title*	*Scoring, comments*
77	*Ah che pur troppo è vero*	S
80	*Allor ch'io dissi: Addio*	S
	Amore uccellatore – see *Venne voglia ad Amore*	
84	*Aure soavi, e lieti*	S; copied for Ruspoli, 1707, 1708, 1709
86	*Bella ma ritrosetta*	S; com. London, *c*.1717–18
	La bianca rosa – see *Sei pur bella, pur vezzosa*	
88	*Care selve, aure grate*	S
90	*Chi rapì la pace al core*	S; copied for Ruspoli, 1709
91	*Clori, degli occhi miei*	A (HWV91*a*); S (HWV91*b*)
93	*Clori, ove sei?*	S
94	*Clori, sì, ch'io t'adoro*	S; no autograph, earliest source *c*.1738–40
95	*Clori, vezzosa Clori*	S; copied for Ruspoli, 1708
100	*Da sete ardente afflitto*	S; copied for Ruspoli, 1709
101	*Dal fatale momento*	S (HWV101*a*); B (HWV101*b*); spurious, by F.Mancini
102	*Dalla guerra amorosa*	B (HWV102*a*); S (HWV102*b*); copied for Ruspoli, 1709
103	*Deh! lasciate e vita e volo*	A; text Paolo Antonio Rolli; com. London, *c*.1722–5
104	*Del bel idolo mio*	B; copied for Ruspoli, 1709
106	*Dimmi, o mio cor*	S
107	*Ditemi, o piante*	S; copied for Ruspoli, 1708
108	*Dolce mio ben, s'io taccio*	S; no autograph, no source attributed to Handel
109	*Dolc'è pur d'amor l'affanno*	A (HWV109*a*), com. London,

		*c.*1717–18; S (HWV109*b*), com. London, ?after 1718; ?text by Rolli
111	*E partirai, mia vita?*	S (HWV111*a*); S (HWV111*b*), com. London, *c.*1725–8
112	*Figli del mesto cor*	A; no autograph or Italian-period copies
114	*Filli adorata e cara*	S; copied for Ruspoli, 1709
115	*Fra pensieri quel pensiero*	A
116	*Fra tante pene*	S; copied for Ruspoli, 1709
	Il Gelsomino – see *Son Gelsomino*	
117	*Hendel, non può mia musa*	S; text Benedetto Pamphili; copied for Ruspoli, 1708, 1709
118	*Ho fuggito Amore anch'io*	A; text P.A. Rolli, com. London, *c.*1722–3; printed without final aria in *HG*
120	*Irene, idolo mio*	S (HWV120*a*); A (HWV120*b*); no autographs or Italian-period copies
121	*L'aure grate, il fresco rio [La Solitudine]*	A (HWV121*a*, fragment), com. London, *c.*1722–3; A (HWV121*b*), com. London, before 1718
	La Lucrezia – see *Oh numi eterni*	
125	*Lungi da me, pensier tiranno*	S (HWV125*a*); A (HWV125*b*); no autographs or Italian-period copies; 1 version copied for Ruspoli, 1709
126	*Lungi da voi, che siete poli*	S (HWV126*a*); S (HWV126*b*); A (HWV126*c*); HWV126*c* probably com. London; 1 version copied for Ruspoli, 1708
127	*Lungi dal mio bel nume*	S (HWV127*a*), cd. Rome, 3 Mar. 1708; A (HWV127*b*), ?com. London; S (HWV127*c*), com. London *c.*1725–8; 1 version copied for Ruspoli, 1709
128	*Lungi n'andò Fileno*	S; copied for Ruspoli, 1708
129	*Manca pur quanto sai*	S; copied for Ruspoli, 1708
130	*Mentre il tutto è in furore*	S; copied for Ruspoli, 1708
131	*Menzognere speranze*	S; copied for Ruspoli, 1707
132	*Mi palpita il cor*	S (HWV132*a*), com. ?London; version of HWV106 with new opening; see also other settings in Section (a) above
133	*Ne' tuoi lumi, o bella Clori*	S; copied for Ruspoli, 1707, 1709
135	*Nel dolce tempo*	S (HWV135*a*); A (HWV135*b*); no autographs, and no early Italian copies of HWV135*b*
136	*Nell'africane selve*	B (HWV136*a*), com. ?Naples; B (HWV136*b*); no early Italian copies of HWV136*b*
137	*Nella stagion che di viole e rose*	S; copied for Ruspoli, 1707, 1709

138	*Nice, che fa? che pensa?*	S; ?com. Hanover, 1710
139	*Ninfe e pastori*	S (HWV139a), copied for Ruspoli, 1709; A (HWV139b), probably com. London; S (HWV139c), com. London, c.1725–8
141	*Non sospirar, non piangere*	S
144	*O lucenti, o sereni occhi*	S
145	*Oh numi eterni [La Lucrezia]*	S; copied for Ruspoli, 1709
146	*Occhi miei che faceste?*	S
	Partenza di G. B. – see *Stelle, perfide stelle*	
147	*Partì, l'idolo mio*	S; no autograph or early Italian copies
148	*Poichè giuraro amore*	S; copied for Ruspoli, 1707, 1709
149	*Qual sento io non conosciuto*	S; only source c.1738–40
151	*Qualor crudele, sì ma vaga Dori*	A; no autograph or early Italian copies
152	*Qualor l'egre pupille*	S; copied for Ruspoli, 1707
153	*Quando sperasti, o core*	S; copied for Ruspoli, 1708
154	*Quel fior che all'alba ride*	S; com. London, c.1739–41; not in HG; pub. in Handel (ed. Burrows), *Songs and Cantatas for Soprano*
155	*Sans y penser (Cantate Française)*	S ('Silvie, Tircis'); copied for Ruspoli, 1707, 1709; not in HG; pub. (ed. Percy Young) 1972
156	*Sarai contenta un dì*	S
157	*Sarei troppo felice*	S; text B.Pamphili; incomplete in HG; copied for Ruspoli, 1707, 1708
158	*Se pari è la tua fè*	S (HWV158a); S (HWV158b), probably, com. London; S (HWV158c), com. London, c.1725–8; HWV158a copied for Ruspoli, 1708, 1709
159	*Se per fatal destino*	S; copied for Ruspoli, 1707, 1709
160	*Sei pur bella, pur vezzosa [La bianca rosa]*	S (HWV160a), copied for Ruspoli, 1707, 1709; S (HWV160b), com. London, c. 1725–8; S (HWV160c), com. London, c.1738–41
161	*Sento là che ristretto*	S (HWV161a); A (HWV161b); S (HWV161c), com. London, c. 1725–8; 1 version copied for Ruspoli, 1709
162	*Siete rose ruggiadose*	A; com. (with variant), London, c. 1711–12
	La Solitudine – see '*L'aure grate, il fresco rio*'	
163	*Solitudini care, amata libertà*	S; no autograph or early Italian copies
164	*Son Gelsomino [Il Gelsomino]*	S (HWV164a), com. London, c.1725–8; A (HWV164b), com. London, c.1717–18

167	*Stanco di più soffrire*	A (HWV167*a*); S (HWV167*b*); 1 version copied for Ruspoli, 1708
168	*Stelle, perfide stelle [Partenza di G. B.]*	S
169	*Torna il core al suo diletto*	S
172	*Udite il mio consiglio*	S; copied for Ruspoli, 1707
174	*Un sospir a chi si muore*	S
175	*Vedendo Amor*	A
176	*Venne voglia ad Amore [Amore uccellatore]*	A
177	*Zeffiretto, arresta il volo*	S; ?copied for Ruspoli, 1709

(c) English cantatas

85	*Behold where weeping Venus stands [Venus and Adonis]*	S, obbligato for treble instrument (?vn); text John Hughes. Two arias only, *c*.1711, from Hughes's cantata *Venus and Adonis*. No autograph: authenticity uncertain. Not in *HG*: pub. in Handel (ed. Burrows), *Songs and Cantatas for Soprano*
124	*Look down, harmonious saint*	T, str; text Newburgh Hamilton, from Cecilian Ode 1720. Recitative and aria: probably a discarded fragment for *Alexander's Feast*, 1736. HG 52*a* (also with shortened aria in *HG* 23).
44	*There in blissful shades and bow'rs*	see Section 2, above (= music for *Comus*)

For the *Deutsche Arien* ('German Arias') HWV202–10, see Section 7 (c), below.

5 ITALIAN DUETS AND TRIOS WITH CONTINUO

Pub. in *HG* 32 (rev. 2/1880), and HHA (V/6). Texts for some of the Hanover duets are probably by O. Mauro.

(a) Duets

HWV	*Title*	*Scoring, comments*
178	*A mirarvi io son intento*	SA; ?com. Hanover, *c*.1711
179	*Ahi, nelle sorti umane*	SS; cd. London, 31 Aug. 1745
180	*Amor gioje mi porge*	SS; com. Italy, *c*.1707–9
181	*Beato in ver chi può*	SA; Italian version of Horace, 'Beatus ille'; cd. London, 31 Oct. 1742
182	*Caro autor di mia doglia*	ST (HWV182*a*); probably com. Italy, *c*.1707–9; AA (HWV182*b*), com. London, *c*.1742
183	*Caro autor di mia doglia*	SS; spurious, by R. Keiser
184	*Che via pensando, folle pensier*	SB; com. Italy, *c*.1707–9

185	*Conservate, raddoppiate*	SA; ?com. Hanover, c.1711
186	*Fronda leggiera e mobile*	SA; cd. London, c.1745
187	*Giù nei Tartarei regni*	SB; com. Italy, c.1707–9
188	*Langue, geme, sospira*	SA; text by G.D. de Totis (from opera, 1690), com. London, c.1722
189	*No, di voi non vuo' fidarmi*	SS; cd. London, 3 July 1741; thematic ideas from 2 movements used in *Messiah*
190	*No, di voi non vuo' fidarmi*	SA; cd. 2 Nov. 1742
191	*Quando in calma ride il mare*	SB; com. Italy or Hanover, c.1707–11
192	*Quel fior che all'alba ride*	SS; cd. London, 1 July 1741; 3rd movement uses theme from HWV154; thematic ideas from 2 movements used in *Messiah*
193	*Se tu non lasci amore*	SA; com. London, c.1722; thematic idea from first movement used in *Messiah*
194	*Sono liete, fortunate*	SA; ?com. Hanover, c.1711
195	*Spero indarno*	SB; single movement, known only from copies; authenticity uncertain
196	*Tacete, ohimé, tacete*	SB; text by F. de' Lemene (1692), com. Italy, c.1707–9
197	*Tanti strali al sen mi scocchi*	SA; ?com. Hanover, c.1711
198	*Troppo cruda, troppo fiera*	SA; ?com. Hanover, c.1711; autograph lost
199	*Va', speme infida*	SS; ?com. Hanover, c.1711; autograph lost

(b) Trios

| 200 | *Quel fior che all'alba ride* | SSB; ?com. Italy, c.1707–9; 2 versions, slightly different texts |
| 201 | *Se tu non lasci amore* | SSB; cd. Naples, 12 July 1708; first movement longer in Naples autograph (HWV201b) than in most copies |

6 ARIAS AND SONGS

(a) Italian arias

All except HWV219 and those immediately following HWV217, 223 survive in Handel's autograph; some may be discarded opera arias. Items from c.1749 may be copies of arias by other composers.

HWV	Title	Scoring, comments
211	*Aure dolci, deh, spirate*	A, str; com. London, c.1722–6
215	*Col valor del vostro brando*	S, bn, str; com. London, c.1711–13
212	*Con doppia gloria mia*	S, str (no va); com. London, c.1722–6

213	*Con lacrime sì belle*	A, obs, str; com. London, *c.*1717–18
214	*Dell'onda instabile*	A, fl, bc; com. London, *c.*1749
216	*Impari del mio core*	S, bc; com. London, *c.*1749
217	*L'odio, sì, ma poi ritrovò*	A, str (no va); com. London, *c.*1722–6
—	*Lusinga questo cor*	S, ob, str; ?com. London, *c.*1712–17
—	*No Kossi presto nò*	S, bc; ?com. London, *c.*1749–51; text apparently macaronic Italian-German
219	*Non so se avrai mai bene*	S, bc; com. London, *c.*1710–18
220	*Per dar pace al mio tormento*	S, bc; com. London, *c.*1749
221	*Quant'invidio tua fortuna*	S, bc; com. London, *c.*1749
222	*Quanto più amara fu sorte crudele*	S, str; com. London, *c.*1721–3
223	*S'un dì m'appaga, la mia crudele*	S, str (no va); com. London, *c.*1738–41
—	*Sa perchè pena il cor*	A, ob, str; ?com. London, *c.*1712–17
224	*Sì, crudel, tornerà*	S, str (no va); com. London, *c.*1738–41
225	*Spera chi sa perchè la sorte*	A, obs, str; com. London, *c.*1717–18
227	*Vo' cercando tra fiori*	S, str (no va); com. London, *c.*1726

(b) **English songs** (see also Section 2, 'Music for English Plays')

* = autograph material survives

226	[*Hunting Song*]: *The morning is charming***	T, bc; text by Charles Legh; autograph presented to Legh in 1751; voice in treble clef; (*HHA* V/5, 6)
228[18]	*Stand round, my brave boys**	T, bc; sung by Lowe at DL, 14 Nov. 1745; pub. as 'A Song made for the Gentlemen Volunteers of the City of London' (1745)
228[9]	*From scourging rebellion*	T, bc; sung by Lowe at Vauxhall Gardens, 15 May 1746

Many other individual songs attributed to Handel were pub. in London during his lifetime. Some may have been original and authentic (e.g. those listed in *HHB* as HWV228[1–24], but HWV228[12] is by T.A. Arne): others were spurious, or pirated arrangements.

7   CHURCH MUSIC

No German church music from Handel's early years in Halle and Hamburg survives.

(a)   Latin and Italian

LATIN PSALM-SETTINGS, ANTIPHONS AND MOTETS

HWV	*Title*	*Scoring, comments*
231	*Coelestis dum spirat aura*	S, str (no va); motet for Feast of St Antony of Padua, com. ? Rome,

232	*Dixit Dominus Domino meo*	1707; fp. ? 13 June 1707, Vignanello; pub. ed. Ewerhart (1957); (*HHA* III/2) S, A, chorus, str; Psalm cx (Vulgate cix); com. Rome, Apr. 1707; *HG* 38; *HHA* III/1
—	*Gloria in excelsis Deo*	S, str (nova); com. ? Rome 1707; survives in copy from 1730s; (*HHA* III/2)
235	*Haec est regina virginum*	S, str; antiphon, com. ? Rome, 1707; fp. ? 16 July 1707, Rome, for Carmelite service; pub. ed. Dixon (1990)
236	*Laudate pueri dominum* (F)	S, str (no va); Psalm cxiii (Vulgate cxii), com. *c.*1706; *HG* 38; (*HHA* III/2)
237	*Laudate pueri dominum* (D)	S, chorus, obs. str; Psalm cxiii (Vulgate cxii, cd. 8 July 1707; *HG* 38; (*HHA* III/2)
238	*Nisi Dominus*	S, A, T, B, chorus, str; Psalm cxxvii (Vulgate cxxvi); cd. Rome, 13 July 1707; fp. ? 16 July 1707, Rome; *HG* 38 (without final Gloria); pub., with Gloria, ed. Bourne (1898) and Shaw (1985); (*HHA* III/2)
239	*O qualis de coelo sonus*	S, str (no va); motet, com.? Rome, May–June 1707; fp. ? Whitsun 1707, Vignanello; pub. ed. Ewerhart (1957); (*HHA* III/2)
240	*Saeviat tellus inter rigores*	S, obs, str; motet for Feast of Madonna del Carmine; com. ? Rome, 1707; fp. ? 16 July 1707, Rome; pub. ed. Dixon (1990); (*HHA* III/2)
241	*Salve regina*	S, str (no va), obbligato org; antiphon, com. ? Rome, 1707; fp. ? Trinity Sunday 1707, Vignanello; *HG* 38; (*HHA* III/2)
242	*Silete venti*	S, obs, bn, str; motet, com. London, *c.*1724; *HG* 38; (*HHA* III/2)
243	*Te decus virgineum*	A, str (no va); antiphon, com. Rome, 1707; fp. ? 16 July 1707, Rome

ITALIAN SACRED CANTATAS

230	*Ah, che troppo ineguali/O del ciel Maria regina*	S, str; recit. and aria, com. ? Rome, 1707–8; *HG* 52*b*; (*HHA* V/4)
233	*Donna, che in ciel*	S, chorus, str; fp ? Feb. 1707 or 1708, Rome; pub. ed. Ewerhart (1959); (*HHA* III/2)

Misattributed:

234	*[Il pianto di Maria]: Giunta l'ora fatal*	cantata, S, str; by G. Ferrandini

| 244, 245 | *Kyrie eleison; Gloria in excelsis deo* | chorus and orch; by A. Lotti (*Missa Sapientiae*); MS copy by Handel from *c.* 1749 |

Handel also made copies of the motet *Intret in conspecto tuo* by G. Legrenzi, a *Magnificat* by D.Erba and fragments from masses by F.Habermann.

(b) English anthems and canticles

Anthems generally comprise selected verses of the psalms, as translated in the Book of Common Prayer

VERSE ANTHEM WITH (ORGAN) CONTINUO

HWV	Title	*Comments*
251	*As pants the hart*	Psalm xlii, 2 versions: HWV251*a*, com. *c.*1712–13; HWV251*d*, com. *c.*1722. Closely related to HWV251*b* and 251*c/e* (see below). *HG* 34, 36; *HHA* III/9

CANNONS ('CHANDOS') ANTHEMS
Com. 1717–18, fp. St Lawrence, Cannons Park, Edgware. For S, 1–3 T, B (+ A in HWV252, 256*a*), ob, bn, str (no va), org (+ recs in HWV253 and 255). *HG* 34–5; *HHA* III/4–6

246	*O be joyful in the Lord*	see 'Canticles' below
247	*In the Lord put I my trust*	Psalms ix, xi, xii, xiii in the metrical version by Tate and Brady
248	*Have mercy upon me*	Psalm li
249*b*	*O sing unto the Lord a new song*	Psalms xciii, xcvi; partly based on HWV249*a* (see 'Other anthems', below)
250*c*	*I will magnify thee*	Psalms cxliv, cxlv; 2 movements added later
251*b*	*As pants the hart*	Psalm xlii; text and some music derived from HWV251*a*.
252	*My song shall be alway*	Psalm lxxxix; partly derived from HWV280; trio 'Thou rulest the raging of the sea' perf. at Cannons but possibly not by Handel
253	*O come, let us sing unto the Lord*	Psalms xcv, xcvi, xcvii, xcix, ciii
254	*O praise the Lord with one consent*	Psalms cxvii, cxxxv, cxlviii in metrical versions of Tate and Brady
255	*The Lord is my light*	Psalms xviii, xx, xxvii–xxx, xlv
256*a*	*Let God arise*	Psalms lxviii, lxxvi; 1st movement of 'symphony' added later

Misattributed:

| 257 | *O praise the Lord, ye angels of his* | Attrib. Handel in Arnold's edition and in *HG* 36: by Maurice Greene, before 1728 |

OTHER ANTHEMS (approximately chronological order)
For soloists, chorus and orchestra (ob(s), bn(s), str), with fl(s) in HWV262, 266,
tpts in HWV249a, tpts and timp in 258, 260–3, 265–8)

249a	*O sing unto the Lord a new song*	Psalm xcvi; for Chapel Royal, fp. CR, ?26 Sep. 1714; *HG* 36; *HHA* III/9
251c	*As pants the hart*	Psalm xlii; for Chapel Royal, text and music largely from HWV251a–b; fp. CR ?7 Oct. 1722; *HG* 34; *HHA* III/9
250b	*I will magnify thee*	Psalms lxxxix, xcvi, cxlv; for Chapel Royal, some music from HWV250a, 249b, 252, 253; fp. CR, ?5 Jan. 1724; *HG* 34; *HHA* III/9
256b	*Let God arise*	Psalm lxviii; for Chapel Royal, partly derived from HWV256a; fp. CR, ?16 Jan. 1726; *HG* 35; *HHA* III/9

258–61 Four anthems for Coronation of King George II and Queen Caroline, fp.
WA, 11 Oct. 1727; *HG* 14; (*HHA* III/10)

258	*Zadok the priest*	English version of antiphon 'Unxerunt Salomonem Sadoc sacerdos', after *I Kings*; performed at the Anointing
259	*Let thy hand be strengthened*	Psalm lxxxix
260	*The king shall rejoice*	Psalm xxi
261	*My heart is inditing*	Psalm xlv, *Isaiah*; for the queen's coronation
262	*This is the day which the Lord has made* (Anthem for Wedding of Princess Anne)	Psalms xlv, cxviii, *Proverbs, Ecclesiasticus*; fp. French Chapel, St James's Palace, 14 Mar. 1734; *HG* 36; (*HHA* III/11)
263	*Sing unto God, ye kingdoms of the earth* (Anthem for Wedding of Frederick, Prince of Wales)	Psalms lxviii, cvi, cxxviii; fp. CR, 27 Apr. 1736; revised for 'wedding' of Princess Mary, CR, 8 May 1740; *HG* 36; (*HHA* III/11)
264	*The ways of Zion do mourn* (Funeral Anthem for Queen Caroline)	Text from *Lamentations, Samuel, Job, Ecclesiasticus, Philippians, Wisdom* and Psalms ciii, cxii; cd. 12 Dec. 1737; fp. King Henry VII's Chapel, WA, 17 Dec. 1737; probably fully choral, without solo movements; *HG* 11; (*HHA* III/12)
265	*The king shall rejoice* (Dettingen Anthem)	Psalms xx, xxi; com. 30 July–3 Aug. 1743; fp. CR, 27 Nov. 1743; *HG* 36; (*HHA* III/13)
266	*How beautiful are the feet of them* (Anthem on the Peace [of Aix-la-Chapelle])	*Isaiah*, Psalms xxix, xcvi, *Revelation*; uses music from HWV56, 62, 250b; fp. CR, 25 Apr.

Handel

1749; music from discarded 1st movement (HWV267) used for 3rd movement; pub. ed. Burrows (1981); (*HHA* III/14)

268 *Blessed are they that considereth the poor* (Foundling Hospital Anthem)

Psalms viii, xli, lxxii, cxii, *Daniel, Revelation*; based partly on music from HWV56, 66, 264; fp. FHC, 27 May 1749, probably in fully choral version; solo movements probably added *c.* 1751; *HG* 36; (*HHA* III/14)

CANTICLES

For soloists, chorus and orchestra (ob(s), bn(s) and str), with fl in HWV278, 280–2, tpt(s) in HWV278–81, tpts and timps in HWV283. *Te Deum* = We praise thee, O God (Ambrosian hymn); *Jubilate* = O be joyful in the Lord (Psalm c).

HWV	Title, key	Comments
278	Te Deum in D ('Utrecht')	cd. 14 Jan. 1713; fp. SP, 7 July 1713; *HG* 31; *HHA* III/3
279	Jubilate in D ('Utrecht')	com. ?Jan–Feb. 1713; fp. SP, 7 July 1713; *HG* 31; *HHA* III/3
280	Te Deum in D ('Caroline')	com. 1714; fp. CR, ?26 Sep. 1714; r. *c.*1722, 1749 (both CR); *HG* 37; (*HHA* III/8)
281	Te Deum in B♭ ('Chandos' or 'Cannons')	com. and fp. *c.*1717–18, St Lawrence, Cannons; *HG* 37; (*HHA* III/7)
246	Jubilate in D ('Cannons')	com. and fp. *c.*1717–18, St Lawrence, Cannons; based on HWV279; *HG* 34; (*HHA* III/4)
282	Te Deum in A	fp. CR, ?16 Jan. 1726; partly derived from HWV281; *HG* 37; (*HHA* III/8)
283	Te Deum in D ('Dettingen')	com. 17 July–*c.* 29 July 1743; fp. CR, 27 Nov. 1743; *HG* 25; (*HHA* III/13)

(c) Hymns and songs to devotional texts

HWV Title, comments

202–10 Nine 'Deutsche Arien', for S, treble inst. (?fl, ob or vn) and bc; texts by B.H. Brockes from *Irdisches Vergnügen in Gott*; com. London, *c.*1724–6; pub. ed. Roth (1920, 1931) and Siegmund-Schultze (1981). (*HHA* V/5, 6):

202 *Künft' ger Zeiten eitler Kummer*
203 *Das zitternde Glänzen der spielenden Wellen*
204 *Süsser Blumen Ambraflocken*
205 *Süsse Stille, sanfte Quelle ruhiger Gelassenheit*
206 *Singe, Seele, Gott zum Preise*

207	*Meine Seele hört im sehen*
208	*Die ihr aus dunkeln Grüften*
209	*In den angenehmen Büschen*
210	*Flammende Rose, Zierde der Erden*

269–77 Settings of 'Amen' and '(H)alleluja, amen'; S, bc; com. London, *c.*1734–41, 1744–7; *HG* 38 (HWV269–74 only); (*HHA* III/Supplement)

284–6 Three English Hymns, S, bc; texts by Charles Wesley; com. London, *c.* 1747; pub. ed. Burrows in *Handel: The Complete Hymns and Chorales* (1988):

284	*Sinners obey the Gospel word* (The Invitation)
285	*O Love divine, how sweet thou art* (Desiring to Love)
286	*Rejoice, the Lord is King* (On the Resurrection)

8   ORCHESTRAL MUSIC

Works are listed in approximate chronological order in each section

(a)   Concertos and suites

HWV	*Title, key (scoring), edition*	*Comments*
348–50	*Water Music* 3 suites: HWV348, F (obs, bn, hns, str); HWV349, D (obs, bn, hns, tpts, str); HWV350, G/g (pic, fl, str); *HG* 47; *HHA* IV/13	cd. by 1717, perhaps based on earlier suites: fp. River Thames, 17 July 1717; autograph lost: arrangement into suites not explicit in early sources
—	Water Music Chamber Suite, 9 movements for bn, vns, bc	contemporary arrangement, but authenticity uncertain; pub. ed. Burrows (1991)
331	Concerto, F (obs, bn, hns, str); *HG* 47; *HHA* IV/13 (*Anhang*)	2 movements, thematically related to HWV348 (see above); ?fp. DL, 20 Mar. 1723
341	*The Famous Water Peice* [*sic*], D, Ouverture and 4 movements (tpt, str); *HHA* IV/13 (*Anhang*)	Pub. *c.*1733; Ouverture resembles movement from HWV349, but work is almost certainly spurious
312–17	Six Concerti grossi, op.3; *HG* 21; *HHA* IV/11; pub. 1734 by Walsh from earlier music:	
312	op.3 no.1, B♭ (recs, obs, bns, str)	?com. Hanover, *c.*1710; no Handel autograph
313	op.3 no.2, B♭ (obs, str)	com. *c.*1715–18
314	op.3 no.3, G (fl *or* ob, str)	arranged (? by Walsh) from music com. *c.*1717–18
315	op.3 no.4, F ('Orchestra Concerto') (obs, bn, str)	com. for KT opera orchestra's benefit night, *Amadigi*, 20 June 1716; in early copies of 1st edition of op.3 a spurious concerto (*HHA* IV/11, printed as 'Op.3 No 4a') was accidentally substituted

316	op.3 no.5, d (obs, str)	arranged, probably by Handel, mainly from sinfonias to 'Cannons' anthems, 1717–18
317	op.3 no.6, D/d (obs, bn, str, with 'org' in 2nd movement)	2 movements, probably assembled by Walsh from movement in *Ottone* (see HWV338, immediately below) and D minor keyboard concerto movement
338	Adagio, b/Allegro, D (obs, str, with fl and 'archiluto' in Adagio); *HHA* IV/15	originally, with 1st movement of HWV317, a 3-movement orchestral concerto, c.1722: 1st movement used as sinfonia in *Ottone*; theme of last movement reworked for ouverture of *Ottone*.
318	Concerto Grosso, C ('Alexander's Feast Concerto') (obs, str); *HG* 21; *HHA* IV/15	com. 1736, for perf. between the Parts of *Alexander's Feast*

319–30 Twelve Concerti Grossi ('Grand Concertos') op.6: G, F, e, a, D, g, B♭, c, F, d, A, b; *HG* 21; *HHA* IV/15 com. Sep.–Oct. 1739, pub. 1740. Originally for str only: obs added later to some concertos by Handel, probably for theatre perfs. HWV323, 327, 329 partly derived from Ode HWV76 and organ concertos HWV295, 296, respectively; HWV327 also partly derived from ouverture to *Imeneo*

332–4	*Concerti a due cori* (B♭, F, F), using 2 wind 'choirs' (HWV332, obs, bns, str; HWV333–4 obs, bns, hns, str); *HG* 47; *HHA* IV/16 (HWV332 also in *HHA* IV/12)	com. 1747–8 for perf. with oratorios: HWV334 for *Judas Maccabaeus*. HWV332–3 include new orchestral versions of music from oratorios
335a	Concerto, D (obs, bn, 4 hns, tpts, timp, org, str); *HG* 47; *HHA* IV/16	com. c.1748–9: 1st movement related to HWV351 (see below)
335b	Concerto, F (obs, bn, 4 hns, str); *HG* 47; *HHA* IV/16	com. c.1748–9: 1st movement related to HWV351 (see below)
351	*Music for the Royal Fireworks* ('Fireworks Music'), Ouverture and 5 movements (?fls, obs, bns, hns, tpts, timp, str); *HG*, 47; *HHA* IV/13	for celebrations of Peace of Aix-la-Chapelle; fp. Green Park, 27 Apr. 1749

(b) Miscellaneous orchestral, and fragments

344, 354	'Chorus' and Minuet (HWV344) and Suite, B♭ (HWV354) (str); *HHA* IV/19	no autographs; apparently movements from Hamburg opera *Florindo*
352–3	Suites, B♭ G (obs, str); *HHA* IV/19	no autographs; apparently movements from Hamburg opera *Daphne*
339	Sinfonia, B♭ (str); *HHA* IV/15 (as 'HWV338')	no autograph; probably com. Hamburg or Italy, c.1706–7
336	Ouverture, B♭ (obs, bn, str); *HG* 48; *HHA* IV/15	autograph lost; probably com. Germany or Italy

355	Aria (Hornpipe), c(str); *HHA* IV/19	no autograph; ? com. *c.*1710–15
340	Allegro, G (str); *HG* 48; *HHA* IV/19	no autograph; ? com. *c.*1710–15
404	Sonata, g (ob, str); *HHA* IV/15	no autograph; similar style and scoring to Cannons anthem music, 1717–18
337	Ouverture, D (obs, bn, str); *HHA* IV/15	com. *c.* 1722–5, probably intended as introductory movement
342	Ouverture, F (obs, hns, str); *HG* 48 (in G)	version of the overtures used in 1733–4 for *Athalia* (HWV52) and *Parnasso in festa* (HWV73) com. *c.*1736
413	Gigue, B♭ (str); *HHA* IV/19	
345	Marche, D (tpt, str); *HG* 48; *HHA* IV/19	no autograph; com. before 1738
302*b*	Largo, F (obs, hns, str); *HG* 21; *HHA* IV/12	autograph headed 'Suite de pieces' (this was presumably the opening movement), comp. *c.*1738
343	Ritornello for Chaconne HWV435 (obs, str)	see under 'Solo concertos', below
356	Hornpipe, D (str); *HG* 48; *HHA* IV/19	no autograph; com. for Vauxhall (Gardens), 1740
—	'March in Judas Maccabaeus', F (obs, hns, side drum, str); *HHA* IV/16	com. *c.* 1747–8, as addition to *Judas Maccabaeus* or to Concerto HWV334
347	Sinfonia, B♭ (obs, str); *HHA* IV/19	3 movements, also used elsewhere; com. *c.* 1747

(c) Solo concertos with orchestra

287	Concerto, g, ob, orch (str); *HG* 21; *HHA* IV/12	com. ?Hamburg, *c.* 1704–5; no autograph; pub. 1863/4, but 1 early MS copy
288	Sonata a 5, B♭, vn, orch (obs, str); *HG* 21; *HHA* IV/12	com. Italy, *c.*1707, ? for Corelli in Rome
(317)	Allegro, d, org (or harpsichord), orch (obs, str); *HG* 21; *HHA* IV/11	pub. in op. 3 no. 6 (1734); probably com. 1733–4, though based on earlier solo keyboard piece

289–94 Six Organ Concertos, op.4, pub. 1738; *HG* 28; *HHA* IV/2

289	op.4 no.1, g (orch: obs, str)	com. 1735–6; fp. with *Alexander's Feast* 19 Feb. 1736 (CG)
290	op. 4 no.2, B♭ (orch: obs, str)	com. 1735; fp. with *Esther*, 5 Mar. 1735 (CG)
291	op.4 no.3, g (orch: obs, str, solo vn, solo vc)	com. 1735; fp. with *Esther*, 5 Mar. 1735 (CG); variant versions of last movement
292	op. 4 no.4, F (orch: obs, str)	cd. 25 Mar. 1735; fp. with *Athalia*, 1 Apr. 1735 (CG); originally concluded with 'Alleluja' chorus (*HG* 20, p.161), short instrumental

		ending probably written by Handel for Walsh publication
293	op.4 no.5, F (orch: obs, str)	adapted by Handel from rec. sonata HWV369; fp. ? with *Deborah*, 26 Mar. 1735 (CG)
294	op.4 no.6, B♭ (orch: recs, str) (Harp Concerto)	com. for harp, perf. in *Alexander's Feast*, 19 Feb. 1736 (CG); later arranged for org, but solo part not identical to Walsh publication
303	Adagio, d, 2 orgs (orch: ?obs, bns, str); *HG* 48; *HHA* IV/12	com. *c*.1738; end adapted by Handel to lead into another movement; later pub. (for solo org) as 1st movement of op.7 no.4 (HWV309; see below)
343	Ritornello, G (orch: obs, str); *HHA* IV/19	added to Chaconne HWV435 (see Section 10(a) below); part of fragmentary outline of organ concerto, including Chaconne, and followed by cue or sketch for 3rd movement of HWV295; com. *c*.1738–9

295– 300	Six 'Second Set' Organ Concertos, pub. 1740; HWV295–6 original, remainder arranged from op.6 concerti grossi (HWV328, 319, 323, 324), pub. as keyboard parts only; *HG* 48; *HHA* IV/7:	
295	no.1, F (orch: obs, str)	cd. 2 Apr. 1739; fp. with *Israel in Egypt*, 4 Apr. 1739 (KT); variant forms of 2nd movement; music later used in HWV327 (op.6 no.9)
296*a*	no.2, A (orch: obs, str)	fp. probably with *Alexander's Feast*, 20 Mar. 1739 (KT); music later used as basis for HWV329 (op.6 no.11)
301, 302*a*	Two concertos, ob and str, both B♭; pub. London, 1740, in collection *Select Harmony*; authenticity of HWV301 uncertain; HWV302*a* arranged from Cannons anthem overtures; *HG*21; *HHA* IV/12	
296*b*	'Pasticcio' concerto, A, org, orch (obs, str)	arranged by Handel (*c*.1743–6) from HWV296*a*, 294, 307
304	Concerto, d, org, orch (str); *HG* 48; *HHA* IV/12	com. *c*.1746; musical material from Telemann
305	Concerto, F, org, orch (?obs, str); *HG* 48 (with defective text derived from Arnold's edition); *HHA* IV/16 (org part only)	arranged by Handel (*c*.1747–8) from *Concerto a due cori* HWV334 (3 movements) and March in F; rearranged by Handel at same period as solo keyboard piece (HWV305*b*)
306–11	Six Organ Concertos, op.7, pub. 1761; *HG* 28; *HHA* IV/7	
306	op.7 no.1, B♭ (orch: obs, bns, str)	cd.17 Feb. 1740; fp. with *L'Allegro*, 27 Feb. 1740 (LIF); 1st movement includes independent pedal part

307	op.7 no.2, A (orch: obs, str)	cd. 5 Feb. 1743; fp. with *Samson*, 18 Feb. 1743 (CG); last movement based on rejected overture movement from *Samson*
308	op.7 no.3, B♭ (orch: obs, str)	com. 1–4 Jan. 1751; fp? with *Alexander's Feast/Choice of Hercules*, 1 Mar. 1751 (CG); 2 variant autographs of 1st movement
309	op.7 no.4, d/D (orch: obs, bns, str)	probably a compilation, from HWV303, movement 'Allegro così così' (autograph *c.*1743) and last movement of HWV317
310	op.7 no.5, g (orch: obs, str)	cd. 31 Jan. 1750; fp. with *Theodora*, 16 Mar. 1750 (CG); final gavotte in pub. version probably added later by Smith jr
311	op.7 no.6, B♭ (orch: obs, str)	com. *c.*1748–9, perf. 1749; closely related to HWV347

(d) Music for wind ensembles

Pub. in *HHA* IV/19, unless otherwise indicated

410–11	Two 'Arias', both F, obs, bn, hns	com. *c.*1725
346	Marche, F, obs, ?bn, hns	com. ? before 1729; also known as 'March in Ptolomy'
416	Marche, D, obs, tpt, bn	com. *c.*1734 ('Dragoon's March')
418	Marche, G, ?obs, bn	com. ?*c.*1741
424	Ouverture (5 movements), D, 2 clarinets, hn; *HHA* IV/15	com. *c.*1741
—	Marche lentement, C, 3 trombones, timp; not in *HHA*	com. *c.*1741, wind version of *Samson* 'Dead March'; facsimile of autograph in Burrows, 'Handel, the Dead March'
—	Marche, G, obs, ?bn, hns; not in *HHA*	independent wind version of *Judas Maccabaeus* march (HWV63, no.32*a*); com. *c.*1746–7
417	La Marche, D, hns (? + obs), bn	com. *c.*1746–7
422–3	Two Menuets, both G, obs, bn, hns	com. *c.*1746–7
414–15	Two Marches for the fife, C, D, fife, bass instrument	com. *c.*1747

The marches HWV419[1–6] may include 2-stave versions of other wind ensemble marches.

9 CHAMBER MUSIC

For detailed coverage of questions of authenticity and chronology, see Best, 'Handel's Chamber Music'.

(a) Solo sonatas with continuo

Identification of these works has been confused by the numbering adopted in published editions. This list follows HWV order, giving precedence to the instrumentation given or implied in autographs or early MSS. Some bc parts may have been intended for harpsichord alone. References to the early printed editions, retrospectively called 'Op. 1', are given in the forms R/W (= Walsh edition with 'Roger' title-page) and W/W (= Walsh edition with Walsh title-page). *HG* 27 adapted and extended these 'Op. 1' numberings; differences are noted below. Miscellaneous solo pieces are also included.

HWV	*Title, scoring, key, main edition*	*Comments*
357	Sonata, ob, B♭; *HHA* IV/18	com. *c.*1707–10
358	Sonata, ?vn (or rec), G; *HHA* IV/18	com. *c.*1707–10
359	Sonata, vn, d; *HHA* IV/18	com. *c.*1724; R/W and W/W Sonata 1 in e for fl (HWV359*b*), as also *HG* op.1 no.1*b* and *HHA* IV/3
360	Sonata, rec, g; *HHA* IV/3	com. *c.*1725–6; R/W and W/W Sonata 2; *HG* op.1 no.2
361	Sonata, vn, A; *HHA* IV/4	com. *c.*1725–6; R/W and W/W Sonata 3; *HG* op.1 no.3
362	Sonata, rec, a; *HHA* IV/3	com. *c.*1725–6; R/W and W/W Sonata 4, *HG* op.1 no.4
363	Sonata, ob, F; *HHA* IV/18	com. *c.*1711–16. R/W and W/W Sonata 5 in G for fl (HWV363*b*), as also *HG* op.1 no.5 and *HHA* IV/3
364*a*	Sonata, vn, g; *HHA* IV/18	com. *c.*1724; R/W and W/W Sonata 6 in g for ob, as also *HG* op.1 no.6
364*b*	Sonata, va da gamba, g	arrangement of HWV364 (indicated by cue in autograph)
365	Sonata, rec, C; *HHA* IV/3	com. *c.*1725–6; R/W and W/W Sonata 7; *HG* op.1 no.7
366	Sonata, ob, c; *HHA* IV/18	com. *c.*1711–12; R/W and W/W Sonata 8; *HG* op.1 no.8
367	Sonata, ? rec (or vn), d; *HHA* IV/18	com. *c.*1725–6; R/W and W/W Sonata 9 for fl in b (HWV367*b*), as also *HG* op.1 no.9 and *HHA* IV/3
368	Sonata, vn, g; *HHA* IV/4	W/W Sonata 10 (only source); *HG* op.1 no.10; probably spurious
369	Sonata, rec, F; *HHA* IV/3	com. *c.*1725–6; R/W and W/W Sonata 11; *HG* op.1 no.11
370	Sonata, vn, F; *HHA* IV/4	W/W Sonata 12 (only source); *HG* op.1. no.12; probably spurious
371	Sonata, vn, D; *HHA* IV/4	com. *c.*1750; *HG* op.1 no.13
372	Sonata, vn, A; *HHA* IV/4	R/W Sonata 10 (only source); *HG* op.1 no.14; probably spurious

373	Sonata, vn, E; *HHA* IV/4	R/W Sonata 12 (only source); *HG* op.1 no.15; probably spurious
374–6	Sonatas, fl, a, e, b; *HG* 48 (Sonatas XVI, XVII, XVIII); *HHA* IV/3	no autographs; pub. London, *c*.1730 (only source for HWV374–5); authenticity uncertain: sometimes called 'Hallenser Sonaten' (following Chrysander's assumption that they were early works); HWV375 includes movements transposed from HWV366, 434
377	Sonata, ?rec, B♭; *HHA* IV/18	com. *c*.1724–5
378	Sonata, fl, D; *HHA* IV/18	com. ?*c*.1707; no autograph, but probably authentic
379	Sonata, fl, e; *HHA* IV/3	com. *c*.1727–8; *HG* op.1 no.1*a*
406	Adagio and Allegro, [vn], A; *HHA* IV/19	com. *c*.1751; 3-part accompaniment (? orchestral short score)
407	Allegro, [vn], no bc, G; *HHA* IV/19	com. *c*.1738
408	Allegro, [vn], c; *HHA* IV/19	com. *c*.1725–9
409	Andante, [?rec], d	com. *c*.1725–6; variant of movement from HWV367
412	[Andante] [vn], a; *HHA* IV/19	com. *c*.1725–6
417	La Marche, D; *HHA* IV/19	com. *c*.1747; 2-stave version of March for wind ensemble (see Section 8 (d), above), instrumentation unspecified
419¹⁻⁶	6 Marches; *HHA* IV/19	com. *c*.1710–20; known only from printed sources; pub. as separate treble and bass parts (nos.1–5) or on 2 staves (no.6); instrumentation unspecified, though title-pages mention fl and vn for treble parts
420–1	Menuets, D; *HHA* IV/19	com. *c*.1743–4; 2-stave versions in autograph; instrumentation unspecified, upper stave ?vns

(b) Trio sonatas with continuo

For 2 vns and bc unless noted otherwise, though fl and/or ob are named as alternatives on original publications.

HWV	*Title, scoring, key, edition*	*Comments*
380–5	Six Trio Sonatas [ob, vn]: B♭, d, E♭, F, G, D; *HG* 27; *HHA* IV/9	no autographs: 1 MS source not deriving from Handel's known copyists; authenticity doubtful
386–91	Six Trio Sonatas, op.2, pub. Walsh, 1733 (with successive 'Roger' and 'Walsh' title-pages); no autographs. *HG*27; *HHA* IV/10/1:	
386*a*	?ob & vn, c	com. *c*.1717–19; *HG* op.2 no.1*a*; variant form of op.2 no.1, not pub. by Walsh but found in MSS

386*b*	op.2 no.1, fl & vn, b	com. before 1727; *HG* op.2 no.1*b*
387	op.2 no.2, g	?com. 1699; *HG* op.2 no.2
388	op.2 no.3, B♭	com. *c*.1717–18; *HG* op.2 no.4
389	op.2 no.4, fl & vn (or 2 vn), F	com. *c*.1718–22; *HG* op.2 no.5
390	op.2 no.5, g	com. *c*.1717–22; *HG* op.2 no.6
391	op.2 no.6, g	com. *c*.1707; *HG* op.2 no.7
392	Sonata, F; *HG* 27 (op.2 no.3); *HHA* IV/10/1	no autograph, but probably authentic and com. *c*.1706–7
393	Sonata, g; *HG* 27 (op.2 no.8); *HHA* IV/10/1	authenticity uncertain: if by Handel, probably com. *c*.1719
394	Sonata, E; *HG* 27 (op.2 no.9); *HHA* IV/10/1	authenticity doubtful
395	Sonata, 2 fl, e; *HHA* IV/19	authenticity uncertain

396– 7 Trio Sonatas, op. 5, pub. Walsh (for vns or fls), 1739: A, D, e, G, g, F,
402 B♭. The set includes movements derived from earlier music, notably Cannons anthems, operas of 1734–5 and (for op.5 no.4) the ouverture to *Athalia/Parnasso in festa*. Handel composed new music *c*.1737–8 for nos.5 and 6, and possibly for nos.1 and 3, presumably in prospect of the publication. *HG* 27; *HHA* IV/10/2

403	Sonata, C; *HHA* IV/19	com. *c*.1738; music also used as basis for Ouverture and Sinfonia in *Saul* HWV53.
404	Sonata, ob, g	see under Section 8(b), above
405	Sonata, 2 recs, F; *HHA* IV/19	com. *c*.1707–10

10   KEYBOARD MUSIC

Mainly for harpsichord (possible exceptions are noted). There are no autographs of Handel's keyboard music from his pre-Italian years.

(a)   Suites

The two collections of suites published in London during Handel's lifetime, HWV426–33 and 434–42, went through a number of forms as Handel ejected, added to or replaced movements. For the early publication history of the suites, see the preface to *HHA* IV/5, neuausgabe 1999.

HWV   Title, keys, comments

426–33 Eight *Suites de Pièces*, 'printed for the Author', 1720; com. or assembled by Handel in the preceding period: A, F, d, e, E, f♯, g, f. Suite HWV430 includes the 'Air con Variazioni', later known as 'The Harmonious Blacksmith', which is also found in early MS sources as a 'Chaconne' in G (at least 2 variant forms) *HG* 2; *HHA* IV/1

434–42 *Suites de Pièces*, pub. Walsh as 'Second Volume', *c*.1733–4, but most com. earlier than HWV426–33; *HG* 2; *HHA* IV/5:

434	[Suite], B♭	com. ?1710–17; the Menuet, g (HWV434/4), is independent and not part of the suite
435	[Suite], Chaconne (21 variations), G	stage 4 from 5 versions of the Chaconne, com. *c*.1705–17; see

		Handel, ed. Best, *Chaconne in G*, and also Ritornello HWV343 in Section 8(c), above
436	[Suite], d	com. *c*.1721–6
437	[Suite], d	com. *c*.1703–6
438	[Suite], e	com. *c*.1710–17
439	[Suite], g	com. *c*.1703–6
440	[Suite], B♭	com. *c*.1703–6, revised *c*.1717–18
441	[Suite], G	com. *c*.1703–6
442	Prelude and Chaconne (62 variations), G	com. *c*.1703–6; 2 different Preludes in sources (HWV442/1*b* in Walsh)
305*b*	Ouverture, F	see Section 10(c) below
443	Suite, C; *HHA* IV/17	com. *c*.1700–3; includes Chaconne (26 variations)
444	Partita, c; *HHA* IV/17	com. *c*.1705–6
445	Suite, c; *HHA* IV/17	com. *c*.1705–6
446	Suite, 2 harpsichords, c; *HG* 48; *HHA* IV/19	com. *c*.1703–6; music for only 1 harpsichord survives
447	Suite, d; *HG* 2; *HHA* IV/6	com. *c*.1738–9, for Princess Louisa (see also HWV452 for companion suite)
448	Suite, d; *HG* 48; *HHA* IV/17	com. *c*.1705–6
449	Suite, d; *HG* 48; *HHA* IV/17	com. *c*.1705
450	Partita, G; *HHA* IV/17	com. *c*.1700–5
451	Suite, g; *HHA* IV/19	com. *c*.1703–6; allemande and courante only
452	Suite, g; *HG* 2; *HHA* IV/6	com. *c*.1738–9, for Princess Louisa (see also HWV447 for companion suite)
453	Suite, g; *HHA* IV/17 and IV/19	com. *c*.1705–6
454	Partita, A; *HG* 48; *HHA* IV/6	com. *c*.1703–6
455	Suite, B♭	com. *c*.1706; keyboard version of orchestral Ouverture HWV336 and Suite HWV354

(b) Fugues

605–10 Six fugues, pub. *c*.1735 as *Six Fugues or Voluntaries for the Organ or Harpsicord, Troisieme Ovarage* [*sic*], following the 2 collections of suites; com. *c*.1711–18: g, G, B♭, b, a, c; *HG* 2; *HHA* IV/6

611	Fugue, F; *HHA* IV/17	no autograph; com. *c*.1705
612	Fugue, E; *HHA* IV/19	no autograph: single source is from MS of organ voluntaries; probably authentic, though text of final bars defective; fugue subject related to *Water Music* overture.

Other fugues, com. at the same period as HWV605–10, were incorporated by Handel into his suites. The 'Six Short Fugues' in *HG* 48 are spurious.

(c) **Authentic keyboard arrangements (or versions) of music from stage and orchestral works**

* = autograph survives

456[1-5]	Overtures:* *Il pastor fido, Amadigi, Flavio, Rodelinda, Riccardo Primo*; HG 48 (*Il pastor fido* only); HHAIV/19	com. *c*.1720–7
482[1-5]	Arias from *Rinaldo,** *Floridante,** *Radamisto, Muzio Scevola*; HHA IV/19	com. *c*.1720–5
305*b*	Ouverture,* f; HHA IV/16	com. *c*. 1747; solo keyboard arrangement of Concerto HWV 305

Another 15 authentic overture arrangements pub. in Handel, ed. Best, *Twenty Overtures*. Ouverture movements also occur in other keyboard works: that in the Suite HWV432 derives from the orchestral overture in the cantata HWV96, later used by Handel for *Oreste* (HWVA[4])

(d) **Individual movements**

HWV	Title, key, edition	Comments
457	Air, C; *HHA* IV/19	com. *c*.1720–1
458	Air, c; *HHA* IV/17 (*Anhang*)	com. ?*c*.1710–1720; authenticity uncertain
459	Air, c; *HHA* IV/17 (*Anhang*)	com. ?*c*.1710–1720; authenticity uncertain
460	Air (March), D; *HHA* IV/19	com. *c*.1720–1
461	Air (Hornpipe), d; *HHA* IV/19	com. *c*.1717–18
462	Air en menuet, d; *HHA* IV/19	com. *c*.1724–6
425	Air (Saraband), E; *HHA* IV/19	'compos'd by Mr. Handel at St Giles extempore'; autograph *c*.1740–50 includes Handel's transcription of opening melody in tablature
463	Air, F; *HHA* IV/19	com. *c*.1707–9
464	Air, F; *HHA* IV/13 (*Anhang*)	com. *c*.1724–6; version of Air from *Water Music*
465	Air and 2 Doubles, F; *HHA* IV/17	com. *c*.1710–20
466	Air for 2-rowed harpsichord, g; *HHA* IV/17	com. *c*.1710–20; for 2-manual harpsichord (or possibly organ); for other 2-manual pieces, see HWV470, 485, 579
467	Air Lentement, g; *HHA* IV/17	com. *c*.1710–20
468	Air, A; *HHA* IV/6	com. *c*.1727–8
469	Air, B♭; *HHA* IV/19	com. *c*.1738–9; re-used in orchestral form in HWV347 and 311
470	Air for 2-rowed harpsichord, B♭; *HHA* IV/17	com. *c*.1710–20; for 2-manual harpsichord

471	Air, B♭; *HHA* IV/17	com. *c*.1710–20
472	Allegro, C; *HHA* IV/17	com. *c*.1705
474	Air, G; *HHA* IV/19	com. *c*.1736–8; based on music of 1st chorus of *Acis and Galatea*; possibly for org
475	Allegro d; *HHA* IV/17	com. *c*.1710–20
476	Allemande, F; *HHA* IV/6	com. *c*.1730–5
477	Allemanda, A; *HHA* IV/6	com. *c*.1724–6
478	Allemande, a; *HHA* IV/17	com. *c*.1705
479	Allemande, b; *HHA* IV/15 (*Anhang*)	com. *c*.1721–2
480	Chorale, *Jesu meine Freude*, g; *HHA* IV/19	com. *c*.1736–40; chorale melody in middle part; possibly for org; 2-bar epilogue may indicate a planned variation
481	Capriccio, F; *HG* 2; *HHA* IV/6	com. *c*.1703–6
483	[Capriccio], g; *HG* 2; *HHA* IV/6	com. *c*.1720–1
484	Chaconne with 49 variations, C; *HHA* IV/17	com. *c*.1700–5; version of the Chaconne in Suite HWV443
485	Chaconne for Harpsichord with 2 Sets of Keys, F; *HG* 2; *HHA* IV/17	com. *c*. 1705; for 2-manual harpsichord
486	Chaconne, g; *HHA* IV/17	com. *c*.1705
487	Concerto, G (2 movements); *HHA* IV/17	com. *c*.1710–20
488	Allegro [Courante], F; *HG* 2; *HHA* IV/5 (in G, for HWV442)	com. *c*.1717–18
489	Courante, b; *HHA* IV/17	com. *c*.1722
490	Fantasie pour le clavecin, C; *HG* 2; *HHA* IV/6	com. *c*.1703–6
491	Gavotte, G; *HHA* IV/19	com. *c*.1705
492	Gigue, F; *HHA* IV/6	com. *c*.1726–7
493	Gigue, g (2 versions); *HHA* IV/6 (*Anhang*)	com. *c*.1704–5
494	Impertinence [Bourée], g; *HHA* IV/17	com. *c*.1705
495	Lesson, d; *HG* 48; *HHA* IV/1 (2nd ed.), *Anhang*	com. *c*.1705–10; early form (2 variants) of HWV428, movement 6
496	Lesson, a; *HG* 2; *HHA* IV/6	com. *c*.1715–20
497–558	Menuets, various keys; *HHA* IV/19	mostly printed, with others, in *HHA* IV/19; 2-stave pieces, probably for keyboard; some related to menuets in other works
A 15¹⁻³⁷	Menuets, various keys; *HHA* IV/19	arranged from music of opera arias
559	Passepied, C; *HHA* IV/19	com. *c*.1721–2
560	Passepied, A; *HHA* IV/19	com. *c*.1705
561	Prelude, d; *HG* 48; *HHA* IV/5 (2nd ed.), in Suite HWV437	com. *c*.1705–6; version of Prelude to HWV437
562	Prelude [Harpeggio], d; *HHA* IV/6	com. *c*.1711–12

563	Prelude, d; *HHA* IV/17	com. *c.*1700–3
564	Preludio, d; *HHA* IV/17	com. *c.*1705
565	Prelude, d; *HHA* IV/1 (2nd ed.), *Anhang*	com. *c.*1710–20; early version of Prelude to HWV428
566	Prelude, E; *HHA* IV/17	com. *c.*1710–20; associated in some MSS with HWV430
567	Preludium, F; *HHA* IV/17	com. *c.*1710–20
568	Preludium, f; *HHA* IV/17	com. *c.*1710–20; associated in some MSS with movements in HWV433
569	Preludium, f ('Arpeggio del Cook')	?com. *c.*1710–20; authorship uncertain
570	Prelude (Harpeggio), f♯; *HHA* IV/6	com. *c.*1717–18; originally associated with HWV431
571	Prelude and Capriccio (2 movements), G; *HG* 48; *HHA* IV/17	com. *c.*1703–6
572	Prelude, g; *HHA* IV/6	com. *c.*1710–17; originally associated with HWV432
573	Prelude (Harpeggio), g; *HHA* IV/17	com. *c.*1705
574	Prelude and Allegro (Sonata), g (2 movements); *HG* 2; *HHA* IV/6	com. *c.*1705
575	Prelude (Harpeggio), a; *HG* 2 (coupled with HWV496); *HHA* IV/6	com. *c.*1717–18
576	Prelude and Allegro (2 movements), a; *HHA* IV/17	com. *c.*1705–6
577	Sonata (Fantasia) pour le clavecin, C; *HG* 2; *HHA* IV/6	com. *c.*1703–5
579	Sonata (Fantasia), for a Harpsichord with Double Keys, g; *HHA* IV/6	com. ?*c.*1707–10 for 2-manual harpsichord
580	Sonata (Larghetto), g (1 movement); *HHA* IV/17	com. ?*c.*1707–10
581	Sonatina, d (1 movement); *HG* 48; *HHA* IV/17	com. *c.*1705
582	Sonatina ('Fuga'), G (1 movement); *HHA* IV/6	com. *c.*1721–2
583	Sonatina, g (1 movement); *HHA* IV/17	com. ?*c.*1721–2
584	Sonatina, a (1 movement); *HHA* IV/17	com. *c.*1706–8; authenticity uncertain
585	Sonatina, B♭ (1 movement); *HG* 2; *HHA* IV/6	com. *c.*1721–2
586	Toccata, g; *HHA* IV/17	com. *c.*1710–20

The 2-stave marches and menuets HWV417, 419[1-6] and 420–1 (see Section 9(a), above) may have originated as keyboard works.

11   MUSIC FOR MECHANICAL ORGANS IN CLOCKS

HWV	Title, key, edition	Comments
473	Allegro, C; *HHA* IV/19	com. 25 Aug. 1738
578	Sonata (Allegro, Trio, Gavotte), C; *HG* 2; *HHA* IV/6	com. *c.*1750; music related to HWV277, 467, 318
587–97	Eleven pieces in C, F, G; *HHA* IV/19	com. *c.*1735–40, '10 [*sic*] Tunes for Clay's Musical Clock'; includes arrangements of opera airs
598–604	Seven pieces in C, a; *HHA* IV/19	com. *c.*1730–40; HWV600 (a version of HWV588) entitled 'A Voluntary or a Flight of Angels'

Also other authentic pieces and arrangements possibly for clock-organ

12   EXERCISES IN FIGURED BASS AND FUGUE

24 exercises in figured bass, com. *c.*1724–6; 6 exercises in fugue, 13 fugal expositions (arranged by modes) and miscellaneous fugal examples (all com. *c.*1728–34). These are illustrated in facsimile in Mann, Alfred, *G.F. Handel: Aufzeichnungen zur Kompositionslehre* and are mostly printed in Ledbetter, David (ed.), *Continuo Playing according to Handel* (Oxford, 1990). There are also a few fragments of fugal writing from other periods, possibly for demonstration or teaching purposes, in Handel's miscellaneous autographs.

Appendix C

Personalia

Amadei, Flippo (*fl.*1690–1730), an Italian cellist and composer, came to London with the Earl of Burlington and served with the Royal Academy of Music 1720–3, contributing Act 1 to *Muzio Scevola*.

Arbuthnot, John (1667–1735), a mathematician, physician and author, was a supporter and friend of Handel during his first years in London. As one of the royal physicians, he may have been influential on Handel's behalf at Queen Anne's court. He was a visitor (possibly a resident) at Cannons during Handel's time there and may have contributed to the libretto of *Esther*.

Ariosti, Attilio (1666–1729) was an Italian composer, resident in Berlin 1697–1703 and established in London from 1716. He composed *Tito Manlio* for Heidegger's company, and seven operas for the Royal Academy of Music, 1723–7. He belonged to a monastic order, and also spent some time as an international diplomat.

Arne, a family of London musicians, included the composer Thomas Augustine Arne (1710–78), whose wife and sister sang for Handel (*see* 'Young' and 'Cibber, Susanna'). His father, Thomas Arne, an upholsterer, promoted performances at the Little Theatre, Haymarket, in 1732, which included *Acis and Galatea* and may have stimulated Handel's revival of the work.

Avolio [Avoglio], Christina Maria (*fl.*1727–46), a German soprano, was married to Giuseppe Avoglio, a musician at the court of Hesse-Kassel. She sang in Hamburg (1729), St Petersburg (1731–8) and in Italy before coming to London. She accompanied Handel to Dublin for the 1741–2 season and continued in his London company the following two seasons.

Bach, Johann Sebastian (1685–1750) was Handel's greatest German-born contemporary, his junior by only 26 days. Bach followed his mature career in the same area of Germany where Handel had grown up (and where many of his relations still lived), but the two never met. Bach's eldest son, Wilhelm Friedemann, became organist of Halle's Liebfrauenkirche in 1746, a post for which Johann Sebastian had competed unsuccessfully in 1713.

Beard, John (*c.*1717–1791) was a chorister at the Chapel Royal under Bernard Gates and sang in the chapel's 1732 performances of *Esther*. Two years later he made his stage début at Covent Garden as a tenor soloist in *Il pastor fido*, which began an association with Handel that lasted until the composer's death; he sang more parts in operas and oratorios under Handel than any other singer, and Handel must have composed many oratorio roles with Beard in mind. In 1759 he married as his second wife Charlotte, the daughter of John Rich, whom Beard succeeded as manager of the Covent Garden theatre. He had a successful career as an actor-singer, independent of his association with Handel.

Berenstadt, Gaetano (*c.*1690–1735) was born in Italy of German parents. He had a varied career as a castrato singer in Italy and Germany, and two periods in London, singing for Heidegger's company (1716–17) and for the Royal Academy of Music (1722–4), where, as a 'second man' to Senesino, he sang Tolomeo in *Giulio Cesare*. He maintained a lively correspondence with contacts in London and was a partisan of Bononcini in operatic politics. His 'huge unwieldy figure' (Burney) probably gave him considerable stage presence.

Bernacchi, Antonio Maria (1685–1756) enjoyed a considerable career in his native Italy as a solo castrato and, latterly, as a teacher. He sang in Heidegger's Haymarket company (1716–17) and was the leading man in the first year of the Handel-Heidegger operas (1729–30).

Bernardi, *see* 'Senesino'.

Bertolli, Francesca (*d*.1767), an Italian contralto singer, sang for Handel in the Handel-Heidegger company (1729–33) and at Covent Garden in 1736–7, having in the meantime appeared with the Opera of the Nobility. She sang in 15 Handel operas (including nine first productions), in which she took several male roles.

Bononcini, Giovanni (1670–1747), an Italian composer, had established a European reputation by 1705, notably through the popularity of his tuneful opera *Camilla* (*Il trionfo di Camilla*). The earlier part of his career centred on Rome, Vienna and Berlin (from 1702). The Earl of Burlington secured his services for the Royal Academy of Music; Bononcini came to London in 1720. His new Academy operas proved popular, especially in 1721–2, but he attracted unfortunate controversies and withdrew from the Academy in 1724, remaining in London until 1732. His one subsequent Academy production (*Astianatte*, 1727) was curtailed by a disturbance caused by partisans of the leading ladies.

Bordoni, *see* 'Faustina'.

Boschi, Giuseppe Maria (*fl*.1698–1744), an Italian bass singer, sang at Venice in *Agrippina* (1709) and was a member of the Haymarket company by the time Handel came to London: the part of Argante in *Rinaldo* was written for him. He sang in Dresden (1717–20), where Handel engaged him in 1719 as a prospective member of the Royal Academy. Though he missed the first short Academy season, Boschi sang in all 32 Academy productions between 1720 and 1728.

Boyce, William (1711–79) was educated at St Paul's Cathedral under Charles King and Maurice Greene. From 1736 he held leading offices in the Chapel Royal, and in 1755 succeeded Greene as Master of the King's Musick: he composed for the London theatres from 1746 onwards. From 1752 he seems to have been in charge of the Chapel Royal boys, in the period before Gates's retirement, and he assisted with their participation in the Foundling Hospital *Messiah* performances.

Brockes, Barthold Heinrich (1680–1747), a German poet, studied law at Halle University where in 1700–2 he organized weekly concerts in his room, but most of his career centred on his native Hamburg. His passion oratorio libretto (*Der für die Sünde der Welt gemarterte und sterbende Jesus*) was published in 1712 and was subsequently set by Keiser, Telemann, Mattheson and Handel (among others): parts of it were also used by J.S. Bach in his *St John Passion*. He is an important figure in German poetry, notably for his nine-volume collection *Irdisches Vergnügen in Gott* (Hamburg, 1721–48); Handel set poems from it in the mid-1720s, the so-called 'Deutsche Arien'.

Brydges, James (1674–1744) was educated at Westminster School and Oxford University, entered Parliament in 1698 and won fortune as Paymaster of the Army during the period of Marlborough's wars. He resigned his office in 1713 but maintained favour (though with a less active political role) during the turbulent period of transition into the reign of George I. Soon after the new king's accession he procured the titles of Viscount Wilton and Earl of Carnarvon for his father, only to receive them himself on his father's death a day later. He devoted the next years to developing his estate at Cannons, Edgware (his wife's inheritance), where Handel was associated with him (*c.*1717–18), but he also had houses in St James's Square and in the west of England. In 1719 he was raised to Duke of Chandos, but his wealth was attenuated soon afterwards by the South Sea Bubble.

Burney, Charles (1726–1814) is chiefly remembered for his *History of Music* (4 vols., 1776–89) and his 'official' history of the Handel Commemoration of 1784. In 1744 he became an articled pupil of T.A. Arne and worked among London's professional musicians in the period before he moved to King's Lynn in 1751. He later recalled several incidents relating to Handel and his circle, no doubt enlarging some of the stories in the telling.

Buxtehude, Dietrich (*c.*1637–1707) succeeded Franz Tunder as organist at the Marienkirche, Lübeck, in 1668, whereupon he married Tunder's daughter. The decision of Handel and Mattheson not to pursue the succession to Buxtehude on their visit in 1703 may have been influenced by a similar condition attaching to Buxtehude's daughter. J.S. Bach travelled to Lübeck in 1705 to hear Buxtehude's evening concerts.

Caffarelli [Majorano, Gaetano] (1710–83), an Italian castrato singer, from the mid-1730s combined a successful opera career with a place in the Naples royal chapel. He appeared as 'first man' in the Haymarket company of 1737–8, singing the title roles in *Faramondo* and *Serse*.

Caldara, Antonio (*c.*1670–1736) began his career in Venice, his birthplace, where he was a cellist at St Mark's, and composed operas and chamber music. Between 1699 and 1707 he was *maestro di cappella* to the last Gonzaga Duke of Mantua. The effects of the war in Italy limited his opportunities for composing operas and he moved to Rome, serving as *maestro* to the Marquis Ruspoli from 1709 to mid-1716, probably overlapping the end of Handel's association with Ruspoli. For Ruspoli he composed mainly oratorios and cantatas. From 1736 he served the imperial court in Vienna, where his opportunities for operatic production were restored.

Carestini, Giovanni (*c.*1704–*c.*1760), an Italian castrato singer and pupil of Bernacchi, began his operatic career in 1721, when he sang in Rome. He succeeded as the leading man in Handel's company when Senesino joined the Opera of the Nobility: he sang for Handel in 1733–5, taking virtuoso leading roles in *Arianna*, *Ariodante* and *Alcina*, and performed in the oratorios of 1735. He returned to London in 1739–40 to sing in Lord Middlesex's season at the Little Theatre, Haymarket, but met with indifferent success. Burney speaks highly of his accomplishments as a musician and actor.

Cibber [née Arne], Susanna Maria (1714–66) made a successful début in the Arne-Lampe season in 1732 at the Little Theatre, Haymarket, as a singer, and took a minor role in *Deborah* for Handel in 1733, but thereafter she concentrated on an acting career, specializing in tragic roles. The scandal surrounding the break-up of her marriage to Theophilus Cibber interrupted her career, which resumed with a season at Aungier Street Theatre, Dublin, in 1741–2. She also joined Handel's concert series in Dublin, probably for the second subscription in 1742, and sang in the first performances of *Messiah*. She sang for two further seasons with Handel in London and re-established her acting career there. In 1732 she sang Galatea, presumably as a soprano; Handel's music for her a decade later was written in the alto clef.

Clive [née Raftor], Catharine ['Kitty'] (1711–85), of Anglo-Irish descent, was primarily an actress, and particularly successful in ballad operas. Handel wrote two songs for her, for plays at Drury Lane in 1737 and 1740, and she was a member of his company for the 1743 oratorio season at Covent Garden, singing in the first London performances of *Messiah* and creating the role of Dalila in *Samson*.

Conti, Gioacchino (1714–61) made his operatic début as a castrato in Rome in 1730. He made his London début in *Atalanta* in 1736 and sang at Covent Garden as 'second man' to Annibali in Handel's company in 1736–7, taking leading roles in the new operas *Arminio*, *Giustino* and *Berenice*. His tessitura was unusually high, and Handel wrote for him in the soprano clef.

Corelli, Arcangelo (1653–1713) established a career as a violinist and composer in Rome from *c*.1675. From 1687 he was employed by Cardinal Pamphili; he led the orchestras for Handel's Roman oratorios in 1707–8. Corelli's concerti grossi op.6, published the year after his death and regarded as 'classic' works in their genre, were popular in Britain: their status and style probably influenced Handel's own op.6.

Croft, William (1678–1727) was educated at the Chapel Royal under John Blow and, as the leading London church musician, was the obvious successor to Blow and Clarke in 1708. He wrote orchestrally accompanied church music before and after Handel's arrival in London, and strengthened his own style after contact with Handel's 'Utrecht' music. He also composed instrumental music, and secular odes and songs.

Cuzzoni, Francesca (1696–1778) had established a substantial musical reputation before reaching London, where she was a principal soprano for the Royal Academy between 1723 and 1728, for the last two years in rivalry with Faustina. She had outstanding success as Cleopatra in Handel's *Giulio Cesare*, and took leading roles in ten other Handel operas. She sang for the Opera of the Nobility in 1734–6 and returned to London for farewell concert appearances in 1750–1, by which time she had clearly lost the vocal attractions that had moved her audiences when she was in her prime.

Delany, Mrs, *see* 'Granville'.

Dubourg, Matthew (1703–67), a violin pupil of Geminiani, made his first solo appearance at Lincoln's Inn Fields Theatre in 1715. In June 1727 he married Frances, the daughter of Bernard Gates, and the next year he left London for Dublin (which he had visited in *c*.1724) to become leader of the Lord Lieutenant's musicians. He subsequently divided his time between Dublin and London, leading the orchestra during Handel's Dublin season of 1741–2 and that for the Covent Garden oratorios of 1743. He received a bequest of £100 from Handel.

Duparc, *see* 'Francesina'.

Durastanti, Margherita (*fl*.1700–34) was a soprano, the path of whose career coincided with Handel's in his early maturity. As the leading woman at the S Giovanni Grisostomo theatre in Venice, she sang the title role in *Agrippina* in 1709. Ten years later she was singing in Dresden when Handel visited to secure singers for the Royal Academy: she sang in the Academy's opening productions in London (Porta's *Numitore* and Handel's *Radamisto*), in their next season and, after a break, returned in 1722–4. She was displaced as first lady by Cuzzoni. Durastanti returned to London for Handel's 1733–4 season at the King's Theatre, following the defection of most of his cast to the Opera of the Nobility: she was then second woman in the company to Strada. The varied roles in which she was cast indicate her versatility.

Farinel, Jean-Baptiste [Farinelli, Giovanni Battista] (1655–c.1720), a French violinist and composer, was Konzertmeister at the Hanover court while Handel was Kapellmeister there.

Farinelli [Broschi, Carlo] (1705–82) was an Italian castrato whom Handel tried unsuccessfully to secure for the Handel-Heidegger company in 1729. Farinelli sang for the Opera of the Nobility in London between October 1734 and June 1737, displacing Senesino as 'first man', but he never sang for Handel. After 1737 he left the stage and served the Spanish court.

Faustina [Hasse; née Bordoni, Faustina] (1697–1781) was born in Venice and brought up under the protection of the Marcello brothers. Following a successful early career as a soprano in Italy, Germany and Vienna, she sang in London for three seasons (1726–8), taking major roles in new operas by Handel, Ariosti and Bononcini. Her personal and professional rivalry with Cuzzoni in the Academy company was encouraged by the London audience: the two had already performed together in Venice during 1718–19. In 1728 she returned to Italy and in 1730 married the German composer Johann Adolf Hasse (1699–1783). She shared in the success of his subsequent operatic career (mainly in Dresden and Italy), which involved a close working relationship with the librettist Metastasio. Her singing had clarity and agility.

Francesina [Duparc, Elisabeth] (*d.*1773), a French soprano, was trained in Italy. Employed by the Opera of the Nobility in their last season (1736–7), she was retained for the next at the King's Theatre, with parts in *Faramondo* and *Serse*. Thereafter she became Handel's leading soprano (1739–46), apart from his Dublin season and the immediately following London season of 1743. She thus created leading roles in Handel's operas (*Imeneo* and *Deidamia*), oratorios (*Joseph* and *Belshazzar*), secular dramas (*Semele* and *Hercules*) and odes (*St Cecilia's Ode*, *L'Allegro*). In his English works Handel gave her extended arias, making the most of what Burney described as her 'lark-like execution'.

Frasi, Giulia (*fl.*1742–72) was taught by G.F. Brivio in Italy and Charles Burney (as repetiteur?) in London. She was engaged as a soprano by the 'Middlesex' opera company at the King's Theatre in 1742 and continued with the various Italian opera companies there, singing also in English works at other theatres. She was engaged in 1749 by Handel as his principal soprano and remained so for the rest of his life (and in oratorios under his immediate successors). Burney referred to her 'smooth and chaste style of singing'. Handel composed major roles in *Solomon*, *Susanna*, *Theodora* and *Jephtha* for her.

Galli, Caterina (*c.*1723–1804) came to London in 1742 to sing as a mezzo-soprano for the 'Middlesex' opera company (1742–3, 1744–5, 1747–8). She sang in Handel's oratorio seasons, 1747–54, attracting favourable attention in *Judas Maccabaeus* (1747). In operas she often took male roles: Handel wrote the name parts in *Alexander Balus* and *Solomon* for her. Like Frasi, she probably received a considerable part of her training from Handel.

Gates, Bernard (1686–1773) was born in The Hague; his father (also Bernard) accompanied William III to England in 1688. Gates was educated in the Chapel Royal and became a Gentleman there in 1708, subsequently combining this with similar posts at Westminster Abbey and Windsor. He succeeded Croft as Master of the Children at the Chapel Royal in 1727, also becoming Master of the Boys at Westminster Abbey in 1740. His Chapel Royal performance of *Esther* in 1732 began a process that led Handel to introduce oratorio into his London theatre seasons. Thereafter Gates co-operated with the provision (and probably training) of trebles for Handel's oratorio chorus. Handel regularly named him as a bass soloist in his English church music.

Gay, John (1685–1732), a member of the same literary circle as Pope and Arbuthnot, probably created the major part of the libretto for *Acis and Galatea*. In collaboration with Pepusch, he produced *The Beggar's Opera* (Lincoln's Inn Fields Theatre, 29 Jan. 1728), which proved very popular and established the new genre of ballad opera. It included incidental references to the contemporary condition of Italian opera in London, but its satirical aspects were mostly directed at politicians.

Granville family were friends and supporters of Handel. Bernard Granville (1689–1775) assembled a manuscript collection of Handel's music in the 1740s; he received gifts of music from Handel, and two pictures through his will. His sister Mary (1700–88) was a fairly close social acquaintance of Handel's in the 1730s, when she lived nearby in Brook Street. She was married twice: to Alexander Pendarves (*d.* 1724) in 1718 and to Patrick Delany in 1743. Delany was appointed Dean of Downpatrick in 1744, and he and his wife lived near Dublin thereafter. Mary's letters, particularly to her younger sister Ann [Mrs Dewes] (1707–61), contain many references to musical life in London and Dublin.

Greene, Maurice (1696–1755) was educated at St Paul's Cathedral, where he was appointed organist in 1718. In 1727 he succeeded Croft as Composer and Organist to the Chapel Royal and in 1735 Eccles as Master of the King's Musick. The leading English-born musician of his generation, he composed oratorios as well as the church music and court odes that were part of his formal duties. In the early 1730s he was, with Bononcini, regarded as being in opposition to Handel, though the degree of personal antipathy between them is uncertain and Greene never presented a serious challenge to Handel's theatrical career.

Grimani, Vincenzo (?1652–1710), a cardinal and (from 1708) Viceroy of Naples, owned the S. Giovanni Grisostomo theatre in Venice for which *Agrippina* was written, and wrote the libretto for the opera.

Guadagni, Gaetano (1729–92) sang as a castrato on the stage in Venice, which led to his dismissal from a post in the *cappella* at Padua in 1747–8; he then went to London as the leading singer in an Italian *buffo* opera company. He was in Handel's company for the oratorio seasons of 1750–3, and 1755, in which he achieved some success under Handel's guidance. He was the first Didymus in *Theodora*, and Handel wrote new music for him for oratorio revivals: the 'Guadagni' version of 'But who may abide the day of his coming?' in *Messiah* is the one most often performed. His subsequent career included the name part in the first production of Gluck's *Orfeo ed Euridice* (1762).

Hamilton, Newburgh (*fl.*1712–59), an author and librettist, had dramatic works performed in London from 1712. In 1720 he provided the composer Robert Woodcock with the text for a Cecilian ode, *The Power of Musick*. He was steward to the 3rd and 4th Earls of Stafford, *c.*1725–54. He arranged the text of Dryden's *Alexander's Feast* for Handel, adding some text from his own Cecilian ode, and wrote the librettos for *Samson* (1743) and the *Occasional Oratorio* (1746). Handel left him a legacy of £100.

Harris family were friends and supporters of Handel. James Harris (1709–80, father of James, 1st Earl of Malmesbury) wrote on aesthetic criticism and philology: Handel features in his letters and in those of his brother William (1714–77, Prebendary of Sarum). Another brother, Thomas (1712–85, Master in Chancery), witnessed the first three codicils to Handel's will and received a bequest of £300 in the last one. Anthony Ashley Cooper (1711–71, 4th Earl of Shaftesbury) was a cousin to the Harrises and was himself married to a daughter of the Earl of Gainsborough. The Harrises also intermarried with the Knatchbull family: Sir Wyndham Knatchbull was a friend of Handel's.

Hawkins, John (1719–89), an attorney and antiquarian, wrote *A General History of the Science and Practice of Music* (1776), which naturally invited comparison with Burney's history of music. In about 1750 his *Memoirs of the Life of Sig. Agostino Steffani* were printed for private circulation: this was probably the first such biography of a composer and, though on a smaller scale, may be regarded as a precursor of Mainwaring's *Memoirs* of Handel. Hawkins's first-person descriptions of Handel in his *History* imply that he visited the composer in his later years. He was a friend of Samuel Johnson, but Hawkins's social relationships were difficult: Johnson described him as 'a most unclubbable man'.

Haym, Nicola Francesco (1678–1729) was active as a cellist, composer, poet and theatre manager. After six years in the service of Cardinal Ottoboni in Rome, he came to London in 1701, initially to serve the Duke of Bedford. A leading figure in the successful establishment of Italian opera in London, he adapted words and music for two operas that were produced in 1706 and 1708. As wholly Italian performances became the norm, his literary services became more extensive: at least four 'house' operas for the Haymarket opera company (1710–17) were his work, and for Handel he arranged the librettos of *Teseo* and *Amadigi* from French dramas and prepared that for *Radamisto*, Handel's first Royal Academy opera. For six seasons (1722–8) Haym served as secretary of the Academy, working as stage manager for all productions and adapting the librettos (including at least seven for Handel): as a practical musician (he served as continuo cellist and was presumably regularly involved in rehearsals) and a native Italian, he was ideally placed for these tasks. His adaptations are sometimes ruthless in their shortening of recitative (partly to suit London conditions) but musically effective. He also had an interest in coins and medals, and at the time of his death was preparing a history of music for publication.

Heidegger, John Jacob (1666–1749) was born in Zürich, the son of a professor of theology from Nuremberg. After an unfortunate love affair he travelled in Europe, finally settling in London. He was involved with the production of opera in London by 1707–8, selecting arias for pasticcios. He was assistant manager at the Queen's Theatre, Haymarket, by 1711 and succeeded Owen Swiney as manager in January 1713: he rescued the current season and maintained the normal precarious life of the company until 1717. Vanbrugh informally let the theatre to him in 1716, and he remained in joint or sole control of it for the next 30 years. He was active in the formation of the Royal Academy and was Handel's partner in the operatic enterprise that followed during 1729–34. After the occupancy of the theatre by the Opera of the Nobility, Handel composed for the theatre again in 1737–8 and hired it from Heidegger for his 1744–5 oratorio season.

Hill, Aaron (1685–1750), a playwright and theatre manager, was manager at Drury Lane and, from 1710, at the Queen's Theatre, Haymarket. Though he survived only one season there, he was responsible for producing *Rinaldo,* Handel's first

London opera, the libretto of which he compiled with Giacomo Rossi. Rossi was presumably responsible for the final Italian text: the incorporation in the scenario of elements from English music-theatre traditions may have been Hill's contribution. After 1711 Hill gave up theatre management. In December 1732 he wrote to Handel, urging him to write English operas.

Humphreys, Samuel (*c*.1698–1738) was the English literary collaborator for Handel's performances from 1730 to 1733. He recast the text of *Esther* in 1732 and supplied the librettos of *Deborah* and *Athalia* in 1733 and English translations for the word-books of the Italian operas (and presumably of the Italian movements added to *Acis and Galatea*) at the King's Theatre.

Jennens, Charles (1700–73), literary scholar and editor of Shakespeare's plays, was educated at Balliol College, Oxford, but did not proceed to a degree because he was a non-Juror. His name appears on every subscription list of publications of Handel's music after 1725, and he was present in Oxford during Handel's visit in 1733. He came from a prosperous family, and inherited his father's estates in 1747: the regular pattern of his life involved residence in London in the winter and spring, and at Gopsall (Leicestershire) for the remainder of the year. He was Handel's principal oratorio librettist, 1738–44: they worked closely together on *Saul* and *Belshazzar,* though their relationship over *Messiah* was less happy. He built up an extensive collection of music, including a comprehensive library of manuscript copies of Handel's works, later subsumed into the 'Aylesford' Collection; scores of operas that Jennens acquired from Italy were used by Handel as a source of musical 'borrowings'.

Keiser, Reinhard (1674–1739) was brought up near Weissenfels and entered the Thomasschule, Leipzig, in 1685. His first major operas were written for Brunswick, 1693–5; by 1696 he had begun a lifelong association with the Hamburg opera house and became its director in 1702. His family links to the area of Germany in which Handel was brought up may have been influential in establishing Handel's career in Hamburg. Handel was certainly influenced by Keiser's music, from which he 'borrowed' considerably. In *Almira* and the *Brockes Passion* he perhaps deliberately invited comparison by setting texts previously used by Keiser.

Krieger, Johann Philipp (1649–1725) and Johann (1652–1735) were brothers, born in Nuremberg. Johann Philipp became organist at Halle in 1677 and moved with the Saxon court to Weissenfels in 1680, where he was in charge of performances of an extensive repertory of German and Italian cantatas and dramatic works (including more than 2000 of his own cantatas). These performances may have been among Handel's formative musical experiences. Handel also acknowledged his debt to a collection of Johann Krieger's music published in Nuremberg in 1698–9.

Lampe, John Frederick (*c*.1703–1751) was a German composer and bassoonist who settled in London in the mid-1720s. He collaborated with the Arne family in a series of English performances at the Little Theatre, Haymarket, in 1732, and wrote for Drury Lane in 1733: his greatest success came, however, in 1737 with the burlesque opera *The Dragon of Wantley* (Little Theatre, Haymarket; later at Covent Garden; libretto by Henry Carey). In 1738 he married Isabella Young, sister of Cecilia Arne. In the 1740s the Lampes were associated with the early Methodist movement; a collection (1746) of hymns by Charles Wesley to Lampe's music was the source for the Wesley hymns that Handel set soon afterwards.

L'Epine, (Francesca) Margherita (*c*.1680–1746), an Italian soprano, was in London from 1702, joined the company at the Queen's Theatre, Haymarket, in 1708 and sang there until 1714, taking part in a revival of *Rinaldo* and the first productions of *Il pastor fido, Teseo* and possibly *Silla*. In 1715 she transferred to Drury Lane, where the musical director was Pepusch, whom she subsequently married. Through Pepusch's association with Cannons, she may have sung Galatea in Handel's first version of *Acis and Galatea*. She retired in 1719, but returned to sing in three performances (including *Radamisto*) in the Royal Academy's first season.

Lotti, Antonio (*c*.1667–1740) began his career in Venice, where he became principal organist of St Mark's in 1704. From 1706 he was active as an opera composer, notably at the S Giovanni Grisostomo theatre in the same season as Handel's *Agrippina*. From 1717 to 1719 he directed the Dresden Court opera, which Handel visited in 1719 in order to hire singers for the Royal Academy, and then returned to Venice, where he composed mainly sacred music. His madrigal *In una siepe ombrosa* was the subject of an authorship controversy in London in the early 1730s. His fluent musical style contained a number of features that stimulated 'borrowings' by Handel.

Lowe, Thomas (*d*.1783) was a tenor and actor in the London theatre companies from 1740, successful in ballad opera and in Arne's more serious stage works. He joined the Covent Garden theatre company in 1748 and was Handel's principal tenor, 1748–51: in 1743 he had also been second tenor to Beard in Handel's London oratorio company. Burney's description suggests that Lowe had a fine voice but was a less intelligent musician than Beard.

Mainwaring, John (*c*.1724–1807), a clergyman, was the author of a substantial biography of Handel, published in 1760, the year after the composer's death. A graduate and Fellow of St John's College, Cambridge, he was appointed rector of Church Stretton, Shropshire, in 1749. His *Memoirs* of Handel were published anonymously, but their authorship is established by subsequent letters between Mainwaring and the publisher. As early as 1761 Mattheson produced an expanded German translation of the *Memoirs* in Hamburg. Much of the biographical section of the *Memoirs* is taken up with Handel's early career and must have been derived from a source close to the composer or at first hand from Handel himself.

Mattheson, Johann (1681–1764), a composer, theorist and musical author, joined the Hamburg opera company as a treble. By the time Handel went to Hamburg, Mattheson was established as a composer, tenor soloist and musical director there. Their initial relationship was close and cordial: a dispute over precedence at the harpsichord (leading to the famous duel) was patched up quickly, but in later years Handel seems to have been guarded in his responses to Mattheson's letters. Their association probably influenced the development of Handel's creative career in Hamburg. An early number of Mattheson's journal *Critica Musica* in 1722 included the first published reference to Handel's habit of 'borrowing' from other composers.

Merighi, Antonia Maria (*fl*.1714–40) followed a successful career in opera from 1714. She sang as a contralto during the first two seasons of the Handel-Heidegger company (1729–31), and Handel gave her substantial roles in the new operas (*Lotario, Partenope* and *Poro*), parts that clearly contrasted with those taken by Strada, the leading soprano. Merighi returned to London to sing in the last season of the Opera of the Nobility, and remained to take part in the 1737–8 season at the King's Theatre, where she sang in *Faramondo* and *Serse*.

Metastasio [Trapassi], Pietro (1698–1782) was brought up in Rome in a poor family; his early education was arranged by his godfather, Cardinal Ottoboni. After diverse experience at various Italian courts, where he gained some recognition as a poet, his operatic career began in 1723, and his first original libretto, *Didone abbandonata* was staged at Naples the next year. His well-ordered, cunningly contrived texts for 'dramma musicale' quickly achieved classic status, and he seems to have achieved a happy working relationship with some important musicians, including the castrato Farinelli and the composer Hasse. From 1730 his main base was the imperial court in Vienna. Handel set three Metastasio librettos (in London adaptations) in the period 1728–32.

Middlesex, Earl of [Sackville, Charles; later 2nd Duke of Dorset] (1711–59), an enthusiast for Italian opera, was the leading force in attempts to maintain it in London from 1739 onwards, notably at the King's Theatre, 1739–45, where the composers Galuppi and Lampugnani and the castrato Monticelli were the main attractions. He was probably also responsible for bringing Gluck to London. Unfortunately, he lacked the financial acumen to secure his operatic ambitions, and his principal venture ended with suits in the law courts. After Middlesex finally withdrew from operatic management in 1748, Francesco Vanneschi, his poet and assistant manager, took over as impresario in the 1750s. Handel successfully resisted personal involvement in Middlesex's ventures.

Montagnana, Antonio (*fl.*1730–50) was a bass singer in Handel's company at the King's Theatre, 1731–3, and then defected to the Opera of the Nobility, singing through all their seasons. He continued with the King's Theatre company in 1737–8, performing in *Faramondo* and *Serse*. He then joined the royal chapel in Madrid. In his early years with Handel he had a striking voice, with a resonant low register which Handel exploited fully in the part of Zoroastro in *Orlando*.

Morell, Thomas (1703–84), a clergyman, Fellow of King's College, Cambridge, and the author of a Greek lexicon, was apparently introduced to Handel as a potential librettist by the Prince of Wales in the mid-1740s. From 1747 he became Handel's principal oratorio librettist, supplying *Judas Maccabaeus*, *Alexander Balus*, *Jephtha* and probably *The Choice of Hercules*: he was also responsible for adapting *Il trionfo del Tempo* into an English oratorio text in Handel's last years. He apparently enjoyed a good social and professional relationship with Handel, who left him a legacy of £200. His librettos, though less distinguished than Jennens's, were serviceable enough. He was also a friend of Garrick and Hogarth.

Nicolini [Grimaldi, Nicolo] (1673–1732) made his initial career as a castrato in Naples, where he was particularly associated with the operas of Alessandro Scarlatti. In London from 1708, he was decisive in swinging taste there in favour of Italian opera. At the Queen's Theatre for three seasons from 1709 he sang in all the operas of the period, including the name part in *Rinaldo*, and arranged some of the pasticcios himself. He returned in 1715, remaining until the company closed in 1717: Handel wrote the title role in *Amadigi* for him. Unsuccessful attempts were made to re-engage him for the Royal Academy in the mid-1720s, but he ended his career in Italy. He was the foremost male singer of his generation: Burney described him as a 'great singer, and still greater actor'.

Ottoboni, Pietro (1667–1740) was a cardinal and a major patron of the arts in Rome. As Vice-Chancellor of the Catholic Church, he lived in splendour at the Palazzo della Cancelleria, where his weekly concerts were famous. He employed a huge household, including musicians, who from 1690 were led by Corelli. According to Mainwaring, Ottoboni brought Handel and Domenico Scarlatti together for a 'trial of skill' in Rome.

Pamphili, Benedetto (1653–1730) was a cardinal, a patron of music in Rome and a librettist. Probably Handel's first patron in Rome, he provided the text for some Italian cantatas and for *Il trionfo del Tempo*, presumably first performed at his palace.

Pendarves, Mrs, *see* 'Granville'.

Pepusch, Johann Christoph (1667–1752) settled in London from Germany in the first decade of the eighteenth century. He was a viola player and later harpsichordist at the Drury Lane theatre, and a harpsichordist and first violinist at the Queen's Theatre, 1708–10. In 1713 he became a Doctor of Music at Oxford University and in 1715–16 he composed English masques for Drury Lane. By December 1717 he was associated with James Brydges's musical establishment at Cannons, of which he became the director in 1719: in 1718 he married the opera singer Margherita de l'Epine, who may have sung Galatea in the Cannons *Acis*. For Cannons, where his period of activity overlapped with Handel's, Pepusch composed mainly church music. He later returned to a theatre career; the peak of his success was *The Beggar's Opera* (1728). In later years he was better known as a teacher, theorist and antiquarian.

Po [del Po], *see* 'Strada'.

Pope, Alexander (1688–1744), the poet and satirist, was a leading literary figure in Handel's London. His sympathies, particularly after the death of Queen Anne, lay with such 'Tory' writers as Arbuthnot, Swift and Gay. He was associated with the Burlington House and Cannons circles, and may have been a part-contributor to the librettos of *Acis and Galatea* and *Esther*. Though short passages from his works entered Handel's English librettos (e.g. *Semele* and *Jephtha*), Handel never set a complete major text by him.

Porpora, Nicola (1686–1768) had by 1730 an established reputation as an opera composer in Italy and was invited to London to direct the new Opera of the Nobility in 1733, a post he retained until 1736, when he returned to Italy. He wrote five operas and various other works for London.

Porta, Giovanni (*c*.1675–1755) held cathedral posts in Vicenza and Verona and was active as an opera composer in Venice from 1716, studying and collaborating with Francesco Gasparini. The Royal Academy of Music commissioned the opera *Numitore* from him for their first season in 1720; this was his sole operatic venture outside Italy. The 1720 libretto describes him as being under the patronage of the Duke of Wharton.

Reinhold, Henry Theodore (*d*.1751) was a bass singer in Handel's Covent Garden company in 1736–7, appearing in operas and oratorios, and he continued to sing for Handel (King's Theatre, 1739; Lincoln's Inn Fields, 1739–41). From 1743 until his death he was Handel's principal bass, and substantial roles were composed for him. He also maintained a successful independent career as a theatre singer in London, playing the Dragon in the original 1737 production of *The Dragon of Wantley* (Carey/Lampe). He died between Handel's two Foundling Hospital performances of *Messiah* in 1751.

Rich, John (1692–1761) was the elder son of Christopher Rich (*d*.1714), who had been patentee of the Drury Lane theatre in 1709 and built Lincoln's Inn Fields

Theatre (though he died before it opened). John Rich took up the management of the new theatre and ran it with success. Pepusch was its musical director, and Rich himself danced as Harlequin in a series of pantomimes. Soon after the success of *The Beggar's Opera* there in 1728, Rich turned his main attention to establishing a new theatre at Covent Garden, which opened in 1732. Between 1734 and 1737, after the Opera of the Nobility had moved into the King's Theatre, he made it available to Handel; from 1743 (except for 1744–5) Covent Garden was also the venue for Handel's regular oratorio seasons. Handel left his 'Great Organ' (presumably used for the oratorio performances) as a legacy to Rich. In 1759 Rich's daughter married the tenor John Beard, who succeeded Rich as principal manager at Covent Garden in 1761.

Riemschneider, Johann Gottfried (*fl*.1720–49) was the son of the Kantor of the Halle Marienkirche and is said to have been a schoolfellow of Handel's. He sang as a bass soloist in Hamburg during the 1720s, and Handel engaged him for the 1729–30 season at the King's Theatre, after which Riemschneider returned to Hamburg. The parts that Handel wrote or adapted for him were fairly modest.

Robinson, Anastasia (*c*.1692–1755), an English singer born in Italy, joined the Haymarket opera as a soprano in 1714 and remained until the company closed in 1717: among her roles was Oriana in the first production of Handel's *Amadigi*. She sang major roles (now as a contralto) in the first seasons of the Royal Academy of Music, and she retired from the stage in 1724, following her secret marriage to the Earl of Peterborough. Her social circle was associated more with Bononcini than with Handel: her diffidence in approaching Handel over aspects of her role in *Ottone* resulted in some interesting letters to an intermediary.

Robinson, Ann Turner (*d*.1741), a soprano, was the daughter of the composer and choral singer William Turner (1651–1740) and wife of John Robinson, organist of Westminster Abbey, whom she married in 1716. Her early theatrical career, 1718–20, included the first short season of the Royal Academy of Music, in which she played Polissena in Handel's *Radamisto* (1720). She left the stage to raise a family, returning in the mid-1720s. As a member of the King's Theatre company in 1732–3, she took minor roles in Handel's first theatre versions of *Esther* and *Acis and Galatea*. Handel's soloist 'Miss Robinson' for the King's Theatre season of 1744–5, probably her daughter, received substantial parts in *Hercules* and *Belshazzar*.

Rolli, Paolo Antonio (1687–1765) came to London from Italy early in 1716, initially to teach Italian, and became involved with the Royal Academy of Music four years later. In Rome, librettos by him had been set by Bononcini. His Italian made him a useful secretary to the Academy, 1720–2, during which time he wrote or adapted all but one of the librettos performed. After 1722 his contributions were sporadic. He provided texts for the Opera of the Nobility (1733–7) and for Handel's last opera, *Deidamia*. He found favour with Queen Caroline, taught Italian to the royal princesses and was elected Fellow of the Royal Society in 1729. He left London in 1744. His surviving correspondence, though expressed through his own refractory personality, is a major source of information on contemporary operatic politics in London.

Rossi, Giacomo (*fl*.1710–31) settled in London from Italy soon after 1700 and in 1710 was employed by Aaron Hill on the libretto for *Rinaldo*. He continued his association with the Queen's Theatre company until 1713, with the pasticcio *Ercole* and, for Handel, *Il pastor fido* and *Silla*. After Haym's death in 1729 he was apparently pressed into service by Handel and Heidegger: he probably adapted the libretto of *Lotario*, among others, and revised *Rinaldo* for the 1731 revival.

Roubiliac, Louis François (1702/5–62) was trained as a sculptor in Paris and possibly Dresden. He came to London in the 1730s, and his first major commission, a large marble statue of Handel for Vauxhall Gardens, was completed in 1739. His last work was Handel's monument in Westminster Abbey, completed after the sculptor's death in 1762. At least one significant bust of Handel is also attributed to Roubiliac. His work, along with the portraits by Mercier and Hudson, provides some of our best images of Handel.

Ruspoli, Francesco Maria (1672–1731) was a Roman nobleman (a Marquis, Prince from 1708) and a patron of the arts. Handel stayed in his household for considerable periods in 1707 and 1708, during which time he composed church music, secular cantatas and *La Resurrezione*, which was luxuriously presented in Ruspoli's Bonelli Palace in Rome; other works may have been performed at his country estate at Vignanello. Ruspoli was a leading member of the Roman 'Arcadian' Academy.

Scalzi, Carlo (*fl*.1718–38), an Italian castrato, was engaged by Handel as second man to Carestini for his 1733–4 opera season at the King's Theatre, in competition with the Opera of the Nobility's first season. Scalzi had a considerable reputation on the continent, but he seems to have made little impression in London. Handel made substantial revisions to the operas performed that season to suit his high tessitura.

Scarlatti, Alessandro (1660–1725) was particularly associated with Naples, where he worked between 1684 and 1702; during that period he claimed to have produced 80 operas, as well as serenatas, oratorios and cantatas, though not all of them in Naples. He spent considerable time in Rome and Florence with his son, 1702–8, and was associated with the same patrons as Handel: Grimani, as Viceroy of Naples, eventually persuaded him to return there as *maestro di cappella*. Handel's style was probably much influenced by his contact with Scarlatti in Italy. Scarlatti's Neapolitan opera *Pirro e Demetrio* was performed with considerable success in London between 1708 and 1717.

Scarlatti, Domenico (1685–1757), son of Alessandro Scarlatti, was a composer and keyboard player who was brought up in Naples. After an excursion with his father in 1702 in pursuit of a post with the Medici family in Florence, he returned to Naples and was active as an opera composer, but in 1705 he moved to Venice (travelling with the castrato Nicolini). In Venice and Rome during the period 1705–9 he undoubtedly met Handel, and also Thomas Roseingrave, who subsequently promoted his works in England. Scarlatti worked in Rome for ten years from 1709, before taking up posts in Portugal, and then Spain, where, released from his father's influence, he developed the genre of keyboard *Essercizi* for which he is best remembered today.

Schmidt, Johann Christoph, *see* 'Smith'.

Senesino [Bernardi, Francesco] (*d*.1759) was an Italian castrato with so great a reputation that Handel was specifically directed to secure his services for the Royal Academy of Music at its formation in 1719: Senesino arrived in September 1720 and was leading man in every production until the company closed in 1728. Though initially unsympathetic to the Handel-Heidegger management, he returned to London in 1730 and sang for Handel until 1733, when he joined the Opera of the Nobility, apparently maintaining a reasonable professional relationship with Farinelli. In 1736 he left London and continued his career in Italy. His singing was one of the principal artistic assets of the London opera companies. Handel wrote much fine music for him, though their personal relationship may have been rather strained.

Shaftesbury, Earl of [Anthony Ashley Cooper], *see* 'Harris'.

Smith, John Christopher, the elder (1683–1763) and the younger (1712–95) were musicians, father and son, from Ansbach, who settled in London. The elder Smith came to London *c*.1718, reportedly at Handel's invitation, and developed a career as a music copyist, possibly also playing the viola in the opera house. Eventually he became Handel's principal copyist and possibly also manager of Handel's orchestra. The remainder of Smith's family probably came to London in the early 1720s. The younger Smith was taught by Handel. He may have served as second harpsichordist to Handel in the opera orchestra, and he undertook a little music copying, but he soon branched out as a composer in his own right, in English theatre and concert genres. In the 1740s he went to the Continent but he was recalled to London by Handel to manage the oratorio performances as the composer's blindness advanced. By 1754 Smith was effectively in charge of the practical arrangements for Handel's performances both at Covent Garden and at the Foundling Hospital, where he was appointed organist, he continued the oratorio seasons after Handel's death. Handel's scores passed as bequests successively from the father to the son; the latter presented Handel's autographs to King George III when he retired from London to Bath.

Steffani, Agostino (1654–1728) served for 21 years at the Bavarian court in Munich before becoming Kapellmeister of Duke (later Elector) Ernst August of Hanover in 1688. Between 1689 and 1697 he composed eight operas for Hanover, and developed a career in international diplomacy. After a period at the Düsseldorf court, he was appointed Apostolic Vicar in northern Germany in 1709, and his church duties came to dominate the rest of his life. He was in Rome from November 1708 to April 1709 and may have met Handel there. As Apostolic Vicar he was based in Hanover and is believed to have supported Handel's appointment as Kapellmeister at the electoral court. By 1706–7 Handel owned a manuscript of movements from Steffani's Italian duets. The Academy of Vocal (later, Ancient) Music in London elected Steffani their first president in 1727, and he responded by writing some new music for them.

Strada [del Po], Anna Maria (*fl*.1719–40) was engaged as a soprano in 1729 for the Handel-Heidegger company at the King's Theatre, Haymarket. She remained the leading lady of Handel's company until 1737, although her companions joined the Opera of the Nobility in 1733. Strada performed in at least 24 operas under Handel's direction and sang (in English) in his oratorio performances, including those at Oxford in 1733. Burney attributed her success to Handel's training, but she seems to have had a reasonable operatic career in Italy in the 1720s before coming to London. Handel was apparently not able to secure a place for her in the 1737–8 company at the King's Theatre, and she returned to the continent in 1738.

Strungk, Nikolaus Adam (1640–1700), a composer, violinist and organist, held appointments in Hamburg (1678–82), where he composed operas, and Hanover, where he was court composer. After visits to Italy and Vienna, he became vice-Kapellmeister to the Saxon court at Dresden in 1688. In 1692 he obtained permission to found an opera house in Leipzig, which opened in 1693: he composed a further series of operas for Leipzig and moved there permanently in 1696.

Telemann, Georg Philipp (1681–1767) was a student at Leipzig University from 1701, ostensibly studying law, but his time there was dominated by musical activities: he arranged cantata performances in the Thomaskirche (to the chagrin of Kuhnau, the Director Musices), founded a Collegium Musicum that gave concerts, and became musical director of the Leipzig opera. A firm friendship with Handel seems to have been established at this time. Following appointments in Eisenach and Frankfurt, he moved to Hamburg in 1721 as director of music in the city's five principal churches. In spite of initial opposition from the city authorities, he was allowed to widen the scope of his activities and became musical director of the Hamburg opera in 1722. His career remained in Hamburg for the rest of his life. He was a prolific composer, and warm personal friendship did not inhibit Handel from borrowing ideas from Telemann's works.

Theile, Johann (1646–1724) received his initial musical training at Magdeburg and subsequently studied with Schütz. In 1673 he was appointed Kapellmeister at Gottorp, but political instabilities forced Duke Christian Albrecht and his entourage to flee to Hamburg, where Theile helped establish the Hamburg opera house, for which he composed the inaugural opera in 1678. In 1685 he took up a post at Wolfenbüttel and six years later entered the service of Duke Christian I at Merseburg, near Halle.

Vanbrugh, John (1664–1726), an architect, playwright and theatre manager, achieved success in the London theatres with his plays in the 1690s and in 1703 began the construction of a new playhouse, the Queen's Theatre in the Haymarket, which opened in 1705 with an opera by Greber. Theatrical politics conspired to concentrate opera in the building, and from the end of 1707 it became the principal venue for Italian opera in London. After four months' experience of the problems of managing an opera company, Vanbrugh transferred his performing licence to Owen Swiney and turned his attention to other interests, including the design of Blenheim Palace.

Vinci, Leonardo (*c*.1696–1730) was based principally in Naples, where he eventually succeeded Alessandro Scarlatti as organist of the royal chapel. His operas became popular on account of their elegant musical style and melodiousness, and Vinci, though short-lived, was influential in shaping late Baroque style. In London in the 1730s Handel produced pasticcio versions of Vinci's operas, probably in an effort to give his theatre programmes a modern flavour. Although he borrowed musical gestures from Vinci for his own music, the influence of that style on his mature works was slight.

Walsh, John (1665/6–1736) and (1709–66), father and son, were music-sellers, publishers and instrument makers. The elder Walsh founded his music publishing business in 1695 and soon came to occupy the leading position in London that had formerly been held by Playford. During his first 20 years in London Handel seems deliberately to have avoided a monopolistic relationship with a single publisher and, indeed, protected his independence with a copyright privilege; from the mid-1730s onwards, however, Walsh became in effect Handel's exclusive publisher, partly as a result of the younger Walsh's dynamism. The Walshes also seem to have run a music shop, selling music, instruments and probably manuscript paper.

Waltz, Gustavus (*fl*.1732–59) was presumably from a German family. He appeared as a bass in the 1732 Arne/Lampe season of English dramatic works at the Little

Theatre in the Haymarket, where his roles included Polyphemus in *Acis and Galatea*, as well as in English operas at Lincoln's Inn Fields the next season. He joined Handel's company at the King's Theatre for the 1733–4 season and moved with Handel to Covent Garden for the next two seasons, singing in both operas and oratorios. He subsequently resumed his career in the English theatre. Burney and Hawkins both state that Waltz was for a period Handel's cook, and Burney describes him as a rough singer, though that is not suggested by the music that Handel wrote for him.

Young family. Cecilia, a soprano (1712–89), was a pupil of Geminiani and sang in the Arne/Lampe English season at the Little Theatre in the Haymarket in 1732. She sang opera and oratorio with Handel's Covent Garden company in the seasons of 1734–6 (possibly also oratorios in 1733) and sang again for Handel in 1739 at the King's Theatre: she created the roles of Dalinda in *Ariodante*, Morgana in *Alcina* and Merab in *Saul*. In 1737 she married T.A. Arne, appearing in many of his stage works in London and accompanying him to Dublin in 1742. She was one of the cast of the projected production of *Alceste* in 1749–50 for which Handel wrote the music. Her sister Esther, a contralto (1719–95), had early success in Lampe's *The Dragon of Wantley* in 1737 and sang regularly in the London theatres for nearly 40 years. She was in Handel's company for the 1744 Covent Garden season, when her roles included Juno and Ino in *Semele*: she was also one of the cast of the projected production of *Alceste* in 1749–50. Another sister, Isabella, a soprano (*d*.1795), who also sang in *The Dragon of Wantley*, married the composer Lampe but never sang for Handel. A younger member of the family, also named Isabella, a mezzo-soprano (*d*.1791), sang in Handel's last Covent Garden seasons, from 1756. She had studied with Waltz, the bass, and made her concert début with him in 1751. She achieved a distinguished career in the London theatres and in provincial concert performances, retaining her maiden name after her marriage to the Hon. John Scott in 1757.

Zachow [Zachau], Friedrich Wilhelm (1663–1712) received his early education in Leipzig (his birthplace) and Eilenburg. In 1684 he was appointed organist at the Marienkirche, Halle, and retained the post for the rest of his life. His surviving cantatas and keyboard music probably represent only a fraction of the works that he wrote for Halle. His style is fluent and pleasing, though it lacks the breadth of the 'High Baroque' manner of Bach and Handel. The latter was probably fortunate in finding in him a conscientious and effective teacher.

Appendix D

The ruling houses of Hanover, Britain and Prussia

This table shows relationships relevant to Handel's biography. British monarchs are shown in capital letters.

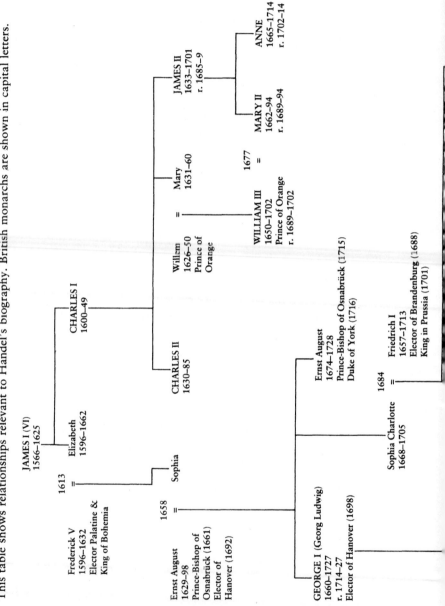

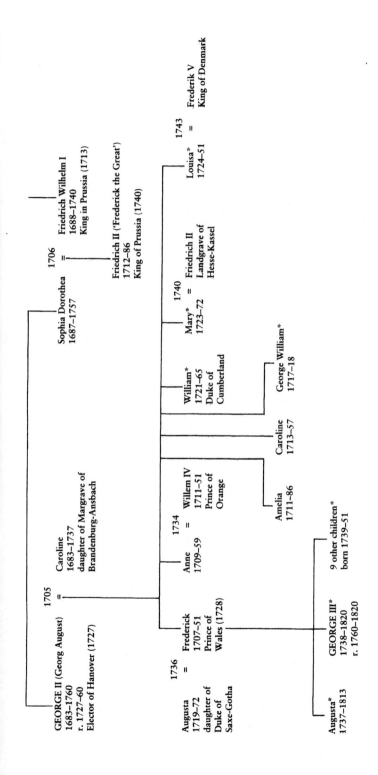

GEORGE II (Georg August)
1683–1760
r. 1727–60
Elector of Hanover (1727)

1705
=

Caroline
1683–1737
daughter of Margrave of
Brandenburg-Ansbach

Sophia Dorothea
1687–1757

1706
=

Friedrich Wilhelm I
1688–1740
King in Prussia (1713)

Friedrich II ('Frederick the Great')
1712–86
King of Prussia (1740)

1734
=

Anne
1709–59

Willem IV
1711–51
Prince of Orange

Amelia
1711–86

Caroline
1713–57

William*
1721–65
Duke of
Cumberland

George William*
1717–18

Mary*
1723–72

1740
=

Friedrich II
Landgrave of
Hesse-Kassel

Louisa*
1724–51

1743
=

Frederik V
King of Denmark

1736
=

Frederick
1707–51
Prince of
Wales (1728)

Augusta
1719–72
daughter of
Duke of
Saxe-Gotha

Augusta*
1737–1813

GEORGE III*
1738–1820
r. 1760–1820

9 other children*
born 1739–51

* = Issue from Hanover line born in Britain

Appendix E

A London opera-goer in 1728

[The following passage is translated from a section of the fifth letter of 'Voiage d'Angleterre' by Pierre-Jacques Fougeroux. The source of the letter is described, with a transcription of the original French text, in Dean, 'A French Traveller's View of Handel's Operas'. The original includes the footnotes given here.]

The Opera, which was once negligible, has become a spectacle of some importance in the last three years. They have sent for the best voices [and] the most skilled instrumentalists from Italy, and they have added to them the best from Germany. This has made the cost so great that when I left London people were saying that it would break the Opera. There were only six solo voices, three of whom were excellent – the famous Faustina from Venice, Cuzzoni, and Senesino the famous castrato; two other castratos, Balbi [Baldi] and Palmerini [a bass], and Boschi for the bass, who is as good as an Italian can be for that voice, which is very rare with them. I had previously heard the three good voices in Venice, and as [that was] 12 years ago they were even better than at present. Faustina has a charming voice, with quite a big sound, though a little rough, [but] her face and her looks are very ordinary. Cuzzoni, although her voice is weaker, has an enchanting sweetness, with divine coloratura, in the manner of the famous Santine of Venice, who no longer appears on the stage. Up to now Italy has had no finer voices than these two women; Senesino is the very best they have ever had, is a good musician, has a good voice and is a reasonably good actor. They are paying Senesino £1600 sterling (equal to 35 000 francs in French money), and £1600 to each of the two actresses, even though the opera plays only two days a week, on Tuesdays and Saturdays, and stops during Lent. It is an enormous amount, and is the way they acquire all the best voices from Italy.

The orchestra consisted of 24 violins led by the Castrucci brothers, two harpsichords (one of which was played by the German Indel [Handel], a great player and great composer), one archlute, three cellos, two double basses, three bassoons and sometimes flutes and trumpets. This orchestra makes a very loud noise. As there is no middle part in the harmony, the 24 violins usually divide only into firsts and seconds, which sounds extremely brilliant and is beautifully played. The two harpsichords [and] the archlute fill in the middle of the harmony. They use only a cello, the two harpsichords and the archlute to accompany the recitatives. The music is good and thoroughly in the Italian style, although there are some tender pieces in the French style. Handel was the composer of the three operas that I saw. The first was Ptolemy King of Egypt, the second Siroe King of Persia, the third Admetus King of Thessaly. These used old Italian librettos for the texts, and the words had been translated into English verse [and printed] alongside the Italian for the benefit of the ladies. As there is nothing spectacular by way of dancing, scenic decoration or stage machinery, and there are no choruses [i.e. movements for independent choral singers] in the performance[1] nor that crowd of actors who should adorn the stage, one might say that the name of opera is ill-suited to this spectacle: it is more like a fine concert on the stage.

The auditorium is small and in very poor taste; the stage is quite large, with poor scenery.[2] There is no amphitheatre, only a pit, with large curved benches right down to the orchestra, where the gentlemen and the ladies are crowded uncomfortably together. The boxes are rented for a whole year. At the back of the auditorium is a curved gallery, which is supported by pillars reaching down to the pit, and is raised to the height of our second tier boxes. This is for the ordinary citizens, and yet you still have to pay 5 shillings, which is 5 francs in French money. Seats in the pit cost half a guinea, equivalent to 11 francs 10. The king has two boxes at the side of the stage, and he came twice with the queen. The princesses were opposite, in another box. Everyone applauds when the king arrives, and cheers when they [the royal party] leave: he had only a couple of guards to protect him. The sides of the stage are decorated with columns, which have mirrors fixed along them with brackets and several candles; the pillars supporting the gallery at the back of the auditorium are similarly fitted. Instead of chandeliers there are ugly wooden candlesticks suspended by strings like those used by tightrope walkers. Nothing could look more wretched, yet there are candles everywhere.

As you are not a lover of Italian music, I hardly dare to tell you, sir, that, apart from the recitative, and the graceless way of accompanying it by cutting short the sound of each chord, there are arias with string accompaniment and wonderfully rich harmony which leave nothing to be desired. The overtures to these operas are what you might call sonatas in fugal style, and very fine they are. I heard a 'sleep' number which imitated those you are familiar with in our operas. One of these overtures included hunting-horns, and so did the chorus at the end,[3] and this was marvellous.

The Concerts. While we are on the subject of music, I must tell you about the public concerts in London, which are poor stuff compared with ours. We heard one[4] which took place in a low room, decorated throughout but with dirty paint, which is usually a dance-hall; there is a platform at one end that you climb a few steps to get on to, and that is where the musicians are placed. They played some sonatas and sang English and German ballads: you pay 5 shillings, worth 5 francs 10, for these inferior concerts. We attended another concert on the first floor of a coffee-house, where the violins from the opera house play every Thursday. They were all Germans, who play very well but rather inexpressively; one of them played the German flute excellently. We also saw a clergyman playing the cello.

You will be surprised, sir, at what I am going to say, that among people of quality, gentlemen and ladies, there are few who are keen on music. They do not know what it is to play together, their only pleasure is drinking a great deal and smoking; you know, sir, how the practice of music in France is turning young people away from debauchery, and how it is being more and more taken up by everyone...

---

[1] There is only a trio or a quartet at the end and [there are only] two duets in the whole opera.
[2] For the scene-changes they use a bell instead of a whistle.
[3] The chorus consists of only four voices.
[4] Next to the fire-pump.

Handel

They also performed [at Lincoln's Inn Fields Theatre] a kind of comic opera, called the Beggars' Opera, because it is about a band of highwaymen with their Captain; there were only two good actors, and a girl called Fenton who was quite pretty. The orchestra is as bad as the other [at Drury Lane]. It is all ballads with worthless music. People were insisting that the librettist had made references to the present government. They drink all the time, they smoke, and the Captain with eight women who keep him company in prison kisses them a great deal. They were going to hang him in the fifth act, but with money he manages to save himself from the gallows. The opera finishes with that. I would bore you if I told you about the country dances at the end.

Appendix F

Select bibliography

This bibliography lists printed materials only; relevant manuscript references are given in footnotes to the main text.

I MUSIC EDITIONS

(a) Collected editions

HG – G.F. *Händel's Werke: Ausgabe der Deutschen Händelgesellschaft*, ed. Friedrich W. Chrysander and Max Seiffert, i–xlviii, l–xcvi (Leipzig and Bergedorf bei Hamburg, 1858–94, 1902); see also below, under 'Music by other composers'.
HHA – *Hallische Händel-Ausgabe im Auftrage der Georg-Friedrich-Händel Gesellschaft*, series I–V and suppl. (Leipzig and Kassel, 1955–); for suppl. i, see General Bibliography, below (under 'Mann, Alfred').

(b) Separate editions of Handel's works referred to in the text

Best, Terence (ed.), *Chaconne in G for Keyboard* (Oxford, 1979)
——, *Twenty Overtures in Authentic Keyboard Arrangements*, 3 vols. (London, 1985)
Burrows, Donald (ed.), *Alexander's Feast*, vocal score (Sevenoaks, 1982)
——, *Foundling Hospital Anthem* (London, 1983)
——, *As Pants the Hart* (*HWV251 c/e*), vocal score (London and Sevenoaks, 1988)
——, *Songs and Cantatas for Soprano and Continuo* (Oxford, 1988)
——, *The Complete Hymns and Chorales: Facsimile Edition with Introduction* (London and Sevenoaks, 1988)
——, *Belshazzar* vocal score (London and Sevenoaks, 1993)
Dean, Winton (ed.), *Three Ornamented Arias* (Oxford, 1976)
Dixon, Graham (ed.), *Three Antiphons and a Motet for Vespers*, with introductions by Watkins Shaw and Graham Dixon (London and Sevenoaks, 1990)

(c) Music by other composers from which Handel 'borrowed'

Roberts, John H. (ed.), *Handel Sources: Materials for the Study of Handel's Borrowing*, 9 vols., with introductions (New York and London, 1986) [incl. facsimile scores of complete works]
Scores of other works from which Handel borrowed were published in 6 supplementary volumes to *HG*, ed. Friedrich Chrysander and Max Seiffert (Leipzig and Bergedorf, 1888–1902)
References to collected editions of music by other composers relevant to Handel's

biography may be found in Stanley Sadie (ed.), *The New Grove* (see Catalogues and reference works, below).

II   CATALOGUES AND REFERENCE WORKS

Burrows, Donald and Ronish, Martha, *A Catalogue of Handel's Musical Autographs* (Oxford, 1994). A comprehensive survey of Handel's autographs.

Clausen, Hans Dieter, *Händels Direktionspartituren ('Handexemplare')*, Hamburger Beiträge zur Musikwissenschaft, vii (Hamburg, 1972). This describes Handel's performance scores which, after the autographs, are the most important MS sources for his music.

Deutsch, Otto Erich, *Handel: a Documentary Biography* (London, 1955; reprinted, New York, 1974). An important collection of transcriptions of documents relating to Handel. It was supplemented and revised for publication in *Händel-Handbuch*, iv, but Deutsch's original remains useful for a few documents (and English translations) that were not included in *HHB*.

Eisen, Walter and Eisen, Margret, *Händel-Handbuch, herausgegeben vom Kuratorium der Georg-Friedrich-Händel-Stiftung*, suppl. to *HHA*, 4 vols. (Leipzig, 1978–85). Vols.i–iii contain the *Thematisch-systematisches Verzeichnis* to Handel's works prepared by Bernd Baselt, which lists Handel's works by HWV numbers and gives musical incipits for individual movements, as well as information about instrumentation, sources, musical borrowings and secondary literature for each work; a short form of the catalogue, without musical incipits, is published as Baselt, Bernd, *Verzeichnis der Werk Georg Friedrich Händels: Kleine Ausgabe* (Leipzig, 1986). Vol.iv, *Dokumente zu Leben und Schaffen*, is a revised and supplemented version of Otto E. Deutsch, *Handel: a Documentary Biography*. References in this book to *HHB* (*Händel-Handbuch*) are to vol.iv unless otherwise stated.

Harris, Ellen T. (ed.), *The Librettos of Handel's Operas*, 13 vols. (New York and London, 1989). Facsimiles of the original printed word-books for Handel's opera performances, with commentary.

Larsen, Jens Peter, *Handel's 'Messiah': Origins, Composition, Sources* (London, 1957, 2nd edition with additions and minor revisions, New York, 1972). The foundation work for many subsequent studies of Handel sources: Larsen's classifications of watermarks have been overtaken by Clausen and by Burrows and Ronish (see above), but his classification of scribal hands by 'S' numbers is still in use, supplemented by material in Clausen, *Händels Direktionspartituren* (see above) and Dean, 'Handel's Early London Copyists' (see General bibliography, below).

Parker-Hale, Mary Ann, *G.F. Handel: a Guide to Research* (New York and London, 1988). An annotated bibliography arranged by topics. It is more accessible and more up-to-date, though less comprehensive, than Sasse, Konrad, *Händel Bibliographie* (2nd edition, Leipzig, 1967); a modern bibliography along the lines of Sasse's is planned for publication in *Händel-Handbuch*, v.

Sadie, Stanley (ed.), *The New Grove Dictionary of Music and Musicians*, 20 vols. (London, 1980). This contains many essential articles about topics germane to Handel's biography. Handel's operas and their performers, and his librettists, are also extensively covered in Sadie, Stanley (ed.), *The New Grove Dictionary of Opera*, 4 vols. (London, 1992).

Smith, William C., *Handel: A Descriptive Catalogue of the Early Editions* (London, 1960; 2nd edition, Oxford, 1970). A comprehensive survey of early printed editions.

III EIGHTEENTH-CENTURY SOURCES

Boyer, Abel, *The History of the Reign of Queen Anne digested into Annals*, 11 vols., 1702–12 (London, 1703–13); probably drawn from contemporary newspaper reports
Burney, Charles, *A General History of Music from the Earliest Ages to the Present Period*, 4 vols. (London, 1776–89); references are to the edition by Frank Mercer, 2 vols. (London, 1935; repr. New York, 1957)
——, *An Account of the Musical Performances . . . in Commemoration of Handel* (London, 1785; facsimile Amsterdam, 1964)
[Coxe, William], *Anecdotes of George Frederick Handel and John Christopher Smith* (London, 1799; facsimile with introduction by Percy M. Young, New York, 1979)
Downes, John, *Roscius Anglicanus, or An Historical Review of the Stage* (London, 1708); ed. Judith Milhous and Robert Hume (London, 1987), indicating the original pagination
Hawkins, John, *A General History of the Science and Practice of Music*, 5 vols. (London, 1776); references are to the edition published by J. Alfred Novello, 2 vols. (London, 1853; repr. New York, 1963)
Hervey, Lord, *Memoirs* – see General bibliography, below (under 'Sedgwick').
Hill, Aaron, see *See and Seem Blind* below
[Mainwaring, John], *Memoirs of the Life of the Late George Frederic Handel*, published anonymously, (London, 1760, facsimile Buren, 1964, 1975)
Mattheson, Johann, *Critica Musica*, 2 vols. (Hamburg, 1723)
——, *Grundlage einer Ehren-Pforte* (Hamburg, 1740)
——, *Georg Friderick Handels Lebensbeschreibung* (Hamburg, 1761; German translation of Mainwaring, *Memoirs*, with additional material by Mattheson)
See and Seem Blind: or, A Critical Dissertation on the Publick Diuersions, &c (London, n.d.; facsimile, The Augustan Reprint Society Publication no.245, with introduction by Robert D. Hume, Los Angeles, 1986); possibly by Aaron Hill, the pamphlet refers to events of 1732 (and was probably published then)
References from contemporary London newspapers and periodicals (when not in Deutsch or *HHB*) are given in the notes.

IV MODERN LITERATURE

(a) Collections of essays

Abraham, Gerald (ed.), *Handel: a symposium* (London, 1954)
Burrows, Donald (ed.), *The Cambridge Companion to Handel* (Cambridge, 1997)
Dean, Winton, *Essays on Opera* (Oxford, 1990). This includes reprints, some of them revised, of articles by Dean that are listed in the General bibliography, below.
Fortune, Nigel (ed.), *Music and Theatre: Essays in Honour of Winton Dean* (Cambridge, 1987)
Hogwood, Christopher and Luckett, Richard (eds.), *Music in Eighteenth-Century England: Essays in Memory of Charles Cudworth* (Cambridge, 1983)

Handel

Hortschansky, Klaus and Musketa, Konstanze (eds.), *Georg Friedrich Handel, ein Lebensinhalt: Gedenkschrift fur Bernd Baselt (1934–1993)* (Halle, 1995)

Sadie, Stanley and Hicks, Anthony (eds.), *Handel Tercentenary Collection* (London, 1987)

Strohm, Reinhard, *Essays on Handel and Italian Opera* (Cambridge, 1985)

Williams, Peter (ed.), *Bach, Handel, Scarlatti: Tercentenary Essays* (Cambridge, 1985)

(b) General bibliography

The list includes the most essential materials relevant to Handel's biography. No attempt is made to give a balanced coverage to the vast literature on Handel, but all items cited in this book are included here (or above). The following abbreviations are used for frequently cited journals and periodicals:

EM – *Early Music* (London, 1973–)

GHB – *Göttinger Händel-Beiträge*, ed. Hans Joachim Marx (Kassel, 1984–)

HJb – *Händel-Jahrbuch* (Leipzig, 1928–33; 2nd series, Leipzig, 1955–91, Cologne, 1992–5, Kassel 1997–)

ML – *Music & Letters* (London, later Oxford, 1920–)

MT – *The Musical Times* (London, 1844–)

Baldwin, David, *The Chapel Royal: Ancient and Modern* (London, 1990)

Baselt, Bernd, *Thematisch-systematisches Verzeichnis (HWV)*, see Catalogues and reference works, above (under 'Eisen').

——, 'Miscellanea Haendeliana II', *HJb*, xxxii (1986), p.67

——, 'Handel and his Central German Background', in Sadie and Hicks (eds.), *Handel Tercentenary Collection*, p.43.

Becker, Heinz, 'Die frühe Hamburgische Tagespresse als Musikgeschichtliche Quelle', in H. Husmann (ed.), *Beiträge zur Hamburgischen Musik-Geschichte*, i (Hamburg, 1956), p.22

Beeks, Graydon, 'Handel and Music for the Earl of Carnarvon', in Williams (ed.), *Bach, Handel, Scarlatti*, p.1

—— ' "A Club of Composers": Handel, Pepusch and Arbuthnot at Cannons', in Sadie and Hicks (eds.), *Handel Tercentenary Collection*, p.209

Best, Terence, 'Handel's Solo Sonatas', *ML*, lviii (1977), p.430; see also *ML*, lx (1979), p.121

——, 'Handel's Harpsichord Music: a Checklist', in Hogwood and Luckett (eds.), *Music in Eighteenth-Century England*, p.171

——, 'Handel's Chamber Music: Sources, Chronology and Authenticity', *EM*, xiii (1985), p.476

——, 'Handel's Overtures for Keyboard', *MT*, cxxvi (1985), p.88

——, 'Two Newly Discovered References to Handel', *The Handel Institute Newsletter*, ii/1 (1991), p.2

Blanchard, Donald, 'George Handel and his Blindness', *Cogan Opthalmic History Society* (Conference Report, June 1999), i, p. 37

Boydell, Brian, *A Dublin Musical Calendar 1700–1760* (Blackrock, 1988)

Braun, Werner, 'Georg Friedrich Handel und Gian Gastone von Toskana', *HJb*, xxxiv (1988), p.109

Buelow, George, 'Handel's Borrowing Techniques: some Fundamental Questions derived from a Study of "Agrippina" (Venice, 1709)', *GHB*, ii (1986), p.105

——, 'The Case for Handel's Borrowings: the Judgement of Three Centuries', in Sadie and Hicks (eds.), *Handel Tercentenary Collection*, p.61

Burrows, Donald, 'Handel's Peace Anthem', *MT*, cxiv (1973), p.1230

——, 'Handel's Performances of "Messiah": the Evidence of the Conducting Score', *ML*, lvi (1975), p.319; see also *ML*, lviii (1977), p.121

——, 'Handel and the Foundling Hospital', *ML*, lviii (1977), p.269

——, 'Handel and the 1727 Coronation', *MT*, cxviii (1977), p.469; see also *MT*, cxviii (1977), p.725

——, 'Sources for Oxford Handel Performances in the First Half of the Eighteenth Century', *ML*, lxi (1980), p.177

——, *Handel and the English Chapel Royal during the Reigns of Queen Anne and King George I*, 2 vols. (diss., Open University, Milton Keynes, 1981)

——, 'Handel and "Alexander's Feast" ', *MT*, cxxiii (1982), p.252

——, 'The Composition and First Performance of Handel's "Alexander's Feast" ', *ML*, lxiv (1983), p.206

——, 'Walsh's Editions of Handel's Opera 1–5: the Texts and their Sources', in Hogwood and Luckett (eds.), *Music in Eighteenth-Century England*, p.79

——, 'Handel and Hanover', in Williams (ed.), *Bach, Handel, Scarlatti*, p.35

——, 'Handel's "As Pants the Hart" ', *MT*, cxxvi (1985), p.113

——, 'The Autographs and Early Copies of "Messiah": some Further Thoughts', *ML*, lxvi (1985), p.201; see also *ML*, lxvii (1986), p.344

——, 'Handel, the *Dead March* and a Newly Identified Trombone Movement', *EM*, xviii (1990), p.408

——, *Handel: 'Messiah'* (Cambridge, 1991)

——, 'Handel's 1738 *Oratorio*: A Benefit Pasticcio' in Hortschansky and Musketa (eds.), *Georg Friedrich Händel*, p. 11

——, 'Handel's Dublin Performances' in Patrick F. Devine and Harry White (eds.), *Irish Musical Studies 4: The Maynooth International Musicological Conference (1995). Selected Proceedings, Part 1*, (Dublin, 1996) p. 46

Burrows, Donald and Hume, Robert D., 'George I, the Haymarket Opera Company and Handel's "Water Music" ', *EM*, xix (1991), p.323

Burrows, Donald and Shaw, Watkins, 'Handel's "Messiah": Supplementary notes on Sources', *ML* lxxvi (1995), p. 356

Channon, Merlin, 'Handel's Early Performances of "Judas Maccabaeus": some New Evidence and Interpretations', *ML*, lxxvii (1996), p. 499

Chisholm, Duncan, 'Handel's "Lucio Cornelio Silla", its Problems and Context', *EM*, xiv (1986), p.64

——, 'New Sources for the Libretto of Handel's "Joseph" ', in Sadie and Hicks (eds.), *Handel Tercentenary Collection*, p.182

Colley, Linda, *Britons: Forging the Nation, 1707–1837* (London, 1992)

Crawford, Tim, 'Lord Danby's Lute Book', *GHB*, ii (1986), p.19

Cudworth, Charles, 'Mythistorica Handeliana', *Festskrift Jens Peter Larsen* (Copenhagen, 1972), p.161

Dean, Winton, *Handel's Dramatic Oratorios and Masques* (London, 1959; 2nd ed. Oxford, 1990)

——, *Handel and the Opera Seria* (London, 1970)

——, 'Charles Jennens's Marginalia to Mainwaring's Life of Handel', *ML*, liii (1972), p.160

——, 'A French Traveller's View of Handel's Operas', *ML*, lv (1974), p.172

Handel

Dean, Winton, 'An Unrecognized Handel Singer: Carlo Arrigoni', *MT*, cxviii (1977), p.556

——, 'Handel's Early London Copyists', in Williams (ed.), *Bach, Handel, Scarlatti*, p.75

——, ' "Rossane": Pasticcio or Handel Opera?', *GHB*, vii (1998), p. 143

Dean, Winton and Knapp, John Merrill, *Handel's Operas 1704–1726* (Oxford, 1987; 2nd ed. 1995)

Derr, Ellwood, 'Handel's Procedures for Composing with Materials from Telemann's "Harmonischer Gottes-Dienst" in "Solomon" ', *GHB*, i (1984), p.116

——, 'Handel's Use of Scarlatti's "Essercizi per Gravicembalo" in his Opus 6', *GHB*, iii (1989), p.170

Dunhill, Rosemary, *Handel and the Harris Circle*, Hampshire Papers viii (Winchester, 1995)

Ewerhart, Rudolph, 'Die Händel-Handschriften der Santini-Bibliothek in Münster, *HJb*, vi (1960), p.111

Fritz, Paul S., *The English Ministers and Jacobitism between the Rebellions of 1715 and 1745* (Toronto and Buffalo, 1975)

Frosch, William A., 'The "Case" of George Frideric Handel', *New England Journal of Medicine*, vol.321, no.11 (14 Sep. 1989), p.765

Gibson, Elizabeth, 'Owen Swiney and the Italian Opera in London', *MT*, cxxv (1984), p.82

——, *The Royal Academy of Music (1719-28): the Institution and its Directors* (New York and London, 1989)

Greenacombe, John, 'Handel's House: a History of No.25 Brook Street, Mayfair', *London Topographical Record*, xxv (1985), p.111

Gudger, William D., 'A Borrowing from Kerll in "Messiah" ', *MT*, cxviii (1977), p.1038

Hatton, Ragnhild, *George I, Elector and King* (London, 1978)

Herbert, Trevor, 'The Sackbut in England in the 17th and 18th Centuries', *EM*, xviii (1990), p.609

Hicks, Anthony, 'Handel's Music for "Comus" ', *MT*, cxvii (1976), p.28

——, 'Handel's Early Musical Development', *Proceedings of the Royal Musical Association*, ciii (1976–7), p.80

——, 'The Late Additions to Handel's Oratorios and the Role of the Younger Smith', in Hogwood and Luckett (eds.), *Music in Eighteenth-Century England*, p.147

——, 'Handel, Jennens and "Saul": Aspects of a Collaboration', in Fortune (ed.), *Music and Theatre*, p.203

——, 'A New Letter of Charles Jennens', *GHB*, iv (1991), p.254

Hodgkinson, Terence, 'Handel at Vauxhall', *Victoria and Albert Museum Bulletin*, i/4 (1965), p.1

Holden, Amanda, with Kenyon, Nicholas and Walsh, Stephen, *The Viking Opera Guide* (London, 1993)

Hume, Robert D., 'Opera in London, 1695–1706', in Shirley Strum Kenny (ed.), *British Theatre and the Other Arts* (Washington DC, 1984), p.67

——, 'Handel and Opera Management in London in the 1730s', *ML*, lxvii (1986), p.347

Hunter, David, 'Patronising Handel, inventing audiences: the intersections of class, money, music and history', *EM*, xxviii (2000), p.32

Hurley, David Ross, ' "The Summer of 1743": some Handelian Self-Borrowings', *GHB*, iv (1991), p.174

Johnstone, H. Diack, 'The Chandos Anthems: the Authorship of No.12', *MT*, cxvii (1976), p.601; see also *MT*, cxvii (1976), p.998 and cxxix (1988), p.459

Keynes, Milo, 'Handel and his Illnesses', *MT*, cxxiii (1982), p.613

King, Richard G., 'Handel's Travels in the Netherlands', *ML*, lxxii (1991), p.372

——, 'On Princess Anne's Lessons with Handel', *Newsletter of the American Handel Society*, vii/2 (1992), p.1

——, 'New Light on Handel's Musical Library', *The Musical Quarterly*, lxxxi (1997), p.109

—— and Willaert, Saskia, 'Giovanni Francesco Crosa and the First Italian Comic Operas in London, Brussels and Amsterdam, 1748–50', *Journal of the Royal Musical Association*, cxviii (1993), p.246

Kirkendale, Ursula, 'The Ruspoli Documents on Handel', *Journal of the American Musicological Society*, xx (1967), p.222 and p.517

Lindgren, Lowell, *A Bibliographic Scrutiny of Dramatic Works set by Giovanni and his Brother Antonio Maria Bononcini* (diss., Harvard University, 1972)

——, 'The Three Great Noises "Fatal to the Interests of Bononcini" ', *ML*, lxi (1975), p.560

——, 'Parisian Patronage of Performers from the Royal Academy of Musick (1719–28)', *ML*, lviii (1977), p.4

——, 'La carriera di Gaetano Berenstadt, contralto evirato (c.1690–1735)', *Rivista italiana di musicologia*, xix (1984), p.36

——, 'The Achievements of the Learned and Ingenious Nicola Francesco Haym (1678–1729)', *Studi musicali*, xvi (1987), p.247

——, 'The Staging of Handel's Operas in London', in Sadie and Hicks (eds.), *Handel Tercentenary Collection*, p.93

——, *Musicians and Librettists in the Correspondence of Gio. Giacomo Zamboni*, RMA Research Chronicle, no.24 (London, 1991)

Loewenthal [Smith], Ruth, 'Handel and Newburgh Hamilton: New References in the Strafford Papers', *MT*, cxii (1971), p.1063

McGeary, Thomas, ' "Warbling Eunuchs": Opera, Gender and Sexuality on the London Stage, 1705–42', *Restoration and 18th Century Theatre Research*, 2nd Ser. VII (1992), p.1

——, 'Handel, Prince Frederick, and the Opera of the Nobility Reconsidered', *GHB*, vii (1998), p.156

McLean, Hugh, 'Bernard Granville, Handel and the Rembrandts', *MT*, cxxvi (1985), p.593

Mann, Alfred, *G.F. Händel: Aufzeichnungen zur Kompositionslehre*, HHA, suppl. i (Leipzig and Kassel, 1978)

——, 'An Unknown Detail of Handel Biography', *Bach: the Quarterly Journal of the Riemenschneider Institute*, xvi/2 (1985), p.3

Marx, Hans Joachim, 'Händel in Rom-seine Beziehung zu Benedetto Card. Pamphilj', *HJb*, xxix (1983), pp. 107–18

——, 'Ein unveröffentlicher Brief Händels in Harvard', *GHB*, ii (1986), p.221

——, 'Italienische Einflüsse in Händels früher Instrumentalmusik', *Studi musicali*, xvi (1987), p.381

——, ' ". . . ein Merckmahl sonderbarer Ehrbezeigung" – Mattheson und seine Beziehungen zu Händel' in Christoph Wolff (ed.) *Über Leben, Kunst und Kunstwerke: Aspekte musikalischer Biographie* (Leipzig, 1999), p.76

Meyric-Hughes, Alison and Royalton-Kisch, Martin, 'Handel's Art Collection', *Apollo*, September 1997, p.17

Milhous, Judith and Hume, Robert D., 'New Light on Handel and The Royal Academy of Music in 1720', *Theatre Journal*, xxxv/2 (1983), p.149

Handel

Milhous, Judith and Hume, Robert D., 'Handel's Opera Finances in 1732–3', *MT*, cxxv (1984), p.86

——, 'The Charter for the Royal Academy of Music', *ML*, lxvii (1986), p.50

——, 'Heidegger and the management of the Haymarket Opera, 1713–17', *EM*, xxvii (1999), p.65

Monson, Craig, '"Giulio Cesare in Egitto": from Sartorio (1677) to Handel (1724)', *ML*, lxvi (1985), p.313

Nichols, R.H. and Wray, F.A., *The History of the Foundling Hospital* (London, 1935)

Ober, William B., 'Bach, Handel and "Chevalier", John Taylor, M.D., Opthalmiater', *New York State Journal of Medicine*, lxix (1969), p.1797

Powers, Harold S., 'Il Serse transformato', *Musical Quarterly*, xlvii (1961), p.481; xlviii (1962), p.73

Roberts, John H., 'Handel's Borrowings from Telemann: an Inventory', *GHB*, i (1984), p.147

——, 'Handel's Borrowings from Keiser', *GHB*, ii (1986), p.51

——, 'Handel and Vinci's "Didone Abbandonata": Revisions and Borrowings', *ML*, lxviii (1987), p.141

——, 'Kaiser and Handel at the Hamburg Opera', *HJb*, xxxvi (1990), p.63

——, 'A New Handel Aria, or Hamburg Revisited', in Hortschansky and Musketa, *Georg Friedrich Handel*, p. 113

Schröder, Dorothea, 'Zu Entstehung und Aufführungsgeschichte von Händels Oper "Almira" ', *HJb*, xxxvi (1990), p.147

Sedgwick, Romney (ed.), *Lord Hervey's Memoirs* (London, 1952; revised edition London, 1963); page references are to the revised edition

Shaw, Watkins and Dixon, Graham, 'Handel's Vesper Music', *MT*, cxxvi (1985), p. 392 [(1) Watkins Shaw: 'Some MS Sources Rediscovered'; (2) Graham Dixon: 'Towards a Liturgical Reconstruction']

Silbiger, Alexander, 'Scarlatti Borrowings in Handel's Grand Concertos', *MT*, cxxv (1984), p.93

Simon, Jacob (ed.), *Handel: a Celebration of his Life and Times, 1685–1759* (London, 1985)

——, 'New Light on Joseph Goupy (1689–1769)' *Apollo*, cxxxix (1994), p.15

Smith, Ruth, 'The Achievements of Charles Jennens', *ML*, lxx (1989), p.161

——, *Handel's Oratorios and Eighteenth-Century Thought* (Cambridge, 1995)

Smith, William C., 'George III, Handel and Mainwaring', *MT*, lxv (1924), p.789

Streatfeild, R.A., *Handel* (London, 2nd edition, 1910; reprinted, New York, 1964)

Taylor, Carole, 'Handel and Frederick, Prince of Wales', *MT*, cxxv (1984), p. 89

——, 'Handel's Disengagement from the Italian Opera', in Sadie and Hicks (eds.), *Handel Tercentenary Collection*, p.165

——, 'From Losses to Lawsuit: Patronage of the Italian Opera in London by Lord Middlesex, 1739–45', *ML*, lxviii/1 (1987), pp. 1–25

Thomas, Günther, *Friedrich Wilhelm Zachow*, Kölner Beiträge zur Musikforschung, xxxviii (Regensburg, 1966)

Timms, Colin, 'Handel and Steffani: a New Handel Signature', *MT*, cxiv (1973), p.374

——, 'George I's Venetian Palace and Theatre Boxes in the 1720s', in Fortune (ed.), *Music and Theatre*, p.95

Tovey, Donald Francis, 'Handel: "Israel in Egypt" ', *Essays in Musical Analysis*, v (London, 1937), p.82

Vitali, Carlo and Furnari, Antonello, 'Händels Italienreise – neue Dokumente, Hypothesen und Interpretationen', *GHB*, iv (1991), p.41

Werner, Edwin, *The Handel House in Halle* (Halle, 1987)
Young, Percy M., *Handel* (London, 1947)
——, *The Oratorios of Handel* (London, 1948)

Index

Abbott, John, 189
Académie Royale de Musique, 102
Academy of Ancient [originally Vocal]
  Music, 166–7, 203n, 455
Addison, Joseph, 73, 85, 357
Aix-la-Chapelle, 195–7, 350n, 371n
Aix-la-Chapelle, Peace of, 297–8, 327,
  342n
Alberti, Johann Friedrich, 8n
Alvito, Duke of, 34–5
Amadei, Filippo, 106, 109, 113, 442
  Muzio Scevola (Act 1), 109, 442
Amelia, Princess, 74, 161n, 188, 334,
  Appx D
Amsterdam, 342n
Amyand, George, 367
Andreoni, Giovanni Battista, 211–12
Andrews, Mr, 75
Anecdotes of George Frederick Handel
  [by William Coxe], 75n, 352n
Angelini, Antonio Giuseppe, 27n, 35n
Anne, Princess (Princess Royal,
  subsequently Princess of Orange),
  74, 117, 165, 180–2, 192, 208n, 211,
  216n, 249, 274, 343, 368, Appx D
Anne, Queen of Great Britain, 66–7,
  70–1, 72–4, 92, 373, 442, 452,
  Appx D
  Birthday Ode for Queen Anne, see
  Handel, Works, Eternal Source of
  Light Divine
Annibali, Domenico, 189, 192, 198n, 445
Ansbach, 79, 455
Arbuthnot, John, 73, 80, 90, 94, 97, 103,
  105, 120, 442, 447, 452
'Arcadian' Academy, Rome, 27, 53, 454
Archbishop of Canterbury, see Wake,
  William

Ariosti, Attilio, 11, 78, 113, 115, 120–1,
  124–5, 130, 216, 442, 446
  Coriolano, 113, 132; Pl. 3
  Elisa (pasticcio), 120
  Teuzzone, 121, 124–5
  Tito Manlio, 78, 442
Ariosto, Ludovico, Orlando furioso, 216
Arne, Cecilia, see Young, Cecilia
Arne, Susanna, see Cibber, Susanna
Arne, Thomas, 265n, 369, 442
Arne, Thomas Augustine, 172, 265, 267,
  274n, 285n, 442, 444, 450, 456, 457
  Artaxerxes; Pl. 7
  Comus, 285n
Arne family, 168, 170, 172, 268, 442, 444,
  449, 457
Arnold, Samuel, edition of Handel's
  works, 250
Arrigoni, Carlo, 171, 188
Arsace (pasticcio), 198n
Atterbury, Francis, 116
'Atterbury plot', 113n, 116
August (Augustus of Weissenfels), Duke
  of Saxony, 2
Augusta, Princess of Saxe-Gotha (Princess
  of Wales, wife of Frederick), 189,
  192–3, 203, 212n, 300, 359, 377,
  Appx D
Austrian Succession, War of the, 38, 297
Avison, Charles, 353n, 378
Avoglio, Giuseppe, 442
Avolio [Avoglio], Christina Maria, 262–
  8, 276, 305, 311–12, 345, 442
Aylesford, Earl of, 331
'Aylesford' Collection, 449

Bach, Carl Philipp Emanuel, 346
Bach, Johann Christian, 346

Edinburgh Musical Society, 370
Edwards, Miss, 212, 268
Egmont, Earl of, *see* Percival, John
Eilenburg, 6, 7, 457
Eisenach, 1, 456
Elford, Richard, 91, 93
Elgar, Edward, 95
Elisa (pasticcio), *see* Ariosti, Attilio
Erard, Mr, 187
Erba, Dionigi, 248
Ernst [Ernst August], Prince of Hanover
  (*d* 1728), 38, Appx D
Ernst August, Elector of Hanover (*d*
  1698), 40, 455, Appx D
Ettinger [Oettinger], Anna, *see* Händel,
  Anna
Exton, 285–6, 296

Fabri, Annibale Pio, 130, 155
Fabrice, Friedrich Ernst von, 112n, 114n
Farinel, Jean-Baptiste [Farinelli, Giovanni
  Battista], 30n, 40, 56, 446
Farinelli [Broschi, Carlo], 40n, 126–9,
  176, 189, 194, 198n, 446, 451, 454
Faustina [Hasse; née Bordoni, Faustina],
  119–22, 125–9, 154, 172, 446, 460;
  Pls. 4, 5
  rivalry with Cuzzoni, 120–1, 445
Fenton, Lavinia, 462
Feustking, Friedrich Christian, 45
Fielding, Henry, 194n
  The Lottery, 201n
Flanders, 288
Fleming, Count, 112n, 114n
Flörcke [Floercke], Johanne Frederike,
  see Michaelsen
Florence, 21, 23, 29–32, 34–6, 46, 454;
  Fig. 3
  Civic (Cocomero) theatre, 30
  Pratolino theatre, 30, 32
Fontenoy, Battle of, 290
Fougeroux, Pierre-Jacques, 140n, 151, 460–2
Founding Hospital, 167n, 299–301, 304,
  327, 331, 333, 339–40, 342, 351–4,
  360, 362–3, 365–6, 366n, 367–8, 443,
  452, 455
Fox, Stephen, 122n
France, 115, 287, 290, 372
Francesina, La [Duparc, Elisabeth], 199n,
  202, 205, 208, 211–12, 264, 276–8,
  280, 288, 305, 313, 446

Francke, August Hermann, 2, 299
Frankfurt am Main, 456
Frasi, Giulia, 305, 324, 341, 345, 354, 366,
  376–7, 446
Frederick, Cassandra ['Frederica'], 365–6
Frederick, Charles, 297
Frederick, Prince of Wales (Electoral
  Prince of Hanover), 74n, 132, 171,
  180, 182, 185n, 189, 192–3, 198, 203,
  206, 208n, 210, 212, 213, 228, 250,
  273, 276, 288, 300, 322, 345, 351,
  377, Appx D; *see also* Augusta,
  Princess of Saxe-Gotha
Fre[e]man, William, 330–1
'French' Baroque musical style, 7, 17, 45,
  55–6, 84, 93, 137, 255
Friedrich [Frederick], Prince of Prussia
  (Friedrich II, 'Frederick the Great',
  King of Prussia), 197, Appx D
Friedrich August, Crown Prince of
  Saxony, 104
Friedrich August I, Elector of Saxony,
  104
Friedrich [Frederick] Wilhelm I, Elector
  of Brandenburg and King in Prussia,
  11, 38–9, Appx D
Freylinghausen, Johann, 2
Froberger, Johann Jakob, 9
Fund for Decay'd Musicians, *see* Decay'd
  Musicians
Furnese, Henry, 176

Gainsborough, Earl of (Baptist Noel),
  285, 448
Galerati, Caterina, 105
Galli, Caterina, 293, 305, 318, 324, 341,
  345, 352, 354, 366, 446
Galliard, Johann Ernst, 64n, 65, 77n, 118
  Calypso and Telemachus, 65
Gallus [Handl], Jacob, 251
Galuppi, Baldassare, 273, 451
  Penelope, 263
Gambarini, Elisabetta de, 292, 296, 305,
  318
  Lessons for the Harpsichord, 296
Garrick, David, 267, 280, 341, 352, 451
Gasparini, Francesco, 23, 32, 36, 153, 452
Gates, Bernard, 93, 165–7, 189, 278, 341,
  442–3, 445–7
Gay, John, 75n, 80, 96–7, 112–13, 126n,
  447, 452

Handel

Handel, George Frideric (*cont.*):
Daphne (HWV4), 20, 46, 56n, 57n
Deidamia (HWV42), 211–13, 229, 446, 453
Didone (HWV A¹²), 193, 195, 233n
Elpidia, L' (HWV A¹), 119–20
Ezio (HWV29), 132, 155–6, 215
Faramondo (HWV39), 197, 199, 226, 229, 444, 446, 450–1
Flavio (HWV16), 113, 115, 133–4, 136n, 142n, 152, 157; *Pl. 3*
Floridante (HWV14), 110–11, 121, 134, 151–2, 161, 173
Florindo (HWV3), 20, 46, 56n, 57n
Genserico (HWV A²), 125
Giulio Cesare (HWV17), 113, 119, 130, 132, 135–50, 153, 216, 230, 294, 320, 323, 443, 445; Fig. 4
Giustino (HWV37), 190, 192–3, 195, 229, 445
Imeneo (HWV41), 202, 205, 211–12, 229–32, 256, 258, 261, 265, 446
Jupiter in Argos (HWV A¹⁴), 105, 204–6, 208, 229, 233n
Lotario (HWV26), 129–30, 135, 155, 364, 450, 454
Lucio Cornelio Silla, see *Silla*
Lucio Papirio (HWV A⁶), 133, 233n
Muzio Scevola, Act 3 (HWV13), 109, 134, 151
Nero (HWV2), 19–20, 45
Olibrio, see *Genserico*
Oreste (HWV A¹¹), 183, 233, 234, 342
Orlando (HWV31), 172–3, 215–19, 223n, 229, 232, 234, 314, 338, 451
Ormisda (HWV A³), 130–1
Ottone (HWV15), 105, 111–13, 115, 120–1, 134, 152, 155, 161, 178, 183, 215, 253n, 453
Parnasso in festa (HWV73), 178–9, 192–3, 212–13, 250, 342, 364
Partenope (HWV27), 130–1, 155, 162, 215, 226, 450
Pastor fido, Il (HWV8), 70, 87–8, 89n, 99, 136n, 179, 183–4, 365, 442, 450, 453; Fig. 10
Poro (HWV28), 131–2, 155, 192, 215, 234, 450
Radamisto (HWV12), 106–10, 113, 125, 134, 138, 143, 151, 162, 215, 256, 445, 448, 450, 453; Fig. 7

Riccardo Primo (HWV23), 124–5, 135, 154, 232n
Rinaldo (HWV7), 65–70, 75, 77, 79, 83–8, 111, 130–1, 137n, 172, 215, 222, 224, 337, 443, 449, 450–1, 453–4; Figs. 5, 6
Rodelinda (HWV19), 119–20, 131, 135, 136n, 153–4, 215–16
Rodrigo (HWV5), 29–32, 56–7, 66; Fig. 3
Scipione (HWV20), 120, 131, 153–4, 232n
Semiramide riconosciuta (HWV A⁸), 178
Serse (HWV40), 199, 225–7, 373n, 444, 450–1
Silla (HWV10), 70, 88, 450, 453
Siroe (HWV24), 125, 128, 132, 154–5, 215n, 376, 460
Sosarme (HWV30), 132–3, 156, 179, 215
Tamerlano (HWV18), 119, 132, 135–6, 153–4, 157, 182n, 215–16, 338
Terpsicore (HWV8), 183, 256
Teseo (HWV9), 70, 87–8, 215, 448, 450
Titus l'empéreur (HWV A⁵), 132
Tolomeo (HWV25), 125, 130, 154–5, 172, 460
Venceslao (HWV A⁴), 131
Vincer se stesso è la maggior vittoria, see *Rodrigo*

Oratorios, German Passion, odes, and English theatre works
Acis and Galatea (HWV49), 54, 77n, 80–1, 96–8, 133, 143, 170–3, 179, 188, 194, 206, 209, 210, 212, 233, 242, 264, 265n, 275, 303, 307, 322n, 363–4, 369, 442, 444, 447, 449–50, 452–3, 457
Alceste, incidental music (HWV45), 158, 331–2, 342, 354, 457
Alchemist, The, see **Orchestral music**
Alexander Balus (HWV65), 293–5, 302, 318–23, 331, 334, 362, 372, 446, 451; *Pl. 10*
Alexander's Feast (HWV75), 187–8, 190–4, 203–4, 205–6, 209, 236–40, 243, 255, 265, 274n, 275, 303, 323–4, 341, 345, 351, 360, 363, 369, 447

partnership with Handel, 124n, 126–9, 131, 161–2, 171, 179, 197, 207, 243, 443, 446, 450, 454
Heidelberg, 60n, 104n
Herodotus, 226n, 314
Hervey, Lord John, 122, 178n, 180–2, 187n, 374n
Hesse-Cassel, 442
Hese-Cassel, Prince (Landgrave) of, 210, Appx D
Hetherington, John, 367
Het Loo, 343
Hickford, Thomas, 207
Hicks, Anthony, xii
Hill, Aaron, 64n, 65–7, 83, 85, 172, 448–9, 453
Hill, John, 266
Hinsch, Heinrich, 19–20
Hogarth, William, 299, 451
Holdsworth, Edward, 46n, 189n, 241n, 259n, 260n, 271n, 272n, 277n, 282n, 286n, 289n, 378n
Holland, *see* Netherlands
Holmes, William (Vice-Chancellor of Oxford University), 174
Holyhead, 260
Homer, 113, 361
Horncastle, F. W., 46n
Hudson, Thomas, 339, 369, 454; *Pl. 11*
Huggins, William, 165, 173
Hughes, Francis, 93, 158
Hughes, John, 64n, 69, 96, 100
Huguenots, 2, 10, 372
Humphreys, Samuel, 166, 173, 234–5, 238; Fig. 9
Hunold, Christian Friedrich ('Menantes'), 17
Hunter, James, 339, 374

Idaspe fedele, L' (pasticcio, after Mancini), 64, 75
Innsbruck, 38
Innsbruck, Prince Karl of, 38
Inspector of Stage Plays, 320n, 342n, 354
Ireland, Lord Lieutenant of (William Cavendish, 3rd Duke of Devonshire), 260–1, 263, 266, 445
Irwin, Lady, 173n
Isted, Mr, 67

Jacobites, 77, 115–16, 152, 175, 287–90
James II, King of England, 115, 123, Appx D
coronation liturgy (1685), 160
Jennens, Charles, 43, 46, 99, 120, 175, 185, 187, 189, 192, 202–4, 206, 209, 240–6, 259–60, 262–3, 267, 271–2, 277–80, 282, 283, 284, 286, 289, 303, 312, 314, 315, 322, 330–1, 345, 363, 377, 449, 451
Jews
in Halle, 2
in London, 204, 292n, 294, 334–5, 371
Johann Adolf, Duke of Saxony (Saxe-Weissenfels), 2, 6
Johann Wilhelm I, Elector Palatine, 60, 61, 67, 104n
Johnson, Hurlothrumbo [?Samuel], 179
Johnson, Samuel, 179n, 316, 448
Jonson, Ben, 66
Jordan, Abraham, 283–4
Judges, Book of, 355
Justinian, Emperor, 180

Keiser, Reinhard, 17–19, 21, 45, 47, 50, 365, 443, 449
Almira, 17, 45n
Claudius, 17, 45n, 144, 365
Nebucadnezar, 17
Octavia, 19, 50n, 52, 59
Salomon, 17
Kensington [Palace], 116, 129n, 162, 192
Kent, William, 204
Kerll, Johann Kaspar, 9, 248, 308
Kew, 321
Kielmansegge, Johann Adolf, Freiherr von, 38, 60, 72–3, 77
Kielmansegge, Sophia Charlotte von (subsequently Countess of Darlington), 78, 112
King, Charles, 443
King's Lynn, 444
Knatchbull, Wyndham, 182, 263, 448
Kreyenberg, Christoph Friedrich, 72–4
Krieger, Johann, 8–9, 449
Anmuthige Clavier-Übung, 8
Krieger, Johann Philipp, 7, 13, 449
Kuhnau, Johann, 10, 17, 456
Kytch, Jean Christian, 65, 87, 157, 163, 201

Miller, James, 274–5, 277–8, 313–14
Milton, John, 209, 240–2, 277, 285, 312, 317n, 357, 361
  L'Allegro, Il Penseroso, 240–1
  Comus, 285
  Samson Agonistes, 312
Minato, Nicolò, 227n
Mizler, Lorenz Christoph, 287
Montagnana, Antonio, 132, 155, 167, 199n, 216, 232, 451
Montagu, Elizabeth, 333n
Montagu, John, Duke of, 277, 297
Montanaro, Antonio, 25
Monticelli, Angelo Maria, 259, 451
Monza, Maria, 212
Morell, Thomas, 291, 292, 293–4, 312, 319–22, 331, 333–5, 338, 342, 349, 355, 356–7, 363–4, 366, 451; *Pl. 10*
Morris, Gael, 373
Morse [Moss], Jonathan, 202, 331, 339
Mozart, Wolfgang Amadeus, 135, 346
Muffat, Gottlieb, 240, 328
Munich, 455
Münster, 55

Naples, 23, 34, 37, 54, 66n, 129, 444, 447, 451, 454, 456
National Anthem, British, 291n
Naylor, Francis, 198n
Neale, William, 261
Negri, Maria Caterina, 177, 189, 192
Negri, Maria Rosa, 177, 192
Netherlands, 61, 192, 202, 211, 343, 350n, 368
Neumeister, Erdmann, 7n, 42
Newcastle, Duchess of (Henrietta), 78
Newcastle, Duke of (Thomas Pelham-Holles), 129
Newton, Michael, 176
Nicolini [Grimaldi, Nicolo], 64, 66–7, 77, 86–7, 89, 119, 451
Nobility Opera, *see* Opera of the Nobility
Noel, James, 285
Non-Jurors, 115, 175, 289, 449
Novello, Vincent, 324n
Nuremberg, 7, 448–9

Oettinger [Ettinger], Anna, *see* Händel, Anna
Oettinger, Christoph, 3
Old Ford, 339, 374
Oldmixon, George, 32, 51, 364

Opera, Baroque
  forms and style, 43–4, 134–6, 140n, 141
  'simile' aria, 53, 126, 149, 229
Opera and oratorio, patronage in London by royal family, 66–7, 74–5, 102, 124, 180–2, 185n, 198, 203, 213, 269
Opera of the Nobility, 171, 175, 178–80, 182, 187, 192, 194, 197–9, 202, 216, 219, 372, 443–6, 448, 450–5
'Opera Register', *see* Colman, Francis
Orange, Prince of, *see* Willem IV
Oratorio, characteristic forms, 25; *see also* Handel, Life, Oratorios in London
Orkney, Earl of (George Hamilton), 78
Orlandini, Giuseppe Maria, 119
Orsini [?Ursini, Gaetano], 105
Osnabrück, prince-bishopric of, 40
Ottoboni, Pietro (Cardinal), 24, 28, 32, 448, 451–2
Ouverture, *see* 'French' Baroque musical style
Ovid, 34, 96, 314
Oxford, 173–5, 205–6, 275, 317n, 369–70, 443, 449, 452, 455
  Christ Church, 173, 206
  Music Room, 331
  Sheldonian Theatre, 173–5, 206
  University, 'Public Acts' and degree ceremonies, 173–4, 369

Pacini, Andrea, 151
Padua, 447
Palatinate, Upper, 290
Palatine, Elector, *see* Johann Wilhelm I
Pallavicino, Stefano Benedetto, 152
Palmer, Mrs, 367
Palmerini, Giovanni Battista, 460
Pamphili, Benedetto (Cardinal), 24–6, 27n, 32–3, 50, 445, 452; *Pl. 1*
Paris, 113, 174, 454
Pasquini, Bernardo, 7
Passerini, Christina, 344, 365–6
Passerini, Giuseppe, 344
Pasterla, *see* Posterla
Pasticcio operas presented by Handel, 119–20, 130–1, 133, 172, 178, 183, 193, 195, 199, 233, 234
Pendarves, Alexander, 447
Pendarves, Mrs, *see* Granville, Mary